*An Edwin Arlington Robinson
Encyclopedia*

An
Edwin Arlington Robinson
Encyclopedia

ROBERT L. GALE

McFarland & Company, Inc., Publishers
Jefferson, North Carolina, and London

Selected lines from the following poems are reprinted with the permission of Scribner, an imprint of Simon & Schuster Adult Publishing Group, Inc., from *The Collected Poems of Edwin Arlington Robinson* by Edwin Arlington Robinson, copyright © 1935, 1937 by The Macmillan Company, copyright renewed © 1963, 1965: "Afterthoughts," "Amaranth 1934," "Annandale Again," "As It Looked Then," "Cavender's House," "Christmas Sonnet," "Demos and Dionysus," "Dionysus in Doubt," "En Passant," "Fortunatus," "The Garden of the Nations," "Glass Houses," "The Glory of the Nightingales," "Hannibal Brown," "Haunted House," "Hector Kane," "If the Lord Would Make Windows in Heaven," "Karma," "King Jasper," "The Laggards," "A Man in Our Town," "The Man Who Died Twice," "The March of the Cameron Men," "Matthias at the Door," "Maya," "New England," "Nicodemus"; "Not Always," "Ponce de Leon," "The Prodigal Son," "Rembrandt to Rembrandt," "Reunion," "Roman Bartholow," "The Sheaves," "Silver Street," "Sisera," "Talifer," "Toussaint L'Ouverture," "Tristram," "Why He Was There," "Young Gideon."

LIBRARY OF CONGRESS CATALOGUING-IN-PUBLICATION DATA

Gale, Robert L., 1919–
An Edwin Arlington Robinson encyclopedia / Robert L. Gale.
p.   cm.
Includes bibliographical references and index.

ISBN 0-7864-2237-8 (illustrated case binding : 50# alkaline paper) ∞

1. Robinson, Edwin Arlington, 1869–1935 — Encyclopedias.
2. Poets, American — 20th century — Biography — Encyclopedias.
I. Title.
PS3535.O25Z459   2006   811'.52 — dc22   2005024674

British Library cataloguing data are available

On the cover: Edwin Arlington Robinson, from a painting by
Lilla Cabot Perry *(courtesy Colby College, Waterville, Maine)*

Manufactured in the United States of America

*McFarland & Company, Inc., Publishers
Box 611, Jefferson, North Carolina 28640
www.mcfarlandpub.com*

To
Danny D. Smith

Table of Contents

Preface

Edwin Arlington Robinson, now firmly established as one of the world's finest poets, is unique in American literary history. He is the man who from the age of about 10 said that he wanted to be a poet and nothing else—win or lose. He is the man who once wrote that he expected little recognition during his lifetime, but that if he could write verse that would live beyond his lifespan, he would happily live in an attic and eat crusts. He is the man who remarked that he would have more to say after his death. In between his early-expressed ambition to write and his death, he was the man who said that he wore his skin inside out. He said that he did not believe we live in a prison house, as one reviewer accused him of thinking, but that we are children in a kindergarten trying to spell God with the wrong blocks. Writing poetry did not pay during his early maturity; so the wolf—as well as the bottle—was often at both sides of his door. When poverty was threatening to destroy him, Theodore Roosevelt* learned about his plight by chance (or was it fate?) and secured him a sinecure with the federal government. Later, when poverty was snapping at his heels again, Marian MacDowell,* founder of the MacDowell Colony in New Hampshire, became his abiding angel. Yes, this poet was, and remains, unique.

E. A. Robinson was unpopular, pop-ular again, and later less so, in cycles. When he got no respect from his boyhood chums in response to his sharing some juvenile verses with them, he burned the precious sheaves. During the twilight decades of American verse, when the likes of William Vaughn Moody,* Ridgely Torrence,* Josephine Preston Peabody,* and Percy MacKaye* held sway, Robinson published bleakly and was often reviewed demeaningly. During the First World War, he began to glitter when the public sun shone warmly on his "The Man Against the Sky." Immediately after the Armistice, his alleged pessimism attracted renewed attention. When the Literary Guild made a best-seller of *Tristram*, the third of his long Arthurian trilogy, its success puzzled and even frightened him. He felt that any poet's increasing popularity, especially in a materialistic democracy, meant that the poetry was increasingly weak. After such celebrity, what forgiveness? His sales necessarily diminished during the dry years following the Big Crash. Before World War II exploded, ominous signs of the coming of which he saw and wrote about in his continuing role as an American Cassandra, cancer struck Robinson in the pit of his stomach, and he (a trifle gratefully) died. He said he was glad he'd be leaving the world before Adolf Hitler grew any more diabolical.

Robinsonian as well as world cycles have continued. A few of Robinson's short poems

---

*Throughout the text an asterisk denotes an entry in the encyclopedia.

1

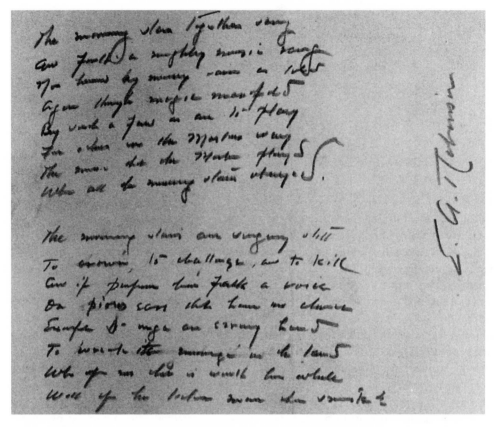

Sample of Robinson's handwriting, from his poem "Atherton's Gambit," reproduced at full size. Used with permission of the Watkinson Library, Trinity College, Hartford, Connecticut.

appear in updated anthologies of American literature and in sensible, modern-day collections of poetry in English; but their appeal has accompanied critical neglect of his longer efforts. All of his poetry remains challenging — to critics, students, and lovers of fine writing alike. Specific petty criticisms and airy generalizations about him can be refuted — always. His popularity among the knowing will never diminish. A general Robinson renaissance, long overdue, is occasionally predicted. I hope that this book will help such an upsurge. Forthcoming biographies, one of which is on the horizon, and perhaps the publication of his collected letters — 3,552 of which are known to be safely institutionalized — will or would do far more.

My friend Henry Wilson Allen, the late author who fashioned some of our best "western" fiction under the pen names Will Henry and Clay Fisher, wrote to me years ago that a Canadian reader of his had recently thanked him for explaining life in a passage from one of his novels. The solution was this: "The truth has no hope in it whatever." Robinson would qualify this dark remark by saying that light-seeking people's disparate views of "truth" produce conflict, to be sure, but that transcendental "Truth" radiates "Light." Would that Allen had studied Robinson, and may other doubters profit by doing so in due time.

Decades ago, when as a youngster I first read Robinson's "Isaac and Archibald," I was struck by the stalwart courage of those two memorable codgers. At the time, I imagined myself the narrator and Robinson an Isaac-and-Archibald amalgam verbosely lecturing me. Later, when I was "teaching Robinson" (as though anyone could teach him), I vowed aloud to my ethereally young students that when I grew old and darkness approached I would apply to myself a terse comment of Archibald. And by Apollo, I have been doing so for some years now. The bracing passage?

> ...there's a light behind the stars
> And we old fellows who have dared to live,
> We see it — and we see the other things...

In addition to the perilous quest for the light, Robinson's themes also include nagging pessimism overcome, or almost, by muted optimism; inevitable mutability, coupled with love too often less than it ought to be; and — perhaps most notable — the failure of those who are seemingly "successful" eyefuls, and the success of those who are observable "failures." These successful failures are uniquely Robinsonian anti-heroes, loners, losers, outsiders, and persons with secret lives trying to make the most out of blown opportunities.

Robinson was also stylistically versatile. One cannot say that he experimented in various verse forms. He meticulously wrote and revised drafts until they either were discarded or became finished works of art, in several modes. Best, surely, are his sonnets. Next, his character studies, some of which are sonnets. Next, his short narrative poems, often in supple blank verse. Next, perhaps, his octaves. Last, but not always lagging, his long narratives, also in iambic pentameter. His mimicking of several French forms, for example, the villanelle, were mainly finger exercises. With some exceptions, so, I feel, were his laborious translations.

Joyce Kilmer, the poet famous as a casualty of the First World War but more famous for his "Trees," greatly admired "The Master," Robinson's poem extolling Abraham Lincoln. In his 1912 review of *The Town Down the River*, in which the poem appears, Kilmer quoted eight lines from it

and asked, "Can any part of this be translated into words of the same language without injury to the meaning?" After singling out the words "shopman," "rancor," and "galling crown" from the lines quoted, he issued this challenge: "Try to paraphrase . . . and the finality of the wording is at once apparent." Nonetheless, in this encyclopedia I must often paraphrase Robinson's exquisite phrasings, as well as his critics' prose, for two reasons: to try to be an efficient aid to many puzzled readers when our subject becomes Robinson the Obscure; and to obey the restrictions on quoting imposed by holders of copyrights of Robinson material.

When I quote or paraphrase anyone other than Robinson, I indicate my sources at end-of-entry "Source" or "Sources." I trust that my citing specific page numbers, or using "passim," makes sense given my use as contextually evident. I use contractions because they can relax academic-critical prose a little. (Asterisks indicate cross-referencing.)

In my penultimate draft, I included several adjectival and adverbial mini-praises and mini-jibes at the maxi-multiple critics quoted or paraphrased. Then, for two reasons, I removed most of them. It seems best to let my astute readers judge for themselves each critical aperçu; and, almost universally, let's say, those critics seem sharper than I am.

I wish to extend my profound thanks to many people and agencies that have helped me complete this reference book. Danny D. Smith, librarian and research source extraordinaire at Gardiner, Maine, answered many biographical questions I posed, and anticipated and answered several other queries. In matters concerning Gardiner folks, where I incompletely site "Sources," Mr. Smith also is owed credit after silent credit. Patricia Burdick, special collections librarian, the Miller Library, Colby College, was gracious with her time, knowledge of Robinson, materials shown, and books generously given to me. Dr. Brian Rines of Gardiner and Augusta, Maine, provided valuable information about Robinson's haunts. Dr. David S. Nivison, Robinson's great-nephew, offered invaluable family data, encouragement, and permission, legally limited, for me to quote certain materials. Dr. Scott Donaldson, Robinson critic and biographer, sent much information and encouragement. Dr. Nicholas Ayo of Notre Dame University generously permitted me to quote from and make detailed references to his dissertation on Robinson and the Bible. Dr. Michael Joe Skupin allowed me to read his dissertation on Robinson's *Merlin* (University of Houston, 2003). Eric J. Esau, Baker Library, Dartmouth College, supplied information about Percy MacKaye and his family. Sara Upton, Amherst College, provided details concerning Harry de Forest Smith. Thelma Seifer, of Seifer Handwriting Consultants, West Hempstead, New York, analyzed Robinson's obscure handwriting with uncanny expertise. The following helpfully advised me about permissions to quote copyrighted writings by or about Robinson: Stacey Bone (University of Georgia Press), Dr. George F. Butler (Greenwood Press), Scarlett R. Huffman (Harvard University Press), Dr. David Garrett Izzo (author of *W. H. Auden Encyclopedia*), Jeniqua Moore (Simon & Schuster permissions supervisor), Dr. Rayburn S. Moore (University of Georgia), Sabrina R. Paris (Pearson Education, Upper Saddle River, New Jersey), Rose Robinson (University of California Press), and Linda Tashbook, Esq. (University of Pittsburgh). Although I am solely responsible for any improper use of materials still copyrighted, I did make diligent efforts to secure permissions and will correct reported oversights in future editions of this work.

Librarians at the University of Pittsburgh, Carnegie-Mellon University, Pittsburgh, and the Carnegie Public Library, Pittsburgh, have been helpful, patient, and fun when I appealed for help. It is a remembered joy that I was granted interloper's privilege to visit the buildings and scout the grounds of the MacDowell Colony, Peterborough, New Hampshire, one summer Sunday afternoon, and to reflect on Robinson's often having been right there. Finally, my love to Maureen (my beloved wife for 61 years now) and to our energetic family — John, Jim, Christine, Bill, and Lisette, and faroff Diana, Caroline, and Stephanie, too.

The following have generously permitted me to quote materials for which they hold copyrights or other rights: University of California Press, Berkeley (Edwin S. Fussell, *Edwin Arlington Robinson: The Literary Background of a Traditional Poet*, 1954); University of Georgia Press (*Edwin Arlington Robinson: Centenary Essays*, ed. Ellsworth Barnard, (c) 1969). In addition, grateful acknowledgment is expressed for data and leads provided by annual issues of *American Literary Scholarship* (Durham, NC: Duke University Press, 1965–); annual *MLA Bibliography* issues; *American National Biography* (24 vols., New York: Oxford University Press, 1999); cracked-back older biographical series, which are often the partial basis of more recent biographical entries; Lillian Lippincott, *A Bibliography of the Writings and Criticism of Edwin Arlington Robinson* (Boston: Faxton, 1937), Nancy Carol Joyner, *Edwin Arlington Robinson: A Reference Guide* (Boston: G. K. Hall, 1978), and earlier, built-upon bibliographies of Robinson by Lucius Beebe and Robert J. Buckley, Jr. (1931), Charles Beecher Hogan (1936), and William White (1971). The Bacon Collamore collection of Robinson's works and related published materials, in the Watkinson Library, Trinity College, Hartford, Connecticut, also contains biographical and bibliographical information of unique value.

Chronology

1818 Edward Robinson, Jr., father (Edward Robinson*), born.

1833 Mary Elizabeth Palmer, mother (Mary Robinson*), born.

1855 Edward Robinson and Mary Palmer marry.

1857 Horace Dean Robinson (Dean Robinson*), brother, born (May 30).

1865 Herman Edward Robinson (Herman Robinson*), brother, born (January 6); Emma Loehen Shepherd (Herman's future wife [Emma Robinson*]), born (April 19).

1869 Edwin Arlington Robinson born (December 22) at Head Tide, Maine.

1870 Family moves to Gardiner, Maine (September).

1881 or 1882 Teacher hits Robinson's ear, causing infection and mastoid damage.

1883–84 Aranson Tucker Schumann* starts teaching Robinson how to write poetry.

1884 Enters Gardiner High School (September), choosing the scientific course of study, to avoid having to study Greek.

1885 Is invited, probably this year, by Dr. Schumann to participate in a club of local poets who read their works at meetings.

1888 Graduates from Gardiner High School (June 17); meets Emma Shepherd.

1888–89 Studies Horace and John Milton during a high-school postgraduate year (September 1888 to June 1889), does odd jobs, continues to write verse.

1890 Herman and Emma marry.

1891–93 Is special student at Harvard (September 1891 to June 1893).

1892 Robinson's father Edward Robinson dies (July). Robinson has operation (October) for inner-ear necrosis, a disease that was to cause permanent partial deafness.

1893 Family experiences financial reverses.

1893–96 In Gardiner, works at odd jobs, writes poetry, writes but fails to sell short stories.

1896 Publishes *The Torrent and The Night Before* at his own expense; Robinson's mother Mary Robinson dies (November); Herman and Emma Robinson move into Robinson family home in Gardiner.

1897 Robinson breaks with Herman (autumn), lives briefly in New York City (December); *The Children of the Night.*

1898 Lives in Cambridge, New York, and in Gardiner and Winthrop, Maine.

1899 Serves (January–June) as secretary on administrative staff of Charles William Eliot,* president of Harvard; brother Dean Robinson dies (September); Robinson returns to New York (October).

1900 Robinson family estate begins to decline (summer).

1901 Robinson family fortune vanishes (November).

1902 *Captain Craig.*

1903 Gardiner family home sold by Herman Robinson; Herman and Emma Robinson often reside separately.

1903–04 Herman sells family house; Robinson works as time-checker during construction of New York's first subway (Autumn 1903 to August 1904).

1905 Works in drygoods store owned by the father of his friend William Edward Butler in Boston (January–May).

1905–09 Is appointed by President Theodore Roosevelt* as nominal employee in New York office of Collector of Customs (June 1905–June 1909).

1906–13 Writes plays (not produced) and novels (later destroyed).

1909 Herman Robinson dies in Boston (February); Robinson briefly visits Emma in Farmingdale, Maine (Autumn); she refuses to marry him (September).

1910 Lives in Chocorua, New Hampshire (July–October); *The Town Down the River: A Book of Poems.*

1911 Begins to spend summers at MacDowell Colony* in Peterborough, New Hampshire (through 1934).

1914 Receives anonymous legacy of $4,000 (from John Hays Gardiner*); *Van Zorn: A Comedy in Three Acts.*

1915 *The Porcupine: A Drama in Three Acts.*

1916 *The Man Against the Sky*; critics begin to recognize Robinson's true stature as a poet.

1917 *Merlin: A Poem*; begins to receive financial gifts from anonymous donors.

1918 Emma again declines to marry Robinson (December).

1919 *The New York Times Review of Books* (December 21) celebrates his 50th birthday.

1920 *Lancelot: A Poem*; *The Three Taverns: A Book of Poems.*

1921 *Avon's Harvest; Collected Poems.*

1922 Awarded first of three Pulitzer Prizes;* honorary degree, Yale.

1923 Visits England (April–July); *Roman Bartholow.*

1924 *The Man Who Died Twice*; second Pulitzer Prize.

1925 Visits Gardiner for last time; honorary degree, Bowdoin; *Dionysus in Doubt: A Book of Poems.*

1927 Emma again declines marriage; *Tristram*; *Collected Poems* (5 vols.); third Pulitzer Prize.

1928 *Sonnets: 1889–1927.*

1929	Awarded gold medal by National Institute of Arts and Letters; *Cavender's House.*
1930	*The Glory of the Nightingales.*
1931	*Selected Poems; Matthias at the Door.*
1932	*Nicodemus: A Book of Poems.*
1933	*Talifer.*
1934	*Amaranth.*
1935	Dies of stomach cancer (April 6), in New York hospital; *King Jasper* (published posthumously).
1996	Edwin Arlington Robinson Poetry Festival organized by Mark Melnicove and held at Gardiner.
1997	Robinson Poetry Festival again held, Gardiner.
2001	*The New York Times* publishes Robinson's "The House on the Hill" (October 1) to console Americans stunned by terrorists' 9/11 strike.

THE ENCYCLOPEDIA

"Aaron Stark" (1896). Sonnet. Aaron Stark is "meager," and in addition "Cursed and unkempt, shrewd, shrivelled, and morose." He is a miser, with "eyes like little dollars in the dark," and he barks and snarls his words through "fang"-like teeth. This "loveless" man enjoys adverse gossip about himself as he "shambled through the town." Only when he hears piteous words does he laugh.

Paul Zietlow regards Robinson as a regional poet because he often "creates the impression of a whole society inhabiting a specific place which can be identified with a particular part of a real country." Zietlow says that "Aaron Stark," along with several other poems, helps to create Robinson's Tilbury Town. Gardiner gossip must have had it that Aaron Stark was based on a deceased town miser named Nathaniel M. Whitmore, because Robinson wrote to Laura E. Richards* (March 9, 1902) to deny it. Still, Emma Robinson* and Ruth Nivison* say that "Aaron Stark" was a partial character sketch of Nathaniel Whitmore, of Kingsbury Street, Gardiner. Robinson didn't need any literary source for his brilliant character sketch, but it is true that he wrote his friend Harry de Forest Smith* (April 16, 1893) to recommend *L'Avare* by Molière, calling the play "easy and . . . magnificent." William C. Childers points out that Moses's brother Aaron has a rod that when cast becomes a serpent (Exodus 7:9–10), while Robinson says that Aaron is "A loveless exile moving with a staff."

Ellsworth Barnard notes that "every word expressive of a physical trait [of Stark] has spiritual overtones." Glauco Cambon feels that "[i]n those eyes of his [Aaron's] 'like little dollars in the dark' we find a Dantean critic of character and culture, telescoped into the flash of one image." Denis Donoghue says the reader's response is subtly altered by the contrary adjectives Robinson uses to describe Stark.

As for Robinson and the sonnet, of which his "Aaron Stark" comes first alphabetically, Richard Cary conveniently summarizes Robinson's attitude toward the sonnet, perhaps Robinson's favorite poetic form: "Thalia," the first poem he published, is a sonnet. He could write a sonnet in 20 minutes or could labor over one for 20 days, or even for six weeks. He said that a single sonnet line might come to him out of nowhere but that the other 13 lines often proved arduous. He once described the sonnet as a shackling mode. He opined that there were only 50 good sonnets in existence. He once complained that a sonnet taking a week to create might earn him only $10. (Sources: Barnard, 160; Cambon, 57; Cary [1974], 58; Childers [1955], 227; Donoghue, 36; E. Robinson, 11; *Selected Letters*, 51; *Untriangulated Stars*, 93; Zietlow, 188)

"After the War" *see* **"Battle After War"**

"Afterthoughts" (1928). Sonnet. The narrator and his friend walked together, then proceeded separately "Into the dark," as was their custom. If his friend hadn't returned, the narrator might have remained "unaware" of the man's distinct qualities. But he returned and said something. It was brief; but it was close to "the sublime." The two never met again.

Throughout the text an asterisk denotes an entry in the encyclopedia.

"Alcaics" *see* "Late Summer"

Alcoholism and Robinson. Many writers, as well as countless millions of other people, turn to drink in search of relief from a myriad of personal troubles or for alleged inhibition-freeing stimulation and even inspiration. For whatever reasons, Robinson seems to have started consuming alcohol early, though moderately at first, to be sure. Laura E. Richards* reports that Robinson in high school associated with a few small clubs of boys, one of which met and occasionally drank "beer of doubtful origin and more doubtful flavor." She adds that while at Harvard, Robinson liked "a goblet of stout, or another of the dusky-brown beverages that he affected, for his solace." Like the titular character in "Miniver Cheevy," Robinson surely thought he "had reasons" to explain why he often "kept on drinking." His brother Herman Robinson* drank too much. When their father Edward Robinson* grew ill and lingered, he turned to alcohol and spiritualism for surcease, and died slowly. Their mother Mary Robinson* died so horribly of black diphtheria that her sons had to prepare her for burial and bury her themselves. Robinson's brother Dean Robinson,* who also drank, committed suicide. These and other family miseries must have seemed unbearable at times to the initially unsuccessful poet. He also suffered all of his mature life from a chronic earache, which surgery failed to help and the pain of which liquor lessened, if only temporarily. Poverty and fear of professional failure also combined to aggravate his misery during his middle years. In addition, non-literary work, especially from 1902 to 1911 or so, tempted him to hit the saloons in lower Manhattan and Greenwich Village, where, he once said, he could strike up temporary little glowing friendships, smile serenely, and talk with unwonted fluency. He called his bar-hopping "shopping," sometimes bought a bottle of rum on the way back to his rented room, and rocked, drank, and recited poetry with any handy friend. He drank enormously many evenings after work in the subway and returned the next morning with a hangover. He once told a friend that he flirted with the idea of killing himself with drink.

Robinson swore off for a while, beginning in 1911, to please his patroness Marian Nivens MacDowell;* he rationalized that he could not write and drink at the same time. Her influence, and that of the MacDowell Colony* in general, according to Bacon Collamore,* saved Robinson "from the deleterious effects of heavy drinking," and that "many [friends] were surprised at his recovery." At least once, Robinson explained to friends that he carefully abstained before 6:00 p.m. Using the third person, he confessed by letter (August 29, 1918) to Richards that for 10 years he consumed more rum than he should have. When Prohibition began, Robinson took to drinking again, in protest, as he explained. Earlier, he also rationalized in a letter (July 31, 1924) to Richards, that it is foolish to classify alcohol as a drug and that it is less dangerous than other forms of necessary stimulants. Hermann Hagedorn,* who observed and described Robinson's monumental capacity for alcohol, said that it did little for Robinson but bring out pink spots in his cheeks and make him more fluent in conversation. Chard Powers Smith* said that although Robinson specialized in straight whiskey, outdrinking four to one any and all friends on given evenings, he could easily quit at any time; therefore, Smith managed to conclude that Robinson was not an alcoholic. Estelle Kaplan remarks flatly that "*Dionysus in Doubt* is too vivid a portrayal of inebriate experience to find its source in anything but reality." (Sources: Barnard, 38, 182, 279; Collamore, ix, 21; Dardis; Franchere, 95; Hagedorn, 198, 201, 205–06, 235–36, 247, 332–34, 356; Kaplan, 7; Neff, 218; *Selected Letters*, 111, 137–38; Richards [1936], 31, 36–37; C. Smith, 27, 33–34)

"Alma Mater" (1910). Sonnet. A man knocks at the narrator's door. He is divinely handsome, and strangely attractive though "battered." The narrator wonders if they ever met before and asks. But the man moans, cries out, and falls "shapeless on the floor." The narrator wonders when he knew this man, why he came here — "Love, warning, malediction, hunger, fear?" Also from what abysmal "scum" come "these rags of memory?"

Emery Neff remarks that it "was the almost unrecognizable wreck out of his [Robinson's] past who knocks at the door in the powerful sonnet 'Alma Mater.'" Scott Donaldson more specifically suggests that the dishevelled stranger Robinson is portraying may be "Joseph Lewis French,[*] dilettante and congenital sponge who often 'borrowed' money and clothing from Robinson," who knew and tolerated him. (Sources: Donaldson [1969], 47; Neff, 156)

"The Altar" (1896). Sonnet. The poet dreams about an altar with a persuasive flame promising so much that love, though warned by sadness, impelled a stream of people toward that furious flame. The poet, though hesitating, is thrilled the way the others are, until he awakens. He thinks about insects flying toward flames, which "must burn somehow for the best."

Robinson suggests that we are all caught in a naturalistic world in which our instincts impel us to trouble despite our being warned by experience. Edwin S. Fussell relates the "desperate optimism" expressed here to similar thoughts in *In Memoriam* by Alfred, Lord Tennyson. Ellsworth Barnard hears "the note of redemption sounded . . . strongly" in "The Altar." (Sources: Barnard, 201; Fussell [1954], 94)

Amaranth (New York: Macmillan, 1934). Narrative poem, in four parts.

I. Fargo, 45, has painted for 10 years, badly. Then he heard a voice telling him to quit, since an art career is a "misfit burden," "a cross . . . not his to carry." He burned all of his works except one mediocre effort. He naps and dreams.

Now he is back at a wharf he knew and is once again tempted to drown himself. The voice returns. Its owner is a coalescence of "All who have been, / And all alive and all unborn," with dangerously sunbright eyes. He tells Fargo that he is still in the wrong world, must now follow him, and calls himself "Amaranth — / The flower that never fades."

They enter the Tavern of the Vanquished, a dark, ancient place. Fargo saw it before, when ignorant. Amaranth divides its occupants into those who avoid "the mirrors that are in my eyes" and those who freely look at them. Evensong, the flute player, warns Fargo about Amaranth's eyes, plays his flute awry, and is smiled at by his companions. Edward Figg is a misguided lawyer. A "playful fate" led Doctor Styx into the wrong work. The Reverend Pascal Flax joined the clergy because he was loquacious; but after looking into Amaranth's eyes, he quit, now drinks too much, and still talks. Pink and Atlas sponge on him. Pink is a deliberately ambiguous poet, who

> . . . cuts and sets his words
> With an exotic skill so scintillating
> That no two proselytes who worship him
> Are mystified in the same way exactly.

Atlas quit being a stevedore, became addicted to painting, and also therefore drinks mightily. Evensong summarizes thus:

> We are the reconciled initiates,
> Who know that we are nothing in men's eyes
> That we set out to be — and should have been,
> Had we seen better. We see better now.

Members of the group argue about the importance of roots. Young Pink criticizes the past. Flax, older, disagrees, and Styx says Pink is "sick of more / Than roots." Figg is depressed. Pink says he has desires. Atlas swaggers off to paint. Although Amaranth warns Pink to stay naively busy and continue dreaming, Pink first tells Amaranth to get lost, defies his eyes, but when he looks at them announces he'll go hang himself. Styx avers that Pink will survive a while since "Poets are of a toughness, / And they are slow to kill." Evensong honors Pink with an elegiac dirge, unpraiseworthy and smiled at. When Evensong says Fargo, their "new friend," must and will remain in the Tavern, Styx lauds Evensong's astuteness. Evensong proposes "drink to all we should have been, / Telling ourselves again it is no matter."

II. Fargo walks past silent houses along familiar streets. He hears his name and some vicious mocking. Complaining people hold picks and shovels and have "clay / Upon their feet." They say Fargo has returned to "the wrong world." Amaranth silences them, warns them to clean up or they will fall into the next graves they dig. He advises Fargo to avoid these gravediggers, instead to prefer the Tavern occupants and come along.

They enter a house from which many depart, including theologians, philosophers, economists, "deceived inventors," and "spine-weary gardeners." All have led themselves astray. Fargo says he knows nothing but that he is here. In a room, they encounter Evensong, Atlas, Flax, Figg, and Styx, and see Pink hanging like a picture. When Evensong toots another dirge, Pink's eyes flutter and he criticizes the music and remarks that Atlas "repudiated and betrayed" his talent as a stevedore. Figg complains that if Pink isn't dead the others are complicit. Denying this, Pink comprehensively insults all the others for being "dry rot walking"; he insists that there is better music than Evensong's, there is a different divinity than Flax can know, and there is a "correct elusive juice" Styx can't find to cure indecisiveness. Praising Fargo's honest uneasiness, Pink asks them all to leave since he is as dead as he can be. Flax complains that

> Poets, whatever the end,
> Should know a little more than most of us
> Of our obscurities.

Fargo sees wanderers, who, Amaranth says, are lost if they don't hear him. He wonders why Fargo listened to him but still came back to this wrong place.

They enter a different, very old house; in it are Evensong and his friend Miss Elaine Amelia Watchman, who is perpetually writing. She has a cat named Ampersand, who talks ugly, is shaped like "&," and hisses at Amaranth. Evensong says Amaranth whispers what many wrongly call doubt. He says that God made Fargo a splendid builder of water pumps, but then "the free thread of his fate" got permanently knotted with another thread. Evensong wishes he and Miss Watchman had never been walled apart by art. She gets him to play more music. He says Amaranth will be uneasy until he learns why Fargo returned here and asks Watchman to query Fargo. She tells the others to leave since she must keep writing. Evensong advises her not to "see / Too far before you, or too far behind." When Watchman boldly says she plans to see ahead, Ama-

ranth and then the others, except Fargo, ask her why. Figg warns her that they took "the wrong road." Styx tells her to get a life, to enjoy her tea, her reading, and her cat. Flax says God Himself is surely apprising her of her limited vision. Laughing but worried, Watchman says Evensong agrees that she has a "little spirit," which protects her from "Love, doubt, regret, or fear," and that her writings will survive after she is dust. When they tell her Pink looked into Amaranth's eyes and has hanged himself, she criticizes Pink for his puzzling, "enameled words / . . . [that are] dead." Then she grabs Amaranth, peers into his eyes, but then staggers and turns cold. Evensong opens "the book of yours that you like best," and says it "will be read / when you and I are dust," but finds the pages to be dust. Screaming, she also becomes dust. Gathering everything into an envelope, Evensong says that there was no surrender in her and that if truth visited her "Where she was living" it would have killed her slowly. Ampersand follows him out. Amaranth advises Fargo to accompany Evensong to muse in seclusion and to beware of those gravediggers.

III. Fargo walks past more graves and wonders why he is still there. He must escape illusions and "return / To his right world." Suddenly an old man appears, calls himself Ipswich, has eyes with burned-out fires in them, and says he dreamed about inventions that more practical scientists put into reality. Ipswich laments the fact that his wife, now at rest here, was uncomplaining but that her voice rebukes him now. Beyond the wharf is a rusty ship full of old men singing and old women voicing "thanksgiving and release." They hold up Lethe-like beverages. Ipswitch offers such a drink to Fargo, saying, "Since I made this drink, / We are the souls of our misguided selves." Fargo is tempted, because

> There was a diabolical bouquet
> Enveloping and intoxicating him,
> As if a siren that he could not feel
> Or see were breathing in his arms.

But, warned by a power (Amaranth), Fargo discards the glass, and it breaks. Ipswitch, weeping, boards the ship, which sails off, groans, clanks, hisses, and then burns and sinks. Amaranth appears and tells Fargo this: Joyful exits such as the vain boat people planned fail; if Fargo had gone along, he would have been doomed too; he should leave.

Fargo enters another house, where he finds Atlas drinking and confidently painting. Figg contends that Atlas's picture is of a blue horse. Flax, sipping in peace, theorizes that today's "Sinners in art believe there are short roads / To glory without form." Altas warns everyone that he is both indignant and strong. Styx agrees to call his picture a horse, wishes it included some recognizable lines, but says the more he drinks the more the horse appears. When Evensong says they should agree it's a horse, Atlas refuses to accept the fellow's sugary compliments and wants no pity from the wretched fellow.

Working on a fresh bottle, Atlas boasts about his unique artistic vision. So what if he was once a stevedore? A Carpenter once changed professions. Atlas, saying he is fearless, might toss everyone out the window — except Amaranth, who puzzles him. Amaranth says he would query Atlas only if the man became timid. Atlas reckons he will be numbered "among the masters." When Amaranth wishes him peace, Atlas boldly gazes into Amaranth's eyes, falls into a chair, and wonders whether he's just looked at God or the Devil. Amaranth calls Atlas a stranger to himself, whereupon Atlas slashes all his paintings to shreds, hopes Amaranth lives to curse everyone, exits, and collapses with a thud. Amaranth again warns Fargo about those gravediggers.

IV. Fargo enters another room, both familiar and not, with Evensong, and starts to paint again. Evensong wishes he had built a place "In the right world," to lock out the past, which brought him here. He had to tell his "small offspring" that he wasn't their father but that their mother was devilish. He asks Fargo why he returned. But Fargo instead paints Evensong's portrait, compulsively. He says he once painted freely, intelligently, but erroneously. Evensong reminisces about a friend with his heart in his work but so unfocused that he took to drink. When Fargo says Atlas lived for art, Evensong says Atlas lived

for paint, used colors, but never learned to draw. Fargo says if he is here much longer, he may drown himself. Evensong says Amaranth won't let this happen. Ampersand enters to see Fargo's painting, says many people desert responsibilities to view art work, and concludes that "Art is cruel, / And so is nature," and so is everything else. When asked, Ampersand says he doesn't like Fargo's work because it lacks "crinkles." He says Miss Watchman "liked writing more than she liked truth, / Or life." Catching a fly, Ampersand ruminates on "nature's law," the fly's fate, and his own "problematical free will," then concludes that

> the same God
> Who sees a sparrow on the ground shows us
> The way to catch him, and we [cats] cannot choose.

He asks Fargo why, if he has free will, he's here painting. Amaranth, now present with Figg and Styx, announces that they came to pay homage to the monstrously ambitious Atlas. All attend his funeral. When Fargo looks at the many graves, they are

> Like waves, interminably motionless
> And held by some unnatural command
> In solid calm upon a sea of earth,
> Where there was never to be storm or change,
> Or a sun shining.

One of the gravediggers, who are pounding Atlas under, says that Fargo was too stupid to stay away and they'll get him. Amaranth orders the verminous diggers to shut up and eat. Evensong says he's still here, undeceived now. Amaranth counters by noting that he whispers messages to all but that he's mostly unheeded. Figg expresses regret for following another's example instead of his own flame, now extinguished; at least he doesn't suffer pains like these others. Styx rebukes Figg, says he would rather see with Ampersand's Egyptian eyes than with Figg's eyes, and concludes that the dead are dead. Flax is comforted to know that his God lives within him, even though he formerly told obvious lies from his pulpit because he once "thought words were life." He believes that at a later reunion Pink, being a poet, will have "a gauge for us that we have not."

Amaranth comprehensively addresses the group thus: Pink's stings, with acidulous truth in them, left each itching differently; he hopes they won't be sorry, even in this "wrong world," that they were ever born; Styx has much to learn yet; Fargo should say that Amaranth's eyes no longer terrify him, should, when he permanently leaves, recall what he left behind here, shouldn't look for Atlas, gone, shouldn't "be sorry for the dead," should instead "Lament them as you may, or treasure them." When Fargo looks up, Figg, Styx, Flax, and the graves are all gone and the gray sky has color. Evensong says he "saw too late to go away," bids Fargo goodbye, and hopes his pumps "Pour strength and blessing" over him, but no paint. Amaranth then says this: He would prefer to have his eyes please "those who see too late"; Fargo, who heard his voice without understanding the source, is free; most who hear him remain vain, choose badly; there is a master superior to Amaranth; "only the resigned / And reconciled will own me a friend"; with more wisdom, Fargo will now leave. Fargo notices that Amaranth and Evensong are fading into a mist, a comforting light flares, and his well-known room is becoming visible. He awakens from his long dream, is joyful and grateful at being delivered, but regrets that Amaranth and Evensong are gone.

Robinson in *Amaranth* demonstrates what happens to people when, having chosen wrong careers, they either face or avoid the truth. Fargo saves himself. But lost are Atlas and Pink, whom Robinson skewers as arty modernists, while Watchman's works collapse, and Evensong, Figg, Flax, and Styx hang on as unredeemed misfits. Robinson, however, not only dramatizes the consequences of wrong choices these losers made but also is caught himself, as his characters' comments make clear, on the horns of the age-old philosophical dilemma of free will vs. predestinarianism. Bacon Collamore* quotes from a letter (November 20, 1933) in which Robinson says that the theme of *Amaranth* is the problem one has if one aims at professional accomplishment without being equipped mentally and spiritually to succeed, and that Amaranth himself embodies related characteristics of conscience, fate, and God.

Chard Powers Smith* lauds Robinson's success in *Amaranth* for combining tragedy, comedy, and nightmare within a strict framework more artistically than any author had succeeded in doing since Henrik Ibsen wrote *Peer Gynt*. Jay Martin sees *Amaranth* as "fantastic and surreal, . . . a Dantean journey through the vividly-lighted rooms, streets, and houses of the mind." Elements in the journey also allude to trips down into the Hades depicted in classical literature. Martin adds that "Fargo wanders through the levels of his self . . . ego, super-ego, and id, exploring aspects of himself by projecting them as personages. . . . He passes through representations of alienation, faithlessness, egotism, despair, and the pleasure-principle . . . in preparation for looking into the eyes of Amaranth . . . [after which] he will see the process of his own remaking, his revivified self." Hyatt H. Waggoner notes that the allegorical nature of Robinson's characters in *Amaranth* causes them to resemble characters in two stories by Nathaniel Hawthorne, "The Great Carbuncle" and "The Christmas Banquet." Earlier, however, Arthur Edgar DuBois (b. 1904, author of a 1934 book on tragic comedy in nineteenth-century drama) had likened his friend Robinson to Hawthorne, arrestingly calling each "a wallflower rather than a dancer, a coroner rather than a doctor," both highly observant in each category. The name Evensong must derive from "Evensong," the name of a poem by Robinson's friend Alfred Hyman Louis.* The name Ipswich could derive from something as close as Ipswich, New Hampshire, a few miles south of the MacDowell Colony* at Peterborough, New Hampshire. Ellsworth Barnard sees Ipswich's powerful potion as alcohol, opium, or perhaps "a spiritual drug" akin to "extreme religious revivalism." Although many critics are effusive in their praise of *Amaranth*, Denis Donoghue regards it as the only "mere failure" among Robinson's often prolix long poems. Ivor Winters regards Pink's general insult leveled at the "dry rot walking" to be "one of the best passages of the poem" but feels that later incidents drag. (Sources: Barnard, 293; Collamore, 57; Donoghue, 32; DuBois, 12; Martin, 148, 149; C. Smith, 367; Waggoner, 291; Winters, 121)

"Amaryllis" (1897). Sonnet. The narrator is wandering in some woods when an old fellow totters up and persuades him to come see the grave he prepared for Amaryllis. The narrator is soon standing for a long time looking at the skin and bones of an old woman. Far outside the woods, happy sounds of successful work only contribute to the narrator's sense of loneliness and sorrow that Amaryllis had become so old.

Using simple rhymes, Robinson relates the old man's "tone" to the old woman's "bone[s]," and contrasts "glad" commerce outside and the narrator's inner "sad[ness]." Amaryllis here be simply represent old age. William C. Childers, however, suggests the following: "Ever since Theocritus first used the name *Amaryllis* in his *Idylls*, it has been a favorite one for shepherdesses and country lasses in classical poetry." Childers therefore concludes that since Robinson read the works of many poets, including Ovid, Virgil, Edmund Spenser, Robert Herrick, and John Milton, all of whom use the name Amaryllis, he may be employing it here to represent poetry in general; also, when he calls his Amaryllis "ancient," he may be alluding to "the longevity of the poetic tradition." Being more specific, Emma Robinson* and Ruth Nivison* identify Amaryllis here with Lydia Ann Palmer, the wife of Seth Palmer* and the sister of Mary Palmer, Robinson's mother. (Sources: Childers [1956]; E. Robinson, 11)

"And So It Was" *see* **"Not Always I–II"**

"Annandale Again" (1929). Poem. The narrator is thinking about Annandale when, bang, the fellow knocks on the door. He is unchanged despite years of having been far away. He begins talking. He says that the places he has visited and the people he has seen are of little importance, since everything is pretty much alike. He thought life was ended when his wife Miriam died. But then he married Damaris. God doesn't want us to ask very often the why about events. Damaris is home with Annandale now, and the narrator is welcome to see her effect in Annandale's eyes. She understands him. Annandale generalizes that we are all in a pleasant enough cage, with God our keeper. Damaris may regard the trap as a home. Noting that the narrator is a

physician, Annandale says that those of a scientific bent ought to pray to discern the essence of life. Annandale dreads the day when Damaris, who knows so much about him, reveals it. He is beginning to guess about her discoveries. He wrote a book when Miriam was alive; it concerned another woman. Damaris wept while reading it, for she saw discernments in it of herself, although she hadn't yet met Annandale. She found recompense by hurting him casually, then turned contentedly passive again. All now proceeds calmly. At this point, the narrator explains that Annandale, in harmony with Damaris, didn't return home again. Fate may have felt offended. Annandale was destroyed in a street accident. The narrator was a witness. He visited Damaris, was evidently kind, and will ask whether Annandale knew more than he might have said to her. The narrator has no answer yet. Women often indefinitely forget what they gain by loss. Wise Damaris may still be wondering.

This poem may contains hidden allusions to Robinson's relationship with his widowed sister-in-law Emma Robinson.* Robinson probably encountered the name Damaris in the Bible; Damaris, an Athenian woman, was converted to Christianity by Paul's preaching (Acts 17:34). Robinson may also have associated Damaris with the Damariscotta River, some 20 miles east of Gardiner, Maine. (See also *The Book of Annandale*, "How Annandale Went Out," and "My Methods and Meanings.")

"Another Dark Lady" (1914). Sonnet. The narrator advises his female addressee not to think he cares where she is, so long as she doesn't come back to him. She is as dreadful as evil persons in any horrible story, as bad even as the diabolical Lilith. He once loved her; so he can't hate her now. In a forest he once compared her feet to beech roots. Yes, but unlike them, "yours are cloven."

Family rumor had it that Robinson was both spiritually and physically attracted to a pleasant young lady from Boston Brahmin society. She was well educated, wrote a little poetry and fiction, and admired his poetry. In the summer of 1898, she was visiting her friends John Hays Gardiner* and his wife in Gardiner, Maine, and walked in the nearby woods — of beech, maple, and oak — with Robinson. He was sad when nothing satisfactory came of their brief relationship. She may have been in his mind when he wrote "Another Dark Lady," the title of which suggests that he was aware that a dark lady had troubled an earlier sonneteer, namely William Shakespeare. In a letter (1914) to Edith Brower,* Robinson said he composed his sonnet in 20 minutes, in a little contest, and got $20 for winning. Hermann Hagedorn* says that Robinson wrote this poem partly to throw off curious readers' speculation about his private life. Edwin S. Fussell relates this sardonic sonnet "to the Elizabeth railing lyric" and cites examples. (Sources: Brower, 160; Fussell [1954], 61; Hagedorn, 296)

"The *Antigone* of Sophocles" (1894–1895). Fragmentary translations. Robinson persuaded Harry de Forest Smith* to provide him with a close literal prose translation of Sophocles's *Antigone*, which he would then render in metrical form. The incomplete result, in five unnamed sections, is mainly in blank verse.

1. Creon's pleasure meshes with that of the speaker.

2. Man is a marvel, sailing, plowing, and trapping, training, and making use of birds, fish, horses, and bulls.

3. The worst thing man ever made is money, which hurts cities, families, and souls; it teaches people to be both clever and evil.

4. Man has learned to think, be wise, speak, and avoid the cold. But he can't defeat either the future or death. Man is shrewd, and acts both rightly and wrongly. He is best when honoring the state and the gods. What about Antigone, wretched daughter of wretched Oedipus?

5. The guard faithfully but reluctantly brings Antigone to Creon and reports that he found her burying the corpse of Polynices, her brother, in violation of Creon's order. The guard and his assistants first saw her beside it and crying, "With a bitter wailing, like a bird / Over an empty nest." She put dust on the body, reverently poured an offering from a brass urn, and then calmly submitted to arrest. Creon dismisses the guard and orders Antigone to explain. She says that his laws are less than those of heaven, that the real sorrow would have been to leave "The child of my own mother to lie dead / Without a mound above him," and that, if her action be folly, why "Then I am charged with folly by a fool."

Robinson knew little Greek but undertook the eventually unsuccessful project of translating Sophocles's classic with the utmost seriousness. He makes use of bits of his translation in *Captain Craig*, the hero of which mentions Sophocles occasionally. However, it seems extravagant of Ellsworth Barnard to contend that Robinson regarded his "translation of *Antigone* as the cornerstone of his career." James A. Notopoulos wrote in 1944 that Smith said that Robinson "believed" that his *Antigone* manuscript "was . . . destroyed." Lewis E. Weeks Jr. relayed in 1969 an indirect report from Ruth Nivison* that "the contents of the box [containing Robinson's *Antigone* papers] were used by the children [Ruth's] to play and consequently destroyed." Wallace L. Anderson reported in 1980 that in a letter (September 13, 1916) Robinson sent to Harry Smith, he says that when he visited Gardiner in 1909 he found that Ruth's children had opened a box containing some of his books and his *Antigone* and scattered the contents. (Sources: W. Anderson [1980], 54; Barnard, 139; Cary [1975], 18–23; Notopoulos, 109; *Untriangulated Stars*; Weeks [1984], 150)

"Archibald's Example" (1920). Poem. The poet sits with Archibald, who is regularly to be seen in his chair frowning away would-be trespassers. He looks beyond his clover to his green hill. He explains that his trees were there once, but they scratched the sun and made "him" (the sun) bleed as it went down behind them. Since they wouldn't rot in 50 years, he cut them down. They did neither God nor anyone any good and moreover were "thieves of light." He adds that Nature approved his action. Archibald generalizes that "Trees are like men, sometimes." Continuing to look, he remembers the time when the trees were still there.

Robinson lets Archibald's callous disregard of nature and of the pleasures nature can give others speak for itself. Emma Robinson* and Ruth Nivison* identify the scene that inspired this poem as an avenue of larches at the Palmer family residence in Whitefield, Maine. Horace Gregory and Marya Zaturenska praise Robinson's "scrupulously unadorned understatement" in "Archibald's Example" and compare it to "The Garden Seat" by Thomas Hardy. (Sources: Gregory and Zaturenska, 129, 130; E. Robinson, 17)

Arthurian Trilogy. In order of publication, Robinson's *Merlin* (1917) was followed by his *Lancelot* (1920) and then *Tristram* (1927). In the chronological order of their events, *Tristram* is first, followed by *Merlin* and then *Lancelot*. James T. Tryon,* Robinson's fellow student at Harvard, reports that when they discussed literature, Robinson "was interested in the Arthurian legends." Tryon adds that "[a]lthough he did not say that he intended to make these legends subject for verse, I was not surprised to find that in after years he had written on them." Glauco Cambon, calling Robinson "Knight of the Grail," compares him to "[t]he knights of the Grail [who] are the heroes of time; they lose when they think they are conquering it, they [like Robinson] conquer when they acknowledge its law."

Laurence Perrine (December 1969) contrasts *Idylls of the King* by Alfred, Lord Tennyson with Robinson's trilogy, concluding that "[w]here Tennyson's is a rigid moral conventionalism, in which judgments are made by a legalistic application of rules, Robinson's is a complex morality, in which judgments are based on a consideration of all aspects of a unique situation." Later, Perrine (June 1974) discusses sources and analogues with which Robinson was familiar and also his varied opinions of them; they are Malory's *Le Morte d'Arthur*, *The Vulgate Merlin*, Tennyson, "The Defence of Guenevere" by William Morris, *Le Roman de Tristan et Iseult* by Joseph Bédier, *Tristan und Isolde* by Richard Wagner, "Tristram of Lyonesse" by Algernon Charles Swinburne, *Tristram and Iseult* by Matthew Arnold, the fragmentary and posthumous *The Holy Graal* by Richard Hovey, *Tristan and Isolt* by

John Masefield, "The Vision of Sir Launfal" by James Russell Lowell, *The Great Maze* by Hermann Hagedorn,* and *Gawain and the Green Knight*.

Charles Cestre* praises Robinson's approach to the Arthurian legend for this reason: "Conscious of having discovered new virtualities of beauty, truth and human pathos in the old tale, he would abstract himself from what had been done before, and set to giving expression to his own sense of the grandeur of the theme, its emotional appeal and symbolic value." Henry W. Wells says that "[a]n idealistic philosophy and an innate nobility preserve Robinson's Arthurian romances from the tragic darkness with which their stories threaten us." Louise Dauner comments that "[t]he problem of what exactly Robinson added to the traditional characters of the Arthurian women is . . . an interesting one; we know that he endowed them with tremendous passion and intellect. He himself noted that he tried to make Guinevere 'interesting.'" Nathan Comfort Starr [1954] writes splendidly about the whole trilogy. He says that, as an Arthurian, Robinson "aimed to reconcile traditional characters and situations with the pragmatic twentieth century." Starr reasons that *Lancelot* was easier for Robinson to write than *Merlin* was, mainly "because it called for less invention." Starr conjectures that "probably . . . never before has the collapse of Arthur's kingdom been described with such emotional intensity." He regards *Lancelot* as "perhaps more sharp and exigent in its emotions" than *Merlin*, which, however, "is a little more moving of the two." As for Tristram and Isolt of Ireland, he says that "[i]n no other version of the legend has the suffering of the lovers been so movingly and even harrowingly portrayed"; but he adds that *Tristram* succeeds least, and that "[t]he reasons probably lie in the modern change of emphasis on Tristram's place in the story and in Robinson's stress on the conflicts of love rather than its rewards." As for the heroines in the trilogy, "the final estimate" for Starr [1977] is that they are powerful because they are mentally strong. Except for Isolt of Brittany, they dispute masterfully, "even while breaking their arguments against the immovable rock of their lovers' objections." They don't surrender; "they only die, either literally or in the spirit. Their whole strength lies in the dialectic of frustrated desire." When Irving Howe adverts to the Arthurian cycle in an essay often demeaning Robinson with too-faint praise, he expresses fear that "I am aware of straining my readers' credulity in saying that *Merlin* and *Lancelot* . . . are profound explorations of human suffering." Scott Donaldson likes the trilogy less than that. He quotes a letter (September 29, 1894) to Harry de Forest Smith* in which Robinson gripes about his "old fault of over condensation" which he "hope[d] to overcome . . . someday"; then Donaldson concludes that the result of Robinson's overcoming that fault was "usually unhappy . . . , as in the case of the Arthurian cycle of long verse novels." Louis Coxe negatively dogmatizes that

> to demythologize his [Robinson's] basic [Arthurian] plot and fabric was a fatal flaw. . . . We cannot accept these poems as natural emanations from the past, the profound, the evocative, nor can we see any more relevance to the lives of people living in the earlier decades of this [twentieth] century than the general notion of worlds breaking up and the death of God and so forth. Robinson does not give his actors anything to *do* [Coxe's emphasis].

Disputing Coxe, Celia Morris says that, in *Merlin* and *Lancelot* at least, Robinson "conceives that human worth and dignity lie not . . . in youth, purity and innocence but rather in grappling with guilt and loss. Integrity means fully . . . recognizing, among other things, the way deep needs can make one hurt others and cripple oneself." Morris concludes, poignantly, that "Robinson's poems [here] . . . become almost meditations, both by the poet and by the characters themselves, on . . . responsibility . . . [following] the attempt to live a life both full and wholly admirable [which] will fail." Ronald Moran generalizes about all three Arthurian narratives to the effect that "[i]n detailed observation that often is tedious and conversations that are often lifeless, Robinson presents characters on the verge of or just after a trauma." Louis Untermeyer* asserts, too assuredly, that in Robinson's Arthurian trilogy "[t]he thoughts are his but not the emotions — the conflicting passions

were disturbances he either did not understand or could not master." John Hurt Fisher suggests the following three chivalric dilemmas: in *Merlin*, love vs. duty; in *Lancelot*, earthly love vs. divine love; in *Tristram*, love conflicted. Richard P. Adams regards Robinson's long narrative poems, beginning with *Merlin* and including, among other works, *Lancelot* and *Tristram*, as "weak in structure, sparse in imagery, and monotonous in tone and style." See also "The Arthurian Trilogy and 'Rabbi Ben Ezra,'" *Merlin*, *Lancelot*, and *Tristram*. (Sources: R. Adams, 119; Cambon, 71; Cestre, 67–68; Coxe, 137; Dauner, 152; Davis [1969]; Donaldson [1966], 221; Fisher; I. Howe, 107; Moran [2003], 3234; Celia Morris, 88–89, 97; Perrine [December 1969], 417; Perrine [June 1974]; Starr [1954], 21, 31, 34, 36, 37, 76, 81; Starr [1977], 258; Tryon, 11; Wells, 319; Winters, 61–96; Untermeyer, 16; *Untriangulated Stars*, 166–67)

"The Arthurian Trilogy and 'Rabbi Ben Ezra'" (1930, 1940). Essay. Robinson was asked by Helen Grace Adams, a young student who was writing a master's thesis, for comments on his theory of poetry and on his philosophy of life. He generously replied in a brief letter (January 1, 1930). In it, he says that his *Tristram* is simply a story without symbolism, that in *Merlin* and *Lancelot* Camelot symbolizes the disappearance of the world before the First World War, and that those two poems may both be best read as narratives. In his poetry, he suggests that the universe is orderly, that so-called rational thinking can be deterministically negated, and that rather like a mystic he cannot prove his sure and certain beliefs. He closes by saying that "Rabbi Ben Ezra" by Robert Browning presents a simple optimism likely proceeding from the poet's temperament, not his experience or personal observation of others. Robinson didn't like it when critics compared his poetry to that of the earlier Browning and in the process suggested an influence. (Sources: Cary [1975], 102–03, 192–93; *Selected Letters*, 160)

"As a World Would Have It" (1902). Poem. Alcestis, having returned from the grave, wonders why her husband King Admetus won't look at her, won't speak. Will he give a sign if she takes his cold hands in hers again? She begs him to look at her, speak, recall their heavenly love. You're still only mourning for me? Tell me the truth. He responds, half choking, that, yes, he still mourns, is aware she's alive, but cannot prove his abiding love yet by looking at or by embracing her. Alcestis waits, slave-like, knowing he will say more. And he does. He tells her everything, looks at her, sees her tears, and also weeps. They kiss, cling to one another, their eyes now closed. Aware that "No man can understand," she wonders why he suffered because she willingly sacrificed her life, why he couldn't trust her action; it wasn't "so strange." She would have given all, have descended into silence, have died, so that he could live — "was it very strange?" Understanding ends suffering.

The poem is in 19 unrhyming quatrains. The first three lines of each quatrain are mainly in iambic pentameter; the fourth, in abrupt iambic trimeter, suggesting the hesitant, interrupted half-understanding of the married pair.

In the *Alcestis* of Euripides, King Admetus of Thessaly has been told by the gods that if he can find a substitute willing to die in his place, he may continue to live. His wife Alcestis agrees to do so and dies. Hercules rescues her and brings her back to Admetus. Characteristically, Robinson is creatively concerned with the back-to-life relationship of the husband and wife here, and implicitly praises superior female awareness of marital sacrifice and true love. (It should be added, in defense of men, that Hercules and Orpheus, both males, braved Hades on missions to save the fair sex.) Chard Powers Smith* restrictively compares Alcestis in Robinson's poem to the self-sacrificial devotion of Mary Robinson,* the poet's mother, in her conduct toward her husband and the poet's father. (Sources: Fussell [1954], 143–44; C. Smith, 195)

"As It Looked Then" (1924). Sonnet. The narrator walks where an ugly spruce casts a shadow over what had once been a path "from nowhere . . . to nowhere." He plans to quit

being "a pioneer" and return, but he suddenly sees a bird-like "flash of blue." It was like a spoken message. Then the beautiful sea appears; it resembles a sky that arches over emptiness.

Ruth Nivison* identifies the scene as the Capitol Island cove after Avon's cabin had disappeared (see *Avon's Harvest*). She adds that her family used to call the "scrub that once had been a pathway" in the poem "Stub-toe Alley." (Source: E. Robinson, 20)

"Atherton's Gambit" (1910). Poem. When the master plays, celestial music is heard, if only by a few who can appreciate it. Atherton observes the master's performance, thinks he can do as well, tries. His friends like him, encourage him a bit, but also tolerantly smile a little. They shouldn't scoff and feel superior.

"Atherton's Gambit" opens thus: "The master played the bishop's pawn, / For jest, while Atherton looked on." In all, the poem contains five eight-line stanzas, in easy iambic tetrameter and with simple, almost monotonous rhyming couplets. Emery Neff, regarding Atherton as a would-be poet, writes this about the poem: "Stanzas of invariable structure manage to convey, by variation of pauses, both Atherton's literal superficiality and the heights of poetry that loom above it." (Source: Neff, 157)

"Au Revoir" (1910). Poem. Robinson wonders why "libellers of destiny" are afraid of nameless things, certain "malefic brew[s]," distant lions. Such people should do their work, face "what may come," and thus "from a nation . . . be missed / As others are from home."

"Au Revoir," parenthetically dated "March 2, 1909," celebrates the departure of Theodore Roosevelt* for a big-game shoot in Africa. It appeared in *The Town Down the River* (1910). In a letter (November 10, 1921) to Edith Brower,* Robinson explains that he omitted the poem from his 1921 *Collected Poems* because people failed to appreciate the humor in everything in it but the final two-line message, "And from a nation [he] will be missed / As others are from home." (Sources: Brower, 178; Cary [1975], 48, 182)

"Aunt Imogen" (1902). Poem in blank verse. Jane, Sylvester, and Young George eagerly await Aunt Imogen's annual visit, which makes "all September a Queen's festival." The children's mother understands their delight when her sister arrives. Jane explains matters: Aunt Imogen is there only one month a year, "While she, the mother,—she was always there." Imogen is puzzled "that she could be / So much to any crazy thing alive," including these "little savages." They besiege her, hug her, cause her something close to pain because of her joy and their raucous love. Jane half strangles her. Sylvester pounds his drum. Young George howls until she gives him a piggy-back ride. From a room Imogen gazes at the fields, is girlishly glad to be with people "who knew her," is relieved to have "cabs and clattered asphalt" far away. She makes everyone laugh. But note

> the feminine paradox — that she
> Who had so little sunshine for herself
> Should have so much for others.

She hungers through being incomplete and regretful. She "ache[s] for something of her own, / For something of herself," even as she is aware that she can make others "Believe there was no other part of her / Than her persistent happiness." Does Jane realize this? Young George is "jubilantly satisfied," knowing that everyone has plenty to do and eat. He tells Aunt Imogene that life is "a good game," especially when she is a participant. This carefree comment seems merciless to Imogen. A child has uniquely thrust this truth upon her. This newly acquired wisdom conquers any lingering dreams for personal joy. So she concludes that "there was no love / Save borrowed love: there was no might have been." Her sister and her children are there but are "not hers, not even one of them." She is simply the aunt. Accepting what the stars have granted her, she blinks back at Young George and hugs the laughing lad tightly.

Robinson's "Aunt Imogen" has been compared to "Daguerreotype" (1901) by William Vaughn Moody,* to Robinson's advantage. As Richard Cary puts it, "Moody was writing in memory of his mother . . . [and his] poem is shot through with the rhetoric of anguish and imploration as against Robinson's controlled utterance and tone."

Robinson's working title for "Aunt Imogen" was "The Old Maid." In many ways, Robinson was an old-maid uncle to Ruth Robinson,* Marie Louise Robinson,* and Barbara Robinson,* the three daughters of his brother Herman Robinson* and Emma Robinson.* His nieces welcomed "Uncle Win" ecstatically when he left noisy New York to visit them. Laura E. Richards* reports that Robinson told Emma that "it was himself that he was revealing — or concealing, as you will" — in his portrayal of the childless Imogen. Writing more generally — and bravely, given the current political-correctness frenzy — Louis Coxe comments on the familial entrapment of New England "spinsters and maiden ladies" of Robinson's era and says that "No poet today would write about such a thing, yet the thing still exists though we do not like to think so." True enough.

Bliss Perry (1860–1954), educator and author, was the editor of the *Atlantic Monthly* (1899–1909) when Robinson submitted "Aunt Imogen" for his consideration. Perry wrote the following in his autobiography:

> Only the other day, when I was praising Robinson's "Aunt Imogen" to his face as one of his finest poems, E.A.R. gently reminded me that I had once rejected it for the Atlantic, on the ground that it was too difficult for a magazine reader to grasp at one reading. Perhaps I was too timid about "Aunt Imogen," but at least I atoned for that blunder by persuading the sceptical House [Houghton, Mifflin] to publish Robinson's *Captain Craig*.

Cary, who quotes these remarks by Perry, corrects the record by presenting evidence that Perry had reservations about *Captain Craig*, regarding it as "[a] volume of obscure verse" to be accepted only because Robinson might write "a more popular book [for them] later." Howard George Schmitt,* Robinson's busy correspondent, met Perry and discussed his poetry with him. Later, Perry made the choices for *Selected Poems* by Robinson (1931) and provided a preface for the book. (Sources: Cary [1974], 121–22, 110; Coxe, 72; Perry, 177; Richards [1936], 59; E. Robinson, 12; Schmitt, 26, 29)

Austin, Lizzie. Robinson's high-school algebra teacher. She was a cousin of Alanson Tucker Schumann* and may therefore have come from Waldoboro, Maine, as he did. Hermann Hagedorn* says that Robinson was not interested in algebra, but that "Lizzie Austin, for all her squinty blue eyes and her spectacles, had a charm which overcame his resistance." Hagedorn also reports that a little later Robinson used to read *Paradise Lost* by John Milton with Miss Austin. (Source: Hagedorn, 30, 45)

"Autobiographical Sketches: Harvard" (1915, 1920, 1925). Essays. Robinson in 1915 filed information about his birth, parents, school, years in college, occupation, address, and membership in the "Institute of Arts and Letters." He lists his book publications, including his play *Van Zorn*, which he humorously says he mistakenly called a comedy, which people of the theater praised, but which nobody has sought to produce. He contends that he has been called a pessimist, which any reading of his poetry would disprove. In 1920 Robinson added little except to say that his two major hatreds are prohibition and free verse. In 1925, editors added the following: Robinson won Pulitzer prizes in 1922 and 1924; he himself wrote the editors to complain that he no longer can eat and drink as much as formerly, and he said that he vacationed briefly in London. (Sources: Cary [1975], 68–69, 187–88)

"Avenel Gray" *see* **"Mortmain"**

Avon's Harvest: Tragic Drama in Verse (1921). Narrative poem in blank verse. The narrator says that fear has long consumed his reticent friend Avon, in New York. Then, suddenly, for more than a year he seemed different. Avon's wife has become fiery eyed. Avon now wants to reveal something to the narrator. So they meet in what Avon called his "Library." When his wife says he learned little in school, Avon agrees he should have learned more there. Avon tells the reluctantly listening narrator that someone may still be alive who knows his secret. Then he begins.

It seems that Avon, when he was 16, was a middling student at a boarding school, had the normal few fights with others, soon forgotten. Suddenly a strange, loathsome boy appeared, like

> the black tiger
> That many of us fancy is in waiting,
> But waits for us in fancy only.

Who sent him? Did God, chance, "invidious . . . stars," the narrator's debt-ridden ancestors do so? Anyway, this stranger deprived Avon of peace forever. He felt caught in an evil net with the stranger, so "undulating" and wormy that God would have had to create a unique monster to exterminate him. Avon asks the horrified narrator to peek out and check the street, and says he has been tortured 20 years. What made Avon injure the stranger? He pitied the lizard-like fellow, let him lounge on Avon's couch, and sensed that he would willingly die trying to save Avon, who, however, mainly longed for a Christian's ability to feel remorseful for such hatred.

When spring came, the stranger, confiding in Avon, "Told of a lie that stained a friend of mine / With a false blot that a few days washed off." But first, the narrator knocked down the strange creature, who got up with "vengeance in his eyes, and a weird gleam / Of desolation," but also tears. Gossip among fellow students made Avon a hero. When the stranger, expelled, was leaving next day, he said, ""If you are silent, / I shall know where you are until you die." Avon found himself incapable of saying anything then but now constantly hears those fateful words. The narrator says Avon could have shaken the stranger's hand and said the truth. Avon replies that if he said anything the two would have fought again and that 20 years of time have cured nothing. There is no antidote for his three diseases (identified later). He says that the narrator's fee for listening like a doctor will be "my gratitude and my affection."

Ten years passed. The stranger sent Avon an unsigned card for each birthday, with that same message, about knowing his location until he dies. Avon saw the stranger in Rome, and the fellow spoke only with vengeful eyes. Avon saw him in London, that time with a woman — God help her. Relief came when Avon saw the stranger's name listed among those who had perished when the *Titanic* sank (April 15, 1912), especially since no more birthday cards followed.

Avon spent "a frosty fortnight" last October with his friend Asher, "an odd bird" who had a lodge in Maine, by a lake, with a village miles away. One night Avon watched Asher and a friend whom they called "The Admiral" go off boating. "Then it was / That hell came." Avon sensed "hidden presences" coalescing into one entity. He felt utterly alone, yet not alone. He lectures the narrator: "Beware of hate, / And listen. Beware of hate, remorse, and fear." Avon implies that the stranger is coeval with Satan himself. The narrator hears Avon's wife pacing outside. Avon resumes. He felt fear at that lake, felt he was the last man left on earth by a wrathful, forgetful God. Well, what happened "ruined good Asher's autumn." Avon entered the lodge, locked the door, lit a soon-fading fire, lay down, slept fitfully, then saw "it." The narrator glances at Avon's covered eyes and hears his wife's footsteps outside. Avon says he saw the stranger's face, expressing the same "sad, malignant desperation" as when Avon had slugged him. The stranger squeezed himself, "half erect," into the room. Avon felt like a man pinned down by a tiger. The stranger looked fierce, vengeful, and struck with something metallic the moonlight revealed. Asher and The Admiral found Avon later. He adds only that tomorrow will be his birthday.

The narrator goes home, doesn't know whether Avon's wife slept that night, and theorizes about Avon. Just before dawn, Avon's wife summons him. A doctor is there. Avon is dead in his room. The doctor, aware of Avon's condition for some months, suggests calling it "a nightmare and an aneurism." He adds that Avon suffered from something beyond fear, that the authorities broke Avon's locked door to enter, but that "she heard him when it came." The doctor concludes:

> If I were not a child
> Of science, I should say it was the devil.
> I don't believe it was another woman,
> And surely it was not another man.

Ruth Nivison,* the daughter of Robinson's brother Herman Robinson,* calls Avon's harvest simply her father's harvest of dislike, terror, and hallucinations, and reports that her mother Emma Robinson* described the dialogue between Avon and his nemesis as based on conversations between the two brothers. Mrs. Nivison also provides the following identifications: the camp is based on Leonard Camp, on Capitol Island; Asher, based on a man named Ruel Dunlap; The Admiral, a Boothbay Harbor druggist named E. L. Porter.

Amy Lowell* contends that Robinson occasionally overuses melodrama and thus obscures "the human element," and cites *Avon's Harvest* as "[t]he worst example," among many she names, of this fault. In the original poem, the dagger is real, and others later find it. This bothered early reviewers. Conrad Aiken, for example, ridicules "a knife of ponderable enough reality, which the ghost, in evaporating, left behind." Signaled by these reviewers, Robinson, when he revised *Avon's Harvest* for inclusion in his 1921 *Collected Poems*, reduces the dagger to a mere " moon-flash of metal," which, as David Brown points out, "becomes an item in the story which may be legitimately regarded as a hallucination of Avon, since he alone sees it." Brown also shows that Robinson's change generously helped to legitimize some early reviewers' slightly mistaken interpretations of the poem. Ellsworth Barnard points out, however, that the revision still contains some obscurity. He feels that *Avon's Harvest* is "the most baffling of Robinson's longer poems," but theorizes that it dramatizes "the intrusion into human life of evil that is uncaused, inexplicable."

It may be of interest that Robinson uncharacteristically rather weaseled out of the controversy regarding the knife, when he explained by letter (June 29, 1934) to Howard George Schmitt* that since "Almost everybody [before the revision] thought the knife was left by a ghost," he removed it to "leave the whole thing 'psychological.'"

Harriet Monroe* says that Robinson's presentation of Avon's "gradual burrowing insanity . . . is done with a kind of cold thrift, as effective in its way as Poe's lush and shadowed eloquence." Henry W. Wells notes that "*Avon's Harvest* is by modern standards almost a perfect short story." Floyd Stovall defines the poem as "a psychological study of the devastating effects of hate and its twin shadows, remorse and fear." Chard Powers Smith* reads *Avon's Harvest* as "exclusively a study of this perverse element in Herman [Robinson*]," the element being a destructive, possibly fiendish personality quirk. (Sources: Aiken, 16; Barnard, 287–88, 300; D. Brown, 346 and passim; Lowell [1922], 136; Monroe, 273–74; Moran [1963]; E. Robinson, 17; Schmitt, 27; C. Smith, 199; Stovall, 11; Wells, 180)

Avon's Harvest (New York: Macmillan, 1921). Collection of 15 poems, including the title poem. Robinson dedicated the book to his childhood friend Seth Ellis Pope.*

Badger, Richard G. (1878–1937). Publisher. Born in Roxbury, Massachusetts, he founded the Gorham Press (1894), run as Richard G. Badger and Company at 157 Tremont Street in Boston. He moved to 194 Boyston Street in about 1900 and pioneered as a profitable vanity press exploiting poets of minimal ability. Hermann Hagedorn* reports that William Edward Butler, Robinson's friend from Boston, paid Badger to publish Robinson's *The Children of the Night* (1897), and also that it was through knowing Badger that Joseph Lewis French* and Edmund Clarence Stedman* first sought out Robinson in New York (c. 1898–1899). Richard Cary states that Badger went bankrupt (December 1900) and that Butler persuaded his father to purchase the remaining stock of *The Children of the Night* and display everything for sale in his department store in Boston. Badger soon was publishing other highly competent authors. For example, he issued Willa Cather's *April Twilights* (1903) and Eugene O'Neill's *Thirst* (1914). Badger moved to 100 Charles Street (c. 1922); suffered further reverses in the 1920s, partly because he was indicted and convicted for publishing obscene items (1923); bought Arthur Vinal's publishing firm of New York (1928); and sold out to the Boston publishing firm, Bruce Humphries, Inc. (1932), which soon became mainly a vanity press itself. (Sources: Cary [1974], 106; Dzwonkoski; Hagedorn, 112, 149, 163)

Baker, George Pierce (1866–1935). Educator. Born in Providence, Rhode Island, Baker graduated from Harvard (1887), taught in the English department there (1888–1924), and in 1906 established and began to conduct his "47 Workshop" to teach playwriting and produce experimental plays. His most successful students were Philip Barry, Esther Willard Bates,* Frederick Lansing Day, John Dos Passos, Sidney Howard, Eugene O'Neill, Edwin Carty Ranck,* and Thomas Wolfe, who patterned Professor Hatcher in *Of Time and the River* (1935) after Baker. Baker also knew and helped Hermann Hagedorn* and Josephine Preston Peabody.* Hagedorn says that Baker told him in 1911 that he ought to ask Robinson to consider becoming a guest in the MacDowell Colony,* in Peterborough, New Hampshire, founded and supervised by Marian Nivens MacDowell,* Baker's friend. Baker transferred to Yale, taught the history and technique of drama, and directed Yale's theater (1925–1935). His publications include *The Development of Shakespeare as a Dramatist* (1907), *Dramatic Technique* (1919), and editions of several plays by his students. (Source: Hagedorn, 261)

"Ballade" *see* **"Ballade of Broken Flutes"**

"Ballade by the Fire" (1896). Poem. The poet sits by the fire, smokes, stares at the glowing embers, and sees a cavalcade of phantoms. He wonders what the years will bring, before various graves are dug. Let the three fates "Around me ply their merry trade," he says boldly. "Be up, my soul," he adds, cautioning himself, however, to keep his debts paid. In an "Envoy" following the poem, he tells his friends to be advised that life is a game we must play and to fear no phantoms.

Earlier than 1890, Robinson had joined the poetry club of Alanson Tucker Schumann,* and was introduced to French poetic forms, then popular in England and the United States. "Ballade by the Fire" was a youthful result, among others. References to Charon and Styx in it demonstrate Robinson's early love of classical literature. "Be up, my soul," Robinson's self-adjuration in the poem, probably owes something to "A Psalm of Life" by Henry Wadsworth Longfellow, whose works Robinson staunchly admired.

"Ballade of a Ship" (1891). Poem. A king's son and a king's daughter, with 300 others along, were aboard the bird-like "White Ship." Seen by the eye of a spying ghoul, the vessel and its roysterers were soon clutched by a "pitiless reef" and hurled to a watery grave, "to slumber and sway / Where the bones of the brave in the wave are lying." This last line, twice slightly modified, constitutes the refrain of this vigorous four-stanza ballad. This poem was originally titled "Ballade of the White Ship" and was published in *The Torrent and The Night Before*, with one line missing. (Sources: Brower, 45; Cary [1975], 171; Justice)

"Ballade of Broken Flutes" (1896). Poem. The poet dreams that he is traversing a distant, desolate, silent "land of ruin." It used to be the music-filled Arcady, but now it reveals only broken flutes, skeletal trees, and a bit of spray from "an unforgetful sea." Iron has crushed the flutes. The poet, dreaming on, determines to try to revivify the place. You are reading the result. An "Envoy" follows, in which the poet says he is going to abandon the destroyed flutes and "fight where Mammon may decree."

"Ballade of Broken Flutes" suggests that the Industrial Revolution, or perhaps the materialistic consequences thereof both in America and abroad, resulted in the ruin of pastoral and romantic verse and all that it represented in the way of easier, more gracious life. In this poem, the rhyme scheme of each of its three eight-line stanzas is *ababbcbc*; moreover, all *a*-rhymes, *b*-rhymes, and *c*-rhymes rhyme identically. That is, Robinson employs only three rhymes throughout. For example, the busy b-rhymes are "away," "decay," "dismay," "lay," "sway," "array," "spray," "aye," "gray," "clay," "to-day," and "play"; for good measure, "fray" and "may" are in the "Envoy." Robinson dedicated this poem to Alanson Tucker Schumann,* his Gardiner physician-

friend who encouraged him early in his career to study and emulate French ballade-style verse. Richard Cary details Robinson's study and use of the ballade form. Edwin S. Fussell cites as sources or analogues for Robinson's ballade here "With Pipe and Flute" by the earlier Henry Austin Dobson (1840–1921) and "The Song of the Happy Shepherd" by Robinson's contemporary William Butler Yeats (1865–1939). Hermann Hagedorn* suggests that Robinson is directly addressing Schumann when he says he will join Mammon worshippers — which he never did. (Sources: Cary [1974], 57; Fussell [1954], 181–82; Hagedorn, 89)

"Ballade of Dead Friends" (1896). Poem. Time laughs at and ignores our prayers, questions, tears, and sighs, even as we lament departed friends. Pepping up, life defies "Age and death," but only until we learn that "All but Love is dying." Meanwhile, we buy shrouds for lost friends. We yearn for what is evanescent. Men turn to dry dust, and that dust looks for new faces resembling absent friends. In an added "Envoy," it is explained that we approach and yet fear the truth, but that death will put an end to our weeping for dead friends. Each of the three eight-line stanzas has identical rhymes, in an *ababbcbc* pattern, with every *b*-rhyme feminine.

When first published, in *The Children of the Night*, this poem was entitled "The Ballade of Dead Friends." It was republished, without "The" in the title, in *The Torrent and The Night Before*; but Robinson kept it out of his 1921 *Collected Poems*. However, Edmund Clarence Stedman,* the businessman-editor, had liked the poem well enough to include it in his *An American Anthology, 1787–1899* (1900), which amused Robinson. (Source: Cary [1975], 28, 177–78).

"Ballade of Dead Mariners" (1893). Fragmentary poem. Robinson enclosed in a letter (October 5, 1893) to Harry de Forest Smith* what he called the envoi of "Ballade of Dead Mariners." The five-line piece says that days and years come and go, leaving neither hopes nor cares. The message the waves pound out is that unspoken love is strongest, while "women wait for ships that never come." Robinson evidently never completed this poem. (Sources: Cary [1975], 16, 172; *Untriangulated Stars*, 111)

"Ballade of the White Ship" *see* "Ballade of a Ship"

"The Balm of Custom" (1900). Editorial.

Robinson sides with William McKinley (1843–1901), 25th president of the United States, in his 1900 Republican Party campaign for re-election. Robinson reasons that many fine Democrats will vote for McKinley's opponent, William Jennings Bryan (1860–1925), not because they believe in his ethics or in his monetary, anti-imperialistic politics, but because they no longer fear him and have become used to him. Such voters "have relaxed themselves into a state of intellectual captivity." Robinson livens this half-column piece by aptly adverting to Michelangelo and Lord Byron, and by saying that "Custom has . . . staled his [Bryan's] infinite monotony," thus paraphrasing Shakespeare's famous comment about Cleopatra: "Custom hath not staled her infinite variety" (*Antony and Cleopatra*, II, ii, 241–42). Robinson published this, his only piece of journalistic writing, in the *New York Daily Tribune* (October 7, 1900), being able to do so only because Edmund Clarence Stedman* recommended him to several editors, to help him earn a little needed income. (Sources: Cary [1975], 66–67, 187; Williams)

"Barbara." A song Robinson wrote about

1896 but asked a friend to destroy. (Source: W. Anderson [1980], 58)

"Barcarolle." A short story Robinson wrote

in the early 1890s, could not sell, and destroyed. (Source: Hagedorn, 102)

"Barney's a Coming Home." A song

Robinson wrote about 1896 but did not preserve. (Source: W. Anderson [1980], 58)

Barstow. This is the last name of four broth-

ers — Nathaniel, George, Joseph, and James — who were among the several boyhood and early-youth Gardiner friends of Robinson.

Robinson enjoyed visiting the Barstow family and often read works by William Shakespeare aloud in their presence. Joseph, an expert hunter, supplied the family and friends with rabbits. James S. Barstow (1876–1941) graduated from Harvard (1898). His sister taught school in Kansas City, and through connections was able to offer Robinson a job as literary editor of the *Kansas City Star*, at $2,000 a year. When Robinson declined, James Barstow took the position (1899–1901). He republished six of Robinson's short poems in the *Star* (1899) to help popularize him in the Middle West. The two met again in New York (from 1902) when Barstow was tutoring an opulent lad in Tuxedo, New York; Barstow in Manhattan hosted lavish dinners in Greenwich Village and often pub-crawled with George Burnham,* Torrence,* Ridgely, and Robinson. When Barstow headed a tutoring school, he offered Robinson a position for $3–4 an hour (1909) but was turned down. In later years, Robinson revisited Gardiner and always sought out remnants of the Barstow family. Laura E. Richards,* who knew the Barstows, wrote in her autobiographical *Stepping Westward* about James Barstow and his brothers. After Robinson's death, James Barstow wrote a tender memoir entitled *My Tilbury Town* (1939). (Sources: Barstow; Cary [1974], 108, 270; Hagedorn; Lowe; Richards [1931], 377; *Untriangulated Stars*, 312)

Bates, Esther Willard (1884–?). Drama-

tist. She was a prolific author of plays and pageants, usually short, devoted to religious and historical subjects, and directed to youthful audiences. She wrote at least 38 such works between 1908 and 1945. She also wrote *The Art of Producing Pageants* (1925). She taught playwriting at Boston University and was head of the Department of English, Rhode Island School of Design, Providence. For six years she also wrote a column for the *Providence Journal*.

Bates met Robinson at the MacDowell Colony* (c. 1913). She became one of his most devoted friends and from 1913 typed most of his manuscripts, many of which he invited her to comment on and even edit slightly. Chard Powers Smith* records many anecdotes concerning Robinson that Bates relayed to him. Smith also suggests that Bates must have been devoted to Robinson, since she would sometimes prepare transcripts of his compositions for an entire year in return for one dinner-and-theater date. (Sources: Bates; C. Smith)

"Battle After War" (1924). Sonnet. The persona rises out of darkness as though spewed out of Erebus into a nameless kind of light. He remembers a kind of sight. But faces and eyes like his and also like what he formerly feared aren't there any more. Once lost, he now shines like a sturdy Roman following Pentecost (see Acts II: 5–11), and feels that he and his friends can partly mitigate terror. Now he has a companion.

Dean Sherman explicates this obscure poem thus: "Robinson is here equating light with Reason and Intelligence and darkness with Chaos and Death." Also, what the persona eluded was the son of Chaos, whom Hesiod personifies as Erebus. Furthermore, in Plato's *Republic*, the journey from the cave to the light resembles the soul's rise to the world of the intellect. Additionally, leaving darkness to shine like the post-Pentecostal Roman may be likened to a human acquiring the Christian light of newly acquired knowledge. The original title of "Battle After War" was "After the War." (Source: Sherman)

Beatty, Frederika (1897–?). Author. She met Robinson at the MacDowell Colony* in the summers of 1933 and 1934. In her reminiscence about their friendship, entitled "Edwin Arlington Robinson as I Knew Him" (*South Atlantic Quarterly*, October 1944), she touches on Robinson's favorite poets (George Crabbe, Thomas Hood,* John Keats, William Shakespeare, and William Wordsworth), his attitude toward money, his playing pool (ineptly), his addiction to mystery stories, his love of music, his trouble finding the exact word, his punctuality, and finally his integrity and kindness. When Beatty, a Bryn Mawr graduate (1919), told Robinson she was writing a book on William Wordsworth, he expressed great interest in reading it when it was finished. The book, completed after Robin-

son's death, was Beatty's Columbia University Ph.D. dissertation, published as *William Wordsworth of Rydal Mount; An Account of the Poet and His Friends in the Last Decade* (1939).

"Ben Jonson Entertains a Man from Stratford" (1915). Dramatic monologue in blank verse. Ben Jonson (1572–1637), Elizabethan playwright, speaks in London (1609) to a visitor, an alderman from Stratford, about William Shakespeare (1564–1616), Jonson's much-admired friend and colleague. Jonson praises him for "put[ting] an ass's head in Fairyland" and for populating several plays cast in "Ilion, Rome, or any town you like / Of olden time with timeless Englishmen." But at the outset, Jonson says Shakespeare wants to be "the Duke of Stratford" and defines his friend's opposing elements: "there's the Stratford in him; he denies it, / And there's the Shakespeare in him." While touching on Shakespeare's lack of knowledge of Greek, Jonson adds that "neither God / Nor Greek will help him." This because "the fates have given him so much, / He must have all or perish." When Shakespeare was a dusty, sweaty actor, various aristocrats laughed at him; yet "half the world, if not the whole of it, / May crown him" uniquely. Oddly, he yearns for a house in Stratford.

Jonson's visitor must have known Shakespeare as a boy. What a scary, "uncommon urchin" he must have been, with discerning eyes even then. If he had a dog, he must have asked it "'what's it all about?'" With proper indifference, Shakespeare dismisses talk of the Aristotelian dramatic unities, by saying, "'I have your word that Aristotle knows, / And you mine that I don't know Aristotle.'" Lately "inclement devils" have surely enflamed Shakespeare's heart, because he now "itches, manor-bitten to the bone," even though he well knows that he is

The lord of more than England and of more
Than all the seas of England in all time
Shall ever wash.

When Shakespeare meets Jonson of a Sunday, he says, "Ben, you're a scholar, what's the time of day?" This with a mysterious "light" shining out of him as he laughs both at his easy-won fame and at jealousy in others, including "Poor [Robert] Greene," their fellow dramatist (1560?-1592), and others who have "scanned Euripides and Æschylus" to little purpose. When his friends will visit Shakespeare in Stratford, "his wife won't like us." When he now says most women aren't worth trying to figure out, "there's a worm at work." After all, he danced with plenty of women, "put one [woman] there [in his sonnets] with all her poison on," and was sent "scuttling . . . to London" by that wife (Anne Hathaway, 1557?-1623) who had "decoyed him." Though partly aloof from would-be cronies, he could analyze them well when he spoke. "Talk? He was eldritch at it; and we listened." He was aware of a natural law that could ruin everyone.

> To me it looks as if the power that made him,
> For fear of giving all things to one creature,
> Left out the first,—faith, innocence, illusion,
> Whatever 'tis that keeps us out o' Bedlam.

An idea is fermenting within Shakespeare like something in "a keg of ale." Something on Cleopatra will cause "a roaring at the Globe [Theatre]." His need to write vies with his desire for a "grand new House."

Jonson theorizes that "something happening in his boyhood / Fulfilled him with a boy's determination" to become a home-town hero. Soon after arriving in London, "the poised young faun / From Warwickshire" quickly became legendary; that was, Jonson adds, well "before I came / To blink before the last of his first lightning." Once back in Stratford, he may write again, but not the same, since "The coming on of his old monster Time / Has made him a still man," and also since "He knows how much of what men paint themselves / Would blister in the light of what they are." Aging now, he knows that " his lark may sing / At heaven's gate"; however,

> *he* sees no gate,
> Save one whereat the spent clay waits a little
> Before the churchyard has it, and the worm.

Jonson encountered Shakespeare at Lambeth one afternoon, and he philosophized that we are either spiders or flies, and described what nature impels the former do to the latter and what nature impels the broom-swinging servant to do to the former. Concluding that it is "'all Nothing,'" he adds that

> It's all a world where bugs and emperors
> Go singularly back to the same dust,
> Each in his time . . .

and the stars will keep on singing. At such times, Jonson encourages Shakespeare to drink, which he does, "for love of me." But then he gets sick, which is regrettable, because "The great / Should be as large in liquor as in love." Jonson predicts that if Shakespeare lives a while longer,

> there'll be a sunset spell
> Thrown over him as over a glassed lake
> That yesterday was all a black wild water.

As a joke, Jonson once called Shakespeare "a mad mountebank," which saddened him by reminding him of his former acting. Repenting, Jonson says, "I love the man this side idolatry." Shakespeare may not write much more, because of "The full brain hammered hot with too much thinking, / The vexed heart overworn with too much aching." But he may still play his lyre wondrously; in truth, "He might have given Aristotle creeps, / But surely would have given him his *katharsis*."

Jonson offers one conclusion and implies a contrasting one at the very last:

> was [there] anything let loose
> On earth by gods or devils heretofore
> Like this mad, careful, proud, indifferent Shakespeare!"

But finally, "O Lord, that House in Stratford!"

Robinson, like Ben Jonson, also admired Shakespeare "this side idolatry," as numerous passages in his letters reveal. He first published "Ben Jonson Entertains a Man from Stratford" in the *Drama Quarterly* (November 1915), for the Shakespeare tercentenary, soon republished it, and saw it anthologized. It may be loosely compared to various dramatic monologues by Robert Browning. Richard Cary presents much evidence that Robinson read and liked only some of Browning's poems, but says he did not consciously pattern his own on them. It is true that in each poet's dramatic monologues, the speaker seeks to describe his subject but often tips his hand about himself.

Here, however, Robinson, while surely revealing much about Ben Jonson, may be showing a few cards of his own.

Emery Neff, finding submerged autobiographical currents in this poem, writes: "In the failure of Jonson, the Londoner, to understand the Stratford in Shakespeare, we may read Robinson's awareness that his roots in Maine were hidden from his New York friends." Earlier, Emma Robinson* and Ruth Nivison* went further. They saw many parallels in this poem to elements in Robinson's life, and often to events touching on their relationship with Robinson. They find these parallels: Naiads' "white arms" and Emma's arm; the reference to Shakespeare's dancing and Robinson's having met her in dancing school; his having Shakespeare put "her poison" in a sonnet to Robinson's brief animosity toward her; Shakespeare's shyness in talking to Robinson's taciturnity with others; Shakespeare's boyhood determination to make Stratford aware of him to Robinson's attitude toward residences in Gardiner, Maine; and Shakespeare's stated plan to write about Cleopatra and Robinson's reading and taking notes for a poem on the same subject, though never written. Jay Parini, in an essay mainly devoted to Robert Frost and in the process implicitly diminishing Robinson, avers that "Robinson was a poet of considerable gifts whose dramatic lyrics are still underestimated by critics," but then admits that Robinson "pioneered an American version of the dramatic monologue that had been popular in England throughout the [nineteenth] century."

Bacon Collamore* published part of a letter (November 10, 1915) from Robinson to William Stanley Braithwaite,* in which he implies that he regarded "Ben Jonson Entertains a Man from Stratford" as one of his finest poems. Collamore castigates a few carping critics who complained that in the poem Robinson has Jonson give Shakespeare's age as "five-and-forty" when he was composing *Antony and Cleopatra*, whereas he was actually just short of 40.

An early critic to praise "Ben Jonson Entertains a Man from Stratford" was Amy Lowell,* who says that in it "the words never stand out . . . to show how well chosen they are, but the whole is as vigorous as everyday conversation." Ellsworth Barnard notes that between the publication of *Captain Craig* (1902) and the Ben Jonson poem (1915), Robinson published no blank verse; he adds that by 1915 Robinson's blank verse began to include more feminine endings and more anapestic and trochaic feet. Though much esteemed and taught, the poem does have its detractors. Ivor Winters, for one, opines: "The portrait of Shakespeare, the ostensible subject of the poem, is diffused among the mannerisms [of Jonson] . . . The blank verse is in some ways quicker and more limber; but the substance of the poem is slight." Robert D. Stevick doesn't like the limber quality of the blank verse, much of which, he complains, is "not easy to sight-read." It should be stated here that virtually every line of Robinson's poetry is better understood and enjoyed when read aloud, and further that his poetic syntax does not reward quick-eyed sight-readers. (Sources: Barnard, 81–82; Cary [1974], 48–49; Collamore, 19; Lowell [1917], 55; Neff, 179; Parini, 260, 261; E. Robinson, 3–4; Stevick [1969], 60; Winters, 134)

"Ben Trovato" (1921). Sonnet. A Presbyterian deacon talks to a friend about some people whom the deacon "know[s]" and whom the friend has "heard of." They, the deacon indicates, are strange. He advises his friend to believe what he heard and not criticize "The benefaction of a strategem / Like hers." He continues. It seems that the man, blind and dying, felt the fur coat his wife was wearing but also felt "the other woman in the fur." The delirious man concluded that his wife had apparently "forgive[n] / All that." When he found that his wife's rings were gone, "He smiled — as he had never smiled at her."

All but a few critics have shied away from the enigmatic "Ben Trovato." Scott Donaldson believes that the wife in the poem "dons the furs of her blind and dying husband's mistress and removes her rings," and thus "create[s] at least a moment of false happiness" for him. Louis Coxe places the poem in the company of a few other poems about "the wife or woman who endures the thoughtless disregard of a husband or lover, the woman who, taken for granted, either finally breaks or goes on enduring." Ellsworth Barnard summarizes the action: "the wife in *Ben Trovato* removes her rings and puts on unaccustomed furs in order to bring a last hour of happiness to her blind and dying husband"; then generalizes that "[n]o woman in Robinson's poems makes a sacrifice comparable to that of the wife in *Ben Trovato*."

However, given Robinson's delight in challenging his readers with obscurity and his presentation of women as often cruel, isn't a contrary explication possible? The betrayed wife sought out her husband's mistress, traded her discardable rings for the envied fur coat the husband purchased for the mistress, put it on, and visited her husband wrapped in it. Or did the neglected wife sell her rings and buy herself a fancy coat and go gloat? At any rate, the husband felt woman and fur, fumbled for and found no rings, and grimaced "as he had never smiled at her [his still-missed mistress]."

The Presbyterian deacon doesn't specify what he and his friend knew about the persons in this predestined triangle. Nor need readers assume, as some probably do, that the dying man's name is Ben Trovato. Robert Mezey points out that the phrase "ben trovato" comes from the Italian saying, "Si non è vero è ben trovato," and translates it thus: "If it isn't true it ought to be." Actually the saying, "Se non è vero, è molto ben trovato," meaning "If it is not true, it is very well invented," was used in literature as early as 1585, in *De gli eroica furori* by Giordano Bruno (1548–1600). Maybe Robinson's hospitalized codger tardily discerned gumption in his wife. We may not be privy to what is *vero* here. Laura E. Richards* describes an odd word game called "'Tionaries' Ball" that Robinson and her other salon-like guests played. Each would name contestants with punning names, for example, Dr. Tix and his daughter Polly. Mrs. Richards said Robinson "introduced Mr. and Mrs. Aritan and good Sam Aritan[,] . . . Bennie Fitz . . . and . . . Mr. Ben Trovato." (Sources: Barnard, 165, 251; Coxe, 133–34; Donaldson [1966], 226; Mezey, 236; Richards [1936], 51)

Betts, Craven Langstroth (1851–1941) Businessman, author, and translator. Born in Nova Scotia, Betts moved to New York, where he became a book dealer, lawbook salesman, and writer of sonnets and blank-verse poems. He knew Titus Munson Coan,* who introduced Robinson to Betts (1897). The two became friends at once, enjoyed drinking together, and occasionally shared living quarters and even the occasional mess of baked beans. Betts's ebullience, which included an infectious devotion to women (his best poem may be "The Perfume-Holder: A Persian Love Poem"), was good for Robinson. Hermann Hagedorn* and Chard Powers Smith* quote many revealing, often morose letters from Robinson to Betts. In one (April 18, 1905), Robinson, while touching on other topics, praises Betts's "joy of living" and urges him not to crucify himself to please sponging relatives. Robinson often wrote to Edith Brower* about Betts, whom she also knew. In one letter (August 27, 1900), Robinson describes an unidentified poem by Betts as "not . . . transcendant or splendiferous, but . . . likely to live if ever it gets into print." Hoyt C. Franchere reports that Betts's incomplete, unpublished memoir of Robinson is in the Williams College Library. Brower in "Memories of Edwin Arlington Robinson" suggests that Killigrew in *Captain Craig* is based on Betts. Robinson dedicated *Dionysus in Doubt* to Betts. (Sources: Brower, 212, 126; Franchere, 40; Hagedorn; *Selected Letters*, 60–61; C. Smith)

"Bewick Finzer" (1916). Poem. At one time Bewick Finzer had $500,000, invested at six percent. But he wanted "what-was-not." He lost out, after which "something crumbled in his brain." Now he is pretty much ignored. The poet and others can't believe how wrecked he seems, with his weak voice, scrawy neck, poor clothes, appearance of desperate "indigence," and remnants of "dreams / Of affluence." A loser "in the race" now, he can hardly bear to face "one who might so easily / Have been in Finzer's place." He will keep turning up and borrowing money that "We give and then forget." He is "Familiar as an old mistake, / And futile as regret." But what does Finzer regret? His lost money or his lost self-respect?

The curious name Bewick may have derived from that of Thomas Bewick (1753–1828), the English wood engraver. Robinson admirably meets the challenge of a difficult *abcbdb* rhyme scheme in this popular five-stanza poem. It is best read aloud to emphasize its galloping fourteener hymn lines, i.e., duh DAH duh DAH duh DAH duh DAH / duh DAH duh DAH duh DAH. Hoyt C. Franchere appropriately notes that "[t]here is nothing enigmatic about Finzer: he stands like a monument to failure." (Source: Franchere, 75)

"Bokardo" (1915). Poem. The poet welcomes Bokardo into somewhat shrunken quarters but soon starts criticizing him. What made you forget "What was yours and [what was] mine"? Why abandon our friendship? He gains Bokardo's attention by remarking that "Friends . . . are small things / In an age when coins are kings." Why hide? So, you tried suicide last week? Well, you'll always find occasion to try again. Despite all this, "the laws" cannot be defeated. Xerxes learned as much when he whipped the sea and at most frightened some fish. Although you called your action courageous, you hurt yourself and not "the laws." Feel free to ask for what you want, but be reasonable and be honest. "Learn a little to forget / Life was once a feast." Don't worry about making up losses.

The poet continues relentlessly. Oh, so you now feel remorseful and near death? Be comforted by having confessed a little bit. Have some fun; forget remorse; realize death can bide his time. Twin devils sit right beside you, distressing you more than you deserve. Still, your last act was somewhat "low." Educative, though. Do realize that "Time will have his little scar, / But the wound won't last." Troubles come, but life goes on. We could talk, tiresomely, about the troubles others have been burdened by. Don't worry, Bokardo, you aren't destroyed yet. Better arrangements and more welcome sights will appear in due time. "Bokardo" closes with a striking, comforting metaphor: "When long-hidden skies are clear, / The stars look strange." This comfort, however, comes only after the poet's slashing rebuke: "But your fervor to be free / Fled the faith it scorned"—lines which Ellsworth Barnard says present "contempt so concentrated as to be not less than cryptic in expression." Robinson's eight-line stanzas here rhyme *ababcccb*, with each eighth line being a terse iambic dimeter.

Chard Powers Smith* interprets this puzzling poem in autobiographical terms. He reports that in December 1904 or so Herman Robinson,* the poet's brother, in poor shape physically and financially, accosted Robinson in New York and appealed to him for help. He probably sprang for a meal for Herman and then surely took him to his small fourth-floor room, was critical of him, and listened to him whine about honor and the temptation of law-breaking suicide. Robinson then rebuked him about alleged remorse, mentioned two devils (which Smith explicates as guilt for stealing from Robinson and for excessive drink to drown the guilt), and tried to assure him that the stars would shine again (which they never did for Herman). Robert Mezey thoroughly glosses the word "Bokardo." In brief, he says that an Oxford prison was named Bocardo and was named after a syllogism; the syllogism is that since some Bs aren't Cs, and all Bs are As, it follows that some As aren't Cs; finally, that a logic professor at Harvard allegedly told Robinson Bokardo was a never-understood figure, which Robinson reckoned symbolized life's many mysteries. (Sources: Barnard, 30; Mezey, 231; C. Smith, 212–15, 402)

"Bon Voyage" (1906). Poem. The subject being bid goodbye is a "wild alloy" of the new and the old, as "old [even] as Troy." The fellow took his ease, sang joyfully, mocked everyone, laughed alike at "Feast or . . . funeral." Whether he was criticized for being juvenile and impolite, or for being tempted by the unknown, "He played the twinkling part / That was his lot." When his "twinkle died," he escaped forever.

This unnamed subject is another of Robinson's unjudged failures or at least misfits. Hints make him out to be singer, poet, or actor. After saying the fellow sang "like a linnet," the poet also calls him "Child of the Cyclades / And of Broadway." This jamming together of unlikes is, according to Edwin S. Fussell, another of the poet's many "juxtapositions of myth and modernity for shock" and "anticipates the revival of 'metaphysical' wit in the 'twenties." Emery Neff praises Robinson's versifying technique here thus: "trochaic trimeters tripping beside iambic dimeters . . . heighten the graceful frivolity of 'Bon Voyage.'" Hermann Hagedorn* hints that Theodore Roosevelt* successfully pressured the editors of *Scribner's Magazine* to publish "Bon Voyage" (January 1906). (Sources: Fussell [1954], 142; Hagedorn, 223; Neff, 157)

The Book of Annandale (1902). Narrative poem, in two numbered parts, unequal in length.

I. George Annandale has just watched the burial of Miriam, his wife, "Under the leaves and snow." He curtly ignores his friends and goes upstairs to a solitary room. The monotonous furniture seems different. He feels a "soul-clutch[ing]," scary void. He sits down, calmly. He must learn to live more expansively again. He has written a book, hidden from everyone, now "covered with red leather." Not even Miriam knew about it. "There was the book, but it was not for her, / For she was dead." He seems to hear a loving voice, not hers.

He remembers that his pallid wife looked up at him faintly at the end, but he cannot weep, although he wishes he could. He feels lost, but less so than "astray." As he enters another life, he sees a "searching face." "[W]ith a speechless promise [it] uttered words / That were not like the world's words." Ungrieving now, perhaps he can become happy. He feels released by Miriam's death, much as he would if his friends were finished with life. Are these thoughts "self-cajoling sophistries"?

Watching Miriam die unmanned him. Once, to be sure, the two were pillowed together, held hands, kissed; she stroked his hair. All this is gone. His "paradise" with her has vanished. Without remorse, he thinks about his puzzling book. Something in it numbs him and makes him drowsy, as though it were "a strange thought-cordial." Too tired now to think or even feel sad, he sleeps.

II. Damaris has been a widow for five years, ever since Argan, her good husband, died.

They were "like lovers to the last"; so she has no regrets, although as a widow she wept more than her "smiles had ever told of other joy." A "new life" beckons; but she is not free, is held back, is "starve[d]," by thoughts near a tomb and by "Argan's ghost."

Laughing and crying, she realizes she must escape "primeval doubts and fears." She senses that something is approaching. She must bravely confront the future. His arrival will free her, unless she remains imprisoned by the past. In such case, he will seek another love — to gain and lose. The poisonous freedom of continuing to live with ghosts would bring wisdom but also a merciless attack by love. She must grasp true love now, for

> should a death-bed snare that she had made
> So long ago be stretched inexorably
> Through all her life, only to be unspun
> With her last breathing?

She should love again, now that this "new life" is sunlit.

Dying, big-boned Argan had grasped her hands and asked her to promise "she would love no other man." Ignorant then of "the love that was to be," she agreed. Argan then smiled, tried to speak, but died. Her foolish, faithless, proudly painful grief now ties her to his tomb with cobwebby threads, and "vampire thoughts . . . suck the coward blood, / The life, the very soul of her."

For these long years Damaris was aware that "The Light itself" was trying to pierce her dark, blind gloom, and was seeking to bring life, love, and glory, although she had been petting and pitying the woman she continued to be, all the while grousing about her. Why not, instead, "quench in her[self] / The woman's fear — the fear of her not fearing?" Annandale, with her now, could easily be told the truth, but instead she laughed nervously. He has brought his leather-bound book, written, he says, "Six years ago, when he was waiting for her." She can read its very words without even opening it, because the words are for her. She knows her face appeared between a life he would have lost without her and the old life represented in a clod from a grave. The spirit therein could then soar on "unimprisoned wings" beyond its "appointed shadow" and into "its own light."

Memories quiver through her, like familiar songs, the consequences of "passion's innocence" so mighty and dangerous that she felt they could never be experienced anew — until Annandale came today with his book. What to do now she sees, wisely, cruelly, "with eyes that had in them / No gleam but of the spirit." She feels like a person in a cave with bats and then suddenly emerging into sunlight. No longer a martyr with dead thoughts, she has found a new and happy life. The warm, strong, questioning, thoughtful, meaningful, friendly, loyal words Annandale wrote are all for her. They "harmonized with love's enduring cords / Like wisdom with release; triumphant words." They feed "love's hunger in the spirit." They explain the nemesis she had long hugged. She feels a freeing, humanizing, magic joy, with Annandale at its center.

Damaris can now find a definite, enduring love. Her autumnal season glitters, is crimson, with a silver river. She is now released from "The grave-deluded, flesh-bewildered fear / Which men and women struggled to call faith." The truth about herself has come fast. She forgets bat-like thoughts about Argan's "flameless dust."

> The shield of love
> Was clean, and she had paid enough to learn
> How it had always been so. And the truth
> Had come to her, and she had found it out
> As if it were a vision.

And a new world blossoms for her.

Ruth Nivison,* the daughter Herman Robinson* and Emma Robinson,* says this: Robinson began writing *The Book of Annandale* during the night of the day when his mother Mary Robinson* was buried; further, in it he is examining his love both for his mother and for Emma, but he disguises this fact by calling the women Annandale's two wives; and, written later, the last part features the death of Argan, who is based on Robinson's recently deceased brother Herman.

It was so hard for Robinson to get *The Book of Annandale* published that he included it in *Captain Craig*, which was accepted by the Houghton Mifflin Company of Boston only after his friends John Hays Gardiner* and Laura E. Richards* financed its publication,

the latter secretly. Reviews and early criticism were not enthusiastic. May Sinclair* merely says that *The Book of Annandale* presents a "burning analysis of the conflict between scruple and desire." Emery Neff expands thus: It concerns the rash promise a wife made to her ill husband not to marry after his death, and then "follows the slow and delicate process of the breaking down of her scruples against remarriage." Chard Powers Smith* details these facts: Shortly before his death in 1909, Robinson's brother Herman persuaded his wife Emma, with whom the poet was spiritually in love, to promise never to remarry. Robinson, however, wrote this poem between 1896 and 1900. It is possible, of course, that his brother, jealously aware of Robinson's affection toward Emma, goaded him well before 1900 by asserting that he would wangle this promise from her. More significant than fraternal animosities, however, is Robinson's subtle attitude toward love expressed and implied in *The Book of Annandale*. Annandale's physical love for Miriam does not prevent him from imagining idealistic love elsewhere. Damaris's loneliness in widowhood nudges her to intuit Annandale's expression of ideal love in his book; but then she meets him, senses the vibrant harmonies in his writing, and wants "the man within the music," evidently, that is, a male's love. With Emma, Robinson had to content himself with spiritual consanguinity, whereas he makes Annandale's and Damaris's future so obscure that there is no critical agreement as to when Annandale first met Damaris or whether they will wed at last. Ivor Winters asserts that Annandale asked the widowed Damaris to marry him, that he then wrote the book, that she refused, that he then married Miriam, that after Miriam's death Damaris becomes aware of his profound love for her, and that life starts anew for her. On the other hand, Smith says that conventionally minded readers regard the poem as "a mere delicate love story ending in a marriage and two people living happily ever after." Charles V. Genthe grimly attempts to demonstrate that "Annandale is murdered either by Argan, Damaris's 'dead' husband, alive and turned physician, or by a doctor who is a symbolic representation of Argan and his point of view." (See "How

Annandale Went Out.") Genthe also believes that the name Argan comes from that of the main character in *Le Malade Imaginaire* by Molière, whose works Robinson relished.

Robinson doesn't help readers much by structuring the poem as he does. But doing so makes it more likely that Annandale married Miriam, loved her physically, wrote about a spiritual lover, buried Miriam, and then called on Damaris, who guesses at the contents of his book. What follows remains obscure. But Richard P. Adams regards the conclusion of *The Book of Annandale*, with a new world being born for Damaris, as "perhaps the most triumphant conclusion Robinson ever arrived at." In a letter (April 12?, 1901) to Josephine Preston Peabody,* Robinson writes reductively that "The Book of Annandale" is about a dying man whose wife promises not to re-marry but who half a dozen years later "pledged herself" to a man who not only recorded odd thoughts in a diary but took a nap on the very day his wife was to be buried. Just what "pledged herself" meant in Robinson's mind is anyone's guess. Ellsworth Barnard suggests that Annandale's book may be "a symbol of life's onward surge" impelling people to escape stagnation by being defiant of conventions. (In "Annandale Again," Annandale and Damaris are married.) (Sources: R. Adams, 122; Barnard, 286; Genthe, 394; Neff, 120; *Selected Letters*, 39; E. Robinson, 13; C. Smith, 191, 192, 193; Winters, 133)

"A Book of Verse That Is Poetry" (1899). Unsigned review. Robinson moderately praises *The Wayfarers* by his friend Josephine Preston Peabody.* He calls its contents "real," says the book isn't "great," but suggests it's acceptable when compared to most contemporary American verse. It will appeal neither to those who read simply for thoughtful content nor to those who subscribe to what is vaguely called art for art's sake. Peabody combines substance and form, displays steady imagination and spirituality, and has other good features if also temporary "feminine vagaries of rhetoric." Robinson quotes from the title poem and from "Jongleur," says he could but needn't quote from other poems, and concludes despite reservations that Peabody has "something to say"

and "an artist's ability to say it." This piece is evidently Robinson's only formal book review. (Source: Cary [1975], 62–66, 186–87)

"A Book of Verses Underneath the Bough" (1893). Poem. Parody of the famous lines from *The Rubáiyát of Omar Khayyám*. Robinson sent this little quatrain to Harry de Forest Smith* in a letter (October 5, 1893), in which he says it would be paradise "enow" if he had a book of poems, a blazing fire, some corn, and his friend smoking with him. (Source: *Untriangulated Stars*, 110)

"Bores" (1887). Unsigned essay. As time advanced beyond the Dark Ages, punishments for often minor offenses ceased. People should benefit themselves but also others, should stop interfering in other people's affairs, and should stop criticizing their behavior or influencing them. Many preachers at funerals are wordy and boring. Trivial literature is a waste of time. It's better to accept reality than to be as gloomy as a shadow. Such pessimists should be tied and sent up the river.

"Bores" is the first item by Robinson to appear in print. It was published in *The Amateur*, issued by the Gardiner high-school class of 1888, a short time before July 1, 1887. (Sources: Cary [1974], 21; Cary [1975], 61–62, 186)

"Boston" (1896). Poem. Although the poet is content with his "northern pines," he fondly remembers a friendly town, especially when it is viewed "in the sunrise by the sea." Seen from above, the light reveals "something new and fierce." Still, light cannot clear away a sense of dim, "charmed antiquity."

This eight-line poem starts like a Petrarchan sonnet (which it originally was), with a slightly off-rhyme *abbaabba* rhyme scheme. The *b*-rhymes are "uprears," "appears," "fierce," and "clears." In the original sestet, the poet adds that although his "Boston is a counterfeit," stripped of reality, it is there for him, like a name on letters from an absent friend. In a letter (May 17, 1897) to Harry de Forest Smith,* Robinson says that ever since he "lied so like the devil" that his northern pines were good enough for him, he "had visions of Auckland" and wanted to go to New Zealand, where he might be able to write a sonnet. (Sources: Cary [1975], 27, 177; *Untriangulated Stars*, 287)

"Boys" *see* "Romance"

Bradford, Gamaliel (1863–1932). Man of letters. Bradford was born in Boston, moved with his family to what is now Wellesley Hills, Massachusetts (1867), traveled in Europe with his family (1878–1879), and attended Harvard College briefly (1882). He married Helen Hubbard Ford (1886); they had a son and a daughter. Bradford's first publications were somewhat unimportant essays, poetry, and fiction (1895–1904). Tragedy hit his family when his son committed suicide (1910) and his father was killed in a trolley accident (1911). Bradford published *Lee the American* (1912), the first of his major "psychographs." The psychographer is a scholar who does careful research on a usually well-known person and then presents basic, significant, and dramatically characteristic data as a study of the essence of that person. Although Bradford wrote much else, he was at his best when creating psychographs, on a variety of subjects, including, for a few examples among dozens, Mark Twain and James McNeill Whistler (in *American Portraits, 1875–1900,* 1922), Charles Darwin (in *Darwin,* 1926), Daniel Webster (in *As God Made Them: Portraits of Some Nineteenth Century Americans,* 1929), and Theodore Roosevelt* (in *The Quick and the Dead,* 1931).

Little appears to be known about Robinson's relationship with Bradford, but Bradford's method of concentrating on the essence of a personality appealed to Robinson, who dedicated *Talifer* "To the Memory of Gamaliel Bradford." (Source: Wagenknecht)

Bradstreet, Anne (c. 1612–1672). First poet of New England. She was born in England, the daughter of Thomas Dudley (1576–1653) and Dorothy Yorke Bradstreet (d. 1643). Dudley was often the deputy governor or the governor of the Massachusetts Bay Colony (1630–1650) and also served as an overseer of Harvard College (1637–1653).

Anne Bradstreet married Simon Bradstreet, settled with him and her father in Ipswich and then North Andover, Massachusetts, bore eight children, and wrote a great deal of important, attractive poetry.

Anne Bradstreet's sister was Mercy Dudley Woodbridge, whose husband was the Reverend John Woodbridge. Their son Thomas Woodbridge married Mary Jones. They had a son named Benjamin Woodbridge. He married Sarah Gerrish and had a son also named Benjamin Woodbridge. He married Susanna Tappan and had a son, Thomas Woodbridge. Thomas married Lydia Ayer and had a daughter, Mary Ayer Woodbridge. Some of these Woodbridges lived near the Damariscotta River, east of Gardiner, Maine. Mary Ayer Woodbridge married Edward Palmer. One of their children was Mary Palmer, who married Edward Robinson,* and thus became Mary Robinson,* the poet's mother. Robinson was therefore indirectly descended from Anne Bradstreet, America's first poet. (Sources: Hagedorn, 4–5; Richards [1936], 4)

Braithwaite, William Stanley (1878–1962). Man of letters and teacher. William Stanley Beaumont Braithwaite was born in Boston. His grandfather, a British admiral and a governor of Barbados, married a black woman. Braithwaite's father, William Smith Braithwaite, was a medical student in London but quit, moved to Boston, and married Emma DeWolfe, whose family had been slaves. William Stanley Braithwaite was homeschooled until his father died (1886). The family became so poor that Braithwaite went out to work (from 1890). Employment as a typesetter acquainted him with poetry by John Keats, Robert Burns, and William Wordsworth. Braithwaite determined to become a poet but not restrictively labeled as an African-American one. He married Emma Kelly (1903); they had seven children. He published his *Lyrics of Life and Love* (1904) and *The House of Falling Leaves* (1908). He wrote reviews and critical essays for the Boston *Evening Transcript* (beginning 1906). As its literary editor, he assembled poems by others into his *Anthology of Magazine Verse and Year Book of American Poetry* (1913–1929). In his

1913 *Anthology*, Braithwaite republished Robinson's "The Field of Glory." In his 1914 volume, dedicated to Louis V. Ledoux* and Robinson, he republished "Eros Turannos" and "The Gift of God." Braithwaite's 1915 issue includes Robinson's "Cassandra," "Flammonde," and "Old King Cole." In 1919 he included "Demos," "The Flying Dutchman," "The Mill," and "The Valley of the Shadow." Braithwaite's 1919 anthology entitled *Victory* featured 38 American poets, and included Robinson's "The New Jester." Braithwaite persuaded Theodore Roosevelt* to write the introduction, which may well represent the former president's last publication. Braithwaite's 1920 *Anthology of Magazine Verse* featured Robinson's "Tact" and "The Wandering Jew." In his 1920 volume, Braithwaite included "The Long Race" "Lost Anchors," "Many Are Called," "Monadnock," and "Vain Gratuities." In 1922 he included "Caput Mortuum." Braithwaite's final volume, that of 1929, includes "Hector Kane." Among the many emerging poets he encouraged, Robert Frost ranks highest. Bacon Collamore* reports that Braithwaite also favorably reviewed Robinson's two plays, *Van Zorn* and *The Porcupine*, as well as his *Avon's Harvest*, in the *Transcript*. Braithwaite's being a quadroon led to his leaving Boston and teaching at Howard University (1935–1945). Retiring in Harlem, he published *Selected Poems* (1948) and a book about the Brontë family (1950).

Soon after Braithwaite wrote a perceptive essay-review of *The Town Down the River* ("Books of the Day: The Spiritual Qualities of an American Poet," *Evening Transcript*, October 29, 1910), Robinson sought him out, and the two became fast friends. Richard Cary reports that Robinson told his Boston friend, the sculptor Truman Howe Bartlett (b. 1835), that Braithwaite's essay-review was the best ever written about his poetry. In at least nine later pieces (notably "America's Foremost Poet," *Evening Transcript*, May 28, 1913), Braithwaite continued his praise of Robinson. Robinson alerted Edith Brower* to Braithwaite's skillful reviews of *Van Zorn* and *The Porcupine*, Robinson's two published plays. Hermann Hagedorn* says that Braithwaite introduced Robinson to Frost and that Braith-

waite persuaded Robinson to publish what became Robinson's 1921 collection of his poetry. (Sources: Brower, 159, 166; Cary [1974], 217–18, 251–55, 289–92; Collamore, 17; Hagedorn, 339, 325)

Briggs, LeBaron Russell (1855–1934). Dean of Harvard College and English composition teacher there. He was revered by the students. When Robinson began studying at Harvard, he took Briggs's course in composition (1891). (Source: Morison, 403)

"Broadway" (1918). Poem. At night, Broadway is "a gay leviathan"; by day, a million-eyed unseeing monster, masked to conceal its true nature. It tears souls, wrecks "men and avenues," and "feeds on hopes and dreams." Its flaming length can "cheer" and "dazzle," but "scorch / . . . wingless moths." If it chances to associate itself with something admirable, it quickly puts on an alluring but evanescent glitter. (Sources: Cary [March 1974]; Cary [1975], 50–51, 182)

"The Brothers" *see* **"Romance"**

Brower, Edith (1848–1931). Writer. Edith Brower, born in New Orleans, was moved at nine months to Wilkes-Barre, Pennsylvania, which was thereafter her permanent residence. She was educated at home, in public schools, and at the Wilkes-Barre Female Seminary. Although nominally a Presbyterian, Brower became an eclectic thinker in religion and a progressive in politics. She adored the arts, gave piano recitals, lectured on music, and published poetry, fiction, and essays in nationally respected periodicals. She commuted occasionally to New York to read manuscripts for Titus Munson Coan,* who had an agency to help would-be authors. When Robinson sent a copy of his *The Torrent and The Night Before* to Coan, he referred it to Brower (1897). She saw its value instantly and wrote Robinson to ask for a personal copy, which he sent. He soon admired Brower, whom he described in a letter (June 17, 1897) to Harry de Forest Smith* as "the most sagacious female that I have ever run across." Brower published an acute review of

Robinson's *The Children of the Night* in the Wilkes-Barre *Times* (December 20, 1897). Robinson visited her in Wilkes-Barre (January 8–9, 1898), this journey being the farthest west he ever went. Their correspondence lasted until a year before her death. She preserved 189 of his letters. Robinson liked to refer to Brower as his "great aunt." She began to write her informative "Memories of Edwin Arlington Robinson" (March 1890) and continued working on it for some time, until it grew to 54 manuscript pages. Four months after Edith Brower died, a memorial service was held in her honor at a women's club in Wilkes-Barre. Along with other tributes, one was read which Robinson had sent. Unfortunately, the text was never preserved. Richard Cary provides an excellent, detailed introduction to his 1968 edition of Robinson's letters to Brower. At the time Hermann Hagedorn* was writing his biography of Robinson, published in 1938, permission to use the poet's letters to Edith Brower was withheld. Cary, who says her Wilkes-Barre *Times* review was the longest concerning Robinson to its date, summarizes her decades-long friendship with Robinson. (Sources: Brower; Cary [1974], 84–86; *Untriangulated Stars*, 288)

Brown, Rollo Walter (1880–1956). Essayist and educator. Robinson met Brown at the MacDowell Colony* (1923). In his 98-page *Next Door to a Poet* (1937), Brown reminisces about his association with Robinson, his observation of him, and his affection for him. Brown makes many, many points of interest: Robinson regarded himself as a poor conversationalist; Robert Frost, a fine one. Robinson was fond of the *Literary Supplement* of the *Times* of London. He was so unusual that he seemed to dominate the colony; while playing pool there, he applauded when someone else won. He composed poetry slowly, restlessly, rocking, pacing, staring at Mt. Monadnock. He often talked about old age. He combined physical quietude and mental churning, slept poorly, and read detective fiction to relax. He was overly sensitive to sights, sounds (especially piano chords and whippoorwill squawks), and smells. He disliked crowds, meetings, big dinners, teas, being asked to explain his poetry, and gossipy journalism. He was downcast by stupid reviews of his work, elated by penetrating reviews, uniquely by Charles Cestre.* He was addicted to coffee. He called certain men he had known at Harvard stuffed shirts, then asked Brown to forget the remark. He often apologized after being dogmatic. He greatly admired Thomas Hardy and Alfred, Lord Tennyson, but Walt Whitman, Elinor Wylie, and Amy Lowell* much less. He revered Johann Sebastian Bach, Johannes Brahms, and especially Gilbert and Sullivan. His humor was wry, piteous, grim, and twined with the tragic. He felt that most people are essentially alone. When able to be so, he was generous with money. He was happy at the early success of other writers. The élan vital of beetles, caterpillars, and pine trees fascinated him. His reading often centered on books trying to explain the meaning of existence. Though hating to be classified, he called himself an optimist. He was fascinated when Brown applied to *The Firemakers: A Novel of Environment* (1931), his novel about coal miners, the theory of Miguel de Unamuno (1864–1936) that all fictional characters are partly autobiographical. Brown reports Robinson's comments on his methods of writing and rewriting, his production of lines per day, criticism of his works, his sales figures, his pleasure at awards, his discontent with Harvard's iciness toward him, and his theory about dreams. Brown concludes that Robinson's "entire mind was always in a fruitful state of self-leavening, always on the track of something which required an awareness that was integral and continuous."

Since Robinson hadn't known Rollo Brown early, it is a coincidence that he named Rollo Brewster, a character in *The Porcupine*, as he did. Brown wrote *Lonely Americans* (1929), in which he discusses Charles William Eliot,* Charles Eliot Norton, and Edward MacDowell,* among other eminent Americans. (Source: R. Brown, 26 and passim)

Burnham, George (c. 1867-?). George Edwin Burnham was an adventuresome person. At 17, he quarreled with his father and left New England, went to the Western frontier, was a ranch hand in New Mexico, a hotel worker, and a bartender, drifted to Wyoming, and was caught there one January night on his way to Butte, Montana. He suffered frozen feet, which turned gangrenous, were amputated, and were replaced with wooden legs. Burnham then studied law at Harvard, became friends with and roomed with Robinson there (1891–1893), and very briefly practiced law with the firm Lord & Day in New York until he became disaffected by corporate greed and political influence, quit and suffered a nervous breakdown, after which he worked for a while early in the new century as a ticket agent in the Boston office of the New York, New Haven, & Hartford Railroad.

Robinson maintained an intimate relationship with Burnham. They were fellow roomers, boarders, and drinkers in New York (1897–1898) and later. Burnham, whose brother-in-law was a construction engineer when the New York subway was being built, suggested that Robinson apply for the job as a subway time-checker (1903). Burnham offered Robinson overnight hospitality when he went to Boston, and visited him frequently at the MacDowell Colony* (from 1911). In "The Burning Book" (1916) Robinson had Burnham in mind as the burner, perhaps only figurative, of his writings. Robinson dedicated *Merlin* (1917) to Burnham. Rollo Walter Brown* reports that Robinson toward the end of his life told him he could endure spending winter months in Boston only if he could stay with Burnham. When Burnham lost his job in Boston because of a bout with influenza, Robinson grew concerned, sent him some money (1931), and promised to send more on a regular basis. When Robinson was in the hospital and close to death, he dictated to Lewis M. Isaacs* his last letter (March 25, 1935). It was to his niece Marie Louise Robinson,* then a nurse in Boston. In it, he suggested that she ask her friend Dr. Arthur Thornton Legg, an orthopedic surgeon, to examine Burnham's pained legs and offered to pay for medical treatment and new prostheses. (Marie married Legg in 1936.) After Robinson's death, Burnham was the curator of the Robinson House at Head Tide, Maine, for a while. (Sources: W. Anderson [1980], 52; R. Brown, 88; Hagedorn; E. Robinson, 9; C. Smith)

"The Burning Book" (1916). Poem, subtitled "Or the Contented Metaphysician." This man envisioned something special, but tonight his eyes are weary. He burns all of his writings, in which he discussed "an end of the world." The pages "are crinkled and curled," and turned into "his ashes of glory." He smiles, free now from the task of explaining "God's face." His dream of teaching others about finalities is ended. Silent joy follows.

Chard Powers Smith* identifies the disappointed author who burned his book as Robinson's friend George Burnham.* Smith writes that the poem "portray[s] . . . Robinson's best friend Burnham the mystic who, having been emptied of self, is destroying his lifework, watching its still glowing ashes." Not actually a writer of sustained works, Burnham was a mystical philosopher who appealed to Robinson's mystical predilections. More generally, the book-burner represents, says Ellsworth Barnard, a person freeing himself from "the self-created tyranny of a mistaken ambition." (Sources: Barnard, 165; C. Smith, 242)

Burton, Richard (1861–1940). Author and educator. Richard Eugene Burton was born in Hartford, Connecticut, where his ministerial father was a frequenter of literary circles that included Mark Twain and Charles Dudley Warner. Among Burton's childhood friends was William Lyon Phelps,* future Yale professor of literature. Studying literature, Burton obtained a B.A. from Trinity College, Hartford (1883), and a Ph.D. at Johns Hopkins (1888). He did editorial work (1888–1897), and taught at the University of Minnesota (1898–1925), with interruptions to be an editor again and to teach briefly at the University of Chicago. He lectured on contemporary literature widely and enthusiastically, while also freelancing (1925–1933) and teaching at Sarah Lawrence College (1928–1931). He became an immensely popular professor at Rollins College (1933–1940). He wrote some 20 books — poetry, fiction, literary criticism, and on linguistics. He served on committees to award Pulitzer prizes. He was married twice — to Agnes Rose Tingley (1889) and to Ruth Guthrie Thomson (1931) — and had no children. He suffered a fatal cerebral hemorrhage as he began what proved to be his final class at Rollins.

Burton maintained a summer residence in Dublin, New Hampshire, and first met Robinson at the nearby MacDowell Colony.* In a reminiscence, Burton affectionately remembers Robinson, who, he says, made some "tolerant comments" on Burton's poetry, displayed "a kind of quiet, deep-down friendliness that [often] took the place of fluent speech," and introduced him "unobtrusively . . . [to] a number of writing folk" at the colony. Burton reports that the two met twice later, in New York, when Burton was giving a private reading, and when the two as committee members of the Book League of America had occasion to talk over possible book choices. (Source: R. Burton, 9)

"But for the Grace of God" (1910). Poem. Under the title is "There, but for the grace of God, goes . . ." The poet asks why a certain man masked a secret hunger. On a certain miserable day, the poet could have spoken helpfully to the fellow but didn't. The poet remembers the day, but the man never returned. He may now be wandering desperately. He briefly illuminated the room when he was in it. The poet wonders why the person remains away. He must be commanding "imps invisible" to speak forlornly. Strangely, wherever he is he sends a message of his loneliness. Will the poet always be trapped by the fellow's "sorry sunbeam"?

The location of the departed man is doubly obscure, because Robinson writes with characteristically enigmatic negatives near the end of the poem: "Why will he not be where he is / And not with me?" Robinson is surely suggesting that God might have reversed the roles of the poet and the other man and made the poet a wanderer, instead, far from his appointed home, bereft of home-town friends, and missed.

"Calvary" (1897). Sonnet. The persona, a long-surviving witness, says that "We gibed" Christ the Master while he, without friends, martyred, weak in body though free in spirit, slowly "toiled along to Calvary." He answered our hound-like curses with tears "for us." Nineteen hundred years later, the persona resumes his commentary. Shame clings to us because "we have not made good the loss / That outraged faith has entered in his name." When will courageous love make us strong? The persona concludes by asking "how long / Are we to keep Christ writhing on the cross!"

Laura E. Richards* reports that "Calvary" was "the fruit of a night-long discussion with a [not named] friend who still treasures the manuscript [as of 1936]." Emery Neff says that after Robinson's mother died, he found solace in "the gospel according to St. John . . . and wrote 'Calvary.'" Edwin Mims oddly begins a brief treatment of Robinson by saying that "[a]mong American poets Robert Frost, Edwin Arlington Robinson, and Robinson Jeffers wrote, in the main, as if no Christ had ever lived." Grudgingly, Mims admits that "[n]o one has more poignantly expressed the significance of Calvary than has he [Robinson] in his ['Calvary'] sonnet." Although Mims then touches on Robinson's "Nicodemus," it is clear that he skimmed through Robinson's poetry superficially. Sister Mary James Power, subscribing to the theological position that Christ was crucified to defeat evil, not either to pay a debt or to be a role model, asserts that in "Calvary" Robinson, after asking "how long," "intimates the time: Christ will not be vindicated until the last day when His enemies shall be made His footstool." (Sources: Mims, 19, 223; Neff, 254–55; Power, 79; Richards [1936], 56–57)

"Calverly's" (1907). Poem. Two of us pay no more visits to Calverly's, where lights are low and strangers are now present. We couldn't call our dead friends back with fiddle music or the clinking of tankards. They survive, though, if we could only "read the book of scattered lives." It tells about Leffingwell, "with his eerie joy"; about Lingard, a "Mooncalf"; about Clavering, who perished "because he couldn't laugh." Since they can't return to tell what happened, let them rest in "one estate / With ashes, echoes, and old wars." When republished in *The Town Down the River* (1910), this poem and "Leffingwell," "Clavering," and "Lingard and the Stars" were all presented under the master heading entitled "Calverly's."

Hermann Hagedorn* says that Robinson "in 'Calverly's' enshrined the romance of the fellowship" he enjoyed in his bohemian days in New York with George Burnham,* Craven Langstroth Betts,* Titus Munson Coan,* and Alfred Hyman Louis.* Robinson may have chosen the name Calverly because, as he said in a letter (January 26, 1898) to Edith Brower,* he liked "The Cock and the Bull" by Charles Stuart Calverley (1831–1884), whose poem is a parody of Robert Browning's *The Ring and the Book*. Spelling the parodist's name "Calverly," Robinson said he preferred "Calverly's version of it much better" than Browning's original. Clavering, Leffingwell, and Lingard will reappear in "Clavering," and Lingard and Clavering in "Lingard and the Stars." As for that "book of scattered lives," Ellsworth Barnard suggests that Robinson's mission in life was "to retrieve and reunite . . . pages" from it; and Scott Donaldson entitled one of his essays on Robinson "The Book of Scattered Lives." (Sources: Barnard, 23; Brower, 71; Donaldson [1969]; Hagedorn, 238)

Captain Craig (1902; rev. ed., 1915). Narrative poem in three numbered parts.

I. The unnamed narrator is a close friend of Captain Craig, a resident of Tilbury who probably had fewer than 10 friends altogther. Like many other people, Captain Craig tried at one point to make himself into something he wasn't. Soon, dizzy on the streets, he had to beg, often unsuccessfully, and would then return to his room cold — "without a curse." He gradually slowed down. Many indifferent citizens repeated the old idea: "trust in God, and let the Captain starve." He laughs and gibes with biblical and poetic quotations. The narrator and four or five others, surprised by his "lettered nonchalance," go visit him. Throned in his one chair, he eulogizes until only the narrator is willing to remain.

Captain Craig's "tuneful ooze / Of rhetoric" changes, and he opines that receiving a gift makes us, first, happy that we get and, second, happy that we give; further, that God remembers and that "his language has no adjectives." Craig tells about a soldier who saved an abused urchin from suicide by a little friendly, soothing talk, then — born to die — did so, and was brought home with "a brass band at his funeral, / As you should have at mine." Craig says that God let men build unsubstantial churches before "Science was . . . born," and now we must learn to appreciate God's laughing music, which is full of wisdom and joy. Craig laughs; and the narrator shakes his hand, departs, and regards Craig as merely another "smug-faced failure on God's earth." However, since the old fellow had tears in his eyes, the narrator figures he might learn something. Still, by morning the narrator has turned a bit cocky.

At a tavern called the Chrysalis next night, the narrator meets some friends. They include Morgan, who fiddled, Killigrew, who drowsed and grinned, and Plunket, who talked learnedly. They kid him for wasting time with that windbag Craig. Though feeling they are missing a point, the narrator merely smokes some pipes. Restless that night, he feels that he is being rebuked — by fate, by God. It dawns on him that he and Craig ought to laugh together, like bright children. Through March and April, the narrator nonplusses his pals by listening to Craig's life story. He and others even arrange some "humorous provision" for the fellow. The narrator must leave Tilbury Town for six or seven months, tells Craig so, and sees in his response an unmistakable, unforgettable look.

Aboard the departing train in May, the narrator feels free of Craig but sluggish, smokes one of Plunket's vile cigars, and outside the windows sees where he and his pals played at being Indians in the woods.

II. Far away, the narrator receives letters from Craig, now in a "renewed estate." In the first letter he writes as follows:

> I cannot think of anything to-day
> That I would rather do than be myself,
> Primevally alive, and have the sun
> Shine into me.

He goes on. He feels peppy, enjoys the light, forgets the darkness, and relishes children's laughter because it "redeems the man." Adults hurt each other and then gripe that God has made them wretched. The mildest breeze totally delights him. He used to think of sick men, wounded soldiers, women working too hard, and abandoned children eating refuse. But Spring makes him forget that the happy half of "humankind" might be drawn into darkness by trying to help the half "here in hell."

Craig sends the narrator long epistles about his former glory days, "When I had hounds and credit, and grave friends / To borrow my books and set wet glasses on them." When he was out riding once, a male friend pointed to a healthy, beautiful, rich woman and described her as "cursed with happiness," forgetful of life's dark side, and with servants who rush when she claps to summon them. She unwraps "an eighteen-carat crucifix" at church, offers "pretty . . . prayers," and is charitable, "but what is giving like hers worth?" She sews on an altar cloth for a minister she calls Jerry and praises his lovely sermons making "life seem so sweet!" In reality, this spinning world, all apple blossoms to her, screams and drips pus.

When this lady rode with Craig, he writes, she pointed out his male friend, and said that he "feeds his very soul on poison," should have been encouraged to read some romance literature, told her when he was about 19 that he had heard she was in love but added it wouldn't last, says roses wilt, doesn't respect kids' laughs, and doubts George Washington was great. Craig concludes that the man and the woman are both right and also both wrong through being one-sided. But is it better to be rendered ignorant by too much light or by too many shadows? Neither of these two people could have profited by self-analysis. How can we test sunshine? It is a devil, dangerously transparent. Split it into its component parts, "ignorance, / Hypocrisy, good-heartedness, conceit, / Indifference," and it does no good to laugh or hold to "obsolescent creeds" in this present dungeon. Trust the child to find the light. Craig adds that while writing all this he imagines seeing "Clotho, Lachesis, Atropos," the three Fates, "with a faintness never fading," with changeless, changing colorless colors.

The narrator's answer to Craig's first letter was a letter combining humor and anxiety, which upset Craig and made him write a sec-

ond letter, in July, mixing the "facetious and austere." Feeling challenged, he says he is not a poet, musician, or painter, but only a wastrel wit who has glimpsed through hell's apertures bits of heaven of the sort to inspire poets. He has thought along through difficult times, once resembled "a frog on a Passover-cake in a streamless desert," but has earned enlightenment, and therefore has received it. He cautions the narrator neither to shake his head nor to laugh and nap; the truth won't sleep. Craig recalls a fat, drunk, sponging low-life — call him Count Pretzel von Würzburger, the Obscene — who though loathsome was still "a free creature with a soul," and not to be condemned. Craig defines Count Pretzel as a self-confessed sinful poet, skeptic, and critic, but also one who found and held down a job to play the piano in a saloon. He knew many compositions, could improvise, and once, 10 years ago, memorably turned "The *Träumerei* into a Titian's nightmare." Pretzel, Craig adds, had a beer and then read his one and only sonnet. It concerned Carmichael, who had three china frogs on a wall, called them Aristophanes's frogs, and laughed and was laughed at when he said so. Pretzel begged more beer but said he was in truth the one who did the giving, which was to preserve Craig and his friends. Craig liked Pretzel and suggests that the narrator might put him in a metered book. One friend might relish it — Killigrew, whom Craig likes despite his smiling too much during visits.

Killigrew wrote the narrator these details: Sagacious old Craig was eating and smoking regularly, was as egoistical as God; Killigrew will wed this December; Killigrew wrote a poem to the effect that Augustus Plunket, Ph.D., got the bishop's pippin-pretty daughter; Killigrew may write an epic sometime; then what?

Craig's third letter bodes ill. Three birds have visited him. He entices them with apples and corn to approach. They are the three Fates, whose bills he pinches. But his "ancient levity" about them "is the forbear of all earnestness." He says he dreamed he was in a strangely lighted forest, unwilling to sleep for fear of dying. "The Mystery, the Child," approached and smiled. When Craig explained that he was a carpenter but with nothing to do, the Child told him to sharpen his tools and "go learn your trade in Nazareth." Craig writes that this dream was as curious as many to which he refers. One such man dreamed he was the new Æschylus, wrote about "the new Eumenides" in America, but woke up with only a phrase remaining. Initially frustrated but finally good-natured, he died young. However, "the rhythm of God" sounds through such unwritten works. Craig reports that Killigrew has "committed" a poem called "A Ballad of London," which, though asked, Craig feels too old to pass judgment on. In it, the balladeer accompanies a man who sports a golden feather, is going to London to get married, but, when asked if he too is going there to wed, declines to answer. Craig obliquely decries the ballad and asks when the narrator is returning to Tilbury Town.

III. In October the narrator finds Craig ill, sitting in bed, having a little physician-prescribed broth. He says that the narrator's smile is forced and that we remember Christ's poetry but fear his prose. He promises the narrator that tomorrow he'll read all the young fellows his testament, clings to his hand, then dismisses him. Next day his eyes seem small, hard, and dry, and he chants with a "lordly quaver" his proudly worded will as though bequeathing great estates. Instead, he gives these heirs "God's universe and yours." If he had been a materialistic success, lesser gifts would have made them speciously happy. Occasionally a writer of tragedies expresses a "fragment of God's humor." Craig opines that "What men lose / Man gains." Like Icarus and others, we aim for the sun, sometimes fall, but must try, must never doubt the elevated truth, must remain sincere. Craig asks his auditors to smile on him and be glad his joke was worthy, be glad he remained inactive and thus prevented their becoming sluggish. He quotes a puzzled poet, to the effect that behind the rough ocean is the calm sea, and further that ages tell of regrets which Time nullifies. Neither criticize nor revere the flesh, but seek the light. No one falls alone. One deep-rooted flower, ever surviving and called love, is really "Selfishness." Craig alludes to an unnamed pompous poet, then recommends "discordant,

hard, grotesque" expressions from more reticent writers instead. At one time, Craig boldly progressed by denying the value of "specious . . . words," turned to the sun, realized he was climbing with the truth, and became serious.

Killigrew tries to interrupt but fails. Craig continues. Once a person "read[s] the book of wisdom in the sun," there is no turning back to read works by the bewildered. Once again, Killigrew is bothersome. Craig, continuing undeterred by Killigrew's sigh, avers that you can't "teach caterpillars how to fly." Still, don't feel superior, with your so-called wisdom, your money, your lovers. Ordinary "bloody-knuckled scullions" and their companions are more like you than you think; help them, don't hurt them. Hide in crowds or alone, and you will still be exposed, perhaps by a Socrates-like humorist. Craig concludes by describing his own funeral, complete with a brass band, some wondering why the fuss, and others answering that Craig kept his humor. He asks for funeral music by Handel, not Chopin.

Craig drops his testament. His mouth trembles. His guests leave, return next day, and find Craig frowning unusually and his eyes glittering like "a glad fish." He explains that he dreamed that he and Hamlet were near Lethe. And Hamlet was rooting a weed by order of the Fates, glared, then laughed at Craig, then with him. The two stepped onto a crocodile, killed it, and ate it.

The friends all make small talk. Egged on by Craig, Killigrew says he dreamed about a sad man who sang but didn't speak. Craig likes that. Killegrew continues. The first song, though sad, had a "mystic cheerfulness," and the singer shed bullet-like tears. The song concerned "Ten men from Zanzibar." Craig is pleased but soon asks to be allowed to sleep. As his guests are about to leave, however, he beseeches them to stay. He seems near death's shore. He wonders what death is and hopes his guests "find / Your promise of the sun." He wants them to look bravely on him now. November rain pelts outside. Stern words follow. He says that their minds must believe in the light. Like Socrates, Captain Craig now asks for the cup. Just before "the long drowse came to give him peace," he says, "Trombones."

Before a fire of beech logs at the Chrysalis that night, the narrator and the others mourn Craig and drink to him out of gratitude that he esteemed them. Morgan plays the Lohengrin march (by Richard Wagner) on his fiddle — most memorably.

Well, separated though they are now, they recall the night the inspiring old captain died. They also remember his funeral procession, over frozen ruts of roads, and Tilbury's brass band playing "the Dead March in Saul." (He requested George Frederick Handel's oratorio *Saul* and, please, not Frédéric François Chopin's piano-sonata funeral march.)

When Robinson started in 1898 writing what became *Captain Craig*, he called it "The Pauper." His friend Josephine Preston Peabody* tried in 1900 to get Small, Maynard and Co. to publish it. Instead, after delays the manuscript went mysteriously missing; it finally surfaced in a Boston brothel, where a publishing assistant had left it during an unprofessional visit, returned crestfallen for it, and accepted it back from the surprisingly careful madam (1901). Rejected thereafter elsewhere, it was eventually combined with other poems into a volume entitled *Captain Craig: A Book of Poems* (1902), published in 500 copies by Houghton, Mifflin, in Boston. This firm was agreeable because of the good offices of the poet's friends John Hays Gardiner* and Laura E. Richards.* They guaranteed it against financial loss, Mrs. Richards secretly doing so.

The titular hero of *Captain Craig* is based in part on Alfred Hyman Louis,* Robinson's brilliant, indigent, often tiresome New York friend, and also on Robinson's brother Dean Robinson.* Theodore Maynard* boldly asserts that "the lettered, broken vagabond, Captain Craig, is Robinson's projected vision of himself." James G. Hepburn is in accord, "except," he says, "for his [Craig's] garrulity." Edith Brower* in "Memories of Edwin Arlington Robinson" contends that Killigrew is based on Robinson's friend Craven Langstroth Betts.* Emma Robinson* and Ruth Nivison* have identified Morgan as based on Robinson's friend Arthur Blair, Killigrew (*contra* Brower), on his friend Linwood Barnard, and Plunket, on his friend Seth Ellis Pope;* and the

Chrysalis, where the friends met, Emma and Ruth say was patterned on a room above Brown's Dry Goods Store, Water Street, in Gardiner, Maine. Emma is specific concerning aspects of Dean's life as reflected in Craig's last days, saying that toward the end Dean was a spiritual beggar addicted to opium despite three voluntary visits for a curing regimen in Dwight, Illinois. She adds that Dean toward the end stayed in a small room in his house on Lincoln Street, in Gardiner, attended to by a man named Wakefield; further, that Robinson's presentation of Craig as intellectually brilliant was a tribute to his brother's wisdom. According to Hermann Hagedorn,* Count Pretzel von Würzburger, the Obscene, is partly modeled on Robinson's sponging friend Joseph Lewis French.* Robinson makes a latter-day Sophocles out of his philosophical hero, who makes slight use of Sophocles's *Antigone.* Evidently the Knight Templars' Band that played during Dean's funeral procession in 1899 included trombones of the sort Captain Craig craved for his funeral. In a letter (March 29, 1903) addressed to Charles Eliot Norton* and published by Bacon Collamore,* Robinson explains that in *Captain Craig* he was interpreting America rather than life.

C. Elta Van Norman details parallels between Captain Craig and Robinson: Both worked only sporadically, found it hard to adjust to regular employment, were more than casually attracted to alcohol, and liked the conviviality it encouraged. Van Norman also observes that the captain's "consciousness of . . . light manifests itself no less than twenty times throughout the poem"; notes that "there is nothing cruel in his laughter"; and concludes that he "has learned to know misery, to face it undaunted, and to refuse to submit to its power or to circumstances over which he has no control."

Henry Rushton Fairclough demonstrates Robinson's wide-ranging knowledge of the classics, which he put to service in characterizing Captain Craig. That seasoned old reader is shown to be aware of Latin pronouns, Cicero, Greek mythology, Trojan War heroes, Hippocrates and Aristophanes and Socrates, the Platonic dialogues, Virgil's *Aeneid*, Plutarch, Aeschylus, Sophocles's *Antigone*, Lucretius, Juvenal, Tacitus's *Annals*, and several less-known mythological bits and pieces as well. Warner Berthoff lauds *Captain Craig* highly. Although he says that "[s]pace is lacking to suggest the variety and energy and sheer surface interest of the line-by-line fashioning of the poem," what follows is a considerable analysis.

In a letter (March 9, 1902) to Laura E. Richards,* Robinson conveniently defines what he calls *Captain Craig*'s "theory": "it is possible to apply good natured common sense even to the so-called serious events in life."

Reviews of the 1902 edition were mixed, but there was enough praise to justify a second printing, of 270 copies (1903). May Sinclair* says tersely that "'Captain Craig' is a philosophy of life, taught through the humorous lips of a social derelict, a beggared Socrates, disreputable as the world counts reputation." She offers this as the advice embedded in the poem: "Be true to the truth that lies nearest to you; true to man; true to yourself; true, if you know no better truth, to your primal instincts; but at any cost, be true."

A second edition of *Captain Craig* was published (1915, number of copies unspecified), with several passages revised — for the purpose, it has been alleged, to please some adverse critics.

After discussing the career of Robinson's hero and Robinson's treatment of him, Charles Cestre* concludes as follows:

> Thus passed away Captain Craig, a humorist who had more wisdom in him and spoke more truth than many a capped and gowned don mouthing sanctimonious homilies. Although the poem is not perfect, it keeps up in most of its parts the difficult alliance of serious purpose and humorous characterisation. Robinson happily resisted the temptation to make humor the vehicle of sarcasm or satire . . . The poison of pessimism is absent . . . When his inspiration wraps itself in darkness, it is the darkness of tragedy . . . not despondency or despair.

Horace Gregory and Marya Zaturenska discuss the "high and serious comedy" in *Captain Craig*, place the tiny poems written by Pretzel and by Killigrew in the tradition of works Robinson has them parody, evaluate "the slow progress of self-knowledge which transcended his [Craig's] failure and the failure of those around him," and touch on the symbolic values of "light" and "darkness" running through the poem. As for that important word "light," Floyd Stovall generalizes thus: "He [Robinson] frequently represents truth by the symbol of light. Written with a capital it is the ineffable Word, the transcendental reality that endures within and behind this phenomenal world. Without the capital it is knowledge, or truth in its pragmatic sense." Louis Coxe lauds the good captain's "mock-serious style" of talk, with its "touches of Mark Twain, Yankee deadpan and put-on culture," but deplores its occasional "flaccidity."

Other commentators, beginning with Amy Lowell,* have disliked *Captain Craig*. She says that "Mr. Robinson's obscure, sometimes positively cryptic, method of expressing an idea . . . degenerated [in *Captain Craig*] into a confusion so intense that the reader wearied in tracking the poet's meaning. In fact, it may very fairly be said to have ruined the poem." Chard Powers Smith* opines that the poem "is, but for a few passages, not an imaginative transcription of imaginatively perceived emotional experiences, but a conscious versification of much deliberately concocted wisdom. Most of it, therefore, is not poetry at all but rationalistic pseudopoetry." Bernard Duffey also generalizes that "from *Captain Craig* [on,] . . . he [Robinson] was to have difficulty with the long poem. He could seldom give it effective structure of its own. Anecdote was added to anecdote and Robinson's ruminative cast of mind tended out of control toward a muddle of observation that was too often lost in confusion whatever it sought in free implication." Wallace L. Anderson speaks for many readers when he succinctly defines *Captain Craig* as "that crazy-quilt of a poem"; aware that Robinson probably inserted otherwise discardable "tavern songs," Anderson adds that the work was "Robinson's phoenix poem." (Sources: W. Anderson [1980], 58, 59; Berthoff, 125; Brower, 212; Cestre, 183; Collamore, 9; Coxe, 68, 73; Duffey, 152; Fairclough, 18–20; Gregory and Zaturenska, 116, 121; Hagedorn, 194; Hepburn, 267; Lowell [1917], 60–61; Maynard [1924], 155;

Notopoulos; E. Robinson, 2, 5–6; *Selected Letters*, 51; Sinclair, 332, 333; C. Smith, 176, 186; Stovall, 5; Sutliffe; Van Norman, 468, 469, 474)

Captain Craig: A Book of Poems (Boston and New York: Houghton, Mifflin, 1902). A collection of 18 poems, under 16 titles, and including the title poem. By 1902, when this, Robinson's third book, saw print, he had earned only $7 by his pen. That sum was paid by the editors of *Lippincott's Monthly Magazine* back in 1894 for his sonnet "For a Copy of Poe's Poems." Bliss Perry (1860–1954), author-educator, was a literary adviser to Houghton, Mifflin. According to Richard Cary, Perry reported to the owners of Houghton, Mifflin that some of the "verse" in *Captain Craig* was "obscure," "eccentric," and "prosaic," but advised acceptance on the grounds that Robinson might compose poems for "a more popular book later" which they could issue. A second edition of *Captain Craig: A Book of Poems*, was published in 1903. The third edition, published by Macmillan in 1915, was expanded by the addition of "Variations of Greek Themes" and "The Field of Glory," and was dedicated "To the Memory of John Hays Gardiner[*]." Robinson gratefully remembered that publication of the 1902 edition had been guaranteed against financial loss by Gardiner; Laura E. Richards* had also secretly promised her aid. Malcolm Cowley seems doubly incorrect when he generalizes that "After the failure of *Captain Craig* he [Robinson] never again displayed the resilience and high spirits of that volume. His humor became a subdued irony and he lost his eagerness for making experiments." (Sources: Cary [1974], 110; Cowley, 29; Perry, 177)

"Caput Mortuum" (1921). Sonnet. (The Latin title means "head of the dead.") The poet says that if he could have magically called anyone to sit with him by his fire, he wouldn't have called the man who surprisingly and happily did come. His visit was "useful." A failure and lacking money, "he paid with golden rhyme." He was an "obsolete" gambler "In Art's long hazard, where no man may

choose / Whether he play to win or toil to lose."

Robinson makes this sonnet profoundly personal by thus asserting that the author's vocation is fraught with danger. Robert Mezey helpfully explains that "caput mortuum" was "what alchemists called the residue remaining in a flask after distillation," hence, "any worthless residue, or even a worthless person — a poet, for instance," demeaned by a materialistic and status-conscious society. (Source: Mezey, 237)

"Cassandra" (1914). Poem. The persona while in a crowd hears someone offer a prophesy — to mere children. He (or she) begins: "Your Dollar is your only Word, / The wrath of it your only fear." The sarcasm continues. You build altars to money but can't see from their tops because you lack vision. You laugh when told to listen to reason, and you offer the excuse that you haven't grown up yet. Don't get cocky and complacent just because time and fate have pampered you thus far. You are ignoring history if you think you have seen "Millenniums and last great wars." Something uniquely prescient follows:

> Your Dollar, Dove and Eagle make
> A Trinity that even you
> Rate higher than you rate yourselves;
> It pays, it flatters, and it's new.

Ignorant of what the Eagle is thinking, you praise it even as it is consuming "your very flesh and blood." You have strength but don't see what you're stepping on. Can't you see what the world is like? The harsh interrogation ends thus: "Are you to pay for what you have / With all you are?" The crowd laughs, moves off, heedless, and in doing so proves that Robinson's criticism of America's cocksure materialism was justified.

Emery Neff says that (as of 1948, at least) "'Cassandra,' probing deeply into the weaknesses of our national character and phrasing them unforgettably, is the finest of our political poems." Archibald MacLeish praises Robinson because "he made for himself a Voice . . . His poems were new poems under the sun not because form or theme or style were new but because the speaker was: new as a man and new too as a man of his time and country." MacLeish uses as his first example a quotation from "Cassandra."

Robinson's "Cassandra" is as timely today as it was the moment it was composed. (Sources: MacLeish, 218; Neff, 259)

Cavender's House (New York: Macmillan, 1929). Poem. Narrative in blank verse, in three numbered parts.

I. After 12 years of wandering, Cavender, once strong and rich, returns to his silent, dark, and empty house, inhospitable now and with dusty, grave-like rooms. He senses that a woman (later given the name of his wife Laramie Cavender) who defeated him there has called him back. He had fears, doubts, and a death wish, but also "one unanswered question." Images from the past seem projected on the floor. She appears, is silent, but her eyes are full of "The look that never told him anything, / But what he told himself." Now he seems to hear her speak. The voice says that she will lift no veils, that she wants not to scare him, that he is "a lord of ruins," that women's feelings are beyond some people's awareness, that suspicions can "be worse than truth and ruin together," and that he is going to learn endurance.

To Cavender, Laramie is inscrutably beautiful, but her eyes are sadly smiling. Had he studied her "changelessness" before, he might have concluded that "there was no evil in her eyes / That was not first in his." He says he has no right to ask her anything, says he's been in hell, and begs her not to leave him. She replies at great length. She is no dream, would like him to forget that certain night but knows he can't, and hopes he knows he has been created by nature but also by himself. Faith for some people is part doubt, part fear. She was born with faith; he wasn't. If she left now, he might forget and be happy.

When he wonders if God, purpose, law exist, and says he feels hopeless, she replies that there is hope, that she is merciful, but that he might continue to suffer. He watches evil in her eyes change to a bereft and unhateful sorrow, tries to touch her but finds he cannot, and shivers. She says that if he dared to embrace and kiss her now and ask forgiveness,

she might almost forget. She concludes that he might have saved his house if he had judiciously weighed his faith concerning her and her faith concerning him. She chides him for his light opinion of women. He would embrace her now but for her derisive, reproachful look. He says that if he touched her he couldn't let her go.

II. Darkness, silence, and death conspire against Cavender and accusingly alter everything in the house. Laramie is there, inviting him nonchalantly to "rapture or despair." Dressed nicely as of yore, she might be asking for praise, forgiveness, his death. She once left him ruined but now has mentioned hope she brought for him.

Next, she says all this to Cavender. Things in this house seem familiar to her, like old songs, old smells, regretted pictures. He treated her like an image "in a twisted mirror." If he had changed it for the better, which he didn't, she would have been waiting pleasantly here for him. But no, he was too skillfully exacting. If she should sing one of her nice songs now, he might stop doubting and regret what he did to her. She couldn't sing now, with him making faces at her. Women see time in bits, the way a bird does while grabbing a worm, or the way a man does while he "takes a woman when his love / Prevails more in his blood than in his heart." Nature makes both sexes this way. "Love is not vengeance, though it may be death, / which may be life," as he may soon learn. God should have enabled her to read Cavender's heart and locate the small place for her in it. He mainly liked her face and body. Ah, but she remembers him as he was at first — promising, accomplished, vital, and "playful and persuasive" enough to make a woman want "to be bent / A little, but not broken."

She could go on whipping him thus; but if he cringed, as he might, it would be worse than if he cursed her. Cavender reckons in this manner. He made his own prison but wasn't wholly responsible. If Laramie lashes him now, she must be the agent of God; therefore God exists, or perhaps some "purpose or . . . law" does. Otherwise, the world's living creatures are all "seeming-endless incident[s] / Of doom." She counters by saying that he must be assigning an intellect to a fate that is alternately vicious and helpful. She reminds him that he used to wreck commercial rivals with a smile, then rationalized, but then stepped into darkness. Why didn't he realize that she quietly objected to such behavior?

For a time he can't reply and instead looks at her gentle hands but then remembers that they are strong enough to mangle and toss him aside. When he finally speaks, it is to ask her why she smiled encouragingly. He would like to retread those roads back to where he left her. Were they constructed before his birth? Were devils along the way? She may know and not answer, or she may not know. She was mysterious enough to be dangerous, and unaware of his near madness. Fuller knowledge would have made their ending different. He pleads with her to remain and says God wills it.

Her hands remain the same, but her eyes and mouth express slow scorn. She reminds him of his masterful selfishness, his erect, authoritative walk, and his notion that the world was made simply for him. But he was wicked and wasteful. When she laughs briefly, Cavender sweats, trembles, and grows afraid that the hope she brought may not materialize. She continues gently, saying that, if he had only known, they could have been as happy as a pair of loving squirrels needing little but acorns. Squirrel-like loyalty could have been easy. He poured "vinegar of suspicion" on their once tasty food and soured it. His remorse seems to generate her recriminations, and all the while he had quite rightly "adored and prized her / As an unmatched possession." But then she ridiculed him offensively, and his world stopped and everything turned dark and he didn't know what he did until afterwards. Has Laramie returned now simply to say he'll go on suffering until fate ends his life? He hears those words of hers again that he should have known.

Now Laramie expresses wonder as to why he is trying to bury himself behind his memories and hoping to find an explanation for what he did to her. You have to die to learn the truth but may not even then, she says. Twelve years ago all was wrecked; your life stopped there; "your time begins" there now. If you had told the law what you did, you wouldn't have endured this slow dying and might have learned something. Maybe we are cursed to suffer painful remorse.

Cavender yells for the truth, even though it would condemn him to hell.

> Tell me that I was mad for doubting you,
> Or that a poison that was burning in me
> Was truth on fire, as I believed it was.

His hope, for her, is only that she will tell him the truth, with no forgiveness, and let him die. Turning hard and pitiless, she answers that she can't help him know "whether or not / My freedom was a sin," but adds that his knowing is more important than his life or her death. This is so, because she doesn't know the answer to what he has just asked.

III. Frightened by looking at her hands, he tells her to say no and leave him burning, or say yes and start him toward the freedom of death. Her answer: Hasn't he heard yet that "Biologists / And bolshevists" are busy killing "Love and poor Romance?" If she had confessed sinning, wouldn't his commercial mind have simply recorded her "destruction" as a loss in his ledger? He asks if he "had reason to be mad that night" and now claims he was out of his mind then. She won't comfort him but does have a plan. He thinks half of her tricky words are "not hers." Some seem like his.

She suggests that they take her "drops of hope" and go outside to the cliff. They were happy there. He warmed her, there, in the cloudy, cold moonlight by embracing her. He said she "was too beautiful to think." But she was careless not to do some thinking. His love for her was gloating. Women ought to believe they don't care. She goes on:

> If I transgressed
> In desperation or in vindictiveness
> At last, as fear inflamed you to believe,
> I wonder when it was your avocations
> Had first recess and leisure to find out,
> And then to be disturbed.

After he "defect[ed]," he should have "scuttl[ed]" only himself.

She beckons him to come "to the old place" by the cliff. With a smile, she asks him to open the door for her. Through darkness they go to a certain seat. She tells him to sit but to keep his "distance yet." He "offend[ed] the Holy

Ghost." The distance to the cliff bottom is shadowy even in the present moonlight. She tells him it wouldn't do him or her any good for him to look down. Nor should he lean suicidally on the rusty iron rail right now. When he learns what time really is, he'll "almost laugh." Is it worse seeing or not seeing the woman down there that he killed? Any remorse? She goes on. In the morning workers "found me." Gossipers wondered why such an envied woman could have killed herself. Cavender should have made sure he was really wounded before killing her. He should have waited until tomorrow. "Tomorrow" is a frightening word. If he jumped down there now, doing so would scare him but not hurt him. He wouldn't like it, but, then, "there's nothing for you to like / In this life any more." She tells him not to touch her and also to stop asking questions. "If other arms than yours have had me in them, / What does it matter now?" God knows if you'll die just now.

Cavender feels sick. What he has been hearing isn't Laramie, though she's here. Does she hate him? She must have lied to him that night. He must know for certain, regardless of consequences. He speaks to her. He won't touch her. She needn't forget. She must tell him whether he had reason to doubt her. Once he has her answer, he will do whatever she requires — kill himself, remain in his dark house, find something hidden behind doors in it not opened before.

She answers "in a voice / That never in life could have been Laramie's." She has no answer for him. All she has is what he brought here and made her to be. She says that if Laramie's eyes see him now they probably do so with pity. She continues:

> There is a love stronger than death,
> Time says; and Laramie's love may have a life
> Stronger than death. I should not be surprised.
> It would be like her.

She says that he has now created Laramie's voice but that he must still hear one more voice before she gives him those "drops of hope" and departs. Making an end may not be an end. Doubt follows "a disordered curiosity." Maybe his injuring her contained his answer. Maybe her "evasion [was] her revenge."

Maybe her behavior was a response to her long-lasting disgust. Finally, "Love, would you call it? / You jealous hound, you murderer, you poor fool! / You are listening to yourself now, Cavender!" After the voice adds that he has time to think but little time not to, it turns silent.

Cavender sees her face turn into something different, and a different voice speaks. It tells Cavender that he must believe in "laws and purposes," that he doesn't fear death but does fear life and fears this distinct voice. Only he can open those locked doors. Will something invaluably meaningful be hidden there? Well, Cavender, alone, with none to pity him, must "cast out the lie within him, / And tell men what he was." In the dark house he finds light enough now

> Where men should find him, and the laws of men,
> Along with older laws and purposes,
> Combine to smite him.

He now fears only unearned, uncontemplated peace. What frightened him had come like a shapeless, unnamed, unannounced stranger, as though through a door he had known nothing about and behind him.

Cavender's House, which Robinson dedicated to the memory of William Vaughan Moody,* was published early in 1929 (limited edition, March; trade edition, April). This was not long before the Big Crash, after which sales of narrative poems naturally diminished.

Emma Robinson* saw much in the plot of *Cavender's House* paralleling aspects of her own unhappy marriage to Herman Robinson,* the poet's brother. She likened herself to Laramie, whose murder by Cavender she equated with Herman's breaking her heart, and Cavender's 12 years of wandering to her own 12 years of unhappy married life. Chard Powers Smith* also diagrams an autobiographical basement under *Cavender's House*. In its domestic triangle, for Cavender he practically reads Robinson's brother Herman; for Laramie, Herman's wife Emma; and for Laramie's non-appearing, possible, impossible lover, Robinson himself. Edwin S. Fussell notes the influence of Edgar Allan Poe, with "strong elements of horror — chiefly pathological — the blurred boundaries between natural and supernatural, the constant tendency toward allegory, the indefiniteness of the natural and social milieu, the formal reliance upon melodrama." Hyatt H. Waggoner notes that there are similarities in *Cavender's House* to works by Nathaniel Hawthorne: "The two themes of the poem, that the answers to our most urgent questions cannot be given us from outside ourselves but must be found within, and that when we stand in the darkness we are better able to see the light, are good Hawthorne as well as good Robinson."

From the outset, though, reviewers and then readers and some critics were puzzled as to Laramie's identity. Many thought she was a ghost, available and willing to haunt and pain her murderous husband upon his return to the house. (But wouldn't any self-respecting ghost of a demeaned wife either, if "guilty," boast of a lover replacing an ice cube of a husband or, if "pure," tell him his groundless doubts ruined what might have been ecstatic love?) Perceptive critics soon recognized that what seems to be a dialogue between Cavender and Laramie's spirit is really, as Emery Neff puts it, "a monologue, a colloquy of the businessman [Cavender] with himself." Back on June 24, 1929, Robinson wrote this to Edith Brower* (in a letter not published until 1968): "Laramie isn't a 'spook,' but a projection of C's uncomfortable fancy." Robinson proceeds to the effect that Laramie resides within Cavender, returns with him to the house, and tells only what he already knows but isn't wholly cognizant of. Robinson might have added that the "house" in which the couple are confined is the ghastly, dark, portable house of the husband's psyche. Robinson took umbrage at readers who evidently were uncertain as to Laramie's cause of death. He wrote (August 7, 1932) to Howard George Schmitt* to quote Laramie to Cavender —"you seized me and then threw me / Down on those rocks a hundred feet below"— and added that "Of course he killed her, but there was no evidence against him."

The long, 1,551-line *Cavender's House*, supple though its blank verse often is, has many negative critics. Yvor Winters, who is representative, opines that "*Cavender's House* is perhaps the most nearly perfect example of

Robinson's worst vices as a narrator," concentrates unduly on Laramie, and asserts his impatience with the slowness of revelations about her. The family of Robinson's friend Thomas Sergeant Perry* believed that the poet took the name Cavender from the name of a railroad station near Hancock, New Hampshire, where the Perrys had a summer home. (Sources: Brower, 196–97; Fussell [1954], 20; Harlow, 208; Neff, 229 ; E. Robinson, 23; Schmitt, 22, 23; C. Smith, 64, 74, 94, 263; Waggoner, 291–92; Winters, 108)

Cawein, Madison Julius (1865–1914). Poet, born in Louisville, Kentucky, to German-speaking parents. Cawein loved rural life, read widely and wrote poetry while still a youngster, and was influenced by his mother, who believed in and practiced spiritualism. After graduating from high school (1886), he worked in a poolroom, and published a book of verse (1887) which William Dean Howells commended. While holding various jobs, Cawein issued seven more such books (to 1894). By this time his kindly disposed readers included James Whitcomb Riley and Robinson. After producing a book of translations from German poets (1895), Cawein issued seven more volumes of his own verse (to 1901). He attracted the attention of Edmund Gosse, British man of letters, who assembled some of his better efforts into what became Cawein's *Kentucky Poems* (1902); Gosse introduced them, by a lapse of judgment, as the best of his times. Cawein married Gertrude Foster McKelvey (1903); they had a son. Four more volumes followed (to 1905), then a five-volume collection of his poetry (1907), which occasioned his election to the National Institute of Arts and Letters. Cawein continued to write too much, including eight more volumes (1909–1913) plus a posthumously published book (1915). The San Francisco earthquake (1906) and a New York stock market crash (1912) debilitated his finances so dreadfully that he had to sell much of his extensive library and also accept charity from the Authors Club of New York City (1914). He died in Louisville.

If not earlier, Robinson became acquainted with Cawein's verse when he read a review of *Captain Craig* (*Critic*, March 1903) by the prolific poet Clinton Scollard (1860–1932). In it, Scollard praised the fiery poetic passages he spotted enlivening Robinson's otherwise too-prosy blank verse, praised Robinson's "The Sage," and also called attention to Cawein's "lovely nature effects." Robinson found himself linked again to Cawein when Theodore Roosevelt* in his review of *The Children of the Night* (*Outlook*, August 12, 1905) praised Cawein, Scollard, and Bliss Carman, in the process of pointing out that, whereas they were well known, Robinson had sadly attracted little attention. Richard Watson Gilder,* the influential editor, knew Cawein and invited Robinson to meet him. Robinson, who composed meticulously, found Cawein's rapidity of production ludicrous. Still, in 1913, when a Boston Sunday *Post* pressed Robinson for an interview, he named Ralph Waldo Emerson as America's greatest poet, praised William Vaughn Moody* as currently the best, spoke favorably of Josephine Preston Peabody* and Cawein, and was distressed when his comments on Cawein were excluded. (Sources: Gregory and Zaturenska; Neff, 127–28, 141, 145, 168; Rothert)

Cestre, Charles (1871–1958). French literary critic. He published "L'Oeuvre Poétique d'Edwin Arlington Robinson," *Revue Anglo-Américaine* (April 1924), an important early study of Robinson. Cestre lectured at Bryn Mawr and Harvard on Robinson's poetry specifically. He published *An Introduction to Edwin Arlington Robinson* (1930), about which Robinson wrote (August 13, 1930) to the wife of Louis V. Ledoux.* Robinson says that this amiable French critic writes much that he long waited to read by some reviewer; he accepts Cestre's relatively unimportant complimentary words while more highly valuing his clearly expressed comments concerning Robinson's poetic intentions. Hermann Hagedorn* reports that Cestre's attention to Robinson "was a source of satisfaction to him." Other works by Cestre dealing with American authors include *Antologie de la littérature americaine* (1926), *Les États-Unis* (1927), *Les Américains* (1945), and reviews of and essays on Willa Cather, William Faulkner, Robert Frost, Lafcadio Hearn, Amy Lowell,* and Walt Whitman. Cestre was also a translator and a compiler of French-English dictionaries. (Sources: Hagedorn, 366; *Selected Letters*, 162)

"Charles Carville's Eyes" (1897). Sonnet. The persona and his friends regarded Charles Carville as having a melancholy face, with a "glad" mouth but "insufficient," passionless eyes. They didn't pay much attention to the little he said. But after his death, his eyes seem to have expressed his "whims" and "theories," and then his friends heard every word of them.

Chard Powers Smith* repeats the family "legend" that Carville's sad eyes were patterned after those of Dean Robinson,* the poet's brother, during his physical decline. Ellsworth Barnard notes that in many of Robinson's poems "snatches of [character] revelation . . . center in the eyes." (Sources: Barnard, 163; C. Smith, 130)

Chase, Lewis Nathaniel (1873–1937). Educator. Chase was born in Maine, and earned three degrees at Columbia University. He published his Columbia Ph.D. dissertation, which was entitled *The English Heroic Play: A Critical Description of the Rhymed Tragedy of the Restoration* (1903), also *Poe and His Poetry* (1913), and much on Thomas Holley Chivers (1809–1858), Poe's professional associate. While Chase was a lecturer on contemporary poetry at the University of Wisconsin, he wrote Robinson to ask him to reply by letter and explain his methods and meanings in writing poetry. Robinson answered on July 11, 1917. See "My Methods and Meanings" and "On the Night of a Friend's Wedding." (Source: Cary [1975], 189)

Child, Francis James (1825–1896). Harvard professor. Boston-born, Child graduated from Harvard (1846), tutored there in mathematics (1846–1848) and in history and political economy (1848–1849), studied in Germany (1849–1851), and returned to Harvard and taught literary criticism and balladry (1851–1896). Child married Elizabeth Ellery Sedgwick (1860; they had four children). He became a renowned editor of standard British poets, and published books on linguistics and prosody, but is best known for his scholarly editions of English and Scottish ballads (8 vols., 1857–1858; 5 vols., 1883–1898). He is said never to have missed a class he conducted in 50 years.

Robinson, who found Child dry, withdrew from his Anglo-Saxon class (1891), attended his lectures on William Shakespeare, but often cut them. Robinson occasionally wrote to his friend Harry de Forest Smith* about Child. (Sources: Hagedorn, 63, 71; Morison, 278–79; *Untriangulated Stars*)

"The Children of the Night" (1896). Poem. Those who live in sullen darkness are "the Children of the Night." Some remain strong; but others, who are weak, might just as well never have been born. God regards as "a soul gone mad" anyone who feels that only chaos lies ahead. Since God "is Love," we must use common sense and glorify Him. Twilights are charming not because of grays in them, but because of their crimsons. Starry skies are beautiful because they augur daylight. "It is the faith within the fear / That holds us to the life we curse." We should remove scar-hiding cloaks and reveal to "the ages" that we are "Children of the Light."

Robinson included "The Children of the Light," with minor changes, in *The Torrent and The Night Before* (1896) but omitted it from his 1921 *Collected Poems* on the grounds that it was embarrassingly immature. Juvenile or not, its imagery of light and darkness is a precursor of one of Robinson's major figurative patterns. (Source: Cary [1975], 25–26, 176)

The Children of the Night: A Book of Poems (Boston: Richard G. Badger,* 1897). Collection of 87 poems under 57 titles, many being reprinted from *The Torrent and The Night Before*. Robinson left out two from it but added 43 new ones. The collection is dedicated "To the Memory of My Father and Mother." Theodore Roosevelt* pressured the editors at Charles Scribner's Sons, New York, to issue a new edition (1905). Since the book sold poorly and some of the reviews were unpleasant, Robinson was discouraged enough to write Edith Brower* in a letter (December

29, 1898) that a second edition probably wouldn't be published. However, as Richard Cary reports, the work reappeared in 1905, 1910, 1914, 1919, and 1921. (Sources: Brower, 87; Cary [1974], 105.

"The Chorus of Old Men in 'Ægeus'" (1896). Poem. Ægeus, King of Athens, was Theseus's father. Theseus promised that he would exchange the regular black sail on his ship for a white one if he returned home victorious from his adventures. Though successful over the Minotaur on Crete, he forgot to unfurl the white sail. On seeing the black one, Ægeus flung himself off a rock to his death. Therefore, celebrations honoring Theseus's safe return were always marred by much lamentation.

Robinson was aware that Sophocles and Euripides had written lost plays about Ægeus; so he wrote this chorus as though it were a translated fragment of what one of them might have included. In it the old men ask the gods to look with favor on the king, now caught in "the mist of death." Death, "the black master," levels strong youths and frail elders alike. "Woe for a father's tears." That wind from Crete was "the saddest." Better had Zeus let Ægeus "die as an old man dies," at the end of a clear day and under a starry sky. However, "the fates are ever the fates and a crown is ever a crown."

Effusive in his praise of the prosodical variety Robinson demonstrates in this sonorous work, Emery Neff notes its Matthew Arnold-like trimeters, its "majestic alteration of hexameters and pentameters," and the "poised rhythm of joy" in this line: "Better, by the word of Zeus, with a golden star." Ellsworth Barnard also lauds this chorus, for its "union of somber dignity and delicate lyricism with which ... Sophocles pronounce[s] man's physical, but not his moral, subservience to fate." (Sources: Barnard, 80; Neff, 69)

"Christmas Sonnet" (1928) Sonnet, subtitled "For One in Doubt." To the many who see little evidence of "love and brotherhood" nowadays, Christ would reply, if possible, that there are many types of crosses. Although there is still plenty of ignorance and pride around, the uncrucified Christ remains near us.

"The Clam-Digger: Capitol Island"
(1890). Sonnet. Neptune planted a watery "garden" in a certain cove. When the ocean water subsides, "oozy lives" fancied by hungry "reasoning mortals" become available. At such times, a clam-digger, like a dreadful king, in boots and with fork and basket, heads for the place and "plays the devil with his bubbling dears / All through the bounteous ottoitic tide."

As a youth, Robinson vacationed with his family on Capitol Island, off the coast of Maine. Richard Cary praises this early sonnet, first published in the Kennebec *Monthly Reporter* (April 26, 1890), for its "tautness, tone, vigor . . . [and] diction." He explains that "ottoitic" derives from a type of bicycle, with wheels parallel-mounted (not in line), invented by Nikolaus A. Otto (1832–1891); the ottocyclist's up-and-down pedal motion must have intrigued Robinson, who clearly relished the word "ottoitic," which he evidently felt suggests the ebb and flow of tides — and which is also an early proof that Robinson was attracted to cockamamie words. (Source: Cary [Dec. 1974])

"Clavering" (1910). Poem. The persona will say little about Clavering. The man was like a sea captain who couldn't sail his damaged ship home, like one who focuses on things somewhere between "to-day" and "the eternities," like one who tries to play on a cracked instrument, like one indifferent to the "mirages of renown." Clavering was gracious to Lingard, wrote a poem for snakelike Cubit before that fellow's death, praised dead Calverly too kindly, and might well have imitated dead Leffingwell's "fiery-frantic indolence." The poet wonders if Clavering pitied him and the others for their pragmatic advice and also wonders what made them conceited. Well, Clavering "clung to phantoms and to friends, / And never came to anything."

It has often been both suggested and disputed that Robinson at the time he wrote "Clavering" regarded himself as also dangerously combining dreams, friends, and failure.

Beyond doubt is what Ellsworth Barnard describes as Clavering's (and by extension Robinson's) "undemanding, all-forgiving, never failing loyalty to his friends." Calverly, Leffingwell, and Lingard, but not Cubit, were introduced in "Calverly." (Source: Barnard, 245)

"The Clerks" (1896). Sonnet. Returning to town, the poet is initially surprised to find some friends still clerking in the same place where they formerly were, back when they were young and handsome. They look "shop-worn" now, to be sure; but they remain "just as good, / And just as human as they ever were." The poet asks people who are ambitious or conceited what it's all for. "Poets and kings are but the clerks of Time," and everyone is troubled and sad. (See "The First Seven Years.")

In a letter (July 11, 1917) to Lewis Nathaniel Chase,* Robinson says he "tinkered . . . for a month" with "The Clerks." Wallace L. Anderson interprets the poem as implicitly autobiographical, presenting Robinson's humbling reaction upon returning to a drygoods store where he once briefly clerked and where friends were still stuck in boring jobs. Gardiner legend has it that the store in question was at 215 Water Street, occupied by J. T. Stone's Dry Goods (1862–1884). Ruth Nivison* further identifies two of the clerks as James Stone and John Stone, of Gardiner. Robert Mezey adds that clerks Cusick & Lincoln, a boot and shoe store that also occupied the site, were also known to Robinson.

Henry W. Wells observes that "The Clerks" "combines in its movement the colloquial and the eloquent: a personal idiom with an impersonal gravity." Irving Howe opines that "[t]he finest of Robinson's sonnets of character is 'The Clerk,'" quotes some of its "perceptual and verbal refinements," but adds that he won't "pretend . . . to close analysis." Louis Coxe suggests that Robinson here "involved himself in the human disaster of living [and] . . . all of us, high, low and in between, are 'clerks of Time.'" Emery Neff says this sonnet demonstrates that "Men we have all seen 'shop-worn' by years of monotonous employment become symbols of the triumph of time, one of the supreme themes of poetry." Timothy Steele says that the point of "The Clerks" is to show "the vanity of human pride" and contends that the last three lines of "The Clerks"— each beginning with an inverted foot (trochaic, not the expected iambic)— "convey a heartfelt emphasis that drives home the point." (See also "My Methods and Meanings.") (Sources: W. Anderson [1968], 82–84; Coxe, 55; I. Howe, 102; Mezey, 218; Neff, 66; E. Robinson, 11; *Selected Letters*, 103; Steele, 71, 72; Wells, 150)

"Cliff Klingenhagen" (1897). Sonnet. Cliff Klingenhagen invites the persona to dinner. The pleasant meal is topped off with drinks. Cliff gives his guest wine and easily has a glass of bitter wormwood himself. The persona asks for an explanation, to which Cliff merely says "it was a way of his." The persona, long a friend of Cliff's, wonders when he'll ever "be / As happy as Cliff Klingenhagen is."

William C. Childers notes that the German verb "klingen" (to ring, clink, sound) may have been in Robinson's mind when he named Klingenhagen, who surely must have clinked glasses with his bibulous guests. Charles Cestre* advises that Cliff's reserving the wormwood for himself "is a symbol, from which one may learn the lesson of self-discipline." (Sources: Cestre, 124; Childers [1955], 229)

"The Clinging Vine" (1914). Dramatic monologue. A wife rebukes her unfaithful husband, thus: You say I should be calm. I am calm now, now that I no longer have a master. I won't make any commotion. Nor will I "kill her." Her face already betrays her fear. You'll leave her soon. Don't bother denying anything. You're barred from my life. Oh, so you'll forgive my blundering speech? I would blindly "creep with you to glory," if you hadn't been faithless even prior to her. You laugh now, but "all your laughs are lies." If, as you say, most men are like you, then most women will "all be mad some day." Now hear this. Once, a man got married, but he had misjudged his fiancée and suffered; "But you — you came clear-sighted, / And found truth in my eyes." Then you lied about me; so I can't

endure you any longer. Don't gripe. Don't pretend. "I'm going. I'm like ice."

The affronted wife speaks in 12 eight-line stanzas, each rhyming *ababcdcd*, with the *a*-rhymes feminine. This well-sustained poetic form reflects the woman's cool, mechanical conversational control. Emma Robinson* and Ruth Nivison* say that the marital difficulties of Herman Robinson* and Emma, and even bits of their conversations, are reflected in "The Clinging Vine."

In an essay concerning aspects of Maine in Robinson's poetry, Lewis E. Weeks, Jr. cites specific words dealing with nature which Robinson uses in "The Clinging Vine" to present "the relationship of the wife and husband, past, present, and future . . . with a finality as complete, as distant, and as vast as space and as substantial as rock, sand, and sea." Emery Neff calls this monologue "ironically styled." There is irony in its title too; Robinson's monologist is anything but a clinging vine. Hoyt C. Franchere notes that in "The Clinging Vine" Robinson reverses the situation in "My Last Duchess," the famous dramatic monologue by Robert Browning; in it, "the Duke reviles his latest partner for . . . her failure to appreciate him." Ellsworth Barnard challenges the reader to wonder whether the wife here is displaying "righteous anger or hysterical delusions." (Sources: Barnard, 47; Franchere, 105; Neff, 178; E. Robinson, 2; Weeks [1969], 320)

Coan, Titus Munson (1836–1921). Coan was the son of Titus Munson Coan (1801–1882), a missionary to Hawaii, where young Coan was born, in Hilo. He became a Yale graduate, a physician, a poet, and a collector of pornographic pictures. He married Leonie Pauline Morel (1877) in New York City, where he was a manuscript doctor and headed a "Bureau of Criticism and Revision" to help would-be writers. Robinson sent him a copy of *The Torrent and The Night Before*, which Coan turned over for evaluation to Edith Brower,* a reader of his from Wilkes-Barre, Pennsylvania, but often commuting to New York. She ecstatically praised Robinson's poems to Coan, wrote to Robinson urgently requesting a personal copy, and his sending her one initiated one of his most pleasant and long-lasting friendships. When Robinson first began to live in New York (1897), he reported to Coan, who helped him, introduced him to many Manhattanites, including Craven Langstroth Betts* and Alfred Hyman Louis,* and drank at times with all of them. (Sources: Brower, 1; Hagedorn; C. Smith)

Cohen, Morris Raphael (1880–1947). Philosopher and educator. Cohen was born in Minsk, Russia, and migrated (1892) with his mother and sister to join his father, already in New York City. Cohen obtained a B.S. at City College of New York (1900) and a Ph.D. at Harvard (1906). He taught philosophy at CCNY (1912–1938) and at the University of Chicago (1938–1942). In his philosophical works he combined naturalism and rationalism, in order to posit law as a social system embodying the use of ideas backed by facts. His publications include *Reason and Nature* (1931), *Law and the Social Order* (1933), *The Meaning of Human History* (1947), and, posthumously issued, an autobiography entitled *A Dreamer's Journey* (1949) and *Reason and Law: Studies in Juristic Philosophy* (1950).

Robinson met Cohen at the MacDowell Colony* when Cohen first went there (1924). Cohen admired Robinson's poetry and sent a copy to his friend Oliver Wendell Holmes, Jr. In his autobiography, Cohen writes that, in considering how "the enjoyment of nature is largely motivated by art" (but is it?), he was stimulated by "discussions with Edwin Arlington Robinson and other fellow colonists at the McDowell [sic] and Yaddo colonies." David H. Burton briefly describes the friendship of the two men. (Sources: D. Burton [1978]; M. Cohen, 196)

Collamore, Bacon (1894–1975). Businessman, and book and manuscript collector. Harry Bacon Collamore, born in Middleton, Connecticut, got a job with the National Fire Insurance Company of Hartford, Connecticut (1912), and rose in the ranks until he became president (1948), a position he held until he retired (1956). He was also chairman of the board of the Pittsburgh Steel Company (1956–1976) and sat on many other boards

as well. During the First World War, he served in the U.S. Army Air Corps. He and his wife Dorothy had two sons. During his intensive active business career, Collamore found time and energy to be an avid collector of books, including first editions and inscribed copies, and of literary manuscripts. Of special value are his items relating to Emily Dickinson, Robert Frost, A. E. Housman, D. H. Lawrence, Edna St. Vincent Millay, Beatrix Potter, Sara Teasdale, Edith Wharton, and Robinson.

During the early 1920s, Collamore began a warm literary friendship with Robinson. He collected books by Robinson, established an amiable correspondence with him, sent him detective fiction, and in return received inscribed first editions. In due course, he donated many of his Robinson books to Colby College, Waterville, Maine, and many Robinson letters to Trinity College, Hartford, Connecticut. (Source: Collamore.)

Collected Poems (New York: Macmillan, 1921; 2 vols., 1921; 5 vols., 1927; 1929, 1937; 1 vol., with additional poems, 1937, etc.).

"The Companion" (1910). Poem. The man may answer almost as he wishes, but not with injurious commonplace and tricky words. Yesterday he lied, and although she laughed she also began to doubt him. Regardless of his blandishing talk now, she will have doubts.

Lawrance Thompson suggests that the titular "companion" may well be the unfaithful husband's close friend but, just possibly, only the wife's ever-present "doubt." (Source: L. Thompson, 138)

"The Corridor" (1902). Poem. The poet remembers a man whom he may have patronized. But the man's "hungry face" haunts him. The man may be dead by now, and the poet remembers only a few words he spoke and even occasionally forgets his name. The two recognized their incipient friendship, but silence kept them apart. Now, the poet cannot "stop that hunger for a friend."

Unless the title "Corridor" is figurative, it suggests that the two men paused briefly in a hallway, spoke, and separated forever.

"Cortège" (1902). Poem. It begins thus: "Four o'clock this afternoon, / Fifteen hundred miles away," and then rings changes on those two lines through the rest of the poem. It seems that a young couple loved, maybe married, and died. Mention of "the grave today" indicates that this day, at that time, and at a distant place, a funeral is now being held or soon will be. Further, it is for the best that they have died.

Robinson met a big challenge when he decided on the rhyme scheme of this six-quatrain poem. Each stanza has identical *abab* rhymes; thus, the word at the end of every line rhymes either with "afternoon" or with "away."

Hoyt C. Franchere reports that this "death may be only a figurative one," that early in 1890 Herman Robinson,* the poet's brother, and Emma Robinson,* recently married, boarded a train in Gardiner for St. Louis, some 1,500 miles away. In light of this information, Franchere adds, the poem may be Robinson's lament at his lost-love Emma's leaving his immediate environs. Franchere also notes that one line of the poem begins "Had she gone," whereas no male is specifically mentioned. Franchere concludes that Robinson is "moaning over the departure of the woman he loved" and over the fact that she "was irretrievably lost," thus figuratively dead, to him. To Gardiner residents, all of this is obvious. Robinson, standing in imagination or otherwise at Depot Square opposite the Gardiner-Randolph bridge, would have sadly seen Emma abandoning him. In his youth (and until 1911), the station of the Maine Central Railroad was in Depot Square. (Sources: Franchere, 65, 66; E. Robinson, 13)

"Credo" (1896). Sonnet. The poet can't find his "way," since there is no star in "the shrouded heavens" to help him, nor any voice except one so distant that he "can hear it only as a bar / Of lost, imperial music." Also, "angel fingers wove, and unaware, / Dead leaves to garlands where no roses are." Negative words and negative suffixes continue, totaling eight through line nine; but in line 10 a change begins. The poet "welcomes, welcomes where he fears, / The black and awful chaos of the night." Why welcome chaotic darkness? "For,

through" and above this powerful blackness, he is cognizant of a message and "feel[s] the coming glory of the Light." In a different context, Warner Berthoff also notes Robinson's "trick of negative identification (not this, not this, not even this, but possibly that, though perhaps not that either)."

W. R. Robinson observes that this "sonnet ... has all the right rationalistic qualities — a tightly formal stanzaic structure, meter, and rhyme scheme — to embody an utterance by a reflective mind." On the other hand, Randall Jarrell quotes the passage about "garlands where no roses are" and feels obliged to aver that it is an example of "poetic rhetoric" that is "embarrassingly threadbare and prosaic." Hyatt H. Waggoner believes that Ralph Waldo Emerson's poem "The Poet" was probably the source "for ... images of music and light and darkness" in "Credo." Evidently agreeing, Irving Howe then trivializes "Credo" by saying that "Robinson ... felt obliged to end with an Emersonian piety." More positively, Edwin S. Fussell concludes that in "Credo" "the poet 'welcomes when he fears, the black and awful chaos of the night ... ' [because] The night is proof of the coming of the light, though it is fearful in itself. 'For,' then, introduces a final modification and explanation of 'welcomes when he fears' in terms of an expansion of the earlier star imagery." Fussell complains that "the syntactical organization [of the poem] ... contributes ... to ... obfuscation." Richard G. Landini regards Robinson's use of journey and Nativity imagery in "Credo" as suggesting his partial affirmation of Christian faith. (Sources: Berthoff, 124; Fussell [1951], 400; I. Howe, 100; Jarrell, 2; Landini; W. Robinson, 65; Waggoner, 269)

Daniels, Mabel (1879–1971). Composer. Mabel Wheeler Daniels was born in Swampscott, Massachusetts, into a musical family. Her mother took her, when she was a child, to a performance of Giuseppe Verdi's *Requiem*; its "Dies Irae" moved her so much that she cried and asked to be taken home. Mabel Daniels played the piano, composed pieces at age 10, and sang soprano. While attending the Girls' Latin School in Boston, she published a few short stories. She entered Radcliffe

(1896), and sang in its Choral Society and in operettas, some of which she composed and others she conducted. After graduating (1900), she studied composition and orchestration in Boston and then for two years in Germany (1903–1905). She published a memoir of her time there (1905). Back in Boston, Daniels joined the Cecilia Society and sang in its mixed-voice chorus, with orchestral accompaniment. This experience was of technical help when Daniels began to compose. She was associated with Radcliffe in several capacities (1911–1945) and was chair of the music program at Simmons College, Boston (1913–1918). Thereafter, she concentrated on composition. She created a choral and orchestral *Exultate Deo* (1929) to celebrate Radcliffe's 50th anniversary; it enjoyed national celebrity and is still performed at educational events. Marian Nivens MacDowell,* who with her husband the composer Edward MacDowell* established the MacDowell Colony* to support working artists, heard Daniels' *The Desolate City* (1913), a choral composition for baritone and orchestra, asked her to direct a performance of it at the colony, and invited her to be a colonist the following summer and later. Doing so enhanced her love of New Hampshire's woods, resulting in her *Deep Forest* (for chamber orchestra, 1931; full-orchestra revision, 1934). Among her other works are *Pirates' Island* (1932, a humorous orchestral suite, later adapted for ballet), *Three Observations for Three Woodwinds* (1943, satirical skit), violin pieces, and an overture for orchestra. Daniels was lauded professionally for blending tradition and innovation, and personally for supporting younger and often needy students. She never married.

Robinson made Daniels' acquaintance at the MacDowell Colony. Chard Powers Smith,* who also met her there (1924), describes her as "critical and consciously broadminded," "[s]trong-faced," and "judicial." Many critics consider Daniels' *The Song of Jael* (1935, performed in 1940) her finest composition. Based on Robinson's "Sisera," it is a well-orchestrated triumphal cantata with modern handling of chorus and effective solo soprano. Some years after Robinson's death,

Daniels published an essay about their friendship; his love of music and of certain instruments, especially flutes and bassoons; and his knowledge of music, especially as revealed in *Captain Craig* and *The Man Who Died Twice*, the last part of which he told her was an outline of a symphony. (Sources: Daniels; C. Smith, 5, 15)

"The Dark Hills" (1920). Poem. At sunset, the hills are dark. Earlier, sunlight flashed like battle flags. The diminished light now "hovers like a sound / Of golden horns" bugling above soldiers' buried bones. The advancing darkness seems to indicate that "the last of days / Were fading" and that "all wars were done."

In this eight-line masterpiece Robinson writes that wars are "done" rather than "won." Either word could be used to rhyme nicely with "sun," which ends the sixth line. He is clearly implying that there are no victors in war. Pseudo-prophecy of eternal pacifism echoes an identical message in Robinson's "Cassandra."

Charles Cestre* highly esteems "The Dark Hills," in which he says "thought, image and mystical vision unite, at the bidding of a powerful emotion, and call to their service lofty language in sumptuous array." Ellsworth Barnard lauds Robinson's word-painting here of "the peculiar poignancy of a fading sunset." G. Thomas Tanselle praises "The Dark Hills" for its teachable simplicity, easy grammar, and diction, and adds that it is composed of a single sentence. Richard Cary informs his readers that "a somber rendition of Robinson's 'The Dark Hills'" by his friend the painter Franklin L. Schenck is in the Colby College Library. Louis Untermeyer* reports that "The Dark Hills" was set to music six times between 1924 and 1958. (Sources: Barnard, 59; Cary [1975], 192; Cestre, 32; Tanselle; Untermeyer, 29, 30)

"The Dark House" (1916). Poem. The poet invites all to avoid asking why he stays in this house but instead to leave him. A Demon gazes at and embraces the poet, who is stuck here. A friend within knows the poet is damned. Supposedly helpful words are quieter than the sound of time's thread being sheared. There is some music, but unheard until the Demon closes a door. The poet's friend may hear it. Then the door will open, and the friend, formerly dead, will live again.

This disarmingly serene poem has 10 stanzas, each rhyming *aabbb*, and each with five crisp tetrameter lines. The poem may be best interpreted as relating to Robinson's problems with demon alcohol.

"The Dead Village" (1896). Sonnet. Children used to play here, people were happy, and there was music. Now nothing remains but ghosts, because "The music failed," after which "God frowned, and shut the village from His sight."

Music was so important to Robinson that, according to Emery Neff, he used it here (and often elsewhere) "as a synonym of the spiritual world." Emma Robinson* and Ruth Nivison* interpret "The Dead Village" thus: When Dean Robinson* and Herman Robinson,* the poet's brothers, failed to carry on and thus caused the family fortunes to begin to evaporate, the "music" of the household stopped. (Sources: Neff, 71; E. Robinson, 11)

"Dear Friends" (1896). Sonnet. The poet urges his friends not to reproach, counsel, and pity him, and not to tell him he is foolish to blow bubbles, i.e., to write poems. He challenges them to blow bigger bubbles. The various games they play create "glasses . . . to read the spirit through." If his friends read his works, they may become skillful themselves, quit being scornful, and actually start praising him. The poet concludes memorably: "The shame I win for singing is all mine, / The gold I miss for dreaming is all yours."

Thus, early in his career, Robinson opts for the poet's life. In the second line of this sonnet, Robinson uses "nor," one of his favorite words, three times: "Nor counsel me, nor pity me; nor say." Emery Neff regards the last two lines of "Dear Friends" as containing "ironic urbanity worthy of Horace." (Source: Neff, 73)

"Demos" (1919). Double sonnet. Sibyl-like, the poet warns ordinary people to cherish his gift, not lose it by succumbing to false desires. He cannot persuade them to realize that they must be led. They have a "fevered glimpse of a democracy / Confused and foiled" by notions of equality. They "See not the great . . . for the small," whereas it is truly "the few [that] shall save / The many." Otherwise, "the many are to fall" while arguing in what will amount to "a noisy grave."

Chard Powers Smith* suggests that Robinson was motivated to compose this antidemocratic poem by his preference for "the culture of preindustrial New England." Floyd Stovall says that in "Demos" Robinson first addressed the danger of "the dissolution of the individualistic civilization of the modern world by the combined forces of mechanization, utilitarianism, and equalitarianism." Emery Neff more specifically locates Robinson's discontent in his adverse reaction to "the vague enthusiasm for democracy engendered by wartime slogans." Ellsworth Barnard reminds readers that the Greek philosophers regarded "Demos" to mean "the uninformed, insensitive, arrogant, mass-minded majority," whose unguided actions Robinson always viewed with alarm. (Sources: Barnard, 32; Neff, 199–200; C. Smith, 295; Stovall, 20)

"Demos and Dionysus" (1925). Dramatic duologue in blank verse. Dionysus, who represents Robinson's passion for individualistic development, greets Demos, the populace. Demos replies, "I thought you were dead," and continues thus: Dionysus, you are irrelevant so far as I'm concerned. Dionysus: Without me, you'll become attractively imprisoned, and won't understand "love and art." Demos: I see no prison. Dionysus: The prison will fill and need to be blown up; you have a disease no physician can cure; you resemble an octopus hiding its evil by squirting ink. Demos: Reason and equality are ever-growing, domineering twins. Dionysus: If those twins work together, they'll reduce themselves and their underlings to collapsing machinery and the country to a "slave-ridden state." Demos: The thought is laughable that any soured, potentially pro-individualistic opposition will do more than labor obediently, have fun, take it easy, shrug, yawn, and "be subdued to studious procreation." Dionysus: Before you become the king bee of drones, it would be better for you to go on a binge and then die. Demos: Not so; better to stop playfully feeling and fancying, to end individuality and spirit now, "for the good of the machine"; those who are "peculiar" and would sabotage the machine will be ground up or exiled. Dionysus: What if in the process the machine breaks down or the exiles return? Who'll repair the machine, who'll stop me from returning with "some honey"? Demos: The machine won't ever fail; honey won't please "palates . . . duly neutralized"; this reconstructed world will have neither hell nor honey. Dionysus: You may have one while desiring the other; if you tyrannize, you'll create a monster that will fall into an "unlovely mess"; later, those inspired by thought and ability will cannister your ashes and re-create a world worth living in. Demos: No one has an "ingenious right to be himself"; I'll clamp down, put everyone in his place, keep him there; all will be "Punctual, accurate, tamed and uniform, / And equal"; your fancy-free "love and art" will be a memory of those once feeble but now reasonable. Dionysus: Instead of going to the hell you think I deserve, I'll be around, I'll challenge you to unmask yourself, or I'll do it. Demos: "Wait and see."

Emery Neff sees in "Demos and Dionysus" Robinson's "uneasiness over the political immaturity of his countrymen . . . and his indignation at the egregious expression of it in National Prohibition." More generally, Ellsworth Barnard regards Robinson's target here as totalitarianism rather than democracy. Richard P. Adams contrasts the principals in "Demos and Dionysus" thus: "Dionysus represents the free creative spirit of man as an individual and the opposing Demos is a false image, wrongly identified with mechanization and conformity." Regardless of refinements in interpretation, "Demos and Dionysus" is not a first-rate poem. (Sources: R. Adams, 117–18; Barnard, 259; Neff, 220)

Detective Fiction and Robinson. In later years, Robinson found it mentally relaxing, and helpful when he suffered from insomnia, to read detective stories. Ridgely Torrence*

reports that Robinson, who often read two such novels in a single night, said that "His only stipulation in regard to them . . . was that they have no pretension to literary quality." In a letter (August 20, 1927) to the wife of Louis V. Ledoux,* Robinson recommended *The "Canary Murder" Case: A Philo Vance Story*, by S. S. Van Dine (Willard Huntington Wright, 1888–1939), for being "highly stimulating and very valuable." In a letter (September 27, 1927) Robinson thanks Bacon Collamore* for sending him three thrilling mysteries. When Howard George Schmitt,* one of Robinson's most assiduous correspondents, learned that he liked detective novels, Schmitt sent him at least four (September 1929, May 1930, June 1934). (Sources: Collamore, 52; Schmitt, 11, 14, 27; *Selected Letters*, 191, 152)

"Dionysus in Doubt" (1925). Poem. The narrator while faraway sees the god Dionysus, who was born of Zeus and "a burning mother." He appears weary and incredulous. His response is partly humorous when he looks down on the narrator's young nation and sees "complacent yet impatient folk." They seem to be expecting "millennial ecstasies." Dionysus complains that the people are childish, legislate too much, are licentious, and are perplexed by their freedom, which "spreads . . . her claws" to "inflict . . . more liberty." The result? Immature tyrants mislead moronic millions along poisoned paths. When the narrator labels the group merely "an unransomed kidnapped juvenile / Miscalled Democracy," Dionysus smiles and says that whatever hope and intelligence the nation has are overcome by "Hypocrisy, timidity, and sloth," as well as envy of others' possessions. Since anyone predicting the coming debacle would be disbelieved and stoned, it's better to keep quiet. The ignorant will forget that "when a sphere is hammered square / All that is hammered is still there," that a humbug all dressed up is still a humbug. Too many people resemble sleeping watchdogs here. Rambling on, Dionysus says too many half-wise people rely on "legioned innocence" and avoid disputes by shutting their mouths —"Except to drink." The result will be standardization, even of pleasures, and an inevitable blind uniformity. Such free efficiency might well be called a kind of hell; in it, everyone is sized up or down in a Procrustean bed so that all men become brothers. Out of the book of truth will come a snake to do some unpleasant biting. Dionysus says that his methods "Are gentle [compared] to those of Him that you revere / So blindly while they rend you" until the end — if end there be. Dionysus closes by urging the narrator to consider his hitherto "unregarded" statements and stop seeking despicable, dishonorable, worthless so-called "benefits." Realize that "Bad laws" are sightless guides carelessly leading the people nowhere. When the narrator responds by asking Dionysus to clarify his puzzling comments, lightning flashes, a hot silence follows, and the god has vanished.

"Dionysus in Doubt" is mainly in blank verse, often, however, varied by lines in tetrameter, trimeter, and even dimeter, and occasionally rhyming. As in "Demos and Dionysus," Robinson is specifically inveighing here against Prohibition but more generally, as in "Cassandra," presenting valuable but puzzling and therefore unheeded advice for Americans after the First World War — to avoid Jazz Age stupidities and grow up. Henry Rushton Fairclough says that both "Dionysus in Doubt" and "Demos and Dionysus" "contain amusing and somewhat subtle reflections on the spirit prevailing in this democratic age, when people are made virtuous by legislation." Estelle Kaplan feels that "*Dionysus in Doubt* is . . . a portrayal of inebriate experience." Ellsworth Barnard downgrades it for "failure of structure," since it lacks any "logical or rhetorical" advance toward any emotionally satisfying conclusion. (Sources: Barnard, 113; Fairclough, 15; Kaplan, 7)

Dionysus in Doubt: A Book of Poems
(New York: Macmillan, 1925). Collection of 21 poems. Robinson dedicated the book to Craven Langstroth Betts.*

"Discovery" (1919). Sonnet. The persona and his friends think that a certain man, briefly away, is as wise as Amos, the prophet who transmitted the Word to complacent Zion to beware of Hamath's power. But the surprising message offered by that man when he returns is simply that the "earth has not a school where we may go / For wisdom, or for more than we may know."

Robinson may have been not only remembering Amos's relayed prophecy that "An enemy shall surround the land, and strip you of your strength, and pillage your castles" (Amos 3: 11), but also equating it to the consequences of America's perilous non-isolationist future.

Dissertations on Robinson *see* **Ph.D. Dissertations on Robinson**

"Doctor of Billiards" (1910). Sonnet. This master of "three spheres of insidious ivory," to which his life is reduced, has fallen from a veritable kingdom. But he smiles and seems self-reliant until his "false, unhallowed laugh" makes others wonder.

Emma Robinson* and Ruth Nivison* equate this gambling "doctor" and Robinson's brother Herman Robinson.* (See also "My Methods and Meanings.") (Source: E. Robinson, 15)

Dodge, Mabel (1879–1962). Wealthy patron and memoirist. She was born Mabel Ganson, in Buffalo, New York, was nicely educated, made a proper social debut, but then became a rebel. She married Karl Evans (1900) and had a son with him. Karl Evans died in a hunting accident (1902). She married Edwin Dodge, an American architect, in Paris (1904), lived in Italy with him, returned to New York (1912), established a salon, and helped Isadora Duncan* establish a ballet school (1914). Divorced (1916), she married Maurice Sterne, a painter (1917). In and near Taos, New Mexico, she fell in love with a Pueblo Indian named Tony Luhan, divorced Sterne (1922), and married Luhan (1923). *Intimate Memories* (1933–1937), her four-volume autobiography, is replete with anecdotes about illustrious writers whom this engaging, energetic woman knew and befriended.

In 1903, while Robinson was staying on Staten Island in La Tourette, the lavish home of Clara Davidge Taylor, one of his benefactresses, and her artist husband Harry Taylor, Mabel Dodge visited them from her Greenwich Village apartment. She was captivated by what she called Robinson's "burning" eyes, enjoyed lunch with him, visited again, but ran away because of allegedly encountering the ghost that supposedly haunted the Taylors' home. She took Robinson to lunch several times in New York. She showed him her portrait. She proudly let him read "Portrait of Mabel Dodge and the Villa Curonia" (1911) by her friend Gertrude Stein. Mabel took no offense when Robinson rightly wondered how she could tell that she was the subject. In later years Robinson corresponded with Mrs. Mabel Dodge Sterne, as he addressed her. On March 12, 1919, for example, he shared his gloomy view of Europe after the First World War with her. In response to her sending him the first volume of her memoirs, in draft form, he wrote to her (November 15, 1933) that he could find nothing objectionable in it so far as the writing itself was concerned, but expressed his fear that she would regret publishing any personal revelations during her lifetime and that of others involved with her, and suggested planning for posthumous publication instead. Obviously, the attention-gathering woman took no notice. (Sources: Frazer; Hagedorn; Rodnick; *Selected Letters*, 115, 173; C. Smith)

Dole, Nathan Haskell (1852–1935). Editor, author, and translator. Dole was born in Chelsea, Massachusetts. His father was a Congregational minister from Maine, then an editor in Boston. He died when young Dole was about three, whereupon his mother took her three children to Norridgewock, Maine. Dole graduated from Harvard (1874), taught Greek and English various places, began a career in journalism and authorship (1880–1887), married Helen J. Bennet (1882; they had four children), and was literary adviser (1887–1901) to the Boston publishing firm Thomas Y. Crowell. Dole, a versatile and prolific author, created or was responsible for dozens of anthologies, biographies, fiction, history, poetry, texts, and translations from French, German, Latin, Russian, and Spanish. He coedited the 10th edition of John Bartlett's *Familiar Quotations* (1910) and included four

short quotations from *Captain Craig* in it; this was Robinson's first appearance in Bartlett. While living in Boston, Dole often summered in Ogunquit, Maine. Among his many professional friends was Harriet Monroe.*

In a review of *The Torrent and The Night Before* (*Bookseller, Newsdealer and Stationer* [January 1, 1897]), Dole names and praises several poems for their "strength and passion," says that they are "too healthy to be really pessimistic," and predicts (correctly) that copies of the little book will one day be extremely valuable. Shortly before his review appeared, Dole wrote Robinson to express a desire to meet him in Boston. Long remembering the 1897 review, Robinson wrote to Dole (April 22, 1928) to express gratitude for his being an early critic finding something meritorious in his poetry. (Sources: Cary [1974], 36; *Selected Letters*, 155; *Untriangulated Stars*, 268)

"Doricha" *see* **"Variations of Greek Themes"**

"Doubts" (1894). Poem. A fragment. Robinson wrote a letter (April 22, 1894) to Henry de Forest Smith* and enclosed stanzas five and six of a projected 10-stanza poem, to be called "Doubts." In the fragment, he says that one may "find tragedy writ in a rose" and wrongly forget that others can "teach mankind to struggle and wait / Till life be over and death forgiven." (Sources: Cary [1975], 17, 172; *Untriangulated Stars*, 146)

Duncan, Isadora (1878–1927). Dancer, born in San Francisco. She was a teen-aged entertainer in New York, went to London, lived in poverty, but soon gained fame there and then in Paris, where she studied and terpsichoreanly replicated the flowing postures of figures on Greek vases in the Louvre. She won both supporters and critics by her innovative dancing, patterned after the natural movements of wind, water, and birds and insects in flight. She established a school for female dancers near Berlin (1904), returned for controversial performances in the United States (1908), expatriated herself again, started a school in Paris (1914) and in Moscow (1921), married the Russian imagist poet Sergei Esenin (1922), who committed suicide in 1925, and was killed when her scarf was caught by a moving automobile that dragged her and caused her to be strangled.

Percy MacKaye,* who knew Duncan, took Robinson, William Vaughn Moody,* and Ridgely Torrence* to meet her one evening (1908) after she had danced to the accompaniment of Ludwig van Beethoven's *Seventh Symphony* at New York's Metropolitan Opera House. They trouped along to her studio in Carnegie Hall and were variously impressed. Robinson saw her at least two more times. On Christmas Eve (1908), Duncan gathered the four poets into her hotel suite, plied them with champagne and sensuously expressive movements, sent MacKaye and Moody home, and tried to seduce Robinson, who though intoxicated maintained an unclimactic reserve. (Source: Hagedorn, 230–32)

Eliot, Charles William (1834–1926). Boston-born, Harvard-trained educator. Eliot taught mathematics and chemistry at Harvard, then chemistry at the Massachusetts Institute of Technology, then was president of Harvard (1869–1909). His policies influenced Robinson's studies at Harvard (1891–1893). Requested by John Hays Gardiner* to do so, Eliot employed Robinson in a menial clerical position at Harvard (January-June 1899). Eliot infuriated Robinson once by asking him if he were married and, upon learning that he wasn't, thoughtlessly averred that being single was a mistake and that every young fellow should wed. (Sources: Hagedorn, 62, 71, 148; Morison, 329–33)

"En Passant" (1924). Sonnet. The narrator says that he should have walked past a certain wild-eyed man, who, however, stopped him and revealed this: He had watched a long while along highways and was now going to the seaside to make sure of something. That evening, reports from the shore explain only this: Someone shot a strange man but before doing so said, first, that a certain person should have come when he was called, and, second, that an unknown "gentleman," properly polite to those who are "accurst," came

from the grave — and not a bit too soon.

The action of this poem may be explained, according to Bernice Slote, as *en passant* moves on a chess board. If a pawn (say white) moves straight forward toward an opposing pawn (black) and stops beside it as though to go straight on soon, the black pawn can capture it by a diagonal forward movement called *en passant*, as though white had paused one space less forward — seemingly to speak. The narrator, who is both the "I" and the "gentleman," did stop thus, met, and spoke to "him," who, also identified as the "one," shot the "stranger" for passing him by, instead of answering his call. The "gentleman," by showing "deference" to the killer, avoided being killed and buried.

Emma Robinson* said that this unpleasant poem referred to her husband, Herman Robinson,* the poet's needful brother, during his sad 1906–1909 years. Emma added that George Burham* told her that Herman told Robinson one evening in New York that he intended to drown himself and that thereafter Robinson sent Herman a check each month until Herman's death. Another interpretation is that the poet is suggesting his own emergence from a quasi-grave through willingness to care for Herman about 1904–1905. In truth, the darkly obscure "En Passant" defies definitive biographical explication. But its moral is clear: You better speak when an *isolato* accosts you. (Sources: E. Robinson, 21; Slote; C. Smith, 402–03)

"L'Envoi" (1897). Sonnet. A thought, a word, a voice presage "some transcendent music I have heard." It is neither timid nor crashing, but harmonious, like nothing any "brief mortal touch has ever stirred." This music is unworldly, not transcribable, and to be played but by one instrument; and "yes," "after time and place are overthrown, / God's touch will keep its one chord quivering."

This poem was reprinted in "Spanish-American War Songs," edited by Sidney A. Witherbee (Detroit, 1898), without Robinson's knowledge and retitled "The One Chord." Correspondence between Robinson and Howard George Schmitt,* as annotated by Carl J. Weber, provides details.

The critic Sister Mary James Power discusses "L'Envoi" and dogmatizes about "[t]hat music one enjoys through the faithful observance of God's Laws." (Sources: Power, 79; Schmitt, 25)

"Erasmus" (1900, 1902). Sonnet. Irregular in form. When he gently protested against "Sick Europe['s]" veneer of religiosity, church officials called him heretical. But when he published his thoughts, conservative leaders positively shook, because they "knew that he was right."

Robinson admired Erasmus (1466?-1536), the leading humanist of the Renaissance, for his emphasis on Christian piety and his desire for reform of Catholic Church rigidities. W. R. Robinson points out that in "Erasmus" the poet's "target was society and sick America rather than the church and sick Europe: he protested against the crust of overdone socialization." Wallace L. Anderson discusses changes in three versions of "Erasmus" and shows that they reveal Robinson moving "in the direction of greater precision and tonal unity." (Sources: W. Anderson [1980], 60; W. Robinson, 90)

"Eros Turannos" (1914). Poem. She was always afraid of him, should have refused him, but preferred him to loneliness. She knew he was a Judas, but love overcame her pride. Meanwhile, the patient fellow looked around and liked what he saw. Her wooded place was near the seaside. She overcame her doubts and got him. By the time the leaves fall, the pounding ocean is tolling the death of her romantic dreams, her home has become a refuge to hide in, and her imperfectly understanding neighbors gossip about her and regard her as demented. Well, if you contend with a god, you have to take what the god gives; that gift may be like a breaking wave, a changed tree, "a stairway to the sea / Where down the blind are driven."

Ruth Nivison* contends that this poem dramatizes the despotic love that occasioned the downfall of her parents, Herman Robinson* and Emma Robinson.* Robert Mezey, however, disagrees with this family interpretation. Jeffrey L. Spear suggests that a possible source of the poem is "Wives in the Sere," a 1901 poem by Thomas Hardy, since both poems are alike in form and content.

Each of the six stanzas of Robinson's "Eros Turannos" rhymes *ababcccb*, and together the stanzas divide into two equal parts. Christopher Beach notes that "[e]ach stanza functions somewhat like a chapter in a short novel or a scene in a tragic drama." Richard P. Adams points out two parallel tensions in the poem: first, "tension arises . . . out of the opposition of reason and emotion"; second, "a profounder tension . . . might be defined as stretching between life and not-life." Laurence Perrine says that the poem depicts Eros "as a tyrant who blinds, maddens, and whips"; the first three stanzas feature the love-maddened, love-blinded woman before her marriage, the last three, the marital tragedy, during which "Fall leaves and pounding waves intensify her disappointment." Robert Mezey, pouncing on the adjective "engaging," which Robinson uses to describe the "mask" of the man in the poem, says that it "contains a thrilling dissonance of several different meanings." Benjamin W. Griffith says the word "Turannos" in the title means an unconstitutional ruler, one achieving power without birthright; hence the husband here may have grabbed love falsely with no right of birth or even any "kindred" devotion; the comment that "passion lived and died" could mean that she was decently aroused but that her usurper was impotent or even homosexually inclined. C. Hines Edwards, Jr. suggests that Robinson's use of restless ocean and leaf-losing tree imagery should tell the reader that the woman is sexually eager but frustrated because the man has lost his potency and that the woman has therefore determined to commit suicide. After analyzing the style of "Eros Turannos," Roy Harvey Pearce concludes, "So it goes: the figurative language, the rhymes (especially the feminine [*b*] rhymes, which have the effect of easing the epigrammatic bite, making the lines subside rather than end sharply), and the stanzaic structure — each has this powerfully memorializing effect." Irving Howe calls "Eros Turannos" "one of the greatest poems on the tragedy of love in our language." Ronald Moran regards it as "the most accomplished of Robinson's shorter poems." Robert D. Stevick compares and contrasts "Eros Turannos" and "The Unforgiven," to the distinct advantage of "Eros Turannos," on which Harold Bloom affixes his imprimatur thus: "Robinson's masterpiece, to me, is 'Eros Turannos.'" Joan Manheimer theorizes that readers are mistaken if they think the speaker, intense though he is, in "Eros Turannos," which is characteristic of many of Robinson's poetic narratives, will, or even can, explain everything with any certainty; hence, part of the readers' pleasure, and duty, is to ponder the limitations of Robinson's speakers. (Sources: R. Adams, 146, 147; Beach, 12; Bloom, 809; Edwards; Griffith; I. Howe, 104; Manheimer; Mezey, 230, 228; Moran [2003], 3231; Pearce, 263; Perrine [December 1949]; E. Robinson, 4; Spear; Stevick, 55–59)

"An Evangelist's Wife" (1919). Sonnet. In this dramatic monologue, a wife admits that she is not herself since God gave her to her religious husband to puzzle over his problem with him. She denies that she is jealous of that other woman, pink-cheeked though she is. If he even briefly thought things through, he might see he has little to forgive his wife for doing. She agrees that he has rarely been cruel and adds that when he was mean she applauded and sang. She says that he hasn't learned much from the Bible. She concludes by letting him go ahead sanctimoniously and think she was actually jealous of God.

"An Evangelist's Wife" is the only Shakespearean sonnet Robinson ever wrote. Each quatrain and the final couplet are spaced as though to disguise its form.

"Exit" (1910). Poem. We praised him dangerously, and now he can't speak for himself. Since we envied him, let's keep quiet in our present ignorance. Because he wouldn't do penance for failure after triumph, let's try to be kind.

The death of Robinson's brother Herman Robinson,* alone in a Boston City Hospital ward (1909), prompted the poet to pen this compassionate requiem in six simple couplets. (Source: Hagedorn, 248)

"The False Gods" (1919). Poem. The False Gods warn their worshippers. These Gods confess that they are "false and evanescent," are composed of straw and clay, will repay the service of neophytes with ashes, are weak, will accept adoration indulgently, will show their true faces only if earnestly asked, and should really be killed off since their "Art . . . [is] inorganic and . . . anything you please." They say that their followers' latest work may soon fall, be "unregarded," be hidden by a newly sprouted forest. Regardless of how innovative the followers think they are, their artistic creations "Are a long way from Athens and a longer way from Troy." The Gods' easy promises, if accepted, will result in grief. They conclude: "If you doubt the only truth in all our perjured composition, / May the True Gods attend you and forget us when we go."

"The False Gods" is Robinson's roundabout rebuke of modernist art, specifically formless free verse. When in 1896 Robinson read "The Lesson of the Master," the 1888 short story by Henry James (1843–1916), he was thrilled by James's repeated use of the phrase "the false gods," meaning the lures of profit, social success, sexual love, and children — all beckoning the true artist away from his appointed task. Emery Neff first traced the title "The False Gods" to James. Ellsworth Barnard identifies Robinson's unusual metrical form here as "long, tripping lines (heptameter and octameter, some iambic and some trochaic)." Edwin S. Fussell defines the form as "paeonic measure . . . — three unaccented [syllables] and one accented." The rhyme scheme of each stanza is a difficult *aaba*. Quoting Robinson's passage about Athens and Troy, Henry Rushton Fairclough says that "[t]he poet who wrote [it] . . . holds up the classics as exemplars for the moderns to follow, and is out of sympathy with the principles and ideals of the *poetae novi* of today." (Sources: Barnard, 70; Fairclough, 24; Fussell [1954], 140; Neff, 63)

"The Field of Glory" (1913). Poem. When war stirs the nation, Levi is distressed to be dreaming while at work supporting his bitter old mother. At this very time, others gain glory by fighting. A couple of veterans return, "Rough, bloody, ribald, hungry, lame." They laugh at Levi's gripes but still make him jealous. When he reads about momentous battles to his mother, she merely "looked him up and down, / And laughed," then carefully warns him. He gets nowhere seeking advice from friends; so he maunders on. The poet concludes about this congeries of people: "And who's of this or that estate / We do not wholly calculate."

Ellsworth Barnard says that the couplet quoted above expresses Robinson's "acceptance of the equivocal nature of all that we apprehend outside ourselves." Robinson wrote Hermann Hagedorn* (December 15, 1913) to describe Levi as "a poor devil, totally miscast," and not very intelligent. Robinson adds that he depicted him "in the light of contemporary materialism." He wrote Edith Brower* (December 21, 1915) that he was happy she "did not think he [Levi] was one of the Twelve Tribes, or an East Side Jew ... I made him merely to let the Race-Optimist explain his optimism, and to justify it ... from a materialistic point of view." If so, why did Robinson name his hero manqué Levi? Edwin S. Fussell says that there seems to be no reason Robinson gave the poem "a setting so suggestive of Old Testament history." (Sources: Barnard, 49; Brower, 154, 155; Fussell [1954], 202; *Selected Letters*, 80)

"Firelight" (1918). Sonnet. In the octet, the poet describes a loving couple, happy for 10 years in cozy seclusion within their four firelit walls and blessed because of thoughts "neither says aloud." In the sestet, the poet notes that the wife would be sad if she interpreted the sorrow "graven" on a certain lonely man's "wan face," while the husband would be upset if he knew the thoughts of a certain woman "who shines / Apart" but who wanted him.

This poem may have been suggested by Robinson's unsatisfactory emotional tangle involving his brother Herman Robinson,* his wife Emma Robinson,* and the poet himself; but he complicated it by adding a second uneasy woman, whose identity presumably remains unknown to biographers.

"The First Seven Years" (1930). Autobiographical essay. When Robinson finds in his bulky *Collected Poems* a section entitled *The*

Children of the Night, he realizes that it was 40 years ago that he began to be an angler in "the squirming sea of language" for special words that often got away. But after both patience and rejections, he began to land some words. Many of his early short poems, including sonnets, were faulty and yet meritorious for being unlike other poems. They did seem too much like "technical exercises." He was sad to realize that John Milton wrote well at an early age but was comforted by the report that British minds mature faster than American minds.

When about 17, Robinson began to delight in blank verse. So he experimented by putting a page of Cicero's first speech to Catiline into blank verse. Although lacking Latin resonance, his version had music, rhythm, and "punch." Translating longer passages from Virgil taught him much about English blank verse. Later, his friend Harry de Forest Smith,* now teaching at Amherst College, gave him a prose translation of Antigone, which Robinson struggled one summer to put into blank verse. He asks that, if found, it not be published. (But see "The *Antigone* of Sophocles.")

About 1889 Robinson realized that he was fated to be a poet. He explains how worried his parents would have been if they had known about this grim necessity; tells about the invaluable encouragement and advice of his neighbor Alanson Tucker Schumann,* a physician-poet who was a master of metrical techniques; says he made good friends during his two years at Harvard (1891–1893), returned to Gardiner and wrote there, and then went to New York (1897); and discusses his subsequent three-year lack of success in getting many of his "wares" published. He sent his sonnet "The Clerks" to several outlets, the last being the New York *Sun*, from which it was returned with a slip oddly saying "Unavailable. Paul Dana." (Dana [1852–1930] worked at the *Sun* and was editor from 1897 to 1903.)

At about this time, Robinson says he decided to try to make a book out of 40 or so poems. Publishers rejected it too. Convinced that his "poems had nothing worse than a new idiom to condemn them," he issued the book at his own expense. For $52 he received 312 copies of what he called *The Torrent and The*

Night Before. Copies now fetch more than $52 apiece. Robinson sent out many copies to editors for possible notice, to friends, and to strangers he knew by reputation. He received responses from all but 10 or 12 recipients. (Thomas Hardy never acknowledged receipt.) Robinson says he had confidence enough to be indifferent alike to "hostility or neglect." Often asked, Robinson says he doesn't know how many copies of his "obscure pamphlet" still exist but would guess that only about half do. (Source: Cary [1975], 104–10, 193)

"Flammonde" (1915). Poem. That fellow Flammonde in Tilbury Town was attractively mysterious, foreign perhaps, aristocratic in mien, neither wanting nor wasting, and he graciously borrowed "what he needed for his fee / To live." Was he a prince, or did he just act like one? He seemed to have inherited what others had to strive for, and without succeeding. He soothed people, allayed suspicions concerning himself, and was certainly attractive to women of all ages. He helped a fallen woman regain the respect of petty townspeople. He saw to the financing of a brilliant lad's future. He settled a quarrel between two people squabbling "over nought." But the townspeople could never figure out the "small satanic sort of kink / . . . in his brain" that kept him from achieving something grand for himself. His charm hid something from his associates. Rarely does nature so endow someone and yet let him live. Gone now, Flammonde is missed and sought.

Emma Robinson* and Ruth Nivison* believe that in "Flammonde" the poet is limning his brother Herman Robinson,* even to the extent of their relating Flammonde's helping a talented boy get an education to Herman's persuading their father Edward Robinson* to send Robinson to Harvard. Perhaps; but Flammonde's mysteriously great past, combined with his parasitic present, certainly makes him seem to be a shadowy sketch of Robinson's friend Alfred Hyman Louis.*

Robinson, who liked to pseudo-deprecate his own writings, in a letter (January 1915) to Edith Brower* said "several people insist upon liking" his "Flammonde," and added "I'm not sure that I don't like it myself." John Drinkwa-

ter quotes the four lines in "Flammonde" beginning with the image of the "satanic . . . kink" and concludes that they "seem . . . to be consummate in their mastery, touching the farthest difficulties of poetic writing." William C. Childers says this: "Flammonde" may come from the French *flam* and *monde*, translated together as "light of the world"; Jesus says, "I am the light of the world" (John 8:12, 9:5); when Robinson says not only that Flammonde is "from God knows where" but also that he is almost miraculously helpful to others, he may be giving Flammonde virtually unique Christ-like powers. Hilton Anderson, also seeing parallels between Flammonde and Christ, says that both denied themselves, did for others, and are now searched for by many.

Amy Lowell* accords general praise to "Flammonde" because in it "is a mellowness of soul, a gentle commiseration for the follies of the world." Yvor Winters, however, criticizes the poem for its "empty mannerism" and brands it "repulsively sentimental." Warner Berthoff, before citing "Flammonde" as an example, generalizes that "Robinson is the poet . . . of separateness . . . [m]ore . . . than isolation: his most compact monologues and analyses invariably assume a listener or observer, the irony of whose uncomprehending presence intensifies dramatically the suggested emotion." (Sources: H. Anderson; Berthoff, 120; Brower, 161; Childers [1955], 226; Drinkwater, 258; Lowell [1917], 55; E. Robinson, 2; Winters, 52)

Flandreau, Charles Macomb (1871–1938). Author. He was a student at Harvard, whom Robinson knew when he also studied there (1891–1893). A few years after graduating (1895), Flandreau wrote about his college experiences in *The Diary of a Freshman* (1901). (Sources: Hagedorn, 68; Morison, 402; C. Smith, 119)

"Fleming Helphenstine" (1897). Sonnet. This fellow, with a shining but not persuasive face, identifies himself to the poet as Fleming Helphenstine, chats, laughs, then frowns. The two gaze at each other awkwardly. They "cringe and wince." With a gutteral apology, Helphenstine dodges off. The poet never saw him again. Robinson's poem dramatizes the chancy capriciousness of often sadly brief encounters.

Richard Cary reprints an unsigned 1898 review of *The Children of the Night*, in which "Fleming Helphenstine" first appeared. The reviewer says that the name "Helphenstine" comes from the German word "helfenstein" (stone of succor). (Source: Cary [1974], 94)

"The Flying Dutchman" (1918). Poem. The defiant sailor voyages alone. He neither commands nor is commanded. He is supposedly seeking "the Vanished Land," that place "from which we came." Dawn comes, but no sun. Then, when a cloud lifts, he abandons yet another island and — maybe cursing the deathless "Power" — sails off again.

One legend has it that a certain Dutch sea captain blasphemed God when He warned him to avoid trying to round the Cape of Good Hope during a terrible storm, and therefore condemned him to sail on but never find a harbor again. Robert Mezey regards Robinson's treatment of the subject as allegorically dramatizing "the poet's unblinkered vision of the individual will in isolation from the community and its perhaps fated damnation," further, as "a judgment of the modern sciences . . . [and] of all human suffering that appears to arise from blind ambition and hubris." (Source: Mezey, 234)

"For a Book by Thomas Hardy" (1895). Sonnet. Robinson says that he had been vainly looking around and faltering in the darkness, amid "hordes of eyeless phantoms," until by the grace of God he suddenly felt "a human atmosphere" and heard a strong, plain "murmur . . . / Flung from a singing river's endless race." The "grand, sad song" was about "Life's wild infinity of mirth and woe." Then it seemed to him that he saw through its flowing music "the cottage lights of Wessex."

Thomas Hardy (1840–1928) was a major force in Robinson's intellectual and professional development. In the course of various letters to his friend Harry de Forest Smith,* Robinson indicates that he has read at least 15 works by Hardy. Ellsworth Barnard concludes that "Hardy was one of the few writers to

whom Robinson was devoted from first to last"; Barnard further reports that the specific book by Hardy to which Robinson alludes in his sonnet is *Jude the Obscure*. When the sonnet was reprinted in *The Torrent and The Night Before*, Robinson sent a copy of the book to Hardy, who evidently never acknowledged receipt of it by any letter to Robinson. Amy Lowell* praises Hardy at Robinson's expense, theorizing that "Hardy touches his characters reverently, even as he dissects them; Mr Robinson is not reverent, his nearest approach to it is a dry-eyed pity." Richard Cary provides thorough evidence of Robinson's response to Hardy over the years. (Sources: Barnard, 106; Cary [1974], 91; Cary [1975], 24, 175; Lowell [1922], 140; *Untriangulated Stars*)

"For a Copy of Poe's Poems" (1906). Sonnet. Robinson says that Poe came from a magical land, stayed here a while, then left. He viewed life's troubles through a dark glass. His "frail . . . hand" sought for hints of joy in "utter night." He left us a few inexplicable songs of great wonder. His poetry expressed a combination of idealism, music, sadness, longings, hopelessness, ghostly dreams, "and one — Lenore."

When the editors of *Lippincott's Monthly Magazine* paid Robinson $7 in 1894 for his sonnet on Poe, the sum was the first the poet had ever been paid for his work; but it did not appear in *Lippincott's* until just short of a dozen years later. Bacon Collamore* quotes a letter (June 6, 1897) from Robinson "to a friend," in which he says that only the sestet of this sonnet is passable. In Robinson's play *Van Zorn*, Mrs. Lovett has Weldon Farnham run an errand for her; it is to get photographs of an Edgar Allan Poe bust. (Sources: Cary [1975], 17, 172–73; Collamore, 13; Hagedorn, 98, 212; *Untriangulated Stars*, 203)

"For a Dead Lady" (1909). Poem. This is an elegy for a woman whose eyes were once brimming with light, who wore roses, who laughed a little harshly, and who trembled not only "at applause" but also "over children" as they were sleeping. Her beauty has been destroyed "by the laws / That have creation in their keeping." Philosophers "who delve in beauty's lore" can never understand why "Time [is] so vicious in his reaping."

Richard P. Adams calls this poem "Robinson at his best, and his best is about the best there is." Each of its three stanzas, in iambic tetrameter, rhymes *ababccab*, with each *b*-rhyme feminine. Floyd Stovall says that in this poem Robinson "sums the incredible sorrow of poets of all ages before the sight of beauty [']shattered by the laws [/] That have creation in their keeping[']." Ellsworth Barnard feels that the woman trembled when she viewed children asleep "because her own innocence and purity responded to theirs." R. H. Super contends, however, that the statement about the lady's "breast where roses could not live," though usually interpreted to mean that "the breast was so lovely that roses faded in comparison," may instead mean that the withering of flowers on a girl's breast signifies she's a flirt. There seems no reason to believe, as Harold Bloom, Hermann Hagedorn,* Robert Mezey, and Chard Powers Smith* do, that the poet exclusively has in mind the desire to memorialize his mother in this universally appealing poem.

When Edith Brower* found "The laugh that love could not forgive" to be a puzzling line, Robinson replied by letter (March 15, 1914) that he meant nothing "more than her way of presuming on her attractions and 'guying' those who admired her." Clyde L. Grimm summarizes and responds cogently to much of the early commentary this poem attracted. (Sources: R. Adams, 142; Barnard, 166; Bloom, 809; Brower, 155; Grimm; Hagedorn, 238; Mezey, xxxi, 226; C. Smith, 221; Stovall, 5; Super)

"For Arvia" (1908). Sonnet. Subtitled "On Her Fifth Birthday," this poem is addressed to the daughter of Robinson's friend Percy MacKaye.* The poet asks the little girl's eyes why they "look so dubiously" at him. What does her scrutiny discover? Is he a mystery? just a friend? She has lots of time in which to answer but has more important things to think about just now, as she awakens to much of value.

This sonnet was originally composed to cel-

ebrate the sixth birthday of Ruth Robinson,* the poet's niece. Ten years later, it was dusted off, retitled and readdressed as indicated, and published. (Sources: Hagedorn, 237; C. Smith, 149–50)

"For Calderon" (1896). Poem. A man soon to die is dictating a letter for Francisco, his younger brother, to write down and send to their brother, named Calderon. The man says he poisoned Mona so slowly that she never realized it. She loved Calderon. The murderer loved her also, but only a little bit until he saw that Calderon possessed her. That ruined the murderer. He pauses a moment, fancying that he hears Mona singing. He tells Francisco not to worry about their family honor, that only his courage matters. He bids Francisco farewell and dies. Francisco doesn't weep, but his heart holds grief and his hand grasps "a written leaf" to send across the ocean to Calderon.

"For Calderon" appeared in *The Torrent and The Night Before*, but Robinson omitted it from *The Children of the Night*. In a letter (April 21, 1897) to Edith Brower,* he calls the poem "a little childish." Emery Neff labels it an "immature piece." Why Robinson chose the name Calderon is puzzling. It is tempting to theorize that it was inspired by that of Pedro Calderón de la Barca (1600–1681), the Spanish dramatist and poet. Calderón had two hot-tempered brothers (Diego and José). All three were fined for killing a servant's son. Calderón is said by some authorities to have been stabbed in the face during a quarrel over a woman. In addition, many of his tragedies are about love, jealousy, and the code of honor. Two such plays of his are *El Médico de su Honra* (The Doctor of His Honor) and *El Mayor Monstruo Zelos* (Jealousy the Greatest Monster). (Sources: Brower, 39; Neff, 87)

"For Harriet Moody's Cook Book" (1938). Essay. Robinson says we should doff hats, consider kneeling, and praise good cooks. The world would be a bad place without good cooks to prepare good meals for people to eat and become good. Without a lot of good people around, many would prefer to leave the world. Robinson insists that his remarks are both true and temperate. Some people think we resemble "our alleged arboreal ancestors" and can survive on uncooked fruit, nuts, and vegetables. Appealing though this assertion may be, it's untrue. You can't cut short the process of learning, being artistic, or dining well. Yes, you can survive on bread and milk, but few try. If you want to, be sure to ask for good bread, which requires good work to make. A good cook is a kind of greater king, who, without having a good cook, would gripe like the rest of us.

Harriet Converse Moody (1857–1932), the widow of William Vaughn Moody,* asked 16 prominent authors to write essays on the importance of good food. She intended to assemble their comments as an introduction to a cook book. Robinson, among others, obliged; but Scribner's editors disapproved and the essays weren't included when the 475-page book was published (1931). Olivia H. D. Torrence, the wife of Ridgely Torrence,* published Robinson's little essay in "The Poet at the Dinner Table" (*Colophon* n.s. 3, Winter 1938: 93–99). (Source: Cary [1975], 110–11, 194)

"For Some Poems by Matthew Arnold" (1896). Sonnet. His firmly playing "the chords of Hellas" arouses classical echoes, the cadences of which offer age-old heroic romances to a land now "cramped and fettered with a band / Of iron creeds." He also sings about Valhalla, Balder, Lok, Frea, and "the hushed sands of Oxus" where Sohrab died "in his father's arms."

Valhalla, Balder, Lok, and Frea are all mentioned in Arnold's narrative poem "Balder Dead"; Oxus and Sohrab, in his narrative poem "Sohrab and Rustum."

The writings of Matthew Arnold (1822–1888), especially his poetry, were a major influence on Robinson from his early adult years. Arnold was required reading in at least one course at Harvard while Robinson was there (1891–1893). James L. Tryon,* Harvard's fellow student at Harvard, says that "[a]mong his [Robinson's] favorite poets were Swinburne, Tennyson, and Arnold; but Arnold he liked best of all and from him he most frequently read aloud, usually selecting

a short poem or sonnet. He liked *Sohrab* and *Rustum* and was interested in the Arthurian legends." Arnold's *Tristram and Isolt* exerted at least a slight influence on Robinson's *Tristram*. In a letter (January 27, 1894) to Harry de Forest Smith,* Robinson expressed criticism of Arnold which has become an academic truism: "His 'mission' [as a critic] stopped his poetry and I have always regretted it." (Sources: Tryon, 11; *Untriangulated Stars*, 123–24)

"Foreword to *The Mountain*" (1934). Essay. *The Mountain* (1934) is a published play by Edwin Carty Ranck (see Ranck, Carty), who asked Robinson to write an introduction. Robinson begins it by suggesting that romance, which is costly and bothersome, is beginning to disappear. Romantic love surely is, in literature anyway. Romantic hate is also declining, even in the Kentucky mountains, because of "education, compromise and prosaic common sense." Perhaps too much conformity and too much sense becoming too common in our so-called democracy will one faraway day trigger a desire to return to romance — though not if it includes traditional old "feuds and furies."

Readers in the North know little about Southern mountaineers except through literature. We admire their courage, feuding, pride, moonshine, dislike of federal revenuers, and annoyance with anyone making a distinction between corn for meal and corn for whiskey. Both of these fine products God made possible. Sadly, however, these mountain folks also fail to understand why unacceptable neighbors should be allowed to live.

The inability of some mountaineers even to read written laws leads to perplexities which Ranck, Kentuckian born and raised, makes the subject of his important, authentic, and well-written drama. Careless readers of it may call its hero, Zeke Holston, bad, whereas he is pure according to his atavistic vision. Zeke regards law-and-order ideas as an intrusion into his bailiwick, and his son, despite his modern talk and fancy ways, as a traitor better off dead. The play, which is dynamic, not static, rightly lacks an expansion of its love subplot and properly concentrates on the bewildered, disillusioned father's response to approaching tragedy. (Source: Cary [1975], 115–17, 195)

"Fortunatus" (1928). Poem. The poet addresses a typically fortunate person. Twice the poet advises him to "Be as you are." The poet continues: No chance or destined event will hurt your complacency. By remaining ignorant, you serve the world nicely. You needn't explain mysteries you don't see. You're unaware of "the drama of dead lives" of people showing you only "calm faces and closed doors." You don't know what burdens others take off your shoulders. You're ignorant of violent history and regard the status quo as all right. You rule over a fiefdom the tiny size of which you couldn't measure. By needing little, you have a sufficiency.

Bacon Collamore* provides details of the publication of this dour little six-stanza poem, rhyming *abcb*. Some 171 copies on white paper, signed by Robinson, were printed by the Grabhorn Press in San Francisco, issued for James Raye Welles, who owned the Slide Mountain Press. It was a 24-page booklet. In addition, 12 copies were printed on brown paper, reserved for Robinson to present as he wished. (Sources: Cary [1975], 52–53, 185; Collamore, 40–41)

"Fragment" (1910). Poem. Briony, rich and idle, lives in his secluded, isolated home, with its fancy white pillars, in a well-shaded forest of beech, oak, and hickory. He might better have used some of "the Briony gold" to please the gods. Instead, he "knew too much for the life he led," became neurotic, was frightened by his sun dial, and said ominously, "Sooner or later they strike." Yes, indeed. Time is a patient ghost, and now more than the wind whispers over Briony's trees and his broken fountain.

Glauco Cambon says that "Fragment" offers a "classically firm style . . . well climaxed by the final stanza." Briony is one of Robinson's many egocentric, non-communicating figures. Roy Harvey Pearce says of Briony and others like him that "the poet can only report his discovery that something unanalyzably vital is involved, and then wonder at it." The fifth line begins "Now many a man"; the thought

continues to the effect that such men would reason that gods would need to be pleased and invisible houses built. Lawrance Thompson, in his 1953 edition of Tilbury Town poems, changes "Now" to "Not," to correct what he regards as a likely typographical error. He contends that whereas Robinson did let the erroneous "Not" stand, many envious observers of Briony's house indeed (to continue quoting the poem), "Would [now, not not] have said, 'There are still some gods to please, / And houses are built without hands, we're told.'" Indeed, Thompson concludes, Robinson was doubtless wishing us to recall that "we know that if our earthly house of this tabernacle were dissolved, we have a building of God, an house not made with hands, eternal in the heavens" (II Corinthians 5:1). The title "Fragment" suggests that, even if Robinson could go on a little, he chooses to break off his poetic admonition early. Emma Robinson* and Ruth Nivison* suggest that this poem is a tribute to Robinson's father, Edward Robinson.* (Sources: Cambon, 78; Pearce, 259; E. Robinson, 9; L. Thompson, 135)

"Franklin Schenck (1856–1927)" (1928). Essay. When some of the paintings of Robinson's friend Franklin Schenck were exhibited at the Macbeth Gallery in New York City (February 28–March 12, 1928), an eight-page catalogue entitled *Paintings by Franklin L. Schenck 1826 : 1927* was distributed to patrons. Included was Robinson's one-page essay. In it, Robinson points out how strange it is that Schenck, "predestined poet and idealist," was once the favorite pupil of Thomas Eakins (1844–1916), the realist painter. The pictures shown now, Robinson continues, were painted in the last 20 years of Schenck's life, in the small house he owned at East Northport, on Long Island, where he died. Although he followed his own bent in painting, he admired "Beauty and genius" in art work by others, whose "methods and tenets" in many cases were unlike his own. Robinson says that he finds beauty and genius in Schenck's "quiet pictures," which may be revered when more obviously appealing ones by other painters are forgotten, despite their current "noise." (See also "A Tribute to Franklin L. Schenck.") (Sources: Cary [1975], 93–94, 192; Collamore, 44)

Fraser, James Earle (1876–1953). Sculptor. Fraser was born in Winona, Minnesota, accompanied his parents when his father moved on various railroad construction jobs, and lived on a ranch with his parents in South Dakota, where he came to know and respect Native Americans, loved the prairies, and modeled small statues in clay. He attended public schools in Minneapolis, studied art in Chicago, and went to Paris (1895) to study at the École des Beaux-Arts. A prize-winning work of his, exhibited at the American Art Association in Paris (1898), attracted the attention of Augustus Saint-Gaudens (1848–1907), the renowned American sculptor, who employed Fraser in Paris and then at his studio in Cornish, New Hampshire (1900). Success for Frazer soon followed. He made a portrait of Saint-Gaudens (1901); worked and taught in New York (1902–1935); was a member of the National Academy of Design (from 1912); the next year married Laura Gardin, one of his students, who soon was also a distinguished sculptor (the couple had no children); with her bought a summer home in Westport, Connecticut; produced the official vice presidential bust of Theodore Roosevelt* (1910) and other works celebrating Roosevelt after he had become president; designed the U.S. nickel featuring an Indian head and a buffalo (1911); created the prize-winning *End of the Trail*, based on a small, teen-aged work of his, redone life-size in plaster (1915) and bronze (1929); was president of the National Sculpture Society (1924–1927); and moved with his wife to Westport (1935). Beginning in 1934, Fraser designed architectural and monumental statues for several government buildings in Washington, D.C., and elsewhere, concluding with a statue of General George Patton (1950, at West Point).

In 1902, James Moore, in whose house on 450 West 23rd Street, in New York Robinson lived (1901–04), introduced the poet to Fraser. The two became friends. Robinson also knew and liked Fraser's wife, attended the theater in New York with them, borrowed money from them when necessary, played poker with them, and roomed with them in Westport and in New York. Robinson dedicated *The Man Who Died Twice* (1924) to Fraser and his wife. The Frasers, with whom he was living when his final illness took him to the New York hospital, visited him loyally there. They were also friendly with Robinson's friends Joseph Lewis French* and Louis V. Ledoux,* among others. Fraser gathered and printed at his expense 54 newspaper and magazine articles about Robinson in a 90-page booklet entitled *In Tribute* (1935). (Sources: Hagedorn; C. Smith)

French, Joseph Lewis (1858–1936). Journalist, editor, and salesman for Richard G. Badger.* When his father lost his New York import business in the Panic of 1873, French lit out for the West. He journeyed along the Santa Fe Trail, visited Mexico, became a newspaperman, founded the *New West* in Kansas City, helped establish the short-lived *Wave* (1895–1901) in San Francisco, and wound up in Boston and then New York. Over many years, at least between 1918 and 1933, French assembled and edited 27 books of all sorts, about airplane pilots, detectives, escapes, ghosts, humor, pioneers, pirates, psychics, riddles, rogues, the sea, and terror.

When Robinson in 1899 was in Cambridge, Massachusetts, as a staff worker for Charles William Eliot,* president of Harvard, French sought him out obsequiously. French was then employed by Richard G. Badger, whose firm had recently published Robinson's *The Children of the Night*. French also associated with Robinson in New York (from c. 1902). French persuaded the editor Edmund Clarence Stedman* to publish "A Poet in the Subway" (New York *Sunday World*, May 15, 1904), an essay by French about Robinson, against Robinson's wish. Richard Cary points out eight factual errors in this otherwise exemplary review and also reprints French's later review, "The Younger Poets of New England" (*New England Magazine*, December 1905), which, though full of more praise of Robinson, contains five errors. (In his review, French also discusses poetry by Robinson's friends William Stanley Braithwaite* and Josephine Preston Peabody.*) French cadged money and clothes from Robinson and his friends, reviled him on occasion, but also valiantly tried for seven years, without success, to get the Nobel Prize for him. At times Robinson thought that the unstable French might kill him, once when he invaded the MacDowell Colony* on the prowl. A few weeks before Robinson died, French entered his hospital room, begged money from him, and departed with $5. French may be defined as a failure of the sort Robinson often sympathized with and wrote about. Shortly after Robinson's death, French died in a sanitarium. (Sources: Cary [1974], 157–63, 191–93; Coxe; Hagedorn; C. Smith)

"The Galley Race" (1890). Translation of Virgil's *Aeneid*, V: 104–285. At sunrise crowds approach the shore, prizes are displayed, and four Trojan galleys appear. They are the *Pristis* (captained by Mnestheus), the *Chimera* (captain, Gyas), the *Centaur* (Sergestus), and the *Scylla* (Cloanthus). Aeneas put an oak on a distant rock to mark the turning point. The crews ready their oars, hear the trumpet, and begin. Their ships plow the frothy waves. The heavy *Scylla* lags somewhat. The *Centaur* and the *Pristis* approach the rock. The *Chimera* is piloted more safely by blind Menoetes, until Gyas throws Menoetes overboard and orders the ship toward the rock, onto which Menoetes, "spew[ing] the swallowed brine [salsos . . . revomentem]," climbs. The *Centaur* goes too close to the rock and snaps its oars on a reef. The *Pristis* rounds the rock and passes the *Chimera*, but *Scylla* leads. Cloanthus promises a white bull to the sea gods and is victorious. Aeneas awards lavish prizes to Cloanthus, to second-place Mnestheus, and to third-place Gyas. Sergestus sails his crippled *Pristis* to port, and Aeneas gives him a Cretan slave.

Robinson wrote a letter (April 17, 1890) to Arthur R. Gledhill,* enclosed a copy of his translation, complained that the work though fun was difficult, and said that it took him two days to translate acceptably "illa Noto citius volucrique sagitta / Ad terram fugit et portu se condidit alto [she flies to the land swifter than the south wind and swift arrow and hid herself in the deep harbor]." Robinson's free version: "Swift as the wind, in arrowy flight she speeds / And rides triumphant in the land-locked port." (See also "Menoetes.") (Sources: Cary [1975], 9–14, 170; *Selected Letters*, 3)

"The Garden" (1896). Sonnet. "The Gardener" and the poet found themselves alone in an unfenced garden full of varied growth. "He" pointed to where the poet scattered his early fennel. It had developed into a "riot of sad weeds," the result of his life. Yes, his, but also those of all humanity. It was like a book of signed leaves, inspired by everlasting thought, rooted by love in the garden-like divine mind. This poem was entitled "God's Garden" when first pubished in book form.

Sister Mary James Power says that "our dependence [is] wholly upon Him [God], Robinson tells us in 'The Garden.' Life, he knows, is a garden. And in his introspection, in company with the Gardener, he has gone through it, seeing all the many flowers and the weeds[,] . . . his own deeds[,] . . . the lives of everybody[,] . . . [p]ropagated . . . from the seeds of eternity . . . rooted . . . in God's Love and tended by His guidance." Charles T. Davis regards "The Garden" as an early, nearly "pure statement of Emersonian transcendentalism." Davis says that Robinson suggests here that his life is an uncontrolled "growth" amid "a riot of weeds," and becomes awesomely aware of "the economy of the life process," in which "'every leaf, miraculously signed,' has 'Outrolled itself from Thought's eternal seed.'" The garden becomes the world, resting finally "on spirit or God." Davis generalizes to the effect that in poems after "The Garden" Robinson employs garden images to indicate the individual's "completed growth" and his "mature nature," and writes less "about an origin in Thought." Instead, he emphasizes "roots," the present's dependence on the past, and the ability of the tiniest of actions to affect "the course of life." (Sources: Davis [1961], 383; Power, 78)

"The Garden of the Nations (1923)" (1923). Sonnet. We are going to be "the bitten flower and fruit" of time, hurt — as it always happens — by blight above and evil from the depths. Dead by then, we won't need to worry about embarrassment or ill repute. Perhaps we'll be replaced by something stronger and more valuable. Let's hope our replacement in God's garden won't be weeds and bugs.

Gardiner, John Hays (1864–1913). Harvard professor of English, and editor and director of the *Harvard Bulletin*. He was a cousin of Laura E. Richards.* The home of the Gardiner family in Gardiner, Maine, was called "Oaklands." Gardiner wrote a splendid review of *The Children of the Night* (Boston *Evening Transcript*, December 24, 1897). He also wrote four books — on composition, prose forms, rhetoric, and the Bible as English literature. He pioneered a course at Harvard on the Bible as literature. He helped Robinson to obtain his 1899 administrative job at Harvard in the office of Charles William Eliot,* its president. Gardiner and Laura Richards both helped finance the publication of *Captain Craig* (1902), the revised edition of which Robinson dedicated to Gardiner's memory (1915). When Gardiner died, Laura records that he "left him [Robinson] a substantial legacy" but does not specify the sum. Rollo Walter Brown* summarizes Robinson's ecstasy when, absolutely impoverished, he received word that in Gardiner's will was a gift to him of $4,000. Brown adds that Robinson said that, given his rate of spending then, he could have lived a million years on the bequest. (Sources: R. Brown, 68; Cary [1974], 90; Richards [1936], 53)

Gates, Lewis E. Harvard professor of English literature. Robinson admired Gates, faithfully attended Gates's lectures during his freshman year at Harvard (1891–1892), and often wrote to his friend Harry de Forest Smith* about the amiable professor. Hermann Hagedorn* describes Gates as a "fluttering gray moth." James L. Tryon* adds that "[w]hat appealed to Robinson most in his study of English were the courses given by Professor Lewis E. Gates in eighteenth and nineteenth century prose writers, and of these he liked best and reacted most to the nineteenth century course which came in the first year of his admission." (Sources: Hagedorn, 70, 71; Tryon, 9; *Untriangulated Stars*)

Genevieve and Alexandra (1917). Dialogue in blank verse. Genevieve, who is pretty, has been unhappily married for six years and has just sent for her rather plain younger sister Alexandra. Two weeks pass before they start to discuss matters seriously. Alexandra says that Genevieve's husband before his marriage saw in Alexandra only the $600 she controlled and, further, that some other woman, whom Genevieve is imagining to be a rival for the husband's love, is simply a challenge to Genevieve. Alexandra adds that some men accept a wife's frigidity, while others don't. When Genevieve cries and says she feels caged, Alexandra retorts that "a rather furry man / . . . likes a woman with a dash of Eve" and tends to look around for satisfaction. The husband kissed Alexandra only in a whiskery welcoming way, and Genevieve should accept him for what he is, faithful, and careful with money. Genevieve says she'd like to change but fears she neither knows enough nor cares to do so. Alexandra tells her to put her "bogey" fear in the sort of darkness she likes. Genevieve says that she futilely gave her all to "his hungry love and hungry mind," which misunderstood the gift. She refuses to be humored when Alexandra says that his eyes are kindness itself for Genevieve. Genevieve says that he is welcome to a veritable harem, and would prefer his violence or a self-inflicted torture to kindness from him. Alexandra says that other women have had such fancies and that only her nerves are talking now. Genevieve says Alexandra must stop calling her "Poor Genevieve!"

The married pair are fatally mismatched, but the pallid conversation the nervous wife has about her so-so husband with her perceptive sister ends nowhere because she won't settle for more than life has dished out for her. Hoyt C. Franchere contends that *Genevieve and Alexandra* "falls short of Robinson's usual level of accomplishment because it dwindles and falls into inconclusiveness at its close." (Source: Franchere, 106)

"George Crabbe" (1896). Sonnet. Robinson says that we can assign George Crabbe's works to a dark book shelf or a lonely attic, but doing so won't keep us from still feeling the force of his strong, stubborn, bravely truthful message. His reputation may have dwindled, but his light is a flame, not a flicker.

George Crabbe (1754–1832) was a Scottish physician, chaplain, and poet. One of Robinson's favorite poets, Crabbe is notable for his grim sketches of ordinary people made unhappy by poverty, narrowing circumstances, and mental unbalance. Amy Lowell* says she prefers Robinson to Crabbe "because Crabbe saw only what is, while Mr Robinson has a deep insight in why it is." Richard Gray says that "[l]ike Crabbe, he [Robinson] implies [in this sonnet], he is concerned with the loneliness of country people, the austerity and sheer poverty of their existence." Robinson found in Crabbe the same dedication to poetic excellence and skill that he strove for himself in handling similar subjects. This solid, unrelenting sonnet is Robinson at his terse best. (Sources: Gray, 142; Lowell [1922], 139)

Gibran, Kahlil (1883–1931). Symbolist poet, artist, sculptor, and philosophical mystic, born Gibran Khalil [*sic*] Gibran, in Besharri, Lebanon (now Syria). Gibran's father, Khalil, was a lazy farmer, violent gambler, and criminal. His mother, Kamila, was a lovable, peppy peddler. The family were Maronite Catholics. The father shamed the family by getting arrested for embezzling (1891). Kamila, finally disgusted, abandoned her husband and took Peter (her son by a wandering first husband), young Khalil, and his two sisters, Marianna and Sultanato, to America (1895). Earlier, her husband's cousin Melham Gibran, his wife, and their two daughters had emigrated to Boston (1890). Kamila and her brood began to live with them there. Only at this time did Khalil begin to learn English. In Quincy, Massachusetts, teachers registered him as Kahlil Gibran, which he later took as his pen name. His drawings attracted patrons, among them wealthy women, in Boston and New York (1896). He went back to his homeland to study Arabic literature in Beirut (1898–1902), returned to Boston (1902–1912), then lived in New York (1912–1924) and finally Boston again (from 1924). His first writings are all in Arabic (1905–1918); his

later ones, mostly in English (1918–1931). Among his eight books, including two posthumously published, *The Prophet* (1923) proved to be the most successful, though only after his death; it ultimately sold several million copies and has been translated into more than 20 languages. *The Prophet* contains 28 often aphoristic prose poems about beauty, death, goodness, independence, love and marriage, family values, nature, religion, and work.

Josephine Preston Peabody* knew the overly ardent Gibran in Cambridge, Massachusetts, probably introduced him to Robinson by 1903 if not earlier, and included a poem about him entitled "The Prophet" in *The Singing Man*, the 1911 collection of her poetry. Gibran gave Robinson a copy of *The Prophet*, inscribing it "with highest admiration." Nicholas Ayo conjectures that the two men must have associated with one another in Manhattan in 1923, since they lived only a couple of blocks apart and shared similar intellectual interests. Robinson, however, must have found Gibran's works somewhat shallow and overly sensual, and so popular that something had to be amiss in them. (Sources: Ayo, 60–61; Gibran, 123, 145)

"The Gift of God" (1914). Poem. This dear woman can "scarcely bear the weight." God has given her a positively anointed son. It seems irreligious of her to acknowledge the fact that she is his mother. He is a shining soul, not to be touched by troubles of any sort. If townspeople were polled, they might smile and gossip crudely about the fellow, but that wouldn't bother the mother. She plans for his enormous greatness, gratefully regards him as worthy of a crown, and dreams on about his ever-rising fame.

Emery Neff says that Robinson is successful when in "The Gift of God" he "ventures . . . to describe maternal love, proverbial for leading American writers into the maudlin, because his humor can temper his tenderness." Ellsworth Barnard praises the poem as "a matchless study of the irony and pathos mingled in the mirages wrought by a mother's love." One extreme example of misinterpretations of Robinson by obtuse critics is the analogy some have expressed linking the mother here with the Blessed Virgin and her child with Jesus. Nor does there seem to be any reason to believe, as other critics have done, that the mother here will inevitably be bitterly disillusioned when in due time her son fails. Emma Robinson* and Ruth Nivison* reductively relate this mother's unwarranted worship of her son to that of Mary Robinson,* the poet's mother, with respect to his brother Herman Robinson.* (See also "My Methods and Meanings.") (Sources: Barnard, 27; Neff, 180; E. Robinson, 2)

Gilder, Richard Watson (1844–1909). Editor and poet. He was born in Bordentown, New Jersey, was assistant editor of *Scribner's Monthly* (1870–1881), and when it became the *Century Magazine* was its editor (1881–1909). He married Helena DeKay (1874; they had a daughter). Gilder traveled to Europe on three occasions (1879–1880, 1895, 1900). Once also an immensely popular poet, he published 16 books of his own verse, notably *The New Day* (1875), *The Poet and His Master* (1878), and *Five Books of Song* (1894). He also wrote biographies of Abraham Lincoln (1909) and Grover Cleveland (1910). His letters were published (1910).

In March 1905 Gilder was conferring with Theodore Roosevelt* in the White House about an essay on Roosevelt's reading habits, when the president incidentally recommended Robinson as a fine poet. A little later, William Vaughn Moody* was dining with Gilder in New York and suggested that the president should assign the needy Robinson a job. Moody asked Ridgely Torrence* about it, and Torrence told Moody he should get Gilder to write Roosevelt to ask him to find a job for Robinson. Roosevelt did so. Meanwhile, Gilder accepted Robinson's "Uncle Ananias" for publication in the *Century* (August 1905) but demeaned it by placing it in his humor department called "In Lighter Vein."

Herbert F. Smith quotes from a letter (December 22, 1908) from Robinson to Gilder in which he praises Gilder's poetic technique and expresses admiration for his refusal to be a simple optimist, as proved in his poem "Non Sine Dolore." Smith feels it incumbent upon him to define Robinson as one of "the lesser writers of the period [1880–1900]" whom Gilder encouraged by publishing a few of his poems in the *Century*. Smith also blithely concludes that when Robinson accepted Gilder's change in one of Robinson's poems, he was showing "his position as suppliant to a whimsical editor . . . [and] also deference to a mature judgment." (Sources: Cary [1974], 163; Hagedorn, 211–14; *Selected Letters*, 65; H. Smith, 27, 45)

"Glass Houses" (1924). Poem. The persona tells his auditor not to ask him to repeat what the fellow's neighbor says privately about his appearance, actions, value, and morals. He can go learn all this elsewhere. If the fellow and his neighbor can enjoy each other's laudatory opinions, fine. The persona adds that he knows about two other people whose "pungent" private opinions, each about the other, came back and stung "the wrong ears." Be aware that people often don't have time enough to repair what gossip injures. Enough said.

Gledhill, Arthur R. A close friend of Robinson during their boyhood and early youth in Gardiner, Maine. The two sang in the Episcopal Church choir. Gledhill's father, the Rev. Joseph S. Gledhill, was pastor of the Universalist Church. In the 1890s, Robinson often wrote from Gardiner and Harvard to Gledhill.

The Glory of the Nightingales (New York: Macmillan, 1930). Poem. Blank-verse narrative in six numbered parts.

I. Malory is returning to a city called Sharon, and plans to go beyond it, to get revenge on Nightingale, who lives in his palatial mansion by the sea and who ruined Malory's life several years ago. Nightingale now has nothing, is lonely, and for a long time fancied that Malory brought on his own fate by meddling. Nightingale used to liken himself to a tree made noble by nature, and likened Malory to a worm trying to bore into it.

Malory trudges on, through changed old neighborhoods near Sharon, aware that former friends would feel he betrayed them. He must show Agatha, in her house on the hillside, that he was doing well, must hear her gratitude, and must let her know that fate is proceeding toward Nightingale. But does he hear mocking murmurs?

II. Malory is close to the city now. Nobody observes him. He proceeds toward Agatha's place, feeling death ahead of him and behind him, and reaches a cemetery. The dead there are probably grateful. He discovers Agatha's name on a tombstone, at sunset. He tells her that he has lost faith in God and in friendship, and that he warned Nightingale to beware of stepping on a serpent in the dark jungle of his life. A crippled victim might be waiting to sting him. Darkness falls, and he tells Agatha that all should be complete within a day. Another name — Absalom Spinner — attracts his attention, and he thinks of Agatha's smiling.

On to Sharon, where fifty thousand residents might be so many strangers' names on headstones to him. He passes a house that used to be his and Agatha's. He intended to glance at it, whoever occupied it.

III. Malory spends his last silver for a predawn breakfast in dead-looking Sharon and then proceeds toward Nightingale's mansion. Symbol of the man's ambition, it is now a kind of stony shell for the "pernicious mollusc" God installed there and then forgot. Malory represents the fate of the place. The flaming sunrise endorses Malory's desire to incinerate two deserving of death. He strides eastward until noon, looking unapproachably distinguished, and on toward Nightingale, who is real enough, like a snake or a wolf. By afternoon, Malory spies the towers of his enemy's castle, around which is "an empty wealth of loneliness." When he gets himself inside, he hears Nightingale's voice from another room. It greets him by name as though they were still young friends. But years have aged and wrecked Malory.

IV. With the deadly weapon he has arrived to use, Malory hesitantly walks in and encounters Nightingale, whom he once loved and trusted, but then hated. Behold Nightingale, imprisoned in a wheel chair in a room walled with books and a window with the sea beyond. His eyes still burn, but less. His body, once strong, is mostly bones. He looks like "skin and death." An unfair fate has turned to dross Malory's desire for the gold of revenge.

Nightingale says with joy that Malory may kill him now. Malory says that Nightingale may be in hell, here, already, and surmises that the tiny bacteria shattering his enemy surely prove the enmity of Nature, and perhaps the existence of God. Aware of an unexpected "warfare of inept negations," Malory now wants to live to see the outcome of events. Nightingale now points two pistols at Malory, asks to see his rival's concealed weapon, and wonders if it might resemble Absalom's.

Malory is unnerved and dismayed by his enemy's debility, sits when asked, and listens as Nightingale says that Malory stole something beautiful from him and that Absalom also came by, once, to shoot him but was dissuaded by accepting some rum and a bribe. Malory calls Nightingale dishonorable and says he saw Absalom's grave. Nightingale says this: Absalom's wife was a chicken-brained, immoral "fruity sort of Cyprian fungus," created by God to be eaten up; Absalom accepted money and lived happily for three years and then died in a dray accident. Malory tries to remonstrate, rises, but falls back, exhausted by his long walk.

V. Malory (now identified as a doctor) has rested in a comfortable room and has eaten some necessary food sent to him by Nightingale, who speaks of turning a Christian cheek, asks Malory to stay one final day since their time is running out, and mentions some deserved money he has settled on Malory, who wonders why he should stick around to witness a vicious but helpless invalid's demise. But, all right, he'll stay to hear about Agatha and her child, whom Nightingale diabolically destroyed. They reminisce about their schoolboy days together. Nightingale saw ability in Malory and aided him to become a bacteriologist.

When Malory pours himself a stiff whiskey, Nightingale recalls that Malory drank too much in Sharon. Now, no matter. Nightingale adds that he himself bribed his free-living father's victims into silence, brightly varnished over his own "fluid conscience," aided other townspeople by his domineering wealth, but wrongly thought he — an "approachable Maecenas" and "The Glory of the Nightingales" — was above the law. While Malory concludes that neither power nor revenge is worth much,

Nightingale rambles on: Townspeople revered him, made him dangerously feel second to none. The lovely Agatha appeared and soon became his ultimate, dangerously adorable goal. He introduced his regal friend Malory to her, and Malory kept him from an amorous paradise. Malory, bridling, says two knaves can fall in love with one decent woman, says Agatha preferred him and was merely sorry for Nightingale, and says Nightingale's "ulcered understanding" prevented awareness of the fact then.

Nightingale replies. He is humble now but back then losing Agatha let the devil, powerful but not omnipotent, inoculate him with hate — perhaps like Malory's for him now. Nightingale felt betrayed by two friends, hid his misery from everybody in Sharon, and would apologize now to Malory except that doing so would bemean them. Back then, Nightingale persuaded Malory to sink his sizable legacy in a stock venture in which he himself was investing. But to ruin Malory's and Sharon's happiness together, Nightingale, when warned while across the sea of an imminent fall in the stock, "sold all mine / For someone else to lose, which is finance," but didn't warn Malory and thus let him lose all. Nightingale wanted to destroy Malory but destroyed only Agatha. He returned to Sharon, stood at her grave, and was happy she was lost to Malory, was thus as much his as Malory's at that point. He says he wanted only her, couldn't have her, Malory took her away; tells Malory to go get his gun in a nearby drawer and take a beach stroll. Malory sees the unceasing waves, the result of "power." They tell him to live and serve, which adjuration is unlike Agatha's smiling, final message to him.

VI. Malory promises to stay until tomorrow. He is tired of the "emptiness of hate," will forget it, will be forgotten by it, and figures on accepting "intimations of a coming light," but also loneliness. He stands near the sea, beside rocks with weeds resembling drowned women's hair. Waves and clouds come and go. After walking amid steadier trees, he returns to sit silently with Nightingale, until that puzzling man orders two servants to put him in a car. He and Malory have a ride. Nightingale calls it pleasant. Back

again, Malory looks out the window and sees in the quickly dying waves an analogy to his longer but also finite life.

Nightingale says he regrets investing as he did and also getting Malory to do so. It was an indecent and dishonorable act, but it also resembled a streptococcus's fated work, or that of the devil he shouldn't have invited into his house. He says that when his "blemishes / And evils" are whisked away, Malory will be free to return and provide professional help to sick millions, since he will have a laboratory here — with staff, patients, whatever.

A lawyer, experienced but ignorant of Nightingale's evil doings, has been summoned earlier. He now enters and prepares Nightingale's will. It bequeaths funds enabling Malory to serve others and not continue wasting his life. Nightingale feels relieved of his longtime burden, asks to be alone, and tells the two to go for a pleasant little drive and then return. Malory and the lawyer, puzzled that a "shining fortune" has been showered on Malory, ride past the ocean and through a forest, chat harmlessly, and return to find that Nightingale has killed himself with Malory's pistol.

Nightingale remains there to ponder, alone. He feels sentenced by his sleeping enemy to a life of service, can thank the vision of the enigmatically smiling Agatha, whom he wouldn't recall to painful life even if he could, queries where light comes from and how it is intended to guide, knows that the "dark glass" of the once-blind Nightingale "is broken." The waves outside are now cold and quiet, like Nightingale, whose present light, however, as well as that of Malory himself, will guide him in his now-funded hospital work.

The Glory of the Nightingales is curiously titled and must put many readers irrelevantly in mind of the famous ode by John Keats, one of Robinson's favorite poets. Robinson's poem was dedicated to the memory of Alfred Hyman Louis.* Its plot is difficult to fathom, partly because Robinson starts it in medias res. Hoyt C. Franchere says that the poem "seems contrived." Ruth Nivison* reports that her mother Emma Robinson* annotated several passages in *The Glory of the Nightingales*, for the purpose of showing that Nightingale may be equated with her husband Herman Robinson* (and Robinson's brother), Malory with Robinson himself, Nightingale's seaside mansion with Herman's cabin at Capitol Island, and so on. Chard Powers Smith* after also trying to equate Nightingale with Herman, makes nothing of any real-life payoff in the presumed Herman-Emma-"Win" amorous triangle. Smith also reports that Robinson told him that a banker once advised his father Edward Robinson* to liquidate some stock the banker knew was soon to collapse, but that Edward preferred to hold it, knowing that, if he sold, an ignorant buyer would later lose money. Smith does not, however, contrast Edward and Nightingale, who gloated that he cleverly sold all his stock to a sucker and called the deal financial.

Readers of *The Glory of the Nightingales* are not privy to enough details about Absalom Spinner and his "fruity" wife, being told merely that Nightingale's egotistic actions involved ruining the nameless "fungus" and paying off the aggrieved husband until death squashed him. Yvor Winters misses some points. First, Winters hints that "Spinner may have been Agatha's husband," although it seems obvious that Malory's being her husband triggers his ruin at the hands of the deprived, hence depraved, Nightingale. Second, Winters says that Nightingale (while in his wheel chair) literally "disarms" Malory, who in truth has quickly preferred talk to gunplay. Emery Neff finds "the fullness of Robinson's powers" on display in *The Glory of the Nightingales*, and reminds readers that in 1930, the year it was published, Robinson gave money to establish a diagnostic laboratory for the Gardiner Hospital, to memorialize his brother Dean Robinson*— which charitable action resembles Nightingale's tardy bequest. Virginia Harlow reports that the family of Robinson's friend Thomas Sergeant Perry* believed the poet took the name Nightingale from that of a guest of the Perrys. (Sources: Franchere, 110; Harlow, 207–08; Neff, 231, 228; E. Robinson, 23; C. Smith, 71–72, 74; Winters, 112)

"God's Garden" *see* **"The Garden"**

"Golden Hair to Gray." A song Robinson wrote but never published. (Source: W. Anderson [1980], 58)

"The Growth of 'Lorraine'" (1902). Two sonnets. First, Lorraine tells the persona that some people are born lucky while others are destined "to be slaves." She remembers that he told her she shouldn't be saying these things, but she adds that she has "gone too far," can't "be content" continuing in the way "some girls" do, but instead is "going to the devil." Second, the persona doesn't believe her when she says he will never see her again; but when he receives a letter from her, he is neither "surprised [n]or grieved." The letter announces her intention to kill herself with quick poison and expresses her continued love for him, even though he cast her "worn-out . . . flesh" aside.

In awe at the compression of this "pair of sonnets," the French critic Charles Cestre* says that "[i]t is marvellous that so much terror, pity and truth can be enclosed in so little space — and expressed so poignantly." That "truth" about her, however, has been subject to varied interpretations. Although Cestre quaintly calls Lorraine "a fast girl" alternately "defiant" and "pitiful," she and her whilom lover have more profoundly disquieted many later commentators. Emery Neff, Hoyt C. Franchere, and others believe Lorraine left her male friend because his socially constrained emotional acts couldn't satisfy her enslaving passion. Still others agree with Chard Powers Smith* and Ronald Moran that she was an abandoned but partly admirable loser. Why otherwise is her name offered pseudonymously in quotation marks? (Sources: Cestre, 15; Franchere, 88–89; Moran [2003], 3230; Neff, 121; C. Smith, 116)

Hagedorn, Hermann (1882–1964). Man of letters. Hermann Ludwig Gebhard Hagedorn was born on Staten Island, New York, the son of a German-born New York Stock Exchange member and his wife. They all spoke only German in their home. Hagedorn learned English at the first of several private schools he attended. He temporarily abandoned his ambition to attend college when his father insisted on his being an office boy, and thus begin a rise in the business world. After contributing to a literary magazine (1903), Hagedorn attended Harvard (1903–1907), from which he graduated as class poet. He married Dorothy Oakley (1908; they had three children), studied at Columbia University (1908–1909), and taught English at Harvard (1909–1911). He began to succeed as a professional writer with a novel and a play (1914). During the First World War he was thoroughly patriotic although his father was pro-German. Hagedorn published *Where Do You Stand?* (1918), in which he urged fellow Americans of German extraction to be loyal to the United States. Theodore Roosevelt* admired Hagedorn and while lunching with him virtually demanded that he write what became *The Boys' Life of Theodore Roosevelt* (1918). When the ex-president died the following year, Hagedorn and others formed the Theodore Roosevelt Memorial Association, which, largely through Hagedorn's efforts, eventually established the first American presidential library. In addition to other biographies, Hagedorn wrote eight books on Roosevelt, the most popular being *The Roosevelt Family of Sagamore Hill* (1954).

In 1910, Robinson was the guest of a friend in Chocorua, New Hampshire, and through him met Hagedorn. Once Robinson had established his routine at the MacDowell Colony* near Peterborough, New Hampshire, he often bracketed summers there by spring and autumn visits to various friends. Hagedorn and his wife, then living in Westport, Connecticut, provided rest stops of that sort. Robinson dedicated his play *Van Zorn* to Hagedorn when it was published in book form (1914). In a letter (October 17, 1918) to Hagedorn, Robinson generously comments that the form of Hagedorn's *The Great Maze* (as part of *The Great Maze, and The Heart of Youth; A Poem and a Play*, 1916), a narrative poem about Aegisthus's murder of Agamemnon, suggested the form of his own *Merlin*. Laurence Perrine finds this unlikely, beyond the fact that both works, as he notes, use "legend for psychological portraiture and philosophical interpretation of life."

Hagedorn's *Edwin Arlington Robinson: A Biography* (1938) was sanctioned by the poet's executors and is his first biography. Horace Gregory and Marya Zaturenska write of it as follows: "Hagedorn's 'official' life . . . can be read with a moderate degree of satisfaction. Like many 'official' lives, the book is not the definitive biography; Hagedorn lacked the orderly diligence of a James Boswell, but one feels that no essential details of Robinson's life have been willfully distorted, and it seems, since a number of Robinson's friends and acquaintances are still alive, that Hagedorn accomplished his difficult assignment with a fair if unbrilliant exercise of tact and propriety." Gregory and Zaturenska probably never knew that permission was not given Hagedorn to use Robinson's informative letters to Edith Brower,* which would have enriched the biography.

Many residents in Gardiner, Maine, where Robinson grew up, resented not only misstatements of facts but also inappropriate emphases in Hagedorn's book when it first appeared; some continue to do so to this day. For one example, James S. Barstow, who was a Gardiner resident, was at Harvard when Robinson was there, and remained one of Robinson's life-long friends, deplores Hagedorn's comments on the Robinson family's early troubles. Barstow writes thus: "It is a great pity that Mr. Hagedorn could not have . . . used more restraint in dealing with the misfortunes of the family. I am told that Mr. Hagedorn felt that if he did not cover this aspect in his biography some one else would at a later date and with less understanding. One may regret that he did not take this chance." Barstow adds that upon reading Hagedorn's indiscreet book, he regretted having supplied him with information concerning certain Gardiner residents still living (as of 1939). (Sources: Barstow, 8; Gregory, 108; Perrine [1974], 346)

Handwriting, Robinson's. Robinson's handwriting was a challenge to friends, typists, and editors (see page 2 above). Esther Willard Bates,* who met Robinson at the MacDowell Colony,* became his friend and typed many of his manuscripts for submission to publishers. She describes his handwriting as "microscopic," with the letters "n," "r," and "v" hardly distinguishable. She says that William Vaughn Moody* called Robinson's hand an "immoral fist." Robinson surely joked in a letter (October 11, 1891) to Harry de Forest Smith* that he was thinking of teaching penmanship to earn money to buy tobacco. Louis Untermeyer,* admittedly no "professional chirographer," knew Robinson's handwriting and said of it that "[h]ere . . . is the way a man takes himself; modestly definite but unassertive, reserved, restrained, and reticent to the vanishing point." Carl J. Weber, editor of Robinson's letters to Howard George Schmitt,* simply calls the handwriting "poor."

To one professional graphologist Thelma Seifer, Robinson's handwriting provides evidence said to reveal that he had articulate speed, rapidity of thought, and fluency of vocabulary. It reveals impatience, individuality, stubbornness, and firm convictions. It shows that he expressed his opinions strongly, and was highly verbal and vocal. He was intelligent and held himself in high regard. He appreciated music and other cultural pursuits. He was ambitious and had drive. (Sources: Bates, 2; letter to author, October 3, 2003, from Thelma Seifer, of Seifer Handwrit-ing Consultants, West Hempstead, NY; Schmitt, 21; Untermeyer, 23; *Untriangulated Stars*, 31)

"Hannibal Brown" (1936). Poem, parenthetically subtitled "*An Alcaic.*" Hannibal Brown's dolichocephalic head, with a hat size of seven, reached only halfway to heaven.

Such a head as Brown's is unusually long, with a cephalic index of less than 75. Robinson, who never intended to publish this ditty, sent it in a letter (October 11, 1918) to Lilla Cabot Perry, the wife of Thomas Sergeant Perry.* An alcaic is a poem written in a complex variation of dominant iambic meters. "Late Summer" (*which see*) is a more serious alcaic. (Source: Cary [1975], 50, 183)

"Haunted House" (1923). Sonnet. The poet and his friend visited this eerie place only to get out of the rain. Once inside, they did-n't see a ghost or anything else except gloom and some skeleton-like chairs. Nor did they hear anything. But they thought about an axe that, a long time ago, was "in the air / Between us and the chimney," near the spot where the men from town said they found her.

"Hector Kane" (1928). Poem. All of us wondered about Hector Kane, who at 85 was youthful and fair in appearance. He had curly white hair, rosy cheeks, and a belief that questions about him were almost worthless. However, "one convivial night" he addressed a group of us, whom he called "children of threescore or so," to explain that he avoided "a world of pain" by going after what he wanted, by getting it, and then by going for more of the same when he wanted to. He said that time was a harmless four-letter word having to do with something unseen. He kept "the worm away" by being cheerfully diligent. He said that thinking can be more dangerous than food or drink. He offered a toast to what's ahead: "*Cras ingens iterabimus.*" Suddenly something wondrous grabbed his tongue, and he said nothing more. He simply lay there, calmly, challenging us to figure out his "mortal trick" and leaving us to fathom what we could from what life had taught him.

Edwin S. Fussell incorrectly cites the source of Robinson's Latin quotation as Horace's Book I, Ode XI. But is from Book I, Ode VII, and reads more fully thus: "O fortes peioraque passi / mecum saepe viri, nunc vino pellite curas: / cras ingens iterabimus aequor" (O you strong heroes, who have frequently suffered worse misfortunes with me, banish care with wine now: tomorrow we will take again our course over the vast ocean). The earlier line in Latin mentions "vino" (wine), which was perhaps as stimulating as whatever was served during the "convivial night" Hector enjoyed with his friends. The last word in the Latin line Hector doesn't complete is "aequor," which, as modified by "ingens," means "the vast ocean." Robinson surely intended irony in misnaming Hector Kane. He is no brave hero, like Achilles's foe, and no killer either, like Abel's brother Cain, for that matter; additionally, he plans no literal voyages, or any strenuous, jealousy-inspired combat, either. (Source: Fussell [1954], 153)

"Her Eyes" (1896). Poem. The inexorably aging, sadly dreaming artist lives alone, frustrated despite his international renown. When he returns to that same room, it still holds an old dream and is the place where "he buried his days." With "a passionate humor," he begins to paint again. A face appears on his canvas, angelic but for her eyes. The work seems "like a soul half done." So he skillfully adds the eyes — those "of a deathless woman." A touch of heaven "make[s] them pure," another of hell "make[s] them human." He adores her again, seemingly "his wife." He wonders how it could be that since she loved him she punished him, even after their time of strife. The truth returns to him ever more plainly "the longer he lives with her eyes to see."

Hoyt C. Franchere says of this artist that, "[l]ike another Pygmalion, he worships her as though she were his wife." Franchere declines to suggest that Robinson is here portraying himself as one who sacrificed personal love for professional success, because, as Franchere notes, Robinson "wrote this poem long before he had achieved fame." Nevertheless, Emma Robinson* and Ruth Nivison* say that "Her Eyes" is Robinson's superb estimate of Emma's worth to him. Discontent with earlier scholarship, John H. Miller lauds "Her Eyes" as containing "a key to understanding how deeply the early Robinson believes in living an engaged life among other[s]." (Sources: Franchere, 102, 103; Miller, 352; E. Robinson, 15)

"Hillcrest" (1916). Poem. In September this place resembles a quiet "island in a sea of trees." Here, in sunshine and in shadow, one can forget "ruins and regrets." If he should think he is ready to explain reality and "to unroll / His index of adagios" in a consoling manner, he will learn otherwise here and set aside vanity. Here he will quit predicting the future, will accept change, will avoid taking a falsely childish delight in the glowing world, and will find peace. His wisdom, being only tentative, will come through humility.

Robinson dedicated "Hillcrest" to Marian Nivens MacDowell,* whose home in Peterborough, New Hampshire, was named Hillcrest. This poem is a tribute to her and to her MacDowell Colony.* Yvor Winters lauds "Hillcrest" for moving gracefully from an expression of humility to that of "stoical endurance," but then undercuts his admiration of Robinson by saying that apart from "Hillcrest" he "probably never succeeds very brilliantly with the didactic or philosophical." Donald E. Stanford, who calls "Hillcrest" "one of the most beautifully written poems of this century," regards it as an example, among several, demonstrating that Robinson was solidly in the continuing "Anglo-American . . . classical tradition" (in which he included Winters, as well as Robert Bridges and J. V. Cunningham). Clauco Cambon also accords "Hillcrest" high praise, saying that "the versification . . . is sustained and flexible, the diction untainted by padding, sagging softness, passive echoes, or rhetorical gestures." Louis Coxe defines "Hillcrest" as "[a] calm, true and lived poem, autumnal as to tone, feeling, imagery and setting," says that its subject is "life and death and change and growth and their interaction," and concludes that its advice is "to accept a world of pain and uncertainty, without fear and without recrimination." Gerald E. Graff demonstrates that "Hillcrest" successfully exemplifies discursive, non-dramatic poetry. Steve Kerby explains that "[o]n one level, 'Hillcrest' is a poem that demonstrates the folly of romanticism. But on a deeper level, it is a gentle meditation about the pain of truth and about the way we humans delude ourselves about that truth." (Sources: Cambon, 63; Coxe, 106, 109, 175; Graff; Kerby, 172–73; Stanford [1969], 486, 490; Winters, 30, 36)

"Horace to Leuconoë" (1896). Sonnet. This is a free translation from Horace, Book I, Ode XI. Horace implores his friend Leuconoë not to worry about what the gods have planned. Better to concern yourself with the present day, which may be "the last." Take care of your wine. Avoid foolish hopes. Even now "time is narrowing." "So seize the day, or ever it be past, / And let tomorrow come for what it will."

In an earlier version, a copy of which Robinson enclosed in a letter (May 21, 1891) to Harry de Forest Smith,* his penultimate line reads "So seize the day, be merry ere 'tis past," which seems better. Horace's famous original goes thus: "Carpe diem, quam minimum credula postero" (Seize the day, trusting as little as possible what is to come). The challenge of "turning an ode of Horace" into English verse was a common task for well-trained undergraduates in various colleges and universities; when Robinson was at Harvard, this exercise was frequent. Ellsworth Barnard points out that this sonnet and "The Torrent" are the only sonnets in which Robinson does not have the eighth line end a sentence. (Sources: Barnard, 65; *Untriangulated Stars*, 19–20)

"The House on the Hill" (1896). Poem. Villanelle. Since "They are all gone away," that is, the inhabitants of the house on the hill, "There is nothing more to say."

The poet rings tuneful changes on these pronouncements, as though to suggest that there is no point in wondering what happened. Or, for that matter, even why one should bother to read this sad message about common enough, inexplicable human loss.

Louis Untermeyer* reports that "The House on the Hill" was rejected by a dozen magazines before the little-known *Globe* printed it without paying Robinson. In a draft, Robinson subtitled it "A Villanelle of Departure." A villanelle, which Robinson enjoyed trying when he was first starting out as a poet, is a complicated French form, usually running on two rhymes (here beginning with "away" and "still"), with five tercets and a quatrain, in which lines one and three of the first tercet are repeated alternately (as quoted above) at the end of the other tercets, and together as the last two lines of the quatrain. Emery Neff notes that "The tune of the villanelle, suffusing desolation with beauty, helps keep 'The House on the Hill' from sentimentality." Louis Untermeyer observes that its villanelle form provides an "echoing repetition ... to project a sense of nostalgia linked with loneliness." Stephen J. Adams cites "The House on the Hill" as one of "many fine examples of the villanelle in the twentieth century."

It has been suggested that in this poem Robinson is deploring the loss of the family house following the disastrous investments by his father, Edward Robinson,* in western real-estate and mining ventures. Lawrance Thompson explicates "house" here as not merely a physical dwelling but also both "a

human body from which all the attributes of life have departed" and even "a graveyard ... from which the spirit has departed." Laura E. Richards* brands as incorrect the statement by Amy Lowell* that the model for the house in this poem was "Oaklands," the family home of John Hays Gardiner;* Richards adds (and inaccurately quotes him) that Robinson, when she asked for his response to Lowell's assertion, replied, "Good heavings, no! the House on the Hill is no house that ever was, and least of all a stone house in good order. I don't know why people will say such foolish things, but they do, and they will do so for evermore." Implicitly negating much critical commentary, Richard Gray quotes the bleak three lines that open "The House on the Hill" and then says, "[t]o try to attach words to vacancy, to clothe transcience and loneliness in language, is a futile gesture, the poem suggests." (Sources: S. Adams, 94; Gray, 139; Neff, 71; Richards [1936], 53; *Selected Letters*, 161; L. Thompson, 141; Untermeyer, 3, 5)

"How Annandale Went Out" (1910). Sonnet. Dramatic monologue. The speaker, a physician and Annandale's compassionate friend, says that Annandale was a ruined "apparatus," never to be mended and facing hell before he would die. The speaker has "a slight kind of engine." He used it and shouldn't be hanged for doing so. Right?

Hoyt C. Franchere boils down evidence from biographers of Robinson and his family and concludes that "'How Annandale Went Out' is unquestionably a fictional representation of the manner in which [Robinson's brother] Dean [Robinson*] died — by a deliberate, self-administered overdose of morphine." Louis Coxe notes that "How Annandale Went Out" is one of several of Robinson's "'trick' poems" with O. Henry surprise endings. Emma Robinson* and Ruth Nivison* suggest that the poem is a dramatic monologue in which Dean Robinson, who probably killed himself with a deliberate overdose of morphine, is talking to himself; however — to be perhaps too literal — if the speaker plans to die by injection, he wouldn't likely worry about also being hanged. Ronald Moran theorizes that the narrator is a suicide-assisting physician who is speaking obliquely, ironically, and, at first, evasively, at his actual trial for murder. Charles V. Genthe believes that Annandale is murdered by Argan or a physician symbolically representing Argan's point of view, in "The Book of Annandale."

When Bliss Perry (1860–1954), educator and author, made choices for *Selected Poems* (1931) by Robinson, the two men, according to Perry's preface, agreed to include a sonnet Robinson liked better than Perry did. Bacon Collamore* provides evidence that this sonnet may have been "How Annandale Went Out." (Sources: Collamore, 54; Coxe, 84; Franchere, 73; Genthe, 394; Moran [2003], 3234; E. Robinson, 15)

"I Make No Measure of the Words They Say" (1896). Sonnet. The poet says that he pays no attention to those who "mellifluously" predict that his "roving whims" will lead him to hell. Such people are coolly forgetful and merely waste his time. On the other hand, when a "rare old master," whose eyes shine "with a living sunset," takes him home "To his long-tutored consciousness," the poet will feel warm, serene, and hopeful that in later years he will know "The true magnificence of better things." (Source: Cary [1975], 26–27, 176–77)

"The Idealist" (1947). Octave. The poet says he is indifferent in the matter of labels. So, call him an idealist. What he wants for himself and others, though, is simply the truth, not "Fame, glory, gold."

Robinson sent a copy of this poem, for which he never sought publication, in a letter (April 2, 1897) to Edith Brower.* (Sources: Brower, 36; Cary [1975], 44, 180)

"'If the Lord Would Make Windows in Heaven'" (1924). Sonnet. His wife "had eyes" but lacks the insight to recognize that "he was doomed to his own way." When she is outside, she appears angelical, even saintly; but at home she dishonors him, calmly sews, and awaits disaster. She suspects that evidence of his idealism won't be seen by others but also professes fear that it may carry him totally out of sight.

Chard Powers Smith* says that in this sonnet Robinson "celebrates satirically" the love Emma Robinson* had for her husband Herman Robinson,* "in his pathetic, failing years." Ellsworth Barnard castigates the wife in the sonnet, "who pretends in public to honor her husband whom at home she torments by systematic and sadistic disparagement." The title of this poem may be ironically suggesting that it's too bad this saintly wife, practically in heaven, can't look down through an aperture in the clouds and see her poor, mortally misguided husband for what he is. Or does the title mean — less likely, to be sure — that under better meteorological conditions she might observe her husband's meritorious radiance well above her? (Sources: Barnard, 251; C. Smith, 254)

"In Harvard 5" (1891). Poem. Rondeau. Studying in a class devoted to the works of William Shakespeare evokes many emotions, and concerns kings, murders, and gloomy Elsinore.

During the time Robinson was at Harvard, he attended a class in 1891 conducted in the Harvard 5 lecture hall by Professor Francis James Child.* A perfect rondeau has 13 eight- or 10-syllabled lines, comprising three stanzas of unequal length, and unified by two rhymes and one refrain. In the accepted 17th-century French form, the first stanza had five lines, the second, four, and the third, six. Robinson's rondeau here conforms exactly. His two rhymes begin, respectively, "lore" and "strain." His refrain is "In Harvard 5." (Source: Cary [1975], 171)

Income, Robinson's. When Robinson's father Edward Robinson* was in his mid-50s, he had accumulated assets worth perhaps $80,000. But at his death (1892), he left a tied-up estate of about only $15,000. The family was in such financial straits that Robinson had to withdraw from Harvard (1893). His brothers Dean Robinson* and Herman Robinson* then mismanaged remnants of family holdings. Robinson received $600 from his father's estate (November 1897) and went to New York City. He lived hand-to-mouth there, tried odd jobs back home in Gardiner, and then worked for a salary called moderate in Cambridge (1899) under Harvard's president, Charles William Eliot.* Robinson's financial hopes were further dashed when Dean died (1899). From Dean's estate, Robinson received $500 (1901) and thereafter a total of $285.65 more (1902). When the family home in Gardiner was sold (1903), Robinson evidently received no share. Robinson was a time-checker of loads of stone at $2 per ten-hour day during the construction of the New York subway (1903–1904), worked briefly in a Boston department store for $10 a week (1905), was a porter in the saloon in Yonkers, and enjoyed a sinecure at the New York office of the Collector of Customs at $2,000 per annum (1905–1909). When Herman died (1909), Robinson inherited nothing except the moral obligation of occasionally helping Herman's widow, Emma Robinson.*

Meanwhile, before, during, and then long after working at moderately paying positions, Robinson wrote poetry. He had paid $52 for the publication of *The Torrent and The Night Before* (1896). He sold "For a Copy of Poe's Poems" for $7 (1895). *Captain Craig: A Book of Poems* (1902) was issued when John Hays Gardiner* and Laura E. Richards* promised the publisher they would guarantee it against financial loss. Richard Watson Gilder* paid Robinson $20 for "Uncle Ananias" (1905). Robinson lived and wrote, without expense to himself, at the MacDowell Colony* in Peterborough, New Hampshire, for 24 successive summers (1911–1934), through the unparalleled generosity of Marian Nivens MacDowell* and her well-to-do friends. Scribner's wisely refused to publish Robinson's *Van Zorn* or *The Porcupine*, either in drama or novel form, but did advance him $100 for future poems he would send (1913). After Gardiner died (1913), lawyers for his estate informed Robinson that he was the beneficiary of a $4,000 legacy (1914). He also received gifts of $100 a month from anonymous donors who, remaining unnamed at first to Robinson, were in reality Lewis Isaacs* and 11 other friends (1917–1921). Robinson's *Lancelot* (1920) won the Lyric Society prize of $500. Bacon Collamore* says

that for his "Pilgrims' Chorus" (1921) Robinson was paid $100. His 1921 *Collected Poems* gained him $1,000 when it was awarded the Pulitzer Prize. For *The Man Who Died Twice* (1924) he won his second Pulitzer. He was also paid $100 for "A Note on Myron B. Benton (1834–1902)" (1925). Then came *Tristram* (1927). Robinson reported by letter (July 27, 1928) to Lewis Isaacs that Macmillan to that date had paid him $12,907.90 for sales of 57,475 copies of *Tristram*. Ultimately, the poem earned Robinson not only his third Pulitzer Prize but also ultimately at least $80,000 altogether in royalties. When he was able, and often when he scarcely was, Robinson gave money to friends and strangers in need.

Robinson must have had more than ample spare money late in his life. He wrote (January 3, 25, 1934; September 22, October 3, 1934) to his pen-pal Howard George Schmitt,* then in the Harvard Graduate School of Business Administration, to ask about Wrigley, Woolworth, Ohio Oil, and railroad investments. (Sources: Benét, 54; Brower, 174; R. Brown, 68; Cary [1974], 67, 218, 272; Cary [1975], 173, 191; Collamore, 16, 31; Hagedorn, 147, 202, 315–16, 345; Neff, 136, 142; Richards [1936], 53; Schmitt, 24, 26, 27; *Selected Letters*, 157; C. Smith, 153–54, 207, 208, 215, 238, 397, 400–02; Winters, 12)

"Inferential" (1920). Sonnet. I gaze at the face of a man in his coffin. When he was alive, I honored him little, and I "deemed him unessential to the race." Nor would I now want him to be elsewhere. He seems to fit his coffin gracefully. He is more important now, and I am somewhat awestruck. Maybe he's telling me not to mind, that "If some of us were not so far behind, / The rest of us were not so far ahead."

The message of this elegy is surely that after a person succumbs to the great leveler called death, his or her character is often made clearer to those who survive.

"Intermezzo" *see* **"The Return of Morgan and Fingal"**

"Introduction to *The Letters of Thomas Sergeant Perry*" (1929). In 1929 Robinson edited *Selections From the Letters of Thomas Sergeant Perry* and included an introduction. He says that friends of Perry's and those who never knew him will, alike, recognize in these letters "a reflection of a personality that was as engaging as it was unusual, as facetious as it was ferocious, and as amiable as it was annihilating." Perry was a boatman, swimmer, and world traveler, but preferred to study the "sublime and magnificent" ocean, though only while he was on land. He walked, played tennis, and rode the bicycle, but preferred books to action. He was a fine reader, wrote well, but never became a great writer, preferring instead to read the literature of others, and like "an experienced and insatiable spider — beneficent or terrible, as the case might be —" suck the vitality out of books that flew his way. He sighed when he found a respectable but not personally engaging book, because he was aware of the vast effort that went into creating something lifeless to him. Such books resembled people that were nice enough but not welcome in his home.

Books were like people to Perry. A world without them would be a hell. They "were the next thing to the breath of life to him." Uncomplainingly, he saw life as a mystery so far from human guessing about that philosophers were mainly amusing to him. As for religious people, he was mainly glad that their beliefs comforted them. He valued a person's character and behavior more than his fame. If a genius's personal conduct were reprehensible, he could not admire his creativity; hence he disliked the operas of Richard Wagner. Though aristocratic in many ways, Perry was democratic in his responses to reality. He was cognizant that the First World War had swept away many aspects of Boston Victorianism. He knew Greek and Latin, and surprised everybody by late in life learning Russian and reading the Russian masters in the original. He revered Anton Chekov for his honesty and competence. He seemed sorry to have been born after Victorian times, since he felt that his ancestors had had all the fun. He expressed dislike of *Salammbô*, the novel by Gustave Flaubert, but never read it. He admired Henry James, his friend, but boycotted his late novels for being too wordy. He generally found novels depressing if true to life, silly if not, and too long always; still, published volumes of letters he never regarded as too long. He relished *Judaism in the First Centuries of the Christian Era, the Age of the Tannaim* (3 vols., 1927–1930) by George Foot Moore (1851–1931) so much that he actually "caressed" the "two mighty volumes" he had access to (the third volume had not yet been published). Perry took an interest in T. S. Eliot, Van Wyck Brooks, and the St. Louis journalist William Marion Reedy (1862–1920). He enjoyed pleasant vulgarity and nonsense, but disliked Aristophanes and François Rabelais.

Perry was profoundly pessimistic about enigmatic human existence, felt sad for humans, especially women, was incuriously agnostic, but regarded "atheism [as] ridiculous, if only for its assumption of knowledge that no human being could possibly possess." His conversational talents were almost unmatched. He remained silently sorrowful because of an unspecified "injustice" done him, and there was also a certain "bereavement" he seldom mentioned. When Robinson told him that Torquato Tasso while imprisoned was denied knowledge of the whereabouts of the manuscript of his *Gerusalemme Liberata*, Perry replied with fire in his eyes that the incident proved the human heart's illimitable endurance.

Perry wrote well, perhaps would not have been a great poet or novelist, but if he had wished could be been a splendid literary critic. He felt that extensive writing would have taken time from his reading. He appreciated great writing, liked writing letters, disliked writing books; his not being ambitious to do so bothered his friends. Robinson believes that Perry wanted to be a professor but by a certain freak of fate was denied the opportunity. He could have given much to young students.

Robinson closes by saying that readers seeking biographical information about Perry should consult the 1929 biography of him by John T. Morse Jr. (1840–1937). (Source: Cary [1975], 94–102, 192–93)

"Introductory Letter to *Wind in the Grass*" (1931). Essay. Robinson was asked to comment on a collection of poems, still in manuscript, written by Christy MacKaye (1909–2002), the daughter of his friend Percy MacKaye.* (Christina Loring MacKaye married Henry Barnes in 1939.) Robinson's response took the form of a letter (September 21, 1930), in which he says that the poems evince a quality for which there is no word. He adds that they show unique imagination and represent a real achievement, and closes by admitting that all this is saying a great deal about a book so early in a poet's career. His letter was published as the introduction to Christy MacKaye's *Wind in the Grass*, which followed her first book, *Out of Chrysalis* (1930). (Source: Cary [1975], 103, 193)

"Isaac and Archibald" (1902). Poem in blank verse. The persona remembers Isaac and Archibald fondly. When he was only 12, he walked with old Isaac from Tilbury Town to check on Isaac's old friend Archibald's oats, five miles away. Oats didn't matter to the boy, but these old men surely did.

As they walked along the River Road, Isaac commented on the glory of the August day, with flashing leaves and hot, hot sun. The boy was sweating and wondered how long Isaac's "ancient legs" would hold out, but the old fellow appeared "cool to his hat-band." Even so, the boy suggested that they sit down in the shade for a time. Agreeing, Isaac rambled a bit but then asked the child if he had "noticed things" about Archibald. No. Upon which, Isaac tolerantly told his "young friend" that he had eyes all right but not yet "The sight within." Further, it wouldn't be right for him yet to experience "The twilight warning of experience, / The singular idea of loneliness." But Isaac for seven years had been noticing a change in Archibald, was aware that he had gone through so awfully much with him, had seen so much good in him that others "have shared and have not seen," that his own heart was pained in a manner the boy hadn't "yet lived enough to know about." Despite the boy's present sense of freedom and confidence, coming to him in due time would be an awareness of loss and of "being left behind." At that far-off time, his "long contempt of innocence" would resemble a half-forgotten

childhood book, "remembered for the pictures." Isaac hoped that God would bless the little boy but quickly added that it was terrible to be losing a "best friend," and knowing it by that friend's "slackening," "common word," "trivial act." Isaac was sure that Archibald "is going" while he himself would be "staying." Isaac beseeched his young companion to remember him, just as he was this day, after he had followed Archibald.

The persona recalls Isaac's word with a dryness in his throat, then continues. He thought of some comforting words but didn't speak them to Isaac then. Restless, Isaac walked on again, too rapidly for the boy's comfort. After a mile, they stopped at a water pump, where Isaac "thanked God for all things / That He had put on earth for men to drink." Again, Isaac walked so fast that the boy voiced fear of learning right then and there about "The bitterness of being left behind," which Isaac had just mentioned. Isaac got a big kick out of this. After two more miles, they saw Archibald's cottage and noticed that the oat field had been mowed. Archibald came limping out, greeted Isaac fondly, and shook the boy's hand. Archibald quickly responded to Isaac's smile and request for some cider by inviting him to go down cellar and observe eight barrels. One "newly tapped" was "An honor to the fruit," he averred. Isaac escorted the boy into the cellar, found the sentinel-like barrels, neatly turned out a live cricket from an old fluted glass, skillfully removed the pine spile from the tapped barrel, and, pouring himself several quick samples, remarked, "I thank God for orchards." When they went back outside, Isaac said he would go have a look around and asked Archibald to sit, rest his back, and tell the boy about how the two of them and two others were snowbound for 10 days, 40 years ago.

Archibald chortled through a curiously wrinkling nose, sighed, and led the boy to the orchard. While munching worm-ripened astrakhan apples, he listened as Archibald half-absently recounted his snowbound tale even while his mind seemingly writhed with unspoken thoughts. Then he addressed his youthful auditor carefully. He and Isaac were old, he said. Whatever they gained, lost, discarded, they were old, were looking back, were in the shadows. But sunlight was still ahead, on their road. They remained "children of the sun," the boy likewise, the weed there likewise. He went on:

> The shadow calls us, and it frightens us —
> We think; but there's a light behind the stars
> And we old fellows who have dared to live,
> We see it — and we see the other things,
> The other things.

Archibald said that the boy must have noticed a change in Isaac. Archibald had been noticing it for eight or 10 years now. He himself had knee pains, but Isaac made him nervous because he was "not quite right" in his head. Archibald advised the boy, whom he hoped God would bless, not to think about such things yet but to be aware that he would do so later. Archibald said that although he was "in the shadow" now, he remembered "The light, my boy, — the light behind the stars. / Remember that: remember that I said it." Don't be confused, distrustful, regretful. "Live to see clearly and the light will come / To you, and as you need it."

The lad, grown now, remembers the scene: Archibald's cracked laugh, merry little eyes, clay pipe; the fragrant orchard, river, baked hills, forest, mighty sun — all fusing into an Homeric scene, a biblical scene, with Agamemnon, Ulysses, Trojans, Jericho, and a glorious future in "the world beyond" — for "I was young." The spell was broken when Archibald said Isaac might get a sunstroke. Isaac appeared, in search of tobacco, wondered why the boy was laughing so, and remarked that Archibald cut his oats a bit too early. At which, Archibald's nose wiggled again. The old men went to the cellar for some cider-laced card game. The boy followed, drew some pictures of Trojans, and one of "Ulysses, after Isaac, / And a little after [the *Odyssey* illustrator John] Flaxman," and amused Archibald by saying his beard was not Homeric. After they all had a comfortable supper, Isaac and the boy walked home again, with the sea, ships, and a sunset all beyond the forest. That night the boy dreamed of "two old angels." They had wings, were bathed in "a silver light," were playing cards, and one proclaimed "high, low, jack,

and the game." He remembers the two, now in "the silence of the loved and well-forgotten." His laughter for Isaac and Archibald, who were too old to make sport of him, was honorable laughter, because he knew them.

Robinson dedicated "Isaac and Archibald" to "Mrs. Henry Richards." (See Richards, Laura E.) At one point, Robinson regarded "Isaac and Archibald" and "The Man Against the Sky" as his two best poems.

Admiring Robinson's treatment of old Isaac and old Archibald, Glauco Cambon concludes that "[s]ince they have faced time without cheating, they do ideally conquer it and thereby allow the poet himself to breathe a mythical aura of timelessness where the past is recoverable." The originals of the two old friends, according to Emma Robinson* and Ruth Nivison,* were Robinson's uncles, one of whom they identify as Seth Palmer,* with whom young Robinson sometimes walked along the River Road out of Gardiner to the home of Kingsbury Palmer, the other uncle. Yvor Winters categorizes "Isaac and Archibald," Robinson's version of rural reminiscence, as "a kind of New England pastoral, . . . extraordinarily lovely." Henry W. Wells, ever on the outlook for literary influences on Robinson from the classics to poets of the 1920s, says this: "E. A. Robinson's *Isaac and Archibald* is stylistically in all respects, notably in the leisurely blank verse and bucolic style, an imitation of Wordsworth's *Michael*." Theodore Maynard* lauds "Isaac and Archibald," saying "it is hard to imagine very much better blank verse could be written than that found in this poem." Louis Coxe, agreeing, opines that "[n]o American before this [poem] had written a blank verse so sinewy." Coxe also defines the poem as "a masterwork, a small miracle of tone, control, speaking voice, and self-effacing description." Harvey Gross and Robert McDowell detect in the blank verse an occasional "lilt of New England speech," and praise Robinson's description of Isaac's tender handling of the cricket in the cider glass for having close syntax, "smooth enjambment and grammatical precision." Ellsworth Barnard notes that in this poem, as elsewhere, Robinson reveals "the breadth of his sympathy and the depth of his charity," and, further, his "perception . . . that life is self-justified." J. C. Levenson demonstrates that "[w]alking . . . becomes a constant underlying movement in the narration" of "Isaac and Archibald," and does so by pointing out "the imagery of movement" throughout — Isaac setting the pace, the boy keeping up, their pausing for water only briefly, their descending into the cellar for cider, and, finally, "man and boy walking altogether naturally together towards the night." Irving Howe wrongly categorizes "Isaac and Archibald" as one of several poems (which he names) "about lost and aging country people." They are aging, yes, like most oldtimers; but, Oh, to be so "lost" in light-fringed darkness as that twosome. (Sources: Barnard, 188; Cambon, 58–59; Coxe, 70; Gross and McDowell, 58, 61; I. Howe, 106; Levenson, 178, 181; Maynard [1924], 167; E. Robinson, 12; Wells, 165; Winters, 132)

"Isaac Pitman" (1890). Sonnet. He traps frenzied thoughts and walls up spoken cadences. When he is dead, he will be famous and will stride through gardens in which new blooms will supplant the old — all "through his life-work sown."

Sir Isaac Pitman (1813–1897) invented an original system of shorthand, which he based not on spelling but on phonetics, and which he described in his book *Stenographic Soundhand* (1837). After he graduated from high school (1888), Robinson took lessons in stenography. (Source: Cary [1975], 170)

Isaacs, Lewis Montefiore (1877–1944). Lawyer and amateur musician. Isaacs received a law degree at Columbia University and also a master's degree in music, having studied composition there under Edward MacDowell.* When Robinson went to the MacDowell Colony* for the first time (1911), he met Isaacs, who was there as a composer. He later was the treasurer of the Edward MacDowell Association. Isaacs instantly detected not only Robinson's genius but also evidence of his financial limitations. Isaacs, along with Louis V. Ledoux* and others, arranged for $1,200 a year to be available to Robinson at the New York Trust Company, starting January 1,

1917, and possibly to continue for three more years. The sum, which Robinson called a gift at the time but repaid later, freed his mind to work more happily on *Lancelot*, which he dedicated to Isaacs (1920). Robinson enjoyed visiting Isaacs, his charming wife Edith, who was the editor of *Theatre Arts Monthly*, and their children, in their home in Pelham, New York. Isaacs in the 1920s became Robinson's financial adviser. Robinson often commented about his poetry in letters to Isaacs. Hermann Hagedorn,* who knew both men well, reports that Isaacs introduced Robinson to the English poet and playwright John Drinkwater (1882–1937) in New York, and that Drinkwater squired Robinson around when he went to London (1923). Isaacs set to music Robinson's "John Evereldown" (in 1924) and "The Dark Hills" (1929). Shortly after Robinson's death, Isaacs provided a piano accompaniment for a tune Robinson had composed much earlier; Robinson mentioned it in a letter (April 21, 1897) to Edith Brower.* Ledoux wrote the lyrics; the work, entitled "Slumber Song," was published in 1935. Isaacs and Ledoux were Robinson's literary executors. (Sources: Brower, 39, 41; Hagedorn, 334; C. Smith; Untermeyer, 29)

"An Island" (1910). Poem, subtitled "(Saint Helena, 1821)." Dramatic monologue. Napoleon speaks fiercely, with occasional use of "*ai*," "Bah," "Faugh," "Ha," "Ho," "Man," and "*Voilà*." He tells his jailer to take away his poor food, complains of rats everywhere, and says that God made rats, rain, and on the seventh day, while resting, added pain. Napoleon says he was once puissant but now counts himself among the dead. With his ears roaring, he is now far from the world, war, and women, and in something like a "lowering outland hostelry." By his failure he consecrates this vermin-infested island. The sea will eventually embrace him. Like a gardener, he planted, tilled, and reaped his desires. Should he be obliged to review his history, to show how a devil guided him to an island? All right. Fate, which he rebukes as "the mistress of iniquities, / The mad Queen-spinner of all discrepancies," dyed his tricolor and converted it to one color. In truth, kings get overthrown.

In time, "learned little acrid archive men" will dig up data about him, but vainly unless they find "another Island." 'Twixt heaven and the sea are islands, rats, and rain. All combine to produce pain. He wonders about his queen. Praise in the form of hag-lipped laurel comes to him after surrender. Promising to remember Fate, he says that posterity will realize that his fate was to know praise but without rest. "The Old Physician," death, cures praise following one victory after another. Napoleon's demon laughs at him this minute. Other demons laughed at Hannibal, Alexander, and Cæsar. Napoleon addresses his demon: "Thing, do I not know them all?" Some leaders die. Others are captured and exiled, "To mould on islands." Fate takes credit for Napoleon's victories, but his failures are his own fault. Suddenly his physician brings what Napoleon calls "pills and toast." He refuses to swallow what may be poison.

"An Island" is cast in a curious form. It is basically in iambic meter, with most lines in pentameter but others in trimeter and a couple dropping to dimeter. Five lines are in French. The rhyme scheme is highly irregular, and a few lines lack rhymes or have off rhymes. This jumpy prosodical uncertainty is perhaps intended to reflect Napoleon's disordered mind, which is, however, not well rendered by Robinson. Critics have pretty much ignored "An Island," and rightly so. Amy Lowell* dislikes it, saying tersely that it "is false to its original in every line." More cogently, the French critic Charles Cestre* says that Napoleon here "is pilloried by the poet in the wild attitude of the frenzied loser at the game of chance, maddened to be penned on a seagirt rock, while the wide world, which he purposed to conquer, settles to forgetting his baneful empire." (Sources: Cestre, 184; Lowell [1922], 135)

James, William (1842–1910). Psychologist, philosopher, and educator. James graduated from the Harvard Medical School (1869), and taught science courses (from 1872) and philosophy (from 1881) at Harvard. While Robinson studied at Harvard (1891–1893), James was not, according to Hermann Hagedorn,* able to "overcome his [Robinson's] re-sistance to the demand for systematic, abstract thought." Nor in later life was Robinson able to appreciate any of James's many books, especially when they concerned pragmatism. Robert D. Stevick, however, valuably compares Robinson's "The Man Against the Sky" and James's "Is Life Worth Living."

As for Robinson's opinions of fiction written by James's brother Henry James (1843–1916), he wrote Harry de Forest Smith* (February 7, 1896) that when he read "The Lesson of the Master" he recognized that "H. J. is a genius"; however, *The Bostonians*, according to a letter (February 22, 1901) he sent to Edith Brower,* mainly showed "what a man is capable of when his logomania gets the better of him." (Sources: Brower, 136; Hagedorn, 78; Morison, 353–54, 377–78; Stevick [1959]; *Untriangulated Stars*, 239)

"James Wetherell" *see* **"Romance"**

"Job the Rejected" (1921). Sonnet. We saw what was inevitable. A certain man met a woman. She didn't trust him; but when he was penitent and complimented her, she accepted him and they got married. Job said his successful rival would "wreck the temple" in a short while. Sure enough, the fellow did, then "hungrily" tried to make amends, but failed and was left "in the dust." Job encountered him there, bided his time, but in his turn hardly proved to be "The confirmation of her heart's desire."

Esther Willard Bates reports that Robinson told her this sonnet never did please him. (Source: Bates, 16)

"John Brown" (1919). Dramatic monologue in blank verse. John Brown, on the eve of his execution, speaks to his absent wife. He says this: God made it necessary for me to "grope," "serve," and "suffer." My bones, heavy now, will "shout the truth" when buried. Some men while hanging me will weep out of pity that in God's name I "pitied millions." May armies come soon to shed blood so that many may live. War is the only solution known to this new land, "this stranger to itself," this "prodigious upstart." An occasional madman or seer shakes up such people. Hangings follow, as burnings formerly did. After I am buried as "an unripe fruit of treason," a harvest of "riper fruit . . . waits." If hell, which I fear not, waits for the dawn, let hell come soon. I have been tempered by hell fire to do what I had to do. My name won't "sleep in history." Nothing will douse the coming fires until they "cleanse and shake a wounded hemisphere, / And heal it of a long malignity." I sought no glory, had few friends, was vilified, was uniquely able "To do my work," now done with. Dear wife, don't mourn for me or for our sons. Should souls mourn in heaven, "done with evil and with earth"? Endure your remaining time without fear. In the approaching silence, I will be nearer you in faith than I am, physically, now. Grieve for me but briefly. I am grateful to those who bestowed "scared allegiance" to me in acts currently named treason. Christ Himself lacked a name until one was given Him. Men have insulted Him with evils that, "with His aid," will be expunged "with fire and blood." Dear wife, I comforted you "in the north" that summer day, by saying the cost in blood might be small. If I had known then what I was soon to know, "I might have wavered; and I might have failed." Now, unlike many, I have little to lose and much to gain. A harvest is coming, and "I shall have more to say when I am dead."

Few critics have commented in detail on Robinson's "John Brown." Robert Mezey notes that Robinson's main source for the poem was several letters Brown wrote in November 1859, especially his last letter, November 30, to his family, which expresses, Mezey observes, Brown's justification of his deeds, his thoughts about his death, and his awareness of his post-mortem prophetic role. Yvor Winters accords the poem high praise, mainly for the passage in which the doomed reformer tenderly implores his absent wife not to grieve for him or their sons. Without any doubt, Robinson, like John Brown, felt that his own words would be more meaningful to readers after his death — though, obviously, he never regarded himself as a latter-day martyr. Robinson was born only a decade after Brown's execution. (Sources: Mezey, 234; Winters, 137)

"John Evereldown" (1896). Poem. Someone sees old John Evereldown standing outside by the gate, in the dark and in the cold, away from the comforts of wherever he abides, which include a cozy fire. That same someone asks him repeatedly where he's going. John answers that he's going to Tilbury Town. Why? Because the women keep calling him to do so. He would like to be free of them, to avoid clouds, rain, creepy shadows, and crawling dead men. But the women keep on calling him; so what's a fellow to do?

Josephine Miles quotes the first stanza of "John Evereldown" and then notes that "[m]any characteristics of Robinson's poetry are found in these [eight] lines — the strong formal use of repetition, the conversational tone, the ballad-like mysteries and assumptions, the language of dreariness." William C. Childers suggests that Robinson may be punning with the name "Evereldown" and "*ever*, *held*, and *down*" — meaning that the poor fellow was once so sexually repressed that in later years he "has become a slave to passion and his life is spent on the treadmill of desire." "John Evereldown" contains Robinson's first reference to Tilbury Town, which he was gradually to populate with numerous memorable dramatis personae. Many critics have noted that Robinson's poems about residents of his Tilbury Town appeared many years before Edgar Lee Masters (1868–1950) began epigraphizing various people in his *Spoon River Anthology* (1915). Despite his regular assertions that the subjects of his character sketches are fictional, Robinson did write Laura E. Richards* (March 9, 1902) that John Evereldown was based on an acquaintance named John Tarbox, whom she also evidently knew. Emma Robinson* and Ruth Nivison* second this identification and add that Tarbox lived on the River Road, south of Gardiner, and that his house later burned down. Ellsworth Barnard says that the repeated "where" and "why" queries, along with old John's repeated answers, "Build for the reader an image of the treadmill of desire on which the man is doomed to wear out his life." (See also "My Methods and Meanings.") (Sources: Barnard, 90; Cary [1974], 94; Childers [1955], 225; Miles, 110; E. Robinson, 10; *Selected Letters*, 50)

"John Gorham" (1916). Dramatic dialogue. John Gorham and Jane Wayland meet again one chilly moonlit night. Jane begins by asking John why he has come here to see her and is pretending to feel sorry for himself. John answers that he wants to tell her what she is and to make her feel sorry. Jane: Be frank now, or you won't see as much of me as my ribbons any more. John: I'm the one who'll be leaving. Jane: Lighten up, let me make you smile. John: You flutter around me like a butterfly over roses, like a cat that catches a mouse "and lets him go and eats him up for fun." Jane: I wouldn't want to be like a cat or a butterfly to you. John: For a year now I remember your ways. Jane: Can't you see me for what I am and forget "the foolishness and all I never meant?" I'm a woman. Find that out. Would it help if I proved it and repented? John: It's too late. We have nothing much to say.

Robert Mezey contends that "John Gorham" is composed "in a folk meter, dipodic, which is employed in many nursery rhymes and ballads." He defines a "dipod" as "a double foot with one strong accent and one secondary one." A more standard definition might be that this poem, which is in 10 quatrains, gently rhyming *abcb*, is written in iambic, trochaic heptameter and octameter lines — a rollicking meter ironically used to present sad lovers at farewell.

Should the reader take sides? Should the reader criticize John for staying bitter and rejecting Jane? She loves him, but did she tease him too much? Does he pathetically misunderstand her womanly ways? Does she ruinously misjudge his manly stance? Incidentally, the politically correct would ridicule poor Jane if she were to complain today to her John as she did back then, when she said, "Somewhere in me there's a woman, if you knew the way to find her." Emma Robinson* says that this poem is based on Robinson's declined proposal of marriage to her in 1910, shortly after the death of her husband Herman Robinson.* (Sources: Mezey, 227; E. Robinson, 2–3)

"John Town." A short story Robinson wrote in the early 1890s, could not sell, and destroyed. (Source: Hagedorn, 102)

Juvenilia, Robinson's. Laura E. Richards* reports that Robinson when a youngster was playing in a cellar with some young friends, pulled from his pocket a sheaf of poems he had written, read them aloud, and asked their opinion. When they said they didn't like them, he burned them in a convenient furnace — "and we have no Juvenilia." Chard Powers Smith* calls this "an overstatement," on the grounds that *The Children of the Night* contains some poems that Robinson wrote as early as in the mid–1880s. (Sources: Richards [1936], 25; C. Smith, 85)

"Karma" (1923). Sonnet. It is Christmas time. All is mostly well, in the eyes of an unnamed speculator. He feels no responsibility for a friend whom he wrecked in the wavering stock market. After all, the fellow "would neither buy nor sell." But when the rich man sees a Santa Claus on a cold street ringing his bell for contributions, he kinda wishes his friend were still around. As recompense, "he fished / A dime for Jesus who had died for men."

Note that Jesus fished also, but for men, not money. Ironically used here, the word "Karma" means the belief that every action, good or evil, is followed by due retribution. The self-deluding anti-hero here pays for hurting a fellow human by charitably dropping a 10¢ piece in a Salvation Army kettle or some similar charity receptacle. Ellsworth Barnard notes that not until the last line is the reader provided a "lurid illumination . . . of man's capacity for hardened misanthropy or infirm self-deception." (Source: Barnard, 100)

King Jasper (New York: Macmillan, 1935). Narrative in blank verse, in six numbered parts.

I. Honoria, queenly and beautiful at 50, feels uneasy, as though a collapse is near. She prepares a smile for the appearance of her husband Jasper, who has earned the name King Jasper. He is handsome, small, tough, with piercing eyes, and well over 60. Before the fireplace, the two banter about her time-defeating beauty and about his factory chimneys, those ever-standing fiery symbols of his power. Honoria says that their troublesome son (later revealed to be also named Jasper), back from travels, may be stronger even than tough Jasper and that the young man sees beyond Jasper's factory. Jasper criticizes the woman their son is with, a woman he calls his wife, though not bound to him by "church or state." Honoria advises giving them sympathy. Wondering why "you women, you pernicious ribs, / Make havoc" for men, Jasper says their "elusive sprout" is too cocky and aimless. He asks Honoria what's troubling her. Has she seen a ghost in this new house of theirs? She confesses to feeling destructive hands and asks if he has "an enemy, or a friend, who died, / And might return . . . to be unwelcome." He admits that he is often away but suggests that all she needs is exercise and rest. How about a long voyage together? She says she would still feel those unseen hands. Jasper confesses he too knows about hands. But his inimical ones are "living and invincible." She says the ones she senses are ghostly and can "crush us." She cautions silence. They hear the voices of young Jasper and his girl.

II. In comes their cocky, handsome son, called the prince, with his companion. She appears slight, firm, fair, and amused. He introduces her as his informally pledged wife Zoë, to whom a wise man once gave a needle-like knife. He defines her as "intricate and industrious," capable of seeing through his parents, prophetic, angelic, and half-divine like his own presently scowling mother. Jasper invites both newcomers to sit and talk. Honoria suppresses considerable rage, says Jasper must speak for himself about whose house this now is, and retires.

Half smiling, Jasper observes Zoë narrowly, while she says she will stay only if welcome. Jasper says some chemicals don't combine, nor will Honoria and Zoë probably do so. Zoë says that they won't remain in this rather cramping house, that she is neither perfect nor evil, and that the elder Jasper likes her — at which he laughs but says he fears her. The prince says he's sorry about his mother, comments on the dragon that lives in his father's chimneys, hints that his father could learn much from Zoë, but adds that maybe he should send both the prince and Zoë into the

darkness outside. While the prince speaks of "invisible hands" and laughs amiably at his father, that man is associating Zoë's "laughing eyes" with unsleeping truth. Can she see those very hands filling his house? Zoë says that she prefers hands she can hold rather than hands she can't even see, that if she ruled the world and couldn't see, hands would kill her. Jasper says he doesn't want to see any woman upsetting the world by being crowned and trying to rule. The prince advises Zoë to "stroke" proud Jasper, not annoy him, and never stick him with that wise man's knife. He asks about his father's old friend Hebron's picture, which used to be in the house. He says that Hebron's son was in the factory yesterday and glared at him. Jasper says that old Hebron died, that no crime was involved, that he wants his son to survive. Zoë says she'll help, says she was a foundling without known parents, adds that "Who[ever] knows a child, knows God," and that the prince told her his father read to him about Sindbad the Sailor and the Old Man of the Sea. The prince wonders if his father might be "finished" the way Sindbad destroyed the Old Man, and if one of his chimneys would fall. Before going upstairs, Zoë gives Jasper an extra-warm kiss. She accepts his welcome home but regrets Honoria's "fierce misinterpretations" of her. The young pair retire upstairs, and Jasper feels fearfully alone in the big, cold room.

III. Jasper tosses awake that night from two to five o'clock, then sleeps, and dreams. (The long dream follows.)

His desert-like past appears ahead of him now, and he is climbing endless rocks and seeking hope ahead. He sees a "gaunt frail shape." A voice, Hebron's, combining affection and venom, welcomes him. Death provided his poison. Jasper remembers crushing Hebron, lying to him, and letting him die.

They walk and talk. Hebron: We were friends, talked all night together. You promised gold "to reward my genius" but let me die. You won't let me die again. Jasper: I never hated you then or now, feared you, wasn't greedy. Hebron: I agree. My "dark" son, "somewhere" now, knew and disliked you; you feared him. Jasper, "groaning while he climbed": Unlike you, I was ambitious but neglected you in search not for gold but for power. Hebron, getting weak: You were always a liar. When we cooperated, you never let me see the results; possessing them, you became a king, but the kingdom you built is an uncontrollable, self-consuming machine. The prince knows this, is happy with Zoë, wants "no other crown." Jasper: I'm restless like that machine you mentioned.

Skinny Hebron, too tired to walk, climbs on Jasper's shoulders, and gloats that Jasper must lift his enemy from the grave he put him in when Jasper took their gold without sharing it. Jasper knows he is fated to stagger on, though thus loaded. Hebron: You lied about our imminent financial success, didn't imprudently murder me outright, but let me starve to death instead. Confess it now. Jasper: You dilly-dallied, wanted to improve our procedures, really would have preferred an intellectual "glory / In your accomplishment," not power, not gold. Be merciful and tell me the truth. Hebron: Speed up. If I seem heavier, it's because I'm turning to gold. Jasper: Strangle me with golden fingers; you're as heavy as the world. Hebron: You aren't the king of the world, and what you're carrying is my weighty share of your gold. Are you Sindbad and I the Old Man of the Sea? Now trot right up this hill. Oh, see Zoë there, on the other side of a chasm, and also your son, laughing at you for being a burdened beast. Jasper to Hebron: Be merciful and let me leap over to them, embrace Zoë, and call her mine.

The young couple dance. Zoë to Jasper: Identify unloving Hebron truly and discard him, claim "your kingdom and your power / And glory" for now and the future, come to your loving son and daughter. Hebron to Jasper: If Zoë regards me as malicious, you made me so; jump now, or I'll soon be too heavy. Meanwhile, the prince is beckoning him. Zoë to Jasper: You are my father; your folly, your shrewdness, and your burying "brain and eyes in golden sand" created me for you. Jasper concerning Zoë: "My folly and I together, for centuries, / Have been the forebears of her parentage."

With her hypnotic eyes on him, Jasper leaps without hope, is released from Hebron's weight, lands on a seemingly safe rock, but is jeered by the prince, and feels a cold stab. He now sees anew. The prince is strangely fearsome; Hebron, "A shape of living gold that once was his / And was now hating him"; Zoë's eyes are full of hate. Zoë to Jasper: You should have fallen; your evil ignorance made me alluring to you; come no nearer; I have a knife; listen to me. But Jasper clutches at her, is stabbed, sees three mocking faces, falls into time's dark death, and awakens wounded in his daylit bed.

IV. People visit sick King Jasper in his palace. Some are sorry, others envious; many hope he dies. Honoria, long apprehensive, tells Jasper that she tried to get along with Zoë but cannot, and one woman in his house must leave. Jasper: I am king; both of you must remain; the world would jeer at my kingdom without his queen and his daughter. Honoria: She isn't my daughter; she fears you, honors you, toys with you as a cat does with a mouse. Jasper: You could not live elsewhere; this house is your world, not Zoë's; she weeps in it when alone in it. Honoria: How do you know this? You must peep at her. She has made you "pliable," which I fear more than change. I'm afraid of Zoë, hate her, want her gone. You fear her, therefore love her. Jasper: I could hug you for your braininess. "That's not one of our more volcanic notions / Of love on fire," but it is praise. Zoë pities me, knowing what I fear to discover. Be gentle toward Zoë, or our house might fall. Honoria: Your rule was systematic, not sinful, but is ending. Our time is short. Remember what was pleasant. Hearing someone, Zoë leaves.

Hebron's son enters. He is almost 30, back from travels and smiling coldly. Young Hebron to Jasper: My inventor-father, your partner once, might have had a lavish palace like yours here, but died early, and is housed in a narrow grave. Jasper: "I am no king"; "an uneven sport of circumstance" gave me much and your father —. Hebron, interrupting: Before I could speak, I knew my father was "Marked . . . indelibly for disaster." Jasper: I seek your parents' features in you. Hebron: I never knew my dark mother. She would have liked your house if she and my father hadn't died; I would like it too, or to have your characteristics. Jasper: You are strong; build as you wish. Hebron: My house is the world, not owned, therefore unlost. Jasper: With age, you'll change your view of things; enjoy "the mirage of your desires" while you can. Hebron: Thanks for advising a mere groper. I'll consider your words before we meet again. Jasper: Had your father lived, he would have adored you more than he would my trashy power. You are welcome to return. Hebron: My curiosity practically commanded me to visit my father's friend's residence and to see the king.

Zoë enters, pretends to be apologetic, pierces Young Hebron with "her startled eyes," and is introduced. He stares back "till she wondered / If all her clothes were on," calls her beautiful, and offers to be her slave. When rebuked for his wordiness, he says they'll meet again, asks to be remembered to the prince, and departs.

Bursting in, Honoria wonders who young Hebron was. He is named by Jasper, who tells Zoë that this Hebron is a liar, and asks why she came in a while ago. She says that "My Jasper" recognized Hebron from a window, feared his gift-bearing entrance, and asked her to go sniff him for sulphur. Honoria says that she hates Hebron and adds that her God would be grateful if she could kill him. Jasper: Christ, who died for us, wants us to love our enemies. I don't hate Hebron. Honoria: You don't hate him; you fear him, as I do. Zoë: I both fear him and hate his ignorantly thinking he can improve the world he is hurting. When Zoë diffidently asks for Honoria's friendship, Honoria bites off a smile and leaves.

Zoë to Jasper: I can't call Honoria mother when in her pride she thinks I'm a serpent. Jasper: You are saving my idealistic son. Zoë: I may be savior or woe to men. When that wise man carried me away from "a morass of men," he said I would be alone with men, but now that I have young Jasper I wonder about that "wise one." Jasper: You came a month ago; I feared you; time is standing still; I should call you mother; I know you're ageless. Why must Honoria punishingly convince herself she hates me? She knows something. Jasper: I had a dream "All about you," and in it you stabbed me. Why? Zoë: Your dream was about more than just me. Jasper: Yes, it was also about this foul, man-wrecked world. Zoë: This prophetic Hebron will get others to bleed for his cause. Was this Hebron's old father also in your dream? I didn't stab you; you stabbed yourself. When I first came here, we all laughed, feared time, had too little time to waste it in fear. I get peeved with "destiny," mourn for time-cursed man. Look down at your kingdom of smoking chimneys. They will fall. Don't fear the knife the wise one gave me. You've hurt others with knives enough. A knife naturally enough struck your heart. Look here; laugh and speak of loving me; don't wonder why your chimneys will fall; you know why, in your aching heart; sleep without dreams; Hebron did it; there will be two Hebrons forever.

V. Dreaming no longer, Jasper sees those ceaselessly busy, unappeasable hands. They are pulling at his fire-breathing chimneys, some of which seem to tremble. There will be kings, but none have "power to stay / Those hands," if they are assigned work. Zoë came too late to do more than tell this king he was doomed. He will endure until his kingdom crumbles, accompanied by marching music.

Two weeks "after / Young Hebron's apparition" came, the prince enters, brings Zoë, and warns Jasper: Zoë and I would like you and mother to pack up and leave. Sulphurous smells warn of trouble, and Hebron, that "ophidian visitor," may reappear. Jasper to his son: The chimneys still live; I can see through Hebron. The prince: Let me wear your crown while there's still time. Jasper: You three should go, leave me here. The prince: Sulphur smells blend with disarmingly "heavenly fumes." You have combined handsome and evil deeds, and "are passing." If Hebron comes, listen to "his red rhetoric" and discover that he doesn't know "that millions who know less / Might yet be taught by kings" who have some modern vision. That accursed Hebron is the Man of the Sea. Jasper: This is strange advice. I hope Zoë makes you less intelligent and more tactful. The prince: Will you stay with us or leave with mother? Jasper, saying nothing, only looks at his chimneys, now resembling trees in a forest fire. So, the prince: You might do well to query Hebron aimlessly.

Jasper: It's too late. Hebron visited earlier today and offered a compromise, but with unction lacing his venom. I can't take too much juvenile advice. Zoë feels all this and may still love me a little. You and she may rule a bigger kingdom than mine. Rest, and don't dream.

Zoë kisses Jasper lightly and leads the prince out. Jasper rests, awakens, and addresses Honoria, his queen: I hoped, hopelessly, that you would like Zoë. You were right to say this palace couldn't house both you and her. You must leave for now. I am planted here, with my chimneys, our son, and Zoë. Honoria, defiantly: I will stay here, in "My home, my world." Zoë's affront to me was little. I see "a clear sky" today. I hear the unseen hands breaking things. Jasper: You must go. Honoria, kissing Jasper passionately: You have been kind and loving to me; Zoë and our son may see better structures rise from the ashes of those mysterious chimneys you erected like temples; knowledge makes Zoë lonely; I love you.

Honoria leaves by the stairway. When a voice tells Jasper to follow her, something like God's voice asks why. Jasper remains alone, until the prince and Zoë enter. The prince: Zoë and I believe in God and the Devil; the Devil is here; kings call him God. You, father, adored the Devil's power. Zoë knows this. A restless, mortally sick dragon lives amid your chimneys. What's left if it should perish? Jasper: Absolutely nothing. Shut up for a while.

Jasper leaves them. The prince to Zoë: Some features of this place still puzzle me. Zoë to the prince: Are you certain that you could leave this dragon and your possibly needful parents? "I'm like a child trying to be at home / In the wrong house." That wise one told me that "I must always go my way alone." I wanted you, though, and helped you learn and see. Would you leave this place with me? The prince: This house is not for us. Let's leave. Something happened today. I'll go and ask mother.

Jasper returns, gives a letter from Honoria to their son and Zoë, and says Honoria found silence to be her only friend and is dead.

VI. For a month Jasper sits in his castle, without graceful, coolly beautiful Honoria,

and hoping for a dreamless dark. Zoë to him:

No God,
No law, no Purpose, could have hatched for sport
Out of warm water and slime, a war for life
That was unnecessary, and far better
Never had been — if man, as we behold him,
Is all it means.

She would like him to take it easy, not want what's past, not worry about death ahead. "If it is all, there's nothing to be feared; / If it is nothing, it is not worth fearing." Jasper: But others will suffer because of future kings like me. Zoë: Yes, the Devil is in charge for now. But,

Our bleeding progress upward from the mud
Might have been longer had there been no kings,
Or queens, or other ambitious anthropoids
Without a conscience before history.

She continues: Let Hebron's ghost be gloriously crowned; let God handle the rest. She adds,

I don't say what God is, but it's a name
That somehow answers us when we are driven
To feel and think how little we have to do
With what we are.

Zoë pets poor Jasper briefly, goes into a nearby room, and listens to and answers the prince. Then the prince: I would like to force father to leave here. Zoë: Nature requires you to stay with your father. My real father wisely told me I must go my way alone forever, seeking the answer I already know. The prince: Let's go and not keep watching the clock until my father dies. Zoë: I love you, but leave me out of your unpleasant picture. Forget what was an illuminating fire but is only embers now. Remember your father, your mother, and me. Your mother could not change. The knife in your father's heart was there before my arrival here. The prince: If we went out and found you in your grave somewhere, you'd be alive, you'd say cover it and let's go. Zoë: I found a rock up and beyond the chimneys today, couldn't lift it, wondered what was under it.

They talk of death, her leaving, the dragons; they embrace and rest until it is dark. Jasper returns in darkness to his solitary chair, broods about Zoë's comments about death, but suddenly sees a wild light rising. The prince rushes in, alarmed, with Zoë, who calmly says that Jasper is spellbound and sees nothing but his kingdom burning. He regards the spreading fire as his glorious funeral "pyre / Of life worth dying for," before a humbled world. A tall chimney crashes. Jasper thinks that old Hebron, that buried genius, may have inspired the ruin, but that all the living kings know what's tumbling down. The prince to Jasper: Don't watch the other chimneys fall, leave, don't remain here with Zoë. If I, the negligent prince, went down there, I might be killed. This house is like "a forgotten island / In a forsaken ocean." You are going to stay, though. Jasper to Zoë: You found my son . . . I am ignorant . . . You two . . . The knife . . .

Silence follows. Then a shot rings out and kills the prince. The king, not seeing the remaining chimneys falling, sleeps. Zoë touches, knows her dead husband, knows she must carry his torch, then senses someone behind her. Young Hebron, approaching, boasts of laying "the son and heir" of Jasper's stolen power and glory at his majesty's feet. Jasper sits, indifferent in death. Zoë, fiery-eyed and erect, scornfully addresses Hebron: You have acted too late. I must go. You must leave. Your madness will ease your hate; your soul will suffer and understand, after your death. Visit and blaspheme at the graves of the three here, and at the graves of others you will kill. Why kill me? Hebron: What "a piece of nature's work . . . you are." Realize that you and I are "God's elected," and will enflame the world with "hate and sacrifice," but also warm it "for knowledge and for love." I want your knowledge; with me you will have some real love, not that of puppets.

When Hebron smears a hot kiss across her mouth, Zoë steps back, remains standing, and stares at him the way a scared child would at a prowler in her home. Ignorantly feeling encouraged, Hebron fingers her shoulders and says he'll gently determine whether she is devil, saint, or both. Her misunderstood smile relaxes him, and he says that Jasper's servants were in his pay and that he has mined Jasper's house to explode when he lights it up for its dead occupant. Zoë asks for a moment with father—too old to change—and son—too

young to die. She fondles the prince's face and whispers consolingly to the king. When she says she must go her way alone, Hebron snarls for her to come with him. No. Why not? Would you rather remain behind and die? Hebron rushes at her, only to be met with a "narrow flash of steel" at his throat. He mutters that she must leave, that he knows. At first she thinks he doesn't, calls him time's fool, but then sees he knows but only because death is teaching him.

Zoë rushes out, to where she and her husband once looked down on Jasper's castle. It is exploding. More than it is burning. More than chimneys are falling. Kingdom, king, prince, their destroyer, dragon. Dead or dying. "There was only Zoë—alone."

King Jasper was supposedly inspired by the bank holiday that President Franklin Roosevelt imposed shortly after his inauguration in March 1933. To Robinson, the event signaled the disintegration of the capitalistic system. He called his anti-hero Jasper to remind himself that his brother Herman Robinson* invested dwindling family money in a copper and zinc mine in Jasper County, Wyoming. Robinson dubbed the poem his "treatise on economics." His single-minded devotion to the artistic profession is indicated by the fact that, according to a Macmillan editor named Harold S. Latham, he completed a revision of the galleys of *King Jasper* literally hours before dying in the New York hospital.

King Jasper attracted many reviews, partly because it appeared shortly after Robinson's death and with an introduction by his friend Robert Frost. (Richard Cary neatly summarizes details of what he calls the "at best wary" friendship of Robinson and Frost.) Some reviewers saw it simply as a story of six unhappy people. Others, however, read it as depicting the then-contemporary struggle between "dark" capitalistic materialism and industrialism on the one hand, and incendiary communism on the other. Several singled out the dream sequence for special praise. The work was gradually recognized as an elaborate allegory. For example, the Marxist-socialist critic F. O. Matthiessen was annoyed that the politically allegorical content of *King Jasper* "is at once both bare and obscure." It seems obvious, however, that Robinson found dangerous excesses both in capitalism and in communism. Jasper may be equated with power and money; Old Hebron, with love of truth; Honoria, custom, convention, rigid law; Prince Jasper, liberal change; Young Hebron, vengeful retribution, lust for power, violent revolution; Zoë, life, beauty, truth. Hermann Hagedorn* remarks that Robinson "gave the poem [King Jasper] a triple significance—first, as a story of six unhappy beings, caught in a cataclysm of all that is life to them; then, as a symbolic drama of the disintegration of the capitalistic system; and, last, as an allegory of ignorance and knowledge and aspiration." He adds that Robinson told Esther Willard Bates* that King Jasper represents ignorance, and Zoë, knowledge and not life (as her name would seem to indicate). Harvey Roy Pearce, reluctant to admire the allegory in King Jasper, opines not only that the poem is "to be regretted" but also that Robinson "was simply not equipped to write . . . allegorical poems."

In truth, King Jasper is so prolix that it seems tedious to explicate each action and speech in the light of intricate allegorical significations. It also seems awkward that Robinson has two Jaspers and two Hebrons here. Why not give the sons their own names? They are certainly different from their respective parents. Floyd Stovall concludes that King Jasper "leaves no doubt of Robinson's faith in the intrinsic worth of humankind." However, Estelle Kaplan bitterly contends that "the 'free' intelligence of Zoë is coupled with the younger generation's inability to understand the fear of their elders, with a total disregard of conscience, and responsibility, and in general with the kind of 'emancipation' which springs from vitality than from reason, more from intelligent unconcern than from reflective experience." As for figures of speech, Charles T. Davis notes that "[f]lame or fire is the leading image in . . . King Jasper," in which fire is both miraculously controlled and also menacingly dangerous. (Sources: Cary [1974], 292; Davis [1961], 384; Hagedorn, 369, 370; Kaplan, 141; H. Latham, 46; Matthiessen, 603; Pearce, 268; Stovall, 22)

"The Klondike" (1902). Poem. A doomed adventurer is telling about the tragic end of his search with 11 other men for gold. They said goodbye to their women, who clung to them. They left the safe little town, lured by the devil's song about the golden river. They energetically pursued the lure but at one point took a "wrong road." Only five men remain alive now. One of them, with his feet and hands dead "clout[s]" and his "brain a freezing feather," rambles deliriously. He says that they "took the frozen chance and laid their lives on yellow." They realize now that their girlfriends will marry others. But they are also aware that other men will hear the same alluring call of the golden river and answer it. And "[e]ach will hold an icy knife to punish his heart's lover." At last the dying man sleeps. His comrades, all "stalled here together," finger his eyes shut so he won't stare at the stars the whole night through; and they agree to "hold our thoughts north while we starve here together, / Looking each his own way to find the golden river." The last lines of eight of the 12 stanzas in "The Klondike" end with the word "river," in seven cases "golden river"; two other last lines end with the word "yellow." The lure of gold is thus made manifest.

Robinson wrote to Laura E. Richards* (January 18, 1902), telling her that she could understand his "notion of quantity" by taking note of the "jingle" in his "The Klondike," as well as in "The Wilderness." By prosodic "quantity" is meant the pleasantly varied use of long and brief syllables in lines of verse. (Source: Selected Letters, 48)

"Kosmos" (1895). Sonnet. Men shudder, "falter," and "shrink . . . / To look on death." What would life, which is so full of trials and forgiving, be without "love that finds us when we go?" God doesn't jest and cast us into this sweaty life for "some vague end" that never "arrive[s]." God would tire of such a "show." You wretches, who plan, perhaps idly, and build "on the sand," must realize that love isn't "so small." If you are courageous, you will soon understand "the triumph, and the Truth!" Part of this early work, which Robinson found unsatisfactory, is re-expressed in "The Man Against the Sky." (Source: Cary [1975], 24, 175)

"The Laggards" (1924). Sonnet. The poet addresses those who are "Scorners of earth." Since you have only one foot equipped with wings, you "are not flying yet." You don't see that between what you grope for and "the towers of God" are way stations you first have to plod to. Isn't it odd that you aren't aware of tolls you must pay to get anywhere? You reply that others have paid and then paid more. Yes, they do so for causes that sometimes remain unclear. "They are the laggards among those who strive / On earth to raise the golden dust of heaven."

Ellsworth Barnard calls this sonnet "powerful but obscure." In it, Robinson may be rebuking writers of little genuine talent. Sister Mary James Power finds Robinson's use of the word "groping" here, early among such usages also quoted, to be "[s]ignificant of the poet's search for Truth" and, further, that "[t]his groping for the Truth . . . vindicates Robinson from the position of a fatalist." She goes on to suggest that Robinson's "harmonizing of Divine prescience with human liberty" is proof that such "harmonizing" is "[f]ar removed from pagan fatalism." (Sources: Barnard, 295; Power, 81, 81–82)

Lancelot: A Poem (New York: Thomas Seltzer, 1920). Arthurian narrative, in blank verse, in nine numbered parts.

Several characters appear in, or at least are mentioned in, both *Lancelot* and *Merlin*. For brief identifications of the following, see *Merlin*, where they were introduced in 1917: Agravaine, Arthur, Bedivere, Bors, Gaheris, Galahad, Gareth, Gawaine, Griflet, Guinevere, Lamorak, Lancelot, Merlin, Modred, Percival, Tor, and Vivian.

The following characters first appear in *Lancelot*. Spellings more regularly employed in Arthurian literature are indicated in parentheses.

Aglovale is a knight whose death, during Lancelot's rescue of Guinevere, Lucan reports to Arthur.

Andred (Andret) comes from Cornwall and is Mark's nephew and Tristram's cousin. He ultimately kills both Tristram and Isolt.

Ban is Lancelot's father.

Colgrevance is mentioned as a knight killed by Lancelot

Elaine; in conversation with Lancelot, Guinevere mentions "those two Elaines," both of whom made her jealous and one of whom is dead. One of four Elaines in Arthurian literature is disqualified: Elaine was Lancelot's mother. Guinevere may have been jealous of the Elaine who was Arthur's half-sister. Guinevere certainly had reason to be jealous of Elaine, the daughter of Pelleas, who used a magic potion to lure Lancelot into bed with her and generate Galahad. And she might have been jealous of Alfred, Lord Tennyson's safely deceased Lady of Shalott.

Ettard is a lady Gawaine stole from Pelleas, who wants vengeance.

Gillimer is a knight whose death at Lancelot's hand is reported by Lucan to Arthur.

Isolt is mentioned as Tristram's beloved at Joyous Gard.

Leodogran is Guinevere's father.

Lionel is a knight loyal to Lancelot in France.

Lot of Orkney rules Scotland, and is the father of Gawaine and others.

Lucan is Bedivere's brother and Arthur's arms-bearing butler.

Mark is mentioned as wanting vengeance against Tristram and Isolt.

Pelleas wants vengeance because Gawaine stole the lady Ettard from him.

The Bishop of Rochester is a holy man whom Lionel knows.

Tristram is mentioned as Isolt's lover at Joyous Gard.

(Agravaine, Arthur, Colgrevance, Dagonet, Guinevere, Lancelot, Merlin, and Modred also appear or are mentioned in "Modred: A Fragment.")

I. In King Arthur's garden in Camelot, Gawaine, who is Arthur's nephew, and Lancelot are back from seeking the Grail and are sparring verbally. Lancelot wishes Gawaine and his brothers Gareth and Gaheris well, says that Agravaine, not Gawaine, is circulating lies, and wants to kill Agravaine (who is also Gawaine's brother) and also to kill Modred (who is Arthur's son). Lancelot intends to proceed south and seek "the Light." Gawaine praises Lancelot for fighting and for turning women's heads. Queen Guinevere enters, wonders why Gawaine worries about Lancelot's need of God's help, and tries to hide her fear. Gawaine says Lancelot will forget Camelot.

II. When Lancelot and Guinevere are alone, he worries about her but says he'll fear Gawaine only if that man is crossed. Guinevere tells the downcast Lancelot he has changed since "that unearthly Quest," says she is used to gossip, and asks him to speak candidly. When he says Gawaine has guessed that the two are lovers, she turns pale and needs comfort from Lancelot. He says he'll lie to himself no longer, doesn't fear Gawaine, and remembers when King Arthur sent him that May to visit Leodogran, Guinevere's father, amid crowds. His statement "God Save the King" became a lie when he saw her face. When Guinevere wonders about going back, Lancelot slowly responds: He fears nothing ordinary; Arthur was enamored once of Lot of Orkney's wife and aroused Modred; love for Guinevere causes Lancelot's sole fear; Modred is hellishly whispering to Arthur. She doesn't fear Modred or Gawaine, worries that Lancelot fears the very Light he seeks, and recognizes changes in him and others near the Round Table. When he scowls, smiles, and scowls again, she says he needn't worry about her and regrets burdening him. She kisses him warmly, says Arthur is off hunting somewhere, and asks if he would come to her this night.

III. Lancelot seeks Guinevere unsuccessfully. Feeling both regret and remorse, he soliloquizes: I remember her warm breath, want to give her life in this twilight here before the dark and then the Light; I betrayed King Arthur, who, off hunting, thinks he'll last forever; Guinevere is a "pale witch-wonder of white fire and gold," a woman among many women who toy with men only to find their beauty shriveled by Time.

Lancelot senses both passion and fear, walks away, thinks of Galahad, returns, and sees Guinevere's "phantom face" for a moment only. Camelot shows lights in the dark.

IV. King Arthur, who became ill, quit the hunt, is back in Camelot, and summons old Sir Bedivere and Gawaine to stay near. As dawn breaks, Bedivere says report has it that Lancelot killed Colgrevance and that Gawaine was with Lancelot in the garden. Admitting as much, Gawaine replies thus: A few proper words from him might have aided heart-sore Lancelot; when Guinevere appeared, Gawaine laughed at and left them; later Gawaine met with Modred, and tried to discourage him. Gawaine, Modred's half-brother, revealed the relationship to Bors, who told Lancelot about it. Guinevere learned all this, talked about it with Lancelot, and when she returned to Arthur, Lancelot followed. Bedivere fails to dissuade Gawaine from regretting his conduct but does caution silence now.

Arthur enters, is shaky, sits, and speaks thus: If I could find a new king, I'd find a beautiful false woman for him, reduce his knights to one, and he'd be fortunate enough. Merlin warned me two years ago when he spoke of a " love that never was." Modred has incensed me. Lancelot fought his way with Bors to temporary freedom. We'll catch and burn him. Gawaine, I have ordered your brothers, Gareth and Gaheris, to seek the traitor.

Suddenly there is fire everywhere, and Arthur already imagines that Guinevere, evil though beautiful, is also burning.

V. While King Arthur is praying, Gawaine crouches and Bedivere weeps. Suddenly come sounds of riotous battle outside. Lucan rushes in, unceremoniously, and taxes Arthur's patience by verbosely describing how Guinevere was led to execution by burning, only to be rescued by fierce Lancelot, aided by Lionel and a dozen others. Leaving many dead, the party galloped far away. Ordered by Arthur, Lucan names those dead. Among six slain knights are Gareth and Gaheris. Gawaine, their infuriated brother, asks timorous Lucan for details. Lucan says the tumult was so confusing that Lancelot couldn't see clearly "upon whom his axe was falling." This convinces Gawaine that Lancelot killed his brothers, whereupon he laments that he ever thought he could reason with Lancelot, that "gracious, murderous friend," and could urge him to leave Camelot quietly. Gawaine vows to rid the world of inhumanly glamorous Lancelot.

Arthur orders everyone out except Gawaine. Gawaine remains quiet while Arthur envisions Lancelot and Guinevere already at

Joyous Gard, recalls Tristram and Isolt, earlier lovers there, and imagines the later pair "lying in each other's arms." He weeps for the dead but is glad his queen is still living. A humbling "vision of peace" follows. But observing Gawaine again, Arthur knows there will be no peace, with Gawaine full of hate and Modred viciously ambitious to wreck the Round Table.

VI. Modred bides his time. Gawaine goads King Arthur to lay gory siege to Joyous Gard. Only death will end the dispute and bring peace. One moonlit night, Lancelot and Bors, his loyal nephew, see a burial party of Arthur's army "in the silver distance." Bors to Lancelot: You pity Arthur, grieve for Gawaine's plight; if you and Guinevere were "discriminately dispatched," the slaughter would end; Arthur's realm is dissolving; the glimmering Light you once saw presages a new realm, neither Rome's nor Camelot's.

Unanswered, Bors leaves. Guinevere, misty and gray, enters. Lancelot to her: If I kill Arthur and Gawaine, will we be happy? Guinevere to him: I can't tell you anything that "folly and waste" haven't told you already. Why this slaughter of numberless pawns and a few knights? You must love war. You have told me much; now tell me all. Gawaine reviles you. Arthur ordered me burned because of you. Does that "far-off Light / You may have seen" hold the answer? It "was not the Light of Rome / Or Time." Must more thousands die before Gawaine, Arthur, and I do? Lancelot: Bors talks too much. I fatally axed two heads without recognizing they were Gaheris's and Gareth's. Gareth loved me greatly. Modred's "occult snake's brain" plans ruin. I don't regret saving you. "As for the Light, leave that for me alone." In case I am "done to death or durance," I have written a plea to Arthur to accord you prudent clemency, because of "another King / More great than Arthur." Is that a moonless sky out there, or do we project an image of it from within ourselves?

The next day is rainy. Arthur sends the fat Bishop of Rochester, with two assistants, to talk to Lancelot. The Bishop reports that Rome has ordered Lancelot to deliver Guinevere to Arthur; he will treat her mercifully, and peace will follow. Lancelot tells Bors and Lionel about the message, then relays the order to Guinevere, says the Devil inspired him to conduct this war, and she will be returning "home to Camelot." She faints in his arms.

VII. Six months pass. One rainy night, with graves outside, Lancelot broods before a log fire. King Arthur, Gawaine, Guinevere, and he comprise too many for one world. Some must die, while Modred crouches. Guinevere enters, angry when Lancelot turns solicitous and says Rome has made her safe. Guinevere to Lancelot: Here with you, I wished that time would stop. You should have let me burn. You said you loved my soul? Now my "blue-veined cream-white soul" goes to safety in Camelot, with Arthur. When you said "Camelot," did I swoon in ecstasy? Will you discard me as a child does "a worn-out doll?" I was a queen. Am I a queen here? I should have died instead of those soldiers.

Lancelot frowns, is torn between sight of her radiant white-gold beauty and that unearthly glimmer, says she was the reluctant "Queen of Christendom," contrasts her and dark Isolt, and says, "Your world, my world, and Arthur's world is dying, / As Merlin said it would." He adds that their love, once mighty, will be recorded as legendary, or else he needn't follow the light. She bridles at the notion that their love is now only a bleeding memory; she gave all for him, and off he goes seeking "a Light." They might love longer. Then when she died, he could pursue his "Vision," which didn't concern Rome, that "refuge for the weary and heart-laden," where she might find happiness if by chance she "live[s] too long." She wishes she were God, to grant the two of them more years of joy.

Smiling as though obscurely wounded by her words, Lancelot to Guinevere: Arthur, Merlin, and surely God all knew our path led to "havoc." The power of the Light, which is not from Rome, though Rome freed you, must not be flouted; total horror would follow. War may come. I still suspect Gawaine. Your home is Camelot.

Lancelot needs some wine, hardly aware that "his life-devouring love was now / A scourge of mercy" upon her. Guinevere, in fury, grief, and fear, to Lancelot: This is the only way? You say I'm free? To bed with hated Arthur? Men died for me. Lancelot: Rest; in safe Camelot, you needn't fear Arthur. I say no more. Guinevere: You need no part of me still? Your kinsmen control all of France; hide me there, alone or with you. I wronged Arthur, but he bribed my father Leodogran for me. Order Lionel or Bors to escort me to and leave me in France; you can tell everyone only that I am happy.

Guinevere kneels and holds Lancelot's knees. Lancelot: The Christian world's queen could never hide from Rome in France. Though in a cave together, we would be spied out. Men must cheer their honest queen, and I must find the Light. "We cannot make one world of two, nor may we / Count one life more than one." Guinevere: I would kill Arthur. Let me perish in France.

Next, Lancelot holds the moaning woman. Rain drenches Joyous Gard. He sits, with embers now dust. Guinevere is gone. He is sure only of the unseen Light, to be found when he stops killing.

Seven days later he escorts Guinevere to Camelot, from which Arthur banishes him. He knows that Gawaine will urge Arthur to continue war. Lancelot with many knights goes from Cardiff to Bayonne, and Arthur and his army follow.

VIII. King Arthur prepared for a long siege of Lancelot on the French seacoast, but Modred now foments rebellion in Britain. Gawaine, half-blinded in a rough fight with Lancelot, sends a letter to him: Arthur is returning home to stop Modred, and Gawaine's war against Lancelot is now "old . . . / If you will have it so." Lancelot is apprehensive about "Modred's evil shadow" but also wonders at Gawaine's motive. Next morning, Lancelot boldly seeks him out, for talk. Gawaine to Lancelot: God created Modred, like the crocodile, to prove His omnipotence, then placed him near trustful Arthur as "the Almighty's instrument / Of a world's overthrow." Arthur, back in Britain and fighting ambitious Modred, needs your help there. Guinevere hates Arthur, is hiding in the Tower of London. Merlin predicted Camelot's doom. "The world has paid enough / For Camelot," although Bedivere anticipates a new Camelot. I might have gone with you to see "Your Gleam."

Gawaine rambles on about his deceased mother being Modred's mother too, how Arthur called for Lancelot to save Guinevere at the stake, about his own approaching death. Lancelot takes Gawaine's cold hand, asks him to "forget what you forgive," and requests that his soul be at peace. Gawaine's eyes are closed.

IX. Lancelot assembles an army in France and proceeds to Dover. News greets him: King Arthur is dead, slain by Modred, whom he slew; Bedivere, sole knight to survive the battle at Salisbury, is in a hermitage; Guinevere is somewhere west of London. Camelot has vanished. Lancelot to Bors: Hold our army for a fortnight, await my word, and if none comes return to France; all of us will see the Light. Riding west alone, he realizes he stopped being guided by the Light once he met Guinevere. A cloud reveals no Light, no Camelot, no "white and gold" Queen. A vision of her floats before him, with nuns about her. Needing to trespass once more, he rides wearily to Almesbury, and an inn. He finds food, wine, rest, fear — then Guinevere. She wears no white and gold, but a nun's black hood and habit. She meets his "sad anger" with "sad pity" and calm kindness, pale face, red lips, and shining blue eyes.

Guinevere to Lancelot: A Mother is here. The Queen is now a child. Camelot can be replaced by unearthly palaces. Arthur, Modred, Guinevere are no more. I dimmed your Light; following it away from me might have been wiser. I was worth little and cost you too much. Forgive my holding you too long. "God pity men / When women love too much — and women more." Lancelot, shrugging, to Guinevere: ""Yes, there is that between me and the light." Guinevere: "No, Lancelot; / We are going by two roads to the same end." Memory of your visit here will make me less lonely. Lancelot: May I see your golden hair again? Guinevere: In your imagination, on your return to Dover. We have no world left for us.

They reminisce about that lost garden, Gawaine's words to them, and theirs to each other. Lancelot still wants Guinevere to leave with him for France. She responds: France is for neither of us; you will remember me; I won't obscure the Gleam you "must follow";

be glad I wasn't dark like Vivian and Isolt, hence more attractive, temporarily; when the bell rings, you must go and I am to stay and pray; in time you will be seeing what I cannot see; I may spend time in purgatory for talking thus to you. Lancelot says that when he first saw her here he would have gambled all to repeat one summer with her. Guinevere calls the past gone, fortunately not to be bought back with their souls.

The bell sounds. She wants to be remembered, all white and gold, as she "used to be." She refuses his kiss, says, "I am not alone" and goodbye. "He crushed her cold, white hands and saw them falling / Away from him like flowers into a grave." She faints. He is gone. When nuns whisper to each other that those two were the Queen and Lancelot, "great lovers," the convent Mother says that it is safest here to love God and safest of all to be dead; and meanwhile, pray.

Lancelot rides past reapers in fields and hears far-off thrushes, beyond the convent. He sees Guinevere's lonely face and hands. After "pity and love" bring wisdom, he seems alone on a reef with her face beneath the sea; there is white but no gold. She is trying to say she's not alone. Twilight comes. After making ruinous war, Lancelot feels he deserves no peace. But

a Voice within him said:
Where the Light falls, death falls; a world has died
For you, that a world may live. There is no peace.
Be glad no man or woman bears for ever
The burden of first days. There is no peace.

Lancelot rides on unburdened, following the Voice but not toward Dover. Guinevere's face fades. When he turns his horse back, the Voice, telling him he's not free, adds this: "When the Light falls, death falls; / And in the darkness comes the Light." Onward he rides, seeing Galahad "alive, now in a mist of gold," and on and on, into nothing and into darkness, alone; and the Light comes.

Lancelot is a continuation of the Arthurian cycle that Robinson began with *Merlin*.

Robinson dedicated *Lancelot* to his friend Lewis Montefiore Isaacs,* to whom he wrote (August 25, 1917) that it was probably the finest poem he had ever written. Its working

title was "Lancelot and Guinevere." Sources Robinson used for *Lancelot*, and also for the earlier *Merlin*, and for *Tristram*, which followed both, are *Le Morte d'Arthur* by Sir Thomas Malory, *Tristram and Iseult* by Matthew Arnold, *Tristram of Lyonesse* by Algernon Charles Swinburne, and *Idylls of the King* by Alfred, Lord Tennyson. According to Yvor Winters, Gawaine, here as in *Merlin*, "is conceived . . . as the graceful, intense and mercurial figure of Malory and of Tennyson." To Winters, King Arthur is simply "imperfect humanity." Bacon Collamore* calls "[t]he publication of *Lancelot* . . . a singularly peculiar performance which deserves a word of explanation." He offers this report: The Lyric Society was a group with few members, perhaps only one, namely its chairman Samuel Roth. Roth edited *The Lyric*, a poetry magazine that published a few of Robinson's works. When Roth asked for more poems by Robinson, he answered that he was busy writing a long one on Lancelot. In reply, Roth cleverly announced a prize of $500 for the best book-length poem submitted to his society and induced Robinson to compete. He did so "[i]n all innocence," and Roth promptly declared Robinson's *Lancelot* the winner of what Collamore labels "a 'framed' contest," paid the $500, and published the book he desired.

Merlin and *Lancelot* are best considered as a unit to be read together. Doing so enables one to see that Camelot was built on a rotten foundation and could not survive. *Merlin* sold so poorly, just before the United States entered the First World War that, though completed in 1917 and rewritten in 1918, *Lancelot* awaited peace, and a little beyond, to be published in 1920. Robinson intended the two poems to be not merely, or principally, linked romance narratives but also, and mainly, a political allegory. Camelot is a foreshadowing of endangered Western civilization, especially Anglo-American. Lancelot, as Robinson said in an early letter (September 8, 1918) to Hermann Hagedorn,* is roughly symbolic of Germany in *Merlin* and will also be in *Lancelot*, while Galahad's light (which Lancelot finally sees) symbolizes the radiance of the Grail, "a spiritual realization of Things and their significance." In the same letter, Robinson says that he regards

Gawaine's statement about the world having paid enough for Camelot to be perhaps "the most significant line" in *Merlin* and *Lancelot*. Ellsworth Barnard interprets Gawaine's remark thus: "Robinson regarded World War I as the death struggle of economic nationalism." Emery Neff gets more specific: "Arthur . . . adumbrates the tradition-bound British Empire, and the light-minded, materialistic Gawaine . . . corresponds to the America of 'Cassandra'"; further, that Guinevere envisions "the world's salvation through the instinct of women to abhor war." To James P. Carley, Robinson's having Guinevere finally remove herself from Lancelot's path inspires him (and perhaps other men) to "choose between Woman and the Light." N. E. Dunn theorizes that Robinson in *Lancelot* is recommending that autocratic societies give way to democratic ones, to satisfy all levels of human nature. Less grandly, Chard Powers Smith* suggests that Robinson had his tangled friendship with his sister-in-law Emma Robinson* in mind when he juggled the emotions of Lancelot and Guinevere. Harvey Gross and Robert McDowell theorize that "the monosyllabic word has been a traditional source of power in English blank verse," and cite as one proof a passage from *Lancelot*, including the famous lines: "'Where the light falls, death falls; / And in the darkness comes the Light.'" (Recall that Smith's biography of Robinson is *Where the Light Falls*.) Christopher Brookhouse relates the themes of destruction and salvation in Lancelot to images of color, darkness, decay, fire, jewelry, light, mist, rain, ripeness, and snakes. (Sources: Barnard, 262; Brookhouse; Carley, 5; Collamore, 28; Davis [1969]; Dunn [1971]; Gross and McDowell, 61; Lacy and Ashe; Neff, 194; *Selected Letters*, 106, 113; C. Smith, passim 230–50; Winters, 64, 69)

Languages, Robinson and. Robinson studied Latin in high school at Gardiner, Maine, loved it at once, soon became adept in reading it, and in due time translated parts of Virgil's *Aeneid* into English verse. He did not study Greek in high school but relied on his friend Harry de Forest Smith,* who did so (and later taught Greek at Amherst College), to provide him with careful prose translations of Sophocles's *Antigone*, parts of which Robinson put into English verse. While he was at Harvard, he studied German and French, and soon mastered both languages sufficiently to be able to read novels and plays in the two languages, especially those in French. During his Harvard years and later, he mentions in letters to Smith so many admired works by German and especially French authors that space is lacking to list the dozens of titles he rattles off. He also taught himself enough Italian to be able to read those passages of *La Divina Commedia* by Dante that he chose to savor in the original. When he began to admire various operas by Richard Wagner, he obtained libretti and read them with pleasure.

A fellow student at Harvard named G. W. Latham comments on Robinson and languages: "Robinson brought no knowledge of French or German with him, and in his first year he took elementary courses in both languages. I have never known anybody to develop facility in reading them more rapidly. . . . Most students in such classes read what is assigned to them. This was not Robinson's way. He tackled everything. The number of French novels that he read through was extraordinary. I think he became a sound judge of French style." (Sources: G. Latham, 19; *Untriangulated Stars*)

"Late Summer" (1919). Poem. One early evening by the seashore, a confused man has met a woman. She smiles inscrutably and is "lavishing feminine / Gold upon clay." This horrifies him. Can't she accept the reality of death? She should have faith that he could help her. A ghost has stolen her from him. Out of the dead man's absence she has woven a dream. In a way, he feels she is imploring him to believe and comfort her. Since he is honorable, he finds himself sure of almost nothing. Fitfully hoping, however, he tells her that men are too destructive, while women are too long-suffering, and, further, that their present situation is ridiculous. The incoming little waves seem to signal hopelessness. If she remains silent, he might be unable to remain calm. With night approaching, he wants her to choose: "We cannot have the dead between us. / Tell me to go, and I go." She responds that what he believes is uniting him and her makes it equally "right" that "you are not one of us" and that she prefers what he might call her lies to his form of the truth. She looks away. The shadowy ocean signals "indifference," and she is now alone.

The poem is composed in what Robinson in a parenthetic subtitle calls "Alcaics," that is, verse marked by complex variations of dominant iambic meters. Ruth Nivison* calls this poem Robinson's unsuccessful proposal of marriage (September 1909) to her mother, who was Robinson's widowed sister-in-law, Emma Robinson.* After elaborating on this Robinson family tradition, Hoyt C. Franchere adds that perhaps Robinson regarded himself as exiled from Emma's love as the Greek poet Alcaeus (c. 600 B.C.), who wrote alcaics, was exiled after displaying cowardice in battle. (Sources: Franchere, 69–70; E. Robinson, 17)

"Lazarus" (1920). Poem, in 18 unnumbered stanzas of irregular lengths. Martha and Mary are speaking to each other after "The Master" has brought their brother Lazarus back from death. Martha says that when she went to her brother, living again, he said nothing, wept, and showed no gladness. Mary says that Lazarus, who was dead and then alive, seems dead again. All is uncertain. Lazarus is alone. And the Master, who came slowly from Bethany because He loved them and now hides, for the sake of the world, is being hunted by His enemies. Mary tells Martha: Time has changed; Lazarus is remote, will be silent until the spirit moves him; we are too young to understand him; we might summon friends; I will comfort Lazarus, since I am less fearful than you. Weeping, Martha says that this act was done for her, since Mary was less eager to go see Lazarus just now. Martha sees him, a shadow among dark trees. Mary assures Martha that He loved them all equally and asks Martha to rest.

Martha, waiting at their doorway and looking at a "familiar" flower, urges Mary to encounter Lazarus before darkness conceals him. Mary goes, finds him hiding his face, and asks him to forgive their evident fear. She feels that her words are poor comfort to him. When he is silent and apparently indifferent, she tries

more loving words. His hands are cold. He is trembling in his white shroud. He speaks one word, her name. Then he says he heard others say that He wept for him, asks Mary who asked Him to come. Lazarus's eyes reveal coldness, loneliness, and bitterness, but no cruelty. He says that he would have wept had he been He. Lazarus briefly feels her black hair, which they once joked about. He kindly offers Mary and then the absent Master his forgiveness, says that only He can explain "The burden" on him now. He asks if it was for Mary that He came to do this and then asks where their friends are. When he sees Martha, he says he "must have time for this."

Mary shivers at all these words and is puzzled thus: What about Martha? Why had He waited? What is still to come to Lazarus? What did He see before tardily arriving? Lazarus asks whether "they" have found Him and whether He left Lazarus and wanted not to see him ever again. Mary comforts Lazarus thus: He will come again and see them all as they were; He told us to fear nothing. Smiling wanly, Lazarus suggests that she and Martha load their fears on him. Mary wonders if he is indeed Lazarus and asks if the Master gave him any "sign of a new joy" to come to their home. Lazarus to Mary: Returning to life, I saw His eyes on mine as if with full knowledge. Mary: He "cannot know that there is worse than death." Lazarus: Oh, yes, He can; yes, there is; I feared; never think about these things; my explanation would be incomprehensible to you; let's go and see Martha now. But, pressing to know whether he told Martha nothing, Mary asks if "Nothing . . . [is] all you have for me?" and wonders if nothing is ahead on "the same dark road."

Lazarus replies: God would care if my return were for nothing? The Master would weep for nothing? Should He be a fugitive just a while? He isn't here to serve "an eternal Ignorance / Of our futility." This can't be what you fear and "mean by Nothing." There would be no point in having a garden with "more weeds than lentils." The shadows now around us won't last. I was "evil" to "let you be afraid of me." Lazarus concludes by saying that he knows not what the Master saw in his eyes, or why he is here again, or what lies ahead; nevertheless, he does know that the Master, whose eyes were all he saw, "looked . . . / . . . as if he knew."

The brief story of Lazarus, of which Robinson wrote this follow-up, is in John 11: 1–44.

Nicholas Ayo reminds readers that in the biblical account of Lazarus, Jesus, Martha, and Mary speak, but Lazarus does not. Ayo adds that Robinson gives voice to Lazarus and sharpens the contrast between the more active Martha and the more contemplative Mary, just as the sisters were characterized earlier in Luke 10:38–42. Edwin S. Fussell notes that, "Deprived of the total context that alone could have made the action fully meaningful, Robinson's characters are brought immediately face to face with the essential terror and ambiguities of the situation." Wallace L. Anderson seems certain of the import of "Lazarus" when he writes this: "As Mary and Martha talk with Lazarus, all three gradually become aware that Lazarus' death and resurrection was [sic] Christ's means of foreshadowing the Crucifixion and making them understand its significance." Such was Christ's knowledge, surely; but Robinson's poem ends without the three siblings' fully understanding.

Ayo explicates "Lazarus" in ranging detail, thus: As to why Jesus wept, it was perhaps because He foreknew Lazarus's unhappy future, or perhaps because of His love for Mary, not her brother. The flower Martha sees may be a lily, symbol of death and resurrection. The white-robed Lazarus appearing to Mary and saying only her name parallels Jesus's emerging from the sepulchre and speaking to Mary (Magdalene) (John 20:14–15). The "burden" which Lazarus forgives Jesus for placing on him may be the moral obligation to forgive in order to be forgiven (Matthew 6:14–15). Mary's hoping for a "sign of a new joy" echoes "tidings of great joy," followed by "a sign," in connection with the Nativity story (Luke 2:10–12). As for Lazarus's telling Mary that there is something worse than death, one may note the following biblical passage: "And fear not them which kill the body, but are not able to kill the soul: but rather fear him which is able to destroy both soul and body in hell" (Matthew 10:28). Robinson has Lazarus tell Mary that his explanation would be incompre-

hensible so as to remind readers that Lazarus could not later advise the five brothers of Dives, in hell, to repent in time (Luke 16:19–31). The weedy garden mentioned by Lazarus is related to the tares-and-wheat parable (Matthew 13:34–40). Ayo deciphers Robinson's method in "Lazarus" thus: "to isolate the mystery of death by a series of negatives, often only implied, which, while never revealing the unknown, encircle it with conclusions about what death must not be." (Sources: W. Anderson [1968], 125; Ayo, 112–34 passim, 223; Fussell [1954], 165)

The League of Three. This was a band of friends in Gardiner, Maine, namely Robinson and his boyhood schoolmates Edward Gustavus Moore and Arthur R. Gledhill.* They formed the group during their senior year in high school. All clearly bright, they were granted the privilege of skipping study hall and repairing to the belfry, where they smoked and opened the roof scuttle to avoid detection. To distinguish themselves, they designed and wore little triangular insignias, often met socially, played cribbage, cut capers, gossiped about girls, read Virgil and swore "by the Styx." Robinson timidly liked Ed's sister Mabel Moore. As part of the Gardiner high-school graduation ceremony (1888), Gledhill delivered an address in Greek. Way led on to way; by the early 1890s Moore was isolated by employment and marriage, and Gledhill, a Congregational minister's son, had gone to become a divinity student at St. Lawrence University and then to teach. Robinson kept in touch with Gledhill by faithful correspondence. In letters (October 22, 1893; November 11, 1893) to their mutual friend Harry de Forest Smith,* Robinson reports that Gledhill was teaching at a school in New York and was married. Hermann Hagedorn* and Chard Powers Smith,* in their biographies of Robinson, quote numerous letters Robinson sent Gledhill, as late as 1896. Still later, reunions back at Gardiner were possible but naturally rare. (Sources: Brower, 56; Hagedorn; C. Smith; *Untriangulated Stars*, xx, 114)

Ledoux, Louis V. (1880–1948). Louis Vernon Ledoux was a poet, an authority on

Japanese art, and an executive in the assaying firm owned by his father, a metallurgical chemist. Through Percy MacKaye* Robinson met Ledoux, who occasionally visited Mac-Kaye at the Judson Hotel (1905). Ledoux was a guest at the MacDowell Colony,* where Robinson met him and his bright and charming wife Jean Ledoux (1911). Robinson was a welcome visitor at the Ledoux country home at Cornwall-on-the-Hudson (beginning in 1912). Ledoux wrote "A Discussion of the Exact Value of Robinson's Poetry" (*New York Times Review of Books*, September 29, 1912). It aimed at amplifying ideas expressed in an essay on Robinson by Joyce Kilmer (1886–1918, soldier-author killed in France) published in the September 8 issue of the *Times Review*. Ledoux published another laudatory essay, "Edwin Arlington Robinson" (Minneapolis *Journal*, November 3, 1912). (Richard Cary reprints both of Ledoux's articles.) When Charles Scribner's Sons, who had published Robinson's *The Town Down the River* (1910), declined to publish *Van Zorn*, Ledoux, who had influence with the Macmillan Company, persuaded its editors to issue the awkward play (1914) and thereby get better books by Robinson later. Ledoux dedicated *The Story of Eleusis: A Lyrical Drama* (1916) to Robinson, who had dedicated *The Porcupine* to him the year before. Robinson remained friendly with Ledoux, who ministered to the mortally ill poet until the very end. Ledoux and Lewis Montefiore Isaacs* were Robinson's literary executors.

Shortly after Robinson died, Ledoux penned a "Memoir" about his long-time friend, in which he "remembered . . . the gentleman of quiet humor, of subtle intuitions; the man who could be trusted to be loyal and who in all the give and take of life never failed in that kindliness of judgment which though it was in essence an expression of his own marked personality, yet was based on an intuitive and sympathetic understanding of all that is most pathetically human — the possibilities of good in what seems evil, the thwarted hopes and unfulfilled aspirations of the people he knew or imagined."

Hermann Hagedorn,* who knew Ledoux well, peppers his biography of Robinson with quotations from Robinson's many letters to Ledoux and his wife — about his poetry, his writing regimen, their friends, and his drinking. Ledoux wrote the lyrics for a tune that Robinson had composed much earlier and that he wrote about in a letter (April 21, 1897) to Edith Brower.* Their friend Lewis Montefiore Isaacs* provided a piano accompaniment, and the work, entitled "Slumber Song," was published in 1935. Ledoux wrote the entry on Robinson in *Dictionary of American Biography* (vol. 21, 1944). (Sources: Brower, 39, 41; Cary [1974], 240–42, 244–46; Hagedorn; Ledoux, 10)

"Leffingwell" (1910). Sonnets. There are three, numbered and titled.

"I — The Lure." Although Leffingwell was a sad case, we can't define him as nothing but "parasite and sycophant." Who knows what light lured and then abandoned the "sorry knight"? He probably was "deceived" and "believed." He certainly fibbed.

"II — The Quickstep." He is dead now, and "we do not know / How much is ended or how much begun." When we get buried, others may say the same about us. He played, lost, was loved and disliked, and departed. We don't know what his failures cost him.

"III — Requiescat." He seemed unaware of sorrows and pains — until when dying he blasted "each of us" profanely, vehemently, and unforgettably. He told us we weren't to be puzzled, cry, or want him to return. Maybe he's with happy ghosts like himself. We dare not query. He promised to haunt us if we did.

In "Calverly's," Leffingwell is described as having "eerie joy," and in "Clavering" as being killed by "fiery-frantic indolence." Emma Robinson* and Ruth Nivison* say that the subject of "Leffingwell" is about Robinson's brother Herman Robinson* "and his apparent downfall." Scott Donaldson, however, feels that Leffingwell, "unaccommodated to the demands of this world," may have been suggested to Robinson, as the dishevelled stranger probably also was in "Alma Mater," by his friend and "congenital sponge" Joseph Lewis French.* (Sources: Donaldson [1969], 47; E. Robinson, 14)

"**L'Envoi**" *see* "**L'Envoi**" under E

"**Leonora**" (1910). Poem. Leonora's funeral and grave have been beautifully prepared, with roses, pinks, and lilies, and with cedars walling the site. Her shapely limbs will be attractively clothed. The place will soon be quiet and dark; "But the builders, looking forward," could imagine "only . . . / Darker nights for Leonora than to-night shall ever be."

Emery Neff interprets this elegy thus: "Leonora . . . death saves from an inevitable path of shame." He adds that "the tripping of hexameters and the idyllic description of her grave do their best to disguise and soften her somber story." The poor girl, soon to be hidden in the woods, is even likened to "a little dryad." Although Edwin S. Fussell identifies the meter in "Leonora" as "paeonic[,] . . . three [syllables] accented and one unacccented," almost every line of the poem could be easily read in such a whisper as to turn hexameters into tetrameters. (Sources: Fussell [1954], 140; Neff, 155)

"**Lily Condillac**." A series of short stories Robinson wrote in the early 1890s, could not sell, and destroyed. (Source: Hagedorn, 102)

"**Limericks**" (1937, 1968, 1968). Three limericks. A man in Sabattis (Maine) shot a skunk beyond a lattice but misplaced his hat in doing so. When a certain poor Hindu needs pants, he must make his "skin do." Ransom, an artist, painted his hands green and showed them through his transom. These limericks are more fun when read than when paraphrased. (Sources: Brower, 147; Cary [1975], 46, 181)

"**Lingard and the Stars**" (1910). Sonnet. A bunch of the boys are indulging their friend Lingard at a table-rapping session. When the table lurches at Lingard, it raps out a message: Remnants of Lingard will have to exist after the end of the world. He is grateful but wishes the ghost would name itself. He stands by the window until some bells ring midnight. Then he gets Clavering to walk with him under the stars.

Both Lingard and Clavering appear also in "Calverly's." Scott Donaldson regards Lingard as less interesting than Clavering and Leffingwell, because Lingard "is given to séances and table-rappings and moon-gazing, and walks among the stars in full retreat from the mundane." Shortly before his death, Robinson's father Edward Robinson* became interested in séances, table-rapping, and the like, and his family indulged him by participating. In 1905 or so, Robinson also did some table-rapping at the Judson Hotel in New York City with various friends residing in the hotel or near it, including Olivia Howard Dunbar (later the wife of Ridgely Torrence*). In a reminiscence about Robinson, John Cowper Powys (1872–1963), the British man of letters, mentions telling Robinson of his delight in encountering the rare word "laelaps" (a type of sea monster) in this line in "Lingard and the Stars": "Come out, you lælaps, and inhale the night." (Sources: Donaldson [1969], 46; Hagedorn, 225, 238; Powys, 2)

"**Lisette and Eileen**" (1916). Poem. Lisette is addressing Eileen, who is absent but is the subject of severe rebuke. It seems that a man they both knew is now dead. A timely word from Eileen might have preserved Lisette's friendship with him. Eileen contended that she withheld that word to "save him." She saved him, all right. But the result was that the man heard words damaging to Lisette, who is now something "that has no name," a mere "worn toy." Lisette says that all the man saw in Eileen was her black hair and blue eyes, and concludes that Eileen, though a survivor, has lost her appeal and is now virtually dead.

Louis Coxe feels that the opening line of "Lisette and Eileen"—"When he was here alive, Eileen"—is "tricky . . . , start[ing] off with a burst that seems melodramatic, too calculatedly arresting and hence self-defeating." Emma Robinson* and Ruth Nivison,* however, contend that the word "dead," which ends the first stanza, means simply "silent." Moreover, they assert that the poem concerns Robinson's friendship with Emma in 1900 or so. (Sources: Coxe, 169; E. Robinson, 9)

"**Llewellyn and the Tree**" (1916). Poem. The narrator knew Llewellyn back in Tilbury

Town. He was mild, idealistic, long-suffering. Llewellyn's wife Priscilla was shrewish and constantly "goad[ed] him for what God left out" (of him). If their temperaments hadn't gotten out of balance, he would've stayed put and eventually "gone his quiet way to glory." But every hope he had, she shook down, until their "labored harmony" ended. She nagged him "once too far, / Not knowing quite the man he was." Just in time, "roses . . . in his path" appeared, in the form of a woman the townspeople regarded as mostly "civet, coral, rouge, and years." So, when Priscilla raised her voice, "shriller than the sound of saws," that nice afternoon in October, Llewellyn took off forever. With him went what the townspeople called "The Scarlet One."

After waiting 20 years, Priscilla died. Then the narrator chanced to see Llewellyn on Broadway, selling "fictive merchandise," some of which the narrator bought. Llewellyn says, "I've tried the world, and found it good, / For more than twenty years this fall." After staying "calm too long," he developed "an unholy guile." He decided not to water "the wine of life / Too thin," found strength late and some speed on another track, and couldn't go back. With energy dwindling, here he is. Remembering in Llewellyn's "worn satiric eyes" something like "immortal youth," the narrator is left to wonder: Llewellyn may now be off somewhere trying "to find the Tree / Of Knowledge, out of which he fell"; may still be dreaming of "rouge and coral"; or may be in a nameless grave.

Emma Robinson* and Ruth Nivison* identify Llewellyn as Will Landers, an editor in Gardiner, Maine, who escaped a shrewish wife by running away with a woman who understood him. Edwin S. Fussell notes that Robinson's reference to the Bible in "Llewellyn and the Tree" "starts in the title, and has to do with the Tree of Knowledge and its part in terminating relations between a hard-pressed husband and his sharp-tongued wife." Fussell concludes that "[c]omplex associations of the temptation and fall of man are involved." John Drinkwater (1882–1937), British poet and dramatist, calls "Llewellyn and the Tree" "a poem of perfect dramatic proportions." Ellsworth Barnard defines it as a "comedy . . .

[in which] the laughter becomes almost hilarious, and [which] is only thoughtful at the end." (Sources: Barnard, 185; Drinkwater, 260; Fussell [1954], 158; E. Robinson, 9)

"London Bridge" (1919). Dramatic duologue. It is between a husband and his wife. He: Why ask me if I hear the children? They aren't making a racket. She: Their singing falls on my heart like snow in summer on a mountain peak. Stop them. He: We've returned to town for a dance tonight. Speak plainly. She: I won't hide the fact that "I met him, and I talked with him — today." He: You poisoned him before I knew you. Explain. She: Don't pretend you don't know. He: Be truthful, as though your salvation depends on it. She: Don't try to hide what you must have known earlier. Don't smilingly lord it over me with talk about "possession[s]." My future challenges will be harder for you to bear than your own. I'm not "on your threshold all my life"; let me into your hitherto secret rooms. He: Your gibberish tries my patience. I rescued you from living in an attic with a cat. I admit I know what you were getting at, but say it plainly. She: Is it useless that I said I met him? Why grin and make me despise you? He: Be careful. Maybe I know better than you what that fellow wants that you pretend is "a genius." She: You think I'm making believe about him? Yes, I met him. Now the future is up to you. Listen to me. Doesn't it help that I say I'll try? Nothing much will matter "If you save me, and I lose him." I lied earlier, but I'm not lying now. He: I waited silently while you "dragged an old infatuation from a tomb." Air it, and it will disappear. She: I returned just now, saw you "at your table," figured this would be the final time and I'd tell you what I learned about you since we got married — that while you thought you were teaching me you learned nothing essential about me. I kept awake by playing dumb. You put only dollar values on everything. You can't neglect me any longer. He: I've made sales, caused windfalls. You sound goofy. Let's delete this conversation. She: Don't challenge me. He: I wonder if God really gave women reason. She: I wonder if God

makes believe that women who are giving
All they have in holy loathing to a stranger all their
    lives
Are the wise ones who build houses in the Bible.

He: You're a devil. She: Wouldn't you miss me if I frittered away to nothing? You might not long to embrace me if you knew that "I made you into someone else." You have a considerable future. He: I doubt it. She: What would our children think of you if we die now? Do you hear their singing? He: Damn them. She: Why? Well, go ahead. He: You're a devil. She: No, a prophet. I see and welcome the end of all our illusions, but you ought to look for "a release." Tonight we'll dance like "merry spectres" on the grave of our unspoken lies. Meanwhile, go away a while. Lord, won't the children stop that noise?

For irony, this drawn-out sequence is in cheery iambic and trochaic heptameter and octameter stanzas. The title suggests that while the children sing and play "All Fall Down" upstairs, the emotional bridge linking their parents is in danger of collapse. Chard Powers Smith* equates the unhappy couple with Robinson's brother Herman Robinson* and his wife Emma Robinson;* but Smith is uncertain whether the other man is a suitor Emma almost accepted before meeting and marrying Herman, or whether he is Robinson himself, since the husband in the poem sarcastically calls him a genius, i.e., the brilliant poet-brother. Charles Cestre* implicitly hopes that in "London Bridge" the husband of this woman whose "nerves are not steady" will "keep . . . cool and, with mixed argument and authority [watch out, Frenchman!], bring . . . her back to her senses." (Sources: Cestre, 14; C. Smith, 148–49, 198)

"The Long Race" (1920). Sonnet. An aging man walks painfully up a hill to a house where a friend would be. Soon they would remove the curtain of 50 years that "had hung / Between the two ambitions they had slain." He gets there. They talk little. Before bidding farewell, he remarks that the friend's weather vane, that of a "little horse . . . on the run," is still there. Going down the hill again and figuring "the little horse had won," he awaits

the next train back out of the region.

The reader doesn't even know whether the friend the man visits is a man or a woman; but it is obvious that when time separates two people, a real reunion is often impossible. According to Ruth Nivison,* Emma Robinson,* her mother, marked this poem "Nov. 1909," which was when Robinson proposed marriage to Emma, his widowed sister-in-law, for the last unsuccessful time. He did, however, propose later. Chard Powers Smith* reports that when in 1909 Robinson visited Emma in Farmingdale, Maine, near Gardiner, he could see a Victorian house nearby with a stable that had a cupola topped by a running-horse weather vane. (Sources: E. Robinson, 18; C. Smith, 225)

"Look at Edward Alphabet" (1938). Poem. Four-line jingle. It begins "Look at Edward Alphabet" and continues to the effect that he's on his way home to pray, but he's plenty drunk and it's "the Sabbath day!" Robinson used to recite this ditty in the mid–1890s. Robinson included it in a letter (December 14, 1895) to Harry de Forest Smith.* Hermann Hagedorn* included it in his biography of Robinson. (Sources: Hagedorn, 96, 389; *Untriangulated Stars*, 238)

"Lost Anchors" (1921). Sonnet. An old sailor, long beached, tells about a ship that sank in a harbor a century ago. Divers, aware of a persistent legend concerning it, went down and found in its "dark hulk" numerous anchors that had been "seized and seen no more." The sailor, to enliven his leisure by suggesting an analogy, talks a lot about himself, "whose mother should have had no sons."

"Lost Anchors" is such a difficult poem that Ellsworth Barnard, first, asks several rhetorical questions about the nature of the legend and about who stole the anchors, and what was so sad in the sailor's life, and how these unanswered mysteries can coalesce into an analogy; and, second, concludes that "the puzzle [remains] insoluble." Yvor Winters concludes, with no evidence, that the sailor was illegitimate. (Married women often regret giving birth.) Lawrance Thompson opines that "the old sailor had started his life-voyage with a cargo of spiritual and moral 'anchors' which he regrets having lost." Robert Mezey begins his comments by saying that the poem "is rather oblique in its bits and hints of narrative," and ends by professing that "the appropriation of the anchors is analogous to the old man's life in that he too has lost his anchors," and is "useless," "warped," and "enbittered." S. A. Cohen defines the verb "to seize" as used in the line "Anchors . . . seized and seen no more" in the nautical sense of "to bind," meaning "to secure" the anchor to its cable to make it ready to be used. Cohen then posits that "the ship never cleared the harbor." (Sources: Barnard, 41; S. Cohen, 68; Mezey, 237; L. Thompson, 135; Winters, 39)

Louis, Alfred Hyman. An English Jew who became a Catholic. He was educated at Cambridge, and was versatile in writing, music, editing, politics, and the law. According to Theodore Maynard,* Louis was blocked from political advancement by William Gladstone, prime minister of England, for comments he made critical of the government in his book *English Foreign Policy*. (Maynard, and Richard Cary as well, say that Louis was the model for Mordecai in *Daniel Deronda*, by George Eliot, who repeatedly visited her until he bored her.) Louis migrated to New York, where Robinson met him (1897). At that time, Louis was living in an attic on West 8th Street. Robinson enjoyed his brilliant conversation but eventually found him to be such an aggressive pest and leech that he abandoned him (June 1901), although Robinson was conscience-stricken afterwards. Eventually, Louis returned to England, where he died.

Robinson partly modeled the hero of *Captain Craig* on Louis, later had him in mind when he wrote "Flammonde," and still later dedicated *The Glory of the Nightingales* to Louis's memory. "Evensong," a poem by Louis, is surely the basis for the name of the character Evensong in *Amaranth*. Edith Brower,* who knew Louis in New York, describes him in her "Memories of Edwin Arlington Robinson" as "the most utterly perfect specimen of the raggedy Bohemian variety of high intellectual" and confirms the likelihood that Captain Craig is patterned on Louis.

Bacon Collamore* describes Louis as "a sad wreck of a man," whose "intended greatness" had been "shattered" by "some tragedy," and who sported a "patriarchal white beard" but was "garbed in a long, dirty frock coat, broken boots, frayed trousers, and grimy shirt, open at the throat and always without a tie." (Sources: Brower, 211; Cary [1974], 277–78; Collamore, 11; Hagedorn, 132–36, 183–84; Maynard [1935], 274; C. Smith, 196, 383–84; Sutliffe)

Lovett, Robert Morss (1870–1956). Educator, author, and reformer. After graduating from Harvard (1892), Lovett taught English at the Univerity of Chicago (1893–1936). He married Ida Campbell Mott-Smith (1895; they had three children). Lovett and his friend William Vaughn Moody* co-authored *A History of English Literature* (1902) and *A First View of English Literature* (1905). Lovett also wrote a play, novels, a biography of Edith Wharton (1925), and his autobiography (1948), and did much editorial work over the years. He supported America's entry into the First World War but became disillusioned when his eldest son was killed in action at Belleau Wood (1919). He worked with Jane Addams (1860–1935) at Hull House, her celebrated Chicago social settlement. Lovett was so liberal that conservatives in the Illinois Senate tried successfully to have him dismissed from the university (1935). He remained so unabashed that he got himself questioned by the Un-American Activities Committee in Washington, D.C., and labeled subversive (1943).

Lovett was a casual friend of Robinson at Harvard when Robinson first went there (1891). Robinson occasionally mentions Lovett in early letters to Harry de Forest Smith.* (Sources: Hagedorn, 68; Morison, 430; C. Smith, 119; *Untriangulated Stars*)

Lowell, Amy (1874–1925). Poet and critic. Amy Lowell was born in Brookline, Massachusetts, into a wealthy branch of the famous New England Lowells. She was privately educated, acquired her family home (1900), was involved in community affairs, determined early to become a poet (1902), began what grew into a huge collection of John Keats material, and published *A Dome of Many-Coloured Glass* (1912), the first of her 11 books of verse. Often traveling, Lowell admired imagism in modern poetry (1913), met Ezra Pound (1913) but soon quarreled with him (1914), and began to lead the imagist movement in the United States. She lectured, gave public readings, and published many poems and much criticism. Her *Tendencies in Modern American Poetry* (1917) focused on Hilda Doolittle ("H.D."), John Gould Fletcher, Robert Frost, Edgar Lee Masters, Carl Sandburg, and Robinson. She is said to have been the first woman to lecture at Harvard (1919). Her 1922 essay on Robinson, "A Bird's Eye View of E. A. Robinson," improves on much in her earlier *Tendencies*. Her lifelong devotion to Keats resulted in her splendid biography of him (1925). Work on it hastened her death, from complications of obesity and chronic hernias. Lowell, slightly taller than five feet, weighed 240 pounds.

Laura E. Richards* gently rebukes Lowell for her erroneous comments about Gardiner, Maine, in *Tendencies*. (See "The House on the Hill.") In a letter (November 26, 1915) to Lowell about her *Six French Poets* (1915), Robinson neutrally comments that it demonstrates her "infernal industry" and performs "a good service to the poets and the public." (The six French poets were Paul Fort, Remy de Gourmont, Francis Jammes, Henri de Régnier, Albert Samain, and Émile Verhaeren.) In another letter to her (October 31, 1916), Robinson names six poems (misnaming two) in her *Men, Women and Ghosts* (1916) and says they gave him "the most pleasure." However, only "Patterns" among the six poems is standing the test of time well. Richard Cary presents sufficient facts concerning Robinson's relationship with Amy, whom, Cary notes, "[i]n private . . . Robinson referred to . . . acridly as 'She'—a species of formless, hovering monster." (Sources: Cary [1974], 292, 292–93; Richards [1936], 53; *Selected Letters*, 88, 99)

Luhan, Mabel Dodge (1879–1962) *see* **Dodge, Mabel**

"Luke Havergal" (1896). Poem. The persona's beloved comes out of her grave to urge Luke Havergal to "Go to the Western gate," where he will see "the vines cling crimson on the wall" and where "The leaves will whisper" to him about her. No dawn light from the East will help him. Faith will lead him to her. If he places trust in her, "she will call."

Theodore Roosevelt* in a review in *The Outlook* (August 12, 1905) gave Robinson a presidential push and made himself an all-too-typical Robinson aficionado by saying that he wasn't sure he understood "Luke Havergal" but was certain he liked it. A. A. Raven offers a standard interpretation when he suggests that Luke Havergal is finally inspired by memory and comes to realize that "the way to preserve love is not to struggle against time by living in the past, but to submit oneself to the future, i.e., to have faith." Walter Gierasch regards one puzzling couplet in the poem — "God slays Himself with every leaf that flies, / And hell is more than half of paradise"— to mean that nature's inevitable seasonal death alerts everyone to the fact that there is no perfection by itself but that everything is relative, with pleasure amounting to less than half of life. N. E. Dunn explicates the parts of "Luke Havergal" showing that "Western gate and crimson leaves are central to the imagery" of the poem. Mathilde M. Parlett says that Robinson is discounting the values of Eastern religions and is instead implicitly offering Christian symbolism in "the 'wall' to which clings Christianity," as indicated by "the vine and the branches from *John* XV.1–6." Ronald E. McFarland seeks and seems to find a possible biblical source for "Luke Havergal," noting that "Havergal" sounds like "prodigal," that the parable of the Prodigal Son is found in Luke 15, and that Havergal therefore must also have sinned and will soon repent. McFarland also contends that Havergal resembles Dante in an earlier infernal situation, and that in the story of Havergal, also a wandering sinner, the unnamed "she" may be equated with Dante's ever-sought Beatrice.

Reading suicide into the poem, Ronald Moran argues, first, that "[t]here is every reason to suspect that the woman . . . committed suicide," and, second, that "[t]hrough the refrain and clipped echo techniques, Robinson gives the poem a movement which is instrumental in reflecting the ripeness at the moment for Luke to commit suicide." Echoing Moran, Lawrance Thompson says that this "tantalizingly 'inferential' poem . . . [may be] best understood if considered as a dramatization of a psychological and psychopathic state of suicidal self-delusion, evoked by the man's grief over the death of his beloved"; she seems to be calling him to die, pass through the gate, and join her. John Miller explicates Robinson's "The dark will end the dark" to mean that the dark of death will end the dark of the world. Richard P. Adams splits hairs by saying that the narrator advises Luke to go to the gate but not through it. Robert Mezey tantalizes would-be explicators of "Luke Havergal" by suggesting that "since the voice of the poem speaks in both the first and third persons, . . . there might . . . be a third character, perhaps the other man in a love triangle, who is luring Luke Havergal to join the woman in death."

Despite the good intentions of these critics, and others, it seems reasonable to agree with a statement by Louis Untermeyer* that "Luke Havergal" is a "haunting [poem] . . . which no one quite understands but which everyone likes to hear." (Sources: R. Adams, 132; Dunn [1973], 17; Gierasch; McFarland; Miller, 355; Mezey, 217; Moran [1967], 389, 391; Parlett; Raven; L. Thompson, 139; Untermeyer, 5)

MacDowell, Edward (1860–1908). Composer. Edward Alexander MacDowell, born in New York City, showed musical talent early; so his mother took him to Europe to study piano and composition, first in Paris (1876–1878) and then Germany (1878–1884), where he also taught piano (1881–1882). One of his pupils was an American named Marian Griswold Nivens. The two returned to New York, where they married (1884; see MacDowell, Marian Nivens). After more time in Germany (1884–1887), MacDowell and his wife returned to America, first in Boston (1888–1896) and then New York. Although MacDowell was a competent concert pianist, he became better known as America's greatest composer by the turn of the century. Among

his numerous compositions, the following may be mentioned: *Lancelot and Elaine* (1888; often considered the best of his symphonies), *Second Piano Concerto in D Minor* (1889), and *Indian Suite* (1892, orchestral suite incorporating Native-American tunes). MacDowell established the first department of music at Columbia University (1896) and headed it with time off for tours and vacations until a dispute with Nicholas Murray Butler (1862–1947), Columbia's president (beginning in 1902), led to his resignation (1904). MacDowell had been unsuccessfully trying to offer undergraduate students courses in various arts and to develop a fine-arts faculty. He had studied painting as a youth and published his own *Verses* (1905). Ongoing unpleasant publicity involving Butler and MacDowell in the *New York Times* followed, and MacDowell's disappointment contributed to his tragic mental collapse and early death. The MacDowells, who had no children, relaxed in their summer home, called Hillcrest (see "Hillcrest"), on farm acreage just west of Peterborough, New Hampshire, which from 1905 they planned to convert into a colony supporting summer visiting residents active in the arts. It evolved into the famous MacDowell Colony.* (Source: Hagedorn, 261–63)

MacDowell, Marian Nivens (1857–1957). (Full name: Marian Griswold Nivens MacDowell.) Wife of Edward MacDowell.* Her father was a Wall Street lawyer. When her mother died, Marian, still a child but the oldest of three daughters, became the household leader. Injured as a child, she spent much of her life walking with crutches. She met her future husband when she began studying piano for three years under his tutelage in Germany. The two married in 1884, the year of her father's death. She agreed to the marriage on condition that MacDowell discontinue working, live with her on her substantial inheritance, and devote himself to musical composition. A miscarriage prevented her from having children. They planned the MacDowell Colony* together.

After Edward MacDowell died (1908), Marian resumed piano playing, toured and gave concert performances of her husband's pieces, and developed their summer home west of Peterborough, New Hampshire, into a colony to support writers and artists on summer grants. George Pierce Baker,* the famous Harvard teacher of dramatic composition, knew about the colony and told Hermann Hagedorn* in 1911 that Robinson should go there and write in its secluded and inspiring environs. He reluctantly agreed to give the place a try that summer. It became his salvation, and Marian became his guardian angel. A taxicab accident (1923) oddly reorganized her spine, after which she could walk without crutches. Robinson became profoundly grateful and loyal to Marian, and to her financial contributors. Rollo Walter Brown* reports that Robinson once said, "There's nothing in the world I wouldn't do for Mrs. MacDowell." Brown adds that Robinson "never ceased to express his gratitude to Mrs. MacDowell" and wondered what would have become of him if he hadn't been able to spend summers at the colony. In the many years before her death, Mrs. MacDowell traveled throughout the United States, gave lectures and piano recitals, and raised public awareness, funds, and support for the colony. Laura E. Richards* attended one such lecture in Augusta, Maine (perhaps in the 1920s), and was all atwitter, as were other members of the audience from Gardiner, when Mrs. MacDowell said that "Augusta" must be proud of their native son, Robinson. When Cyril Clemens, cousin of Mark Twain, asked Mrs. MacDowell to contribute a few words to his *Mark Twain Quarterly* for 1938, she graciously wrote this: "It is one of the great joys of my life that we had an opportunity of giving Mr. Robinson something he always said he could not have found save at the MacDowell Colony." She goes on to remember that his "outstanding quality . . . was his great simplicity, to which one might add 'quality of mercy' — his compassion for man and his possible weakness — rather than judgment." When the New England hurricane of 1938 blew down hundreds of trees and damaged several buildings at the colony, Marian MacDowell, aged 82, went on a final concert tour, raised funds, and reopened the place (1939). Mrs. MacDowell wrote *Random Notes on Edward MacDowell and His Music* (1950)

and *The First 20 Years of the MacDowell Colony* (1951). (Sources: R. Brown, 17, 69; MacDowell, 16; Richards [1931], 381–82)

The MacDowell Colony. The composer Edward MacDowell* and his wife Marian Nivens MacDowell* bought a small farm in Peterborough, New Hampshire (1896). They enjoyed summering and working amid its peaceful surroundings. Since MacDowell understood the creative, professional, and social advantages that accrued when artists in different disciplines mingled socially, he and his wife dreamed about converting their property into a community in which artists could retreat, work, relax, and share ideas. Various prominent persons, as varied as Andrew Carnegie, Grover Cleveland, and J. P. Morgan, and also New York's Mendelssohn Glee Club combined to establish a fund to honor MacDowell and to further his and his wife's idea. The first "colonists," however, had hardly begun to arrive when MacDowell died (1908). Before 1911, the only colonists were female. Locally grown food helped feed the colonists.

Inspired by the widowed Marian MacDowell, physical aspects of the colony were expanded from a house, a one-room lodge, and about 60 acres, until the present total of some 32 widely separated artists' studios were built on 450 hilly and forested acres. Mount Monadnock towers majestically nearby.

Robinson first began residing in happy summer months at the colony in 1911. Apprehensive at first but inspired almost instantly in every way, he returned each summer until his final healthy one (1934). For most of these years, Robinson used the Louise Veltin Studio, which was funded by the Alumni of the Veltrin School and built in 1912 and 1913. It is said that in the Veltin Studio Thornton Wilder wrote *Our Town*, his 1938 Pulitzer Prize-winning play. This rustic little cabin, built of fieldstone, has a recessed door under its west gable, log rafters, wall plates with round trunk ends extending under the eaves, a staircase ascending to a window over the door, and a peaked slate roof. The interior has a red cement floor, stucco walls, substantial light from deep-silled windows, and a stone-manteled fieldstone fireplace let into the north wall and giving into an outside fieldstone chimney. A dirt road passes the east end of the studio. This studio, like the others, often similarly designed, is bare almost to Spartan austerity, on purpose to stimulate creative work and minimize distractions. Inside each studio is a wall plaque, inscribed with the names of occupant after grateful occupant. Breakfasts and dinners are served at a big barn called Colony Hall. Picnic lunch baskets are unobtrusively delivered at each artist's front door. Sleeping quarters are available in three nearby buildings, and a library is also close. Meetings, lectures, concerts, impromptu events, and bright chatter promote conviviality, new ideas, and collaborative ventures.

Robinson fraternized with so much modesty, courtesy, humor, conviviality, and camaraderie that he became a legend in his time. In 1922, the colony published a list of its former colonists. Included were 89 writers, 33 composers, 23 painters and sculptors, and 19 performers. *The Peterborough Anthology*, published in 1923, includes works by poets who had resided at the colony. Robinson is represented by "Fragment," "Hillcrest," "Monadnock Through the Trees," "Mr. Flood's Party," "Rembrandt to Rembrandt," and "Veteran Sirens." Back in 1936, Bacon Collamore* cautioned would-be buyers not to believe certain bookdealers' false claims that *The Peterborough Anthology* "contain[s] . . . the first book-appearance of poems written by Robinson," since these six poems had all previously appeared in other books, which Collamore carefully specifies.

Robinson made many new friends in the colony, especially but not always in the dining and recreation rooms at Colony Hall. They soon included Esther Willard Bates,* Percy MacKaye,* Carty Ranck,* and Ridgely Torrence.* Among other colonists less closely associated with Robinson, but still persons with whom he interacted on occasion, the following may be named: Amy Marcy Beach, composer; Frederika Beatty,* writer; William Rose Benét, poet, critic, husband of Elinor Wylie; Maxwell Bodenheim, ill-starred bohemian man of letters; Lilla Cabot Perry,

painter, wife of Thomas Sergeant Perry;* Mary Colum and Padraic Colum, Irish-American husband-and-wife writers; Mabel Daniels,* composer; Frederick Lansing Day, playwright; John Erskine, professor, novelist; Parker Fillmore, educator, banker, fiction writer; Herbert Gorman, critic; Margaret MacLean, educator, composer; Douglas Moore, composer; Lloyd R. Morris,* critic; Frances Patterson, film critic; Grant Reynard, artist; Constance Rourke, author; Robert Haven Schauffler, poet, biographer; Leonora Speyer, violinist, poet, educator; Nancy Bird Turner, author; Louis Untermeyer,* editor, poet; Margaret Widdemer, author; Thornton Wilder, novelist, playwright; and Elinor Wylie, poet, wife of William Rose Benét. In 1955 the colony began to remain open and operational all year.

Talent is all that is required for one to apply. Emerging artists as well as artists already of repute are welcomed. There are no residency fees, but modest ones are accepted if volunteered. To date, more than 5,400 architects, artists, composers, filmmakers, printmakers, sculptors, and writers have come from all parts of the United States and abroad and have benefited from their almost paradise-like time at the MacDowell Colony. Each year as many as 1,200 applications generate more than 200 fellowships, for from two weeks to two months each. In needful cases, grants are available to defray travel expenses. The U. S. Department of the Interior designated the colony a National Historic Landmark (1963), and three years later it was entered on the National Register of Historic Places. In 1997 it was awarded the National Medal of Arts for "nurturing and inspiring many of this century's finest artists" and for offering outstanding artists "the opportunity to work within a dynamic community." The names "MacDowell Colony" and "Robinson" are inextricably intertwined. (Sources: Collamore, 32; Hagedorn, 261–71; C. Smith, 380–87)

"MacDowell's Legacy to Art" (1925). Essay. Robinson says that once in a while something happens to shake the belief that Americans are "an unclassified conglomerate of materialists and money-worshippers." We certainly are more than that, and "proof of our latent idealism" is the fact that the *Pictorial Review* has given Mrs. Edward MacDowell (see MacDowell, Marian Nivens) its Annual Achievement Award for 1923. The sum of $5,000 honors a woman who makes the most distinctive achievement in art, drama, education, industry, literature, music, science, or sociology in a given year. Mrs. MacDowell, through the Edward MacDowell Association (see the MacDowell Colony), has enabled "creative workers" to advance more rapidly than otherwise in various branches of the fine arts. In 17 years, she has overcome difficulties and misunderstandings and has increased three buildings on 60 acres to 30 buildings on six hundred acres, thus fulfilling the dream of her late husband Edward MacDowell* "for the furtherance of American art."

Robinson forcefully advocates the establishment of a $300,000 endowment. First, he says it is necessary to tell those who haven't seen the colony what it does. Usually, 20 to 25 residents are composers, painters, sculptors, and writers already well established. Many, though not most, will contribute greatly to "our cultural development." In a figurative sea are islands of various eminence; in a forest, a garden, are peculiarly developed trees, flowers. All combine to "show what has been going on underneath." Trees and flowers are often cultivated, to their advantage; but talented people are often nurtured less.

Some "artist[s]" will produce, despite difficulties; but, as in the case of Thomas Hood, their creations are often "tragic fragment[s]." Adversity may stimulate to a degree. But Richard Wagner complained about his early "hardships and disappointments," and his work is better for aid from "the long-suffering and magnanimous [Franz von] Liszt and the peculiar King Ludwig of Bavaria." When we listen to Ludwig Beethoven's music, we forget that he was often insulted and that he died "almost friendless, in a verminous bed." Franz Schubert "might well have better disciplined an unfailing inspiration" if he had enjoyed more leisure.

The likelihood that we now lack such geniuses as William Shakespeare, Wagner, and these others just named, doesn't mean that more such won't appear. Nor does it mean that we shouldn't encourage those with less than towering talent. They too help keep our world from being "drab and barren." The MacDowell Colony has carried on for 17 years, and we hope it will continue "indefinitely." In four months, an artist working here, in "quiet and seclusion," can do the work of four ordinary years filled with worry and interruptions.

Robinson concludes what he calls "this brief and inadequate article" by saying that he has written both under adverse conditions and in "the seclusion of the MacDowell Colony in the New Hampshire woods," and that most of his work has been done here. Others have similarly benefited and will say as much "—and more."

Robinson sent a letter (July 31, 1924) to Edwin Markham,* who was one of the judges deciding to whom the *Pictorial Review* editorial board gives its annual awards. In his letter, Robinson tactfully mentions Mrs. MacDowell as someone to consider. (Source: Cary [1975], 84–88, 191).

MacKaye, Percy (1875–1956). Poet and playwright. Percy Wallace MacKaye was born in New York City. His father was the actor-dramatist Steele MacKaye (1842–1894); his mother, a writer. After being educated at home, in New York public schools, and in private schools in Massachusetts and Washington, D.C., MacKaye attended Harvard (A.B., 1897) and in 1898 married Marion Homer Morse (1872–1939). The couple had a son, Robert ("Robin") Keith MacKaye (b. 1899), and two daughters, Arvia MacKaye Ege (1902–1989) and Christina Loring MacKaye Barnes (1909–2002 — see Robinson's "Introductory Letter to *Wind in the Grass*," a book of poetry by Christy MacKaye). MacKaye and his wife traveled in Europe (1898–1900), during which time he studied at the University of Leipzig. When they were home again, MacKaye taught in a boys' school in New York (1900–1904).

An unbelievably prolific writing career followed, during which MacKaye wrote more than 50 books, 30 play productions, four opera libretti, and other works. Especially noteworthy were the following: *The Canter-*

bury Pilgrims (published 1903, produced 1909), a verse play commissioned by the distinguished actor Edward Hugh Sothern (1859–1933); the verse play Jeanne d'Arc (1906, 1907); the musical tragedy Sappho and Phaon (1907, 1907), with music by Albert Augustus Stanley (1851–1932); The Scarecrow (1908, 1909), a prose drama based on the short story "Feathertop" by Nathaniel Hawthorne and enjoying productions in England, Germany, and Russia; and poems and masques, some with casts literally of thousands, in celebration of special American anniversaries (the discovery of Lake Champlain [1909], the founding of St. Louis, Missouri [1914], and William Shakespeare's death [1916, with an opening dance by Isadora Duncan*]). MacKaye occupied the first chair in any American institution of higher learning for creative literature at Miami University, Oxford, Ohio (1920–1924); this honor, together with his essay "University Fellowships in Creative Art" (Forum, June 1921), helped to foster later American writer-in-residence grants. Cecil Sharp (1859–1924), the composer-ethnographer, encouraged MacKaye to live in rural regions for a while and write about their folkways. He did so, and several dramatic and poetic works centered on Kentucky and New England life resulted (1923–1928). MacKaye's last years were marked both by illness and by continued but less significant writing. He wrote a two-volume biography of his father (1927), a masque honoring George Washington (1932), and a verse tetralogy based on Hamlet (1949), and also edited the letters of his friend William Vaughn Moody* to his wife Harriet Moody (1935). MacKaye constantly labored to democratize dramatic and poetic literature, to increase popular involvement. In a 1909 address entitled "The Playhouse and the Play" he points out that ideally the theater is a people's civic temple. Arvia MacKaye Ege wrote a biography of her parents entitled The Power of the Impossible: The Life Story of Percy and Marion MacKaye (1992).

When Robinson was living with other writers at the Judson Hotel, in New York City's Washington Square area, he met MacKaye (about 1905), who occasionally dropped by. The two became friends. Robinson attended the opening performance of MacKaye's Sappho and Phaon with William Dean Howells, William Vaughn Moody,* and Edmund Clarence Stedman.* MacKaye introduced Isadora Duncan to Robinson and their friends Moody and Ridgely Torrence* (1908). Robinson wrote "For Arvia," a birthday sonnet for MacKaye's daughter (1908). He admired MacKaye's Jeanne d'Arc when he heard MacKaye read it aloud, and according to Richard Cary told a Boston Post interviewer (1913) that he regarded MacKaye's Uriel, and Other Poems (1912) "his best work." When Robinson was turning 50, MacKaye organized a tribute entitled "Poets Celebrate E. A. Robinson's Birthday," published in The New York Times Review of Books (December 21, 1919). Bliss Perry (1860–1954), author-educator, wrote the introduction; and the following admirers of Robinson's poetry, among others, contributed columns of praise: Hermann Hagedorn,* Louis V. Ledoux,* Vachel Lindsay, Amy Lowell,* Edwin Markham, Edgar Lee Masters, John G. Neihardt, Josephine Preston Peabody,* Torrence, and MacKaye himself. When MacKaye turned 50, a collection of congratulatory essays was published, in 300 copies, by the Dartmouth Press (1928). Robinson contributed a one-page prose piece entitled "Unquestionable Genius." Years later, when Robinson lay dying in the hospital in New York, he missed among a stream of visitors his friend MacKaye, who was ailing in Florida. (Sources: Cary [1974], 258; Hagedorn)

"The Man Against the Sky" (1916). Poem in 10 unnumbered stanzas.

The poet sees a man against the gloriously fiery sky, standing on a "flame-lit height." He resembles "the last god" heading home.

He is knowing, lonely, meaningful, but apparently "inscrutable." Wherever he is going, pretty much "alone he goes."

He may have striven, dared to go into unknown depths, been purged by fire.

He may have been happy, may have descended easily, may have made his mother's eyes glisten proudly. Don't question those who by "slaughter, toil, and theft" aided his progress.

He may have been indifferent to good and evil, egocentric, "effete[ly]" cynical, escapist, convinced only that "life [is but] a lighted highway to the tomb."

He may have been an indifferent, undoubting dreamer, disillusioned and walking toward death "like a stoic Roman." Perhaps, employing "the swift logic of a woman," he decided to "Curse God, and die."

He may have been a "smiling" physicist, calm, thoughtful, fatalistic, indifferent to a mechanical nature that he partly controls. Maybe he was a shiver-inspiring political leader.

Whatever drove or lured him, "his way was even as ours." Must we choose between Heaven and Hell, those "two fond old enormities"? Still, his enigmatic qualities challenge us to ask why we should go on "a little farther into time and pain," if the end is really nothing but "ashes and eternal night." If that should be the case, why launch children "to voyage again / A little farther into time and pain"? Are we nothing but "brains and bones and cartilege"?

Ah, "an orient Word [see John 1:1] comes to us "in incommunicable gleams / Too permanent for dreams," and cannot be denied. Several theories are unsatisfactory, including ideas of "communal repose," life as a "planetary trap," humans as evolving under "silly stars" from fish and birds into tailed creatures in trees deriding our "immortal vision."

Even though we cannot fathom Eternity, even though Death humbles us, it is still folly to pity ourselves, laugh, and curse, deny our spiritual destiny, or commit suicide. If

> All comes to Nought,—
> If there be nothing after Now,
> And we be nothing anyhow,
> And we know that,—why live?

There must be something beyond "our sunset fires." There must be a satisfying Word.

At one time, Robinson regarded "The Man Against the Sky" and "Isaac and Archibald" as his two best poems. "The Man Against the Sky" is mainly in iambic pentameter, but with many lines shorter by one, two, or even three feet; all but a few lines find rhymes, sometimes to produce couplets but sometimes so many lines later that they chime faintly, if at all.

David H. Hirsch suggests that Robinson alludes to biblical fire imagery and also to the depiction of Adam in *Paradise Lost* by John Milton in such a way as to undercut his own attitude toward faith. David H. Burton feels that philosophical idealism and doubt occasioned by naturalistic science resulted in Robinson's disavowal of orthodox, established Christianity. However, Sister Mary James Power, after quoting the passage about brains, bones, and cartilege, concludes that "Faith, then, lights the poet's path more clearly than science directs his reason." Robert D. Stevick discusses the anti-materialism evident in both "The Man Against the Sky" and "Is Life Worth Living?" (1895) by William James.* (See also "My Methods and Meanings.") Fred Somkin quotes a pertinent passage from "The Man Against the Sky," including "Till down the fiery distance he was gone," and a passage from the chapter entitled "Of some Sources of Poetry Among Democratic Nations," in *Democracy in America* by Alexis de Tocqueville (1805–1859), and then notes that "[t]he parallelism of image and language between Tocqueville and Robinson would seem to be more than a coincidence although there is no direct evidence that Robinson ever read Tocqueville."

Amy Lowell* evidently misinterpreted "The Man Against the Sky," which caused Robinson to write her (March 18, 1916) to explain that its conclusion intends, in "obviously ironic" tones, "to carry materialism to its logical end and to indicate its futility as an explanation or a justification of existence." Yvor Winters helped little when opining that in the poem Robinson "handle[s] 'abstract' language . . . ineptly." James G. Hepburn quotes seven lines in the poem, beginning with "But this we know, if we know anything," and concludes that they "describe the way to salvation." Hepburn hints that a critic might be found who "regards the poem as the equal of any other American poem of equal length." But then Hepburn frets over the distinction between Robinson's meaning here and his voice here, and half-generalizes that "[i]t is tempting to say that the dilemma of Robinson's career was the struggle between true voice and false belief." Let's hope Robinson's formula for "salvation" isn't "false." This, in spite of Malcolm Cowley's strictures against "The Man Against the Sky," in which he contends that Robinson "suggests . . . a sort of Buddho-Christianity too vague to be intellectually respectable."

Hoyt C. Franchere defines "The Man Against the Sky" as "an unequivocal affirmation of life and a denial of eternal death." Louis Coxe calls it "a personal and eloquent assessment of man's possible fates in a certain moment in history"; he admits its metrical and syntactical awkwardness, but lauds its "fine Wagnerian moments, great eloquence," and daring. Ellsworth Barnard regards the poem as "a pageant of human life," in depicting which the poet's "mood is one neither of eagerness nor of endurance, but rather of reflection — a weighing and balancing of appearance and reality, of materialism and idealism, of the odds on extinction and survival." Bernard Duffey peruses the poem and concludes that, "if we cannot ever know or even really imagine any destiny toward which the man descends, we may still extend a will to answer into unknowing itself." Roy Harvey Pearce's comment on the lonely man in the poem is that "[h]is meaning as man lies precisely in his being no one but himself, and [he] must be memorialized as such."

J. G. Levenson demonstrates the modernity of "The Man Against the Sky"—first, by saying that "without explicit mention of world war, this is a poem of 1916"; second, by relating it to the century-long effect on poets and other thinkers of William Wordsworth's "Ode: Intimations of Immortality from Recollections of Early Childhood"; and third, by suggesting that Robinson's poem argues so forcefully that "[d]oubt is certain, disbelief plausible, despair sympathetic, and hope obscure" that his "source of light is below the horizon of consciousness" and yet is still there. (Sources: Bernard, 78; D. Burton [1970]; Cowley, 30; Coxe, 100; Duffey, 181; Franchere, 141; Hepburn, 273; Hirsch; Levenson, 164, 165; Pearce, 266; Power, 75; Somkin, 246; Stevick [1959]; Winters, 36–37)

The Man Against the Sky: A Book of

Poems (New York: Macmillan, 1916). Collection of 26 poems, 14 of which had been previously published. Robinson dedicated the book "To the Memory of William Edward Butler." Butler's father owned a department store in Boston and offered Robinson a job at one time. Instead, he worked briefly (1899) for Charles William Eliot,* president of Harvard. James L. Tryon* describes Butler as one of Robinson's "warm friends" at Harvard, as a uniquely early admirer of Robinson's writings, and "as a champion of the poet in his days of obscurity and struggle for recognition." (Source: Tryon, 11)

"A Man in Our Town" (1924). Sonnet. A man in our town faced indigence calmly. In large part to please ourselves, we sought him out to help him. Although he wasn't marvelous, when he went away some of us shed "many a thrifty tear" and in addition our neighborhood changed. Even if he is forgotten, his having been here was beneficial.

"The Man Who Came" *see* **"The Master"**

The Man Who Died Twice (New York: Macmillan, 1924). Narrative poem. The narrator, a minor composer of music, happened to be on Broadway and by chance saw his friend Fernando Nash, a potentially great though now failed composer, after 20 years of separation. Forty-six years old, Nash was beating a drum with street revivalists and shouting "Glory to God."

The narrator never joined in with others who knew Nash and jeered at him for failing as a composer. However, the narrator, like the others, did suspect that Nash's boasts about his "unproved opuses" wouldn't bear fruit. Now they are "mute as ashes," although Nash said "he praised them" accurately. He repeatedly said, "I had it — once." Nash told the narrator that a year earlier he was close to death, but then came "a more revealing end / Than that."

Somewhat indifferent, though aware of Nash's former gigantic talent, the narrator walked along with Nash to his "barren room." It contained an iron bed, a box of old orchestrations, a gas flame, a chair, and a portrait of

Bach looking down on Nash as a Titan might on a worm once insolent. And there was a mirror, "Filmed with too many derelict reflections." Sitting in front of it, Nash, who once had a massive, semidivine face, glowered and saw what seemed a bleary, heavy, evil-sodden, uninvited stranger.

Nash addressed this "bloated[,] greasy" visitor: You had "a daemon in you, not a devil," were gifted, "had it — once," listened to "drums / Of death" unaware that it was fatal to do so, and remembered being inspired when a schoolboy by unique celestial music. Why were you so fatally impatient that all you eventually heard were your destroyers' drums? If you had waited, "Symphony Number Three. Fernando Nash" would have placed you among the mightiest. Your first two symphonies, soon going nowhere, were merely rungs on a ladder off which you fell. You built, mastered, wrongly doubted, and let your miraculous "new machine" turn to rust. Meanwhile, your lenient daemon was letting your unprotesting soul follow "devil women." You beached jelly-fish, "crapulous . . . lump," "whale of lust and drunkenness," "deficient swine," you knowingly sneaked away from God when still able to serve Him. You are too sane, too thin, too unsure to commit suicide. Try starving yourself and see if your offended God will send you a message.

Thus this once-glorious friend ignominiously, but perhaps half-proudly, flagellated himself for more than an hour beside the narrator, who responded by saying Nash might be faking it. Nash smiled, hinted at his buried genius, and called himself a "king who lost his crown before he had it, / And saw it melt in hell."

Surprisingly, what then transpired enabled the narrator much later to appreciate

> what violent fire had once,
> In such a cracked, abandoned crucible,
> Fused with inseparable obscure alloy
> Celestial music,

to create Nash's wasted genius. Midnight chimes tolled. Nash tore his first two symphonies to tatters, as unrepresentative of his ability, although his competitors, he averred, would have been happy had they composed them; went down "dark stairs again that

night"; began "a last debauch" lasting three weeks; and wound up back in his room with Bach staring at him soberly once more. Nash lay in bed. Bach nodded approvingly as a procession of more than 70 rats, dressed in black and white, came through the key hole, assembled into an orchestra, and played "the first chords of the first rat symphony / That human ears had heard." The music was eerie, sturdy, darkly foaming, "coarse and unclean," with the damned all crying in agony to the accompaniment of death drums Nash had heard before. The rats bowed, leered, and left Nash in an icy sweat. A disapproving Bach resumed his pictorial status.

Nash regarded the rat music as an intermezzo between his drunken prelude and a fugue yet to come. He wanted to tell someone about it all, and the narrator was his handy audience. One afternoon, he said, he remembered the rats and looked up at Bach, who couldn't see the fires, hopes, regrets, and remorse churning within Nash. Suddenly something came. He hoped it was a "new clarity [that] was the light that comes / Before the night comes." His wits seemed clear, like sunshine on once-dirty grain. His "armor of negation" fell off. Shame for having insulted the Holy Ghost seemed curative. He felt like an eager child again. Ugly emotions had martyred him, but now came "the peace / That passeth understanding." A fire drove his once-gnawed heart. His years-long sloth was ending. He should have gone out for food. But he luxuriated in new calmness. Suddenly he heard the death drums, though muffled in clouds that hid "Tumultuous and elusive melodies." He merely listened to them peacefully. More drum beats came from that "same unyielding cloud / Of sound and fire." In it was "A singing flame." It might not last, if this "mocking hour" were to be the only time that, after "smouldering" for years, it "should leap at him and scorch him." Fear replaced peace. He waited for the music to burst out of the cloud and submerge him in ecstatic regret. Wanting death, he heard more muffled drums.

Nash told the narrator that he should have awaited that "flaming rain," those "celestial messengers." But, no. He might have lifted "Olympian gold" instead of "mouldy pottage," except that his home had always been "the dismal valley." How could he have "peace / In the complete oblivion of achievement"? He longed for "unendurable fulfillment" and then all-dissolving lightning out of the cloud. Instead, he found himself listening to "a singing mist," a unique fire, heavenly messengers from afar; and he wore "glory" because of it all. In the midst of supernal joy, though, came the hollow sound from the "chilly reed" of a bassoon, and beauty gave way to "infernal drums," a chorus of offensive "demons, men and women," forcing worshippers out.

Nash lay quiet, well aware of long-ago lamentations and regrets. As a pageant climbed from a deep-down domain up toward the stars, at first not heard but soon singing, he knew he had just missed "seizing immortality" with it. More drums. Then out of his "creative charnal house" Nash told the narrator about a wild "bacchanale of . . . usurpers" of life, who mistook "hell for paradise," tracked dirt onto gleaming floors, and hurled "the dregs of their debaucheries" at the walls of "Life's immortal house." God, tired of them, quieted them with trumpet blasts. Death drums finally ceased.

Next, a march, a hymn, and the exiles returned, chastened and grateful. Their glistening voices made the dome above them shine. More drums, to frustrate this seeming purification. The singers praised freedom, while death's hand pounded malevolently — until more trumpets provided "that choral golden overflow / Of sound and fire, which he had always heard" and yet had never really heard. "All he had known and had not waited for / Was his." Tears gushed, blinded him. Full of praise and tired, Nash stumbled into the dark hallway, beseeching God, a friend, the devil, something, not for food but for composition paper. Which force then hurled him down the stairs?

Two weeks later Nash lay in a hospital ward, with a dreadful lesion and close to death. Remnants of his fiery personality encouraged attendants to condemn him back to life. He would recognize no more celestial messengers. What glories hovering about him were now like unearthly jewels an idiot might hammer into fragments and bury "in darker waters than where ships go down / Hull-crushed at midnight." Nash told the narrator as much. Then he asked to be cremated and his ashes sunk at sea, and said "fear not for my soul. I have found that, / Though I have lost all else. All but those drums." He called them his personal "drums of life" now. Something not a dream followed him, made him a child again, and had him beat the drums joyfully on the street. He asked the narrator to believe that he recognized a harvest he couldn't gather, a harvest more golden than anything gathered by kings. He praised God who gave it and took it back. He knew that the narrator recognized his quality, which his rivals feared. He went on:

> Once, for an hour,
> I lived; and for an hour my cup was full
> With wine that not a hundred, if a score,
> Have tasted that are told in history.

He said that only a final messenger would come next, and soon. He found more than he lost but failed God by not waiting. Still, God saved his soul. When the narrator tried to assuage Nash by saying that other composers had tried to make him conform, Nash smiled indulgently, rejected pity, praised God again, and asked the narrator to believe he "had it — once."

The narrator reports that Fernando Nash is dead. His final drum-beating in loyalty to God is not the issue. The profound story is that Nash, frail, extravagant, with a distinction finally burned, was a giant once communing

> With older giants who had made a music
> Whereof the world was not impossibly
> Not the last note.

He had "the nameless and authentic seal / Of power and of ordained accomplishment"; in the narrator's belief this accomplishment was validated by his telling him the truth. The narrator continued to believe that "the giant / Was always there, and always will be there" in essence, even as he dropped Nash's ashes in the ocean.

Fernando Nash is another of Robinson's gifted "failure-redeemed" characters, to use Hoyt C. Franchere's neat designation. Nash dies twice, thus: Nash, compared to Greek heroes Achilles, Ajax, and Hercules, and seeking gold from Olympus, "had it — once" and should have patiently awaited the fiery sounds the messengers would have brought him from on high. Instead, his turning impatiently and sordidly, for 20 ruinous years, to tin-pan street revivalism, wine and women and then some, killed him once. Then, resting from the mother of all hangovers, he heard celestial music above the constant accompaniment of death drums, rushed to find paper on which to record the varied movements, but tumbled down the stairs. This action killed him a second time. Yet, though unable to scribble what he had heard, he had the satisfaction of knowing he was elatedly moved by divine music and hence died aware of his unlost musical ability.

Scott Donaldson suggests that when Nash "berates himself . . . for not writing the great symphony he knew himself capable of," Robinson was himself "contemplat[ing] . . . what might have been, had he given way to doubt during the long years when his work went largely unrecognized." Emery Neff says that if Fernando Nash had merely boasted about his talent, he would hardly be "distinguish[ed] from thousands of failures who have made extravagant claims"; Robinson therefore validates Nash's assertions by filtering them through a composer-narrator aware of Nash's "early promise." Neff evidently wished to counter Yvor Winters's contention that the narrative "is more grotesque than moving" because readers are "not convinced that Nash is a great man." Robinson's narrator, presumably reliable, was convinced. Chard Powers Smith* reminds readers that Robinson presented *The Man Who Died Twice* in "the grandest manner, the manner of symphonic composition, the only kind of art that he admitted to be grander than his own." Ellsworth Barnard regards the description of Nash's unwritten opus as perhaps "the most stirring passage of blank verse" Robinson ever composed. Barnard calls the music a symphony, and organizes and divides it into four movements. The first movement starts when Nash hears that "singing mist" and the music emerges from chaos as a "quivering miracle of architecture." The second movement becomes a "passionate regret / And searching lamenta-

tion of the banished." The third is the usurpers' crystal-smashing bacchanale. The fourth, preceded by the omnipresent death drums, is the "sound and fire . . . always heard" yet "not heard before." Pleasing to impatient readers who dislike *The Man Who Died Twice* is the comment by James Dickey about the "intolerable amount of poetic hemming and hawing, backing and filling" cluttering it. Nonetheless, Robert Mezey calls *The Man Who Died Twice* Robinson's best book-length poem.

Robinson dedicated *The Man Who Died Twice* to James Earle Fraser* and his wife Laura Gardin Fraser. Shortly after Robinson's death, James Fraser collected and privately printed 54 newspaper and magazine articles about the poet, in a 90-page booklet entitled *In Tribute* (1935). (Sources: Barnard, 60–61, 170, 242; Dickey, xxi; Donaldson [1980], 67; Franchere, 93; Isaacs; Mezey, xxxiv; Neff, 218–19; C. Smith, 321; Winters, 108)

"Many Are Called" (1920). Sonnet. The immortal "Lord Apollo" still rules in his magically "fortified" and hence "impregnable domain." Numerous "melodious multitudes" have tried, "sacred[ly] and profane[ly]," to entice him out, but always without success. "At unconjectured intervals," and by virtue of non-human will and word, "A questing light may rift the sullen walls," after which for the most part "its infrequent rays / Fall golden on the patience of the dead."

Yvor Winters defines "Many Are Called" as "a sonnet on the rarity of poetic genius and the loneliness of its reward." In it, Robinson is implying that his vocation as poet was thrust on him by destiny. The title of the sonnet, derived from the famous biblical warning, "For many are called, but few are chosen" (Matt. 22:14), suggests to Ellsworth Barnard an "analogy . . . between the grace of Apollo and that of the Christian God, which is vouchsafed . . . inexplicably and irresistibly to but a few of the many who seek it." Edwin S. Fussell reports that "Apollo (god of 'light' as well as of poetry) appears more often" in Robinson's poetry than any other god from classical literature. The sixth line of "Many Are Called" — "In ecstasy, in anguish, and in vain" — describing the efforts of those "multitudes" to entice Apollo, is a clever example of zeugma. Robinson regarded "Many Are Called" and "The Sheaves" as his two best sonnets. Robert D. Stevick calls it "probably his best sonnet." (Sources: Barnard, 12–13; Fussell [1954], 147; Stevick [1969], 66; Winters, 40)

"The March of the Cameron Men" (1932). Poem. Narrative mostly in blank verse dialogue. It is twilight in autumn. A man and a woman are in a boat. She asks to be rowed away from the silent house, to the middle of the lake, where no one can see or hear them. He calls her lovely, says looking at her resembles praying, wonders if she is looking into the water for a monster, adds that she is free of her former monster. She counters that funeral arrangements must be made. Although she cautions him to speak carefully, he continues thus: She drove him away once but called him back; back he came like an army of marching men, as though accompanied by some music she was "drumming / On dim keys, in a dark room." She summoned him, a doctor, to save a dying man. She could have driven him off, to drown himself in the lake, but didn't, instead asked him to sing.

Saying songs might comfort sick people, she wonders what that music was she played. He says he made up "playful and equivocal" words about her for her melody. He recites eight lines of it; it tells how her summons, the night, the stars, "And the March of the Cameron Men" combined to recall him, "a king who believed he was dead," to life.

She vaguely remembers the music that had been hidden in her fingers and hopes the stars weren't hidden from him all those years. He responds: More than stars were hidden; she was too, as he was from himself; however, that march back to her included a positive regiment of hopes. They are now free, just as the man in the silent house now is. Formerly "angry and implacable," she called him back, was waiting for him. He recites the next stanza of his "March": Her smile gave him more than scholars learn; no whisper of their former stormy times remained; he found her in the March. Continuing to mention love, he hopes that she will rejoice for the two of them. He

won't be foolish, "with him there, in that house."

She smiles, thinks that the marching men might intend "to kill somebody," then

> wonder[s] why
> So many of our songs and melodies
> That help us to forget, and make us happy,
> Are born of pain, and oftener of defeat
> Than victory.

When she adds that melancholy gives birth to hope, he replies that his song is one of triumph after her dark unhappiness, that her smile made him remain, that she undoubtedly prayed for the release nature has provided. She interprets his song to mean that marchers proceed to freedom, captivity, or death — which may also be freedom.

She says his song shouldn't be left unfinished; so he sings the rest: When he left her, stars were in his path; he wandered by himself, had a mocking dream, awoke to hear only "the sound of the world going round" to the sound to the continuing March. He tries to make her feel undisturbed, says he recited the end only to humor her, says all danger is gone, and asks why she doesn't look at him instead of toward that house, which anyway is blocked from view by trees. He goes on: He is no longer there; "There's only an old garment all worn out — / A body that he was glad to leave behind"; she merely tolerated him "With lies and kindness. It was a wrong knot / You made, you two." He concludes: Her husband will soon be buried in his grave, his first true home; his other one she was never at home in.

She says those marchers might march over her grave. When she says, yes, she married the fellow, her companion in the boat replies that women marry as a seeming duty, then fear letting go, may even resemble freed prisoners he has seen who actually fear their freedom. She thinks some prisoners were plain murderers, whereas the two of them did so with "precaution and finesse." When he is startled, she looks daggers back at him but then smiles. Laughing slightly, he admits to many mistakes but says she wouldn't be on this dark lake with him now if she doubted his better nature. He cares for her, would love her with more than "carnal pride," has more good qualities than bad, has saved the lives of many who might have preferred to die, and hasn't "suborned / The best of me in hastening" anguished deaths, and therefore hasn't killed anyone.

Smiling and feeling the water, she admires his hairsplitting but says that "on a judgment day" God or a tough magistrate might demand a rephrasing of his thoughts. Then she says, "We have not killed him. We have let him die." He isn't going to hear the two of them returning, "But we shall hear those Cameron men, I think," forever marching and singing in response to their words about never killing anyone. Did those words start his marching song?

He admits misgivings, admits staking everything for her fate, admits killing — but for her freedom more than for his love of her. Then: "God — is it you / That I am looking at! Are we alone[?]" What was insufferable is all past; they must realize what their freedom means. She wonders if women ever are free, ever think. If so, her answer to his comments is simply "Horrors — hear that!"

When a loon yells over the waters, the man calls the sound a full-stop punctuation mark on their talk and on their aims, and tells her that after her husband's removal and burial she'll be free. She replies that when two plan havoc together, one is foolish, the other, unseeing. She "paid once for ruin / And once will do." Her belief that all would be well for the two of them was countered by her sudden awareness of "patient nature waiting like a fox / For an unguarded pheasant." Her escape from him, now, will save him too. Her promises to him he will more kindly remember once they are broken.

With a shudder he defines this innocent repulse as "More venomous than contempt." Why did you call me? Why let me embrace you? What did I let him die for, if not for a future with you? Are we both to lose after that gamble? "By God, my lady," he says, if he has understood her then the best place for her now would be under earth with her husband or drowned in this lake now. That house without him in it won't be more likable than it was with him.

She agrees, thus: He was a devil and should

have died earlier. If you drowned me, I would be at peace but you would be sad and would be followed by the marchers. Instead, be wise now and be free soon. Whereas most people only dream of wisdom and freedom, we can achieve it and then look back on this quiet night as a blessing. The loon sounds off again.

Dead cold replaces the once-living triumph in him. He wonders again who she is, this time expecting no answer. She asks to be rowed back, says her husband is harmlessly awaiting them, will be gone tomorrow, as the two of them will be, tomorrow. She will pray for him and forever hear the Cameron Men.

"March of the Cameron Men" is a traditional Scottish song, in praise of the fierce Cameron clan from Lockaber, in the western part of the Highlands. The song begins thus:

> There's many a man of the Cameron clan
> That has followed his chief to the field
> He has sworn to support him or die by his side
> For a Cameron never can yield.

The chorus follows and is repeated twice:

> 'Tis the march of the Cameron men.
> 'Tis the march, 'tis the march,
> 'Tis the march of the Cameron men.

No wonder the hero manqué of Robinson's poem chooses this Scottish song to buck up his courage. Laura E. Richards* says that Robinson's father Edward Robinson* used to sing "The March of the Cameron Men" in a fine baritone voice while Mary Robinson,* his wife and the poet's mother, played his accompaniment on the piano. Chard Powers Smith* theorizes in great detail about the amorous triangle in "The March of the Cameron Men." He suggests that the poem was inspired by the tangled relationship of Robinson, his brother Herman Robinson,* and Herman's wife Emma Robinson.* Herman, more ill in 1908 than he realized, told Emma that he would not remarry if she died first but that if he died first she would doubtless marry her brother-in-law; she promised not to do so; Robinson, who loved her, thought she loved him more than she did Herman; by 1932 (the date of this poem), Robinson had returned to his earlier opinion of Herman as diabolical and therefore used "his unattended death" in the Boston City Hospital (February 1909) as "the basis of the passive euthanasia in *The March of the Cameron Men* where the doctor-friend and the wife of the incurably suffering fiend "'let him die.'" (Who says the husband here was so fiendish?) Hoyt C. Franchere, agreeing with most of Smith's interpretation, suggests that Emma perhaps played and sang the Scottish song for Robinson, and roughly equates the boat trip of the two characters in the poem to a long, stressful walk Robinson and Emma took after Herman's death.

Yvor Winters says that "[t]he conversation [in the poem] is too long and too subtle for the occasion and the writing is nowhere remarkable." He adds that the song within the poem is "symbolic of the woman's remorse" but that the symbolism is "extremely vague" and "wholly unnecessary." Ellsworth Barnard, however, regards the song as "a symbol of the distance that has already been placed between them by the death, not of the woman's husband, but of what they thought was love." (Sources: Barnard, 93; Franchere, 66–69; Richards [1936], 16; C. Smith, 223, 224; Winters, 140, 141)

Marks, Josephine *see* Peabody, Josephine Preston

Mason, Daniel Gregory (1873–1953).

Composer, writer, and educator. Mason was born in Brookline, Massachusetts, studied at Harvard (1891–1895), and continued training in composition privately. He composed his first work in 1894, began writing about music, and published *From Grieg to Brahms* (1902). He married his brother Edward Palmer Mason's widow Mary Lord Taintor Mason (1904) and became a devoted stepfather to their four children. Daniel Mason taught at Columbia University (1905–1942), advanced in rank, took a leave to study in Paris (1913), was appointed MacDowell professor (1929; see MacDowell, Edward) and Music Department head (1929–1940), and retired (1942). Mason was conservative in orientation, was called a Boston classicist, introduced American touches in his compositions, and disliked Impressionism and Modernism. He helped innovate the practice of musicologists to offer commonsense explanations of music to lay readers. He received many honors and awards. Mason's autobiography, *Music in My Time and Other Reminiscences* (1938), discusses, among much else, his many friends in New York and New England.

While working at Harvard (1899), Robinson met Mason, who was then an assistant to Barrett Wendell,* the popular English teacher there. When Robinson went to New York, he and Mason corresponded and soon became close friends. Robinson's letters are full of mordant wit during the early days when professional success was slow in coming. When Edmund Clarence Stedman,* broker, poet, and also editor, chose a few of Robinson's poems for inclusion in *An American Anthology, 1787–1900* (Boston, 1900), Robinson wrote to Mason (May 18, 1900) one of his most famous and characteristic comments on his own works. Calling "Luke Havergal" an "uncomfortable abstraction," he predicts that it will be "soused in anthological pickle — along with two or three others of the forlornly joyous breed." Once Mason was hired at Columbia, the two socialized. Shortly after Robinson's death, Mason published a selection of his letters to Mason (dated 1900–1934). In one letter (September 11, 1900), Robinson says that silence is worse than honesty and therefore feels free to blast, with ultra-courteous ferocity, a sonnet which Mason penned and a draft of which he sent Robinson. It memorialized the premature death of Philip Henry Savage (1868–1899), a promising young poet both men knew. (Mason edited *The Poems of Philip Henry Savage* [1901]; and in his selection of Robinson's letters, he includes the octet of his savaged sonnet.) Mason in *Music in My Time* briefly discusses several persons he and Robinson knew, including Robert Morss Lovett,* Percy MacKaye,* William Vaughn Moody,* Josephine Preston Peabody,* Josiah Royce,* Stedman, and Ridgely Torrence* (and Olivia Howard Dunbar, later Torrence's wife). Mason also quotes from many letters Robinson sent to him and reveals that he wrote a parody of Robinson's "Vickery's Mountain," which he called "Chickory's Fountain" and sent to Torrence (1910). (Sources: Hagedorn; Mason [Spring 1937], 224–25; Mason

[1938], 115–47 passim; *Selected Letters*, 30; C. Smith)

"The Master" (1909). Poem, parenthetically subtitled "Lincoln." The persona explains that at first "we" sneered at his name, only to revere it later. Those who jeered may not be remembered long. He came in perilous times, took "note of us," remained both mild and "untamable." We didn't understand his smile, his wincing, his waiting. He was "The jest of those for whom he fought." He didn't ask much of us, nor did we do much. He was aware that we were learning even as we laughed at him. He knew we had to be taught, like school children. Now we see that his face, which we flung "venom" at, was "never young" and never "wholly . . . old." He was "elemental" when dying and "ancient at his birth." He was "The saddest among kings of earth." He responded to "rancor with a cryptic mirth, / Laconic — and Olympian." His many virtues have soared away with him, far above what we can accomplish "with [our] inept, Icarian wings." We agree now on the sublimity of this Titan, unique in our epoch.

"The Master" was originally called "The Man Who Came." It attracted a great number of comments by reviewers when it first appeared. The poem is composed of eight stanzas, each having eight tetrameter lines and rhyming *ababcbcb*. This challenging pattern may, on first reading, prevent the possibly dazzled readers from fully absorbing the poet's worship of President Abraham Lincoln. At any rate, "The Master" merits many rereadings.

Richard Cary presents evidence that Robinson told a friend that he worked on it for a year and that it proved uniquely difficult to compose. Hermann Hagedorn* reports that Robinson sent a manuscript copy of it to Kermit Roosevelt, the son of Theodore Roosevelt,* who saw to it that the poem was read aloud to the Roosevelt family in the White House. Ellsworth Barnard comments on Robinson's unusual "gift . . . of fusing the lyric and the dramatic," as evidenced in "The Master." Yvor Winters says that Robinson's two poems about presidents, "The Master" and "The Revealer" (concerning Roosevelt), both "indicate . . . Robinson's distrust of the common man and his belief in the superior leader as the only hope for democracy." Coxe notes that Robinson "has that quality he ascribes to Lincoln . . . : that of being "ancient at his birth." (Sources: Barnard, 73; Cary [1974], 220, 223; Coxe, 12; Hagedorn, 238–39; Winters, 53)

"The Master and the Slave Go Hand in Hand" *see* **"Sonnet" ("The master and the slave go hand in hand")**

Matthias at the Door (New York: Macmillan, 1931). Narrative poem in blank verse, in six numbered and evenly spaced parts.

I. Matthias, now 50, is comfortable with his commercial success. He has an estate of lofty, sun-seeking trees, shadowy rocks, and a gorge where he stands and looks at his house. "Matthias was in harmony with his house," and happily thinks of his Natalie in it now. He calls himself God's "good and faithful servant," hence rightly rewarded, even though he is regarded by many hereabouts as distant. Suddenly Garth, a neighbor, approaches. He is bent over from fighting adversity, is tired of life, tells "mighty" Matthias that all his rocks might make him a suitable monument, and confesses he both admires and envies him. In turn, Matthias views Garth as a kind of trick-performing little animal and says the fellow should have listened more. Garth gazes at "a vast square rock / That filled the distance with a difference."

Garth remarks that a biography of Matthias would say this: Matthias was a fine example; he wouldn't bother others in their unimportant "homey" work; no one would dare cross him; he didn't fear his enemies or need his scanty friends; the truth behind his mysterious life might be surprising. Smiling indulgently, Matthias says Garth is always welcome here but should avoid darkness. Garth points out that black rock, says it is big enough to be God's tomb, notes something "Egyptian in it," says he and Matthias might well pray in it since both of them are "in the dark," and Matthias's God might be there where twin pillars carved out of darkness frame "a door / Worth watching." Matthias impatiently and apprehensively follows Garth, who says this:

It is dark here; I have lived a year in the dark; I will knock on this final door; I don't try to kill you; you are strong and "wrapped in rectitude" that films your eyes; you will probably visit this place only briefly. When Matthias upbraids Garth for being both curious and envious concerning him, Garth answers that Matthias will learn more about this "dark hole." Matthias disclaims responsibility for the present poor condition of Garth, his former companion. Garth recalls that Matthias saved Timberlake, and now wonders why; he got burned doing so and might have done Timberlake a favor by letting death end his fruitless life. Unable to get Garth to leave the place, Matthias climbs out, feels a chill, returns to his house, and gratefully sees his beautiful wife Natalie. Uneasy, she asks if he has been "seeing demons . . . or walking / . . . [with] spirits." He says yes, he saw Garth.

II. The next day is a warm Sunday, normally a good day for Matthias to meditate acquisitively on whom to victimize next. But today he worries about shadows and a chill. Natalie, "preoccupied and restive," waits until her husband tells her what she's thinking. Matthias: Why worry about Garth, a failure? Natalie: Why did you send the authorities "to that awful hollow," where they found him, a suicide by poison? What would you think if I poisoned myself? Matthias: You're too brave to do such. I fear only growing old, want to "live on with you, / And always." That's a compliment to you. You don't look happy. Avoid thinking about Garth down there. You're better here with me. You're always too moody.

Timberlake, kind, wrinkled, straight, and with twinkling blue eyes, suddenly enters, and says "melodious[ly]" that he hopes God will now help innocent Garth, whose death he just heard about. Matthias says he's sorry for leaving Garth alone and forgives him for his bitter, contemptuous envy. Timberlake smiles when Natalie says Matthias habitually looks away from criticism, says they should believe Garth turned unbalanced but died friendly toward others, and adds that he won't kill himself. Matthias agrees that Timberlake won't be a suicide and calls Garth "dishonored." When Natalie sarcastically queries this word from her "sovereign," Timberlake remarks that "Ac-

complishment and honor are not the same." Matthias calls a halt to these apologies for Garth, whom he says he tried to help, and calls himself honest, though hard, and no fool. Natalie bothers Matthias by several statements: You put Garth in his place, as Garth did you; you wrongly said Garth could have stopped all critics by stopping the initial attacker; we often can't identify our enemies; Garth, who did much good, shouldn't be labeled a fool; suicide may be bravery; you know how to ignore my moods. Natalie invites Timberlake, offering to leave, to remain and guard them against Garth's return, which Matthias says won't happen. Natalie counters him by saying that men can't "put fate in a cage" but try to. She counters Timberlake, as he leaves, when he says all's well with Garth.

Matthias tells Natalie that Timberlake and Garth may now be equally distant from them. They agree that their departures cause loneliness. She kisses her husband on the nose, which act has been her reassuring habit for years now. He tries to hold her with iron hands; but, saying he mightn't want her to be demonstrative, she evades him. He blames Garth.

III. Natalie, alone next day and envying the dead, muses about Matthias's patronizing Garth, how she told Matthias she loved him "temperately," and how she might have married Garth or Timberlake. Then she goes down to Garth's door-like hole in that rock. Timberlake is there, out of curiosity. Talking, the two agree that Matthias fortunately doesn't know everything but may rightly have called Garth foolish. Just as Timberlake is saying he loves Matthias, partly for saving his life, Natalie rushes into his arms. They kiss fervently. She labels the two of them ghouls and fools to be there. "Like an unhappy witch" with a sexy face, she laughs and sits.

When he calls their earlier restraint "honor," she responds verbosely: Honor triumphed over love and happiness; they should have married and been wild; he could have been faithless and returned; if they had then killed each other, it would have proved they lived before they died; she should tell Matthias that two lives got ruined; Matthias thinks she loves him; he put her in a cage and toyed with her; men should learn "Somethings"; you are foolish.

Timberlake's reply begins with the suggestion that Matthias may have learned something via Garth's "farewell." He continues by remembering that 20 years ago Matthias saved him from drowning in smoke and fire by battering his door down and dragging him out. Natalie wonders why their "malignantly" tangled fates don't cause them to go crazy. Timberlake says that Garth, evidently "a good atheist who believed himself / And life a riot of cells and chemistry," should have killed himself earlier. Natalie agrees that "annihilation" ends all but says she isn't ready for it yet. Timberlake says that Matthias, though scorched himself, was glad he rescued Timberlake, who sensed he was an obstacle between Matthias and Natalie and made himself excessively worthless. This act was more to aid Matthias, who loved Natalie, than to aid Natalie, who, if she had married Timberlake instead, might have found him wanting and might have managed to create an emotional "woman-quake." He asks her to define the degree of her joy in her "safe nest" with Matthias. Natalie's answer is to hold Timberlake's "hot lips with hotter lips / That had alive in them the fire of death." This teaches him his loss. After she points to the door-like hole Garth entered, the two walk out, up, and apart.

Twilight finds Matthias confronting Natalie on their veranda. He says he saw her with Timberlake; they would have had more privacy for lovemaking deep past the door to the cave. Natalie answers directly. All right; so you saw us; I was drawn there; Timberlake was drawn too; if you hadn't bravely saved him from the fire, I would have married him, probably "to my sorrow," because he was a creature of folly; he "gave me to you" in gratitude; "I liked you," and your "real" love didn't deserve the agony of my refusal; also, I had nothing "better . . . to do." When asked, Matthias says he believes her but then leaves.

IV. Days pass. In an uneasy silence, she muses: Matthias's faith in her is dead; Timberlake, who loved Matthias but whose love for her was doubtful, was rightly far away; Matthias would make no "smear[ing]" demands.

Matthias, burdened by his changed world, finally approaches her. He feels awful solitude but regards himself as "always on an emi-

nence." Natalie says this: I prefer patches to holes; ships with unpatched holes sink; I wronged you "only [in] thought"; women do think; shall our ship, having taken in some "dark water," sail or sink? Matthias, though feeling she was his no more, says they should try. She wishes she might find the God that Matthias believes in, to thank him for small mercies. Matthias acknowledges his continuing faith. She says that one day he will thank his God she stayed "clean," which fact would help patch their ship if he could lose his "Olympian pride."

Silence follows. Natalie looks down at the big black rock. Timberlake was once there but isn't any longer, admirably. If Matthias only realized the "deceits" she used to please him, he would "be sorry for all women / Who lie because they live." During much time, Matthias maintains his distance and pride, grows civil, then mellow in an unripe way. His embrace, after silence, she backs away from but then sees remembered sadness in his eyes. When he tells her, "Nothing in you . . . / . . . will be outlived in me," the pity she feels for him hurts her too. She feels she might conventionally love him again but for Garth's death down there.

She lasts two more years with Matthias; but when his fine tarnish wears away, "pagan rawness of possession" emerges and dirties her to illness. Another year passes. She knows "inviolate fire" prevents Timberlake from returning. When Matthias, drunk, calls her a martyr, she replies that she is not, but is a fool, and wants him to leave. He grabs at her. She shrinks away and asks if he has turned her into "chattel," says she was weak to stay so long, says he spoiled himself, not her. He reminds her of her words about his real love and agony at possible loss, adds she sold herself, boasts he has love enough for both of them. But when he gloms her mouth with his, she slaps him hard, then calms down and escapes.

Matthias drinks himself to oblivion in his room, awakens in sunlight, and finds a note — "Matthias, I am sorry. Natalie," Finding courage in another drink, he goes down past the sunlit beauties of nature, to the "rocks and shadows."

V. With a servant's guidance, he finds Natalie dead. Quickly come loneliness, a retreat of faith, the end of mirages. On a chilly October Sunday, declining a maid's offer of food, Matthias wonders "if ever his faith / Was more than a traditional convenience" oddly surviving childhood. He is sustained by "pride of unbelief" and remains seemingly eminent. December gives way to March. Suddenly Timberlake returns — wrinkled, worn, coughing, and wistfully wondering if he's welcome. Matthias is thrilled to be alone no longer. Timberlake has a drink and thinks perhaps Matthias's abstinence is a eulogy to dead Natalie. Matthias says that Natalie doesn't care and doesn't know anything and that Garth properly told him to believe in nothing. Timberlake counters thus:

There's not a man who breathes and believes
    nothing.
So you are done with mysteries. If you are,
You are the one elected and fulfilled
Initiate and emeritus of us all.

Timberlake says he still loves Natalie, harmlessly now, and is delighted to be prepared for the future by this reconciliation with Matthias. Timberlake drinks, maunders about biblical warnings to drunkards, and makes Matthias glad to possess a friend again but uncomfortable when he says that Matthias may think his God is buried but perhaps "you . . . buried him alive."

By the fourth day Timberlake feels weaker. He tells Matthias to drive to town and make more money, and promises not to kill himself but instead to wait "Until my name is called." Matthias tells himself he'll provide for Timberlake, hardly old at 50 and ever unknowable. Returning home in the rain, Matthias notes Timberlake's absence, and with two others finds him exhausted after having gone to the rocky door which Garth and Natalie visited. Matthias is glad the rain keeps Timberlake from seeing his tears. Next day Timberlake, though weak, explains: Natalie called me; down there I thought of the mess our three lives were; nature started to build us, then quit short; others ignorantly "emulate" us; "I have found gold, Matthias, where you found gravel"; you must find your own treasure by looking inward; fate's removing your toys is no curse; some lives thrown away aren't wasted; happy women are easily understood, but no one can "interpret / A woman hiding pain." The puzzled doctors hear Timberlake coughing for three more days and nights.

VI. One night, Matthias sleepwalks into Natalie's room and dreams about her. First, she is laughing and says the two of them are in timeless heaven, their souls and bodies mingling. Then, demonic, she seems to be strangling him in hell and says, "Your God has changed his mind." That second dream follows him like a death smell. Companionless, he unavailingly seeks the truth — in darkness, in books that seem like keys to unfound doors, in the implications of his well-built fortune. But he has only "money and pride." Hearing Garth reminding him that what he built walled others out, he commends Garth.

One Sunday afternoon in August, without his knowing it, seeds of sympathy that Matthias once planted are sprouting in his garden. Tired of his pride but too proud to be found an ignoble suicide, he needs either light or restful darkness. An Egyptian door appears. When he tries to open it, Garth decisively tells him "Not yet." Matthias, flexing his power, responds, "Why . . . wait?" Garth explains: "You cannot die, Matthias, till you are born"; go up again for now; Timberlake and Natalie are together; I am an emissary from the dark. Matthias apologizes for criticizing Garth, who replies: Your generous words won't be wasted; return now; though "unconsciously together" now, we must be "consciously apart, to the same end." Matthias: Says who? Suppose I push? You're dead, and only your voice keeps me from oblivion.

Amid Matthias's queries, Garth explains much: You lack nerve to break down the door, which moved slightly to let you hear me. The others aren't here for you. Natalie went her unique way, is beyond recall, was never wasted. You'll come to the door only when "your name is called." My voice may be yours, may be Cæsar's. A punishment may be a reward. Mysteriously, many unborn live. Go "seek what's hidden / In you." Science won't end your darkness. After evolution, language, which is "chips of brief experience," separates us from grass; some "worms, armadillos, hyenas" are superior to some men. Don't uselessly pound the door; instead, save your hands to return and build, alone and friendless, a safer tower; dedicate it to those needing it. I no longer feel fear or envy. "Good-bye, Matthias."

Matthias breathes, is alive, sees no door in the cold, heavy darkness, hears the musical tinkling of the brook which Natalie, Garth, and Timberlake visited. Matthias has to be born, live, serve, and be useful "in a new world." Those three "strangely lived and died to find [it] for me." Knowing that his new tower will be good, Matthias gropes along, rests in the cold blackness, feels new-birth warmth, and waits patiently and gratefully for dawn to come.

Nicholas Ayo points out that Robinson was writing "Nicodemus" at the same time he was writing *Matthias at the Door*, which "bears a close thematic resemblance with 'Nicodemus,' even though not a Biblical poem." Ayo adds that "Two complex images with biblical roots penetrate this work [*Matthias at the Door*]; they are 'rebirth' and 'death and resurrection.'" Chard Powers Smith* regards *Matthias at the Door* as "the last of Robinson's great autobiographical dramas." Hoyt C. Franchere says that Matthias's finding Natalie and Timberlake embracing "tempt[s] one to regard this poem as a final thrusting solution of the Emma-Herman-Win triangle" (i.e., Emma Robinson,* Herman Robinson,* and the poet).

Whether Emma is responsible for Natalie or not, she is highly complex. Of the brilliantly sketched heroine Louise Dauner says that, "possessing both passion and temperament in a situation which blunts both," she puts on a mask "of a cynical mirthless mirth." Dauner continues: Natalie is tragically flawed because of fine but complexly contradictory character qualities; she tries to explain away "the basically irrational motive of sex"; she suffers because "irrationality triumphs"; and, sadly, "her . . . late-blooming honesty" causes her both to admit "her mistake" and to realize "that its remedy is beyond her."

The reader is made to regard the death door as immemorially old through the use, seven times, of the words "Egypt" or "Egyptian" to describe it. Floyd Stovall concludes that it is in *Matthias at the Door* that "the optimism behind Robinson's tragedies is most clearly seen and stated." Yvor Winters says Robinson ruins the poem by making the door in the rock not only a seemingly practical place for suicide but also a symbolic entrance to a new way of life in an improved world. James Dickey, also negative, calls the excessive "introversion" in the poem "boring." Emery Neff more tactfully says that, as with *Cavender's House* and *The Glory of the Nightingales*, the story of Matthias is about "the chastening of the businessman who thinks himself perfect," but adds that it is less complex, less interesting, than they are.

Foreshadowing is especially well handled in this poem. The blank verse is usually easy rather than obtrusive. Note, for example, that Natalie's five-word farewell note to Matthias is a perfect iambic pentameter line. However, while practically dying, Timberlake is made to speak 247 lines. Robinson dedicated *Matthias at the Door* to Ridgely Torrence.* (Sources: Ayo, 137 n.2, 187; Dauner, 153; Dickey, xix; Franchere, 111; Neff, 235; Parker; C. Smith, 263; Stovall, 15; Winters, 118–19)

"Maya" (1923). Sonnet. Man's soul rises from the insufficient, "complacent mind" and insufficient flesh through the empty night "up to a far height." Flesh and mind can't see there, can feel only terror there. The Soul then meets Will and is "again consigned" to the right, "supreme illusion." The Mind wonders what's happening there that it doesn't already know is true. Enough and more, yet not enough, is the "descending Soul['s]" reply; and it goes on to say that the Mind, "in the dark," and, while there both little revealed and yet greatly admired, "may still be the bellows and the spark."

Robinson frequently wrote about what may be called his transcendental idealism. Ellsworth Barnard dismisses "Maya" as "a transcendental dialogue between Mind and Soul." Denis Donoghue presses further: "[T]he poem affirms . . . that the mind's typical fault is complacency, unless it is prepared to go beyond its own comforts, at which point it becomes imagination, its better self." W. R. Robinson asserts that in this poem "[t]he Mind's arrogance and the Soul's contempt produce an unmitigable hostility." It is likely, however, that Robinson is having the lofty soul of man encourage the necessarily limited mind to believe that it can participate in or at least precipitate spiritual illumination — vital to Robinson's constant call for light.

The word "maya" here means the sense-world of various phenomena which conceals the unity of absolute being. Robinson's "Maya" cries for explication by a critic expert in Indian philosophy of the Vedic Period. An indication of the devotion of Robinson readers is the fact that at an auction in Chicago, on November 15, 1955, a man named Louis H. Silver bought the manuscript of "Maya" and presented it to the Colby College Library. (Sources: Barnard, 32; Donoghue, 38; W. Robinson, 22; "Some Other Recent Acquisitions")

Maynard, Theodore (1890–1956). A Catholic-convert friend of Robinson. He writes critically, and a bit superciliously, about Robinson's poetry in *Our Best Poets: English and American* (1924) and later reminisces about him in "Edwin Arlington Robinson," *Catholic World* 141 (June 1935): 266–75.

"Menoetes" (1892). Sonnet. Who is Menoetes? He was thrown by Gyas from the Trojan galley into the water. This victim of a "raging" sea captain may well represent any one of us. Be aware that "summer suns will never shine / When skies with tyrannous clouds are overblown." This sonnet was inspired by Virgil's *Aeneid* V: 173–75. (See also "The Galley Race.") (Source: Cary [1975], 16, 172)

Merlin: A Poem (New York: Macmillan, 1917). Narrative in blank verse, in seven numbered sections.

The following characters appear, or are at least named, in *Merlin*. (Some reappear in *Lancelot* and *Tristram*.) In some instances, relationships and actions touched on immediately below are not presented in Robinson. Spellings more regularly employed in Arthurian literature are indicated in parentheses.

Agravaine (Agravain) is Lot's and Morgause's son and Gawain's brother. Agravain helps Mordred expose Lancelot's and Guinevere's love affair. Lancelot kills Agravain.

Arthur is King of Britain, husband of Guinevere, father of Mordred, advisee of Merlin, and head of the Round Table in Camelot. Arthur's sword is Excalibur. Lancelot's and Guinevere's love affair and Mordred's revolt contribute to the fall of Camelot.

Bedivere is a knight loyal to Arthur and throws the wounded king's Excalibur into the lake in one version of the Arthurian legend. After Arthur's death, Bedivere becomes a hermit.

Blaise is Vivian's key-holding gatekeeper and becomes Merlin's servant and secretary.

Borre (Llacheu) is Arthur's son. (The legends concerning him are inconsistent.)

Bors is the loyal cousin of Lancelot, whom he warns of Agravain's and Mordred's plot to expose his love affair with Guinevere.

Dagonet is Arthur's knight who acts as his court fool.

Gaheris is Lot's and Morgause's son, and Gawain's and Gareth's brother. Gaheris kills his mother upon finding her with Lamorak. Lancelot kills Gaheris and Gareth during his rescue of Guinevere at the fiery stake.

Galahad is the son of Lancelot and Elaine of Corbenic, and is destined, through descent from Joseph of Arimathea, to achieve success in the quest for the Grail.

Gareth is Lot's and Morgause's son, and Gaheris's and Gawain's brother. Lancelot kills Gaheris and Gareth while he is rescuing Guinevere.

Gawaine (Gawain) is Lot's and probably Morgause's son, and Agravain's, Gaheris's, and Gareth's brother. Mordred is Gawain's brother or half-brother. Lancelot's killing of Gaheris and Gareth causes Gawain to turn against Lancelot, which starts the ruin of the Round Table. Gawain later dies in Lancelot's presence in France.

Griflet (Giflet) is one of Arthur's knights. He throws the wounded Arthur's Excalibur into the lake in one version of the Arthurian legend.

Guinevere is Leodegan's daughter and Arthur's wife. Her dowry included her father's gift of the Round Table. After Arthur sleeps with Morgause, Guinevere, rejecting Mordred, falls in love with Lancelot. He rescues her from execution. War follows. After the fall of Camelot, Guinevere retires to a nunnery at Amesbury.

Kay is Arthur's seneschal, i.e., manager of the royal household.

Lamorak is Pellimore's son, Perceval's brother, and Morgause's lover. Gaheris kills her but spares unarmed Lamorak, whose death Gawain successfully arranges.

Lancelot is Arthur's most splendid knight. His loving Guinevere and killing some of Gawain's brothers during her rescue from Arthur precipitates war. Lancelot takes Guinevere to Joyous Gard, gives her back to Arthur, goes to France, and might have been reunited with Arthur but for Gawain's animosity. Mordred's revolt dooms the Round Table and Camelot, because Lancelot's return to aid Arthur is too late. After Guinevere becomes a nun, Lancelot lives in a hermitage near Glastonbury.

Merlin is a prophet, a magician, and Arthur's advisor. He falls in love with Viviane and lives with her in Brittany for a time.

Modred (Mordred) is Arthur's half-brother, their mother being Morgause. Mordred lusts for Guinevere, with Agravain exposes her love affair with Lancelot, seizes power when Arthur is in France attacking Lancelot, and is killed when Arthur returns to Britain and is also mortally wounded. (In other versions, Mordred is Arthur's nephew.)

Morgause is one of Arthur's half-sisters. Her sons by Lot are Agravain, Gaheris, Gareth, and Gawain. In one version, she and Arthur are Mordred's parents.

Percival is Lamorak's brother and serves Arthur. He figures in the quest for the Holy Grail.

Tor is a minor knight in Arthur's court.

Vivian (Viviane) is a beautiful woman who falls in love with Merlin, who teaches her to be an enchantress and is lured by her away from Camelot to Brittany. (In several versions, she is named Nimue.)

I. Witty Dagonet approaches Gawaine, by himself at Merlin's Rock above King Arthur's "whispering town" of Camelot, to ask if his faraway gaze is seeking Vivian. Rumor has it that Merlin has left her; they had been con-

sorting in Broceliande, his "gay grave / In Brittany." Gawaine replies: I remember when Merlin told me it was just as well neither of us would be a king and try to control a world; I see only Camelot. Dagonet says: That's sight enough to make anyone "go mad"; Merlin's arrival here won't spell either peace or quick war; Vivian has been defeating Merlin's philosophy with fancy lovemaking. Gawaine says he would find that better than old age, until Dagonet warns that if Gawaine bets his "wisdom for a woman" he'll win "a grave." Though aware of his knightly prowess, Gawaine silently suspects Arthur prefers Dagonet, an "ominous clown."

II. Tough Sir Lamorak and his guest Sir Bedivere, the latter King Arthur's favorite after Lancelot himself, reluctantly start discussing Merlin. Lamorak: Merlin warned Arthur about Lancelot; Arthur proceeded to make a great mess of everything; meanwhile, Merlin also warned Arthur about Modred; Modred and Borre are both "strapping bastards," but Modred is more sinful than Lancelot or Queen Guinevere. Bedivere hopes that the queen will become a nun, fears that the bitter wind now blowing over Camelot's castles will soon be sweeping over fallen towers, bones, ashes, a wilderness. He blames Lancelot for that "potent wrong" against Arthur, who is now "broken." Lamorak: You, Bedivere, are iron-fisted but sermonize too much; Arthur married Guinevere knowing she loved Lancelot simply to prove Merlin's predictions wrong; Camelot won't go to hell just because of a beautiful but foolish woman.

Sir Kay, the seneschal, enters and, queried, reports that the troubled queen is silent now, that Arthur's "desperation" is a net stronger than the net Vivian threw over Merlin, and that Arthur has summoned Merlin from his grave and is even now being warned about that worm Modred. Lamorak sarcastically rejects any sympathy for either Arthur or the queen, asks what Merlin thinks of "Queen-fed" Lancelot, and getting no answer blasts women in general. To this Bedivere expatiates on the power of love, unknown yet to Lamorak, and says he sees all ending with his serving Arthur and ultimately "see[ing] the Grail," God willing. Lamorak: I see a "stinking" political mess, stirred by Modred and the equally evil Agravaine; God made neither villain but said "let 'em go, and see what comes of 'em"; the Grail and I never worried about each other. When Kay anticipates ruin because Arthur is in effect dead now, Lamorak snorts that Arthur is plenty alive but that Modred, and Gawaine too, bear watching.

III. Having summoned Merlin, now a beardless, dallying sybarite in fancy clothes, King Arthur sees that the fellow's authoritative wizardry has faded. Arthur fears that Vivian controls Merlin, who, however, tells him to remain a fighting king. Arthur apologizes but says Merlin returned to God his gift of prophecy and laughed in Vivian's arms. Merlin, warning Arthur to the degree possible for him, tells Arthur that no one can "undo" the "coil of Lancelot and Guinevere." Time-wasting regrets and remorse would cause him to lose Camelot and his crown. The pure knight will come to the Siege Perilous that Merlin founded; that knight "is to find the Grail / For you," and is the formerly trusted, "evil-fated" Lancelot's son. More evil is Modred, Arthur's son by his then-unrecognized sister Morgause. Protect Guinevere, although she never loved you, for she is your kingdom. Arthur says he will never see the Grail, since he erected his rule "On sand and mud."

Having arranged for Merlin and a convoy to return to Brittany starting at dawn, Arthur apprehensively begins to regard Bedivere, Bors, Gareth, Gawaine, Griflet, Lamorak, Percival, and Tor as all perhaps untrustworthy. He calls Dagonet and asks for a half-merry song. But Dagonet is too sad to sing; so Arthur gently dismisses him, then bitterly calls himself a worse fool than foolish Dagonet, and stares through the night at his dead illusions.

IV. Arthur is well aware that Merlin thinks more highly of that "small woman," the alluring Vivian of Broceliande, than of Arthur's whole kingdom. Meanwhile, Vivian is in Broceliande, remembering Merlin. When he received Arthur's letter, she couldn't stop him from returning to Camelot. He told her that Arthur from boyhood called him "Fate." But she well knows Merlin will ring at her gate again, as he did "in the spring / Ten years ago."

He reported to Arthur then that Vivian cut off his glory, as happened to Samson.

Still, like a pilgirm, Merlin, 10 years ago, did ring her gate bell and was admitted by Blaise, one of her three hundred male servants. Merlin was led through "shaded ways," past sunlit hedges and a fountain, to her, all clad in green like a slim cedar, with dark hair and a complexion of "blood and olive." Cherry blossoms were all about. While Merlin thought her world was nothing without him, Vivian (then aged 25, having first seen him when she was five) was thinking he probably fancied his "beard and robes and his immortal fame" would be scaring her. In reality, she knows he had "tossed away his glory" for her. She loved no man before Merlin, and, once seeing him at Camelot, could love only him. The two sat and toyed verbally. He disliked her green attire; she, his cloudy beard. She doubted the rumor that her mother was a fairy; he, the rumor that his father was the devil. He boasted that he made kings but added that he never lived until now. When he saw the sunset flaming behind her castle, he thought of Camelot burning. When he said he didn't wish to return there, she asked him to feed her "an ounce of [his] wisdom," then assigned Blaise to help him.

V. The period of 10 years continued. On that first night, Blaise, loyal but somewhat saucy, shaved Merlin, dressed him in purple, and escorted him to Vivian. She was sheathed in twinkling crimson, tingling in triumph, torch-lit, and resembling, he thought, an olive-blossomed, perilous flower, fragrant like "a rose / Made woman by delirious alchemy." Their kiss was a surrender of his "beardless wizardry." Calling him a maneless lion, Vivian gave him food, as from a "magician's oven," and wine, long "quickening" in "Merlin's grave"—all to the tune of flutes, viols, and hautboys. When she chided him for paying the bird pie exclusive attention, he reminded her that she had seen his "great love" and that he must eat or turn to "untimely ashes." She expatiated on his ugly, fearsome, Jeremiah-like beard, was glad when he said he created one kingdom and never any more, told him one Merlin was sufficient for her, and said the golden cups they were drinking from were like ones her father gave kings. Merlin seemed to see "A threatening wisdom" in her eyes. He chided her when she expressed fear of the "specks" she pointed out to him in their golden drinking cups; but then in those specks he saw a black sky, red clouds, and falling towers, then saw nothing, then saw the "slow light of another sky." At last the twittering of birds melted into the sound of a black-headed baby's "breath of innocence" sleeping beside him.

One afternoon beside the sparkling fountain, Vivian told Merlin that she liked fish, ferns, and snakes, and wanted him to join her at a pool where green ferns resemble marching men who stay there always. When they do depart, other crisp ferns come. She hoped Merlin would never go, called him unique, and said he would never grow old. Although Merlin never heard a rude word from her, Vivian feared she might one day buzz incorrigibly at his ears and he would strike her dead in a "philosophic rage." Then he would sit on her grave in remorse. When he protested, she embraced and kissed him, and put her head on his shoulder. She called her head a curse punishing him "for knowing beyond knowledge," and said that like him she "saw too much" but unlike him couldn't make a kingdom. She expressed the hope that her "unquiet soul" will one day go "where souls are quieter." Then:

> Vivian is your punishment
> For making kings of men who are not kings;
> And you are mine, by the same reasoning,
> For living out of Time and out of tune
> With anything but you.

Then, after 10 swiftly passing years, Dagonet brought King Arthur's summons to Merlin, who told Vivian that he made Arthur a king "to be a mirror for the world," was fated to return, but couldn't be more now or do more now than ever before. Not asking Merlin to remain, she watched him go, pitying herself and pitying her "fond Merlin," whom she "had changed" and "who had changed the world."

VI. Now Merlin, who left Vivian for Camelot and returned to her two years later, tells her no kings are pursuing him now. They discuss gossip in Camelot. He hoped to hold his intellectual mirror beside Arthur's for benefit to the future. But, no. Without her, he was lonely; yet doubts plague him here.

"On a golden day in autumn," Merlin and Vivian talk in spurts about Fate and Time. When she asks for a story, he tells, obliquely, about Arthur: his being trapped by Morgause; their dark, reptilian son Modred; Arthur's marrying Guinevere despite her loving Lancelot, Arthur's best knight, and the doom therefore of Arthur's "kingdom builded on two pits / Of living sin." Merlin, who made Arthur king, wanted his reign to be a mirror for the world. Vivian expresses discontent at hearing about kings and sins; she is glad to be away from that clotted, wounded world; it is hardly "a moral for the speckled ages" hence. Objecting to his unfriendly stare, she tells him they can make "this Broceliande a refuge" for "two disheartened sinners" the world doesn't want.

Merlin becomes aware that the potent will of Change has ordained his presence here. When she reminds him of "specks," he accuses her of worrying that word, out of context, like a dog shaking a rag. Saying she could be a finer king than his unlikable, speckled one, Vivian invites him to go bury king, queen, and sins elsewhere; says the world will forget that king "And build for some new king a new foundation"; and laments that, given their present "Tree of Knowledge," they can't call "this forbidden place" Eden.

Alone now, Merlin concludes that a visionary "May see too far, and he may see too late / The path he takes unseeen"; or be lighted by "the immortal flame"; or go beyond twilight to "a nameless light" revealing in death the Grail; or, fooling around with "moths and flowers," be told by Fate to go dig his grave. Aware of his age, Merlin promises himself to tell Vivian a final story.

Days pass. Vivian looks increduously at Merlin, stooped and trembling. Who is he? Not one adored above rulers and jewels. Not her happily terrorizing lover. Not world maker. By the fountain he takes her hands and tells that final story: "I am old." He says he will return to Camelot, return to her, leave her again; he saw too much in Camelot, and beyond, to live; he "played with Time," which will get even with him now. His kiss rests on leaf-cold, unanswering lips.

Next morning Merlin puts on his old pilgrim robe. Vivian, blinded with fear, asks if he is going. Yes, and part of the way with good Blaise. He repeats what he once told Arthur: "I can be no more than what I was, / And I can say no more than I have said." He prays that God will keep her well.

VII. Dagonet, Bedivere, and Gawaine are near Merlin's Rock. Bedivere asks Gawaine to persuade King Arthur to make peace. Gawaine urges death to Lancelot for rescuing Guinevere and killing multiple knights, including Gaheris and Gareth, Gawaine's two unarmed brothers. Bedivere gripes that their kingdom is worth more than revenge. Dagonet brings laughter by saying there'd be no wars if everybody were "rational or rickety" like the three of them. He summarizes: Lancelot wars for love, insane Arthur for hate and love, Gawaine for hate, Modred for his father Arthur's crown and wife; Merlin is "buried in Broceliade!" Bedivere responds that "Another age will have another Merlin, / Another Camelot, and another King."

Gawaine and Bedivere leave to join Arthur's attack on Lancelot and Guinevere at Joyous Gard. Dagonet soliloquizes like a wise court fool on history and human qualities. Merlin, unseen by Gawaine and Bedivere, approaches, in his pilgrim's cloak, with a small beard, and mystical, peaceful eyes that have seen too much. Dagonet says Merlin's offer to pray for him "is indeed the end." Merlin counters: "And in the end / Are more beginnings . . . than men" realize this day; "the Grail foreshowed / The quest of life" which killed many, discouraged others. Dagonet updates Merlin: The Light fell only on Galahad in the Siege Perilous; Gawaine failed to find the Grail, returned, is practically Arthur's king, and hates Lancelot; Bors and Perceval are back; passionate Lancelot has little fun with Guinevere; Arthur's "frenzy . . . has overthrown his wisdom." Merlin: Everyone starts with "a groping thought," which is part "Of an eternal will," becomes illusioned, makes his "self" wilful; Arthur, Gawaine, Guinevere, and Lancelot became "swollen thoughts of this eternal will" and necessarily proceeded to inherit "a wrecked empire." This ruin is

> lighted by the torch
> Of woman, who, together with the light
> That Galahad found, is yet to light the world.

Though admitting his thoughts don't grope much, Dagonet boldly disputes all this by recalling how a woman "with corn-colored hair / Has pranked a man with horns," chanced to be rescued from execution, and caused many combat deaths. If she had been burned as Arthur wanted, his kingdom might be alive. But since that "eternal will says otherwise," Dagonet plans to take his wages to some quiet place with shepherds, now that his beloved Arthur is insane and his beloved Merlin dead. Merlin, saying he is old but not "wholly dead," views Camelot now, and sees it all red and black and crumbling, precisely, he says, the way Vivian looked, "black and red" at that time "her eyes looked into mine / Across the cups of gold," and then, to flute music, "all was black and gold."

Merlin asks Dagonet not to leave him. If he did, he would resemble a fly sent by Fate to sting him and turn his love for Dagonet "to last regret." He tells Dagonet much: "Time overtook" me in Broceliande, where with too many words I warned Vivian. She was warm, kind, and too wise in a world of selfish men. I was joyfully with her in that springtime. I can't see anything to do now but leave Vivian, Arthur, and the world, and to pray for Vivian in this man-made world. In exile now, she knows and cares, yet doesn't know she cares or care she knows. In the future, someone like her will laugh anew and bring helpful fire. I saw all this before. I promised Vivian I would see her again but won't. She may love another man; but my love is "an index of her memories," and she'll remember when my "heart was young."

While Merlin stares at Camelot, which is quiet now but with wind coming, Dagonet expresses fear that Modred, controlling half the kingdom, will grab Guinevere. Merlin answers that if so, it won't be for very long. He asks Dagonet to escort him a little way off and to promise not to mention seing him again for fear people would doubt his loyalty. He hoped

Arthur would be a mirror to others and make them cautious. He saw too much though being "neither Fate nor God," and he uniquely saw "through the dark that lay beyond myself / . . . two fires that are to light the world."

Dagonet calls himself Merlin's fool and the king of no place, says he will take Merlin to a tavern for the night, and after that he will follow Merlin until he dies Merlin's fool. As they leave the deserted Rock and walk into the shadowy night, a cold wind bites them and darkness falls on Camelot.

Among at least 13 sources Robinson used for *Merlin*, and also for *Lancelot* and *Tristram* yet to follow, the main ones are the folllowing: *Le Morte d'Arthur* by Sir Thomas Malory, *Tristram and Iseult* by Matthew Arnold, *Tristram of Lyonesse* by Algernon Charles Swinburne, *Idylls of the King*, especially "Merlin and Vivien" therein, by Alfred, Lord Tennyson, and the summary by S. Humphreys Gurteen of *The Vulgate Merlin*, available in *The Arthurian Cycle* (1895). Owen W. Gilman, Jr. presents textual evidence that "Merlin I" and "Merlin II" by Ralph Waldo Emerson also influenced Robinson's characterization of Merlin. Ruth Nivison,* the daughter of Robinson's sister-in-law Emma Robinson,* presents yet another source, namely her mother, who, she points out, was the close model for Vivian.

The narrative line of *Merlin* seems awkward. Charles Cestre,* normally effusive in his praise of Robinson, finds a little fault here, saying that "[t]he plot of the *Merlin* would be a perfect scenario for a play, but for the retrospective IVth and Vth parts, that take us away from Arthur's court, back to the bower of bliss where ten years before Vivian had drawn the seer by the magic of her siren-song." Theodore Maynard* adverts to the "architectural faults" of *Merlin*. Michael Skupin explains that "these [seven] sections [of *Merlin*] are not in chronological order, which would be IVa, V, I, II, III, IVb, VI and VII." How could Robinson have replied in a letter (June 24, 1917) to Edith Brower,* who had complained of difficulties with *Merlin*, "I thought I had written something that would read straight along"? Amy Lowell* writes, "Can the poem be said really to end? So little rounded it is, that it almost

seems as though it might have stopped before or after the last line without affecting the result." Ben Ray Redman quotes Lowell's abrasive words and says that "they provoke, indeed demand, a downright contradiction"; asserts that "the poem *Merlin* is instinct with a dual vitality: the characters possess the life of epic figures, with all their grandeur and their mystery, and the life of modern individuals, with all their psychological and emotional complexities"; and later specifically lauds the "almost barbaric splendor," "lavish sensual beauty and . . . rich sensual passion" of the scene in which Merlin and Vivian touch speckled cups at table. Yvor Winters points out that Robinson's Merlin is not old, mysterious, and magical as in Malory, nor senile as in Tennyson, nor a subject for parody as in *A Connecticut Yankee in King Arthur's Court* by Mark Twain; rather, Robinson's *Merlin* is middle-aged, mentally and physically powerful, and "given a supernatural air by the fatalism which is central to the theme"—that theme being "human tragedy as the consequence of a falling away from wisdom, and of the falling away as inevitable." Emery Neff refines this idea: "Merlin . . . conceives the experiment of letting Arthur build a kingdom on rotten foundations, so that its collapse may be a mirror in which ages to come may read the doom of every society so based." Ellsworth Barnard says that Arthur's kingdom was rotten because of his affair with his sister (urecognized) and then his loveless union with Guinevere; Barnard then analogizes by saying that "The rotten foundation of Western civilization would have been [*sic*] its economic and political imperialism, . . . the fierce pursuit of personal and national wealth and power." This echoes Robinson's own assertion, in a letter (September 8, 1918) to Hermann Hagedorn* that he converted Merlin into "such a lover of the world as to use Arthur and his empire as an object lesson to prove to coming generations that nothing can stand on a rotten foundation."

Although some readers find disparate stories in Merlin as Arthur's advisor and Merlin as Vivian's lover, Nathan Comfort Starr says this: "Contrary to the opinion of some critics the two strands unite to make a single story of the conflict of virtually irreconcilable forces."

Louise Dauner says that "Vivian illustrates the knowing woman" who "within limits" fashions her own destiny; when, as a youth she first saw Merlin at Arthur's court, she chose him "for her lover." Lyle Domina seeks to refine earlier critical comments and, in that enterprise, "to examine *Merlin* more closely, with particular emphasis on the question of fate, on the nature of Merlin's love affair with Vivian, and on Merlin's 'spiritual defeat,' and the whole problem of pessimism within the poem." Valerie M. Lagorio points out Robinson's use of "three dominant leitmotifs: the mirror, which is central to his apocalyptic purpose, using the Arthurian world as a mirror for all ages to see the causes for the decimation of his and their world; specks, standing for moral and spiritual imperfections; and black and crimson clouds, storms, and ominous darkness." Earlier, Cestre also made much of the word "specks" in *Merlin*, saying that "'specks,' in his [Merlin's] reflective melancholy mood, become the symbol of the gloom gathering over their [his and Vivian's] heads." The devotion of scholars to Robinson is typified by these mind-numbing statistics, developed by Elsie Ruth Dykes Chant and summarized by Skupin: *Merlin* contains 2,629 lines of blank verse, has 26,904 syllables, has 90 trochees substituted for iambs, has 112 anapests substituted for iambs, has three hexameter lines, and 482 lines ending in unstressed syllables. (Sources: Barnard, 118; Carley, 3–4; Cestre, 79, 85; Chant; Dauner, 154; Domina, 472; Franchere, 116; Gilman; Goodrich; Lacy and Ashe; Lagorio, 167; Lowell [1917], 69; Maynard [1924], 167; Perrine [1974]; Redman, 73, 73–74, 79; E. Robinson, 14; *Selected Letters*, 112; Skupin, 29–32; Starr [1969], 111–12; W. Thompson; Winters, 63, 68)

"A Mighty Runner" *see* "Variations of Greek Themes"

"The Mill" (1919). Poem.

"The Mill" (1919). Poem. The last thing the miller's wife heard him say was that "There are no millers any more." She is apprehensively awaiting his return home. The tea has turned cold. The fire is dead. Still, "there might yet be nothing wrong." Dazed by fear, however, she soon finds herself at the mill, which is warm and fragrant and thus reminiscent of the past. Her husband has hanged himself there. She proceeds to "Black water, smooth above the weir / Like starry velvet in the night." The ruffling her body makes is brief.

Esther Willard Bates* reports that the real mill providing a physical basis for the one in this poem was a dark and silent one in West Peterborough, an extinct settlement near the MacDowell Colony.* Ben Ray Redman, adept at defending Robinson against early adverse critics of "The Mill," says that "those who object to its obscurity should realize that it is, in great part, to the indirect method that we owe the drama and the haunting atmosphere which pervade the whole." Two critics have zeroed in on the impact a few words make in "The Mill." Emery Neff says that "The unobtrusive appearance of . . . 'yet' in . . . [']there might yet be nothing wrong['] . . . is beyond praise." Wallace L. Anderson notes that the "double stress at 'Black water' . . . accentuate[s] the finality of her act." Norman N. Holland lists and comments on various readers' responses elicited by questions about this unsettling and challenging poem, responses ranging from objective to subjective. Gloriana Locklear counters standard interpretations when, after analyzing Robinson's use of several past perfect and past conditional verbs, she surmises that the reader has "little text proof that the miller's wife has gone out to the mill and found her husband hanging," and that her "drowning [herself] is a very speculative thing, not something that we are to take as an accomplished fact." (Sources: W. Anderson [1968], 104; Bates, 3; Holland; Locklear, 177; Neff, 197–98; Redman, 41; W. Robinson, 104)

"Miniver Cheevy" (1907). Poem.

"Miniver Cheevy" (1907). Poem. Miniver Cheevy grew skinny griping at everything. He had plenty of reasons to complain. He liked to think of the long-gone times of horses, knights, and their shining weapons. While he was busy sighing about the past, he avoided work and dreamed away about Thebes, Camelot, and the neighbors of Priam. He combined a dislike of present-day successes with a conviction that romance and art were outmoded. He would have committed sins to be a Medici, regarded khaki uniforms with displeasure, and yet missed the gracefulness of "iron clothing." He was both scornful of gold and distressed that he lacked it; in fact, he "thought, and thought, and thought, / And thought about it." All this time, aware of being "born too late," he scratched himself, continued thinking, coughed, blamed fate, "And kept on drinking."

The rhyme scheme of this eight-stanza poem is *abab*, with each pair of *b*-rhymes feminine. Robinson brings Miniver back from the past and down to reality when he writes that his subject "mourn[s] the fact that romance is "on the town" while art is "a vagrant." Ellsworth Barnard regards "Miniver Cheevy" as comic because there is a "disparity" between Miniver's and his viewers' views of "the same experience," namely, Miniver's life. However, nothing seems really funny about Miniver's self-deluded fate. Would anyone like to be his nephew or niece? One might also question the assertion of Hermann Hagedorn* that in "Miniver Cheevy" Robinson "'spoofed' himself." Hyatt H. Waggoner expands this chancy notion: "Miniver *is* [Waggoner's emphasis] Robinson," who like Miniver "dreamed of Camelot," but — more — went on "and wrote three very long, and very tedious, Arthurian poems in which the 'dreaming' is compulsive and unrecognized." Winifred H. Sullivan believes that, in addition to spoofing himself as resembling Miniver, Robinson also "satirizes the age and, especially, its literary taste." Christopher Macgowan points to Miniver as illustrating Robinson's persistent refusal to blame fate for human failures. Macgowan says that Miniver wrongly "called it fate" that he was born past his supposedly preferred medieval times; yet, Macgowan adds, although Robinson "gently mocked . . . [the] self-indulgence that accompanied Miniver's alcoholism," he also expressed "a genuine sympathy for a man unable to live in what his life has made of his personal present."

Robert Frost relished Robinson's use of the word "thought" four times in describing Miniver's inactivity. Frost writes, "I remember the pleasure with which [Ezra] Pound and I laughed over the fourth 'thought.' . . . With the fourth, the fun began." Frost explains that the fourth "thought" "turns up . . . round the corner," helps to "shape . . . the stanza," and effortlessly turns "the obstacle of verse . . . to advantage." Christopher Beach observes that in the last stanza of "Miniver Cheevy" "[t]he rhyme of 'thinking' and 'drinking'—. . . playing with the thin vowel sounds of Miniver's name — encapsulates the difference between what Cheevy is and what he would like to be." (Sources: Barnard, 183, 182; Beach, 11; Frost, xi; Hagedorn, 238; Macgowan, 35; Sullivan, 185; Waggoner, 284, 283)

"The Miracle" (1896). Sonnet. A woman asked the persona, whom she called "brother" and "friend," to do something for her. After her death, let "red roses be the sign / Of the white life I lost for him"; further, pity and forgive him, don't curse and hate him. Then she died "read[ing] / Love's message in love's murder." She was buried beneath red roses, but in the spring white blossoms appeared there.

According to a letter (October 7, 1894) that Robinson sent to Harry de Forest Smith,* he only half liked "The Miracle." The amorous triangle in the poem may have been suggested by Robinson's disappointment when his brother Herman Robinson* and Emma Shepherd (see Robinson, Emma) were married in 1890. The woman's "white life" might be her sexual innocence, miraculously restored after death. (Sources: Cary [1975], 17–18, 173; *Untriangulated Stars*, 170)

"Mr. Flood's Party" (1920). Poem. Old Eben Flood pauses on his walk back from Tilbury Town to "the forsaken upland hermitage" that he calls his final home. No one can hear; so he comments that "we" won't have many more harvest moons because "The bird is on the wing," according to the poet. Eben raises his newly filled jug and invites himself to toast the bird. Standing there "as if enduring to the end / A valiant armor of scarred hopes outworn," he hoists his drink in a way resembling "Roland's ghost winding a silent horn," in a "salutation of the dead." He puts his jug down gently, just the way a mother might lay a child down to rest, "knowing that most things break." Then he plants his uncertain feet carefully, paces off a little, greets himself with a handshake, and announces that the two haven't shared a friendly drop for some little time. His other self willingly has just a bit, "For auld lang syne." The brief drink was just enough, for now; it makes old Eben sing, "with only two moons listening." The song wavers off. He is alone again. He shakes his head, aware that

There was not much that was ahead of him,
And there was nothing in the town below—
Where strangers would have shut the many doors
That many friends had opened long ago.

Emma Robinson* and Ruth Nivison* suggest that this poem was inspired by Robinson's memory of being with his brothers and witnessing an old neighbor named John Esmond treating himself to a solitary drink on Church Hill one night. Esmond lived, they add, on the Brunswick Road in a cottage later perhaps owned by Charles Strehan. Wallace L. Anderson [1980] presents evidence that the model for Eben Flood was an old man named Johnny Hutchings, who, Robinson said in an early letter from Gardiner (February 3, 1895) to Harry de Forest Smith,* liked to go to bed with a bottle of rum and an assortment of dime novels. Carlos Baker reminds readers that "the advent of Eben Flood [*Nation*, Fall 1920] approximately coincided with the passage of the Volstead Act [initiating Prohibition, as of January 16, 1920], which Robinson regarded with extreme displeasure." Although Baker believes that the contents of Mr. Flood's jug was hard cider, one may hope he knew a coastal bootlegger bringing scotch in from Canada.

William C. Childers notes that the name "Eben Flood" sounds exactly like "'ebb and flood,' a variant form of 'ebb and flow,' which refers to the rise or fall of the tide." Childers adds that the expression also alludes to "the rise and fall of human fortunes," clearly, here, including those of Mr. Flood. Chard Powers Smith* says that in the late 1920s Robinson told him that "Mr. Flood's Party" was "the best thing I ever did." Thomas L. Brashear finds parallels between "Mr. Flood's Party" and "Childe Roland to the Dark Tower Came." Baker, after discussing the obvious influence of Omar Khayyám's *Rubáiyát* ("The Bird of Time has but a little way / To flutter—

and the Bird is on the Wing") and *The Song of Roland*, names a possible third literary source—"The Old Man's Carousal" by James Kirke Paulding (1779–1860).

The precise, iambic pentameter lines and the difficult rhyme scheme—*abcbdefe*—of "Mr. Flood's Party" help to create solidity in the structure of this seven-stanza classic. Ben Ray Redman, defending Robinson against critics who dislike his humor, writes this: "Much has been said of his 'astringent humor,' but we must seek another adjective to fit the humor that he reveals in 'Mr. Flood's Party,' let us say, and in a host of other poems. Because of his pity he cannot be cruel, and because of his humor he cannot be sentimental; his scale is balanced well." Emery Neff reports that the poem "arose from . . . a recollection of Harry [de Forest] Smith[*]'s father's story of a Maine eccentric who used to propose and drink toasts to himself." James L. Allen, Jr. suggests that allusions in the poem to the moon and to singing underpin its theme of the wax-wane, rise-fall cycle of the tide-like lives people experience. Although most readers probably reason that Mr. Flood sees two moons because his liquor is causing him to see double, John E. Parish contends that he (Flood, that is) sees two moons because his eyes are suffused with tears. H. R. Wolf tries this: Mr. Flood is "exile[d] from himself—the self that is rooted in the past"; requires the relief of alcohol, which "points to an infantile need"; and therefore, since Robinson combines the image of Flood as "mother" with the jug as a "sleeping child," it "is not farfetched" to explicate "the 'two moons listening' . . . as a breast image."

Ellsworth Barnard comments on the effective use of assonance and alliteration in the third stanza of "Mr. Flood's Party." Roy Harvey Pearce says that "Robinson has no illusions about the fate of this man—not even enough to comment, in the manner of one of [Herman] Melville's narrators [that of 'Bartleby'], 'Ah. Mr. Flood! Ah humanity!'" Pearce adds that neither Mr. Flood, nor any other of Robinson's similarly lonely, deprived subjects, has "the power to say even 'I prefer not to.'" A few critics believe, doubtless incorrectly, that Eben Flood drank so much that his former friends shut their doors against him. He has clearly outlived his cronies and is indeed "enduring to the end," which phrasing, as Anderson (1968) noted, "calls to mind the words of Jesus when he sent forth his disciples, 'he that endureth to the end shall be saved'" (Matt 10:22; see also Mark 13:13). Richard Gray, in explicating the Roland image, comments that "the knight and the drunkard turn out to be very much alike. Both . . . present types of endurance, as men who recall the past while preparing to meet their former companions in another world." (Sources: Allen; W. Anderson [1968], 111; W. Anderson [1980], 54; Baker, 327, 334; Barnard, 56; Brashear; Childers [1955], 225; Gray, 143; Neff, 198; Parish; Pearce, 260; Redman, 35; E. Robinson, 17; C. Smith, 340; *Untriangulated Stars*, 202)

"Modernities" (1921). Sonnet. The knowledge we gain may soon be antiquated. We are simply the latest but not the last to struggle intellectually. We will encounter problems our parents failed to solve. But later we too will leave the "dark" field to others.

"Modred: A Fragment" (1928). Incomplete blank-verse narrative. Leading Agravaine and Colgrevance through a gate into his father King Arthur's palace, Modred professes his desire to show them Lancelot's sneaking into Queen Guinevere's room during Arthur's supposed absence. The three will then kill Lancelot. Surprised at hearing this final detail, Colgrevance declines. Modred blandly urges the two to be loyal to the king, says he saw Guinevere as she "nuzzled and smothered" Lancelot, and forward they proceed. Agravaine whispers to Modred that they don't need Colgrevance along, to which Modred says Colgrevance "was appointed by his fate" to help Modred's "necessity" in case of emergency. They hear Dagonet singing to their smiling prey.

This 164-line section was originally part of *Lancelot*. It was deleted by Thomas Seltzer,* who had a small publishing house and who, before publishing *Lancelot*, thought it was too long. Robinson issued a limited edition, in 250 copies, of "Modred: A Fragment" (New York, New Haven: Edmund B. Hackett,

1929), and sold the manuscript to Howard George Schmitt, in 1929, for something over $50. Ellsworth Barnard describes Modred here as "suave and persuasive, and his egotism and malice are only to be inferred." (Sources: Barnard, 205; Carley; Schmitt, 10)

"Momus" (1910). Poem. Momus gripes, over and over: Byron is passé, Browning has vanished, Wordsworth occasionally "lumbers like a raft," and poets nowadays won't find any subjects. But Momus is then reminded that as long as stars shine blue some themes will be left for poets to write about and, failing, left for Momus to gripe about.

The poem means little unless the reader is aware that Momus in Greek mythology is the son of night, personifies censoriousness, and is often regarded as licensed to grumble and carp and find fault. Although Robinson liked the works of the three poets he named but only with reservations, he implicitly attacks them here a bit but then less implicitly criticizes Philistines of his time for their belief that poetry itself is passé. Robinson deliberately downgrades Momus by writing about him here in three choppy little sing-song stanzas, in dimeter, trimeter, and tetrameter trochees, rhyming *aabbccb*. (Read aloud, this rhyme scheme sounds for all the world like "Mary had a little lamb.") Two pairs of funny rhymes are "become of" and "some of" and perhaps "father" and "ra[h]ther."

"Monadnock Through the Trees" (1921). Sonnet. Before any time-mocking structures such as the Pyramids ever existed in Egypt, you were high "above ancestral evergreens,"old pine trees, and this before anyone ever saw you. And when we have all "done our mortal best and worst," you will still be here in a calm as unaltered as when Assyrians headed south for war.

Robinson undoubtedly had the poem "Monadnoc" by Ralph Waldo Emerson in mind when he began writing "Monadnock Through the Trees." Robinson delighted in his view of Monadnock from his studio at the MacDowell Colony* and once, according to Hermann Hagedorn,* remarked to Marian Nivens MacDowell,* his hostess there, that "I rather think the old fellow will miss me a bit when I'm gone." Ellsworth Barnard extols "Monadnock Through the Trees" when he says it contains "a complex and fluid pattern (past and present, time and eternity, nature and man) by enveloping his poem with allusions to ancient history." (Sources: Barnard, 141; Hagedorn, 371)

Monroe, Harriet (1860–1936). Writer and editor. Born Hattie Monroe in Chicago, she read widely in her lawyer-father's home library. She attended Mosley School in Chicago (beginning 1867–1868) and the Visitation Convent in Washington, D.C. (1877–1879), returned to Chicago, and wrote poetry and was a freelance reviewer of art, music, and drama for Chicago and also New York newspapers (1879–1889). When she visited New York with her sister (1888–1889), she was befriended by editors Edmund Clarence Stedman* and Richard Watson Gilder,* among others involved in literature. Monroe published poetry (beginning 1888) and gained recognition for an ode she composed for the opening of the Chicago Auditorium (1889). She visited Europe (1890) and met several distinguished writers. She was art critic for the *Chicago Tribune* (1890, 1909–1914). Her ode commemorating the World Columbian Exposition held in Chicago (1892–1893) gave her further renown. The first of her several volumes of poems is *Valeria and Other Poems* (1892).

Monroe remained active as a freelance journalist, creative writer, and teacher (1895–1910). She published *John Wellborn Root* (1896), a biography of her brother-in-law, an architect for the Columbian Exposition. She revisited Europe (1897–1898). She secured funds to establish *Poetry: A Magazine of Verse*, America's first journal devoted exclusively to poetry (1912). In the beginning, Alice Corbin Henderson was associate editor and Ezra Pound was foreign correspondent; Monroe remained founder-editor until 1936. *Poetry* enabled her to give early exposure to such often innovative poets as T. S. Eliot, Robert Frost, James Joyce, Vachel Lindsay, Amy Lowell,* Wallace Stevens, and Robinson. Monroe revisited Europe (1923). Her *Poets and Their Art* (1926) includes canny commentary on

Robinson. Always socializing pleasantly, she continued to travel widely, to Mexico (1933) and China (1934), and attended a conference of P.E.N. (the International Association of Poets, Playwrights, Editors, Essayists and Novelists) at Buenos Aires, Argentina (August 1936). While exploring Inca ruins, Monroe suddenly died, and was buried in Arequipa, Peru, at the foot of Mount Misti, in the Andes. Her autobiography is *A Poet's Life: Seventy Years in a Changing World* (1938). Monroe never married.

Harriet Monroe happily published "Eros Turannos" (1914), "Bokardo" (1915), and "Avenel Gray" (1922; see "Mortmain") in her *Poetry*, and in other ways encouraged Robinson. She reviewed five of his books in *Poetry*, preferred his non-Arthurian works, and published three perceptive overviews of his evolving career (1916–1935). (Source: Cahill)

Moody, William Vaughn (1869–1910). Poet and playwright. Born in Spencer, Indiana, Moody soon moved with his family to New Albany, Indiana, where he attended school. After high school, he studied painting, taught, studied classics at an academy in Poughkeepsie, New York, and entered Harvard (1889). He wrote for the *Harvard Monthly*, spent his senior year in Europe, Turkey, and Greece, and returned to Harvard study (B.A., 1893; M.A., 1894; instructor in English, 1894–1895). During his years in and near Harvard, Moody made friends with Robert Morss Lovett,* Daniel Gregory Mason,* Josephine Preston Peabody,* and Bliss Perry, among others. While teaching at the University of Chicago (1896–1898, 1901), Moody wrote poetry, did substantial editing, and began a prolific publishing career cut short by an early death. His poetic-drama trilogy (never produced) is *The Masque of Judgment* (1900), *The Fire-Bringer* (1904), and *The Death of Eve* (1912, incomplete). His prose plays are *The Sabine Woman* (produced in 1906; retitled *The Great Divide* and produced again, 1909) and *The Faith Healer* (produced 1909). He collected his lyrics in *Poems* (1901). Moody was once regarded as America's foremost poet, especially by his friends, later including Percy MacKaye* and Ridgely Torrence.*

Moody is now mainly remembered for a few short poems, including these three: "The Brute" (1900), describing the machine as something to be feared, admired, and mocked; "Gloucester Moors" (1900), combining nature description with an image of the world as a ship of souls; and especially "An Ode in Time of Hesitation" (1900), critical of America's imperialism following the Spanish-American War. Moody diverted his energy from creative writing to prepare scholarly editions of standard English authors, and by coauthoring two books with Lovett —*A History of English Literature* (1902, a money-maker) and *A First View of English Literature* (1905). Moody met Harriet Tilden Brainard (1899), married her (1909), began going blind, and soon died of a brain tumor. Moody is an early example of the now frequently observable scholar-professor-poet.

Robinson undoubtedly saw Moody when both were at Harvard (1891); but Moody, two classes in advance, was popular and sociable, unlike Robinson. Their friendship began in New York (1899). When Robinson heard about Moody's forthcoming "Ode," his endorsement of its message is indicated by a pungent passage in a letter (April 18, 1900) to Daniel Gregory Mason, in which he sarcastically wondered how "our incomparable republic" could ever justify turning the Philippine Islands into "a game preserve." Hermann Hagedorn* believed that Robinson regarded Moody as "his most dangerous rival for poetic supremacy in America." He adds that Robinson was apprehensively "patronizing" in his reaction to Moody's *The Masque of Judgment*, when in a letter (November 25, 1900) to their mutual friend Josephine Preston Peabody he says that *The Masque of Judgment* is "pretty big" but that its fundamental "scheme . . . escaped" him, then opines that "Perhaps Moody's greatest trouble lies in the fact that he has so many things to unlearn." In a letter (January 17, 1901) to John Hays Gardiner,* however, Robinson praises *The Masque of Judgment* as "astonishing[,] . . . almost flawless" in its form. He admired the message of Moody's "Ode" but in another letter to Mason (September 26, 1901) calls the image of "God's ring-finger" in it "really damnable." In

the same letter, he lauds "The Daguerreotype," Moody's 1901 saccharin ode to his mother's memory. Horace Gregory and Marya Zaturenska suggest that "The Daguerreotype" typifies "the lack of sensibility and taste," and even the persistent "faulty diction" of "The 'Twilight Interval'" period of American poetry, dominated, they say, by Moody.

Moody helped Robinson on occasion, not least when he suggested to Richard Watson Gilder,* one of his editorial associates, that President Theodore Roosevelt* ought to assign Robinson to an consular sinecure abroad. The outcome, instead, was Robinson's New York job with the Collector of Customs. When Moody's *The Sabine Woman* was a success on Broadway, Robinson attended the first performance and celebrated his delight by writing "The White Lights." Moody's success helped motivate Robinson to write his own first play, the ill-starred *Van Zorn*. Moody, who always admired Robinson's poetry, may have been, as has often been suggested, a sort of gental spiritual mentor" to Robinson. When Moody died, Robinson wrote (October 17, 1910) to MacKaye that Moody has "his place among the immortals" and it was good that "he is now done with pain." Robinson dedicated *Cavender's House* (1929) "To the Memory of William Vaughn Moody." Maurice F. Brown explains that Robinson and Moody attracted one another by being different in appearance, personality, and action, that they often were affiliated with the 1890s literary tradition, but that Robinson was ambivalent in his attitude toward Moody and indifferent to his philosophizing. Richard Cary expertly summarizes the relationship of Robinson and Moody. (Sources: Brower, 32, 33; M. Brown; Cary [1974], 121; Gregory, 27; Hagedorn, 180; Morison, 430, 433; *Selected Letters*, 29, 33, 38, 44, 69)

Morrell, Mary (1837–1919). (Full name: Mary Osgood Ring Morrell.) She was Robinson's primary-school teacher. Born in Industry, Maine, she was the daughter of Joseph Ring and Sarah Goodridge Ring. Her husband was William Morrell (1836–1920), a Gardiner brick maker and printer. (See "Uncle Ananias.") Mary and William married in

1869, and he died the following year. They had one son, Harry Mellen Morrell (1869–1881), whose premature death by diphtheria affected young Robinson deeply. Hermann Hagedorn* describes Mrs. Morrell as "smooth, white, and rotund," and a good-humored and successful teacher. By terms of her will, Mrs. Morrell bequeathed a set of gold and white china to Laura E. Richards Wiggins (d. 1988), daughter of Laura E. Richards,* whom Robinson knew well. (Source: Hagedorn, 17)

Morris, Lloyd R. (1893–1954). Social historian and literary critic. Morris was born in New York City, obtained an A.B. at Columbia University (1914), was employed in the U.S. Postal Censorship office in New York (1914–1918), edited *The American Exporter* (1919–1923), and during the later 1920s was occasionally an expatriate in Paris. Morris, who never married, was a versatile freelance writer, taught in Columbia's extension division, and worked with New York postal authorities in counter-intelligence censorship (1941–1944). In addition to books on aviation, the American theater, the history of New York City, a play, some fiction, and an autobiography, Morris wrote critical studies of Nathaniel Hawthorne (1927) and William James* (1950), as well as *The Poetry of Edwin Arlington Robinson* (1923), the first book devoted to Robinson.

Chard Powers Smith* says that Morris, who frequented the MacDowell Colony,* wrote Robinson about the death of Smith's wife abroad and got Smith an invitation to the colony. Thus Smith met Robinson, who was both sympathetic and invited him to play pool. (Source: C. Smith, 3–14 passim)

"Mortmain" (1922). Poem. Avenel Gray, 50, has gray hair, gray eyes, and a visitor. She and Seneca Sprague, also 50 and with thinning gray hair, are sitting in her garden this Sunday afternoon. To him, she is graceful like a 30-year-old but timid like a child. He says that he is bringing Time and Destiny along; wonders why this "perishable angel" likes him but doesn't love him; says they once agreed that their lives were going to be a triumph together; warns that what she loves is far away.

When he adds that he might leave her, she seems frightened, then laughs, and wonders where he might ever go. He expresses puzzlement, to which she says she has done nothing to make her a stranger to him. He says, not reproachfully, that she and her brother were born strange; she must speak, since he isn't wise or kind enough to leave silently this time; his hope now resembles dry bones in a desert; he wants her now to recognize that she is an anomaly, an "adorable and essential monster."

Avenel remains silent and merely stares at her flowers, until their "fragrance had almost a sound" which becomes "an accusing voice of color." Seneca looks beyond her many blooms, to the trees and to the blue summer sky that hides stars. He suggests that God first tortures our faith with "harps / Or fires" and then sets up unavoidable laws. Seneca calls Avenel a phantom before which an immeasurable power may be making him bow "for the last time, possibly."

Her eyes fill with tears. Pyrrhus, her old cat, enters. She wonders if what Seneca is getting at is that she is "an old cat" too. When she says she's been reading *Hamlet*, he counters that all of his reading has taught him only that her brother used to be here and still is. She has made him wait, "so long," to say this at last. Pained, she finally replies: I can't forget my brother; I am not mysterious; I've been right here, "all alone." Seneca says that her brother, though gone now for 10 years, has caged her; she has wasted time, is now deceiving the present. She tells him he didn't cause the wait. He worries if, should he take her far away, she would forget the half of her buried here. At this, Pyrrhus leaps into Avenel's lap and regards Seneca with suspicion. Seneca adds that "insight and experience" told him that carting her off would be useless. Further, she is wrong to say she has been alone here; he is "forever near you, and if unseen, / Always a refuge"; however, trying to get her away might have provided him with a timely escape.

Avenel retorts: These statements present more nonsense than you ever said in 40 years. Where would you go? Seneca says they are neighbors, yes, but friends no more. She says he is ignorant to talk of powers and laws, which after all made her the way she is. Praising God that she is not any stranger than she is right now, Seneca adds this: You are wed to your brother's ghost; his cold hand is always on my shoulder; I surrender my dream to him; later fatigue or pity in you won't help. Avenel doesn't believe him, says he may well depart but only for a short time, asks him to leave Time and Destiny behind when he calls again, says the two of them will stay amiable through being aware of their families' never-changing differences.

Pyrrhus yawns as Seneca sighs and leaves. Home again, he improvises the vision of a ship departing from Tilbury Town, being engulfed in mountainous waves, and sinking with everyone aboard.

Esther Willard Bates* says that Robinson asked her whether her mother knew any true "dead hand" (cf. mortmain) stories not already used by writers. Her mother didn't. Bates reports that Harriet Monroe* asked Robinson to contribute a poem for the 10th anniversary issue of her *Poetry: A Magazine of Verse.* He sent "Mortmain," the title of which she persuaded him to change. So, for what proved to be its magazine appearance only, he called it "Avenel Gray."

According to Emma Robinson,* Robinson's widowed sister-in-law, "Mortmain" reflects his unsuccessful proposal of marriage to her, and further, that the conversation between Avenel and Seneca is almost word for word hers and the frustrated poet's. Chard Powers Smith* says that while reading "Mortmain" he visualized Robinson and Emma in her garden in Farmingdale, Maine. Hoyt C. Franchere also reads "Mortmain" as "a dialogue between Edwin and Emma in later years." Emery Neff regards "Mortmain" as "one of the most moving portrayals of New England reticence, whereby speech is only a surface indication of passion and despair." James Dickey writes that Avenel and Seneca "are . . . exemplars of eternal laws that we may guess at but not know." The image of that flower's fragrance taking on a "voice of color" is quite an example of synesthesia. "Mortmain" cries out for someone to explicate hidden meanings in "Avenel," "Pyrrhus," and "Seneca." (Sources: Bates, 10–11; Dickey, xvi; Franchere, 71; Neff, 221; E. Robinson, 21; C. Smith, 226)

"Mulieria, a Metrical Discourse, by Edwin Robinson" (1888). Poem, unrecovered. The poet dreams that he has wandered into a town in which only women live. He is arrested by police persons in petticoats. To escape probable danger, he hands them a copy of the Delineator (which is rhymed here with "their [women's] natur'"). Since it is a fashion magazine, its contents naturally trigger a quarrel among the ladies.

Robinson recited this poem as part of his high-school graduation program, held in a huge building also housing a skating rink, in Gardiner, Maine (June 15, 1888). The *Kennebec Reporter* (June 16, 1888) and the Gardiner *Home Journal* (June 20, 1888) comment on the poem, and Hermann Hagedorn* summarizes it and quotes parts of it. He also evidently interviewed surviving friends of Robinson; their impression of the event was that the young poet was handsome and nervous, and read too softly to be heard above a rainstorm drumming on the roof. (Sources: Cary [1975], xiii; Hagedorn, 44; Richards [1936], 29)

"Music and Poetry" (1916, 1940). Essay. Robinson wrote this in the form of a letter (July 15, 1916) and sent it to Arthur Finley Nevin (1871–1943), a composer and the brother of Ethelbert Woodbridge Nevin (1862–1901), the better-known composer. Robinson complains of the difficulty of saying much about the relationship between music and poetry, since each is also the other. Earlier, he says, he defined poetry as a language expressing through emotional reactions what cannot be said. Words, regardless of their intensity or lyricism, are more subtle with respect to sounds and meanings than combinations of musical tones can be. Many modern composers wrongly try to make tones act like words. Likewise, many poets, for example, Algernon Charles Swinburne and Sidney Lanier, try to make words act like tones. Poetry is harder to analyze than music because poetry is simultaneously both language and music. Programme poetry cannot be, and programme music should not be. Poetry and music are demonstrations of the greatest art. Musicians can happily say that music starts where poetry ends; however, musical tones must proceed beyond what we now have if they intend to overtake poetic tonalities. (Sources: Cary [1975], 69–70, 188; *Selected Letters*. 95–96)

Music, Robinson and. Among all the arts and next to poetry, Robinson was the most intensely responsive to music. Laura E. Richards* invited Robinson to informal musicales at her home in Gardiner, Maine, and notes in her book about him that when one of her daughters would be playing something by Bach or Beethoven he would be "sitting in the deep chair, listening with every fibre of him." In an essay, Lewis Montefiore Isaacs* writes that Robinson's knowledge of music was extensive, that he relished musical interludes which interrupted or followed his intense hours of writing, and even that he played the clarinet. (He also played the violin.) In the course of discussing many of Robinson's poems, Isaacs includes quotations about or mentions the following musical composers, musical compositions, and musical instruments: Bach, bassoon, Beethoven, "The Bohemian Girl," *Bolero*, "The British Grenadier," Brahms, cornet, *Don Giovanni*, drum, *Figaro*, *The Flying Dutchman*, flute, Gilbert and Sullivan, *Götterdammerung*, Handel, *H.M.S. Pinafore*, hautboy, *Iolanthe*, lyre, *Meistersinger[s]*, Mozart, *Norma*, *Parsifal*, Ravel, *Ruddigore*, Scriabine, *Tristan*, trombone, *Il Trovatore*, "The Trumpeteer of Säckengen," viol, violin, and Wagner. In a letter (February 13, 1933) to Laura E. Richards, Robinson says that he finds Richard Wagner "greater and more incredible as time goes on." In several of Robinson's poems, music figures for symbolic value or as background. Richard Cary reprints a Boston *Post* interview (May 30, 1913), in which Robinson says he is "fond of old songs, such as 'My Old Kentucky Home.'"

Louis Untermeyer,* with the help of William J. Studer, presents a list showing that on 17 occasions between 1924 and 1960, 10 different poems by Robinson were set to music, with "The Dark Hills" being the winner with six renditions. Scott Donaldson says that Robinson's "poetry sounds [his emphasis]"; notes that "[r]efrains from nature and the music of the spheres serve throughout to embody image and convey metaphor, to abet

character and lend structure"; points out that Robinson composed a little music and enjoyed listening to a wide range of music; discusses the musicality of *Captain Craig* and *The Man Who Died Twice*; and carefully analogizes *Tristram* and musical forms. (Sources: Cary [1974], 258; Donaldson [1980], 63 and passim; Isaacs; Richards [1936], 50; *Selected Letters*, 170; Untermeyer, 29–30)

"My Methods and Meanings" (1917, 1940, 1975). Essay. Robinson wrote this in the form of a letter (July 11, 1917) to Lewis Nathaniel Chase.* He makes many exciting points. For biographical details, he refers his reader to *Who's Who*. He has hoped his poetry would speak for itself about him. In 1907 he was criticized for being a radical and for using simple language. He depends on context, not vocabulary, therefore was labeled too subtle by "the initiated" and dull by the dull. To understand him, one needs a serious sense of humor. Imagine, someone thought his "The Gift of God" was "a touching tribute to our Saviour." He was once under the influence of William Wordsworth and Rudyard Kipling, but never consciously under that of Robert Browning. Admittedly, like Browning, he uses more colloquial language than "poetic" language. His style was established before his first book was published, in 1896.

He regularly sees the end of one of his poems before he starts writing it. He discards a started poem if he feels disgusted with it and feels it is saying nothing. As examples of ease or difficulty of composition, he says that for a joke he wrote "Another Dark Lady" in 20 minutes but fiddled with "The Clerks" for a month. Often, a first draft must seem worthwhile or the poem will fail; however, something worthwhile "takes any amount of labor" to complete.

He is reluctant to "annotate individual poems." Most of his works have some personal touches, but he can't recall "anything . . . that is a direct transcription of experience." For example, the ringing of church bells, which he doesn't like to hear, triggered his writing "On the Night of a Friend's Wedding"; yet those bells rang for the marriage of a couple he cared nothing about.

He used to sweat over a single line of poetry for days, doesn't now but is grateful for such "grilling experience" and feels that "the technical flappiness of many writers" results from their never forcing themselves to work similarly hard over their lines. Fortunately, few people are committed to writing poetry with sufficient devotion for it to get in the way of their earning money for food.

Evidently responding to a specific request, Robinson reluctantly recommends 13 of his poems which might be read aloud and "possibly give pleasure." He says most of them need no explanation but then adds fragments of commentary on the others, thus: "Vickery's Mountain" concerns "human inertia," stronger than Vickery; "John Evereldown" and "The Tavern" are "fanciful sketches, without ethical or symbolical significance"; "Doctor of Billiards" presents a man wasting a life he mysteriously finds worthless; "The Man Against the Sky" represents "a protest against a material explanation of the universe"; "The Return of Morgan and Fingal" comprises "an episode with overtones." The other poems, named but not discussed, are "The Clerks," "Amaryllis," Cortège," "The Master," "Calvary," "Flammonde," "and The Gift of God."

Republishing this essay (1975), Richard Cary [1974] presents all the needful evidence of Robinson vis-a-vis Browning (he liked Browning's lyrics, couldn't stand his longer works and plays, despised "Rabbi Ben Ezra," and hated being repeatedly linked to Browning); Wordsworth (Wordsworth's "Ode: Intimations of Immortality from Recollections of Early Childhood" was worth all the rest of Wordsworth); and Kipling (he was once influenced by him, preferred his poetry to his prose, and thought him often too journalistic). (Sources: Cary [1975], 78–81, 189; Cary [1974], 48–49, 50, 77, 90)

"Neighbors" (1919). Poem. The persona says that when he and others thought about a certain "wolf-haunted wife" in their neighborhood, they were sympathetic about the problems she bore and the shabby clothing she wore. She was aloof, smiled or maybe only seemed to smile, rarely visited them, and when she did soon distanced herself again. Her suddenly dying should have struck them as a natural change, but instead it seemed strange. It was the same old story: "Love, with its gift of pain, had given / More than one heart could hold."

"New England" (1923). Sonnet. This is the region where the wind always comes from the north-northeast, where "children learn to walk on frozen toes," where people envy others faraway "Who boil . . . with . . . a lyric yeast / Of love." "Passion" is here defined as "a soilure of the wits" and as "a cross . . . to bear." "Joy shivers in the corner" and knits. Conscience gets a kick out of torturing "the first cat that was ever killed by Care."

Robinson once wrote (August 10, 1923) to Laura E. Richards* that New England was in his blood and bones, and won't be denied. Emery Neff suggests that in "New England" Robinson is "caricaturing the . . . disdain" of "a younger generation of writers bent on displaying emancipation from Puritanism" and in the process ridiculing "New England reticence." Glauco Cambon adds that "the mockery here comes through in a terse satirical vein that is, itself, an understatement of love." Louis Coxe defines Robinson's "New England" as "wry and pungent," while Scott Donaldson says that in it Robinson "is having some fun with the [New Englander] stereotype, the kind of fun . . . hard to imagine Robert Frost having." Denis Donoghue calls the poem "one of Robinson's most controlled achievements" and proves his assertion. (See also "On My 'New England' Sonnet.") To mitigate the seeming criticism of New England, Robinson revised "New England" for later republications, beginning in *Dionysus in Doubt* (1925). Richard Amacher suggests that in changing the third line, which originally read "Intolerance tells an envy of all those," to read "Wonder begets an envy of all those," the word "Wonder" became the most important word in the entire sonnet. (Sources: Amacher; Cambon, 58; Cary [1975], 189–91; Coxe, 140; Donaldson [1969], 43; Donoghue, 38; Neff, 221; *Selected Letters*, 134)

"A New England Poet" (1918). Essay.

Robinson says that news of the recent death in Florida of Alanson Tucker Schumann* may be missed by his Boston friends and readers of his poetry. So he offers this tribute, subtitled "Alanson Tucker Schumann's Unostentatious Career" (Boston *Evening Transcript*, March 30, 1918). He gently praises Schumann, his one-time Gardiner neighbor and poetry mentor, for finding time as a physician to write polished, competent, unpretentious ballades, rondeaux, rondelles, villanelles, and especially sonnets "by the hundreds." Robinson quotes Schumann's sonnet entitled "Guidance," about "A lettered board" at a street corner pointing the observer to "The shadow of a Cross upon the snow." He quotes "Deane's Grove," another sonnet, about trees aging but therefore bearing fruit "nearer to the sky." He quotes "The Song That I Shall Never Sing," a poignant ballade, the refrain of which is the thrice-repeated title. Robinson admires Schumann's clarity, patience, and precision, and ventures to predict "that time, with his odd revenges, may give . . . Schumann's name" a higher place than that of many poets currently better known and louder. (See also "The First Seven Years.") (Source: Cary [1975], 81–83, 189)

"The New Jester" *see* "The Old King's New Jester"

"The New Movement in Poetry" (1917).

Essay. Robinson was asked by Lloyd R. Morris* whether he thought a new movement in poetry was underway. Morris published Robinson's reply in *The Young Idea*, of which he was the editor.

Robinson says that of course there is a new movement in poetry, just as there are new movements in everything, but that in his opinion there is no "radical change" in what we call poetry, either in "structure" or in "general nature." If Morris is hinting at *vers libre*, Robinson continues, he feels that "this mode of expression" can provide pleasure but not much for him. Of furlongs of it that he has read, only yards have been satisfying for him. He fears friends will label him "conservative" if not "reactionary" for saying this, even

though he was called "too modern" some time ago. He feels that anything new in poetry is more likely to involve changes not in "metrical or non-metrical form," but in "vocabulary and verbal arrangements," and also in greater "incisiveness and . . . clarity." He continues by asserting that less than one percent of *vers libre* yields pleasure, that its "best days" are behind it, and that *vers libre* poets will in future write better in traditional forms, which still provide much "room for . . . innovation and variety." He closes by praising the sincerity and importance of recently published poetry. (Source: Cary [1975], 77–78, 189)

"The New Tenants" (1919).

Sonnet. The day has come for his inimical tenants to leave. He had built triumphant "barriers" against their efforts to defeat him. Now "new tenants" have slipped in and have made themselves already so much at home that he can easily imagine what "guile[ful] . . . vindictiveness" they might try on him to become insolent.

Critics have almost completely avoided this difficult picture of a man who, according to an odd reading by Ellsworth Barnard, is "in the process of degenerating — one might almost say decomposing — under the assaults of long-tolerated vices." (Source: Barnard, 230)

Nicknames for Robinson.

Robinson as a child and youth was called "Win" and "Winnie" by family members. In primary school, he was called "Pinny." Some friends called him "Rob" and "Robbie." Many referred to him in letters and some in conversation as "E.A." and "E.A.R." His nieces called him "Uncle E.A." He wanted never to be called "Eddie."

It should be a challenge to psychiatrists that Robinson remained unnamed until the summer of 1870. His mother Mary Robinson* was vacationing with her children at South Harpswell, Maine, when the naming of the infant six months old was fated to take place in the presence of others. At the suggestion of a woman from Arlington, Massachusetts, several names were put in a hat. "Edwin" was drawn, and the lady from Arlington offered "Arlington" as a middle name. The future poet's mother was bizarre enough to agree. Robinson's first name was given as "Edward" in print so often — and even "Edgar" now and then — that he grew chronically disgusted. A poet-friend named Florence Peltier (b. 1862, author of *A Japanese Garland* [1902], a story about Japanese manners and customs) reports that when she was dining with Robinson at the hospitable home of Laura E. Richards* in Gardiner, "he remarked that his name sounded like a tin pan rolling down hill! 'And why shouldn't it? Aren't my name's initial's [*sic*], E.A.R., wholly concerned with sound?' he concluded, and then heartily chuckled."

Another challenge — this to those with onomastic interests. Robinson occasionally signed letters to friends fancifully, for example, to Josephine Preston Peabody* (January 26, 1905; March 31, 1917) he signed himself "Hank Felio" and "R. Crusoe," respectively; to Louis V. Ledoux* (August 20, 1910), "P. Vickery, Esquire"; to Ledoux's wife (August 30, 1915), "John B. Gough"; to Laura E. Richards (August 29, 1918; July 20, 1924; and later), "Torquato Tasso," "Appius Claudius," "T.T." Robinson signed one letter to Peabody "Fred Keats." (Sources: Cary [1974], 15–16, 99; Hagedorn, 13, 16; Peltier, 6; *Selected Letters*)

"Nicodemus" (1930). Dramatic duologue in blank verse. It is in 22 stanzas of irregular lengths.

Caiaphas (the high priest of the Jews under Tiberius) complacently welcomes Nicodemus (a Pharisee ruler of the Jews), who he thinks looks more like a fugitive in his long cloak than "a lord / At home in his own city." When asked if he has disguised himself in fear of robbers, Nicodemus answers, "No — not robbers." Caiaphas guesses that Nicodemus was troubled when he demeaned himself to meet that man said to be "a carpenter — / Before he was a . . . [*sic*]" (see Mark 6:3). Nicodemus replies that certain men "dead yesterday, / And alive today," don't care about that man's former trade but about what he is now. When he adds that the man doesn't ask them to become carpenters, Caiaphas smirks, says he's glad because Nicodemus might cut himself, and adds that he wouldn't like to meet men recently dead and now in the concealing night. Nicodemus: Those men came out of dark-

ness; but you and I, so-called worthy ones and now on "shining heights" are the ones in the dark. The lowly may find life and peace. We are dead, "painted shells of eminence," afraid to say so (cf. "whited sepulchres," Matt. 23:27). Caiaphas: I'm not surprised that you hide in a cloak. The carpenter you visited must have been pretty strong not to laugh at your treating him condescendingly. Nicodemus: The man — "if he be man" — admitted that he had been obliged to "vanish" from "good" authorities like us and thus avoid our laws, which "hate" him.

Caiaphas: Come on, say plainly he hates our laws. "Would his be any better?" Laws, ours and Caesar's, keep us safe. "This man is mad" (cf. "He [Jesus] . . . is mad," John 10:20) or a charlatan. I've not heard him but only rumors about him echoing around Jerusalem. It would be perilous for both you and him "if you pursue him." Get him away. He can't be so strong, if we mere "powerless things of earth" can damage him. Accounts of him are like a creaking house of the sort he might have carpentered. Nicodemus: He says he plans to safeguard his body "till there is no more use for it." After that, "a man's end / [is] Awaiting him." Meanwhile, he fears "But . . . the blindness that is ours who fear him." Caiaphas: I'm not scared. I'm not blind. I don't appreciate your calling me a dead shell. Does your carpenter speak in a similar fashion? Nicodemus: No. But let me tell you, both of us are dead, blind, and afraid. Caiaphas: You and your carpenter are insane, and God is aware of what's going to happen. A final indulgent warning — supply "your seditious prophet" and hustle him out of town.

Nicodemus: Don't harp exclusively on fear. This fearless man "foresees . . . [his death] that you and I may live." You are like a child unwilling to read a new book that has strange letters, but they spell "life," not "death." You are an ignorant "priest of death." Our scary old formal laws are lifeless. Caiaphas: I'm tired of your telling me I'm afraid. Our well-established laws are good enough for me; the only death in them is "death itself," which I understand. Point to a law of ours that calls us insane. Nicodemus: We're not mad, only "dying while we are dead." He has told me that light is "coming for the world." We prefer the dark to the light. "He is the light" (cf. John 1:9, 8:12). Those who keep loving ancestral darkness drive him away, laugh at him, thus hurt themselves, not him. We should resemble fruit that falls "from an undying tree," is crushed to blood, dies not, but increases because it is alive forever. The lowly ones, lacking fame, money, influence, and hypocrisy, have been the first to love him, to be his heirs, and — unlike you — to find in his words more than words, "but the Word." We are too lofty to hear those powerful words or to see "the inevitable harvest / Of this eternal sowing" (cf. "He that soweth the good seed is the Son of man," Matt. 13:37). Be braver than I am, Caiaphas; mingle with the crowd, hear him, look around, and see that "the lowliest" resemble you in the eyes of God. I feel ignoble garbed in what you call my "noble robes." I smite the air with the sword of truth. Blood may flow (cf. Jesus "came not to send peace, but a sword," Matt. 10:34) and yet unnecessarily and "against fate," unless his fate is "that his worn body / Shall perish that he may live." His death won't be death. We make truth into a monster, but one never feared by him; "our flawed complacency / Is a fool's armor against revelation." Instead of avoiding it, let's stand together beside him, openly.

But, in the name of friendship, Caiaphas warns Nicodemus that he is demented and urges him to hide the mad carpenter. Nicodemus replies that Caiaphas is hypocritical, and might as well be honestly scornful instead. Nicodemus will soon return to his "cold house" in Jerusalem, aware that Caiaphas can't drown his "misgivings" with wine or remove fear by calling the truth mad. Nicodemus offers "light / For eyes that will not open," and says he won't be seeing Caiaphas again. Caiaphas dismisses the mad carpenter as "an inch of history," whom Nicodemus could save but who can't save Nicodemus. Caiaphas predicts that Nicodemus will eat and drink with that carpenter in secret, not dare be seen with him in public, that when the dangerous Messiah is jailed or safely crucified — as perhaps Nicodemus will let happen — Nicodemus will mourn too late.

In rejoinder, Nicodemus says that panic and not safety would follow and that Caiaphas totally misjudges him. Caiaphas, smiling, repeats his prediction that Nicodemus will remain loyal to "our laws and hearts"; he knows he's correct because he's always correct and if wrong wouldn't be a priest. Nicodemus clutches his black robe and is blinded by tears from seeing Caiaphas, himself, anyone "Save . . . one that he had left alone, / Alone in a bare room, and not afraid."

Hermann Hagedorn* reports that after Robinson had finished writing *Matthias at the Door* (summer 1930), he reread "the third chapter of St. John, which had been his inspiration, and, in three days, . . . at the point of exhaustion, let 'Nicodemus' write itself." It contains 325 lines. He dedicated the poem to his friend Edwin Carty Ranck (see Ranck, Carty). The precise biblical source of the poem is John 3:1–21, 7:50–52 and 19:39–42. For Caiaphas, see Matthew: 26:3, 57. Nicholas Ayo implies that Robinson may have been influenced in writing "Nicodemus" by *Christianity Between Sundays* (3rd ed., 1892) by George Hodges (1856–1919), an Episcopal priest whom Robinson may have met in Cambridge, Massachusetts (1893), and who certainly gave Robinson a copy of his book in 1897.

Ayo dates the action of "Nicodemus" as occurring just after Nicodemus's interview with Jesus, some time before Caiaphas started the plot against Jesus, therefore before Caiaphas knew anything about the miracle of Lazarus's being raised from the dead (see "Lazarus"), and shortly before Jesus's condemnation to death. Yvors Winters opines that "Nicodemus" "is excellent in its plan and is for the most part respectable in style"; but he finds the style "relaxed and a trifle flat," and concludes that it "is hardly one of the important works." Edwin S. Fussell finds irony in "Nicodemus" because Robinson's readers have more different facts and different interpretations thereof at their disposal than were available for Nicodemus and Caiaphas. Emery Neff summarizes the ending of the narrative thus: "Nicodemus departs in tears at the vision of courage and renunciation beyond his capacity." Ayo, who identifies and quotes the biblical cross-referencing cited above (and several others), regards "Nicodemus" as one of the most profound religious poems ever written by an American, and concludes that "[a]s a didactic poem which presents a poignant understanding of the perennial struggle between reason and faith, it has no equal in Robinson." (Sources: Ayo, 57, v, 49, 137–58 passim, 224; Fussell [1954], 168; Hagedorn, 362; Neff, 236; Winters, 140)

Nicodemus: A Book of Poems (New York: Macmillan, 1932). Collection of 10 poems, including the title poem.

"The Night Before" (1896). Dramatic monologue. The speaker, in prison for three hundred days now, is to be hanged tomorrow for murder. He is explaining matters to an understanding friend he calls Dominie. When the narrator was little, he thought everything was wondrous and just for him; but he soon learned about separate individualities and, further, "That a happy man is a man forgetful / Of all the torturing ills about him." He met a woman and soon loved her, "Not for her face, but for something fairer, / Something diviner, I thought, than beauty." He and her spirit would make "soul-music when . . . together." Their passion resembled blazing noontime sunlight, "but . . . / Never a whit less pure for its fervor." His hot, human "baseness" soon "perished" and left him spiritually triumphant.

She laughed as she wronged him; but was it sin, or did "the chains of her marriage" themselves cause the break-up? Toward her he now feels no love, no hate, only "still regret." For a while, though, their life together went on; but then the music stopped, truth appeared, darkness followed, and hope vanished. If he had been stronger or weaker, he might simply have left her. At one point, he forgave her, after which she trembled, cried, clung to him, and kissed him, only to laugh and slip away and sin again; but then she returned to his hot embrace yet once more. At last he upbraided her, and "the farce was over."

He began to feel a strange fellowship with strangers. He pitied them for their own likely sufferings, saw them as "brothers / And sisters," but only until they appeared to be gossiping about him and "laughing / At me and

my fate." When, suddenly, he met the fellow who had turned his wife's "love to his own desire," hell itself seemed to be mocking him, and hate triumphed over glorious good. What can science do to assuage someone scarred at birth or to eliminate "sleeping venom" from someone's soul? Passions can be demonic. The narrator, however, says he isn't shifting any blame to God.

Finally, inspired by the devil he called brother, he followed the man who had cuckolded him. The city gleamed dreamily; the streets pulsated; crowds floated by, laughing, singing. The self-assured "cad," who had "brainless art" and a snake-like "smooth and slippery polish," might have been planning to flirt anew, and sing and drink in a tavern. Anyway, the narrator found him sitting with a frothy drink in "an uptown haunt," shot him in the back, and fainted as though on fire in the eerie place.

He queries Dominie: What are we? Ignorant slaves, puppets controlled by fiends, gods condemning ourselves? He complains that "heaven and hell get mixed" in our bedevilled lives. We miss or laugh at Christ's whispered admonitions, and we fall. The narrator neither curses nor sympathizes with the fallen, whom a power more merciful than he "must shrive." Meanwhile, "I — I am going / Into the light? — or into the darkness?" Should he have hope? Only hours remain now. He wonders if he and Dominie "may meet" tomorrow.

In a letter (August 25, 1898) to Edith Brower*, Robinson says that "The Night Before" was partly inspired by "A Last Confession" by Dante Gabriel Rossetti, and adds a possibly deceptive disclaimer, that it is "absolutely impersonal." A couple of reviewers in 1897, as noted by Richard Cary (1974), found a source, or at least an analogue, for "The Night Before" in the more gruesomely plotted *Giovanni Episcopo* (1892) by Gabriele D'Annunzio (1863–1938); *Episcopo and Company*, a translation, was published in 1896. May Sinclair* admires "The Night Before" because of its "imaginative insight, subtlety, and emotional volume." Cary, however, decries it as "an amateurish effort" and implies that Robinson properly "excluded [it] from his collected works."

Robinson's niece Ruth Nivison,* the daughter of his brother Herman Robinson* and Emma Robinson,* suggests that in this poem Robinson is placing himself, in imagination, as Herman's murderer; she knew that both men were in love with Emma. Agreeing, Chard Powers Smith* reports that Robinson, after falling in love with Emma, only to lose her to his brother Herman Robinson, started a draft of "The Night Before," now lost, on the night of February 12, 1890, the day of Herman's and Emma's wedding ceremony, which the poet did not attend. Boldly calling "The Night Before" "the worst long poem he [Robinson] ever published," Smith, though equating its narrator's rival for the woman's love with Herman, concludes that whereas the narrator's love was largely spiritual, the caddish rival's love was successfully carnal.

While working on the poem and afterwards, Robinson often wrote his friend Harry de Forest Smith* about it. He called it "a queer poem . . . a tragic monologue . . . in unrhymed tetrameters" (May 27, 1894). He defined the plot as "unpleasant, . . . creating a fictitious life in direct opposition to a real life" he knew; and added that in it he was aiming to advise people "not to thump a man" when he is already defeated (June 3, 1894). He reported that for weeks he had been rewriting "The Night Before" in blank verse (December 14, 1895). In his letter of June 3, 1894 to Smith, Robinson also says that "The Night Before" is "founded upon my system of 'opposites,' that is, creating a fictitious life in direct opposition to a real life which I know." James G. Hepburn, using implications of Robinson's so-called system of opposites, explicates "The Night Before" as well as a few other early poems thematically comparable.

After "The Night Before" was published in *The Torrent and The Night Before*, Robinson complained to Smith that a friend said he couldn't understand the story; Robinson defended himself by saying he thought it was perfectly plain except for the possibility that its meter bothered the ignorant friend (December 7, 1896). He summarized reviews of *The Torrent and The Night Before*, groused that some critics called him a pessimist, and said that "The Night Before" "is purely objective,

and may be called anything from pessimism to rot" (February 3, 1897).

J. Vail Foy discusses "The Night Before," which he says is unsuccessful but does represent the young poet's first attempt at a long narrative poem. Ellsworth Barnard sees a superficial influence from Robert Browning in "The Night Before" and adds that he has never seen its verse form elsewhere — "unrhymed, somewhat irregular tetrameter." Edwin S. Fussell calls the form "truncated tetrameters," which means that all but a very few of the 373 lines in the poem end in unaccented syllables. (Sources: Barnard, 98, 285; Brower, 82; Cary [1974], 46, 47, 60, 204; Cary [1975], 33–42, 179; Foy; Fussell [1954], 140; Hepburn; E. Robinson, 7–8; Sinclair, 331; C. Smith, 90, 98–99, 102; *Untriangulated Stars*, 158, 161, 162, 264–65, 273)

"Nimmo" (1916). Dramatic monologue. In a tangled manner, the narrator, who knew the painter Nimmo and knows Nimmo's wife Francesca, is speaking candidly to a friend, and is both directly and indirectly correcting his auditor's impression of Nimmo. The narrator begins by saying he may have led his auditor on but is quitting now and wishes to address former confused nonsense about Nimmo. He says the legend about Nimmo is so established that the speaker "May live on to be sorry for his ghost." He reminds his auditor that they remember "a velvet light" that used to emanate from Nimmo's eyes when he was angry or surprised, or when he was made to laugh, or when "Francesca made them [his eyes] bright." Since the auditor says nothing about those eyes, the speaker wonders if he ought to continue telling about Nimmo.

Anyway, those eyes started to lose their luster and inner fire, and grew smaller; people were sad to think that the couple must have unnecessarily squabbled. But they "never fought." The narrator then remarks, "I say nothing of what was, / Or never was, or could or could not be," warns his auditor that suspicion won't illuminate understanding of their friend, and says that he will explain something not in his auditor's memory of Nimmo. He startles his auditor by this: "The devil has had his way with paint before, / And he's an artist." Now back to Nimmo's eyes, he says. When Nimmo painted a picture of himself, the devil inspired him to paint his eyes, or maybe the devil did it himself. Whatever—this frightened Francesca so terribly that she "fled from paradise."

Although she may have been scared all the time by "evil in their [the eyes'] velvet," the narrator will "trust the man as long as he can smile." Furthermore, Nimmo resides in the narrator's heart now; maybe the narrator has much that's unforgivable to tell him, but the narrator "played" and must "pay." He is aware that Nimmo, "defeated and estranged," displays "The calm of men forbidden to forget / The calm of women who have loved and changed." Nimmo is passive; Francesca, silent; the two are beyond arguing. We need God's help both when women believe they understand and when they do understand. The narrator says he interprets Nimmo honestly and tells Francesca as much. As for Nimmo, he is fruitlessly confused, working as "what he was born to be—a man." The narrator's final comments to his auditor: Don't let my comments tease your memory, which count for zero, into disclosures; Nimmo and I have long trusted each other; "I'm painting here a better man, you say, / Than I, the painter; and you say the truth."

Robinson first published this poem in *Scribner's Magazine* (April 1916), calling it "Nimmo's Eyes." He retitled it "Nimmo" in his 1921 *Collected Poems*, omitting two stanzas at that time. Richard Cary conveniently reprints them. In one of the deleted passages, the narrator catches his auditor laughing and warns him he won't laugh for very long. In the other deleted passage, the narrator says he told Francesca that she wrongly turned a mere "episode" into "an epic."

Questions, not answers, arise regarding this enigmatic poem. Is Nimmo alive only in the narrator's memory, or is he perhaps not dead? Can a painting reveal to a woman something previously hidden about her husband? Can Satan inspire an artist? Did the narrator contribute to Francesca's change of attitude toward Nimmo? Who is the auditor? Francesca? Nimmo?

Chard Powers Smith* relates the behavior of characters in "Nimmo" to Herman Robinson,* his wife Emma Robinson,* and Robinson himself, but in ways not clarified. Many fictional works deal with the influence of expressions in portaits. Examples which might have influenced Robinson are "Prophetic Pictures" (1837) by Nathaniel Hawthorne, "The Liar" (1888) by Henry James, and *The Picture of Dorian Gray* (1891) by Oscar Wilde.

"Nimmo" has almost universally silenced the critics. Ellsworth Barnard mentions its "tangled motives and unclear lights," then calls it "disturbing" and finally "eerie, obscure."

Paul Zietlow provides great help in understanding "Nimmo." He theorizes that the citizens of Tilbury Town, which is a place "socially and spiritually ruined and decayed," lack a "stable perspective" from which to observe accurately and judge profoundly the many supposed misfits about whom Robinson writes many provocative poems. Zietlow finds numerous examples to support his position—best, perhaps, "Nimmo." In it, he argues, "the complexities of judgment, the many levels of insight, the tortured probings of conscience lack the unifying stability of one comprehensive perspective; as a result, the story remains obscure." (Sources: Barnard, 69, 138, 170; Cary [1975], 49–50, 183; C. Smith, 198, 203; Zietlow, 198, 195, 196).

"Nimmo's Eyes" *see* **"Nimmo"**

"Normandy" (1910). Poem. The persona has wandered to icy Switzerland and has also seen gondoliers in Italy. The time has come when his dreams are dreary, his songs cold, his love gone. So he says, three times, that he will return to Normandy, where he was born.

In a subtitle Robinson says that this poem is "(From the French of Bérat)." Frédéric Bérant (1800–1850) was a French composer, one of whose chansonettes is "La Normandie." Robinson's "Normandy," which first appeared in *The Town Down the River*, is cast in a ballade form similar but not identical to the one Robinson used in "Ballade of Dead Friends." (Source: Cary [1975], 47–48, 182)

Norton, Charles Eliot (1827–1908). Author, educator, and editor. Norton was born in Cambridge, Massachusetts, was Harvard-educated, and brilliantly taught art history there (1873–1897). Robinson during his second year at Harvard (1892–1893) attended Norton's course in ancient art, ecstatically wrote (November 29, 1892) to Harry de Forest Smith* that Norton's lectures were "simply magnificent," and, further, that Norton "is by all odds the greatest man in America." Robinson was also a guest at small Sunday gatherings in Norton's home. Robinson gifted Norton with a copy of *The Torrent and The Night Before*, which, according to Richard Cary, Norton acknowledged in a gracious and complimentary letter. (Sources: Cary [1974], 38; Hagedorn, 70, 78, 79; *Untriangulated Stars*, 76)

"Not Always" (1924). Sonnets. Two, both numbered.

I. "He" was alone, felt protected by certainty and obscurity, and for a while beat back fears and doubts. But when nothing happened, he "quailed." He felt as though God had let "the last light go . . . out" and left him in the dark. But finally, "out of silence crept / Invisible avengers" and other helpers, resulting in the arrival of "song[s] . . . as of the morning stars."

II. For days and nights the two said nothing, harbored fruitless "recriminating thought[s]," and were nurtured by proud aversions. They wanted only to separate. Each hoped the other would create their escape. Neither realized how long the wall between them would "frown / And shine for them through many sorts of weather."

These two baffling sonnets are probably a narrative unit about a man who in the first poem loved a woman who appears in the second poem, but, when unrequited, got over it. Then the second poem details the long-lasting misery of that woman, who was married to another man and stayed married to him.

Chard Powers Smith* equates the man in the first sonnet with Robinson and theorizes that he loved Emma Robinson,* the wife of his brother Herman Robinson,* got nowhere with her, and found release only when light stirred his creative imagination. What fol-

lowed in due time, Smith continues, was Emma's and Herman's "love . . . twisted into disgust in the one and surly suspicion in the other." But, in that case, why not say that both felt both disgust and suspicion? Ellsworth Barnard calls these two sonnets "somewhat obscure" but later is on unobscurely shaky ground when he concludes that "both partners in the first story and the wife in the second acquire at least a capacity for endurance and a stoic wisdom." There seems no reason to assume that anyone but the one man in the first poem is helped to a tuneful morning; further, it seems unwise to assume that the wife in the second poem is unique in gaining endurance and wisdom. Does the title "Not Always," which is applied to each sonnet, mean that the couple will eventually reconcile? or die? The title more clearly suggests that the man in the first poem emerged into the light, which Smith says means that the poet's "imagination [escaped] into the light." (Sources: Barnard, 108; C. Smith, 154, 155)

"A Note on Myron B. Benton (1834–1902)" (1925). Essay. In 1925 Joel Elias Spingarn (1875–1939), American man of letters, editor, and educator, privately published in 200 copies a leaflet entitled *Thoreau's Last Letter With a Note on His Correspondent, Myron B. Benton by Edwin Arlington Robinson* (Amenia, NY: Troutbeck Press, 1925). When he was dying, Henry David Thoreau received a complimentary letter from Benton and dictated a reply. By chance, this letter was the last one in Thoreau's voluminous correspondence. Spingarn included "A Poem on the Death of Thoreau" by Benton and quotations concerning Thoreau by the naturalist John Burroughs (1837–1924) and by the clergyman and man of letters Moncure Daniel Conway (1832–1907), and paid Robinson $100 for his 3½-page essay.

In it Robinson opines that, whereas many people work hard for little success, others seem "predestined to a sort of casual immortality." Such was Myron B. Benton. From all accounts, he was a farmer who loved the soil. He also wrote poetry that no one could call great. But he also happened to send Thoreau a let-

ter in which the dying man detected "a mingled quality of sincerity and distinction," and
which contained nothing of the "fulsome or
extravagant." The letter gained Thoreau's "respect and attention." So he found strength to
answer it. Whereas Thoreau, though not then
appreciated, was confident of his great value,
Benton "did not worry ... about his future
fame," and yet avoided obscurity by being the
recipient of a "poignant and unique letter from
Thoreau." Estelle Kaplan quotes Robinson's
comment about "casual immortality" and adds
that "[i]f we could know the whole truth of
the matter, perhaps we should know to our
surprise and possible discomfiture that all so-
called earthly remembrance ... is casual or
accidental, or what you will." (Sources: Cary
[1975], 88–90, 191; Kaplan, 18)

"Octave" (1897). Eight-line poem, in blank
verse. The poet, while loving all saints, prefers
those never "calendered." Their pleasure is his;
their grief, his also, because "Grief that knows
itself / Soon glorifies itself." Nameless saints
may reveal more to him "Of God than all the
tomes of printed prayers."

Robinson reported to Edith Brower* by letter (March 14, 1897) that the Boston *Evening
Transcript*, when it published "Octave" (February 26, 1897), misprinted "all the tomes" as
"any tons." (Sources: Brower, 30, 31; Cary
[1975], 43, 180)

"Octaves [I, III]" (1897). Two eight-line,
numbered poems, in blank verse.

I. The purpose of a poet is to sing vigor-
ously about "the eternal strength of things."
Though often rough and ungracious, the poet
"sings well" if he echoes "the one right chord /
Wherein God's music slumbers," and if in the
process he wakes up "one drowsed ambition"
to the truth. Robinson wrote (April 1, 1914)
to Edith Brower* that he regarded this octave
as the poorest poem he ever wrote.

III. To most people, the simplest word may
sound as weird and untrue as maniacs' prayers.
But if that simple word is "the plain word of
Truth," it will echo and repeat itself. (Sources:
Brower, 156; Cary [1975], 44–45, 180)

"Octaves [I–XXIII]" (1897, 1921). Twenty-

three eight-line, numbered poems, in blank
verse. Robinson wrote (April 10, 1897) to
Edith Brower* that he had written 40 octaves,
planned to write 60 in all, and found them
"wicked things to make — infinitely harder
than sonnets." He wrote her later (January 7,
1901) to report that William Vaughn Moody*
made two mistakes when he judged Robinson's "Cliff Klingenhagen" to be a fine poem
but regarded his octaves as worthless. Louis
Coxe calls them "feeble poetically because ...
of inadequate thought." But Chard Powers
Smith* admires their "impassioned rhetoric"
and calls "the Octaves" Robinson's "first great
poem." Without a doubt, their tangled syntax is initially troubling, and perhaps finally so
as well. (See also "Octaves [I–III]" and "Octaves I–XXV.") (Sources: Brower, 37, 135;
Cary [1975], 180; Coxe, 103; Moran [1969];
C. Smith, 157, 312)

I. We "groan" about mistakes emanating
from our mysteriously large selves, but instead
we should welcome God's accomplished
"touch." Charles Cestre* quotes from this octave to support his assertion that all of the octaves here, which are "philosophical epigrams
... [of] irresistible strength and charm," succeed because of "exact choice of words, ...
freshness arising from ... novel association of
terms, ... vigorous concentration of thought
associated with ... compactness of phrase,"
and rhythmic "elasticity and forcible beat."
(Source: Cestre, 56)

II. Life spurting in "mankind," lacking any
"clean scheme" to build on, rushes around
insanely, like a violent army taught only by
"Ignorance." Emery Neff sees this early poem
as "a prelude to political poems still far distant." (Source: Neff, 86)

III. It seems that "world-worshippers" have
potent enough art but lack "wisdom or ...
will" to recognize their "perversity" and the
value of losing.

IV. We're so used to "error" that we don't
know what "truth and usefulness" are. Fancying ourselves titanic warriors, we fight
proudly, forget God, and aren't really alive.

V. The only place where we can battle and
"fall / Triumphant and unconquered" is on the
unclouded western field where we are clad in
"Thought's impenetrable mail." Part Three of

Where the Light Falls, the biography of Robinson by Chard Powers Smith,* is entitled "Thought's Impenetrable Mail." (Source: C. Smith, 279)

VI. When "the timeless hymns of Love" outclass mere "cradle-songs" and we feel ecstatically released, we will be able to read God's eternally true "runes" recording the "All-Soul." Chard Powers Smith* sees resemblances between the "All-Soul" here and the Over-Soul of the Transcendentalists, mainly Ralph Waldo Emerson, who was a major influence on Robinson. (Source: C. Smith, 302)

VII. When finally serene, the mind realizes that God is available both in immeasurable "excellence" and in a universe manifestly whirling.

VIII. Regardless of seemingly adverse circumstances, "There is no loneliness." Wisdom's light pierces "the darkness here and there" to reveal "complete companionship."

IX. We should realize that when we experience faith-hurting doubts about someone thought to be totally pure, that very "wonderment" is a source of wisdom. Yvor Winters suggests that the disappointment presented here "is offered as evidence of the real existence of the impersonal standard," but then he criticizes the poem as "stiff and insensitive" in its "movement." (Source: Winters, 49)

X. We shouldn't cry but rejoice at someone's death, because the knowledge frees the memory and enables the spirit to become aware of "a thrilled invisible advance." Ellsworth Barnard discusses this "octave" in connection with Robinson's thoughts on "whatever . . . survives the physical death of the individual." In doing so, Barnard quotes two letters Robinson wrote to Harry de Forest Smith* (February 18, 1894; December 7, 1896). In the first, Robinson says that he cannot help believing in immortality; in the second, after the death of his mother, he expresses both relief that she is gone and belief that death represents both deliverance and advancement. (Sources: Barnard, 215; *Untriangulated Stars*, 131, 264)

XI. To the end we seek the start of life, that spark where there isn't any spark, much like frustrated old astronomers, "dream[ing] of un-triangulated stars." Edwin S. Fussell locates the source of this poem in the following lines from "The Task" by William Cowper, one of Robinson's favorite poets:

> we do not find the living spark
> Where no spark ever was; and thus we die,
> Still searching, like poor old astronomers
> Who totter off to bed and go to sleep,
> To dream of untriangulated stars.

Robert Mezey explains that untriangulated stars are stars too remote for their distances to be measured by astronomers using "geometrical calculation." Denham Sutcliffe entitled his edition of Robinson's letters to his friend Harry de Forest Smith* *Untriangulated Stars*, to suggest a person's inevitable difficulty in establishing patterns of social, emotional, and spiritual relationships. (Sources: Fussell [1954], 76–77; Mezey, 220; *Untriangulated Stars*)

XII. The poet cannot see through the clouds of knowledge screening him from "the glorifying light." Wisdom breaks through his "credulity," but do his words help the dead?

XIII. Friends are fine; but when you realize you are your own best friend, you stop scorning your "own wealth and wisdom."

XIV. Despite many troubles, "we are fraught / Forever with indissoluble Truth." Adversities are "dreams / Of wasted excellence" and are indifferent to the passage of time.

XV. We should courageously stay put, instead of returning to old paths, familiar fields, magical "dead things," and speciously moonlit, ruined walls of ancient stone. Apropos of this poem, Ellsworth Barnard notes that "whatever he [Robinson] may think of the future, he deprecates nostalgic gropings toward the past." (Source: Barnard, 265)

XVI. We should bravely look past "this idiot world / Where blood pays blood for nothing," and see the world's "helpless . . ." materialism destroyed by "salvatory steel." Ellsworth Barnard suggests that the point of this poem is that we should "confront the picture [of] . . . 'this idiot world' . . . without flinching and without giving up . . . hope." (Source: Barnard, 270)

XVII. Instead of being held down by sadness and vainly hoping for relief, separate yourself from reality if you expect ever to achieve "repose" in this life or any other. Edwin S. Fussell proves that this poem reveals "Miltonic mannerisms," John Milton being one of Robinson's favorite poets, as Fussell also demonstrates. (Source: Fussell [1954], 68–69 and passim)

XVIII. We boldly criticize ourselves for inadequately grieving, unaware that truth is constant, whereas neither the world nor our lamentations are.

XIX. One "cadence of . . . infinite" music exceeds the best-"phrase[d]," most sweetly "rhyme[d]" poetry. To echo chimes hammered on "God's forge" takes awesome strength. Wallace L. Anderson notes echoes in this poem of "Merlin" by Ralph Waldo Emerson, who says in it that the master poet "Must smite the chords rudely and hard, / As with hammer or with mace." (Source: W. Anderson [1968], 78)

XX. Whoever would write about "the glory of the real" needs tools yet unnamed, and also skill, courage, and "clean wisdom."

XXI. Human "greed" and "blunders" are proved by our cursing limited dawn light, neglecting sorrow's benefits, and preferring "prodigal . . . gold" to the "generosity of thought."

XXII. Always "the clean seer" looks, unappalled, beyond hellish complainers, sees God's shining "highways," and knows that "Love's complete communion" frees man of anguish. Robinson wrote (December 14, 1897) to Edith Brower* to express surprise that she read "clean seer" as "clear seer" but then blamed his poor handwriting for her mistake.

Ellsworth Barnard cites this octave as Robinson's continuing affirmation of purposeful life and ends his superb study of Robinson by quoting it in full. (Sources: Barnard, 271–72; Brower, 65)

XXIII. The wake of the ship taking the poet's friend away stands for love, life's purpose, and wisdom's winning departure "from the crumbled wharves of Time."

"Octaves I–XXV" (1897). Twenty-five numbered eight-line poems, in blank verse, in *The Children of the Night*. When Robinson

published his 1921 *Collected Poems*, he included 23 of them (see "Octaves [I–XXIII]") and omitted two (see "Octaves [I. III]"). (Source: Cary [1975], 180)

"Oh for a Poet — For a Beacon Bright" *see* **"Sonnet" ("Oh for a poet — for a beacon bright")**

"Old King Cole" (1915). Poem. Old King Cole, of Tilbury Town, wisely "anticipate[s]" a simple old age, with his pipe and his bowl, and not in a "Khan's extravagant estate" either. In place of unneeded "fiddlers three," this widower has two "disastrous" sons, Alexis and Evander. They are "Born thieves and liars"; but when gossipers tell Old King Cole about their devilish misdeeds, he extinguishes the tattle-tales' fiery wrath by kindly commentary. With benignant smiles and haloes of smoke rings, he greets one all-night visitor who hopes in vain to hear paternal gripes. Instead, Old King Cole speaks with admirable directness: Alexis and Evander weren't the sons he would have chosen, but he's not about to let their "infirmity" freeze him over. They'll probably meet "a bad end," yes; but he refuses to "groan," because "I can see what I can see, / And I'm accordingly alone." He loves his friends and likes his neighbors, offers welcome to all, and won't offer laborious explanations, because that auditor would then start doubting him. His pipe doesn't calm him, nor does drink drown his grief, for which "there is no balm / In Gilead, or in Tilbury Town." Neither he nor his auditor can blind anyone to an awareness of his situation. He may yet be ruined or find his "wasted love" in ashes; but, just maybe, "like One [Christ] whom you may forget, / I may have meat you know not of." As Old King Cole continues by saying he'd prefer living to weeping, he happily notices that his auditor is asleep.

In the beginning of "Old King Cole," about his hero's not anticipating a "Khan . . . estate," Robinson humorously rings changes on the opening of "Kubla Khan" by Samuel Taylor Coleridge: "In Xanadu did Kubla Khan / A stately pleasure-dome decree." At the end of his poem, Robinson has Old King Cole closely paraphrase John 4:32 about "meat . . . not [known] of."

"Old King Cole" is in 10 eight-line stanzas, the lines being in iambic tetrameter, rhyming *ababcdcd*, with the *b*- and *d*-rhymes feminine. This clear, basic form is well suited for a poem celebrating a clear-headed, unsubtle subject. Iambic pentameter lines would have been a little too solemn. "Old King Cole" has understandably not challenged critical explicators. Ellsworth Barnard adequately defines it as "a tragic-comic picture of an upright father acknowledging the worthlessness of his two sons and refusing to be crushed thereby." Chard Powers Smith* regards King Cole as a prime example of those who "come to regeneration through the Robinsonian self-atonement of endurance." Smith strains, however, when he equates Cole's sons and Robinson's two brothers, Dean Robinson* and Herman Robinson.* (Sources: Barnard, 69; C. Smith, 327, 156, 209)

"The Old King's New Jester" (1918). Poem. Those of you who see only vision-reducing dust in "the coming order" should be cautious about returning to "your dusty places / Where the old wrong seems right." For eons, the elders have discouraged debate with the young. Together we must be led by mighty events to proceed toward "the vague towers of our unbuilded State," even though we can't yet estimate either our pace or the distance. If you are "Haunt[ed] . . . by day" and restless at night because of "the old wrong and all its injured glamour," it's just as well to try "the new wrong." If you yearn for what won't return, you'll experience "qualms" and become discontent.

This poem was first published as "The New Jester" in the Boston *Transcript* (November 23, 1918), less than two weeks after the Armistice of 1918 ending the First World War. According to Bacon Collamore,* this version contained several typographical errors, which by a quick letter (also November 23, 1918) to William Stanley Braithwaite,* editor of the *Transcript*, Robinson asked him to correct before any reprinting. In "The Old King's New Jester," Robinson joshes those naively desiring to regress to essentially lost pre-War conservatism through unwillingness

to confront an admittedly obscure and perhaps perilous future. Wallace L. Anderson suggests that this poem is Robinson's response to an awareness of "[t]he uncertain state of world affairs and the necessity of laying new foundations based on moral principles." In this powerful poem, Robinson meets the challenge of a difficult poetic form. Each of four nine-line stanzas rhymes *abcbddede*, with the *d*-rhymes feminine, and with the lines in irregular iambic pentameters and trimeters. (Sources: W. Anderson [1968], 97–98; Collamore, 23)

"An Old Story" (1896). Poem. The poet ignores a certain critic, doesn't even give him a "friendly sign,"

> But cursed him for the ways he had
>   To make me see
> My envy of the praise he had [from others]
>   For praising me.

Although the persona would gladly have killed him then, he realizes the friend's value now that he's dead.

Robinson neatly manages a challenging rhyme scheme in this poem. Each of its three quatrains rhymes *abab*, each *a*-rhyme being three monosyllabic words. Richard Crowder suggests that the quatrain quoted above makes more sense if the gist of the fourth line is garnered first, that of the third line second, second line third, and first line fourth. Thus, the meaning more clearly is that the critic praised the poet, who envied the critic for gaining praise, whereupon the critic told the poet his jealousy was a flaw, and all this doubly bothered the poet. (Source: Crowder [1945])

"The Old Story" *see* **"Variations of Greek Themes"**

"Old Trails (Washington Square)" (1916). Poem. While walking in Greenwich Village, the narrator encounters an old acquaintance not seen for 10 years and evidently now 40. Calling himself a typical ruin and a ghost whose dreams have failed, he leads the poet to a saloon and is soon laughing into his drink. The two are both aware of the man's lack of fulfillment. It seems perverse that the once-feisty fellow has come into view again. It seems he won't ever "attain . . . his offended share / Of honor" among former peers again. He senses the narrator's silent query and answers by admitting he's a kind of vengeful "confirmation" of something in their past. He guesses that the narrator is sorry about it, even though his ledger-like recollection of the man's "arrears" combines fear and complacency. The man says that for 10 years his incubus-weighted conscience has troubled him; despite the fact that his often-dashed hopes for success have lured him to Broadway. Now he's back home, forgetful of accolades from "foreign worms," but lonely. Something called him to his old Eleventh Street room, to feel alive once more.

The two men leave the saloon and go to the man's room, in which they briefly "shivered in the gloom" and from which they soon emerge to stroll along the well-lighted "Avenue." The narrator agrees to take him to a new hotel, where he laughs, eats, seems to ignore not only a bleak past but also an ominous future, but then says he hasn't "failed; . . . merely not achieved." They attend a performance "at the Metropolitan" of *Boris Godunov* (by Modest Mussorgsky), during which the bells ring and the man responds by "croon[ing]" to the effect that "God lives" and he's "the man!" True enough; he got himself better nourished for some three weeks, worked hard in Yonkers for five years, "and then sauntered into fame." Now he's free to go on any streets he pleases. The old ghosts would still be in his old room, if he ever returned, which he probably won't do. Nor will his ghosts seek him out. Furthermore, his memories now "flicker," get faint, and die. Adulatory applause may be dangerous, but less so "Than growing old among the ghosts." Anyway, we're happy he deceived us. Still, old memories make the narrator "wish those bells in *Boris* would be quiet."

In "Old Trails," Robinson adverts to memories of his years in Lower Manhattan, where he lived in shabby rooms, frequented basement bars, and convivialized with friends of various stripes. Ellsworth Barnard believes that Robinson is expressing a personal worry that his protracted struggle to achieve artistic acclaim was costly, when he has the narrator of

"Old Trails" end by expressing fear of echoes from the past and the unquiet bells of *Boris Godunov*. Louis Coxe, who regards "Old Trails" as a work of major importance, identifies the "disenchanted, cagey, reticent" narrator's friend as perhaps George Burnham,* Mowry Saben,* or, indeed, Robinson himself. Coxe prefers, however, to stress the fictionalizing of the character, who here is "the quintessential American, artist-bohemian variety, vintage 1910 . . . He has roamed the world for ten years looking for — what? Himself? Success? Both. And at last, . . . that he may find that new and . . . true self which shall succeed, he must go back to the place he started from, amid . . . ghosts of . . . failures including his own." Coxe relates Boris Godunov, hero of the opera, to Robinson's returning native. Each ruined his past and pays dearly "for fame and applause"; when the bells in the opera ring, they do so to gather the Russian people against Boris, who murdered for political success. (Sources: Barnard, 147; Coxe, 165–66)

"On My 'New England' Sonnet" (1924). Essay. The complicated story behind this rare example of self-defense by Robinson, as discussed by Richard Cary and also by Leon Satterfield, is as follows. Robinson published his "New England" in the London *Outlook* (November 22, 1923) and republished it in the United States in the *Literary Digest* (December 1, 1923) and *The New Republic* (December 5, 1923). David H. Darling, a Gardiner businessman and part-time poet, took umbrage at Robinson's sonnet and sent a letter (January 25, 1924) critical of it to Major John W. Berry, editor of the Gardiner *Journal*. Berry published the letter (January 31, 1924) together with Darling's jingoistic, three-quatrain "New England Still." In his letter, Darling takes Robinson's sonnet literally, complains that the British have criticized the United States sufficiently without any American giving them more ammunition, and says that he "would prefer to remind the world of the rugged virtues that made New England what it is." His accompanying "New England Still" blasts critics of his beloved region. Next came a defense of Robinson by his friend

Laura E. Richards.* Also appearing in the *Journal* (February 7, 1924), it contends that his sonnet "was supposed to be aimed at those who patronize New England," and hints that seemingly "severe strictures" against New England in the poem disappear upon a more careful second reading. Richards also got the *Journal* staff to reprint, with her letter, Robinson's inoffensive — in fact, magnificent — 1923 sonnet "The Sheaves." Next to be published in the *Journal* (February 14, 1924) were a letter by another anti-British man named H. A. Swanton, also his poem, "New England," and, along with both, Robinson's defensive essay. The *Journal* was not yet finished. It published (February 28, 1924) two more items: "Sam Talbot's Got His Ice," a 36-line poem by Darling praising a Gardiner ice-cutter who minded his New England business; and a final Darling epistolary swipe at Robinson. Soon thereafter came an obituary notice that Darling had suffered a fatal heart attack, at age 53, on April 19, 1924.

Robinson begins his essay by commending Darling for the vigor of his letter and that of his poem, then suggests that he look again at the sonnet, and note its irony and its satirical attack not upon New England but "upon the same patronizing pagans whom he flays with such vehemence in his own poem." Robinson continues by wondering how his sonnet can "be regarded as even intelligible if read in any other way than as an oblique attack upon all those who are forever throwing dead cats at New England for its alleged emotional and moral frigidity." He closes by saying that he quite possibly wrote "an uusually bad sonnet." But before winding up with this mock self-derogation, this superb sonneteer lets fly a zinger: "Apparently Mr. Darling has fallen into the not uncommon error of seizing upon certain words and phrases without pausing to consider just why and how they are used." (Sources: Cary [1975], 83–84, 189–91; Satterfield)

"On the Meaning of Life" (1932). Essay. This essay, in the form of a letter (September 18, 1931) to Will Durant (1885–1981), was in response to Durant's request. He had asked several prominent persons to state their ideas

as to "the meaning or value of human life." He prepared and edited their replies in a book entitled *On the Meaning of Life* (1932).

Robinson begins by explaining his delay in answering. He thought he lacked much of any depth or value to offer. Philosophers would be out of work if one of them found the answer. We have acquired much material knowledge over time, but not much knowledge about truth. Our ancestors broke each other's skulls with rocks and never learned much about their souls they thus freed. We are not closer to the truth about that, either. Some deny, easily, the existence of the soul. But in truth we don't know whether we have souls. If a people believe only in materialistic mechanism, how can they avoid also believing that prolonged, complex, and devilish lives are anything but absurdly futile? Robinson's innate belief is that such an absurd and tragic view cannot be. The prospect of annihilation should be no more terrifying than the idea of a falling asleep at the end of a day either joyful or otherwise. However, if life is nothing but what it seems to be, improvements and enlightenments can never make up for what agonies life has forced upon humankind in the past, nor for what we are now suffering. So, what can we do? Follow our one light, which of course may be false and lead us into a morass.

Robinson doubts that so-called mechanists, though cocky, are intellectually satisfied. They may be appropriately compared to brave explorers standing on a jutting land or rock and peering through an advanced pair of eyeglasses into a fog in an effort to see an invisible ocean, and then announcing to comrades the discovery of the world's finale.

Robinson concludes by saying that these possibly grim-sounding statements result not from personal misfortunes or frustrations but from general observations and reflections. (Sources: Cary [1975], 111–12, 194; *Selected Letters*, 163–65)

"On the Night of a Friend's Wedding" (1896). Sonnet. Robinson says that if he ever grows old and is alone, he won't have to wait "Much longer for the sheaves" resulting from what he has "sown." To be sure, he has been comforted by "six or eight / Good friends" kind enough to prattle about his poems. But tonight everything is turned amiss and seems to suggest that his friends will soon regard him as something "Like a tall ship that floats above the foam / A little while, and then breaks utterly."

Harry de Forest Smith* was the friend whose marriage (June 25, 1895) caused Robinson to write this lugubrious poem. He reluctantly replied by letter (July 11, 1917) to Lewis E. Chase,* who had asked him to annotate some of his poems, by saying that, for example, he was prompted to write this sonnet by some bells he happened to hear ring during the wedding of a pair of strangers. Emery Neff says that in the last two lines, about a ship's breakup, "[m]etaphor and simile combine unforgettably." Would many readers agree with Ellsworth Barnard, who detects in the whole sonnet a "bantering and . . . rather Byronic self-deprecation"? (See also "My Methods and Meanings.") (Sources: Barnard, 84; Cary [1975], 189; Neff, 72; C. Smith, 145; *Selected Letters*, 103)

"On the Way" (1919). Poem. Duologue in blank verse, parenthetically subtitled "Philadelphia, 1794." Aaron Burr and Alexander Hamilton, riding together toward eventually separate destinations, are obliged to halt and stand aside so that President George Washington can ride on ahead of them.

Burr says he's sorry to interrupt Hamilton's thoughts about the nation's credit but must say that a president can put dust on a general and perhaps this one should be called "his Majesty." To these gripes and then Burr's hints that Hamilton fears the multitudes, he replies that America is finished with royal robes but is apprehensive of continued connections to France. Burr expresses annoyance against "compliments / To Monticello." Hamilton praises Washington, for "There was a nation in the man" who just rode by, and adds that Washington made possible the very road Burr finds so dusty. Burr cautions Hamilton to ask John Adams whether they should pin their faith entirely on Washington. Hamilton says Adams would remain silent, as usual, and then praises the majestic Washington again.

Burr says that if America and France "eat each other," Hamilton may be "master of the feast." Hamilton says that if war comes he will remain here and probably Burr will too, and warns that Burr has vision but not will power. Hamilton fondly remembers serving as a "savior" at Washington's side and, though imperfect, gave him advice and "a modicum besides" that he acted on. He says that Washington governs for a needful, ignorant public and suffers "pin pricks of inferiorities," is both "cautious" and "lonely," and from on high inspires ordinary people "That they may view him only through the mist / Of their defect, and wonder what he is." Burr replies that he is content to leave Washington where he is. Washington never injured Burr, although he has patronized Burr, who since then mistakenly figured on being "an atom in the annals / Of your republic." Burr continues by warning Hamilton about "Monticello," doing so by comparing its popular resident to Ahab and Hamilton to Naboth, Ahab's victim. Hamilton retorts that Burr can play up to Ahab but wonders why he "invidiously wield[s] . . . the Scriptures," and warns him to avoid falling like a certain fame-seeking archangel. Burr says he's going to study "our new land's new language," which he says Hamilton, only 37, doesn't like, then cautions that maybe Hamilton, who has won enough, ought to "vanish" before he "fade[s]," and adds that he probably can't enjoy any more "mortal triumph[s]."

Continuing his jibes, Burr says he pursued Hamilton on horseback just now, caught up with him, and thus saved him from making "a pounding piece of news" by getting hurt falling right behind Washington's horse. Retorting, Hamilton describes his adversary as "a friend / . . . jealous for the other's fame," asks whether Burr is going "to diagnose the doubtful case / Of Demos [the common people]," and tells Burr he needn't wield a sword against him because he is leaving government work to practice law in New York. Burr says that he intends to check the pulse of the "ignoble" populace and examine their speech, to report back to Hamilton, and to stay near him and not go away so far that he couldn't ever return but instead would "fare . . . ill," as Alcibiades did by going to far Phrygia. To this Hamilton hints that Burr could go far away successfully, and thus imitate Themistocles, who went to Persia and "fared well." Burr retorts that he has no plan to go any great distance, sees his immediate road ahead, and prepares to take it. Hamilton says all right and goodbye.

Esther Willard Bates* reports that Robinson was inspired to write "On the Way" when he read *Alexander Hamilton: An Essay on American Union* (1906) by Frederick Scott Oliver (1864–1934). The result is a generally unsatisfactory, too-talky, but witty dialogue between two opposing post–American Revolutionary political figures. Robinson characteristically sides with Hamilton, who lauded Washington, distrusted the populace, feared anarchy if too much power were given to it, and therefore favored centralization of governmental authority. Only after this imagined dialogue did Hamilton disagree with Thomas Jefferson, alluded to when Burr names Monticello. And only later did Aaron Burr lose the presidential election to Jefferson, kill Hamilton in a duel, and be tried for treason (and be acquitted) after his failed effort to seize vast lands in Spanish America and create a republic in the Southwest. So the several hints in Robinson's poem make bitter sense to his readers but would not have made much to any contemporary eavesdropper on horseback near the cleverly disputatious duo.

Lamenting Burr's "invidious wielding of the Scriptures," Hamilton half-cautions him against being "inveigle[d] . . . to emulation" of Ahab. In 1 Kings 21:1–16, Ahab takes innocent Naboth's land. When Burr says he won't imitate Alcibiades (whom he first names early in his talk with Hamilton here), he is alluding to the retreat of Alcibiades (c. 450–404 B.C.), the Athenian general-politician (like Burr) who was finally distrusted, was defeated by the Spartans, was dismissed, and fled to Phrygia, only to be murdered. Hamilton snidely suggests that Burr should instead take his cue from Themistocles (c. 515–449 B.C.), an Athenian soldier-statesman who, when he lost favor with the people and was ostracized, fled, was labeled a traitor, but thereafter lived handsomely with the Persians. Wallace L. Anderson contends that the title "On the

Way" suggests that in truth Hamilton and Burr are even here "'on the way' toward the duel 10 years later that resulted in Hamilton's death and Burr's [first] disgrace." (Sources: W. Anderson [1968], 124; Bates, 23)

"The One Chord" *see* **"L'Envoi"**

"Palaemon — Damoetas — Menalcas" (1890, 1940). Translation of Virgil's "Eclogue III." Two shepherds, Damoetas and Menalcas, criticize each other jocosely, then decide to have a singing contest. Menalcas wagers carved beech cups against Damoetas's heifer. When their friend Palaemon approaches, he agrees to be the judge and orders them to sing alternately. Damoetas praises Jove and mentions Galatea. Menalcas lauds Phoebus and Amyntas. Damoetas switches to Phyllis, until Menalcas says he is also attracted to her. Damoetas appeals to Pollis and the Muses. Menalcas counters by praising Pollis and by ridiculing unsuccessful imitators who might as easily seek to "milk a butting goat, or yoke his foxes [iungat vulpes et mulgeat hircos]." Damoetas and Menalcas ramble about flowers, fruits, and livestock, then pose two riddles. Damoetas: "tell me in what land . . . / Only three ells of sky lie open to the sight." Menalcas: "tell me in what land the written names of kings / Are born with blooming flowers." Palaemon judges the contest to be a tie and orders the irrigation sluice closed, since "the fields have drunk their fill [sat prata biberunt]."

Robinson sent a copy of his translation in a letter (April 17, 1890) to his friend Arthur R. Gledhill.* Ridgely Torrence* transcribed the translation, making many errors in the process, and included it in his edition of Robinson's letters. "Pollis" should be Pollio (Gaius Asinius Pollio, 76 B.C.—A.D. 5), Roman orator, historian, poet, and Virgil's protector-patron. In his letter, Robinson told Gledhill that the main part of his translation is in pentameter rhythm, while the singing contest is in Alexandrine couplets (i.e., pairs of rhyming hexameters), his purpose being to make his translation visually resemble the original as closely as he could. According to scholars, the answer to Damoetas's riddle is probably Rome and Rhodes; to Menalcas's, Sparta and Troy. (Sources: Cary [1975], 3, 169; Rand, 83–90; *Selected Letters*, 3, 181–84)

Palmer, Seth (1818–1894). Family relative. Living on his farm near Pittston, Maine, he was a kind, humor-loving cousin, as well as brother-in-law, of Robinson's mother, Mary Robinson.* His devoted wife, Lydia Anne Palmer, was Mary's sister. As a youth, Robinson enjoyed visiting the Palmers' farm and playing with their children. (Source: Hagedorn)

Papers, Robinson's. Robinson's manuscripts, letters, correspondence, and other papers are in more than 70 repositories in the United States. Four locations containing the bulk are the following: Colby College Library, Waterville, Connecticut; the Houghton Library, Harvard University, Cambridge, Massachusetts; Library of Congress, Washington, D.C.; and the New York Public Library, New York City, New York. Among other locations, libraries at the following universities and colleges contain by far the most Robinson material: Boston University, Boston, Massachusesstts; Columbia University, New York City, New York; University of Delaware, Newark, Delaware; Indiana University, Bloomington, Indiana; Middlebury College, Middlebury, Vermont; University of New Hampshire, Durham, New Hampshire; Smith College, Northampton, Massachusetts; University of Texas, Austin, Texas; Trinity College, Hartford, Connecticut; University of Virginia, Charlottesville, Virginia; Williams College, Williamstown, Massachusetts; and Yale University, New Haven, Connecticut. Sizable holdings are also at the following institutions in New York City: American Academy of Arts and Letters; the New-York Historical Society; and the New York Public Library.

When Wallace L. Anderson was at work on an edition of Robinson's letters (left incomplete at Anderson's death), he published the first and last known letters. They were, respectively, to an older cousin named Fred W. Palmer (January 5, 1882) and to his ailing friend George Burnham* (March 25, 1935). In between, Anderson reports, Robinson wrote more than four thousand letters that have survived, in addition to others known about but destroyed or not yet found. (Sources: W. Anderson [1980]; Bates; Robbins, 272)

"Partnership" (1902). Dramatic monologue. The wife of Bernard Palissy (c. 1510–1589), the French potter, is speaking to her husband: What you have produced is beautiful. I am ashamed of succumbing to fatigue before your success. The western sun shines on it over my bed and "Throws a glory on your head." Your determination taught me that our life has culminated in your glorious achievement. Despite your tears, your continuing frown expresses still-unsatisfied "faith and pride." The two of us kept on living, suffering, forgiving, toiling, and crying "For the glory of the clay" and "the gift the gods have kept." Hold high your accomplishment. Forgive my doubting. After all, "we [women] are not men"; so we don't need to specify unduly. "You to triumph, I to rest. That will be the best."

Originally entitled "The Wife of Palissy," this poem became "Partnership" in the 1921 *Collected Poems* and thereafter. By changing its title, Robinson made it impossible to understand the poem fully without someone's footnote that the partners were the Palissys, or at the least a footnote providing the original title of the poem. Richard Cary provides evidence that Robinson regretted renaming the poem. In a letter (October 22, 1893) to Harry de Forest Smith,* Robinson quotes four lines from the potter's song in "Kéramos," by Henry Wadsworth Longfellow. Taking this lead, Emery Neff comments that "Robinson encountered [Palissy] in Longfellow's 'Keramos' as a symbol of 'the prophet's vision.'" Neff adds that Palissy "told in his autobiography of his sixteen-year search for the secret of white enamel, to which he sacrificed everything, even feeding his kiln with his household furniture as a last resort." Neff does not report that Palissy failed in his white-enamel adventure, nor does Robinson do more than concentrate on the wife's self-sacrificial devotion to her husband's egocentric artistic struggle.

The firm structure of the poem reflects the wife's deceptively quiet assurance. Each of the nine stanzas rhymes *aabbb* (none feminine!), with four trochaic tetrameter lines followed by a trochaic trimeter one. Chard Powers Smith* believes that when, in "Partnership," Palissy's wife praises his ceramic piece, Robinson is secretly having Emma Robinson,* his sister-in-law, praise a manuscript of his; Smith then explicates the entire poem biographically. His interpretation seems strained. Smith does valuably point out that in real life Palissy's wife was a cold vixen, and thus the reverse of helpful to him. Probably not knowing that "Palissy" was the original title of the poem, Charles Cestre* interprets it romantically thus: "We infer that an artist's wife, on her death-bed, being shown her husband's masterpiece, lately completed, recognizes his genius which she had doubted." (Sources: Cary [1974], 292; Cestre, 49; Neff, 120; C. Smith, 170–74; *Untriangulated Stars*, 113)

"Pasa Thalassa Thalassa" (1910). Poem. The translation from the Greek, "The sea is everywhere the sea," is beneath the title. Robinson remembers his "sea-faring friend," lost in the ocean a decade earlier. The missing man's garden of roses and vines has decayed, and the trellises "lie like bones in a ruin." Smoke from his chimney no longer rolls into the twilight. Instead are seen puzzling flights of swallows. Finding only "shadows and echoes" here, the poet wonders where along the lamplit streets he might find someone to say where his sailor friend now lies. In the Indian Ocean, the "fields of Atlantis," off stormy Cape Horn? Few people are left to walk the weed-grown "path to his cottage," and few could even remember him. The poet prefers to stroll toward the town and let others sail after his friend, whose "name [is] carved somewhere on the sea."

Henry Rushton Fairclough identifies the source of the title "Pasa Thalassa Thalassa" as Antipater of Sidon, in the *Palatine Anthology*, vii, 639. Emma Robinson* reports that the poem was inspired by the loss at sea in 1885 of the *Washington* and all aboard, including its owner, Captain Israel Snow Jordan, the Robinsons' neighbor at 74 Lincoln Avenue, Gardiner, Maine, when the future poet used to play with Augustus Jordan and Alice Jordan, the captain's children. It is known that the cap-

tain's widow liked Robinson, fed him cookies, gave him apples from her orchard, and even sent him more apples after he had left town. Captain Jordan's portrait is at Colby College.

In unrhymed dactylic and trochaic hexameters, "Pasa Thalassa Thalassa" merits the praise of Emery Neff, who says that its "rhythm is used to reinforce the mood and theme." Ellsworth Barnard admires the poem, traces poetic analogues, and says that Robinson's depiction of late-summer dusk in the lost sailor's garden "invites and sustains comparison with two of the great English lyrics of the nineteenth century, Swinburne's *A Forsaken Garden* and Tennyson's *Tears, Idle Tears*." Louis Coxe feels that the poem, composed "in what he [Robinson] called his 'jingly vein,'" has "a Kiplingesque quality that is derivative, fin de siècle and, though most competent, uninspired." (Sources: Barnard, 239; Coxe, 83; Fairclough, 15; Hagedorn, 237; Neff, 157; Richards [1936], 10–11; E. Robinson, 14)

"The Pauper" *see* **Captain Craig**

"Pauvrette" *see* **"The Poor Relation"**

Peabody, Josephine Preston (1874–1922). Poet and prize-winning playwright. She was born in Brooklyn, New York. Her father encouraged her love of Shakespeare. After her father died (1884), she moved with her family to Dorchester, Massachusetts. She attended the Girls' Latin School there, began to write, and published a poem when she was 14. Horace Scudder (1838–1902), editor of the *Atlantic Monthly*, was so impressed by her juvenile poetry that he persuaded some rich friends to pay her way to attend Radcliffe College as a special student (1894–1896). Peabody moved permanently to Cambridge (1900) and taught English later at Wellesley College (1901–1903). She married Lionel S. Marks, a Harvard engineering professor (1906; they had two children). She was semi-invalided (from 1913), and fought depression by maintaining a profound belief in God.

Peabody published many poems in respectable journals, and also published collections of her poetry, beginning with *The Way-farers* (1898), nine poems of which the editor

Edmund Clarence Stedman* included in his *An American Anthology, 1797–1900* (1900). Her later collections are *The Singing Leaves* (1903), *The Singing Man* (1911, pro-labor), and *Harvest Moon* (1916, anti-war). Peabody also wrote a play about Christopher Marlowe (1901), and wrote about Shakespeare (1900), woman's suffrage (1907), St. Francis of Assisi (1913), and Mary Wollstonecraft (1922). *The Piper* (1910), her most popular play, is based on the legend of the Pied Piper of Hamlin. Dramatizing the conflict between Christianity and Satan, it was performed in Stratford-upon-Avon, elsewhere in England, and in New York and widely on tour in the United States.

Robinson met Josephine Peabody in Cambridge (1899), through her friendship with Daniel Gregory Mason* and Laura E. Richards.* Robinson came to like her but at first feared she cared for little about him but his poetry. The two, however, soon became mutually admiring friends. In an unsigned review (*Literary Review* 3, January-February 1899) of her *The Wayfarers*, Robinson, according to Richard Cary, "praised her lyrics . . . as displaying an imagination 'not of the pounding, pyrotechnic sort.'" (See also "A Book of Verse That Is Poetry.") When Robinson first began to reside in New York (1900), they began an extensive correspondence, which was often about details of their work and which continued intermittently until at least 1919. Back in 1900 she tried unsuccessfully to get Robinson's *Captain Craig* published, by inviting an editor of Small, Maynard and Co. to dinner and then pressuring him delicately. Robinson asked Peabody to edit his "Twilight Song" ruthlessly when it was in draft form. He urged her to concentrate on lyric poetry, for which he felt she was especially gifted. Her diary records their interaction in loving detail. It is likely that by 1903, if not earlier, she introduced Robinson to her close friend Kahlil Gibran,* the mystic poet-artist from Lebanon. (Sources: Cary [1974], 259–60; Current-García; J. Gibran, 123, 145; Hagedorn; Neff; Peabody; C. Smith)

"Peace on Earth" (1919). Poem. On Christmas Eve the persona is approached by a panhandler who doffs his tattered hat, says, "Peace on Earth," asks for "A morsel out of what you're worth," repeats his "Peace" message, calls himself Ichabod, and swears he's "sober now." The persona asks whether he believes in God and whether there will really be peace. The man replies that we're celebrating the birth of the Son of God, wonders whether that God is his or the persona's, and hints at the stinginess of some of God's "anthropoids" this day. He complains that "A One wiser than you" would see a valuable light in him, even though the persona sees him only as "A Christmas curiosity." He says that he might have slugged the persona "from behind" and robbed him of what he could find. The fellow asks whether he will be given money for a new hat if he says he believes in God. But whose God? "Has he commanded that his name / Be written everywhere the same?" God may value both men's lives equally. Each person's world is in him, for his "endurance to the end." Peace on earth is determined by each individual's faithful, honest evaluation of his world. The persona tips the fellow generously and gets as thanks the fellow's statement that he prefers telling the truth to lying, on Christmas Eve, regardless. As he leaves, the persona is pleased that the "droll . . . derelict" has money for a new hat, since

> His unshaved, educated face,
> His inextinguishable grace,
> And his hard smile, are with me still,
> Deplore the vision as I will.

The name Ichabod means "inglorious." Ellsworth Barnard calls "Peace on Earth" a "whimsical warning . . . against smug or hasty judgments on our fellows." Incidentally, Robinson was unusually sympathetic when approached by panhandlers. (Source: Barnard, 170)

"Peaches and Ether." Essay. An unpublished editorial Robinson wrote in 1900, at the suggestion of Edmund Clarence Stedman,* the editor-poet, to try to make a little needed money. It was a satirical piece criticizing much contemporary poetry and was rejected by the *New York Post*. (Source: Hagedorn, 172–73)

Peck, Harry Thurston (1856–1914). Educator and man of letters. Peck was born in Stamford, Connecticut, attended Columbia University (A.B. 1881, A.M. 1882), studied classical philology in Europe, and received his Ph.D. at Cumberland University, Lebanon, Tennessee (1883). While teaching Latin, Hebrew, Arabic, and literature at Columbia (1882–1910), Peck found time and energy to be a wide-ranging author of scholarly books, biographies, poetry, and children's stories. He also was a prodigious editor of works and encyclopedias devoted to classical philology and geography. He also contributed to a variety of periodicals, some of which he edited, including the influential *Bookman* (1895–1902). Peck married Cornelia MacKay (1882). They had two daughters and then were divorced (1906). He married Caroline Hickman (1909). Trouble engulfed Peck when he was sued by a former stenographer for breach of promise and was additionally sued for libel (1910). Although neither case ever went to court, Peck was dismissed from employment and from various clubs, felt humiliated, and committed suicide.

Peck reviewed *The Torrent and The Night Before* (*Bookman*, February 1897) and famously said that Robinson's "humor is of a grim sort, and the world is not beautiful to him, but a prison-house." This image inspired Robinson's even more famous rejoinder, which Peck promptly published: "I am sorry to learn that I have painted myself in such lugubrious colours. The world is not a prison house, but a kind of spiritual kindergarten, where millions of bewildered infants are trying to spell God with the wrong blocks" (*Bookman*, March 1897). Even earlier, Robinson had voiced displeasure with one of Peck's poems, published in Peck's *Bookman*. In a letter (May 5, 1895) to Harry de Forest Smith,* Robinson said that he could tolerate only the thought in the Peck verse. Richard Cary cites as an undoubted source of Robinson's prison-house image these lines from "Ode: Intimations of Immortality from Recollections of Early Childhood" by William Wordsworth: "Shades of the prison-house begin to close / Upon the growing Boy." (Sources: Cary [1974], 50; *Untriangulated Stars*, 223)

Perry, Thomas Sergeant (1845–1928). Scholar, educator, author, and translator. He was born in Newport, Rhode Island. He was the great-great-grandson of Benjamin Franklin, the grand-nephew of Commodore Matthew Galbraith Perry (the early leading negotiator with Japan), and the grandson of Oliver Hazard Perry (the naval hero). After graduating from Harvard (1866) and studying and traveling in Europe (1866–1868), Perry taught French and German at Harvard (1868–1872), did editorial work for the *North American Review* (1872–1877), and taught English at Harvard (1872–1882), until he was dismissed by Harvard's president Charles William Eliot,* whom Perry disliked. Perry married Lilla Cabot (1874). She was a painter and a poet. The Perrys had three daughters. After considerable writing and publishing, Perry taught English as a university professor in Japan (1898–1901). Home again, he continued to read and study, including Sanskrit and Russian. He helped to popularize the works of several French and Russian novelists, and also Edward FitzGerald's translation of *The Rubáiyát of Omar Khayyám*.

Not long after he began going to the MacDowell Colony* (1911), Robinson met the Perrys. They had a summer home called Flagstones at Hancock, New Hampshire, a few miles north of Peterborough. Beginning in 1913, Robinson began to visit the hospitable Perrys there. Thereafter, he spent many weekends at Flagstones each summer. Lilla Perry often read drafts of Robinson's poems aloud to him, which enabled him to evaluate their tones and rhythms. He and numerous other distinguished guests enjoyed parties hosted by the Perrys and livened by splendid conversation, impromptu poetizing, and informal musicales. Lilla painted a splendid oil portrait of Robinson (1916), now in the Robinson Room at Colby College, Waterville, Maine. Amusingly, it features a sizable cigar in the poet's right hand, even though he incessantly smoked Sweet Caporal cigarettes and no cigars. Mrs. Perry and her friend Laura E. Richards* innocently viewed cigars as more masculine. Lilla Perry also painted a fine portrait in 1889 of her husband serenely reading. After Perry died, his family persuaded Robinson to edit what became *Selections from the Letters of Thomas Sergeant Perry* (1929). Robinson also wrote "Perry, Thomas Sergeant," for *Dictionary of American Biography* (vol. 14, 1937). (See "Introduction to *The Letters of Thomas Sergeant Perry*" and "Perry, Thomas Sergeant" [1937].) (Sources: Cary [1975], 192–93, 195; Harlow, 200–08)

"Perry, Thomas Sergeant" (1937). Essay. After his friend Thomas Sergeant Perry* died, Robinson was asked to write a 700-word biographical sketch of him for publication in the prestigious *Dictionary of American Biography* (21 vols., 1927–1937). He undertook the assignment seriously, and wrote Perry's widow Lilla Cabot Perry and their daughter Margaret Perry several times to ask for suggestions and emendations.

Robinson begins by naming Perry's distinguished ancestors, including Benjamin Franklin, Oliver Hazard Perry, and Commodore Matthew Galbraith Perry. He discusses Perry's education, early travels, brief teaching career, and editorial work. He lists and praises Perry's mid-career publications, mentions his three-year teaching adventure in Japan, but concentrates on his gradually demonstrated preference for omnivorous reading and erudite language study. Robinson extols Perry for achieving a hospitable philosophy that was rationalistic, quasi-mechanistic, and fastidious, but also democratic. Copyrighted 1934, Robinson's sketch of Perry was published in 1937 (vol. 14). (See also "Introduction to *The Letters of Thomas Sergeant Perry*" and Perry, Thomas Sergeant [1845–1928].)

"The Peterborough Idea" (1916). Essay. Robinson begins by mentioning a Bret Harte parody of a romantic novel by Alexandre Dumas père. Harte presents a hero who needs a 37-foot ladder and promptly stumbles on one. Similarly, in the spring of 1911, Robinson began to feel the need to escape hot, noisy New York City and find a place in which to write before summer came. The place should be near civilization and provide lodging, food, bed, walk to breakfast, walk to secluded building in woods, fireplace, wood, doorway view of New England scenery, uninterrupted work hours, lunch brought in, sociable dinner, easy evenings, and privacy. He obviously thought destiny would not cooperate, until a friend suggested the MacDowell Colony.* Though troubled by the word "colony," he left New York, timidly stayed in Boston a while, but soon reported to Peterborough, New Hampshire. He figured on trying the place for two weeks, then fibbing about needing to escape; but he remained for 10 weeks, from mid–July to the end of September.

Robinson found more than he had expected and nothing of what he had feared. He discovered that if he loafed there he couldn't rest, and he couldn't rest unless he worked at writing. Earlier, his long-suffering New England conscience got tired of reminding him of lost opportunities; so he was free to take full advantage of this new chance. He worked well and enjoyed nature greatly. He explains that "the Peterborough idea" is not a school, sanitarium, resort, experiment, or extended tea party. It lacks counselors, hours, amateurs, regulations. It does not encourage perennial loafers. It limits the number of guest "workers" to about 20 to 25. The creator of this colony tolerates misconceptions about it with good humor. It does not aim mainly to attract "the impecunious." Fine work has been accomplished here by wealthy writers and by those with "problematical" income. However, "neophytes and wrecks are alike ineligible."

Robinson praises Edward MacDowell,* who had the idea for what became the MacDowell Colony. He was an unusually serious, scholarly, inspired, and sophisticated American composer. The colony provides unique advantages to the poor and to the independent alike, and in the process inspires the "serious worker" to do well, through "isolation, liberty, and opportunity." A certain "mystical touch" is there, as inexplicable as the appeal of MacDowell's "Keltic Sonata." The genius of the deceased MacDowell helps to make the place "a workshop, not a wonderland," or perhaps a shop with such a land "thrown in." The few who come to play are not treated well and mostly don't return. The best among the colony's guests have been "accepted" and recommended by contemporary critics; "that is the Peterborough Idea." The world needs artists working in various genres and is better because of their creations; those artists will fail without opportunities. Persons are wrong who say that artists are selfish and are best when dead.

Robinson explains that Mrs. MacDowell (see MacDowell, Marian Nivens, [1857–1957]) sacrificed much to convert her husband's "thought" into what is now a combination of some five hundred acres of farm and forest land and several well-constructed buildings. Although she is probably tired of being praised, this essay may have value for correcting the many misconceptions that have gained currency about what is a completely "rational, natural and desirable" project. (Sources: Cary [1975], 70–77, 188–89; Payne).

Ph.D. Dissertations on Robinson. Between 1936 and 2003, at least 56 Ph.D. dissertations were written and accepted on the subject of Robinson alone or Robinson in connection with other writers. The first was by Elisabeth Grohs, "Edwin Arlington Robinsons langere Verserzählunger," Vienna, 1936. Nine more appeared in the 1940s; 12 in the 1950s; 15, 1960s; 13, 1970s; two, 1980s; two, 1990s; and two thus far in the 21st century.

Using abbreviations and shortened titles, and in alphabetical order by writer, they are: N. Ayo, "EAR and Bible," Duke, 1966; A. Baumgärtner, "Das lyrische Werk EARs," Mainz, 1952; S. Betsky, "Aspects of Philosophy of EAR," Harvard, 1943; J. C. Bierk, "EAR, Social Critic, Moral Guide," Northwestern, 1969; A. S. Blumenthal, "New England in Poetry, R. W. Emerson, E. Dickinson, EAR," Washington, 1986; E. W. Booth, "New England, EAR, R. Frost, C. Ives, C. Ruggles," Utah, 1974; B. R. Brubaker, "Political Appointments of Writers, Including EAR," OSU, 1966; D. H. Burton, "Christian Conservatism in EAR's Poetry," Georgetown, 1953; F. W. Conner, "Cosmic Optimism, R. W. Emerson to EAR," Pennsylvania, 1944; R. H. Crowder, "Three Studies of EAR," Iowa, 1944; M. L. Dauner, "Studies in EAR," Iowa, 1944; C. T. Davis, "Poetic Drama, W. V. Moody[*], EAR, R. Torrence[*], P. MacKaye[*]," NYU, 1951; P. Dechert, "EAR and A. T. Schumann[*]," Pennsylvania, 1955;

D. C. Downing, "Poetry EAR, Reappraisal," UCLA, 1977; D. L. Durling, "Work of Robinson in Light of American Thought, American Literary History," Queens, 1949; M. Essl, "Arthurian Motif, T. Berger, M. Z. Bradley, EAR, M. Stewart, T.H. White," Salzburg, 1991; F. W. Eckman, "Language of American Poetry," OSU, 1954; O. H. Evans, "Sonnet in America," Purdue, 1972; P. O. Ewers, "*Merlin, Lancelot, Tristram,* EAR's," Loyola, 1966; R. S. Fish, " 'Man Against Sky,' Other Poems, EAR," Oklahoma, 1970; J. V. Foy, "Character, Structure in EAR's Narratives," Cornell 1961; L. D. Fryxell, "EAR, Dramatist, Dramatic Poet," Kentucky, 1955; E. S. Fussell, "Early Poetry, EAR," Harvard, 1949; J. A. Gowen, "Puritan Characteristics, Poetry of EAR," Stanford, 1968; J. E. Horner, "Images of Man, EAR, W. C. Williams, R. Jarrell," Texas, 1982; A. L. Insdorf, "American Strain: Connecting Art and Experience," Yale, 1975; E. Isely, "Imagery in Poetry, EAR," Arkansas, 1967; N. Joyner, "EAR's Theory of Poetry," North Carolina, 1966; E. Kaplan, "Philosophy in Poetry, EAR," Columbia, 1940; T. W. Koontz, "Gentlemen in Poetry, EAR," Indiana, 1970; S. G. L. Lim, "E. C. Stedman[*], T. B. Aldrich, G. C. Lodge, T. Stickney,* W. V. Moody[*], EAR," Brandeis, 1973; E. J. McGregor, "Bible Elements in E. Dickinson, S. Crane, EAR, R. Frost," Brown, 1978; J. F. Malof, "Isolation in Early Poems, EAR," UCLA, 1962; J. Manheimer, "Speaker's Voice, Poetry of EAR," Brandeis, 1974; J. H. Miller, "EAR's Changing Beliefs," Indiana, 1970; G. Mitchell, "EAR's Sonnets," Temple, 1949; E. S. Moon, "Organic Form in Shorter Poems, EAR," Michigan, 1956; R. W. Moran Jr., "Study of Shorter Poems, EAR," LSU, 1966; P. R. Morrill, "Psychological Aspects of Poetry, EAR," Northwestern, 1956; C. B. Morris, "Camelot," CUNY, 1968; R. S. Moseley III, Narrative Form, Long Poems, EAR," Connecticut, 1967; S. L. Mott, "Happy Ending as Controlling Element, EAR," South Carolina, 1965; L. Mulligan, "Mythology, Autobiography, in *Tristram,*" Massachusetts, 1975; L. D. Perrine, "EAR and Arthurian Legend," Yale, 1948; W. R. Robinson, "EAR, Poetry of Act," OSU, 1962; L. J. Satterfield, "Irony in Poetry of EAR," Nebraska, 1969;

M. J. Skupin, "Merlin in EAR and L. Binyon," Houston, 2003; A. A. Stevens Jr., "Shorter Narratives, EAR," Missouri, 1954; R. D. Stevick, "EAR: Principles, Practices of Poetry," Wisconsin, 1956; M. W. Sundermeier, "Concordance, Poetry of EAR [2,781 pages]," Nebraska, 1972; E. A. Weil, "Female Characters in EAR," North Carolina, Greensboro, 1993; W. J. Wilson, "Existentialism in EAR's Pessimism," Nebraska, 1973; "P. N. Zietlow, "Shorter Poems, Hardy, EAR," Michigan, 1965; E. H. Zuk, "Sonnet, EAR, E. Millay, R. Frost, E. E. Cummings," British Columbia, 2001.

Phelps, William Lyon (1865–1945). Educator and literary critic. He was born in New Haven, Connecticut, earned a B.A. at Yale (1887) and then an M.A. at Harvard and a Ph.D. at Yale (both 1891). After teaching briefly at Harvard (1891–1892), he became an immensely popular teacher at Yale (1892–1933), specializing in the works of Robert Browning and Alfred, Lord Tennyson, and innovatively in the modern novel. Phelps married Annabel Hubbard (1892; they had no children). He was an off-campus lecturer (1920s), wrote a monthly magazine column (1922–1936), and conducted a radio program (1934–1935). However, all was not happy with Phelps, for he suffered from insomnia and depression, and also had a nervous breakdown (1924).

Phelps combined graduate studies and writing at Harvard when Robinson first arrived there (1891). Phelps says in his *Autobiography, with Letters* (1939) that he never saw Robinson until Yale awarded Robinson an honorary degree in 1922. Robinson, who may have seen Phelps at Harvard, surely sent him inscribed copies of *The Torrent and The Night Before* in 1896 and *The Children of the Night* a year later. In his enormous *Autobiography*, Phelps finds ample room to comment genially on Robinson, whose *Tristram* he calls Robinson's best poem. (Sources: Hagedorn, 68; Skupin, 38; C. Smith, 119)

"The Pilgrims' Chorus" (1921). Poem. A sound came to us, as from heaven. A light fell where we see it now. A divine fire burned in the west. A voice came that freed us. Others may follow, into fields not yet sown.

This three-quatrain poem is in trochaic octometers, an unusual metrical form. It was written to be a part of *The Pilgrim Spirit*, a pageant celebrating the tercentenary of the pilgrims' landing, by George Pierce Baker,* Harvard professor of dramatic composition. Robinson almost never agreed to write anything to attach to somebody else's work. But he did so in this case because he knew Baker and about him, both through their being at the MacDowell Colony* together and also through several of Baker's students, including Esther Willard Bates.* In addition, he didn't mind accepting $100 for his 24-line poem. According to Bacon Collamore,* Robinson "confessed . . . that this was one of the few pieces of hack work which he ever turned out, and swore that he would never again write poetry to order." Edwin S. Fussell also calls Robinson's effort here "a piece of hack work." (Sources: Cary [1975], 51, 184; Collamore, 31; Fussell [1954], 11)

"The Pilot" (1906). Poem. The persona is sailing with others under the true stars but without their absent comrade's guidance. As they drift, toss, and wander, they yearn for the missing man, who was charming and learned. He "fought . . . [a] foul . . . gale," was victorious beyond their comprehension, but now is gone; and they must sail on, while finding everything different.

"The Pilot" has been explained as Robinson's expression of loss following the death in 1899 of his brother Dean Robinson.* Each of its three eight-line stanzas rhymes *abbaccac*, with only the *c*-rhymes masculine. The trochaic tetrameter meter may remind readers of the sing-song lines of *The Song of Hiawatha* by Henry Wadsworth Longfellow. (Sources: Hagedorn, 237; C. Smith, 73, 315)

"The Pity of the Leaves" (1897). Sonnet. The November wind shrieks from the moors with a message of "ancestral shame" and echoes through the halls of an old man's house. He also hears "Words out of lips that were no more to speak." Their import makes him shake like "old floors" weighted by "dead footsteps." He is "plagued" by "brown, thin leaves" skittering "with a freezing whisper" "on the stones outside" his house. At times, the leaves "stopped, and stayed there," as though to show they were dead. When the old man weeps, they "flutter . . . off like withered souls of men."

Emma Robinson* says that Robinson wrote "The Pity of the Leaves" when his father Edward Robinson* was lingering in his final illness (1891 or 1892).

Harvey Gross and Robert McDowell, contending that Robinson is "the master of the sonnet," cite this powerful poem as one proof. Emery Neff regards it as an "intimate expression . . . of the bereavement and the loneliness of old age." Louis Coxe places "The Pity of the Leaves" in the literary tradition of New England writers, including Robert P. Tristram Coffin, Robert Frost, Nathaniel Hawthorne, Sarah Orne Jewett, and Eugene O'Neill, all of whom wrote about old people's loneliness. What is the reader to make of "ancestral shame" and of "lips that were no more to speak"? Is the old man conscience-stricken? If so, why? Was his behavior caused by some family curse? Are the dead lips his, his wife's, whose? In this sonnet may be found an example of Robinson's rare use of off-rhymes, thus in its octave: "moors," "corridors," "perforce," and "floors." (Sources: Coxe, 51–53; Gross and McDowell, 59; Neff, 86; E. Robinson, 11)

"Plummer Street, Gardiner, Maine" (1951). Sonnet. The poet wonders why row houses have been built where Van Amburgh's circus used to be. Now where are all the animals, the clowns, the giants, the rifle galleries, the stands for drinks and cigars, the tattooed fellow, and the trapeze artists? Robinson included this poem in a letter (May 10, 1900) he sent to William Vaughn Moody.* (Source: Cary [1975], 46, 181)

"A Poem for Max Nordau" (1896). Poem. This poem has three stanzas, the first two with four lines each, and the third with five. It is one of Robinson's funniest works. The first line, "Dun shades quiver down the lone long fallow," is repeated in the second stanza and ends the third. Betweentimes, the poet reports that the owl scares the night, winds rattle reeds and make "frayed leaves flutter," dead stems "shimmer" in the cold dew, stars are pale in the foul air, shadows fly around, and a sorrowful moon awakens "The lewd gloom."

Robinson's intention was to spoof the gloomy fin-de-siècle theory of Max Simon Nordau (1848–1923), expressed in his initially popular *Degeneration* (1895), that for various pseudo-scientific reasons late-19th-century literature should be disliked. Richard Cary (1974) specifically notes that "Robinson's heavy lather of alliteration and assonance clearly indicated a spoof of the Symbolist school of poets . . . trailing Poe's resonant footfalls." Robinson offers a cold satiric frieze of decadent pictures here. It seems possible that in "A Poem for Max Nordau" Robinson pretends to be trying to write a triolet and failing, like a properly disobedient decadent poet. The poem has only two rhymes, as a triolet must. But the first four lines rhyme *abba*, whereas in a triolet they must rhyme *abaa*. Additionally, whereas in a triolet the first, fourth, and seventh lines must be identical, Robinson here has the first, seventh, and thirteenth lines identical. Finally, since a triolet must have only eight lines, Robinson tacks on his third stanza, and gives it five instead of four lines, to boot. (See also "Triolet.") In a letter (October 6, 1895) to Harry de Forest Smith,* Robinson says, "October is the month for me. I like the red leaves. Red leaves makes [*sic*] me think of *Degeneration*."

"A Poem for Max Nordau" appeared in *The Torrent and The Night Before*, but Robinson kept it out of *The Children of the Night*, because, according to Laura E. Richards,* "it was meant to be funny, and he was afraid people might not realize this." Richards lamented its exclusion, because she liked its "incomparable lilt and swing." Indeed, Emery Neff reports that it was a "skit . . . which reviewers and other readers had taken seriously." (Sources: Cary [1974], 37; Cary [1975], 32, 178–79; Neff, 87; Richards [1936], 57–58; *Untriangulated Stars*, 233)

"Ponce de Leon (Havana, 1521)" (1932). Dramatic duologue. It is in blank verse. Ponce de Leon lies wounded by a possibly poisoned arrow that struck him during a battle in lush Florida, a region he named and fought to conquer. His men, loyal though feeling defeated, transported him to Havana, to a sagacious physician he knew there.

The doctor tells De Leon, with a smile, that he is too old to continue perilously exploring. Why should he have left his wife, his house, his wealth? If, he adds, De Leon returns to a child-like, spiritual innocence, "our Saviour" may reward him. Smiling in pain, De Leon replies: I have sinned, lied too long, heard lies too often to be forgiven. The doctor: Rest, close your eyes, recall evidence of your past valor. Doing so may refresh you. We scholars are merely books with faces, whereas you are a mighty man. De Leon: I have few memories that could nourish my soul. You said the arrow was not poisoned, but my flaming memories damn me. How soon will I die? Doctor: God mercifully keeps all who suffer from obtaining knowledge about their demises. Think instead about your glorious victories for Mother Spain. Without victories, can there be dominions? Without a price, can there be victories? De Leon: You're trying to deceive me, though innocently. My conquests have mainly resulted in bloodshed, not wealth. Although you speak of dominions, that arrow dominated me. Doctor: History will provide a lavishly bejeweled record of your "conquest . . . rich and intact." De Leon: My jewels, which I would like to see, are only my wife Ines and our children. Jealous of Cortes, I too sought an unknown world to win and give my name to. I should have quit. I should have been content when I conquered Puerto Rico. God wisely hid that fountain of youth I sought. Finding it would have made me ruthless with my own men. We Spanish were the first to ruin this new world. "Are the first always / The worst?" Or did God "pamper" us simply to provide our "ultimate undoing"? Because of us, a mortal stench may remain throughout these islands. Doctor: This kind of talk, truthful though it may be, gives you no hope. "Truth is not always hope; nor, as we learn, / Is anguish always death." Listen for the hope whispering in the waves just outside.

De Leon, feverish: Be wiser. There is no hope in any sound of any wave. I want "water,

. . . not the sound of it." Those sounds "are the music of time's funeral," apparently endless. Your eyes speak truthfully about my delusory fame, achieved by "tricks and treacheries and exterminations." I recall these islands, fated to be somnolent until I arrived, shook them up, reigned, was adored and called a god so often I believed it. I became a worse devil than their multiple ones. Maybe some Haitian devils were awful, but at least they were native ones. Imagine seeing what I have seen — men and women embracing children and all leaping into the sea rather than confront the white man any longer. Doctor: Come now. I've heard of many atrocities committed by others, including (Nicolás de) Ovando (1460?–1518?), but few by you and your men. It's possible that many dark-skinned natives are grateful for acts of kindness you've forgotten. Go back and listen to their thanks. De Leon: What the natives in my residence in Florida will be happy to hear is the cannon booming an accompaniment to my funeral barge returning home. I hope that in death I don't hear native lamentations that I caused and that are worse than cries in hell. Doctor: It's wise to get these poisonous thoughts out of your system. You're not evil. I do thank God that you didn't find the fountain of youth. De Leon: Yes, God has wisely measured the extent of human lives. When that "old woman from Luquillo" told me about that fountain, she said that I was "thirsting for it" but that she wouldn't drink from it because her one long and happy life was sufficient. What I really sought at first was a new land, not a perpetual life. In your eyes I see peace, wisdom, and — most helpfully — "no fear for the end." But tell me, what is it all about?

Doctor: Some voices hidden in us whisper that we'd "better go the other way." Other voices encourage us to proceed directly but with care. Still other voices would have us believe that, if this world is the only one, we are "animate accidents" created as sacrifices "To an insatiate God" presiding over nothing. But that God isn't ours. Still other voices, once distant, are now close, not recognized but welcome, and hard to understand because "You cannot listen / To more than you may hear" nor interpret what lies beyond your comprehension. De Leon, in pain: True. I'll die soon. Doctor: Yes, and I, being old, will too, and gladly, provided "there are voices." De Leon: There are some I'm happy you don't hear. Your eyes tell me more than your words, more than my 60 years of life convey to me. What I see in your eyes "may be voices." Doctor: Not voices, probably; my eyes, however, have sufficiently observed "this torn world and its infirmities" to have gained "some wisdom," "some forbearance." When you've confessed to your priest, you'll feel peace, be wiser, fear not, have less pain. You seem to me less horrible than, defeated, you have presented yourself. I'll follow you to death in time, which itself will finally die. De Leon: Thank you for saying less than all the truth. I will tell God everything He knows about me that I can remember, and I hope God knows more about me than I now recall.

At this point, Ponce de Leon sighs, feels the doctor's hand cool upon his forehead, and closes his eyes to feel his pain again, alone.

Yet he was not alone, for the same eyes
Were there. He smiled, knowing them to be there,
And opened his to say that he was ready.

W. R. Robinson advances understanding of "Ponce de Leon" by applying its leap-of-faith anti-intellectualism and its anti-mechanistic hints to candid opinions contained in a letter Robinson wrote (September 18, 1931) to the philosopher-historian Will Durant (1885–1981). (See "On the Meaning of Life.") Several Catholic critics have found personal comfort in parts of the poem as well. Sister Mary James Power, for example, says "God's Wisdom is in the order of His mercy. It is infinite. Robinson would have Ponce de Leon realize the Omniscience of God in defeating his plans to discover the fountain that would bring not only perpetual youth, but the fulfilment of evil propensities long a part of him." Henry W. Wells places "Ponce de Leon" in "[t]he long tradition of the [poetic] dialogue" and says that it "stand[s] among Robinson's ripest work in simple dialogue." (Sources: Power, 76; W. Robinson, 23–25; *Selected Letters*, 163–65; Wells, 184)

"The Poor Relation" (1915). Poem. She has doubts, is sad for being a bother to others, and says she should have died long ago. "Beneath her beauty, blanched with pain," is a childish querulousness. Why should she have paid so much for her stainless memories, only to be defeated? She clings to those few visitors who still know where she lives. They talk with her about "roses" in what she quietly knows to be her "grass[less]" past. When they have paid their dutiful minutes with her, they leave her, and then she "count[s]" the "chimneys and . . . spires" outside her window. She knows the brevity of their pity. "But one good friend always reappears, / A good ghost." Welcome memories stir; and she laughs, fearlessly, in recollection of the power she had in her youth. She was once envied for her charm and status. Some "friends" are still alive who meanly rejoice at her "losses." Her memories include "treasure[d]" songs of her childhood. Meanwhile, the harp-like hum of the big city "blend[s]" the never-arriving future and the thoroughly ended past, all accompanied by little drip-drops "Of Time['s]" drum. This poor relative, "Bereft enough to shame a sage," sighs but little, has "no illusion to assuage / The lonely changelessness of dying," and like a comfortably caged bird "sings and watches," all the long time "Unsought, unthought-of, and unheard."

In a letter (August 31, 1915) Robinson thanks Edith Brower* for liking "Pauvrette," the poem he later called "The Poor Relation." He says it should prove effective because most people "must know somebody to whom it will apply to some degree." The poem comprises nine stanzas, each with eight tetrameter lines, and sustains a difficult *ababccab* rhyme scheme. The *b*-rhymes are softly and appropriately feminine; for example, in the last stanza are "long sighing," "dying," and "no more flying."

How old is the subject of this poem? Yvor Winters bluntly calls her "an old woman," while Ellsworth Barnard presents evidence that she need not be so regarded. Scott Donaldson identifies the "good ghost" as "her own self, when young." Glauco Cambon admires the poem enormously, and says that "[t]here are few things in modern verse worth comparing with the 'largo' effect of the final . . . [11 lines], where verbal precision, rhythmical effect, rhyme melody, and functional onomatopeia combine to make the 'small intolerable drums / of Time' an orchestral commentary on the situation." Louis Coxe says that "[t]he last two stanzas of this poem have a nearly intolerable intensity of pathos." Teasing the reader are hints about this heroine's possible former wealth and a possible unrequited love affair. Wallace L. Anderson skillfully explicates the subtle flower and bird imagery in this poem. (Sources: W. Anderson [1968], 113–16; Barnard, 284; Brower, 163; Cambon, 56; Coxe, 113; Donaldson [1969], 51; Winters, 34)

Pope, Seth Ellis (1873–1922). A lifelong friend. Pope was born in Medfield, Massachusetts, graduated from Bowdoin College (A.B., 1895), taught before and after that date at the Highland Avenue School in Gardiner, couldn't maintain classroom discipline and discontinued, attended the New York State Library School (1900–1901), and was a librarian in Hartford, Connecticut (1902–1912). Pope moved to New York City, taught there at the High School of Commerce (1912–1916) and taught and was a librarian at Boys High School in Brooklyn (1916–1922).

Robinson knew Pope when he was teaching in Gardiner, during which time both were members of the Quadruped Club,* which also included Arthur Blair and Linville Robbins. They admired Robinson's early poetry and encouraged him. When Pope was in trouble with the Gardiner school authorities and Laura E. Richards* was critical of him, Robinson defended him. Killigrew in *Captain Craig* is modeled on Pope. In 1918 Robinson resumed their friendship when Pope, abandoned by his wife, was lonely and let Robinson share his dingy Brooklyn apartment. Robinson hung on with him, remote though the location was, in the hope of comforting the fellow, and dedicated *Avon's Harvest* (1921) to him. Pope also made room in his Brooklyn home for the painter Franklin L. Schenck. (See "A Tribute to Franklin L. Schenck.") (Source: Hagedorn)

The Porcupine: A Drama in Three Acts
(New York: Macmillan, 1915). Drama.

Act I. The scene is a comfortable room, with three doors, in the home of Rollo and Rachel Brewster, and their sick son, in Tadmor, a New England village. Alma Scammon, 30-plus years, is Larry Scammon's sister and is living with the Brewsters. She is talking with Stuart Hoover, a lawyer a couple of years Alma's senior and married to Louise. Alma and Stuart are discussing Larry, home again after a 10-year absence. He is playing the violin in an adjacent room, to cheer Rachel's son, who is ill. Alma is upset that Rollo is being "cruel" to Larry, who, Stuart counters, knows Stuart left Alma in the lurch 10 years ago. When Stuart laments his marriage, Alma mollifies him by saying his wife brought something new to the area — her beauty, her singing voice. Stuart replies that Louise found his property alluring, led him into loveless wedlock, and now toys with Rollo. They discuss unhappy Rachel; perhaps Larry's fiddle may be pleasing her, as well as her child.

Rollo emerges from his study. A little younger than Larry, Rollo, who is clerical in appearance, has been writing a religious lecture. When he asks Alma what she and Stuart have been discussing, she says it was about how to make Rachel happy. He says no one can be happy with Larry and his fiddle around. She replies that Dr. Ben Baker says the music is good for the lad, then reminds Rollo that his father married her brother's and her mother.

The music stops. In pops lively Larry, in a pea-jacket and rubber boots. He greets Rollo, then Stuart. Stuart says he's going home; Larry says some people lack homes to go to. Stuart leaves. Rollo upbraids Larry about his wandering and his clownish garb. Larry, saying he has returned in courteous humility, rebukes Rollo for undignified sanctimoniousness.

Louise Hoover, 35, slim, pretty, taps on the door, enters laughing easily, wonders if Rollo and Larry have been scaring each other, and reports she saw her "lost" husband heading for Baker's office, a place full of smoke and drink. Just as Rollo, embarrassed, returns to his study, Rachel enters, timid, wan. Louise remarks that Rachel looks tired, laments saying so, and asks Larry to beat her with his bamboo stick. Rachel says her son is asleep, and adds that she wishes the whole world could sleep peacefully, too. Louise says if she is given life, freedom, and what she wants, then peace and sleep could easily follow on. When Larry says that's a tall order for "the Powers," Louise says some women get what they want; so she should, too. Larry says she must ask "the Powers" properly and tell what she'll pay; they may threaten "double liability." Louise wishes the Powers would hear from this "wilderness . . . Tadmor." Rachel wonders if Louise dislikes the town. Louise asks if Larry does. He says it's good for a short rest of his fagged brain. Alma and Louise laugh; Rachel doesn't. Louise says Rachel needs invigorating and wonders if she ever had fun when she was little, only to fear the Apostles were frowning at her. Alma says Rachel is hurting her child by worrying so much.

Rollo re-emerges, dishevelled from writing. Rachel answers her son's call. Alma leaves. Rollo wants to walk outside. Larry offers to accompany him to Dr. Ben's for a drink. Rollo says he won't go. Louise says she'd like to go with both of them for a drink. Larry exits.

Paying no attention to the child's cry, Rollo reminds Louise that for a year he's been in love with her. She gets nervous, wishes she hadn't come to Tadmor, says she's bored. He says he's sorrowful. She doubts it, says she's seen him like this before. He embraces her, kisses her, asks her to go away, anywhere, with him. She remains passive.

Suddenly Larry returns with Ben, who grins. After minor talk, Rollo exits to continue writing, Louise leaves, Rachel enters, Ben goes in to check on her sick son, and she suddenly beseeches Larry to be kind to the child. He promises easily and re-enters the boy's room. Alone, Rachel takes a vial from Ben's medicine case and hides it in a bookcase. Alma enters, frightening her. Alma says she knows about "Larry's child." Shucking off pity, Rachel blurts out about loving Larry, his leaving without knowing, her insanely marrying Rollo since he wanted her, her wanting Larry now that he's back.

Re-entering, Rollo stares at Rachel. Alma exits. Baker and Larry return. Baker checks his case, says some aconite is missing that he must have left in his office. He pours some

medicine for the child. Rachel takes it to him. Ben tells Rollo he is professionally worried about Rachel, and Alma too.

When Ben leaves, Rollo ignores Larry and unfolds a newspaper. Larry brightly tells Rollo that he has returned to Tadmor to find old friends and to help Rollo, and that Rollo is the subject of gossip. Rollo orders Larry to leave his house. Rachel hears, enters, complains, is bullied by Rollo, but is gently persuaded by Larry to leave him to talk alone with Rollo.

The two men have a long discussion, the gist being all this: Larry, in profitable construction work in a Chicago office, learned about Rollo and his "Blue Lady" from a gossipy associate named Fillson who visited Tadmor. Stuart would have confronted Rollo but for Rachel's feelings. Rollo counters by saying Ben wants to marry Alma, then reveals that Rachel proposed marriage to him; he accepted, but she turned into a porcupine. Larry being puzzled, Rollo explains that he can't go near her "armor of invisible knives"; so it's no wonder he's fooled around with another woman; now he feels doomed. Larry suggests a painful way out, hints that Rollo suspects him of being interested in his "Blue Lady on the Hill," and promises to reveal something tomorrow.

Act II. Next day, Ben and Alma are in the same room. To his complaint that women don't like him, she says she likes him but couldn't marry him. He defines Stuart's wife Louise as an "imported musical houri." Having checked on Rachel's son, Ben leaves. Larry, having talked with Rollo in his study, emerges and praises Ben to Alma. Entering, Rachel asks Alma to leave, so she can talk with Larry.

When Larry mentions their years'-ago "boy-and-girl love-affair," Rachel says she wants to tell him something. Interrupting, he asks whether she's let that memory of him stand between her and Rollo and wonders if she's been fair to Rollo. Her reply is to wish she were dead. His reply is to explain why he left town so suddenly 10 years ago: He quarreled with Rollo's father, who a year earlier killed Larry's mother with "his damned temper"; "half crazy," Larry left home. Rachel says she needed him then; now, only Alma likes her, but also half-pities her. Rachel asks Larry whether what was once between them is forgotten now. His answer: Do you need me still? Her answer: It's too late. He gets around to asking what she was about to tell him earlier. She starts to answer, but her son shouts for "Uncle Larry." Larry boastfully asks her to remember he can do much for people, then goes to play the fiddle for what Rachel says is "Your—the child . . . Go!" He goes.

Rollo enters cheerfully, likes the music, tells Rachel she looks tired. Louise taps and enters, recognizes the music as "Roy's wife . . . / Wot ye how she cheated me[?]" When Rollo oilily reports that he and Larry are now compatible, Louise flittily rejoices but wonders if sorry-looking Rachel helped. Rachel, passive, leaves for a nap. Not finding Alma about, Louise thinks of going home to play with her cat. But, entering, Larry promises her a funny story. Rollo takes a walk outside.

After bantering with Louise, Larry tells her most people shouldn't get married, asks about Stuart and is told that he is a good husband "for somebody [else]," and therefore challenges her to desert him. Louise hints that "circumstances," which sometimes show through as "poverty," restrain her. Larry suggests she might do well singing in operas, in a big city. Their guarded chatter alerts her that a bribe is coming. She should leave so that Alma and Stuart can get happily together. Larry says Stuart and Ben have been apprised, and makes out for Louise the first of an everlasting number of monthly checks — to be paid back when she sings as Richard Wagner's Brünnhilde or Isolde, whatever, or never. She agrees, coyly, to head for her much-missed New York, writes out a "Dear Stuart" letter that Larry dictates, invites him to visit her, and holds his hand alluringly — until Rachel enters, observantly. Louise needles her slightly, says farewell to her and "Mr. Larry," and leaves.

Rachel expresses relief at Louise's departure, then complains that Larry thinks he knows about women and regards life as childish. He challenges her to write a book about life, if she knows its meaning. She says she still wants to tell him something. Turning earnest, he asks her why she said she needed him. Denying this, she hears Stuart's knock and admits him. They talk at odds, until Rachel com-

ments on this curious house and goes to check on her child.

Larry hints about the lady in blue. Stuart, much puzzled, is tempted to leave the country. Larry says Stuart needn't, can try something new, and reminds him that he took Stuart partly into his confidence. Alma appears and says she doesn't much admire Larry. He squeezes her neck. Her squeal brings Rachel, who complains about this disrupted, weird house. Larry mentions gossipy Fillson, which brings Rollo in. Larry makes announcements: Big changes are coming to those assembled here; uncertainty won't rule any longer; Alma must dress better; Rachel must bravely brighten up; Stuart will now walk with Larry. Rachel expresses fear that Larry is trying to orchestrate too many changes. He laughs and departs with obedient Stuart.

Rollo says Larry may be crazy. Rachel fears Larry may be wrong. When Rollo calls Rachel a spiny porcupine, Alma hugs her and calls her, rather, a wiggly seal. Rachel remains passive. Rollo signals Alma to go to the sick boy's room, tells Rachel that he and Larry are friendly again, and suggests that they exchange explanations and mend their marriage. Rachel replies that Rollo and Larry are driving her mad and wants to say nothing more. When Rollo shouts, "The women in this house!" and escapes to his study, she echoes "This house!" and retrieves the aconite.

Act III. The scene is the same; the time, next evening. Ben is there, and Rollo asks him to prescribe something for his "unapproachable" wife's nerves. Demurring, Ben suggests that Rollo consult well-traveled Larry and then tell Larry to talk with Rachel. As Larry enters, neatly dressed, Ben says he's going to bill a patient and leaves.

Rollo suggests a truce with Larry and expresses worry about Rachel. Responding cheerfully, Larry turns the subject to Louise. Alma's entrance interrupts them. Larry tells her Ben has left and she may regret rejecting him. Rachel enters, comments on Larry's presentable garb, and says she has reason to be quiet. Rollo says something's going to happen. Larry says let it. Alma says the house may burn down. Rachel says it couldn't. Larry tries to cheer her up. Stuart enters and reports that his wife Louise has run off. After interruptions, he gives Louise's letter to Rollo, whom he squelches from trying to assert his innocence. Rollo retreats to his study to think. Larry reads Louise's letter aloud: Louise and Stuart lived in Hell a decade and he'll be glad she's permanently out of his life. Stuart says Rollo won't try to get Louise back to Tadmor. Rachel checks on her son.

Larry says Rachel and Rollo have much to ponder, likens her 10-year misery to Stuart's, says everything in life must change, and exits to confer with Rachel. This leaves Stuart alone with Alma, who asks him "how it feels to be — deserted." He confesses to being a failure in law and marriage, then wonders why she never married. She laughs. Larry returns, is worried about himself, but joshes Stuart, who leaves. Rollo re-emerges from his study and asks what Larry and Rachel think about things. Alma retires to bed.

Rollo hesitantly thanks Larry for what he did and expresses confidence in his own future. Rachel re-enters, looking scared. Rollo tells Rachel that there will be gossip in town, but that he relies on her to forgive him and provide moral support for his continued lecturing. Rachel says she's too weak to help him now but "forgive[s] everybody." Rollo says she'll see more clearly tomorrow, asks Larry to cheer her up, and exits.

The long, climactic scene follows. Larry: You're supposed to laugh. Rachel: You're children. Larry: We all are; let's grow up. You're Rollo's wife. Rachel: I can't define myself. Be good to "the child." He likes you more than he does Rollo. Larry: I will, but help me. Rachel: Individuals like you, "apart from the community," are usually disappointed, though you think you're doing right. Larry: One woman (Louise) is gone; Alma will be happy (with Stuart). Why did you marry Rollo? Rachel: You left; I was alone, "mad"; Rollo wanted me; I half-seduced him, wasn't a proper wife; tell Rollo eventually; take "your boy" with you; tell him "when I am gone." Larry: We'll survive. Rachel: I hold only to "my life-long love for *you!*" You never truly left me, though you didn't know. Larry: We'll escape; Rollo needs "a change of air." Rachel: Did you know the depth of my love for you,

then, and now? Larry: What a question! Do you know how much I loved, love you? Rachel: That was an unneeded question, if you now love me. Larry: All I am and have is in your hands; we can be wise, happy, or silly, miserable; there's a way. Rachel: You were thinking about "that woman." Larry: More about you. Rachel: Much later, you must remember me. Marriages are God-heard vows.

Larry is glad to hear the child shouting "Uncle Larry!" and says the child wants both of them. Rachel says she's alone and tells him to go to the child. Telling her to wait, he goes. She finds and drinks the poison. He fiddles.

Robinson was in financial straits in 1905; so he decided to try to write commercially viable plays. For the next four years he struggled. The results were *The Porcupine* and *Van Zorn*. Both failed, as did his effort to convert *The Porcupine* into a novel (1910). It was published as a play in book form (1915), dedicated to Louis V. Ledoux.* Perhaps Robinson and Louis Ledoux joked over the fact that Robinson named Mrs. Hoover "Louise." Robinson wrote (March 9, 1913) to John Hays Gardiner* about his playwriting difficulties: "I cannot hit the popular chord, and for the simple reason that there is no immediately popular impulse in me." According to Bacon Collamore,* production rights for *The Porcupine* were secured by Emanuel Reicher but the play was evidently never staged.

The clumsy entrances and exits of the seven characters in *The Porcupine*, plus the aptly timed cries of the unnamed child, would make for good slapstick comedy but for Rachel's and Larry's tragic actions. Hoyt C. Franchere feels that *The Porcupine* "has moments of suspenseful action and a not inconsiderable dramatic power." Rollo's marriage to Larry's and Alma's mother seems a gratuitous pseudo-complication, unaddressed by the critics. Hyatt H. Waggoner seems not only too kind to Larry Scammon when he labels him a "redemptive character with the power to change people's lives," but also too hard on Rachel, who he says "develops protective quills, refuses to grow, and commits suicide." After all, Larry got young Rachel pregnant, ran off to make his fortune, returns home in funny boots and with a fiddle, and tampers in others' lives, in part imperceptively; meanwhile, Rachel has been married to a windbag who consorts elsewhere, and is offered a rescue by a mumbler but only after being pounded down in an early 20th-century rural community. Irving D. Suss carefully analyzes the style and structure of *The Porcupine*. (Sources: Collamore, 18; Franchere, 49; *Selected Letters*, 79; Suss, 358–60; Waggoner, 287, 288).

Praed, Winthrop Mackworth (1802–1839). English poet. He had Cornish and New England ancestors. He wrote satirical poems, skits, and vers de société. It seems likely that Robinson read some poems by Praed. Robinson may have been influenced slightly by Praed's poems concerning the French lyric poet Pierre Jean de Béranger (1780–1857), George Crabbe, Old King Cole, and a friend called "Clavering"; moreover, Robinson's and Praed's poetic techniques are often similar. Ellsworth Barnard, on the other hand, doubts Praed influenced Robinson much at all. (Sources: Barnard, 283–84; Fussell [1954], 85–88, 195; Hudson)

"The Prodigal Son" (1929). Dramatic monologue. The well-known prodigal son of the Bible (see Luke 15:11–32) is speaking to his long-suffering brother: Come on, laugh with me, and enjoy "the fatted calf." You probably wouldn't have any of it if I hadn't come back home. Let's agree "it is best / For you that I'm again in the old nest." One day you'll be grateful to God and sing about your knowledge gained. You might even understand humanity better. This whole experience "was fate's way of educating us." When I'm gone again, you'll understand life better. When I'm dead, you may tearfully regret your critical comments, while "I, the ghost of one you could not save, / May find you planting lentils on my grave."

"The Prodigal Son" is the only poem Robinson ever wrote in heroic couplets. Does he do so to suggest the supposed heroism of the speaker? Edwin S. Fussell downgrades this retelling of the parable when after identifying Robinson's two-point theme —"the necessity for man's sympathy and understanding," and "the growth of wisdom through error and

humiliation"— he concludes that Robinson "restricted his center too much," thus making "his analysis of the problem seem . . . thin." Nicholas Ayo points out that in this poem Robinson "draws a moral for the story beyond what the Gospel reveals, although not opposed to it. . . . Such a lesson about the richness of mercy, of love that is freely bestowed, had surely escaped the elder brother in the Gospel parable." (Sources: Ayo, 136; Fussell [1954], 166)

Pulitzer Prizes, Robinson's. Robinson won three Pulitzer Prizes; they were awarded for *Collected Poems** (1921, paying him $1,000), *The Man Who Died Twice* (1924), and *Tristram** (1927).

The Quadruped Club. This was an informal association formed about 1893 in Gardiner, Maine. Its members were Arthur Blair, Seth Ellis Pope,* Linville Robbins, and Robinson. The four young fellows rented a third-floor room for $2 a month over a dry-goods store at 279–283 Water Street, which from the back window had a view of the Cobbossee River and its mill pond. Blair toiled in a local bank but wanted to be a violinist and a poet. Pope taught school in Gardiner for a while. Robbins, a geologist, also taught school locally. They occasionally tolerated visitors. The four met almost nightly. They talked, drank, smoked, and heard Robinson read his poems and Blair play his violin, from which Robinson himself sometimes scraped tunes. During occasional days in the Quadruped room, which he called his "eyrie," Robinson also wrote poems, including parts of *Captain Craig* and "Aunt Imogen." The Robbins scholarship fund at Colby College is named after Linville Robbins. (Sources: Brower, 37; Hagedorn, 92–94; C. Smith, 163–64, 178)

"Quatrain" *see* **"A Wreath for Edwin Markham"**

"Rahel to Varnhagen" (1920). Dramatic monologue in blank verse. In a headnote, Robinson explains that "Rahel Robert and Varnhagen von Ense were married, after many protestations on her part, in 1814. The marriage—so far as he was concerned at any rate—appears to have been satisfactory."

Varnhagen, 24, sits on the floor smiling, while Rahel, almost 40, whom he loves, tells him that the letters that she received from a former lover and that he has just read, in part, contain "the cinders of a passion / That was my life." She is glad Varnhagen hasn't simply bolted out of her house on this rainy day. She knows he is strange but hopes not so strange that he will go away and risk becoming perilously gloomy. If he looks up at her again and blinks again, she is going to wonder if she has opened her past to him for nothing. Her "wreckage" of a face will show him evidence of warm love sought, cooled, lost, and paid for. Her whilom boy-lover gave her daily sunshine but inspired no dreams. Once, to be sure, he did play Adam to her Eve-like banishments. The episode "Was brief, but it was eternal while it lasted." Despair soon followed, then floods of tears. She doesn't know where the fellow is now.

After "many days / Dressed all alike" marched past Rahel, she chanced to see him again, this time with a woman. The look in his eyes registered fear and seemed to strike a blow at her. At one time she would have suffered through any of several tortures for him. But she saw that "he was jealous." If only he could have "found out finally / Where the wrong was." But no, he was a combination of evil and honor. When Rahel asks if Varnhagen thinks her ruin of a face masks something, his expressed negative is reassuring. Still, she defines him as youthfully, inconvincibly blind, but cautions him to recall details of their relationship. Otherwise their love might land them in a desert akin to the lava-cratered moon. When he denies that he is laughing, she retorts that he should be crying in response to her "unwomanly straightforwardness." She wonders how best to persuade him that she is being truthful now, knowing he must have doubts because truth lives under water and pops up for air but momentarily. What he takes for her may be a vision of himself. He must realize that what he calls her "divine impatience" is truly a dangerous "bad temper." He might seek to feed on her wisdom too late.

She is alike indifferent to "men's applause / And women's envy." Meanwhile, at home she has been crying and praying. She asks whether he can really be the man to save her from the "flaming language" of men's still-unwritten books; further, whether he is certain that after she waited all these years just for him on this rainy day she might still proceed eventually by herself "To a cold end." "Well," she believes he is aware of all that.

Edwin S. Fussell notes that a passage in which Rahel says she has "seen so many days / Dressed all alike" echoes Ralph Waldo Emerson's celebrated poem "Days," in which "Days" are "Muffled ... like barefoot dervishes" and "march . . . single in an endless file." Esther Willard Bates* says that in conversation with her Robinson defined "Rahel to Varnhagen" as "an interpretive monologue," and, further, that he had access at the MacDowell Colony* to a copy of *Rahel Varnhagen, a Portrait*, by Ellen Karolina Sofia Key (1849–1926), translated from the Swedish by Arthur G. Chater (1913), read it, but said he made no direct use of it in characterizing Rahel.

Amy Lowell* generalizes that "Robinson's forte is [t]wo people and an atmosphere," and cites "Rahel and Varnhagen" as the best example. Chard Powers Smith* contends that the poem has little reason to survive save as a reflection of "Robinson's post–1918 understanding that Emma [Robinson*] does not love him." Yvor Winters asserts that "Rahel to Varnhagen" "is a speech by the elderly lady [under 40 is "elderly"?] to her young lover, which terminates in her acquiescence." Winters adds that the poem "on the whole is excellent, but is marred by moments of Robinson's inept playfulness." Ellsworth Barnard finds Rachel's "recital of her romantic past" partly comic and Varnhagen's bored tolerance thereof exasperating to Rachel but proof to her that he is confident of "the enduring quality of their mutual love." Still, Robinson might have responded to such cocksure manly faith with a dash of his handy occasional antifeminist skepticism. (Sources: Barnard, 143; Bates, 4–5; Fussell [1954], 33; Lowell [1922], 135; C. Smith, 252; Winters, 137)

Ranck, Carty (1879–c. 1950). Edwin Carty

Ranck was a writer. He was a reporter for the *Brooklyn Eagle* (until 1910 or 1911), then attended the "47 Workshop" conducted by George Pierce Baker* at Harvard (1911). Recommended by Baker, Ranck was a guest at the MacDowell Colony* (beginning in 1912), wrote "An American Poet with a Message," an early essay on Robinson (Boston *Evening Transcript*, May 12, 1913 — reprinted by Richard Cary), thereafter cultivated Robinson's friendship, and published enthusiastic reviews in the *Transcript* of book after book by Robinson. Ranck wrote poetry and unproduced plays between 1911 and 1934. He once used Henry Thomas as a pen name. Robinson loaned him money from time to time and dedicated "Nicodemus" to him. Ranck spent much time and energy (from 1913) assembling reams of notes for a biography of Robinson.

Hermann Hagedorn* knew and wrote about Ranck, emphasizing his energy, good humor, crudeness, devotion to Robinson, and Robinson's delighted tolerance of Ranck, whom he regarded as an occasional welcome stimulus. Hagedorn calls him Robinson's Boswell. Chard Powers Smith* knew Ranck well, probably better than Hagedorn did, also observed what he called Carty's Boswellizing, probably better than Hagedorn did, regarded Ranck as an ill-mannered social misfit, and says Robinson worried about his instability, but nonetheless authorized his writing a biography of him under the supervision of the more reliable George Burnham.* According to Smith, after Robinson's death his family spurned Ranck and named Hagedorn as the official biographer. Smith concludes his alternatively sympathetic and critical comments about Ranck with a summary of rumors about him — that he grew mentally challenged, went blind, and destroyed his notes on Robinson along with draft work on a biography. (Sources: Cary [1974], 248–51; Hagedorn, 276–77, 313, 358; C. Smith)

"The Rat" (1920). Sonnet. When a certain "useless and not always clean" fellow appeared, the persona and his friends alternately "pitied . . . or scorned him," and wondered why God hadn't made him a rat "in accord / With any other creature we abhorred." But now that he is dead, is in that "final hole," and won't come back, the townspeople talk less about rats and more about men.

Ellsworth Barnard lists this poem among several he calls elegiac and goes on to say that "[o]nly death . . . elevates [so-called rats] to the level of acknowledged humanity." (Source: Barnard, 107, 131)

"Recalled" (1921). Sonnet. Everyone is now dead near the place. Beside a hole in a wall, "fruitless vines" hug their parental vines, which "survive / In evil thorns." Only "old Isaac" could explain all this, and he did so with either "humor or compassion." Referring to those vines, he explained that God killed off "in the last of them a line / That Satan would have disinherited"; he added that when we are finished with everything but elements of "the Divine," death will follow for us too.

"Rembrandt to Rembrandt" (1929). Dramatic monologue. It is in blank verse, parenthetically located and dated as happening in "Amsterdam, in 1645." It is helpful to recall that by 1645 Rembrandt van Rijn (1606–1669) had recently completed his magnificent but initially controversial *Sortie of the Banning Cock Company* (1642, known as "The Night Watch"), and that his dear wife Saskia had died (1642), as had several of their children (but not his beloved Titus).

Rembrandt is looking at himself in a mirror and also at a self-portrait, and addresses his remarks to himself. He has been discredited by "injured Hollanders in Amsterdam" for his bewilderingly new style of painting. Saskia, with a laugh at both the Hollanders and Rembrandt, warned that they would scorn him.

As Rembrandt admires his portrait, he wonders if by this time he has not achieved and then lost everything. However, seeing how the painting reflects the image of himself in the mirror, he doubts that. Some critics feel that after the deaths in his family "the painter died." Some Hollanders feel that he's a dead man painting in darkness. God and Rembrandt, he says, know differently. So, let Franz (Hals) paint "heads all in a row, and all alike." Franz does it well. Examining his own portrait, Rembrandt says he'll need those firm jaws, eyes, pugnacity, "fire," and then some, to oppose his enemies and even himself. Now he lacks fame and adulation. Saskia foresaw this trouble, and with kind laughter concealing doubt gave him money before she died.

Rembrandt thinks it may have been just as well that Saskia died. Living longer, she might have shaken his faith, seen unadmitted errors in his style, and agreed with the townspeople. She might even have persuaded him to share "A taste that would have tainted everything." It would have

> been for two, instead of one,
> The taste of death in life — which is the food
> Of art that has betrayed itself alive
> And is a food of hell.

Saskia might have agreed with those who were praising work by other artists, only temporarily popular, and might have grown angry when he wouldn't imitate them. She naturally loved joy and might have slipped angrily into poverty for which gossipers would have blamed him. Also, how could he doubt himself and expect her not to do so as well? His "house" fell into "ruins." Yet this left him essentially safe. Happily,

> There's life in you that shall outlive my clay
> That's for a time alive and will in time
> Be nothing — but not yet.

His portrait is secure in its health, although his own "teeth and eyes" are getting infirm. Later, when he can't paint, he might write something and thus "serve . . . [his] stricken soul." When he thinks, his painting cautions him not to "commit your soul / . . . to . . . your denial" thus.

Rembrandt promises to avoid the "dragon-spawn of Holland." This place used to be worse, but even now there are some "slimy tyrants" who are fearsomely, insanely strong. He thanks his image for warning him about his countrymen's dangerous and increasing devotion to commercialism.

Suddenly an "occult abortion" perches on one of his finished pictures and fills the silence surrounding his few remaining friends, by saying in effect "So what?" to his productions and his hope for future fame. The creature contin-

ues: You are an "aspiring insect" doomed to the same soft oblivion reserved alike for good monks and evil killers. And if you believe in immortality, your soul may laugh at your very best ochre and oil smears, even though they contain "mortal eye[s]," the likes of which fish also have. Go paint some herrings or some sides of beef. Why paint human beef-eaters? God made both "beef and human" and only by a whim distinguished between them.

Soon, however, "comes another spirit." To its truthful message "a string" in Rembrandt vibrates in response. And why not, "Since I am but a living instrument / Played on by powers that are invisible"? After all, he is a mortal violin vibrating to invisible, potent fingers. This spirit continues: If you had painted faster, you might not have developed further. The Dutchmen whose faces and "slight identities" you included within the "golden shadow" of your masterpiece may curse you for "pernicious[ly] filching . . . their florins," but your paint gives them continued life when "their names are nothing." Regardless of all this, you know you created that "picture as your demon willed it." So, go right along, and "hold your light / So that you see, without . . . [letting everything] blind you." Then, "if you see right / Others will have to see." Don't worry about your reptilian enemies "in the night / That now is coming on." Nor should you fret because assurances of your eventual great fame are unheard in Holland. What of that?

> Have you the weary leisure or sick wit
> That breeds of its indifference a false envy
> That is the vermin of accomplishment?

Remember that you are one of the fortunate few whose "task" is revealed, whose "skill" is given him, and whose "tool" to work with is "too keen / For timid safety." Consign your enemies to hell; don't worry about time; firmly believe you have some years ahead. You can't tell when oblivion, now riding on your neck, will defeat you. In any event, "Oblivion heretofore has done some running / Away from graves, and will do more of it."

Since his wiser self says all this, Rembrandt is encouraged to stop looking back and instead to realize that Saskia is gone, along with "the old joy and the old roses." So he will paint away, aware that "Apollo's house . . . has no clocks / Or calendars" to tell him his distance from Amsterdam or explain why Holland can't see the light he sees until Holland is apprised of it by others. Unless he prefers to rest easy with his "widowed gold," he should pay no further attention to "his darkness in the dark," and also not react to "Holland scorn." Nor should he worry about unseen, "distant welcome" and unheard "wayside shouting," but instead remain faithful to himself.

Elizabeth A. Howe notes that in this dramatic monologue "the painter addresses himself, looking in a mirror, so that speaker and interlocutor are identical — an arrangement that forms an interesting parallel with Rembrandt's self-portrait." Irving Howe lists several of Robinson's dramatic monologues, "Rembrandt to Rembrandt" being the first, and allows that "Robinson mostly transcends" the difficulties inherent in the genre. Chard Powers Smith* writes that Esther Willard Bates* told him that in the early 1920s Robinson told her that "Rembrandt to Rembrandt" was his best poem. Emery Neff says that in it Robinson "presents his ideal genius, neither spoiled by acclaim nor daunted by unpopularity." Hoyt C. Franchere defines the poem as "the self-portrait of the artist rendered as self-analysis and . . . catch[ing] . . . the Holland painter asking questions that Robinson may well have been asking of himself." The poet now, like the painter then, had achieved success, was solitary, puzzled his critics, questioned himself, wondered about his work, had doubts about achievement, determined to follow his genius, and agreed both to accept present obscurity and to anticipate posthumous acclaim.

John Lucas notes that "Rembrandt to Rembrandt" is indicative of "Robinson's ceaseless curiosity about human nature, his wanting to track down the way a man thinks and suffers and lives in his mind." Robert Mezey says 1645, the date Robinson assigns to the action in his poem, "may reflect the influence on Robinson of the [since-disproved] legend . . . [that Rembrandt was] scorned by his bourgeois countrymen for his honesty and unflinching realism"; in truth he had students and commissions and Saskia's dowry, Hals was

popular well before his bankruptcy in 1652, and Rembrandt was bankrupt in 1656 not earlier. So Mezey concludes that this great poem reflects Robinson's "decades of poverty and neglect," rather than Rembrandt's. (Sources: Franchere, 114; E. Howe, 95; I. Howe, 107; Lucas, 148; Mezey, 238; Neff, 257; C. Smith, 240)

Residences, Robinson's. Robinson was born in the family home in a hamlet then called Head-of-the-Tide, Maine, on December 22, 1869. In September 1870 the family moved to their new house at 67 Lincoln Avenue, Gardiner, Maine. At Harvard, Robinson roomed at 717 Cambridge Street (1891–1892) and at 1716 Cambridge Street (1892–1893). After the death of his father Edward Robinson,* Robinson returned to Gardiner and lived in the family home (1893–1896).

When he first went to New York, he lived for six weeks in a boardinghouse with his friend George Burnham* on West 64th Street (beginning November 1897), returned to Gardiner to care for his dying brother Dean Robinson,* but was soon back to New York and Burnham (January 1898), followed by Cambridge, using spare space of willing friends (1898), then Gardiner again (summer 1898), and nearby Winthrop, Maine (until January 1899). He worked at the college office at Harvard and lived, partly, back at 1716 Cambridge Street (January-June 1899).

Soon after Dean died, Robinson returned to New York (October 1899). Burnham found him a hall-room in the boarding-house where Burnham lived at 71 Irving Place, south of Gammercy Park. Craven Langstroth Betts* let Robinson room with him at 450 Manhattan Street, Harlem (summer 1900). Robinson moved with Burnham to 91 Palisade Avenue, Yonkers (November 1900). Robinson roomed and boarded alone at 29 East 22nd Street, New York (from March 1901). He moved within weeks into a fourth-floor room of a house at 450 West 23rd Street owned by a friend named James Moore; Robinson often delayed paying rent until he began work as a subway time-checker (October 1903–August 1904). He roomed at No. 1 Yarmouth Street,

Boston (January–May 1905) while clerking in the drygoods store of a friend named William E. Butler (later a suicide victim).

When Moore suffered financial reverses and lost his house, Robinson moved to the Hotel Judson, on Washington Square, New York City. While there, he met or renewed acquaintance with the following: Olivia Howard Dunbar and Ridgely Torrence* (later her husband), Louis V. Ledoux,* Percy MacKaye,* Daniel Gregory Mason,* William Vaughn Moody,* and May Sinclair.* At this time, Robinson began his sinecure in the Collector of Customs office, New York (June 1905–June 1909). A widow named Clara Potter Davidge lived at 121 Washington Place, New York, and built a studio in her back yard for Robinson's use (December 1909). Robinson vacationed in Chocorua, New Hampshire (July–October 1910), in the hideaway home of his friend Truman Howe Bartlett (b. 1835), a talented old sculptor and amateur philosopher. When Clara Davidge married Harry Taylor, an artist, and moved with him to Staten Island (December 1912), Robinson went along.

From the time Robinson discovered the MacDowell Colony* in 1911, he was there every summer though 1934. Betweentimes, he resided sporadically with a widening circle of friends in their homes (in Cornwall-on-the-Hudson, Boston, and elsewhere), and returned to New York for productive winters — in one room on West 83rd Street (1918–1922), in the Brooklyn home at 810 Washington Avenue of his old friend Seth Ellis Pope,* who taught and was a librarian in Brooklyn for some years until his death (1922), and thereafter in a room off the studio of his sculptor friends James Earle Fraser* and his wife Laura Gardin Fraser (beginning 1922). During his trip to England (April-July 1923), Robinson took hotel rooms off Pall Mall and then in Mayfair, and spent a brief time in Oxford. When the Frasers moved to 328 East 42nd Street, Robinson joined them (autumn 1925–June 1926, and often as late as 1935). Robinson, who often seemed at home nowhere, was sometimes made to feel at home in a rocker chair in indulgent friends' homes. Robinson's obituaries gave his final legal address as 328 East 42nd Street, New York. (Sources: Cary [1974]; Hagedorn; Mason [Winter 1937; Spring 1937]; Peltier, 13; C. Smith)

"The Return of Morgan and Fingal"

(1902). Poem. Morgan and Fingal came over by boat to spend the night with me. Morgan hoisted a drink while Fingal played his fiddle and sang. It had been 12 years since we were together; so a knock on my door was vexing. Outside I found a pale woman. She said nothing but "You — you three — it is you!" To my puzzled query, she replied that it was God's will for us to ferry a certain dead girl to her home. A splashing sound and the wind frightened the woman, and her yells brought Morgan and Fingal out. Into their boat the four of us piled, and with great difficulty we sailed south "Through the flash of the midnight foam," found and ferried the dead girl to a silent wharf, carried her where there was some light, and soon left "the two to the father there." My friends and I steered back together, saw my light, docked the boat, and went back inside, each "content / With a life that fed no cares." We warmed ourselves, smoked our pipes, and drank Fingall's well-prepared punch — happily together again.

Emma Robinson* reports that the poem was suggested to Robinson by a real though non-fatal incident occurring at Capitol Island. A certain girl needing help was ill, not dead; the two men in the poem were based on Robinson's brothers Dean Robinson* and Herman Robinson,* who had gone to the island to work for the day. To Edith Brower,* Robinson explains by letter (June 1900) that "The Return of Morgan and Fingal" merely depicts "the grotesque way in which mystery, tragedy and joy mix themselves at times on this peculiar and amusing planet." Brower noted in the margin of this letter and in her "Memories of Edwin Arlington Robinson" that the original title of the poem was "Intermezzo." In her "Memories," she adds that Morgan is based on Fullerton Waldo; he was a classmate of Robinson's at Harvard and played the violin and the viola skillfully. To Lewis Nathaniel Chase,* who had asked for explications of some of his poems, Robinson replied by letter (July 11, 1917) that "The

Return of Morgan and Fingal" is nothing but "an episode with overtones." The poem, in ballad form, has 22 four-line stanzas, each in seemingly inappropriate rollicking and galloping fourteeners, rhyming *abcb*, with several *c*-lines having internal rhymes, and begins and ends with "Morgan, Fingal, fiddle, and all."

A Robinsonian moral embedded in this poem and of value to 21st century American readers might be this: When our permissible national domestic tranquillity is interrupted by a request from foreign shores, we characteristically rush to aid, provide help, hope that those in trouble can then fend for themselves, and ought to expect to return finally to our recognizable friends again. (See also "My Methods and Meanings.") (Sources: Brower, 118, 211; E. Robinson, 12; *Selected Letters*, 104)

"Reuben Bright" (1897). Sonnet. Reuben Bright was a butcher, earned his living honestly, and, we are told, "did right." So don't think he was more of "a brute than you or I." When he learned that his wife was mortally ill, he cried all night like a child. Women wept to see him doing so. After his wife died, "he . . . paid / The singers and the sexton and the rest," placed many things that she had made in a chest and added some chopped cedar, "and tore down the slaughter house."

Emma Robinson* and Ruth Nivison* identify Reuben Bright as based on Seth Palmer,* a family relative, and then gratuitously add that although Seth's wife Lydia Anne Palmer and three of their sons died of typhoid fever the family never theorized that perhaps their privy was too close to their well. A typographical error provided some readers a little fun when after "tore down" in "tore down the slaughter house," ending the last line, was mistakenly added the word "to" in the first print run of *Collected Poems* (1921). (In his book on Robinson, Ben Ray Redman unfortunately quotes the incorrect form of the last line.) Bacon Collamore* reports that when Robinson corrected this error, he "commented that this particular instance was the worst kind of typographical error, since it made sense!"

Louis Coxe says that "the rest" whom Reuben Bright paid were persons to whom he owed money, not "undertakers and supernumeraries of what exsequious sort," because, as the narrator has told us, the despairing widower was "honest . . . and did right." Radcliffe Squires regards Reuben Bright's destruction of his slaughter house as "a gesture whereby he destroys the symbol of the world's idea of himself," Squires having just earlier dogmatized that in this poem "we are definitely told that the world would prefer to ignore the essential capacity of a man for grief." (But is this so?) (Sources: Collamore, 29; Coxe, 54; Redman, 15; E. Robinson, 12; Squires, 182).

"Reunion" (1923). Sonnet. By a strange circumstance, we happened to come together after years of being apart. But youth was gone, and time offered no reprieve. We soon left, separately. And now? Pale sunset, whispers in the silence, fireplace cold, chairs near it empty, and less friendly stars overhead.

"The Revealer" (1910). Poem. It is parenthetically subtitled "Roosevelt" and with an introductory quotation from "Judges 14[:8, 18]" about Samson's seeing a lion's carcass with bees and honey in it, and about citizens asking him what is sweeter than honey and what is stronger than a lion.

Opposing discredited Mammon-favoring materialism comes our needed "seer," who smiles at certain lions at the gates. They sniff around, are tempted to roar, are upset and uneasy, but seem not to care "if the gods restore / The lost composite of the Greek." When the shadowed land turns brighter, behold that "The combs of long-defended hives / Now drip dishonored and unclean." We sufficiently know the difference between dead lions and sweet honey therein. Our subject "Is . . . the world's accredited / Revealer of what we have done." If we retrogress after his departure, we will be punished. His power is limited to "seven years," not a hundred. We ought to begin to understand and become "far-seeing." The trouble is that we remain myopic, cocky, and money-mad; and, regrettably, "The Titan" cannot aid us forever.

This poem is in praise of Theodore Roosevelt.* Robinson in a letter (July 20, 1910) to Louis V. Ledoux* discusses "The Revealer" extensively. He expresses annoyance that Lyman Abbott (1835–1922), editor of the *Outlook*, rejected it, and wondered whether Abbott was bright enough to understand it but disagreed with its contents. He complains that imbecilic readers frequently misinterpret his intended obscurity for vagueness.

However, more than obscure in "The Revealer" he certainly is. The poem includes the following words: "Mammon," "Tyrian heritage," "a small cloud in the skies," "Nazarite or Nazarene," "an Angel with a Sword," and "Titan." Even as astute a reader as Edwin S. Fussell brands Robinson's technique in handling "a biblical tradition for a structural symbolism . . . clumsy and ineffectual" in "The Revealer," and labels as "flat" his calling Roosevelt a "composite of the Greek." Ellsworth Barnard asks this: Even though Robinson signaled his readers that he was about to compare Samson and Roosevelt, will many readers fathom "the implications of the references to other biblical passages in 'a small cloud in the skies" and 'an Angel with a Sword'?" After Sisera was defeated by Barak, who along with Samson was one of the six Major Judges, sought refuge with the neutral Kenites, and was killed by Jael, it is said that "the earth trembled, and the heavens dropped, the clouds also dropped water," which rain continued to discomfit the enemies of Barak and Samson (Judges 5:4). When Robinson mentions the armed angel, the allusion may be to the cherubim and the flaming sword preventing the return of Adam and Eve to Eden (Genesis 3:24). Nicholas Ayo, concentrating on Roosevelt as Samson, notes that "Roosevelt, the lion-slayer in many ways, also brings sweetness forth from the defeat of his enemies." Yvor Winters says that both "The Revealer" and "The Master" (about Abraham Lincoln) "indicate, perhaps not very clearly, Robinson's distrust of the common man and his belief in the superior leader as the only hope for democracy." Robert Mezey, after identifying Robinson's numerous allusions, concludes that "doing so can help only so far — 'The Revealer' remains a somewhat obscure poem." (Sources: Ayo, 181; Barnard, 34; Fussell [1954], 160, 200; Mezey, 227; *Selected Letters*, 67; Winters, 53)

"Richard Cory" (1897). Poem. When Richard Cory appeared in town, we were all impressed by his looks and manners. "He was a gentleman from sole to crown, / Clean favored, and imperially slim." He was "richer than a king," well educated, and envied. We ordinary folk worked, waited for enlightenment, and lacked money for much more than bread. "And Richard Cory, one calm summer night, / Went home and put a bullet through his head."

"Richard Cory" is the best-known and most frequently anthologized poem Robinson ever wrote — to his regret. Yvor Winters simplistically calls it "a superficially neat portrait of the elegant man of mystery" but one that "builds up deliberately to a very cheap surprise ending." Denis Donoghue says it "seems . . . a contrived piece" but without explaining why. "Richard Cory" startles every new reader, and gentle ones are surely left, in Hoyt C. Franchere's words, "with a sharp sense of emptiness, of a life wasted, of failure — and of Cory's loneliness." However, Cory's emptiness is other people's challenge. Richard P. Adams, for example, says that the poem "leaves the reader free to decide . . . that working and waiting and going without, and even cursing on occasion, may be a pretty good life after all."

Many critics call attention to the puzzling merits of "Richard Cory," a compressed, 16-line poem. W. R. Robinson says it derives its "power from concreteness, from clarity achieved through sharp observation." Emery Neff notes that "its four quatrains . . . [have] no deviation from prose order." Ellsworth Barnard concludes that the logical movement of its first 14 lines — concerning Cory's appearance, manners, lack of vanity, praise by others — is "a painstaking preparation for the last two [lines], with their stunning overturn of the popular belief." Harry R. Garvin, after thorough research into biographical and critical studies of Robinson then available to him (no later than 1962), and a thorough reading of Robinson's works, became "convinced that 'Richard Cory' is among the many finely good poems that have inexhaustible aesthetic possibilities . . . [, with] a depth of poetic indirection, of insight, and of meaning in the character and in the poem." Garvin concludes that when Cory commits suicide, "the townspeople feel neither a long surprise nor a sadness but rather a retributive satisfaction and finally that the townspeople are being judged by Robinson." Garvin diagnoses Cory's "despair and . . . catastrophe" as the consequence of his "sin of an indifference [to others] that can spread within and destroy." Garvin points out that "the sullen poor" of the town, identified in the poem as "We people on the pavement," are the narrators, uniquely in all of Robinson. Charles A. Sweet, Jr. contends that the narrator is unreliable; that the townspeople have prevented Richard Cory from speaking with them; and that they have, indeed, "erected a barrier around themselves," with the result that "their only reaction to Cory is stasis and silence."

William C. Childers theorizes that the name "Cory might well have been suggested by [Richard] Coeur de Lion," who embodies "the romantic medieval knight but who was in reality spiritually corrupt and dissolute." Robinson's purpose, Childers feels, may have been to "contrast . . . Richard Cory's majestic outward appearance and his inner bankruptcy." Charles R. Morris finds "so many anglicisms" in the description of Richard Cory that Robinson probably had in mind the suicide of "that arch-Tory of the American Revolution, Dr. Silvester Gardiner of Gardiner [Maine]."

Further proof that "Richard Cory" is intriguing is an explication of it by David Kelly et al. almost line-by-line, and their placing it in its cultural context in 10 double-columned pages; they advise that "The poem may be read as an ironic commentary on the American dream of wealth, success and power"; they explain that its hero-manqué's suicide was by way of Robinson's "assuring us that the wealth most of us will never know is not worth having anyway." (Oh?) Jerome Kavka presents a psychoanalytical autopsy following poor Cory's death by self-inflicted gunshot. First, Kavka discounts Cory as victim of symbolic regicide, touches on ruinous pre-genital envy, metapsychologial loss of personal cohesiveness, characterological mental but not body self-disintegration, the absence of inner esteem causing arrogance, one's home as seedbed of personal ruin, and loss of illusions.

Then Kavka concludes that Cory, failing to gain approval of the citizenry, commits the final deed of the propless narcissist.

In his "The Richard Cory Murder Case" (*Ellery Queen's Mystery Mazagine*, February 1963), Manly Wade Wellman has Miniver Cheevy (see "Miniver Cheevy") find that Cory didn't commit suicide but was murdered. Regardless, Paul Simon and Art Garfunkel, the famous rock singers, adapted "Richard Cory," as well as "A Most Peculiar Man," another song about suicide, in their popular album *Sounds of Silence* (1966). (Sources: R. Adams, 110; Barnard, 99; Childers, 1955, 225; Donoghue, 32; Franchere, 86; Garvin, 316, 317; Kavka; Kelly, 115, 123; Charles Morris, 52; Neff, 86; W. Robinson, 62; Sweet, 580; Winters, 52)

Richards, Henry (1848–1949). He was a resident of Gardiner, Maine. His father was the owner of paper mills. His mother was a member of a well-to-do family named Gardiner. Richards, a Harvard-educated architect, married Laura Elizabeth Howe (see Richards, Laura E.) in 1871. Richards and his wife, who ultimately had six children, lived in Boston until the Panic of 1876 caused him to close his architectural firm. He bought the finest colonial-style house in Gardiner, where from 1878 the Richardses lived for the remainder of their lives. Richards managed the family paper mill, which burned (1893), was rebuilt, but then closed (1900). He and his wife established Camp Merryweather, a summer camp for boys on Lake Cobbosseecontee, which became a major source of income.

Richards improved the family home by adding a third-story in monitor form, a bay window over the piazza, and Truscan columns. Located at 3 Dennis Street, Gardiner, called "The Yellow House," and remaining in the family, it was listed on the National Register of Historic Places (1979). Richards's autobiography is *Ninety Years On* (1940).

Richards, Laura E. (1850–1943). Laura Elizabeth Howe was born in Boston, the daughter of Samuel Gridley Howe and Julia Ward Howe. Laura was educated at home and then in private schools in Boston. She married Henry Richards* (1871); the couple had four daughters and two sons, whom the mother dubbed "The Noble Six." She began publishing nonsense poems in 1873 and compiled many of them into *Sketches and Scraps* (1881), which was the first book of nonsense verse written by an American and published in the United States. When she and her husband moved to Gardiner (1876), she felt she was in a backwater, but she soon adapted and became a vital force for civic good. For example, she, her husband, and the Rev. Leverett Bradley (1846–1902) founded the Gardiner Public Library (1881); it was the second such library in Maine. Henry Richards designed the library building in English-Jacobean style. Continuing to write, Laura Richards became known as the "Queen of Nonsense Verse." She edited her father's papers (2 vols., 1906, 1909), wrote a short biography of both parents (1911), and, among other biographies, the 1915 one co-authored with her sister Maud Howe Elliott of their mother that won the first Pulitzer Prize for Biography (1917). Her most popular book was *Captain January* (1890), which was the basis of two movies. More than half of her upwards of 90 books were books for children; they spanned decades and included *Five Mice in a Mouse-Trap, by the Man in the Moon, Done in Vernacular from the Lunacular* (1880); and *Harry in England* (1931). *Stepping Westward* (1931) is her autobiography.

Through her husband's business contacts, Laura Richards knew members of the Robinson family but not Robinson until he sent her a copy of *The Torrent and The Night Before* (1896). She invited him to one of her frequent literary evenings; though initially demurring, he finally strolled over to her Yellow House (1897). Thus began one of the most enjoyable and fruitful friendships Robinson ever knew. When Scribner's proved reluctant to publish what became his *Captain Craig* (1902), Mrs. Richards and John Hays Gardiner* persuaded the editor to do so, by a financial guarantee. The book went into a small second printing. It contains "Isaac and Archibald," which Robinson dedicated "To Mrs. Henry Richards." Later, the Richardses and Gardiner provided regular anonymous stipends to the poet.

Robert J. Scholnick details the fruitful friendship of Mrs. Richards, Edmund Clarence Stedman,* and Robinson. Robinson's poignant poem "The Voice of Age" is undoubtedly a tribute to Laura E. Richards. In turn, her *E.A.R.* (1936), a 61-page memoir, dedicated to Ruth Nivison,* records many charming memories. Chard Powers Smith,* however, labels the bulk of her commentary about Robinson, including much that she also dictated to her daughter Rosalind Richards, "a desperately generous lie." This is interesting in light of the long-standing rumor, now confirmed, that Robinson once "made a pass" at Rosalind, whose many letters from him have not yet been published. According to Wallace L. Anderson, letters from Robinson to Rosalind, in the Houghton Library at Harvard, are under seal until 2007. Undoubtedly they contain details of interest. Henry Howe Richards (1876–1968), one of the Richardses' two sons, was the English master at Groton School, in Groton, Connecticut, when Kermit Roosevelt, the son of Theodore Roosevelt,* became interested in Robinson's poetry and made the president aware of its excellence — with momentous, well-documented results. (Sources: W. Anderson [1980], 52; Richards [1931], 378; Richards [1936]; Scholnick; C. Smith, 167; D. Smith)

Robinson, Alexander. An ancestor of Robinson. Alexander and his brother Archibald Robinson* moved to Newcastle, Maine, about 1760. Alexander later moved to Bristol, Maine. (Source: Richards, 4)

Robinson, Archibald. An ancestor of Robinson. Archibald and his brother Alexander Robinson* moved to Newcastle, Maine, about 1760. Archibald later moved to Head Tide. (Source: Richards, 4)

Robinson, Barbara (1895–1991). The youngest daughter of Herman Robinson* and Emma Robinson,* born in Farmingdale, Maine, just north of Gardiner (and later incorporated by Gardiner). Barbara's sisters were Ruth Robinson* and Marie Louise Robinson.* The three girls became Robinson's beloved nieces. In Boston in 1937 Barbara married Harold Wright Holt (d. 1978). He was the son of Ira W. Holt and Ida M. Sinclair Holt, and became a professor of law and the dean of the law school at the University of Illinois, Champaign-Urbana, Illinois. Barbara and Harold had one daughter, Fanny Elizabeth Holt, born in Urbana (1938). She married and divorced Cabell Calloway, the natural son of the actor, band leader, jazz composer, and singer Cabell ("Cab") Calloway III (1907–1994). F. Elizabeth Calloway, as she called herself, had a daughter, Chevelle ("Shelli") Calloway (1963–2004), and a son, Kevin Calloway.

Shelli, born in New York, spent several of her early years in St. Croix, the Virgin Islands, moved with her parents to Boothbay Harbor, attended high school, graduated from Towson University, Maryland, earned a law degree at George Mason University, practiced law, became an energetic, admired, and generous teacher of English, economics, and social studies (from 2000) at Cony High School, in Augusta, Maine, and resided in nearby Pittston. Shelli and her husband Jon F. Dilley had a daughter, Emma Dilley, and a son, Miles Dilley, but some years later became unpleasantly estranged. In 2004, Emma was nine, Miles was six, and Jon Dilley, aged 51, was an independent electrical contractor in Pittston (from 1996), a mile or so southeast of Gardiner, and also a telecommunications specialist in Portland, Maine. He had a daughter, Ramisi L. Dilley, age 18, by a marriage (1985) to Carla Elliott, age 50, divorced (1992) and living in California; Ramisi had been living in Pittston alternately with Dilley, Shelli, Emma, and Miles.

On August 21, 2004, Dilley, a gun owner and a member of militia groups, ended a tragically escalating family argument by shooting to death both Shelli and his own mother, Sarah ("Sally") Jean Olsen Murray, age 71, in the latter's summer cottage in Boothbay Harbor, Maine. At the time of their murders, Shelli was visiting her mother-in-law Sally, whom she adored and with whom she shared a dynamic business partnership. Emma and Miles, who had accompanied their mother Shelli to their grandmother Sally's home,

witnessed the shooting, fled to a nearby Coast Guard station, and were not physically harmed. The police were summoned by a neighbor and quickly arrested Dilley, who, according to their report, confessed. Emma Calloway, Robinson's great-great-great-niece, was undoubtedly named after his beloved sister-in-law Emma Robinson.* In actions worthy of a Robinsonian plot twist, Jon's two brothers (R. James Dilley and Brian G. Dilley) rapidly filed a civil complaint to attach his property (valued at $979,400); their sister (Margaret E. Beekman) joined the two brothers in a request for funds from Jon's assets to defray part of their mother's funeral expenses, and inevitable legal expenses and estate taxes; Jon Dilley's court-appointed attorney came from Damariscotta, Maine. (Sources: *Kennebec Journal*, August 26 and September 11, 2004; *Boothbay Register*, August 26 and September 23, 2004; Augusta *Capital Weekly*, August 27, 2004)

Robinson, Dean (1857–1899). (Full name: Horace Dean Robinson.) The oldest son of Edward Robinson* and Mary Robinson,* hence the brother of Herman Robinson* and of Robinson the poet. Dean, as he was called, was born in Alna, Maine. He lived with his parents in their home at 67 Lincoln Avenue, Gardiner, Maine (beginning 1870). At his father's insistence, Dean reluctantly entered the Maine Medical School (1877), then part of Bowdoin College. After graduating *cum laude* (1881), he practiced medicine in Gardiner (1881–1884), moved to Camden, Maine (1884–1887), and served patients as a country doctor along the rugged coast and on nearby islands. He was engaged to a young Gardiner woman named Ardell Toby, but she died while he was in Camden. Dean began treating his neuralgia and also his mental distress by prescribing morphine for himself. He became addicted to it and also to alcohol. He returned to Gardiner (1887), practiced in Alma (1887–1889), then returned home again, subject to hallucinations. He was enamored of Herman's wife Emma Robinson,* before their marriage. The night of the wedding (1890), Dean was found near the Kennebec River, unconscious. He was engaged (1891–

1893) to Della Collins, the daughter of Jason Collins, a famous riverboat captain. Dean's being a burden on the family made his father aware that sending Robinson the future poet to Harvard might be financially risky, but he did so anyway (1891). Dean later worked in Gardiner as an ice weigher and a bank clerk. The father's death (1892) converted Dean into the incapable head of the family. When Mary Robinson,* the brothers' mother, died of black diphtheria (1896), Dean supervised preparations for her burial. Dean was appointed her estate administrator (1896); soon Herman became administrator (1897), even though Edwin by this time was in nominal control. From a man in Gardiner named F. M. Noyes, Dean leased a drugstore at 207 Water Street, in which the family had a financial interest (1897–1899). When his condition grew worse, he spent most of his time in the Robinson family home, attended by a male nurse. Dean somehow obtained sufficient morphine from the Water Street drugstore to commit suicide by deliberate overdose. The family sold the lease to the store (1901).

Robinson once said that when Dean was 20 he was more knowledgeable than Robinson the poet ever would be. Aspects of Dean's intellectual range may be part of Robinson's characterization of the hero of his *Captain Craig* (1902). In "The Pilot" (1906) Robinson may be expressing his sense of loss after Dean's death. He was surely thinking of Dr. Dean's morphine-filled needle when he wrote about the "machine" used to euthanize Annandale in "How Annandale Went Out" (1910). Robinson donated $1,000 to the Gardiner Memorial Hospital in Dean's name (1930). Garth, the sadly attractive failure in *Matthias at the Door* (1931), may owe something to Dean. David Shepherd Nivison, the grandson of Herman and Emma Robinson, has written movingly about the indirect depiction of Dean Robinson in "How Annandale Went Out," saying that the poem was "so important to the poet that it was almost a part of his being, to be guarded as though it were a piece of himself . . . and I feel we are poorer if we are unable to consider what this poem meant to Robinson, its intimate connection with a painful memory, a case in his own life

and family of that problem which always absorbed him, of worth in apparent failure, of the man enduring through the ruin. For at the level to which criticism must rise in Robinson we deal with more than just the poem; we deal with the poet as well." (Sources: Hagedorn; Nivison, 184; C. Smith)

Robinson, Edward (1818–1892). (Full name: Edward Robinson, Jr.) Robinson's father. His parents were Edward Robinson, Sr. and Elizabeth Kennedy Robinson. Born in Alna, Maine, Edward was a shipwright in Boston. He married Mary Elizabeth Palmer (see Robinson, Mary) in 1855. Born in Alna were their first two sons, Dean Robinson* (1857) and Herman Robinson* (1865). Edward was a lumber dealer, a grain merchant, and the manager of a general store in nearby Head Tide. Soon after their third and last child, Edwin Arlington Robinson, was born (1869), Edward moved with his family to Gardiner. He invested in mortgages in Western land, was a bank director, a member of the school board, a local politician and civic leader, and a state legislator in Augusta. Edward was interested at home in music and poetry. Worth approximately $80,000 (by 1870), he became semi-retired. He was hurt financially by the Panic of 1877, unfortunately let Herman manage family finances (beginning in 1887), and drank a bit too much. He agreed with misgivings to finance Robinson's attendance as a special student at Harvard (1891); slowly declined in mental and physical acuity; turned to spiritualism and even experimented in levitation; and by his death destroyed Robinson's lingering Harvard dreams. By terms of his will, Edward left a dollar to each son and holdings worth about $17,000 to his wife. (Sources: Hagedorn; C. Smith)

Robinson, Emma (1866–1940). (Full name: Emma Löehen Shepherd Robinson.) The wife of Robinson's brother, Herman Robinson.* She was born in Rengold, New Jersey. Her parents, David Clark Shepherd and Amanda Dietz Rudebock Shepherd, were Pennsylvania Dutch. Emma was a cousin of the Standard Oil Rockefellers. Early in his business career, her father David harvested

Kennebec River ice for a Philadelphia company. He prospered, bought a mansion for himself and his family in Farmingdale, Maine, and with his wife had three daughters. Emma, the eldest, attended the district school at Farmingdale, graduated from the Hallowell Classical Academy, and studied for two years at St. Catherine's Hall, in Augusta. Returning home, she began taking lessons at a dancing school in Gardiner, where Robinson met her (1888). At this time, according to her daughter Ruth Robinson,* Emma was engaged to a man named Fred Moore. Robinson immediately liked her. He was disappointed and distressed when Herman returned from a trip to the West, met her, and soon married her (February 12, 1890). Emma and Herman had three daughters, Ruth, Marie Robinson,* and Barbara Robinson.* Robinson became their devoted and adored "Uncle Win." By 1897, Herman had slid into financial failure and drug addition. Emma, Herman, and their daughters moved into the old Shepherd home in Farmingdale with Emma's mother, recently widowed (1903). Aided by money inherited from her father and by skimpy and irregular cash from Herman, Emma supported herself and her daughters by sewing. At some point (1900?, 1907?), Herman got Emma to promise that when he died she wouldn't marry Robinson. Herman died in February 1909.

After Herman's death, Robinson unsuccessfully proposed marriage to Emma (September 1909) and was again refused, twice (1918, 1927). Biographical theories suggest two contrary interpretations of Robinson's relationship to Emma. One theory holds that she was his only and constant love, even as her marriage to Herman turned from infatuation to duty to pity. Edgar Allen Beem presents evidence of this theory. The other theory contends that Herman was Emma's eternal love, weakened by his drinking, to be sure, but surviving his death; and that she was only bigsisterly in her affection for Robinson. In Robinson's poetry there is direct and subtle evidence to support both theories. According to Emma's daughter Ruth, Emma loved Robinson; according to Barbara, she did not.

In any event, Robinson, according to Hermann Hagedorn,* once shared with Emma the following uniquely heartwrenching and revealing thought: "I don't expect recognition while I live but if I thought I could write something that would go on living after I'm gone, I'd be satisfied with an attic and a crust all my life." (Sources: Beem; Hagedorn,118; Mezey, xxx; E. Robinson, 7–8; C. Smith, 203–04, 227–28, 251, 373–74)

Robinson, Herman (1865–1909). (Full name: Herman Edward Robinson.) The second son, born in Alna, Maine, of Edward Robinson* and Mary Robinson,* and hence the brother of Dean Robinson* and Robinson the poet. Herman was the handsome, stalwart, and popular son. After high school, he worked in a Gardiner savings bank (from 1884) and represented it in land ventures in Kansas, Minnesota, and especially Missouri (1886–1888). Meanwhile, Edward was becoming so weak physically that he appointed Herman to handle the family's finances (1887). Herman married Emma Löehen Shepherd (see Robinson, Emma) (February 1890) and soon took her away temporarily to St. Louis, where he had already bought a small house (1889). They eventually had three daughters — Ruth Robinson,* Marie Louise Robinson,* and Barbara Robinson.* It was Herman, home again when family finances started to disappear (1891), who persuaded their father to let Robinson attend Harvard (1891). That same year, Herman and his family began living in a cottage on Capitol Island, just off the Maine coast.

After Edward's death (1892), Herman was cheated by his St. Louis land-speculating partners. The Panic of 1893 further worsened his business interests. Combining self-destructive bitterness and suspicion, he turned to alcohol and occasionally deserted his family. The death of the Robinson brothers' mother Mary Robinson* (1896) contributed to Herman's defeatist decline (1897). From New York, Robinson was occasionally able, and obliged, to send Emma a little money. Herman sold the family house for a loss (1903), often stayed on Capitol Island, and caught fish and dug clams for money. He sought out Robinson in New York (1904). Herman gave up alcohol (c. 1907) but soon required treatment in Boston for tuberculosis (1907). He tried to seek a new life somehow, somewhere, but died, friendless and alone, in a public ward of the Boston City Hospital (February 1909).

Herman Robinson, the epitome of the appealing success-turned-failure, is in the foreground or background of many poetic characterizations by Robinson. Hoyt C. Franchere finds one example, among a dozen, of a resemblance between Herman, late in his life, and King Mark of *Tristram*. The handsome face of each, Franchere says, "became pouched with 'wine and riot,'" while the "once clear eyes [of each became] red and rheumy." In many other poems, Robinson presents, in poetic disguises, himself as a spiritual lover and Herman as a carnal lover of Emma in her many phases. (Sources: Franchere, 130; Hagedorn 248; C. Smith)

Robinson, Marie Louise (1893–1938). The middle daughter of Herman Robinson* and Emma Robinson.* She was born in Farmingdale, Maine. Her sisters were Ruth Robinson* and Barbara Robinson.* Marie Louise, who became a nurse, was married in Chelsea, Massachusetts, in 1936, to Arthur Thornton Legg (1874–1939). He was the son of Charles Edmund Legg and Emily Harding Legg, and became a renowned Boston orthopedic surgeon. Marie and Arthur Legg had no children, which was a possible factor in her death by suicide.

Robinson, Mary (1833–1896). (Full name: Mary Elizabeth Palmer Robinson.) Robinson's mother. She was descended from Anne Dudley Bradstreet* (c. 1612–1672), the first woman poet in America. Anne's father was Thomas Dudley (1576–1653), governor of the Massachusetts Bay Colony. He had two daughters, Anne and Mercy. Anne married Simon Bradstreet. Mary Robinson, a devout Congregationalist like her Palmer forebears, was a school teacher before her marriage to Edward Robinson.* Laura E. Richards* describes Mary as lovely and delicate, and says that the future poet, when five, read "The Raven" by Edgar Allan Poe to his mother while she was sewing. (Richard Cary states that later Robinson both confirmed and denied reports that when he was a child he read to his

mother.) Mary was quietly concerned, and steadfastly loyal, when one after another of her sons experienced various difficulties. She was widowed (1892) and not very long afterwards died of black diphtheria. Neither preacher nor physician nor undertaker would come near her at the end, and her sons prepared her for burial and buried her. (Sources: Cary [1974], 306; Hagedorn; Richards [1936], 4, 6; C. Smith)

Robinson, Ruth (1890–1971). The eldest daughter of Herman Robinson* and Emma Robinson,* born in Farmingdale, Maine. Ruth's sisters were Marie Louise Robinson* and Barbara Robinson.* Ruth seems to have been Robinson's favorite niece. In Brookline, Massachusetts, she married William Nivison (1884–1944), of Guardbridge, Scotland, the son of Robert Nivison and Margaret Boe Nivison. William Nivison was the chief engineer and superintendent of the Hollingsworth & Whitney Paper Company in Gardiner. When it closed (1940), the Nivisons moved to Mobile, Alabama. They had two sons, both born in Farmingdale, Maine: David Shepherd Nivison (b. 1923) and William Nivison (b. 1924). Ruth often invited "Uncle Win" to visit them in Gardiner. When Robinson was dying in the New York hospital, Ruth, who was then a nurse, visited him affectionately. Ruth became an executrix of Robinson's estate. Laura E. Richards* dedicated *E.A.R.*, her memoir of Robinson's childhood, "To Ruth Nivison."

Richard Cary counters the once-prevailing notion that Robinson was "variously compounded . . . of atheist, pessimist and misanthrope" by presenting evidence from some 50 notes Robinson sent to Ruth, as well as 13 to Marie, and two to Marie and Barbara together. This correspondence, Cary asserts, demonstrates Robinson's "instinctive, unobtrusive generosity to his own family," his "fundamental modesty and self-effacement," his "sober wit and moderate pessimism," his "absolute dedication to the writing of poetry," and his "consistent solicitude for others." (Sources: Cary [1960], 195–197, 199, 201, 202; Hagedorn, 357, 377; C. Smith, 144)

Roman Bartholow (New York: Macmillan, 1923). Narrative poem in blank verse, in eight numbered parts.

I. In early spring Roman Bartholow, a scholar and amateur farmer, looks out from "his ancestral prison," a mere "ivied house of stone," at his lawn and the river beyond. His wife Gabrielle has failed to meet his expectation of combining "beauty, mind, and fire," and in return now regards him as mere living "furniture." So he was almost religiously glad to welcome Penn-Raven, a kind of amateur healer, as their guest. He has been a neighbor for a year and more, and at one point quizzed Bartholow about his grandmother and mother but then added that Roman was "not the son of any father," the father's portrait being visible on the wall. Agreeing, Roman said, "My father was to me a mighty stranger." Penn-Raven stayed on with Bartholow and became "A resident saviour" but has recently spoken of his need to leave soon.

This morning Bartholow fears that if he stamped on his "footworn flags" where he stands, "he should hear a sullen ring / Of buried emptiness." He looks up. Behold, a man with a fishing basket, a rod, muddy boots, and clothes of varied "hues . . . like those on Joseph," and

> a face more made for comedy
> Than for the pain that comedy concealed,
> Socratic, unforgettable, grotesque,
> Inscrutable, and alone.

The fellow is Umfraville, Bartholow's bookish neighbor, who says that two months ago he saw from a distance a cetain sad-faced man (Bartholow) looking as though he were digging in search of his soul. Umfraville has come from his home on the east side of the river to offer breakfast trout in exchange for a drink. Staying for several drinks, he expatiates on the difficulty of finding one's soul. Bartholow praises him for being ageless and then praises Penn-Raven for helping him to see himself anew and become more peaceful. Umfraville runs himself down as impossibly ugly; will express joy if the possibly untrustworthy Penn-Raven, whom he has also observed a bit, can bring peace to another; and offers Bartholow his warm friendship should he need to ask for

it later. When Bartholow agrees to visit him, Umfraville waves, with tears in his eyes, and departs.

II. Bartholow, feeling reborn by Penn-Raven's empowering help, regards Umfraville as unnecessarily defeated, takes an invigorating breath, goes upstairs, and finds his image in the mirror to be that of a happy, tolerant fellow — until, that is, his timelessly beautiful wife Gabrielle enters laughing at him. She says he might have seen Apollo or Antinous in the mirror but calls him Narcissus instead. He gently warns her that David in the Bible exiled his laughing wives. She tells him to go look at his grandfather's portrait and calls him a spider. She escapes his quick kiss. When he tells her of his being reborn, she replies that she knows, is glad, and hopes she has a soul. When he replies that she is mainly concerned about getting breakfast, she agrees, but then soon finds him in his library reading something in Greek. He calls her poor-witted for not understanding the passage and translates it "Let me be worthy of your mysteries" (Aristophanes, *The Frogs*, 1. 887).

They start eating breakfast. Penn-Raven enters singing, then fixes both with his strangely potent violet eyes. Gabrielle has a roll and says she won't touch any trout that the "unhappy monster" Umfraville brought. This bothers Bartholow, who says her beauty should make her more tolerant of Umfraville's ugliness. In retaliation, she offers "Raven," munching his trout, her trout for seconds. Penn-Raven says it's a shame Umfraville's inherited grotesqueness should cause this childish couple to wound each other. After the three do some verbal fencing, Penn-Raven stares at Gabrielle intently, then walks toward the river to have himself a smoke.

At the doorway Bartholow tells Gabrielle that he may have to remove some trees to improve their view of the river. He hopes the two of them can be as harmonious as trees and rivers are, speaks of his escape from hell and of his feeling alive anew, expresses sadness at her name-calling when she caught him at his mirror, and asks whether they can't call the "mystery" in his translation simply "The joy of being." She retorts that she didn't figure much in his "rapture." He suggests destroying their old ruined house of pain and building "With new love a new house." She smiles wanly and doubts his ability to build. He says the two of them could do it together. She says that he still needs "the Raven," that he would prefer him to any children. Indignant and pacing, he calls her ancestors colder fish than any alive today. She retorts that he has inherited traits of his grandfather, whose painted face may haunt her; that any house he could build would be a phantom house, which could still collapse and injure them; that each of them is attracted to the other; that the world envies them their apparent happiness; that if he wants her to go, she'll leave and ask nothing; and then asks his forgiveness. After shrugging, Bartholow says that he'll forgive her "defection," recognizes her suffering and loneliness when he was blind during "those black years"; but he adds that if she goes on remembering and constantly reminding him of "each empty day" he hurt her with, she'd better leave him. Gabrielle merely replies that their same old trouble would lodge itself in any new house, like a rat hiding in the walls. When he asks if she wants him to kneel submissively, she answers that his doing so wouldn't make him wise. She sees Penn-Raven returning and moves away from Bartholow, who admits he's unworthy of her mysteries.

III. Bartholow usually oversaw outside work by his helpers, but now he feels the need of exercise. Gabrielle laughs and tells him to go grab an axe and chop a tree down, while Penn-Raven advises him to relate his body to his soul in the activity, expresses more joy in seeing two-sided rivers than mysterious oceans, places a chair for Gabrielle, and soon listens to vigorous axe blows with her. Whereas she fears Bartholow's arms will quickly ache, Penn-Raven says the toil will help him emerge from his former dark prison, during which time she stayed memorably silent. Gabrielle reminisces aloud about her silence while her husband paced, communed with his house, pretended to be reading, and neglected her. Bartholow told her at that time that he was in hell and without companionship there. When she tells Penn-Raven she was in hell too then, he asks if she wants him to explain the situation. He distinguishes between eternity and her years, long or short, of suffering with Bartholow. She meets Penn-Raven's fiery glare with "her languid and reluctant eyes." He talks about a region betwixt earthly heaven and heavenly earth that we stay in or leave, before helpful death. Her mentioning a desired democracy triggers his comments on the vanity of escapist "illusions and evasions / Like yours." She counters first by wondering what to do after one finds the truth, and then by expressing resentment of his charge of escapism. Meanwhile, they hear Bartholow's axe blows.

IV. One July evening Penn-Raven is brooding outside. He has stayed too long. He reckons the same moon will shine on the same quiet river and on the same trees, minus a few. Bartholow enters, hopes at least someone somewhere knows he is ecstatic at having renewed vigor, and is grateful for Penn-Raven's help. Penn-Raven thanks him for his hospitality, praises his felling that one tree, and says he must leave soon, perhaps before rain comes, and before Bartholow grows impatient. Bartholow says he may be misunderstanding Penn-Raven, walks toward the river, and leaves Penn-Raven puzzled and aware of his own limitations.

First fancying himself away from here and becoming a ghost if he ever returned, Penn-Raven goes inside and interrupts Gabrielle's reading by planting a heavy kiss smack on her mouth. He detects "more fear than anger" when she jumps toward the bare window and glares back at him. She reveals that Umfraville, whom she never saw before, witnessed the two of them embracing a week earlier. Penn-Raven says that when he leaves he can't say he's losing her, because she was never his to lose. She says what she may have yet to give is her life. He says he'll follow her to an end he doesn't see. Telling him to avoid the window, with moths outside banging the screen, and to sit down out of sight, she hopes that he'll remember her generosity, says that when they first met she, like him, had her share of "revelations, disillusions, / Tragedies," was in the dark, blamed none, but, enlightened by him, expects him to feel all right when he leaves. Penn-Raven's reply, intended for comfort, is that when he leaves tomorrow, many may be burdened but she may have reasons to live. To her contention that women are better than men at understanding actions, he says that when he first arrived here she probably regarded him as an "adventurer" or even a "charlatan," whereas he innocently saw her as the answer to his needs, saw everything about her in ruins, and saw her husband as an unimprovable stranger to her.

When Penn-Raven says he observed many changes after his arrival, Gabrielle yawns, then says that those changes may be in him only, that the soul-and-body "medicine" he used on Bartholow may prove of impermanent aid, since Bartholow's "illumination cannot last. / ... I know it never does." Angered, Penn-Raven tells her to believe that her husband's soul was always healthy and that she ought to seize the opportunity for renewed happiness. Gabrielle wonders what he's doing and hints he may be acting like "the converse of a woman scorned." His responsive eyes distress her with their habitual bewildering and accusatory "calm primeval sheen of innocence." He says he did little, belittles his healing powers, and recommends for everyone that "unfailing fountain head / Of power and peace," since, after one drinks from it, everything else is "trashy draughts." Gabrielle bridles in the thought that he regards her as trash. He says this: She'll regret such criticism when he's gone; some never know great, crowning, scarring love at all; if she stays easygoing, she will return to the darkness he found her in; her charms and troubles "overwhelmed his loyalty"; when she ignorantly let die the virtually unique love she let her husband kindle for her, he suffered for both self and her; she felt ruined and therefore careless of "another ruin or two," which might be fun anyway.

Stunned, Gabrielle wonders at his gift of her "emancipation," says she cares so little for life that this special love her husband offered means little, and hears "a rat somewhere" in Penn-Raven's "holy temple." All seems changed. Anger releases fear in her; then she sees, then only feels, the burning of his fanatically fiery eyes. He carefully responds, to this effect: She shouldn't be perversely evasive after what he said. She shouldn't be triflingly charitable, for "Who are the rich to you, and who the poor?" She has nearly wrecked her husband. She can't continue a dream life with him. But if she tells him all, she can't build a new house with him; therefore "Let the worst be the worst." If she doesn't break her shell of loneliness, she'll stay "too beautiful to be alive."

V. Penn-Raven leaves. Gabrielle remains, feels tortured, vainly seeks an answer, hopes there is a reason, looks about at the everlastingly same old things, and regards the rage caused by his "calm and virulen[t] ... / ... invective" to be submerging her wrecked and empty life. Enough. As for Bartholow — if he suffered in gaining "illumination," hadn't she also suffered gaining none? What if each had given to the other but not chained by marriage? She weeps, weary and pained. When Bartholow reappears, can fear lead to pity, pity to her telling him, and that to hope, and hope to "that house of his"? It would have rats. She could have gone "unspotted" to her grave, in "comfort without love," but only "had all gone well," which it hadn't. She feels helpless as Bartholow approaches. He frowns at her accusingly. She says Penn-Raven talked a long while, then left, probably to go toward the river. Bartholow wonders what they discussed that turned her deathly pale, sits, and says his doing so will depict them as homey and sociable again. She feels frozen by his cool gaze. He says this: Penn-Raven has half-wrecked matters; her face seems marked; she might be planning houses without him; propless structures they would be; he may owe apologies to both her and generous Penn-Raven; the Bartholows might build a new house.

Gabrielle says that it's all too late; that Bartholow is free to build a new house with another woman; that if she had, and if he had found in her either more than the mind he flattered her by saying she had or else less than it, then they might have been saved. When he hoped just now to elicit "sorrow and remorse," he finds only pride and is aware that she was lost to him even before Penn-Raven arrived "To save him and filch her from his arms." Bartholow is almost speechless. She feels surprised at her freedom and fearlessness, is aware that his freedom is darkness again for him, and is coldly certain of her future. After staring icily, he speaks. He rebukes her for talk-ing about livable houses others can securely build, when his he ignorantly dreamed of is dust; he won't hurt her, since she's too beau-tiful; but he, her first prey, was really too strong for her to trap in her spider-like web instead of letting him go.

Gabrielle complains about Bartholow's friendship with devilish Umfraville, won't talk more about houses, calls herself destitute, compares herself to a plant wrongly falling onto his soil. Bartholow says that she isn't des-titute and can build for herself elsewhere, that both were wrong to build here, and that any further construction here would be "sand / And moonshine." She sadly notes that she can't live here, has lacked wings to escape, will "soon be gone," and is wistfully glad he'll "soon be free," but not by dying. Softening a little, he says that his debt to her, which, though "vague, is measureless," and general-izes that sometimes leaders are led by those they have led, though on roads leading to "darkness [where] all is dark." This about vagueness she denies, being certain of wasted mercy, limited change, sunshine somewhere for him. She seeks some message for a final time in his eyes; gently kisses his forehead; feels him trembling; concludes his doing so "was less for her / Than for the saviour-friend who had betrayed him." She leaves him watching the moths pounding the window screen and from her room can see the same trees, moonlight, and river he is also looking at. Putting out her light, she feels held by nothing tangible about her, remembers how each of the three of them worked on the other two, reasons that she has only a past while Bartholow has a future, and therefore silently glides through moonlight to water.

VI. Everything Bartholow, alone now but with "his new-found soul," sees beyond the window seems strange now, for which he blames Penn-Raven. That heavy fellow strides in and says he's leaving tomorrow, even before rains come. Bartholow wants him to remain and talk with him, with darkness concealing their faces. Penn-Raven advises him to avoid shipwreck by quickly ending a wrong mar-riage, and then to go forward into life. Seeing a picture with two faces in this room, Bartho-low damns Penn-Raven volubly, knocks him to the floor, starts to choke him, but is soon grabbed, defeated, put in a chair, and lectured to, calmly. Penn-Raven commends him for atavistically showing his grandfather's strength but tells him to settle down. Bartholow calls him "a giant, / . . . a damned parasite and thief," says he won't have murder on his soul, or a carcass to dispose of. He listens to Penn-Raven's tragedian-like recital of humankind's general woes, on Bartholow's sowing fennel while hoping for flowers, and on his present need to summon his new, pride-tinged wis-dom to restrain wild love with dignified reti-cence and to realize some things "Were not to be." Bartholow upbraids Penn-Raven for poaching in others' gardens. But Penn-Raven, first asking forgiveness, rambles on, about his being drawn here, about love abjured, about hate that obscures vision, about his still-unachieved work, and about letting vexing ills fade.

Even though Bartholow laughs malevo-lently, scornfully, at these revelations, Penn-Raven continues: Bartholow shouldn't let one woman wreck his view of the world. She was a mere flower; he, a poor gardener; so let her wither in darkness. She, though partly weed, may just possibly flourish in other soil. Bartholow, with truth rooted in him, is "doom[ed] . . . to be free." Deciding to fight no more, Bartholow says Penn-Raven has been heard now and should leave. But continuing instead, the fellow analyzes Gabrielle critically, as one of little power and little pride, ignorant of the world, with a frozen soul, playing with lies, and surely not Bartholow's for long. Bartholow expresses more scorn. Penn-Raven replies that it is best he say little more than that Bartholow has "played / With life as if it were a mere toy" until he thought he had bro-ken it; but not so; he has inherited great gifts he can't help using now. As an inspired insult, Bartholow gives Penn-Raven a "cheque" for $1,000 and tells him not to pantomime any dishonest pretense of refusal. He defines his adversary as having some truth but also a last-ing "small and rotten residue" to ponder until death.

Penn-Raven examines and pockets the check, tells Bartholow that his magnanimity is now prevailing over his earlier ferocity, says Bartholow is among the few who are obliged to help little people pep up, tells him he'd prefer to leave in the morning rather than on a night train, since such trains are uncomfortable, and adds that mutual friends in town might gossip about his precipitous departure. Totally outraged and flinging another curse, Bartholow dismisses Penn-Raven, who bows and looks up childishly. With their backs turned, the two suddenly hear feet on gravel and a knock on the door.

VII. Two mornings later Bartholow raps on the fisherman-scholar Umfraville's door. The fellow admits his early guest, excuses himself, dresses, apologizes for being ugly, and asks if Penn-Raven, that "sainted scalawag," has robbed him and left. Over steaming coffee, Bartholow elaborately tells "how she died" (Gabrielle has drowned herself) but "not why." Pressed, he adds that if he had been different he might have cherished her diminished self, that their talk of building a new house was mere talk, that "a madness . . . was born in her," and that he won't judge her. Umfraville hints that marriage can be poisonous, thinks maybe Penn-Raven saved Bartholow, but is glad his "saviour" is gone, warns about costly newfound freedom, and says he now has "a choice of ambiguities." This speech Bartholow calls "an early douche of rudiments." Umfraville says that Bartholow has been enlightened, that he and Gabrielle were unsuited, that he wouldn't wish her alive again and back here, and that "she was dead before she died." Adding that he's neither judgmental nor farseeing, Umfraville lists a dozen sorts of selfish, hurtful behavior and continues to the effect that Bartholow's "soul-practitioner" doubtless found much in him to save and that his newfound light probably won't fade. Umfraville theorizes that if we were all frank cannibals, instead of "anthropophagous hypocrites," and gobbled each other's hearts frankly, some of us would "climb / Higher than we are" and the bones of weaklings would be strewn behind us. Umfraville hastens to say he's being general but, specifically, is sure Bartholow is happy that his "omphalopsychite" has left him.

Bartholow goes into considerable detail.

Two men brought Gabrielle's body to him in the moonlight. Penn-Raven left suddenly that same night without seeing her face again. Bartholow hasn't slept for two nights. When he rebukes Umfraville for suggesting he killed his wife, Umfraville, looking like a grinning griffin, says he really said nothing. Bartholow praises Penn-Raven for helping him unlock himself and see light, says he's glad he didn't kill him, then agrees he may have killed his wife. He finally says,

She married without love; and when love came,
A life too late, I should have been a liar
To take it, or to say I treasured it;

this because, when her "remnant" of love for him emerged from their ruined lives it was only because "a beauty scarred / Is beauty still." Bartholow concludes that he couldn't say he forgave the scar, because Penn-Raven was in the house; this was Penn-Raven's "smear," and it blinded Bartholow and caused his attack. But Bartholow will remember the strange man appreciatively. Umfraville says that if Penn-Raven were still in Bartholow's residence, the fellow would punish Bartholow further and get another check for doing so, and that the guy is laughing yet. Denying this, Bartholow says Penn-Raven took the check but wept and insisted he hadn't even asked for gratitude. Silence follows this disclosure. Umfraville waits faithfully, solemnly, full of questions, and finally smiles sadly.

VIII. Three months later, autumn scatters leaves between Bartholow's lawn and the river, more visible where he cut the tree. Preparing to depart forever, he fancies he sees a "shipwreck on the air," and his face, a dead one's, and a forever-absent friend's. His family home is empty, sold. Umfraville, to whom he gave all of his books, is with him. Bartholow wonders what thoughts a new tenant here might have a century hence. Umfraville asks what Bartholow will do if Penn-Raven comes crying and appealing for more money. Bartholow says he won't. Umfraville, with a growl, summarizes the advice Penn-Raven gave Bartholow: Realize others have worse knots to untangle; some evils contain their own solutions; you can give others a remedy but not share it with them; nor necessarily will others, though sometimes benefiting, even know its source; you'll always be solitary. Umfraville, calling Penn-Raven a blackguard, says the fellow knew nothing of Bartholow's past but claimed he could save him.

Bartholow responds gently to Umfraville, saying this: He too called Penn-Raven a blackguard, who then admitted he was; but he was more and helped Bartholow unlock doors; nature now leads him away from Penn-Raven and away from death. Umfraville's reply is a barrage of pedantry. He quotes or alludes to Aristophanes, Cimmerian, Dante, Melpomone, Pindar; apologizes for being so bookish; hopes to be worthy of his friend's mysteries; and says his gist is that Bartholow and Gabrielle were in the dark, where she ended, and that Bartholow should step forward.

Bartholow knows that the phantom house he discussed with Gabrielle is a phantom still, that she was an "alive" woman, but that she is happiest in her grave. He tells Umfraville that he won't pore over his past like a book with "blank leaves," also that what Umfraville calls his giant "Custom" (i.e., strictures of traditional marriage?) might be overthrown, replaced, and its nakedness clothed properly. Umfraville urges him to work to that end, while he'll continue reading his own dead giants. When Bartholow suggests that they read some of those living giants together, Umfraville, ugly and therefore lonely, declines, and then explains that the occupants of his Acropolis of

> scraps and ashes
> Of a lost world that I shall have intact
> And uninfected with modernities

are truly dead. Further, that he and Bartholow wouldn't thrive well together; that the damnable, naturally endowed Penn-Raven correctly said Bartholow would live on and aid others; and that Bartholow tonight will sup with his anxious friends and then depart. The two men shake hands. Bartholow says he'll hear from Umfraville, who, he adds, may read not only his dead authors but also aid "the living / Who are not yet alive."

Umfraville, his best and most loving friend, walks away and disappears. He correctly defined Penn-Raven as both savior and be-

trayer. Bartholow concludes that all their debts were "cancelled in a grave, / Where lay a woman doomed never to live," so that "he who had adored her and outgrown her / Might yet achieve." He regards the ivy that covers his house like a garment and hides the past as growing from "roots of wrong" and tangled too complexly for any gardener to do more than "prune / Or train a few new branches." He fancies a smile from Gabrielle's lips and remembers her final, gentle kiss.

Bartholow locks his door with the new owner's key and walks past the gate and onto the road, well aware that he would not see those "changeless . . . hills," those "changing trees" flaming in the twilight, and that river ever again.

Ruth Nivison* says that her mother, Emma Robinson,* is the basis for Gabrielle; Bartholow is based on Emma's husband, Herman Robinson,* Robinson's brother; that the poet himself is adumbrated in Penn-Raven; and that Herman's house on Lincoln Street, Gardiner, becomes transmuted in the poem into the Gardiner mansion called Oaklands. Laura E. Richards* wrote that Robinson told her that in describing Bartholow's house "he had actually described Oaklands, 'the outside at least.'" To Rosalind Richards, Laura's daughter, Robinson wrote (May 18, 1923) much to the same effect. Ruth adds that her mother identified Ruel Dunlap, with whom Herman fished and camped, as the model for Umfraville. Chard Powers Smith,* participating in this identification game, partially equates Roman Bartholow's father with Robinson's father Edward Robinson,* Roman with Robinson's neurotic brother Herman, Gabrielle with Herman's beautiful wife Emma, and Penn-Raven (at least with respect to his attentions to Gabrielle) with Robinson. Emma agrees, having told Ruth that after a big argument over Emma, Herman banished Robinson. Robinson descendants cannot be pleased that Emery Neff brands Gabrielle "one of the most repellently negative and destructive minds in American verse, even though Robinson gives her a final moment of piteousness . . ."

Francis Murphy laments that when fame came to Robinson with his first Pulitzer Prize (1921), it became "too easy to publish, year after year, the endless procession of psychological narratives that flowed from his pen [beginning with *Roman Bartholow*, which] . . . are, by any frank assessment, almost unreadable." Even Charles Cestre,* Robinson's first non-American admirer, laments that "*Roman Bartholow* somewhat halts in the middle and sags at the end" but adds "[w]hat great poet was always equal to himself?" Yvor Winters also regards *Roman Bartholow* as a mediocre work that fails because of both the unpoetic subject matter and the manner of treatment. In an early review, Dorothy Dudley suggests that the narrative requires more than a single reading for fuller comprehension and appreciation. She says that during her first reading, "stepping over surfaces, I made out not much more than the sides of the triangle — that old, old figure, which now, whether in the employ of the theatre, movie, or magazine page, nearly always succeeds in adding to the panic and superstition surrounding the economic legend, marriage." A subsequent reading persuaded Dudley to conclude that the quotation from Aristophanes "gathers weight and is finally part of the burden of the poem," and that, tragically, none of the three principal characters is allowed to be worthy of the mysteries of either of the other two. Added to this may be the fact that basic imagery running through the poem concerns houses built or imagined, eyes open and closed, different darknesses, different lights, and moonshine. Ellsworth Barnard regards the poem as both unnecessarily drawn-out and as Robinson's most difficult work stylistically. It is so difficult that Emery Neff found more plot details than are truly there. He does ably point out the symbolism of the moths hurting themselves against the window screen; he says that when Robinson calls the moths "clumsy" and "indignantly / Refusing to be free," they resemble poor Gabrielle.

Henry W. Wells praises both Robinson and Robinson Jeffers for being "among the most effective narrative poets in recent years" (to 1940); becomes specific by noting that "[a]lthough the action of *Roman Bartholow* is relatively simple, the story progresses with Shandean leisureliness [cf. *Tristram Shandy* by Laurence Sterne] and, being one of the longest of Robinson's poems, certainly equals a novel in its scope"; adds that Robinson "writes the modern psychological novel in a singularly dry, analytical style"; and suggests that he owes something to the novels of George Meredith and Henry James.

Roman Bartholow tries the patience of the most dedicated reader, especially because of its prolix psychologizing and wordy dialogue. To be sure, Jay Martin finds the last 11 lines of the narrative (which he quotes) to be "elegiac, yet trembling with anticipation, . . . [and] among the best that Robinson ever wrote." Before that irredescent closure, however, *Roman Bartholow* in the standard *Collected Poems* runs to 124 pages, and an awesome 3,958 lines, including the last 11. *Hamlet*, Shakespeare's longest play, is 3,906 lines. *Roman Bartholow* is second in length only to *Tristram*, Robinson's longest poem. Still, Roy Harvey Pearce goes too far when he thunders that *Roman Bartholow* is "to be regretted."

A serendipitous feature in *Roman Bartholow* for superficial readers of Robinson, if there are any, is the quietly uproarious humor he uses to describe Umfraville's ugliness. To some, Robinson may seem intellectually pretentious, not to say offputting, to have Bartholow quote Aristophanes, Umfraville quote Pindar and Dante, and Penn-Raven sing words from one Italian opera and another Italian song. However, explicators welcoming challenges popping up in texts should pursue the following sources: "*tout' aniarotaton*" ("this is most grievous," from Pindar, "Pythian Ode IV," 1. 288); "*nessun maggior dolore*" ("there is no greater sorrow," from Dante, *Inferno*, V, 122); "*Chi mi frena . . .*" ("What restrains me . . . [?]," from Gaetano Donizetti, *Lucia di Lammermoor*, II, ii); and "*Non ti scordar di me*" ("Do not forget me," by Ernesto de Curtis and Furnò). A translation of the whole passage in Pindar from which Umfraville quotes is this: "But they say the saddest fate of all is to know the good but to be necessarily shut away from it." Penn-Raven's singing the Italian love song as he approaches Bartholow is cunning, because the unsung line following is "my life is bound with yours." His adverting to *Lucia di Lammermoor* is also appropriate, since the plot involves a marital triangle, even, one might say, a quadrangle. (Sources: Barnard, 95, 285; Cestre, 27; Dudley, 96, 99; Martin, 154; Murphy, 4; Neff, 214; Pearce, 268; Richards [1936], 54; E. Robinson, 14, 19; *Selected Letters*, 131; C. Smith, 74, 171; 174, 217–18, 256; Wells, 178, 179; Winters, 103–06)

"Romance" (1897, 1975). Poem. It is in two numbered and titled parts.

I. "Boys." Three of us were friends together and were more than brothers. We were boys then.

II. "James Wetherell." We liked James Wetherell well enough and treated him all right. But "some things have come to light," and now he has gone.

"Boys," at first called "The Brothers," appeared in *The Children of the Night*. (Sources: Brower, 43; Cary [1974], 94–95; Cary [1975], 45, 181)

Roosevelt, Theodore (1858–1919). Twenty-sixth president of the United States.

Born in New York City, Roosevelt graduated from Harvard (1880), was a member of the New York State legislature (1882–1884), ranched in North Dakota (1884–1886), and returned to politics. He was a member of the U. S. Civil Service Commission (1889–1895), was president of the New York City Board of Police Commissioners (1895–1897), was U.S. assistant secretary of the navy (1897–1898), served with the U.S. cavalry in Cuba during the Spanish-American War (1898), and was governor of New York (1899, 1900). His being vice president of the United States when President William McKinley was assassinated made him president (1901). Re-elected, he served until 1909. During his administration, Roosevelt saw to it that Panama was recognized and the Panama Canal project was started (1903), businesses were regulated and trusts were curbed, natural resources were preserved, and William Taft succeeded him in the White House (1909). Roosevelt's later career included big-game hunting in Africa and exploring in South America, an unsuccessful bid for the presidency (1912), and great sympathy with the Allied Powers during the First World War. Roosevelt was also a prolific author; his many books began with *The Naval War of 1812* (1882), included other history books, books on hunting, exploring, and war, and ended with *America and the World War* (1915).

Roosevelt had three sons and one daughter. His son Kermit Roosevelt (1889–1943) was a student at Groton School, in Groton, Connecticut (1903), when he happened to encounter Robinson's *The Children of the Night* among the books of Henry Howe ("Hal") Richards. He was the son of Henry Richards* and Laura E. Richards,* Robinson's close friends in Gardiner. At the time, H. H. Richards was the English master at Groton and was also Kermit's hall master. Intrigued by Robinson's poetry, Kermit bought a few copies and sent one to his father (1904). Laura Richards's recollection is that "Hal" read passages from *Captain Craig* aloud to his pupils, including Kermit, whose interest in Robinson was so great that, she adds, he told "his father of the wonderful new poet."

The president, enthralled by Robinson's poems, became his sponsor, conferred with the popular editor-poet Richard Watson Gilder,* wrote Robinson, offered him diplomatic work in Montreal or Mexico City, and finally placed him as a special treasury agent in the New York Custom House at $2,000 a year (June 1905–June 1909). When Roosevelt published his review of *The Children of the Night* (*The Outlook* 80 [August 12, 1905]), the presidential nudge helped Robinson immensely. Roosevelt also browbeat Scribner's editors to purchase rights to *The Children of the Night* and publish a new edition of it (October 14, 1905). Robinson dedicated *The Town Down the River* to Roosevelt (1910). Louis Untermeyer* quotes, without giving the date, from a letter Robinson wrote to Kermit Roosevelt, in which he says he doesn't like to think about where he would be without President Roosevelt's fishing him out of hell by his hair. David H. Burton says that although Robinson and Roosevelt were philosophically unlike, they were both anti-materialistic. George Monteiro shows how in its first issue *The Touchstone*, a short-lived periodical (January–May 1906), satirized, with illustrations, Roosevelt's help to Robinson. Richard

Cary clarifies the time line of events concerning Robinson and Roosevelt, and reprints the presidential review and several reviews partly in response to it. (Sources: D. Burton [1968]; Cary [1974], 165–67, 170–256 passim, 309; Franchere, 47; Hagedorn; Monteiro; Pringle, 474–75; Richards [1931], 382; Roosevelt, IV, 1145, 1193, 1303; C. Smith, 212, 216; Untermeyer, 12)

Royce, Josiah (1855–1916). Born in Grass Valley, California, Royce earned degrees at the University of California at Berkeley (B.A., 1875) and at John Hopkins (Ph.D., 1878), taught philosophy at Berkeley (1878–1882) and then at Harvard (1882–1883, 1890–1916). Robinson was not impressed by Royce's class lectures at Harvard (1893). According to a letter (February 21, 1893) from Robinson to Harry de Forest Smith,* Royce "is not at home in psychology, and I get absolutely nothing from what he says." Nevertheless, Estelle Kaplan tries to demonstrate that Robinson gained philosophically from his contact with Royce. J. C. Levenson contends that "Robinson's cast of mind was critically affected by his two years at Harvard, and by the great philosophic dialogue of William James and Josiah Royce to which he was eyewitness for a time." (Sources: Hagedorn, 78; Kaplan, 25–34 passim; Levenson, 163; C. Smith, 78, 284; *Untriangulated Stars*, 87)

Saben, Mowry (1870–1950). Writer and editor. Saben was born in Uxbridge, Massachusetts. He accomplished university study at Harvard, Oxford, and Heidelberg. After beginning his professional life as a lecturer in Helena, Montana, and sermonizing on independent ethics in New Bedford, Massachusetts, he did editorial writing for the remainder of his peripatetic career. Saben worked for the *Tacoma News*, the *Portland Telegram* (Oregon), the *Denver Republican*, the *Detroit Free Press*, the *Chicago Journal*, and the *Rochester Herald*. He contributed editorials to the Boston *Transcript*, the *New York Times*, and the *Baltimore American*. He was associate editor of the *Washington Challenge* and wrote weekly columns for the *National Republican* and the *Argonaut*, also editing the latter

(1934–1936). He served briefly as an assistant to James J. Davis, who was a long-time secretary of labor in the cabinets of presidents Warren Harding, Calvin Coolidge, and Herbert Hoover. Saben was the author of *The Twilight of the Gods* (1903) and *The Spirit of Life* (1914). He died in San Francisco.

Hermann Hagedorn* gained information about Robinson through correspondence with Saben. Hagedorn reports that Robinson met Saben when the two were students at Harvard (1891–1992). Saben's father was a mathematician and tried to make his son another. But Saben, inept in mathematics and loathing it, preferred literature, history, and Protestant theology. Partly owing to his father's puritanical disciplinary tactics, Saben had a nervous breakdown and thereafter rebelliously enrolled at Harvard, despite his physician's advising against his doing so and also against his drinking. Therefore, Saben drank, ate, smoked, was merry, annoyed the authorities (both faculty and police), but impressed Robinson with his unabashed hedonism and intelligence, and survived. At Harvard, the two, along with George Burnham* and a few others, established the Corncob Club, which Saben dominated by virtue of a combination of loud mouth, total recall of everything he ever read, and alcohol. Saben told their friends to ignore Robinson's melancholy taciturnity and to take note of him, since he was a genius and would prove it in due time. According to Chard Powers Smith,* Saben was dismissed from Harvard for low grades and drunken rowdiness (March 1892).

In later years, Robinson and Saben became more intellectual friends than socializing ones, and remained in contact through correspondence. In early letters (October 1, 22, 1893) to Harry de Forest Smith,* Robinson describes Saben as "a magnificent fellow with all his peculiarities, but not just the one I should go to for an impartial criticism [of Robinson's poetry]," and as "unquestionably gifted with a fine intellect. He is not very well balanced, but that is not to be laid at his door."

Richard Cary (1972) discusses the backgrounds and relationship of Robinson and Saben. Cary (1974) also reprints an unsigned "column article" by Saben entitled "The

Poems of Edwin Robinson" (*Denver Republican* [December 3, 1905]) and summarizes Saben's amusement and Robinson's embarrassment when Robinson learned that Saben wrote it. According to Wallace L. Anderson, except for one 1896 letter, all early letters from Robinson to Saben were lost in a Rochester fire. (Sources: W. Anderson [1980], 52; Cary [1972]; Cary [1974], 193–95; Hagedorn, 64–65, 71, 75, 194; C. Smith, 121; *Untriangulated Stars*, 108, 114)

"The Sage" (1902). Sonnet. The much-esteemed wise man while seeking "Truth" returns to "the Orient" and finds where "Asia" had torn "The curtain of Love's inner shrine" and was thereafter "scarred by the Unseen." In "a treasure chest" he found "a gleam . . . not of gold" but with this flaming message:

I keep the mintage of Eternity.
Who comes to take one coin may take the rest,
And all may come — but not without the key.

The working title of this poem was "Emerson," and it extols Ralph Waldo Emerson, whose transcendental philosophy, and that of his intellectual colleague Thomas Carlyle, were major influences on Robinson, particularly in his early maturity. Robinson always regarded Emerson as America's greatest poet. However, in "The Sage" Robinson concentrates on Emerson's philosophy rather than on his poetic achievement. Hyatt H. Waggoner opines that Robinson "is . . . unaccurate about Emerson historically" in this sonnet "when . . . he describes Emerson as having developed his philosophy by going back to ancient oriental truth for his wisdom." Edwin S. Fussell traces the rent-curtain image in "The Sage" to a "veil . . . rent" in "Sonnet to Homer" by John Keats (not to be confused with his more famous "On First Looking into Chapman's Homer").

The fifth line of "The Sage," "Previsioned of the madness and the mean," troubled Edith Brower,* whose understandable objection to "the mean" sparked Robinson to begin the first of two replies to her (June 10, 1900) by quoting the dictionary definition of "mean" as "intermediate between too extremes." But wouldn't most readers try to synonymize "the mean" to mean the base, ignoble, stingy?

(Sources: Brower, 116; Fussell [1954], 81; Waggoner, 290)

"Saint Paul" *see* **"The Three Taverns"**

"Sainte-Nitouche" (1902). Poem. As for his friend the preacher Vanderberg, the narrator reluctantly offers this "tribute for his memory." The good fellow lost, then found, and then lost himself again. When they all buried Saint-Nitouche, who was Vanderberg's mistress, he said "So what?" in effect, and explained that he had wife, child, and church to consider and wouldn't "leave them in the lurch." On the evening of Sainte-Nitouche's funeral, he said that he would rather talk with the narrator than take either "bromide . . . [or] cyanide." He explained in detail: The past made him glad; life should continue; his home used to sparkle a lot; he'd be free again; he learned much through being a love slave; the narrator was sinful to think ill of him; Sainte-Nitouche made his very future "sweet"; sure, there was an element of bitterness, at first.

You see, Vanderberg wanted to explain what otherwise would be a "broken story." He wept a little when he said he was going to welcome the future. After all, he continued, Sainte-Nitouche put him on the right dark but starry path to lighted heights, though with some inevitable stumbling on his part. She had really been an innocent child.

Vanderberg didn't greatly mind when the narrator smiled, because he did so "in the dark," unable to share Vanderberg's "lonely pride" and his awareness that all would be fine. He said he had his work cut out for him to find "God's pathway through the gloom." When the two men parted, Vanderberg said he knew the narrator would ultimately agree with him and would understand him better later.

Sure enough, the narrator did. And sure enough, Vanderberg, after somehow sanitizing his formerly shrine-like home, continued his profession like a successful actor, but in the process put off many former friends by his obviously "defensive" bursts of "five staccato . . . laugh[s]." Moreover, his sermons were "glacial," long, and "thin." But his home became holy again.

Then one day Vanderberg spoke confidently

to the narrator. We dream. We win glory, lose glamour. Don't pity me. Admit your faith in me. Feel, don't frown. You know I did right. I know I troubled your faith in me and your love for me.

His eyes had that certain gleam. A stroke then killed him. We took him to his grave. But "what was yet to live lives yet." What we learned may be hard to express:

> The fight goes on when fields are still,
>   The triumph clings when arms are down;
> The jewels of all coronets
>   Are pebbles of the unseen crown.

Vanderberg's certainties have survived the reproofs of the narrator and his associates. With limited capacity, the man quested alone to find his light. The narrator and others besmirch his name now, but he seems to have won. The narrator wonders whether Vanderberg found "half truth to be passion's thrall" or whether, when he was with the others, "love [was] triumphant." Finally, at any rate, neither "Saint Anthony nor Sainte-Nitouche / Had ever smiled as he did — quite."

Ruth Nivison* says that Robinson is the St. Anthony of the final line. Chard Powers Smith,* also finding autobiographical import in "Saint-Nitouche," wonders whether in the poem "soul music that opens the 'starry way . . .' is . . . a function of passion" in Robinson's view. In a letter (April 1, 1901) to Edith Brower,* Robinson calls this poem a parable; his doing so indicates both that the poem is intended to teach something and that Vanderberg is a seriously religious person. Emery Neff calls attention to Robinson's "apparent reversal of [the Rev. Arthur] Dimmesdale's experience in [Nathaniel] Hawthorne's novel [*The Scarlet Letter*]." (Sources: Brower, 139; Neff, 122; E. Robinson, 13; C. Smith, 190)

"Scattered Lives." This was to be the title of a book of 15 or so prose tales and sketches Robinson wrote and planned to publish but never did. In a letter (April 14, 1895) to Harry de Forest Smith,* Robinson says the book would appear "even though it be printed on toilet paper with a one-hand press." Wallace L. Anderson, after a thorough study of Robinson's pertinent letters, complied a list of the ti-

tles of Robinson's planned but abandoned and presumably destroyed prose sketches: "Marshall," "Three Merry Gentlemen and Their Wives," "Anxious Hendricks," "Lévy Condillac," "Parable and the Pines," "Theodore," "The Black Path," "Lachesis," "Christmas Eve" (later entitled "The Ruins of Bohemia"), "A Recognition," "Saturday" (later entitled "Alcader"), "The Wool-Gatherers," "John Town," "A Little Fool," and "The House Across the Water." Anderson concludes that these 15 "sketches were studies of character and personal relationships drawn from a philosophical and psychological point of view." (Sources: W. Anderson [1947], 501–03; *Untriangulated Stars*, 219)

Schmitt, Howard George (b. 1910). Friend of Robinson. Schmitt graduated from Harvard (1933) and immediately entered its graduate school of business administration.

When Ray M. Verrill, Schmitt's English teacher at Nichols School, Buffalo, New York, took up Robinson's "Sonnet," beginning "Oh for a poet — for a beacon bright" and read it to the class (fall term, 1928), young Schmitt lagged behind to express his delight. Verrill recommended Robinson's *Tristram*, and Schmitt's fascination intensified. He looked up details of Robinson's life. At Verrill's suggestion, the young man sent Robinson a letter expressing his delight in the poet's work and to wish him a happy birthday. Robinson's gracious reply (January 9, 1929) initiated a correspondence ultimately including at least 66 letters, the last of which Robinson wrote from his New York hospital bed and is dated January 22, 1935.

With youthful zeal, Schmitt asked Robinson to sign copies of his books, find rare copies and provide advice about prices, send a photograph, read a juvenile friend's sonnets, sell him the manuscript of "Modred: A Fragment" (the poet accepted at least $50 for it), etc. Robinson, as one would expect, always replied with friendly, sometimes almost apologetic, patience. He agreed to meet Schmitt at the MacDowell Colony* (August 1, 1929), after which his letters to the lad grow longer and even more accommodating. Schmitt must have had access to money, because Robinson offers guarded comments (February 10, 1930) about his paying $350 for a 1902 *Captain Craig* and (October 20, 1930) about getting an 1897 vellum edition of *The Children of the Night* for $260. Robinson evidently saw Schmitt at the MacDowell Colony in later years. Once (September 8, 1932), he wrote to complain that visitors interrupted his work there. Schmitt published a note in *Saturday Review of Literature* (May 22, 1937) about minor changes Robinson made in *Amaranth* for what became the 1937 edition of his *Collected Poems*. (Source: Schmitt)

Schumann, Alanson Tucker (1846–1918). A native of Waldoboro, Maine, Schumann was a homeopathic physician, poet, ladies' man, and alcoholic neighbor of the Robinson family in Gardiner, Maine. Schumann learned some of the technicalities of versification from his high-school teacher, Miss Caroline Davenport Swan. His cousin was Lizzie Austin,* Robinson's high-school algebra teacher. Miss Swan formed the Gardiner Poetry Group and conducted weekly meetings at 57 School Street, the location of the home of her invalid mother, whom she lived with and ministered to. One evening Schumann introduced Robinson, when he was young and lonely, to the group, which also included Judge Henry Sewall Webster, a local poet. They, and especially Schumann, taught Robinson much about the ballade, chant royal, rondel, sonnet, triolette, and villanelle. James L. Tryon* describes Schumann as "the master mind of his [Robinson's] Maine background." Schumann was soon resolutely praising Robinson's poems as better than his own.

Schumann wrote about two thousand poems, mostly sonnets (including sonnets on sonnets, all in the Petrarchan form, a type he idolized and recommended to Robinson). Their mutual friend Richard G. Badger* published Schumann's one book, *The Man and the Rose* (1911). Later, Robinson modified his formerly high opinion of Schumann, as evidenced in a letter (July 31, 1924) he wrote Laura E. Richards.* In it, he defines Schumann as having been a successful and happy "local doctor until poetry got him at about the age

of thirty," after which he declined and would have died in poverty but for the fact that "he married some money." His first house was located at 49 Lincoln Avenue, Gardiner. His larger Gardiner house, financed by his second marriage, was at 136 Maine Street.

Emma Robinson* and Ruth Nivison* say that Dr. Schumann was the inspiration for Robinson's sonnet "Shadrach O'Leary." (See also "The First Seven Years" and "A New England Poet.") Robinson dedicated his "Ballade of Broken Flutes" to Schumann.

Peter Deckert analyzes Robinson's experiments in French poetic genres and concludes that, "considering Schumann's often overfacile handling of them, it is not hard to believe that the French forms finally seemed too frivolous to Robinson, too lightweight to bear the reflective burden that he was now ready to impose on his verse." According to Wallace L. Anderson, most of the letters Robinson wrote to Schumann have never surfaced. (Sources: W. Anderson [1980], 52; Cary [1974], 21; Cary [1975], 189; Deckert, 398; Hagedorn, 34–36; E. Robinson, 15; *Selected Letters*, 138; C. Smith, 84–85; Tryon, 6)

Seltzer, Thomas (1875–1943). Editor and translator. By 1920 Seltzer was sufficiently experienced as an editor in New York, and also as a publishing translator of German, Polish, and Russian literary works, to establish and head his own publishing firm (1920–1926). His first issue was *Parliament and Revolution* (1920) by the British statesman Ramsay MacDonald (1866–1937). Next came Robinson's *Lancelot: A Poem* (1920). Soon following were books by E. E. Cummings, Henry James, D. H. Lawrence, Gilbert Murray, Marcel Proust, and Stefan Zweig, and a few others. After Seltzer ran afoul of the New York Society for the Suppression of Vice (1922), his successful but costly legal defense so crippled his company financially that he sold it to his uncles, publishers Albert Boni and Charles Boni.

"Shadrach O'Leary" (1910). Sonnet. For a time, Shadrach O'Leary poetized about "ladies frail and fair." Because his creations were tricky and popular, he remained indifferent to the fact that they "limped." However, last year the persona talked with O'Leary, learned that he had "Forgotten . . . the ladies and the lyre," and commended him as more respectable for being "A failure spared."

Shadrach of the Bible was also delivered from a destructive position (Daniel 3:26). Emma Robinson* and Ruth Nivison* say that Alanson Tucker Schulmann* inspired "Shadrach O'Leary." Robinson may be punning in it to the effect that the songs Shadrach strummed out of his imagined "lyre" were untruths. (Source: E. Robinson, 15)

"Shandon Bells." Unpublished poem. According to Laura E. Richards,* it is a parody. The "effusion" begins thus: "With deep affliction / And malediction / I often think of those Randolph bells." Richards explains that Randolph was a town across the river from Gardiner, Maine. (Source: Richards [1936], 15)

"The Sheaves" (1923). Sonnet. A vast field of wheat is turning from green to gold. The vision is a combination of "the body and the mind." Its meaning, totally uncommercial, is the more significant "the more it is not told." Unusually beautiful weather climaxes when, on a certain day,

> A thousand golden sheaves were lying there,
> Shining and still, but not for long to stay —
> As if a thousand girls with golden hair
> Might rise from where they slept and go away.

Robinson regarded "The Sheaves" and "Many Are Called" as his two best sonnets. "The Sheaves" seems unique in Robinson's canon. Read aloud, it is almost unbearably moving. Read silently, it seems to be accompanied by quiet and harmonious music. The expected iambic feet are, once in a while, replaced either by spondees or by three unaccented syllables in a row. The effect is alternately invigorating and calming.

"Shiras." Poem. An abandoned work. Robinson drafted a poem he called "Shiras," probably in 1901, wrote (January 18, 1902; c. February 1902) to Laura E. Richards,* first that he liked it, but second that his "own whim" ran away with him in writing it. (Source: *Selected Letters*, 48, 50).

"Shooting Stars" (1896). Poem. When the stars are shining brightly in summer skies, "He sits and waits for shooting stars." Their sliding "across the night / Like arrows from a Titan's bow" causes him to shout with joy, untroubled by any scientific explanations. He may be not very smart, but he is "Released from knowledge and its woe"; so he sits and watches rapturously. Let's not mock or scorn him.

The difficult format of "Shooting Stars" is identical to that of "Ballade of Dead Friends," except that in "Shooting Stars" the *b*-rhymes are not feminine.

Short Stories by Robinson. When in the mid–1890s Robinson despaired of earning a living as a poet, he briefly tried writing short stories. He especially admired the works of François Coppée (1842–1908), notably his *Vingt Conte Nouveaux* (1883) for their compression, and sought to pattern stories of Americans on Coppée's depictions of French life. He occasionally wrote Edith Brower* to praise and recommend Coppée. Some of Robinson's stories, according to Hermann Hagedorn,* were entitled "Barcarolle," "John Town," "Lily Condillac," and "Those Merry Gentlemen and Their Wives." A few of Robinson's friends read and liked them, but no magazine editor did; so Robinson destroyed them all and returned to poetry. (Sources: Brower; Hagedorn, 102)

"Siege Perilous" (1916). Poem. The young man was warned by many people more experienced than he as to the dangers of taking "The fearful seat." He wondered whether he was "mad or right," and whether he was in truth afraid of "God's fury." Then one day a heavenly light fell upon his vision and cancelled all doubts. He won and remained unscorched; further, his winning means that others will also safely win.

The Siege Perilous, that is, the one chair at King Arthur's Round Table, which sat 150 knights in equal positions, was reserved for the knight who would achieve the quest of the Holy Grail. Thus, Robinson's succinct poem implicitly relates to his Arthurian poems — *Merlin*, "Modred," *Lancelot*, and *Tristram*. The form of Robinson's "Siege Perilous" is simpler than its bracing message. It is in five four-line stanzas. Each line is in iambic tetrameter, perhaps less "serious" than pentameter lines. Each stanza carefully rhymes *abab*, with each *b*-rhyme feminine.

"Silver Street" (1924). Sonnet. Robinson invites the reader to stand with him here on Silver Street and fancy "Where Shakespeare was a lodger for Mountjoy [*sic*]." It was here that Shakespeare created a world, called it his toy, and peopled it with "king, wizard, sage and clown, / Queen, fiend, and trollop." In the process he troubled "friends and [those with] envy" alike. Standing in a graveyard, he wondered what it all could mean. We may do so as well. In any event, "One has to walk up Wood Street and Cheapside."

When Robinson was in London (spring 1923), he visited the cemetery at the corner of Silver Street and Wood Street. He recalled a passage in *A Life of William Shakespeare* (enl. ed., 1916) by Sir Sidney Lee (1859–1962): "In the year 1604 Shakespeare 'laye in the house' of Christopher Montjoy [*sic*], a Huguenot refugee, who carried on the business of a 'tiremaker' (i.e., maker of ladies' headdresses) in Silver Street, near Wood Street, Cheapside." Robinson regarded the region as uniquely exciting because of its associations with Shakespeare. Robinson wrote (August 9, 1923) to Lewis Montefiore Isaacs,* then in England, about Wood and Silver streets, Cheapside, and Shakespeare there. (Sources: Fussell [1954], 66–67; Hagedorn, 336; *Selected Letters*, 133)

Sinclair, May (1863–1946). British woman of letters. She was born at Rock Ferry, near Liverpool, attended a ladies' college at Cheltenham (1881–1882), published poetry (1887, 1892), moved to London (1897), published her first novel (1897), and then another novel (1898), two novellas (1901), and *The Divine Fire* (1904), an allegorical novel about the development of an idealistic London poet. Sinclair was a pioneer in using Freudian insights and stream-of-consciousness techniques in her fiction. She successfully toured the United States (November 1905–January 1906) to promote *The Divine Fire*. Home again, she wrote more novels, provided introductions to works by Charlotte Brontë, published a book about the Brontë sisters for the Women Writers Suffrage League (1912), and early in the First World War volunteered for work with a British ambulance corps in Belgium (1914). As a founding member (from 1921) of P.E.N.—the International Association of Poets, Playwrights, Editors, Essayists and Novelists, a literary club—she was chosen as a delegate to represent England at the second P.E.N. conference, in New York (1924). Ill health began to overcome her (1929). Sinclair was long regarded as the premier British woman novelist until more innovative fiction beginning in the 1920s made her 24 novels seemingly less appealing.

Long an admirer of Robinson's poetry, Sinclair categorized and praised it, along with poetry by William Vaughn Moody* and Ridgely Torrence,* in an essay entitled "Three American Poets" (*Atlantic Monthly* and *Fortnightly Review*, both September 1906). When she was in New York (1906), she was made welcome in the Judson Hotel, in Washington Square, where she associated with Percy MacKaye,* Moody, Torrence, and several others, including Robinson. Hermann Hagedorn* reports that Robinson became reacquainted with Sinclair and also attended a P.E.N. meeting when he was in London (1923). (Sources: Brower, 182; Hagedorn, 335)

"Sisera" (1932). Narrative in blank verse. It is in 17 stanzas of different lengths.

Barak, an Israelite military leader, has routed Sisera, a Canaanite who serves under King Jabin and commanded the now-slaughtered forces that had held Israel in bondage for 20 years. Sisera leaps from his bouncing chariot like an animal escaping a cage to brief freedom. After three hours of running, Sisera seeks sanctuary with Heber, the neutral Kenite whose gorgeous, hot-blooded wife, Jael, both Jabin and Sisera have found attractive. Sisera carelessly forgot she might be pro-Israel. Falling at her feet, he happens not to see her smile. She reckons that by helping Israel she will be fulfilling Deborah's prophecy. So she bathes Sisera's hot face and closed eyes, while he finds her cool hands and heated breath simply unbelievable. When he opens his eyes, she seems a bit too motherly for comfort.

Jael gets Sisera to talk about battle casualties and survivors, reassuring him all the while that Kenites love peace. He says he wants either to have some drink or to die right here with her. She plies him with a special bowl — the very "milk of life" — to make him sleep ever so soundly. Fearing that "some fiend of Israel" might seek him out, he wants her to inform any pursuers that "No man was here." Crouching and with fierce eyes, she replies that no man here will leave here except as food that scavengers might grab, that no man is here now "who has not seen his last / Of Israel."

As Sisera falls asleep, Jael feels his temple. Gloating further, she pillows his head sideways, finds a hammer and a nail in the dark, crouches again, and pounds the nail through both of his temples. He is reduced to a silent face — all this for Deborah, Barak, and Israel. Deborah will urge Barak to celebrate God in resounding songs.

Leading his men, Barak enters, hot after combat. When Jael announces that Sisera is here, Barak replies that he spotted Sisera running desperately and that she must have promised him what no man could give him. Jael tells Barak about prophetic voices she heard, asks for praise, says she was patient, says the chosen serve the Lord, and shows him her victim. Believing that war is man's work, Barak begins to fear Jael's future boasts and lusts. She explains how she held the nail and God drove the hammer, and asks for Deborah to be summoned as witness of her deed. Jael's cockiness disconcerts Barak, who reminds her that in his opinion it took the Lord "More than six days, I think, to make a woman," mutters thoughtfully that he'll have to rewrite "The book of woman," and then stolidly stands before "what women do" — namely Jael's dead prey. Again, Jael tells Barak to inform Deborah that her "hand was God's that held the nail" and shouts that women as well as children and men can now all sing to peaceful Israel's "King of Glory!"

Robinson's source for "Sisera" is Judges 4:17–22 and 5:24–27. Robinson's rendition is notable for irony and foreshadowing, both devices being handled here with an unusual lack of subtlety, given Robinson's unremitting obscurities elsewhere.

Emery Neff remarks that "[t]he speed and fire of 'Sisera' are in the best tradition of heroic verse." In "Sisera," Robinson shows his agreement with many commentators who feel that Jael by killing Sisera fulfilled Deborah's saying (see Judges 4:4–9) and therefore suppose that Jael was actuated by divine influence. However, this interpretation is without biblical justification. Moreover, Edwin S. Fussell points out that Robinson makes Barak apprehensive of cunning Jael, whereas in the Bible Barak "actually joins with Deborah in an unholy hymn of joy at Sisera's treacherous murder." Nicholas Ayo observes that of Robinson's several poems inspired by his careful reading of the Bible, only "Sisera" and "Young Gideon" make use of Old Testament stories and that in these two poems Robinson displays "fewer signs of an accurate and faithful handling of the Bible." In analyzing "Sisera," however, Ayo notes Robinson's skill in handling geographical and military details, his deepening of Heber's personality, his dramatic treatment of Jael's would-be lovers, his stringing out Jael's talk with Sisera, and his imaginative invention of Jael's inner thoughts and of the voices she says she heard. Most significant is Ayo's contention that in inserting un-biblical qualms in the Old-Testament fierceness of Barak, Robinson makes Barak's ethics dramatically clash with Jael's amorality. (Sources: Ayo, 161, 159–72 passim; Fussell [1954], 168; Neff, 237)

"Slumber Song." Sheet music. Robinson composed the simple melody; Louis V. Ledoux* wrote the words; and Lewis Montefiore Isaacs* prepared a piano accompaniment. One issue of a hundred copies was printed on vellum offset; the trade edition, on ordinary paper. (Source: Collamore, 59–60)

Smith, Chard Powers (1894–1977). Writer. Smith was born in Watertown, New York, the son of a prominent attorney and New York Supreme Court judge. After earning a B.A. at Yale (1916), Smith served in the

U.S. Army (1917–1920, finally as an artillery captain). He received an LL.B. at Harvard (1921) and, much later, an M.A. at Columbia (1949). He married Olivia Carey Macdonald (1921; she died without issue when they were in Italy in 1924). He married Marion Antoinette Chester (they had two children, then divorced in 1957). He married Eunice Waters Clark (they had no children). Smith practiced law intermittently (1921–1947), but his heart was in writing, poetry at first. Of his four books of verse (1925–1936), his best perhaps is *Hamilton: A Poetic Drama* (1930). Novels followed, the best being historical reconstructions. In his ambitious *Pattern and Variation in Poetry* (1932), he attempts to reduce upwards of 2,000 poems to subject-and-style formulas. Smith was a lecturer at Northwestern University (1937) and at the University of Kansas (1950). His *Yankees and God* (1950) is a history of New England culture from 1600 to 1950.

An endearing work by Smith is *Where the Light Falls: Portrait of Edwin Arlington Robinson* (1965), which he intended to be a memoir long after he was an up-and-coming poet given a summer grant at the MacDowell Colony* (1924) and met Robinson. *Where the Light Falls* is composed of biographical insights frequently based on material not then published, on repeated attempts to get at Robinson's inchoate "philosophy," and on offputting commentaries concerning Robinson's life-long, never-requited love for his sister-in-law Emma Robinson.* It is reasonable to conclude that Smith wore blinders when he read Robinson's poems featuring two men and a woman and thus missed their beautifully wider, non-autobiographical contents. (Source: C. Smith)

Smith, Harry de Forest (1869–1943). Educator. Smith, born in Gardiner, Maine, obtained a B.A. at Bowdoin College (1891) and an M.A. at Harvard (1896). He married Adela Hill Wood (1895). They traveled in Europe, and he studied at the University of Berlin (1896–1897). When they returned to the United States, Smith taught school briefly in Massachusetts, wrote an essay on Homeric poetry (April 1901, evidently unpublished), and became a professor of Greek at Amherst,

where he taught the Greek language, Greek literature, art, and history, and philosophy (1901–1939). He was also director of libraries and helped improve its collections and physical plant (1934–1939). He was more devoted to his students than to pursuing scholarly renown. His wife and their daughter Barbara survived him.

Robinson first became friendly with Smith when the two shared a common love for Latin in high school. Robinson also admired Smith's parents, who had a farm on the Old Brunswick Road outside Gardiner. During Smith's summer vacations from Bowdoin, the two young men often met, incessantly smoked, ate apples, read, and talked together. When apart, they corresponded regularly. In one early letter (May 21, 1891), Robinson included a draft of what became "Horace to Leuconoë." In addition to other bits of verse, Robinson sent the draft of what became "Supremacy" (on October 1, 1893). By letter (February 4, 1894) Robinson broached the idea of what became their abortive collaboration on a translation of Sophocles's *Antigone*. What he wanted was for Smith to send him installments of a careful prose translation, which he would turn into unrhymed, sonorous, picturesque poetry. In a letter (March 11, 1894) he said he would try to put the play into "regular English heroic verse," with the chorus in "irregular ode" form. Thereafter he sent more renditions, ending with one batch of dozens of lines (November 11, 1894). Meanwhile, Smith got married (June 19, 1895), and Robinson commemorated the event in his lugubrious sonnet, "On the Night of a Friend's Wedding." He reported that the remainder of his work on *Antigone* would be "plain sailing" (October 6, 1895). He wrote of trying "the new version" (September 27, 1896). After sending Smith a letter (April 24, 1897) to the effect that he must finish the work, nothing further came of this ambitious, time-consuming project. Smith published an erudite, unsigned review (*The Nation* 68 [June 22, 1899]) of *Odysseus als Afrikaumsegler und Amerikaentdecker* (1898; Odysseus Sailed Around Africa and Discovered America). The 72-page monograph was by an author using the pen name "Eumaios." Smith calls it a "travesty" compared to "soberer works of learning."

Denham Sutcliffe carefully edited, annotated, and indexed many of Robinson's delightful and often revealing letters to Smith from 1890 through 1900, and one dated 1905. However, Sutcliffe was not permitted to publish all of the Robinson-to-Smith letters. Wallace L. Anderson reports that eight 1892 letters, in which Robinson provides details of some of his racy late-night off-campus capers, as well as many post–1905 letters, were omitted from Sutcliffe's edition.

In his biography of Robinson, Chard Powers Smith* uses the letters and many other sources of information to provide a running commentary on the unwavering affection Robinson had for Harry Smith. For example, Chard Smith quotes most of Robinson's letter of May 20, 1894, which tells "much of the inner Robinson in his outward relations." In it, Smith continues, Robinson expresses pleasure at receiving word of Smith's engagement; says that his view of his own prospects is melancholy, doubts that Smith will ever become wealthy or esteemed by the public, but expects him to achieve "an eminently respectable place as an intellectual American citizen"; fears that memories of the two friends' boyhood together will now seem childish; and closes by saying that he won't attend Smith's wedding ceremony. The two men remained friends until Robinson's death. (Sources: W. Anderson [1980], 54; C. Smith, 138 and passim; *Untriangulated Stars*, 19–20, 109, 125, 140, 232, 255; Weeks [1984])

"A Song at Shannon's" (1919). Sonnet. After a strong but sad and careless "night-bird" delivered a monotonous "old song" at Shannon's well-lighted place, two friends who heard it left, separated, and proceeded into considerable darkness. Each took regret and ignorance with him. Robinson equates light with intelligence here, or at least information, and darkness with ignorance, if not evil.

A simple interpretation of this puzzling poem is that a careless person sang or simply said something which caused two friends to disagree irreconcilably. Robinson frequented saloons in Lower Manhattan at the time he probably wrote this poem and could easily have observed how a comment or a ditty could trigger a dispute between otherwise friendly drunks.

"Sonnet" ("Oh for a poet — for a beacon bright") (1894). Sonnet. Robinson calls for illumination from a poet to split "this changeless glimmer of dead gray"; to bring "back the Muses"; to light up Parnassus; to scare away petty, mechanical versifiers whose works peter out fast. Why is our age so "barren"? We have the same ingredients — "men," "women," "flowers," "seasons," "sunset[s]." Can't a single poet "wrench one banner from the western skies, / And mark it with his name forevermore?"

Edwin S. Fussell notes that when Robinson included this sonnet in *The Torrent and The Night Before*, he changed "Shall not one bard arise" to "Shall there not one arise," and "as of yore" to "as before." In doing so, Fussell feels, Robinson avoided banal and stilted phrasing.

Innumerable literary critics have lamented that the period roughly from 1890 to 1910, often labeled "the twilight interval," was bereft of major poets. Robinson was one of the first poets to appeal for more vigorous and creative efforts by fellow practitioners. (Source: Fussell [1954], 185)

"Sonnet" ("The master and the slave go hand in hand") (1896). Sonnet. Masters and slaves are hand in hand, though without feeling the touch. Kings sometimes envy scullions' joys. But unless "the sonnet-slave . . . understand[s] / The mission of his bondage," he will die without finding "The perfect word, that is the poet's wand." In a sonnet, which is a veritable crown, "the rhymes / Are for Thought's purest gold the jewel-stones." Yet forms and sounds never quite realized by the poet will tease him, causing regrets and longings, and he will hear "The crash of battles that are never won."

"Sonnet" ("When we can all so excellently give") (1896). Sonnet. We prove that we lack "love's wisdom" by giving and taking blows. We can't see "God's . . . light superlative" in the "elemental over-glow" of love. We ought to see in everything "God ever made that grows"— branches, birds, children, roses, etc.— "The glory of eternal partnership."

This sonnet is indicative of Robinson's early admiration for the transcendental thoughts of Ralph Waldo Emerson. Chard Powers Smith* suggests that the "elemental over-glow" may have emanated from Emma Robinson,* Robinson's sister-in-law, or perhaps from Mabel Moore, a girl Robinson knew in high school. (Source: C. Smith, 396)

Sonnets, 1889–1927 (New York: Crosby Gaige, 1928). Collection of sonnets. It was first issued supposedly in 561 numbered copies, after which came a trade edition. According to Bacon Collamore,* Robinson fumed at the printers' dishonest practice of profitably running more copies than were acknowledged in colophon descriptions; so he wrote at least three times to James R. Wells (1928–1930), a business associate of Crosby Gaige, to complain — and with markedly decreasing tact. (Source: Collamore, 46–48)

"Souvenir" (1918). Sonnet. The persona remembers a certain old house that he knew about when he was young. He recalls details: a window, flowers, a bat, and "moths and mysteries." He also remembers that inside the place "were dim presences / Of days that hovered and of years gone by." When all is silent, a "faded noise" emerges — "the voice / Of one whose occupation was to die."

Sparhawk-Jones, Elizabeth (1885–1951). Artist. Born in Baltimore, she studied painting at the Philadelphia Academy of the Fine Arts. She exhibited her works, which often won prizes, in Philadelphia, Washington, D.C., New York, and elsewhere. The Art Institute of Chicago has some of her paintings, inclcuding her popular "Shop Girls."

Elizabeth Sparhawk-Jones admired Robinson immoderately. She contended that in some ways she was a model for Isolt of the white hands in Robinson's *Tristram*. When Robinson was dying in the hospital in New York, she visited him and told him frankly — and to his wan amazement — that she had always loved him. After his death she painted pictures that depict aspects of his evolving career. (Source: C. Smith, 53, 366)

"The Spirit Speaking" (1929). Poem. It is parenthetically entitled "Christmas, 1929." In worshipping the letter of the law, which is "A grief and a malevolence," you go on and on, ever failing to know the true God. In the process, you have created a God that "mock[s] . . . you from the sky." Once a year (at Christmas time), you who regularly think you are high and mighty suspect you aren't.

This bitter, accusatory poem is in disarmingly sing-song, galloping-fourteener ballad form, in four six-line stanzas, mostly rhyming *abcbdb*.

"Stafford's Cabin" (1916). Poem. Forty years ago, old Archibald told the narrator that 50 years before that a certain event occasioned "a legend" about Stafford's cabin. One night Archibald and some others heard "a master shriek" and then saw a fire. All they could find in the morning was an iron bar and something bound up with chains, which they buried. They found no evidence in the ashes concerning "who or what had been with Stafford there." Archibald added that Stafford lived alone, wasn't liked, and caused people to look at their shoes when "he asked you for the news." The narrator remembers Stafford's apple tree, which Archibald said was the only witness to whatever happened at the cabin, visits the site of the incident, and finds it "overgrown with golden-rod as if there were no ghost."

Emma Robinson* and Ruth Nivison* identify the basis of "Stafford's Cabin" as a legend told to Robinson by Kingsbury Palmer, his uncle, at Whitefield, Massachusetts. The poem has seven stanzas. Each stanza has four seven-beat iambic or trochaic lines, rhyming *aabb*. Ellsworth Barnard finds this form, "abstractedly considered, to be singularly unsuited to . . . the bloodshot flame" in the poem. But surely Robinson's conscious purpose is to mismatch form and content for gruesome irony. Yvor Winters regards the poem as Kiplingesque. Emery Neff sees it as an "outline . . . [of] a melodramatic mystery on the order of 'Avon's Harvest,'" which was published five years later. (Sources: Barnard, 70; Neff, 178; E. Robinson, 3; Winters, 22)

Stedman, Edmund Clarence (1833–1908). Man of letters and stockbroker. He was born in Hartford, Connecticut, attended Yale (1849–1851), edited the Norwich *Tribune* (1852–1853), married Laura Hyde Woodworth (1853; they had two sons), and held a variety of jobs. He published *Poems, Lyrical and Idyllic* and became an editor of the New York *Evening World* (1860). During the Civil War years, Stedman was a clerk, a banker, and then a stockbroker. Thereafter, he combined two careers — as a successful Wall Street broker, and as a poet, editor, anthologist, critic, and mentor of young writers. He celebrated the start of his dual career in his poem "Pan in Wall Street" (1867). *A Library of American Literature* (11 vols., 1888–1890), which he coedited with Ellen Mackay Hutchinson, and his *An American Anthology, 1787–1900 . . .* (1900) combine to demonstrate that by 1900 America could boast a splendid literature. Ellen Hutchinson, literary editor of the *New York Tribune*, married Royal Cortissoz (1869–1948), the eminent art critic, in 1897. In *The Nature and Elements of Poetry* (1892), Stedman formulates his decorous aesthetic principles. Though conservative, he helped further the careers of many more forward-looking writers, including Percy MacKaye,* Harriet Monroe,* William Vaughn Moody,* Ridgely Torrence,* and Robinson.

Stedman was the first editor to publish poems by Robinson in an anthology (1900) and did so at the urging of Laura E. Richards.* For his *American Anthology* he chose "The Ballade of Dead Friends," "The Clerks," "The House on the Hill," "Luke Havergal," and "The Pity of the Leaves." The indefatigable Stedman found room for samples of 570 other American poets in this anthology. Through the publisher Richard G. Badger,* Stedman obtained Robinson's address in New York City, visited him, and invited him to his Bronxville home, along with Torrence, whom Robinson met there (1900) during the first of several times he accepted the Stedmans' hos-

pitality. When Stedman introduced the two poets, he (in)famously punned thus: "Torrence — and The Night Before." Stedman recommended Robinson as a possible freelance editorial columnist to several newspapers, including the *New York Evening Post* and the *New York Daily Tribune*. Robinson did publish his one and only such piece, titled "The Balm of Custom," in the *Tribune* (October 7, 1900). Stedman gave Robinson money when he was in bad shape (1902). Carlos Baker summarizes Robinson's attitude toward and friendship with Stedman. Robert J. Scholnick explains the friendship Robinson enjoyed with not only Laura Richards but also Stedman. (Sources: Baker, 333; Cary [1974], 162, 163; Hagedorn, 163–64, 172–73, 193; Scholnick; Williams)

Stickney, Trumbull (1874–1904). Joseph Trumbull Stickney, classical scholar and poet, was born near Geneva, Switzerland. His Harvard-trained father taught classics at Trinity College, in Hartford, Connecticut, but on inherited wealth frequently traveled in Europe (to 1885). After attending a boarding school in England (1886), young Joseph rejoined the family, then studied the classics at Harvard and graduated (1895). During a long European residence (1895–1903), mostly in Paris, Stickney wrote essays, poetry, reviews, and translations; enjoyed many friendships with fellow American expatriates, including the versatile man of letters Henry Adams (1838–1918) and the sculptor Augustus Saint-Gaudens (1848–1907); and earned the first *Doctarat ès Lettres* at the Sorbonne (1903) ever awarded an American student. His thesis title was *Les Sentences dans la Poésie Grècque*. Stickney returned to America, taught Greek at Harvard (1903–1904), tried to write and translate further, but died of a brain tumor.

When Stickney first attended Harvard, he made friends with Robert Morss Lovett,* William Vaughn Moody,* and Robinson, among many others. Stickney wrote a splendid short review of Robinson's *Captain Craig* (*Harvard Monthly*, December 1903), in which he praises Robinson's "plain Saxon" diction and "smooth versification." Moody, and also George Cabot Lodge and John Lodge, sons of the distinguished American political leader Henry Cabot Lodge (1850–1924), collected and published *The Poems of Trumbull Stickney* (1906). (Source: Cary [1974], 156)

"The Story of the Ashes and the Flame" (1897). Sonnet. Wherever she happened to be, regardless of the reason, that "was her place" in his view, and regardless of any gossip that swirled around her. He loved that woman, whether she was faithful or otherwise. Oh, yes, "The story was as old as human shame." But after "that lonely night" when she ran away, books only blinded him, because in them he read nothing but "The story of the ashes and the flame." In that old story, she was always about to return to him again, to deceive him again, with "penitent sad eyes" full of the sort of laughing moonlight that has always puzzled lovers. During such readings, he would momentarily remember once again those kisses of hers that "were the keys to Paradise."

Chard Powers Smith* says that this early poem, according to the Robinson family legend, supposedly "records" the "wiles" of Emma Robinson* in the late 1890s to hold her husband Herman Robinson,* the poet's brother, even as her affection was "cooling." More objectively, Ellsworth Barnard and Wallace L. Anderson place this poem alongside others by Robinson that treat similar subjects objectively. Barnard notes that several such poems deal with "the loneliness [that] springs from some discord between the characters," while Anderson locates this early poem among "a gallery of portraits, not lush with color, but chiaroscuros, vignettes of light and shade, or incisive delineations in dry point." (Sources: W. Anderson [1968], 79; Barnard, 136–37; C. Smith, 170)

Suicide, Robinson and. Robinson's father Edward Robinson* toward the end drank so carelessly that he perhaps deliberately hastened his death. Robinson's brother Dean Robinson* committed suicide. Robinson's niece, Marie Louise Robinson,* committed suicide only three years after his death. No fewer than 13 characters in Robinson's poetry commit suicide. They are Atlas and Pink (in *Amaranth*), Richard Cory ("Richard Cory"), Gabrielle (*Roman Bartholow*), Garth and Natalie (*Matthias at the Door*), Honoria (*King Jasper*), Lorraine ("The Growth of 'Lorraine'"), the miller and his wife ("The Mill"), Nightingale (*The Glory of the Nightingales*), and two unnamed men ("Bon Voyage," "The Whip"). Further, Luke Havergal ("Luke Havergal"), and possibly his unnamed "she," may well add to the total. In addition, Rachel Brewster takes poison in *The Porcupine*.

In a letter (June 23, 1921) Robinson wrote to a friend named Arthur Davison Ficke, he comments thus after hearing that a mutual acquaintance may have killed himself: "A suicide signifies discouragement or despair — either of which is, or should be, too far beyond the scope of our poor piddling human censure to require of our ignorance anything less kind than silence." There must have been times in Robinson's initially frustrating career, as well as when he was suffering first from inner-ear damage and finally from stomach cancer, when he thought he might his own quietus make and see whether after "the darkness comes the Light."

Ellsworth Barnard believes that Robinson "looked upon Christian dogmas, including the proscription of suicide . . . , as man-made and not God-inspired." Harry R. Garvin remarks that "[i]n his poetry, Robinson is never bitter toward suicides, even when a character is morally worse than Richard Cory; for example, in 'The Whip,' 'The Mill,' 'The Growth of Lorraine,' 'Bon Voyage,' *Roman Bartholow*, *Matthias at the Door*, *Amaranth*, and *King Jasper*." Rollo Walter Brown* says that Robinson regarded suicide as often unjustifiable if, for example, one lost money in the stock market, but sometimes perhaps justifiable, for example, if one had an incurable disease and knew it. In an essay on Richard Cory's suicide, Jerome Kavka concludes that Robinson, aware of personal flaws owing to narcissitic tendencies, may well have avoided suicide, unlike his self-destructive brothers Dean Robinson* and Herman Robinson,* because of "his capacity to transform his own feelings of specialness into the creative arena where he became enormously useful to others." (Sources: Barnard, 180; R. Brown, 94; Garvin, 319; Kavka, 159)

Sumichrast, Fréderic César De. From Canada, he was a professor of French at Harvard. Sumichrast, whom Robinson in a letter (September 13, 1891) to Harry de Forest Smith* dubbed "His erudition," was assigned to be Robinson's advisor when Robinson entered as a special student at Harvard. During his first term, Robinson took a French course with Sumichrast, whose wife invited Robinson to their home for evening gatherings with other students. He accepted a few times, was shy and felt uncomfortable, and declined later invitations. At one such gathering, he met James L. Tryon,* who became a good friend. (Sources: Hagedorn, 79; Tryon; *Untriangulated Stars*, 23–24, 34, 42, 319)

"The Sunken Crown" (1909). Sonnet. The persona tersely advises his associates to permit a certain foolish, self-deluded fellow, who is indifferent to their smiles and frowns alike, to go ahead and go down where others have perished, and to let him sink or swim. Let him "plunge . . . for the sunken crown," while they safely "wait for what the plunge may show." The fellow is a fool, a Narcissus playing "truant . . . out of school," a "jest of Ascalon." If he should now be wearing that crown of his, it "may cool / His arrogance, and he may sleep again."

Emma Robinson* and Ruth Nivison* contend that "The Sunken Crown" depicts the "plunge" of Robinson's brother Herman Robinson.* Was Herman's plunge that they mention financial or psychological? Whether either, other family members were probably critical, and this criticism may be reflected in the poem.

Readers are welcome to interpret the poem as Robinson's praise for risk-takers. The poet says that the careful ones on shore "are safe enough." Robinson himself was a truant from then-contemporary schools of poetry. The reference to Ascalon is interesting. Herodotus, the fifth century B.C. Greek historian, wrote that a peculiar sexual class of Scyths whom he names "Enarëes" were afflicted with a so-called sacred disease and were lapsing into degeneracy, owing to their having plundered the shrine of the goddess of Ascalon and thus

having incurred her wrath. Ascalon is mentioned again in *Roman Bartholow* (part V). Robinson may have regarded the narcissistic as degenerate; however, the supposedly condemnatory fulminations of his persona here may be ironic. Emery Neff thought so when he called "The Sunken Crown" a "fine ironic sonnet . . . [which] scorns the world's scorn for the idealist who risks all." (Sources: Neff, 154; E. Robinson, 15)

"Supremacy" (1892). Sonnet. The persona describes "a drear and lonely tract of hell" where he has seen shadowy persons whom he "had slandered" by calling them "churls and sluggards." But after they had vanished, God-given daylight burst in and ended his "dream of . . . glory," and he "heard the dead men singing in the sun."

In a letter (October 1, 1893) to Harry de Forest Smith,* Robinson says that this poem and others he had been writing "must be taken as rather vague generalities: they will not bear, and I never intended them to bear, any definite analysis. To me they suggest a single and quite clear thought."

Readers may be excused if they ignore this once-secret admonition of Robinson's. If the persona in "Supremacy" reflects his personal attitude toward others, Robinson is here rebuking himself for shortsighted and hasty criticism. However, he may be having the persona speak for those people in Gardiner and at Harvard who have been misjudging him along with other persons conventionally regarded as lazy misfits. Hermann Hagedorn,* espousing this interpretation, comments that Robinson's Gardiner neighbors might once have been calling the seemingly lazy would-be poet their linguistic equivalent of churl and sluggard. Agreeing but becoming specific, Emery Neff points out that in "Supremacy," first published in the *Harvard Advocate* (June 16, 1892), Robinson may be beseeching his parents not to misjudge his behavior; Neff adds, sadly, that Robinson "was still far from justifying his way of life to his father," since that man died a month after the poem appeared. Lawrance Thompson suggests that the poem may fittingly summarize many of

Robinson's later Tilbury Town poems that consider "the difference between material failure and spiritual failure; the difference between apparent spiritual failure and actual spiritual triumph." (Sources: Hagedorn, 82; Neff, 33; L. Thompson, 140; *Untriangulated Stars*, 109)

Swanton, Mary (1841–1923). (Full name: Mary Olivia Worcester Swanton.) Mary was a Gardiner neighbor, living at 1 Kingsbury Street, near the Kennebec River. She was the daughter of Henry Aiken Worcester and of Olive Gay Worcester. Olive was a member of a Gardiner Swedenborgian family. Mary followed her mother's religion. She married Walter Scott Swanton (1838–1872). He was born in Bath, Maine, went with Mary to St. Joseph, Missouri, to try to establish a newspaper there, but soon died of typhoid fever, leaving two sons, Walter Irving Swanton (1869–1943) and Henry Aiken Swanton (1870–1944). Mary returned with them to Gardiner and gave birth to a third son, John Reed Swanton (1873–1958). He became a well-known ethnologist affiliated with the Smithsonian Institution.

Robinson shyly relished the hospitality accorded him by Mrs. Swanton and her sons in their home. They made candy, played cards, and read together. Robinson happily remembered playing and swimming in the river with a gang of boys that included the three Swanton boys, Harry Morrell, the son of Mary Morrell,* and a few others. Nor, however, could he forget the Swanton boys' Aunt Dorcas, who was generally confined to an upstairs room and into whose scary presence he could not then be lured. Eventually, the Swanton boys grew up, went off to engineering schools, and pursued their separate lives thereafter. (Source: Hagedorn)

"Tact" (1920). Poem. Without too much vanity, the man pays the woman an appropriate regard as he listens to the truths she mentions. She spares him guileful words, which she could easily have spoken but which he, remaining ignorant, would simply have smiled at. Aware that his imagination might lead him to cause an eruption, he stays there for a while.

When they separate, it is with "a merry word," which he believes is

> as light
> As any that was ever heard
> Upon a starry night.

The woman smiles in the sure and certain knowledge that he wouldn't sense "The ruins of a day that fell / Around her in the dark." Nor would he ever fancy that she was scarred when she was left there "Alone below the stars."

Robinson cast "Tact" in galloping fourteeners, that is, in alternate iambic tetrameter and trimeter lines, all combining to comprise three ironically swinging octaves, each rhyming *ababcdcd*. Theodore Maynard,* who knew Robinson slightly, reminisces thus: "I talked to him once about the ambiguities of meaning in the third and fourth lines of his poem 'Tact,'" at which, "'Good Lord!,' he said, 'if people find that obscure, I wonder what they make of some of my other things.'" (The two allegedly puzzling lines, which Maynard quotes, are these: "No vanity could long withhold / Regard that was her due.")

Ellsworth Barnard places "Tact" among Robinson's "frequent portraits of women bruised in spirit by masculine egotism or imperceptiveness." Reversing genders of the ill-suited pair in the poem, Emma Robinson* and Ruth Nivison* curiously contend that in it Robinson was revealing his tact for not saying "I told you so" when long after the death of his brother Herman Robinson* he tried but soon failed to resume a close friendship with Herman's widow, Emma, who, he always felt (and perhaps she did too), should have married him instead of Herman. (Sources: Barnard, 46; Maynard [1924], 158; E. Robinson, 16)

Talifer (New York Macmillan, 1933). Narrative poem. It is in blank verse, in five numbered parts, and dedicated "To the Memory of Gamaliel Bradford[*]."

I. In the "scattered sunlight" of a day in June, red-haired Althea sits in her tree-fringed ancestral home, sad and angry. Her hoped-for pride is falling. Now she is merely "one / Of the Lord's playthings." A certain man (later identified as Samuel Talifer) has just spoken. Like other women ever since Eve, she's going to be gossiped about. Dr. Quick, an old friend, enters. (It is later revealed that he was an orphan, inherited his "sinful" uncle's house and his money, lives nearby, and is back after wandering Reuben-like in Europe.) Quick notices Althea's sadness, asks why she hasn't married Talifer by now and isn't in the Talifer mansion, and says he's heard some town talk. Althea reveals that Talifer has just told her that he has found "Peace" with Karen, their neighbor, who, Quick comments, "Inherited a face and little else / Than a cool brain." Althea says this: Karen has always hated me, but courteously, for having a family tradition; I have been loyal to Talifer; Karen's "waxed language" is harmful; Talifer inspired "truth and wisdom" in me, but he seems to think my head is hollow.

Cautioning patience, Quick says that Talifer has been venomously bitten, although Karen is less like a serpent than a fascinating "ivory fish." Althea says she won't kill herself but asks whether, if her ship is sinking, she should step out and await another. To this, Quick advises her to forget, wait, and learn. He reminds her that she lost something when she abandoned him. When Althea professes ignorance, Quick advises her, his "dearest friend alive," to believe that time, if she's patient, holds something for her that is inexplicable now, and bids her a temporary goodbye.

II. Quick makes his way through an unimproved section to Karen's cottage. That ultracool brunette beauty, with ivory face and passive smile, is reading Greek, her table loaded with classics. He gives her cool cheek a kiss, admits that he has heard about Althea and Karen, calls them a pair of different cats not lapping "from the same saucer," and asks why in God's name she is "disowning and abandoning" her prized freedom. He says she combines "beauty and brains" but maybe also a little more. She laughs. He tells her he has a place in Wales she could live in and read a lot, and asks why she's breaking his heart. She says a good reason is approaching.

They hear the "velvet crunch" of Talifer's car coming near. Karen says she'll be jealous, because Talifer will look at Quick, not her.

Behold Talifer. He is big, erect, commanding, powerful, showing less of fire than a gleam in his eyes, iron-chinned, and with "a ripe repose" but also "honest warmth" in his voice. He bids a welcome home to Quick. Quick says his wandering days are over, praises Karen, and says Talifer has stolen her illuminating self from the world, leaving only twilight. Beaming, Talifer says he still wonders at his fated good luck, rambles a while about someone in pain, but says he's found "Peace." Quick gently theorizes that whereas Talifer only thought he loved Althea he really loved Karen, found out in time, and is a bit sorry for Karen "down there," lonely, and thinking about Talifer, who smiles and scowls together.

To smooth matters, Quick says that if he were God everyone would be happy and adds that, though only human, he may still do some good. Karen hints that in these times of change, Quick mightn't escape some women, with lighter hair and eyes than hers. Quick contends that fate has guided him to "a grim wall, with a locked entrance." Karen tells Talifer to drive Quick to Talifer's place and mix him a drink — maybe like one given Socrates. The two men leave by car.

Over some refreshing scotch, Talifer rebukes Quick gently, boasts that he has been honorable even while causing "sorrow and pain" elsewhere, says that he passed the manhood test through being taught by Karen, and predicts that Quick will forgive him and wish the happy couple joy. Quick's response: You scarcely saw this place, where you were born, for 10 years, returned two years ago to Althea; she was waiting for you; you would have married her but for Karen, whom you fell for because of her beauty, brains, and "God knows what" else; don't imagine I'll reproach or doubt you; don't mention honor; as for joy, may you find knowledge of it easy when you look back at struggles for it. Quick drinks up. When Talifer asks if Quick has forgotten about Karen, the answer is a sarcastic negative, then a merry laugh.

III. Talifer and Karen got married in August and after a long honeymoon are home again in June, and are arguing — all this according to Quick, now speaking with Althea. He says he hasn't seen the two and hopes they're as unhappy as two spaniels together in the rain, says his prognosis is "not . . . nice," says they're incurably wretched and he's "sinful glad" of it. He rambles on: He should have been a priest to help the wicked; God helps "selfish and infatuated" people like Talifer and Karen, who, lacking self-awareness and being indifferent to time, feel helpless in their prison with "a door / That has no bolt"; Talifer won't forget Althea.

Telling Quick that he talks too much but not frankly, Althea adds that she's sorry for everything imprisoned, including herself, still feels somewhat important, and isn't happy being punished now. Quick: You needn't say anything more, "for the present"; I stress those three words; so be indifferent rather than desperate. Althea: Give me medicine to put my memory to sleep. Quick: I can't; reason can't cure circumstances; so kneel and thank God that "folly . . . / Is not yet absolute"; then sleep. Queried about the word "folly," Quick says his seeing both Talifers yesterday caused it. They agree that one Talifer is enough. Quick laughs at that stale comment by Talifer about finding "Peace" with Karen, puts warm hands on Althea's shoulders, defines Talifer as nicely urbane, lovable, and unenvied while accomplishing nothing, and bids Althea goodbye, "but not forever."

In August, a year after their wedding, Talifer and Karen receive a visit from Quick. Talifer offers "a carved smile on an older face," while Karen, Quick says, resembles a sleepy kitten. He offers her a mouse, that is, a book by Apollonius Rhodius, and requests a drink. Talifer now resembles "a bronze Dante smiling" as he commends Quick for—wonder of wonders—knowing what women want. Countering, Quick says he knows two women who don't want him, despite his obvious virtues, which he amusingly lists. Karen yawns, orders drinks for Talifer and Quick, and goes off for a nap.

The two men talk. Quick recalls their friendship and their earlier quiet frankness, and hints at his present doubts. Desolate and half-angry, Talifer says that Quick, a mere bookworm, can hardly know he has lived 12 monotonous months in, in . . . Quick interrupts by suggesting he means "In an aquar-

ium," and says there are two reasons why Talifer will flop out of it, land safely, and escape, to a place nearby. Dense, Talifer expresses fear that he can't escape from Karen, beautiful, indifferent, reclining like a saint or a child, and that he recently thought of choking her. Quick criticizes his mean, dead uncle; denies that Talifer would ever kill anything, unless maybe a twice-stinging wasp; tells him to drink up and avoid water; and posits that Karen envied Althea, sensed Althea's animosity, therefore went for Talifer. He asks Talifer why has the fellow remained

> in an amatory trance . . . [with]
> A changling epicene anomaly,
> Who sleeps, and finds her catnip in the classics?

He predicts Talifer's "release" soon. Talifer expresses puzzlement, says that he is currently the last of the Talifers, calls Karen sinless, dutifully hears his ancestors' voices, but says that "Time and events" may proceed to silence them.

Quick pours many fingers of whisky for himself, threatens to speak as frankly as his "incisive uncle" ever did, calls Talifer a noble ass foolishly nibbling on dead grass, and orders him to defeat "time and events" and try to find "Peace" elsewhere. Smiling, Talifer says he has been confused for a year and requests his friend's patience.

IV. In September Talifer walks along a familiar path, colored by falling autumn leaves, to an apprehensive Althea. They hold hands. She hopes he and his wife are happy. Talifer observes that her "not ruinously beautiful" face combines "humor, truth, and passion, and . . . love / That outwears time," and also sadness and injury, but no anger. He says that if she honestly hopes he's happy he'll leave at once. She says her reasons are hers privately. He says he was cocky, became a fool, wishes he could return to yesterday, hopes happiness finds her, is glad her eyes are kind and aren't dismissing him, and wants no pity. Althea can't see his hopeful smile, rubs her eyes in fear that he's a spirit, and observes kindness in his once-fierce eyes. He clasps a fallen leaf and asks her to keep it until he returns. She says this: It's my right to keep the leaf even longer, since it came from my tree; your face is merciful looking, unlike last year's; I can't believe you've found "Peace" elsewhere. Talifer again asks the agreeable girl to keep his leaf and, fearful of gossip, departs.

Talifer is joyful as he retraces the familiar but now-changed path to his ancestral, vermilion-ivied home. The place, however, contains the "soul-frozen disillusionment" of a so-called woman "he had bound himself [to] by church and state, / In a blind relapse of pagan turbulence." He finds Karen couched and asleep. He senses Althea beside him. He is doomed unless he makes a target for the town out of his "not yet humiliated name." Some "ancient God" is mocking him by putting in his bed a creature combining a divine "face and form" but also "ice and intellect and indifference." It is foolish for him to remain Karen's "famished prey." Althea is worth more than his legendary family tradition. He wonders aloud why Karen was ever born. Was the cause "God, fate, or nature, or mischance . . . ?"

With hands in air and eyes blazing, Talifer is aghast when Karen suddenly shrieks, jumps to her feet, hands at throat, then sways. Talifer lifts her gently back to the couch, strokes her cold fingers, asks if she could be dreaming that he could hurt her, and says he would never do so. Karen senses truth despite words, evades him, grabs a chair, orders him not to touch her, complains about his eyes, his hands, and his eyes, and cries out that he mustn't look, mustn't speak.

Breaking silence at last, Talifer explains that he had his hands in the air "above . . . your loveliness" when he was calmly speaking; she woke up, and may have heard him. But she must realize this: Our "mishandled" lives together are a comedy; we aren't fools; I'm not mighty, not glorious, not vicious; I don't lie; you may have seen humor in my desperate hands; you are beautiful but "inaccessible and impossible." Karen replies that his eyes spelled death; he mustn't touch her. She cries out for Dr. Quick, runs out of the house like a fox, and heads for town. Talifer, as though held by strong, unseen hands, lacks the will to follow, and even smiles.

While Talifer is thinking of Althea and of her red leaf, and while Quick is reading,

yawning, and thinking he won't leave others any intellectual inheritance, Karen runs past his maid and suddenly stands there before him, pleadingly. Like a child, she embraces him and begs him to take her away from Talifer and Talifer's wild eyes. Unlike a father, Quick begins to dream what loyalty for a year prevented him from envisioning. They hug and have a warm kiss, at which he wonders. Well,

> there she was,
> The loveliest biological achievement
> That his prehensive eyes had yet approved,
> Or that his arms had held.

He seats her down, gives her a drink, asks her to explain, and promises to comment. After she has relayed the details, Quick says that Talifer would seem to be either blessing Karen or bidding her farewell. He wonders if she ever gave herself to her husband, wanted only what Althea desired, and to steal him away used her face, "anatomy," "pied-piper voice," and "quaint learning." Telling Karen that she can't ever return to Talifer now, Quick labels her "a devil" and excuses her misinterpretation of Talifer's hands and eyes by comparing the fellow's actions to that of "a good old dog," which, if she woke him up and saw him close and staring, might have reared on hind legs and barked. Karen agrees she can't go back to Talifer. Quick advises her to regard the Talifer mansion as a burning house to run from, is aware she and Talifer don't "want" each other any more, and tells her he will go explain everything to Talifer, will get her maid there to assemble some of Karen's personal "discreet commodities," and will be back in a matter of minutes.

Karen complains that gossip prevents her remaining in Quick's abode. Agreeing and calling himself her "inveterate slave," he tells her she can soon go to New York, three hours away; expect her things — including her "trinkets," "dictionaries," and library of Greek classics — to be sent after her; board a certain ship; and remember that house of his in Wales he told her about.

V. One Sunday morning two years later, Talifer and Althea, joyfully married and with an ignorantly happy son named Samuel, are joking about how to welcome Quick, their "deliverer," who smashed their "complexities" like an idle clock, and is about to visit them. Althea knots Talifer's cravat until it looks like a dead snake, swings it, and he "watched it as contentedly / As if it had been Karen."

In the afternoon, Althea muses under a tree about her former misery, her present happiness, and her hope that Quick will be pleased to view himself as her savior. Approaching solemnly, Talifer says he has a wormy memory that neither reason nor humor will suppress. In Karen's cottage he told their friend Quick about finding "peace" with Karen. He'd like to forget that memory. Quick aided him for Althea's sake. Her responsive laughter causes Talifer to say she would have been spanked by a Pilgrim ancestor for jibing thus at a man back in those days. Agreeing, she tells Talifer all this: I think that men then were awesomely stern, and that women, more severely devoted, felt "The more they toiled and the less fun they had, / The more God loved them for it"; men chopped trees and moved rocks then; women, for a diversion from housekeeping, bore "twelve to twenty children" then; I wouldn't want to go back to the time of my great-great-grandmother, who died at 90, smiling but sad "to go so soon"; the world is advancing to the point where we'd be "curiosities" soon; when you married me, I was a "proud limpet" and was "clinging to the past"; things changed for the better, and I don't fear your presently domesticated eyes.

Talifer laughs at all this, notes Samuel, Jr.'s "chariot" approaching, says they must make the growing lad work to make the family healthy, feels haunted about Quick's impending visit after two years' absence, and says the fellow will need spirits to pep him up. When a servant wheels the infant in, the happy father, first, watches in wonderment when its confident mother takes up what was and still is a part of herself, and, second, awkwardly taps the mysterious creature's nose.

Quick strides in contentedly, sits, accepts a tall drink from "my children!," commends Talifer's improved face and race-saving baby, and holds up and lectures the face of what he labels "this obscure phenomenon / Of ambulent mortality called man." Quick alludes ver-

bosely to Althea's patience, the omniscience that infants lose as they mature, Talifer's former doomed status, Quick's own generous but unstable genius and his stern uncle, and that curious word "Peace."

Talifer interrupts to say Althea now regards his early unhappiness as "quaint." While her memories make her shake, Quick continues lecturing the baby, more particularly: Your mama is now fulfilling your father's life, despite the brief intervention of a false woman resembling a Lilith or a "Fish-Venus"; your mama would gladly have roasted her; I, your father's "good friend and your mother's faithful slave," was in the town nearby and freed your father from that "learned" fish he had married; I urged your father's fated "Time and Events" to gallop.

Althea tells Quick that since he loves to talk he should keep on. So he tells the baby this: I transported the fishy goddess, together with her toys — books in Greek and Latin — to "a little house / In Wales." What with the nearby musical river, nice trees, and all the books "any normal monster would require / For heavenly bread to feed her and her beauty," you'd think she'd be content. But, no. In October, finding Wales "too chilly and remote," she happily fled to Oxford to accept "A fur-lined assignation with the past." She is harmless there, and yet old scholars might be pursuing her "like dogs" and "forgetting their arthritis." Your father's regular remittances to her constitute "paradise in the bank."

Saying little Samuel has heard plenty, Althea quivers quietly "With a recurrent mirth of reminiscence" that Talifer neither "shared . . . nor indignantly / Reproved." When she takes little Samuel in her arms, Quick warns her that the child may be "a wrathful Julius Caesar" and howl if shaken.

Talifer complacently says that when their baby seems about to cry, he resignedly lets Althea go off, handle matters, then return. He adds that she shouldn't rejoice at his "remorse" but instead, after a few years, become a merciful, sympathetic, obedient, and "agreeable helpmeet." Meanwhile, he must be patient when her memories and fancies go burrowing into the past like a cat in a can of ashes. Althea hands him the boy. He resembles "An insane centipede" but is soon masterfully "compressed" by Talifer, who hears late afternoon bells and smiles. Althea looks at the two men, shakes "Unfeelingly," moans, and chokes on "an accumulation of impressions." Quick laughs. The baby bawls for attention. Smiling again and looking about serenely, Talifer hears only "the mellow bells of peace."

Esther Willard Bates* reports that Robinson was disappointed because readers did not immediately realize that *Talifer* was a "comedy" with "light-hearted ... irony." Although a few critics have called it a comedy, is a disastrous first marriage funny, especially when the wife's motivation is jealousy and a better woman must be patient for a decade and then marry the complacent man? Furthermore, at the end Althea is still so unsure that she moans and chokes. Admittedly, Quick's mercilessly protracted asseverations are occasionally comic.

Yvor Winters seems correct when he defines *Talifer* as "dull," Talifer as "noble and fatuous," and Karen as "impossibly vain and learned"; however, where is the evidence that Karen and Quick ever got married, as Winters asserts? Ellsworth Barnard complains that the story line in *Talifer* has "gaps that the reader ... will find hard to bridge." Louis Coxe believes that *Talifer* "may be the very worst poem he [Robinson] ever wrote." Richard Crowder (1960) gently takes to task a few adverse critics of *Talifer* who cast doubt on the value of the poem, and then illuminates it by demonstrating the "allegorical link between the names of the characters and their functions, the relationship of the times of year to the plot, and, especially, the prevalence and import of certain recurring images." Crowder notes that Talifer regards himself as "a man of iron," that Karen is "'pure'— that is, virtually monstrous — intellect," Althea is "healer," and Quick is "life." Crowder relates to the action the implications of Robinson's setting of events specifically in June, August, and September, and he discusses the import of imagery based on "faith and belief," "light and fire," "pain, drowning, and stealing," and, best of all, trees. In an essay concentrating on Samuel Talifer, Crowder (1962) interprets the narrative as an allegory concerning "the eternally haunting problem of error, consequence, and recovery," in which "Talifer, as a human being, meets and succumbs to the blandishments of the Devil, represented by seductive but fruitless Karen. . . . He is subsequently restored to the healthful, the righteous, and the good, as embodied in Althea, through the wisdom, counsel, and action of a savior, Dr. Quick." Minor allegorical assignments, Crowder notes, feature the name Manfred (from the German Manifred, man of peace), the Hebrew name Micajah (who is like under God?), and Samuel Jr. (heard of God, or name of God) — all of whom are mentioned by the learned Quick.

Robinson, who capitalizes carefully, distinguishes between "Peace" and "peace" in *Talifer*. (Sources: Barnard, 82; Bates, 21; Coxe, 148; Crowder [1960], 242, 243, 244; Crowder [1962], 56, 54; Winters, 119)

"Tasker Norcross" (1920). Dramatic duologue and monologue, in blank verse. The narrator remembers talking, but mostly listening, to Ferguson, who began once by saying that "There were three kinds of men where I was born: / The good, the not so good, and Tasker Norcross." When he hinted that only two kinds remain, the narrator assumed that Tasker was dead — to which assumption Ferguson, who since has died, "Agreed indifferently" but then added that most of his "friends are dead." (This puzzling introduction to the poem makes sense only later, when the reader tardily realizes that Ferguson is describing himself when he discusses someone he calls "Tasker Norcross.")

The narrator persuades Ferguson to continue talking by calling himself a friend. Ferguson expresses a doubt that the narrator will understand but says that the narrator probably is patient to hear about such horrors because they relate to "the slow tragedies of haunted men." When encouraged, he continues. Most of us laugh before we understand, and, because we don't know, we believe in God, and only God knows why Norcross knew too much.

Ferguson's monologue proceeds. He invites the narrator to visualize an ancient house filled with ghosts of ancestors dying honorably, for the most part. Word of such honor passes on down through friends. But, lacking friends, genius, madness, or faith, a person often lives longer than he would like. Imagine a person, he asks, "as a more or less remembered phantom"; would he be thought of much, by anyone, on any given day? When this elicits no reply, Ferguson says he had to use "the personal hook" to get his auditor to pay attention to his "undramatic narrative."

The narrator turns sarcastic and says that upon hearing nothing he doesn't need to say anything. This makes Ferguson's formerly glittering eyes smoulder with a "lonely fire" that neither kindness nor lies could extinguish. Nor would the narrator, remembering dead Ferguson, have pleased him any by mourning him or wishing him to "tread again with an aim / The road that was behind him"—because he lacked his stated requirement of faith, friend, genius, or madness.

After considerable silence, Ferguson says that they shouldn't talk precisely and, further, that he's "incorrigible." He invites the narrator to visualize Norcross's house again: white, square, "chillier than a tomb / To look at or live in"—near trees, a road, a railroad, a river, and hills with more trees. The place would stare through the trees like a pale prisoner through bars. Passersby would say they know him but remember nothing either good or interestingly evil about him. They might say roughly the same about a cat, except that a "cat might have a personality" of the sort God didn't give Norcross. Ferguson confesses that he discovered this missing component in Norcross and adds that God has created many such human zeroes. However,

> Blessed are they
> That see themselves for what they never were
> Or were to be.

When the narrator asks him to focus on Norcross, Ferguson sighs and complains. But then he says that when he found and began to know about Norcross in his very house, he was indifferent, "no better." Yet "'Worse' were not quite the word." He was simply "not anything," was like a worm so dusty that birds would avoid him before breakfast. When the narrator says that it was thus, worm-like, that

Norcross gained "Salvation," Ferguson replies that the worm might do so but that Norcross was a vacuum "in the air" and unable to be filled. The narrator recalls that Norcross died facing a uniquely horrible hell.

Next, the narrator smiles. Ferguson limns details of Norcross's house for him. In that plain box, the man was miserably, tragically conscious of being trapped like a rat. If he hadn't known his fate and had therefore been able to act differently, people might have blessed him, envied him, and honored him when he died. Yes, the generous man had more gold than he needed, but "what he gave said nothing of who gave it." Ferguson challenges the narrator to find a book in Norcross's house worth reading or a picture of any interest. The man cared nothing for music or statues. Art works were alive, unlike him; he knew it. No poet could escape "his tethered range, [which] / Was only a small desert." Art-inspired light that helps others he regarded as "nonsense" in a world best filled only with mortality. "'Art,' he would have said, / 'Is not life, and must therefore be a lie.'" He heard about the Greeks and also about his soul, but shrugged all off. Faith and philosophy he imaged as postwar starving orphans forlornly eating scraps. He saw stars but not "beyond them," heard speech but not silence, tasted food but not "the Bread of Life."

At this point, the narrator recalls he admitted to Ferguson that he was beginning to see but then decided to say nothing. Time caught up with Ferguson, whose death made little news and caused no tears; among female mourners, none mourned for love and none were lovely.

Years later the narrator was traveling and detoured to Ferguson's birthplace. A citizen gladly took the narrator "to his house"—among trees, near a railroad and a river, boxlike, chilly—like a description he had heard. The citizen said that after Ferguson died, he bought the house at auction and was cold in it ever since. Asked if he knew Ferguson, the man said yes, for 20 years, but only the way one would know a tree. Maybe he "held himself / A little high when he was here." Although that citizen, and others too, "remembered Ferguson, / . . . none of them had heard of Tasker Norcross."

In the poem "Tasker Norcross," the name "Tasker" probably derives from the middle name of J. Dana Tasker (1903–1975). Tasker, a Gardiner schoolboy helped by Laura E. Richards,* held editorial posts with the Paris *Times* and *Reader's Digest* before joining *Time* magazine (1937).

Few critics have adequately discussed "Tasker Norcross," which is one of Robinson's most difficult poems. Emery Neff dismisses it as "the portrait of a materialist who suffers from vague awareness of what he is losing from insensitivity to the arts." Wallace L. Anderson, similarly reductive, says this of poem and poet: "In 'Tasker Norcross,' his 'nonentity poem,' he drew a picture of the barren life of a man without faith or philosophy." Ellsworth Barnard places Tasker with other Robinsonian characters as "melancholy examples of what lives are like to which is denied a commanding and fortifying purpose." Charles Cestre* points out similarities in Tasker Norcross and Gervayse Hastings in "The Christmas Banquet" by Nathaniel Hawthorne. Edwin S. Fussell builds on Cestre's observation by noting that Hastings and Norcross both exemplify "the theme of 'death in life.'" (Sources: W. Anderson [1968], 97; Barnard, 236; Cestre, 126; Erskine; Fussell [1954], 41; Neff, 200)

"The Tavern" (1897). Sonnet. When the persona passes the old tavern and looks at weeds and grass around it, and at its torn curtains and broken windows, he is frightened and seems to see the ghost of the old host there. He was Ham Amory, and he was murdered. No one has details of the Tavern's story. The persona and his friends know only that years ago late one night "A stranger galloped up from Tilbury Town" and almost knocked down "That skirt-crazed reprobate, John Evereldown." (See "John Evereldown.")

Emma Robinson* and Ruth Nivison* not only identify the original tavern on which the tavern in the poem is based as Kennebec House, opposite Gardiner's freight house, but also add that Sam Lane, the host there, once entertained President Ulysses S. Grant. (See also "My Methods and Meanings.") (Source: E. Robinson, 11)

The Tavern and the Night Before *see* ***The Torrent and the Night Before***

"Tavern Songs: Chorus" (1894). Poem. The poet reports (three times in this four-line poem) that there is a town by the river, and adds that the river is near the sea. In a letter (October 7, 1894) to Harry de Forest Smith,* Robinson sent this ditty and indicated that he planned to write some tavern songs having special musicality. "Edward Alphabet," "John Evereldown," and "Luke Havergal" may have been part of the plan. (Sources: Cary [1975], 18, 173–74; *Untriangulated Stars*, 170)

"Thalia" (1890). Sonnet. Thalia, the Greek Muse of comedy and pastoral poetry, combines with Morocco and mimicry to mix up something diaphanous that God never intended to create either for "Himself" or for us. Meanwhile, Pollio (Gaius Asinius), the Roman orator and poet, dances with Terpsichore, the Greek Muse of dancing and choral song, while Midas ignorantly wiggles in the nearby mud. We know neither what we'll be like when dead nor what we are while living. "Sorrow's mercenary laugh" links up with credible untruths. But who lives who can "write man's epitaph?"

Richard Cary reports that "Thalia" is Robinson's first published poem and appeared on March 29, 1890, in *The Reporter Monthly* (a literary supplement of the *Kennebec Reporter*). (Source: Cary [1975], 3, 168)

"Theophilus" (1916). Poem. It is in five quatrains. The poet directly addresses Theophilus. I wonder why you were named Theophilus. Cyclops would have kept you out of his games. Thinking of your probably "innocent" dreams makes me shudder. Obviously you prove that "Heredity outshines environment" at times. Traces of Belial are in you. You are best when you are asleep. So, go ahead and sleep, and let us propose that a better name for you would be Caligula, Caliban, or Cain.

Emma Robinson* says that by titling the poem as he did Robinson was suggesting the attitude of their parents toward his older brother, Herman Robinson.* Lawrance Thompson cites Luke 1:3 in support of his seeing irony "in giving this devilish creature a name which means 'Lover of God.'" Edwin S. Fussell notes "the divergent yet complementary areas of feeling . . . juxtaposed by swift allusions to classical and biblical history" in "Theophilus," which Ellsworth Barnard dismisses as a "whimsical portrayal." (Sources: Barnard, 182; Fussell [1954], 151; E. Robinson, 4; L. Thompson, 136)

"There Was a Calm Man in Sabattis" (1937). A four-line poem Robinson calls a limerick in an undated letter to Daniel Gregory Mason.* It explains that a man fatally shot a skunk through a lattice and wonders where his hat is. (Source: Mason [Winter 1937], 63)

"Thomas Hood" (1896). Sonnet. Robinson praises Thomas Hood for wrapping his bitter thoughts in "puns and pleasantries," and says that Hood never looked with ordinary eyes upon "anguish and . . . sin." Amid his jokes Hood mingled "The nameless and eternal tragedies / That render hope and hopelessness akin." Even as his readers laugh because of his wit, they feel uneasy, sense the death of mirth, and fear that pleasure will elude them.

Thomas Hood (1799–1845) was born in London, lived there, became an associate of Charles Lamb and other writers, suffered poverty and illness, was an editor of and a contributor to periodicals often humorous, but is now notable almost uniquely for his anonymously published "Song of the Shirt" (1843), which pleaded for labor reforms. Robinson in 1891 submitted his sonnet about Hood to Robert Morss Lovett,* then a senior at Harvard and the editor of the *Harvard Monthly.* Lovett rejected the poem. Robinson wrote Harry de Forest Smith* (December 8, 1891) about both his disappointment and Lovett's visiting him courteously and with encouragement. No wonder Lovett rejected the poem. In it, Robinson enigmatically mentions "the branded man of Lynn" and someone or something that "sailed away with Ines." It remained for Robert Mezey to publish in a footnote that "Lynn" and "Ines" are named by Thomas Hood in his poems "The Dream of Eugene

Aram" and "Fair Ines," respectively. (Sources: Mesey, 218; *Untriangulated Stars*, 45–46)

"Those Merry Gentlemen and Their Wives." A short story Robinson wrote in the early 1890s, could not sell, and destroyed. (Source: Hagedorn, 102)

Three Poems (1928). Unauthorized publication. It was put together by Lucius Beebe and Bradley Fisk, in Cambridge, Massachusetts. The two were students at Harvard at the time. Beebe, who was analyzing Robinson's handling of Arthurian materials for a master's thesis, learned from Robinson that he had discarded a Lancelot fragment and was given a copy for use in his thesis. Beebe copied it, returned the original, and persuaded Fiske to join him and have a local printer make a copy for each of them. When friends also wanted copies, the idea expanded, and 17 copies of "Lancelot Canto IV," together with Robinson's "Ballade of a Ship" and "In Harvard 5," were printed. To assure timely copyright, Beebe and Fiske deposited a copy in the Harvard Library and sent another copy to the Bodleian Library, in Oxford. An ill-starred Harvard lad sought a copy for himself from some of the printer's abandoned sheets, was unsuccessful, and in spite told Robinson about Beebe and Fiske. The two promptly tracked the informer, beat him up, and sent him to the hospital. To purify themselves from any police-report taint, Harvard authorities expelled Beebe, who never obtained his M.A.

Bacon Collamore,* who provides details of this event, adds the following: Beebe's "Edwin Arlington Robinson and the Arthurian Legend" was eventually published; Robinson included the Lancelot fragment in a later version of his *Lancelot*; in two 1929 letters and one 1934 letter, Robinson says he originally omitted what he called the Modred fragment because it introduced four characters not appearing elsewhere in *Lancelot*; and Robinson says he thinks 25 copies of *Three Poems* were printed, four or five were sent to libraries (including one to Harvard's), 12 were destroyed, and his friend Lewis Montefiore Isaacs* has a copy not for sale. Collamore also reports that

Beebe published *Aspects of the Poetry of Edwin Arlington Robinson* (Cambridge: Dunster House Bookshop, 1928) and included in it a Robinson bibliography by Fisk; and that Beebe published an essay entitled "Dignified Faun: A Portrait of E.A.R." (*Outlook*, August 27, 1930), filled with dishonest descriptions and anecdotes about Robinson. (Source: Collamore, 41–44, 46, 52–53)

"Three Quatrains" (1896). Three numbered quatrains, in iambic pentameter and rhyming *abab*.

I. Poets will mock fame, which "haggard men" will seek.

II. We should toast future splendid accomplishments and not worry about Lucullus and Nero.

Lucius Licinius Lucullus (c. 110–56 B.C.) was a rich, learned Roman general. Nero here is probably the Nero (A.D. 37–68) who was the allegedly fiery and certainly suicidal Roman emperor.

III. Despite our inability to do everything, time will still manage to find "a withered leaf in every laurel."

"The Three Taverns" (1919). Dramatic monologue. It is in blank verse, in eight unnumbered parts.

Near Rome, Paul greets "Herodion, Apelles, Amplias, / And Andronicus" (four of his disciples). He expresses a little surprise that they might be thinking he wouldn't appear, since he said that he would and also that he would proceed farther west. He says he is a prisoner now and must appear before Cæsar. Paul might have avoided Cæsar, as Agrippa told Festes that Paul might, except that God willed otherwise. Paul knows not when the cup of death will be his to drink. He recalls that "the great light came down" on him when, as Saul the "fiery Jew," he was near Damascus; now older, he is no longer afraid of "time and men."

Indeed, when he was Saul, Paul studied not Christ's teachings but the law, saw Stephen stoned to death, and failed to see how "a man be given / To live beyond the Law." Now he knows that one's real self is one's inner spirit. After his own death, his "toil" will be ended but the "work" of his "faith within" will begin.

Paul again reminds these disciples that he promised to be with them in Rome and now warns them that whether his stay is long or short, "wolves are coming." He will speak confusingly to Cæsar, since,

> if I cloud a little with my own
> Mortality the gleam that is immortal,
> I do it only because I am I—

and sometimes speaks stingingly because many a person "feel[s] before he sees." He reports that words expressing their "love and . . . faith" have spread the faith to Antioch, Haran, and elsewhere, but he wonders if their faith is only "the shut fruit of words." The Jews merely have the law, whereas "these Gentiles" now "Have love and law together," unlike what is evidenced "in shrieking history." He suspects that Rome will soon be preparing a fiery, thorny crown for "new masters." So let fall what is to happen. He tells his disciples that they are to plant, gather, go forward, and replant, for they work in eternal fields unburdened. Their "light yoke" will weigh no more than "a clear jewel" shining with a brighter light than the sun or the dazzling stars. Gamaliel, that good Jew, spoke well about men being unconquerable "if they be of God." Mere words, however, are mere words, whereas "the Word . . . lives and is the life." There will be "aches and innovations," without which "Attainment would have no . . . joy." There will also be future creeds and schisms, and deaths from them even—"because a farthing has two sides." But "we have . . . the Cross between two worlds." It will guide them, but it will also blind them and they will suffer until they truly see. Then their former world will seem "a smitten glimpse of ruin."

Paul notices that his friends seem to look at him credulously. He hasn't leaped gigantically, although some of his words "from Corinth may have leapt / A little through your eyes into your soul." Were your eyes alive? To be effective, "a man of words" who is writing "in the Lord's name for his name's sake" must have "in his blood the fire of time / To warm eternity." Such a man will be "destitute" uniquely "if his light be not the light indeed."

Paul confirms the truth of the statement

that "The Kingdom is within us," but only to the degree that faith makes it so. Followers, however, mustn't simply sit around waiting for "the Coming." Paul asserts that his words may puzzle "the hearts and heads / Of nature's minions"; nevertheless, they "will yet be heard." His message must be variously interpreted. Similarly, Christ planted a garden which will be larger later. Christ knew that these disciples would sow seed-like words, which, though strangely mixed, would produce a "foreign harvest of a wider growth, / And one without an end." Sadly, in time to come, Jews, Gentiles, and pagans, all in darknesses as yet unnamed, are going to brandish, "Like heads of captured Pharisees on pikes, / Our contradictions and discrepancies."

Although many do indeed see through glass darkly, they do see something "as dark as a lost fire" become a beacon of salvation to another, in time. "There shall be light," and these disciples are going to light torches first for a few and then for far more. They must fight, speak from the heart, "Give men to know that even their days of earth / To come are more than ages that are gone," and trust that "Eternity will answer for itself." They must think of Paul as a blemished brother. They must watch out for stoics and grammarians. They must never despair.

Paul continues by saying that what is best in life is what is uncertain. These disciples should put their fears to rest among their "faded sins" of times past. Paul asserts that he was once more zealous and foolish than they. A person's body, that "little house of days," may cause him regrets, but they are only temporary. This world is going to last a while; and millions upon millions, with clogged ears and bewildered eyes, will be here to misjudge the world's ills, its ashes, and its seemingly wrathful pitfalls. Many who hate each other "are soon to know that without love / Their faith is but the perjured name for nothing." Paul, who was once hated, now has no time for hate. He has left "Home, friends, and honors" behind him now, and in the process has gained this enriching wisdom, "that out of wisdom has come love," love that "measures and is of itself the measure / Of works and hope and faith." The disciples' final path is something

that they can prepare and that has been prepared for them, right here in this world in which they "have sinned and suffered, striven and seen." Meanwhile, if they take it a little easy, Paul concludes, "Peace may attend you . . . / And me . . . even in Rome."

Well then, Paul is now seven leagues from Cæsar. He told Amplias, Andronicus, Apelles, and Herodion that he could come; but he admits that he didn't think he would be doing so as a prisoner, and just because he saw "beyond the Law / That which the Law saw not." He is grateful that his friends came a distance to see a dangerous man. He expresses the hope that they may meet again, even though no one can tell what he might encounter in Rome.

The title "The Three Taverns" comes from this biblical passage, which Robinson quotes and cites under the title thus: "When the brethren heard of us, they came to meet us as far as Appii Forum, and The Three Taverns. (*Acts xxviii, 15*)." "The Three Taverns" first appeared in *The Lyric*, edited by the controversially liberal Samuel Roth (1894–1974). Robinson's working title for the poem was "Saint Paul," as he indicated, according to Bacon Collamore,* in two letters (March 22 and June 17, 1919) to Roth. Also, in a letter (June 1, 1919) to Edith Brower,* Robinson says "I'm sending you my St. Paul."

Nicholas Ayo cites biblical sources as he explains aspects of the poem as follows. The four named Christians — Herodion, Appelles, Amplias, and Andronicus — would not know about all of Paul's epistles but did know "The Epistle of Paul the Apostle to the Romans," since the four men are directly addressed in it (Romans 16:7–11). Ayo demonstrates that Robinson was thoroughly familiar with the chronology of events in the acts of the Apostles. Paul wrote Romans about A.D. 58, in Corinth, from which he says he wrote the four friends he names in the poem. He promised to preach in Rome and farther west, in Spain (Romans 1:15; 15:24). His reference to Agrippa and Festes came to Robinson from Acts 26:32. The reference to death's cup for Paul echoes Christ's own words (John 18:11) and also other identical biblical imagery. As for Saul near Damascus and the light, see Acts 9:3–4. His former "fiery" anti-Christian actions Robinson finds ample warrant for, as well as the Pauline doctrine of obligatory action contrary to hidebound observance of "the Law" (Acts 7:53; Galatians 1:14, etc.). Briefly, again all according to Ayo, for faith empowering one above legalisms (II Corinthians 10:7); wolves (Acts 20:29); his clouded, necessarily imperfect reasoning (II Corinthians 5:1); Antioch (Acts 11:26); Gamaliel (Acts 5:34–36); the "Word," capitalized (John 1:1); farthing (Matthew 10:29, 31; 22:19–20); the Kingdom within (Romans 3:28); seeing through a glass darkly (I Corinthians 13–12); our little mortal house (II Corinthians 5:1); and so on. Ayo is moved by Robinson's use of seed, sowing, and harvest imagery, because many readers would relate it both to the Garden of Eden and to the Easter-Morning garden immortalized by Christ's rising from the dead there. Ayo reports that "there are about two hundred biblical allusions" in "The Three Taverns," which gives the poem the highest concentration of such allusions of all of Robinson's works. Ayo concludes that "'The Three Taverns' best illustrates Robinson's detailed familiarity with the Bible, the functional accuracy of his borrowings, and his sensitive elaboration of only pivotal — and paradoxical — points in St. Paul's character and teaching, such as the law and freedom, faith and charity, the word and the Word." Robert Mezey also helpfully annotates this complex poem.

Yvor Winters regards "The Three Taverns" as "one of the greatest poems of its kind and length in English." Wallace L. Anderson says that "'The Three Taverns,' a poem of great intensity, is a closely reasoned statement of St. Paul's position interwoven with a theme of the conflict between man-made law and the higher law within." Ellsworth Barnard's high praise for the poem culminates thus: It "perhaps comes as near to translating the essences of the Epistles into modern idiom as will ever be possible." (Sources: W. Anderson [1968], 125; Ayo, 43 n. 50, 69–111 passim, 222; Barnard, 91; Brower, 174; Collamore, 24; Mezey, 232–33; Winters, 136)

The Three Taverns: A Book of Poems

(New York: 1920). Collection of 29 poems, including the title poem.

"Too Much Coffee" (1936). Poem. Without measuring or drawing a line, some people are in shadows challenging the advent of daylight.

Louis Untermeyer,* the minor poet but influential editor and anthologist whom Robinson knew at the MacDowell Colony,* published this four-line ditty in his *Modern American Poetry: A Critical Anthology* (1936) and later explained that Robinson slipped it under his cottage door after the two and others had had a long, convivial, alcoholic night at the colony. (Sources: Cary [1975], 52, 184–85; Untermeyer)

Torrence, Ridgely (1875–1950). Born Frederick Ridgely Torrence in Xenia, Ohio, he attended Miami College (later Miami University), Ohio (1893–1895); was a special student at Princeton University (1895–1896); and wrote for *The Nassau Literary Magazine* (1896) but withdrew from Princeton for health reasons and moved to New York City (1896). Torrence combined rather steady publishing, editorial work, teaching, and being a delightful friend of other writers. His publications include *The House of a Hundred Lights* (1899, poetry), *El Dorado: A Tragedy* (1903, verse drama), *Abelard and Heloise* (1907, verse drama), *Plays for a Negro Theatre* (1917, three groundbreaking dramas), *Hesperides* (1925, poems), and *Poems by Ridgely Torrence* (1941, 1952). He did editorial work for *The Critic* (1903–1904), *Cosmopolitan* (1905–1907), and *The New Republic* (1920–1933). He was a visiting professor at Miami University (1920–1921, 1942) and at Antioch College (1938). His most important literary friends included Robert Frost, Percy MacKaye,* Josephine Preston Peabody,* William Vaughn Moody,* Edmund Clarence Stedman,* and Robinson. Torrence and Moody toured the Mediterranean region together (March-May 1907). Moody's death four months later shocked Torrence, whose "Santa Barbara Beach" is an elegiac verse tribute to his friend.

Torrence met Robinson at Stedman's home (1900), which, as Richard Cary puts it, provided Stedman "his chance to perpetrate the oft-repeated pun, 'Torrence — and The Night Before.'" Torrence soon wrote Peabody to say how much he respected and liked Robinson. Hermann Hagedorn,* who knew all of these people, says that Torrence, the "incarnation of youth," with a combination of fluidity, wit, and social graces, was to all appearances totally antithetical to Robinson, and concludes that this amiable collision of opposites produced an enduring friendship.

Friendship, however, never kept Robinson from judging anyone's poetry with ruthless objectivity. According to John M. Clum, when Robinson read Torrence's "The Lesser Children" (1905), an acclaimed poem against hunting for sport not food, he wrote (September 9, 1905) to Peabody that Torrence's self-assurance was huge but that "The Lesser Children" was inferior to Moody's anti-imperialistic "An Ode in Time of Hesitation." In 1906 Torrence and Robinson began rooming in the Judson Hotel, in Washington Square, New York. Another resident was the beautiful freelance writer Olivia Howard Dunbar. Chard Powers Smith* reports that when Torrence married Olivia (1914), Robinson's letter of congratulation was reserved, saying that he doesn't know how they will value his good wishes but sends them anyway. Smith says Torrence told him that Robinson had been in love with Olivia, but Smith adds his doubts. Marian Nivens MacDowell* invited both Torrences to her MacDowell Colony* (1915), where they again associated with Robinson. He was outraged when Torrence was not awarded the Pulitzer Prize for poetry for his *Hesperides* (1925). Robinson dedicated *Matthias at the Door* to Torrence (1931). Torrence often visited Robinson when he was dying in the hospital in New York and helped him proofread *King Jasper* during that time. Torrence edited *Selected Letters of Edwin Arlington Robinson* (1940). This work, capitalizing on Robinson's considerable popularity, includes representative samples, contains helpful footnotes, but is carelessly edited and lacks an index. (Sources: Cary [1974], 260; Clum; C. Smith, 239, 366; Hagedorn, 164, 338–39; *Selected Letters*)

"The Torrent" (1896). Sonnet. The poet reveres the foaming, flashing, chiming waters of the torrent, which, with "leaf-split" silvery sunlight all about, makes "a magic symphony." At first, he deplores the advent of loggers bent on cutting the "patriarchal trees" and converting the silver of the torrent's spray to gold. But soon he begins to welcome their arrival, because "The jealous visionings that I had had / Were steps to the great place where trees and torrents go." With these two lines "The Torrent" stops.

Emma Robinson* and Ruth Nivison* identify the original "torrent" as Rolling Dam Brook in Oaklands, the Gardiner family estate in Gardiner, Maine. One indication of Robinson's sense of the worth of his poetry is the fact that, according to Hermann Hagedorn,* when the editor of *The Critic* said he would pay Robinson $15 for "The Torrent" if he changed the last two lines (the 14th line is an alexandrine, i.e., has an extra iambic foot), Robinson rejected the offer. Louis Coxe notes that although "the great place" devotedly mentioned in the last line of "The Torrent" is neither described nor in strict truth known, Robinson strongly suggests that we "must either believe it is there and work toward it in belief," or become reconciled to oblivion. For some reason, the last two lines puzzled readers; and their puzzlement, as Richard Cary abundantly demonstrates, distressed Robinson no end. Ellsworth Barnard points out that this sonnet and "Horace to Leuconoë" are the only sonnets in which Robinson does not end a sentence with the eighth line. (Sources: Barnard, 65; Cary [1974], 44; Coxe, 48; Hagedorn, 98; E. Robinson, 12)

The Torrent and the Night Before (1896). Robinson's first collection of poems, containing 46 poems under 43 titles. On the title page Robinson placed this bold quotation and identified its author as "Coppée": *"Qui pourrais-je imiter pour être original?"* (Whom should I imitate to be original?— Richard Cary identifies the source as François Coppée's *Le Trésor*.) John H. Miller carefully demonstrates that when Robinson assembled the poems for this collection, he placed them in groups to lead the reader from insecurity to an awareness of the importance of "learning to live profitably rather than looking forward to death or bemoaning his life in this world."

The book was privately printed, at Robinson's expense, by the Riverside Press, Cambridge, Massachusetts. It contained the following note: "This book is dedicated to any man, woman, or critic who will cut the edges of it.—I have done the top." For 312 copies Robinson paid $52 to the Riverside Press of Cambridge, Massachusetts, where his uncle Edward Proby Fox worked and interceded for him. Line 13 of "Ballade of a Ship" is missing, and should read "They danced and they drank and their souls grew gay," and was corrected by hand by Robinson in some of the copies. He received his shipment of books a few days after the death of his mother Mary Robinson,* made no effort to sell them, and gave many of them away. Cary reports that "the most prominent figure to have publicly recommended Robinson so far" i.e., by 1897, was Edward Eggleston, who did so in an interview published in *Outlook* (February 6, 1897). Eggleston (1837–1902) was an Indiana preacher who gained popularity when he began to write fiction, the best being his novel *The Hoosier Schoolmaster* (1871). Although Robinson groused about initial lack of recognition, reviews were numerous and often complimentary.

Rollo Walter Brown* reports that the copies of *The Torrent and the Night Before* that Robinson sent to Charles William Eliot* (Harvard's president), to Charles Eliot Norton* (eminent professor there), and to Thomas Bailey Aldrich (poet) all wound up in Harvard's archives. Bacon Collamore* notes that Robinson also sent copies to Edmund Gosse, Thomas Hardy, and Algernon Charles Swinburne. Laura E. Richards* reports that a copy (c. 1941) sold for $1,500, but adds that the daughters, when little, of Robinson's brother Herman Robinson* and his wife Emma Robinson* made doll houses of spare copies, before they disappeared. (See "The First Seven Years.") As of 1955, only 66 copies of *The Torrent and the Night Before* had been located. By 1974, 125 were known to exist, according to Cary, who compares the rarity of *The Torrent and the Night Before* to that of Edgar Allan Poe's almost vanished *Tamerlane* (under 10

copies extant). According to *Bookman's Price Index* (Detroit: Gale, 1999, 59:629), a copy of *The Torrent and the Night Before* sold in 1998 for $450, an inscribed copy, for $1,750. (Sources: R. Brown, 63; Cary [1974], 49, 52, 54; Collamore, ix; Justice; Miller, 348; Richards [1936], 46, 47; C. Smith, 348; "'Torrent' Number Sixty-Six")

"Toussaint L'Ouverture: Chateau de Joux, 1803" (1931). Dramatic monologue. It is in blank verse. Toussaint L'Ouverture says that he has been imprisoned for months, or perhaps years, has had no food or water for three days now, but now in his ill-lit cell greets a friend who has dared to visit him. The man must be cautious and not ask questions, as though Tousaint were anything more than "a transplanted shovelful / Of black earth, with a seed of danger in it." Napoleon, "a perfidious victor," shouldn't fear him. What hope Toussaint brought is gone now, and he is far from his island.

His friend is saying nothing. Toussaint knows he is now "an old sick black man" near death. God knows that Napoleon climbed so high that he sees only himself. Toussaint was betrayed but knows he lived with a purpose. Although he is not "a black snake," his blackness is important.

Some lives seem to be nothing but weeds, "to be crushed or cut," or let shrivel, perish, and be forgotten. Toussaint's life was different. His "was a million lives," and he served others, only to be exiled and buried alive. Is he hated because he's black?

Toussaint says that Napoleon cannot starve his name, which will be meaningfully known "in this world's unhappy story." Out of a certain island, where he is remembered, "dreams and deeds may come." Isn't it remarkable that a mere "black commodity" could see so much? God put eyes in his "black face"; he saw good in "multitudes," faced tyranny, recognized people far beyond his island, but knew they would suffer because pompous leaders would gain support from slaves. Their condition will continue until they convert their shackles into swords. Meanwhile, silent capitulation prolongs their misery. Toussaint says he has done all he can against systematic madness, malice, craftiness, and hatred. Ignorance will keep on defeating hope.

Last night, Toussaint says, he saw Napoleon burning alive in hell. His eyes revealed his continued hate for Toussaint, who felt no joy in Napoleon's misery. He wonders if insanity would be preferable for him to his present knowledge. Although Napoleon's hands were burning and he will be on fire again before he dies, Toussaint is aware that death is his own only cure. His story, when told, will be a sad one.

Toussaint cannot hear his friend now. Where is he? Is he dead? Nothing but death is to come here. Toussaint was only a commodity, to be snatched from his island, to France, then here. Isn't it odd that in this darkness he can see better than Napoleon can in his? He asks his friend to help him stand up.

Toussaint senses that his friend's visit was a dream. This prison has been a dream. He remembers the ship. To France? Only partly awake, he sees waves, feels winds and sunlight, sees white breakers on a shore, sees a mountain, people — all welcoming him. Ah, it is his island.

Toussaint queries his friend, unseen in renewed night. "But you are there — / You are still there. And I know who is here."

Wallace L. Anderson reports that Robinson was inspired to write this poem when he read *The Black Napoleon: The Story of Toussaint Louverture* (1931) by Percy Waxman (1880–1948). This biography of Pierre Dominique Toussaint L'Ouverture (c. 1746–1803) details the rise of the heroic slave to black general, liberator of Haiti (1791), able governor there (1801–1802), and opponent of Napoleon, who sought to re-establish slavery and whose army captured and imprisoned Toussaint (1802). Robinson was especially moved by Waxman's incensed account of Toussaint's capture, his being sent to France and separated from family members detained elsewhere, his being denied a trial, his being permanently locked down (beginning August 23, 1802) at Fort de Joux near the Swiss border in a 20' by 12' stone cell with one small high window and no toilet, Napoleon's indifference to his courteous and piteous written pleas, and his being deprived of food and water at the very end (April 7, 1803). Ellsworth Barnard

notes that unity in Robinson's poem about the black hero is enhanced by the repetition of the word "black," used 11 times. It is of interest that when French officials, tourists, or suppliers of relief enter modern-day Haiti, they usually do so by landing at the Toussaint L'Ouverture International Airport just outside Port-au-Prince. (Sources: W. Anderson [1968], 123; Barnard, 91)

"The Town Down the River" (1908). Poem. It is in dialogue, in four numbered parts. Throughout the poem, "The Watcher by the Way" speaks to a number of persons, of various ages and talents and fortune, as they march along, lured by "the Town down the River, / Where the millions cringe and shiver."

I. The Watcher warns some young people, who are ignorant and dreaming. They reply that the Watcher is old and burdened. They say that they may have trouble, but that they "seek the light" and look forward; he can't tell them what to do; he is welcome to "watch or . . . wither."

II. The Watcher tells some "fiery folk" that they are strong, may well befriend each other, and yet may receive gifts from townspeople that might backfire. He wonders if they are being lured by "sirens in the River." These folks admit that the Watcher is "sage and self-exalted," but they say that they must pursue their own path and, further, that the Watcher has no standing in the place they are heading for.

III. The Watcher notes that some marchers are beginning to falter, and he wonders what they have to say now. Maybe they will stay put where they are; maybe they will return home. Their answer is to complain that the Watcher shouldn't scold them, even though they're "Derelicts, . . . / Poets, rogues, and sick physicians." They must follow their leaders, now ahead of them, "out of grayness, / To the light that shone so far."

IV. The Watcher sees some old, withered people approaching him. They warn him, praise him, accept his bitter criticism, and say they won't be beckoned farther by the River. The Watcher, however, wants to join them in continuing on the way, since, as he puts it,

Long have I waited,
Longer have I known
That the Town would have its own,
And the call be for the fated.

He adds that they are all equally old. When one of them replies that he can hear the River constantly calling, the Watcher urges everyone to come along, for "The lights are shining."

Hermann Hagedorn* says that in "The Town Down the River" Robinson "suggested the fascination, the mystery, the ruthlessness of the city [New York] he had [by 1905] come to love." Ellsworth Barnard believes that, although the down-river town "on one level is New York, [its] more inclusive identity is Destiny, or Fate, on whose inscrutable face all come to look with joy, indifference, or despair, answering eagerly or reluctantly her irresistible command." By analyzing "the metrical arrangements" of the poem, Barnard demonstrates that "the movement [in it] is not of marching feet but of flowing waters." (Sources: Barnard, 45, 75; Hagedorn, 237)

The Town Down the River; A Book of Poems (New York: Charles Scribner's Sons, 1910). Collection of 33 poems. Robinson dedicated the book to Theodore Roosevelt.*

"The Tree in Pamela's Garden" (1920). Sonnet. Pamela, really in no way deceptive, feels that men can keep their distance, but also that, "if Apollo's avatar" is one of those nearby fellows, she won't "have to grieve." Nosy Tilbury Town citizens misunderstand her sighing and regard her as unlike Eve except for also being "in a garden." Her gossipy neighbors busily "make romance of reticence" and wish that since "she had never loved a man" she might have a pet, say a cat, or a bird. But they fail to see that she both overhears them and smiles.

Chard Powers Smith* summarizes two different items of Robinson family gossip — one, that Robinson is here touching on his quiet affection for a childhood girlfriend and humorously comparing himself to the incarnation of the god of poetry; two, that he is here implicitly depicting a spinster friend "who had a happy affair with someone else."

"The Tree in Pamela's Garden" may be read as another of Robinson's several poems about genuine success in seeming failure; here, Pamela is sweetly reconciled to quiet, inevitable, acceptable loneliness. Scott Donaldson notes that in "The Tree in Pamela's Garden," "as in almost all of Robinson, it is clear that the majority, the chorus, is mistaken. The Tilbury Townspeople do not understand." After reviewing previous scholarship on this poem, Eric A. Weil applies what seems pertinent to his happy conclusion that "Robinson again [as in 'Aunt Imogen'] trades gender to reveal he was not a stranger to heterosexual love and perhaps . . . not a stranger to sex." (Sources: Donaldson [1966], 228; C. Smith, 181–82; Weil, 232)

"A Tribute to Franklin L. Schenck" (1927). Essay. Robinson describes the funeral at East Northport, Long Island, New York, of his friend Franklin L. Schenck (1856–1927). Robinson says that this man was not successful in any conventional way, but, being "altogether different," will prove irreplaceable. His friends and many townspeople demonstrated their love for him by creating a wonderful "atmosphere of spontaneous tribute and affection" during his funeral. Schenck lived as he purely wished, cared nothing for "wealth and social conventions," loved his home-grown flowers, vegetables, and chickens, and "paint[ed]" when he pleased," indifferent to "any prevailing temporary style" in doing so. He wished the best for one and all, including those who "misjudged him for his informalities and eccentricities." He made the world better. Although it is said that "The dead go fast," he "will go slowly, very slowly from the place where he is so much alive." A monument to his memory is an exhibition of some of his paintings in the Brooklyn Chamber of Commerce.

According to Bacon Collamore,* Robinson's "Tribute" appeared in a Northport newspaper dated February 18, 1927. Hermann Hagedorn* defines Schenck as "a painter of creditable landscapes"; describes his Long Island farm as "a handkerchief of land," with a dog, rabbits, chickens, and vegetables; and says that Robinson helped arrange for the Brooklyn exhibition of his work. Richard

Cary reports that "Schenck's somber rendition of Robinson's 'The Dark Hills' now hangs in Colby College Library." See also "Franklin Schenck (1856–1927)." (Sources: Cary [1975], 92–93, 192; Collamore, 44; Hagedorn, 322, 323)

"A Tribute to Theodore Roosevelt" (1927). Essay. Robinson says that a "casual and incidental" event in the life of "Colonel Roosevelt" was a significant one in his own life. At a time when Robinson's condition was between "precarious" and "desperate," one of his books made its way to Roosevelt. It attracted his fancy and aroused his curiosity as to the "being who had written it." Roosevelt wrote to the editor of *Century Magazine*, Richard Watson Gilder,* who recommended the poet. Roosevelt's supposedly exclusive interest in "biceps and sunshine" was disproved by his manifested interest in characters — "neither strenuous nor sunny" — featured in Robinson's poems. Following their example would more likely "lead one sooner to the devil than to the White House." Already in the White House, the colonel "felt . . . immune." So he "tracked" Robinson to a "dingy room in Boston" and soon got him into the New York Custom House, where he worked with not much "diligence and efficiency." Robinson closes by expressing, "inadequately," his gratitude to "a most unusual man." (Source: Cary [1975], 92–93, 191–92)

"Triolet" (1891). Poem. The poet lugubriously notes that boots are standing by a "wall," no longer answering when duty "call[s]," but instead are rotting and "crawl[ing]" with bugs.

The only virtue of this poem is that young Robinson successfully met the challenge of the triolet form. A triolet must have eight lines, rhyming *abaaabab*, with the first, fourth, and seventh lines being identical, and the second and eighth lines being identical. (Sources: Cary [1975], 14, 170; Hagedorn, 47)

Tristram (New York Macmillan, 1927). Arthurian narrative in blank verse, in 10 numbered parts.

Characters appearing in or mentioned in *Tristram* are as follows: Andred, Arthur,

Brangwaine, Gawaine, Gouvernail, Griffon, Guinevere, Howel, Isolt of Ireland, Isolt of the white hands, Lancelot, Mark, Modred, Morgan, Morhaus, and Tristram.

A few of them appear or are mentioned in *Merlin* and *Lancelot* earlier. For brief identifications of the following, see *Merlin*, where they were introduced in 1917: Arthur, Gawaine, Guinevere, Lancelot, and Modred. For brief identifications of Andred and Mark, see *Lancelot*, where they were introduced in 1920. The following characters first appear in *Tristram*:

Brangwaine (elsewhere spelled Brangaene, Brangwain) is Isolt's loyal maid. In some Arthurian poems, she accidentally provides Iseult and Tristan the love potion intended for Iseult, betrothed to Mark, after which she generously agrees to be Tristram's beloved Iseult's virginal substitute during Mark's dark wedding night.

Gouvernail is Tristram's loyal companion.

Griffon is King Howel's bad neighbor.

Howel is the king of Brittany and the father of Isolt of the white hands.

Isolt of the white hands is King Howel's daughter and forgetful Tristram's patient bride.

Morgan is an amorous vixen who helps Tristram; called Queen Morgan of Gore here, she is not given many of the qualities of the well-known Morgan le Fay.

Morhaus is the uncle of Isolt of the white hands.

I. Isolt, who is 18 and is the daughter of Howel, the King of Brittany, both amuses and distresses her father by gazing ever northward, toward England, across a sky full of white birds flying. She is thinking of Tristram, who praised her when she was a child and who promised her he would return. Howel jests that the north is full of wolves, bears, and ill-mannered, hairy men. He tells her that Tristram's uncle, Mark, King of Cornwall, is tonight marrying Isolt of Ireland. When Howel's Isolt asks about this Isolt of Ireland, Howel repeats reports of her pride and unique beauty. He asks what if Tristram, King Arthur, or our "Saviour" returned?

When Isolt says that Tristram's eyes were truthful and that he gave her an agate, her father counters by asking whether, should Tristram came back only to leave again, she would drown herself, and mentions that he might sell her to Modred, if that reptile's threatened plan to overthrow Arthur should succeed. Saying she wouldn't kill herself, Isolt turns utterly serious, states her devotion to her father, her patience as a woman, and her belief and trust in Tristram and in God. He chides her for dreaming. She will continue to do so, she says, and retires. Howel senses an uncanny maturity in his changeling-like child, but fears for her future, and stares out at distant stars and a cold moon over cold waters.

II. The same moon glimmers on Cornwall, where King Mark of Tintagel is now wedding Isolt of Ireland amid festive music. Tristram broods outside, stares at murderous Cornish waters, and regrets he kept his promise to bring Isolt to his uncle. He remembers that despite his killing her uncle Morhaus, she and he fell into desperate, impermissible love. His soul retches as he imagines his goat-like, salacious-eyed, gaunt-armed uncle with his miraculously beautiful but shuddering wife. Mark will soon

> crush the bloom of her resisting life
> On his hot, watery mouth, and overcome
> The protest of her suffering silk skin
> With his crude, senile claws.

Gouvernail, Tristram's old friend, walks down toward the rocks and says that Mark, though immensely grateful to Tristram, is annoyed that he isn't attending the wedding party. Gouvernail appeals to Tristram for old times' sake to tell him what to say to Mark. Tristram replies that he will answer a royal command but otherwise Gouvernail should go tell Mark he is sick or drunk. First joking that Gouvernail might get a harp and sing Tristram's excuses to the king, Tristram with total seriousness says he is horribly sick. Gouvernail morosely leaves.

Alone again, Tristram hates the thought that Isolt will soon be "the bartered prey / Of an unholy sacrifice," though sanctified by Rome. He weeps, moans, thinks of leaping into the "insensate ocean," and cries out his beloved's name.

Suddenly Queen Morgan, slim, gorgeous, and mock-modest, interrupts him to report

that Mark was "vexed and vicious" when Gouvernail reported Tristram drunk and sick. Tristram tells Morgan to return to the king, say he'll appear if commanded, otherwise say "delicately or . . . directly" that he is melancholy and warns everyone to stop being stupid. Morgan replies that she'll lie to the King for him; she knows why Tristram isn't happy; Isolt should lament marrying "a man old enough to bury himself"; Tristram's heart may bleed but heal, since God made many women. He replies that he must courtously listen to her but that queens ought to behave. Morgan, wiggling closer, admits she is a strange queen, a legend even, among a plenitude of queens. While casting an eye on her "fair and feline face" and her "white bosom," Tristram asks her to tell the king that he "has feasted over much / In recognition of his happiness." He calls this excuse "An error that apology too soon / Might qualify too late," says he plans to save part of his shredded "integrity," and promises servitude to Morgan.

Morgan, grimacing a moment, counters that women are the slaves to men they honor, that men know this, that men sometimes honor women to humor them, that moreover women are men's "slaves and their impediments" both. After Tristram rewraps her opened cloak around her, she repeats his comment about quick apologies and augurs that she and "Sir Tristram, Prince of Lyonesse," may meet again under England's skies.

III. Tristram muses. He was the son of a king and a "forgotten mother" (later revealed as Mark's sister). He sailed from Ireland to Cornwall with that beautiful woman, who made him tardily aware of his callowness. He had pledged himself to another king and saw his doom too late.

Brangwaine, her faithful maid, brings Isolt like a shadow down the stairs to him. She is a combination of majesty, grief, shame, and fear, until

> terror born of passion became passion
> Reborn of terror while his lips and hers
> Put speech out like a flame put out by fire.

They hear no music now. Brangwaine flits off. Time finds no room between their souls, bodies, silences. Words, though, would have broken an earlier silence. Falling back, Isolt wonders what they've done to one another and to fate, and predicts their death.

Tristram excuses her former pride, which couldn't have cured his blindness even had she prayed. After all, he did kill her kinsman Morhaus and was wounded. She says she did pray but without avail; sadly, wars cause "two sides"; nevertheless, she healed his wound, but only to bid him farewell. Yes, Tristram remembers, and also that when he returned from Mark, who made him an adept knight, it was as his ambassador, sworn — ignorant as he then was of any love affairs more than gay and foolish temporary victories — to demand Isolt for Mark. Too late it was that Tristram began to see all other women's faces merely as "silly skulls / Covered with skin and hair." He says he has Isolt this night, yes, but Mark will do so "all his life," and Tristram was the means. He avouches that he could hang the king, then apologizes to Isolt, who leaps and

> Muffled his mouth with hers in a long kiss,
> Blending in their catastrophe two fires
> That made one fire.

With tear-brimmed eyes, she tells Tristram that he was naive, that he mustn't curse himself with vicious names meaninglessly, that it will be awful if Mark orders him to return with them, that he is unlike his cousin Andred or evil Modred, that he couldn't kill the king, and that time may be on their side.

The two sadly discuss their pathetic options: They may hope for heaven; any rescue attempt would fail; Mark's army will drag her to "ignominy"; Tristram and Isolt's father both saw shadows in similar ways. The couple silently embrace again. He reasons that her death would be mercy for her and the best memory for him, until Isolt's renewed kisses end reason. She strengthens his thought of their love with a smile hinting at God's future aid, but he fears the strength of Rome's God. Isolt affirms their unique, eternal, stronger-than-death love, not to be hurt even by Tristram's liking "a new face"; but she also asserts that if free of Mark she would still not be free, that Tristram could have stopped her misery only if he had spoken earlier. When he says that if he hadn't been asleep in paradise he would have defied God

to claim her, she smiles, stops crying, and remembers a moment on the ship taking her to Mark during which she thought Tristram might speak "one true word" to her. Instead, he remained loyal to a nothing, said nothing, never even kissed her. She says God made her "all love," deprived of which, many suffering women become "mostly pride and fire." She urges Tristram to believe that he is all there is in her life, says he can't save her, and wonders if he should remain with her in Mark's house. Tristram says he would prefer death, by rocks and the water, his sword, any poison; says he must leave; says time is on their side.

Their melting embrace is shattered by Brangwaine's shouted warning from the nearby garden. Isolt fears for Tristram, only later for herself. Tristram suddenly finds Andred, spying on them, hurls him head first into a wall, and leaves him badly crumpled.

IV. King Mark appears, orders Gouvernail, also arriving, to get Brangwaine and escort her and Isolt out, and then to return with guards to hold Tristram, whom he asks what happened to Andred. Tristram sees Isolt's "frightened eyes" as she is led off. He turns and answers Mark so sarcastically, so critically of the snake called Andred, and mentioning the word "apology" so evasively that Mark threatens him. Tristram sees his uncle thus:

> two red and rheumy eyes,
> Pouched in a face that nature had made comely,
> And in appearance was indulgently
> Ordained to wait on lust and wine and riot
> For more years yet than leeches might foresee.

Tristram comments to himself that honor is unknown to Mark, who rebukes Tristram for dishonor, says sarcastically that he will spare Tristram because he is his own sister's son, and orders him to accept either exile from Cornwall or death. Tristram asks what he has done, says he wouldn't mind death, and calls Andred his "lizard-cousin," therefore conscious again instead of dead. Andred spits, snarls, says Tristram and Isolt were kissing and pledging themselves to each other, and calls himself loyal to Mark, who signals Andred's removal and Gouvernail's departure.

Mark rages in tears, then reminds Tristram that he tried to steal his queen as though she were the king's gold. To which Tristram says he rid Cornwall of Morhaus, brought Mark his queen, loved her when she couldn't love Mark, and a marriage with "rituals, lies, and jigs and drinking" is ugly. Leering, Mark hints that Tristram may become insane if he lets jealousy, that "reptile with green eyes," eat at his heart. Mark banishes Tristram this instant from Cornwall. If he returns, Mark swears, he will have Isolt watch him be burned alive — his "passion [thus] cooling in the flames." Saying he spares Mark to secure Isolt's safety, Tristram leaves.

Tristram trudges for miles under rains that couldn't cool him, thinks of sending a message to Lancelot and Gawaine at Camelot, imagines Isolt in Mark's foul embrace, regards his own sin with her as "not sin, but fate," but concludes that their love can "be fulfilled / Only in death." Two nights later he sprawls under a tree, where shame, rage, and madness follow and turn him feverish. He murmurs "Isolt," smiles, sleeps, and awakens in a sunlit barn. Gouvernail, who followed Tristram, is caring for his sick friend, carts him onward.

Days later, Tristram finds Morgan hovering over him and pronouncing him "safer here than in your shroud." She alternately feels triumphant and frustrated. She recalls that other men, sometimes mere "willing remnants" or "eager cinders," have succumbed to her; but here's this Tristram now, lonely, lethargic, and still half-dead. In a voice of metal, she taunts him by saying he'll be going soon, leaving her to knit and wither. He "forgetfully" surveys her "studied feline slenderness / Where frugal silk was not frugality." The ravishing face of violet-eyed Isolt flies between them; but sloth created a hunger and a remorseful surrender in him, and he grabs Morgan "like an animal." With her fondling arms like hot snakes around him, Tristram, hating both her and himself, lifts the laughing woman and carries her away.

Gouvernail and Morgan's mute guard wait. After a fortnight, Tristram, having often said he must leave, finally does so. Morgan, angry, injured, venomously proud, and with a steely laugh, calls him blind, hints he'll never find a doctor to cure his heart of "the poison of a lost Isolt," warns him not to try to "put Fate's eyes out," and says they might meet again. Riding out with Gouvernail and extolling his unique loyalty, Tristram worries that the occupant of "that snake's nest" behind them, spurned and hence venomous, and also Andred, weak and malignantly envious "from birth," are both everlastingly evil. He proposes going to Brittany, where there's peace, and also a virtuous king with a white-handed daughter to whom he once gave an agate and whose innocence may make him wise, and then strength may follow. Gouvernail advises Tristram to believe that time's big box of future days may contain one for Tristram to gladden and enlighten him. He calls Tristram a king, whether ever of Lyonesse or somewhere else, and complains that many kings have been born to be anything but. Tristram replies that he must learn to rule himself before ruling anything else. Gouvernail remains patient.

V. King Howel welcomes Tristram to Brittany. Little Isolt of the white hands is there. When Howel says that his bad neighbors, under Griffon, are threatening to attack, Tristram volunteers some new military strategies and quickly disposes of Griffon and his minions. Tristram takes Isolt's harp and sings carelessly about himself to her. He thinks it advisable to save this "small white pawn" from being sacrificed in "the cold game of kings."

One summer Tristram and Isolt are together by the twilit sea. Sorrow becomes pity, and pity a kind of non-love love. They embrace. His "bewildered lips" sense "the sting of [her] happy tears." Although his heart is in Cornwall, he will comfort this Isolt's hope with "kind lies." Her gray eyes signal him not to break silence by words. If he should return to Tintagel, Mark would burn him alive before the violet eyes of the other Isolt. When this child-like Isolt says she persuaded her father that Tristram would keep his word and come again, Tristram, captivated by her gray eyes and obvious need of him, says gently that he might not have returned. He wonders why one Isolt's name is written in red on his heart, another, in white. They walk inside.

Time passes. Tristram sings of wars and love. He wonders, half weeping, whether rose-white Isolt sees enough beyond her fingers to see herself alone again. He smiles at her. Her large eyes are unsmiling in return but express her need. Is she wise past thought, or innocent past wisdom? This "wise fiery thing" now becomes his wife. Howel holds Tristram's hands and tells him this uncomplaining woman-child is his "to keep or crush" and to ask life simply "to be life, and fate." Tristram's response is to see moonlit eyes above Cornish shores.

As though he would inherit the Breton kingdom, Tristram builds an able army, more ships, docks, new housing that distresses conservative critics, and a garden in which his "white rose" wife was more beautiful than any rose — except that "Dark and love-red" one, forever absent.

Two years pass. Rumors rumble far away and roll into silence. Then one afternoon Isolt asks Tristram what she would do if he should die. It would be one thing if he were to go away, because he would return. But die? She says that she senses a fearful shadow on him and adds that she is fated not to have everything. He holds her, equivocates about wisdom and "sick reality," then suddenly sees a ship coming in from the north. He feels Isolt "scorching him / With an unconscious and accusing fire." Although she says she used to watch for such ships but no longer does so, she is soon terrified when he identifies the ship as from Arthur. While she goes inside and waits at her same old window, he greets Gawaine from Camelot.

VI. Gawaine and Isolt of Brittany are sitting in her garden. He wonders what Tristram, here with Isolt, could be griping about. Aloud, he dithyrambically praises her: She is wonderful, not fragile at all, with eyes that could look down on the earth and see it as puny, hair "whiter than gold," little alabaster ears, flower-like face, low voice like singing bells. He "dare not estimate" the rest of her except her perfectly created hands and feet. She emanates divinity. He is happy he didn't woo her unsuccessfully and inevitably be wounded unhealingly.

Isolt praises Gawaine's probably often-used rhetoric and says it still remains sharp for future service. He detects care behind her laughing eyes. She says she can't go after him and save him from harmlessly talking but being taken seriously by others. She senses a concern in him, asks about Tristram's being called by Arthur to be made a knight of his Round Table, and wonders if she should be naive enough to think that, once away again, Tristram would ever return to her. Though doubtful, Gawaine says she must believe he would — anyone would, for such a woman as she. She fears that Mark will kill Tristram. Gawaine says Mark can't, because — and this is confidential — he has been imprisoned for forging the pope's name on an order for Tristram to go fight Saracens, and surely die doing so. Gawaine tries to assure Isolt that Tristram will return either quickly or, if slowly, wiser and still happily hers. Isolt thanks him for his frankness but can't muster a smile. Gawaine is hopelessly fond of her.

Gawaine finds Tristram looking at the ship which is to sail next morning for England. Gawaine can't see ahead to Camelot, a place supposedly stable but soon to be wrecked "by love and fate / And loyalty forsworn." He tells Tristram he should remain with Isolt in her garden through fear of Mark's long arm, but since he won't, he should be knighted by Arthur and return to Brittany immediately.

Tristram, alone now by the lapping sea, hears it whisper the name "Isolt," sees her wild violet eyes, but then enters white Isolt's garden and sees her tear-filled eyes. He tortures himself by wondering

> if such a love as hers
> Might not unshared be nearer to God's need,
> In His endurance of a blinder Fate,
> Than a love shared asunder, but still shared,
> By two for doom elected and withheld
> Apart for time to play with.

He scrutinizes his life ahead, sees no light, and ponders matters of darkness, time, and peace somewhere.

Isolt tells Tristram he can't be annoyed that she is joylessly anticipating loneliness — and for how long? Calling her his "child," he hints that Arthur won't take "for ever" to knight him, then mentions King Mark. At this, Isolt blurts that he shouldn't name him, or one other, at this time, and despite interruptions asks what thieves he plans to bear arms against as a new knight, and wishes he had had that other woman and then reported to her for healing. Tristram corrects her belief that Gawaine arrived here from Mark's Cornwall; it was from Arthur's Camelot. When she apologizes, he is aware of her terror and must soothe her with "cold lies"; even so, he sees violet eyes behind his present sunny garden. Isolt walks away in anger, leaving him to stare at the flashing sea.

Next morning, no longer showing distress, Isolt on the shore waves a white hand for all to see, smiles just for Tristram, now aboard the ship for Camelot, sees Gawaine, his wounded heart already mended, wave his "gay hat," and hears trumpets and grateful citizens shouting farewell to Tristram. Later, at the same window where she watched for a different ship, Isolt sees a ship turning to a speck, then sees white birds flying above the sunlit sea.

VII. In Cornwall, Isolt of Ireland has distanced herself from Mark, now regards him as more common than base, more ruinous to himself and to others than cruel, and wonders why he doesn't sell her. Brangwaine suggests hiring killers to drown Mark, and Andred as well. By almost two years later, Isolt's fiery love and fear have burned her down to a longing for longing to end.

Tristram, remaining in Joyous Gard after Lancelot's departure, broods, looks north, envisions wild-eyed Isolt on the stairs above the Cornish breakers, and half hopes she is dead, hence at peace and sure to visit him in spirit a final time. Suddenly his Isolt is there. They kiss and embrace fervently. She moves back, or did in thought, and "smiled at him as only joy made wise / By sorrow smiles at fear." That smile teaches him enough. Her radiant face reveals utter love and understanding.

It seems that Guinevere profited from Mark's imprisonment and, attended by two loyal persons, proceeded to Cornwall and beyond. Tristram doubts this miracle — wrought by God, death, or fate — until Isolt speaks. She laughs. He shakes like a tower in a storm, then pressures her with his giant strength. The two speak of time, their love, the world lost and perhaps dead elsewhere, their unique reality, death. Soon, her fiery eyes and sad smile foretell what he doesn't see. He says they needn't speak, to know. She says this is their eternal moment; later, if she dies, she wants him to be

happy. He says they are safe this night, in this place. Her warmth in a throbbing embrace warns him that heat can cool. In a voice combining velvet and gold, she says they are caged together and she is reluctant to see beyond it. He sees only Isolt, incomparably finer than — and far from — flame, sunsets, trees after rain, sleeping children. She says God made each of them for the other. Or was it fate? If she dies first, he won't forget her; if he dies first, she won't have long to wait. Conclusively, she adds,

> My life to me is not a little thing;
> It is a fearful and a lovely thing;
> Only my love is more.

His answer is that for many people "Living is mostly for a time not dying — / But not for me."

She chides him a little. Then her flaming kiss makes his power turn helpless until her breathing and her hot beauty are "almost a part of him." He holds her close through fear she'll vanish. They speak of loneliness. She cogently concludes that "If life that comes from love is more than death, / Love must be more than death and life together." Saying love is the most, he expresses such fear of trouble's approach that she wonders if she should dismiss him now. He reassures her that "Gold and glory" are inferior to love, the only reality. They kiss wordlessly. Foamy waves near them whisper an "unceasing sound of doom." She says that nothing is worth fearing "Here between life and death." He cautions her to believe her stars, which don't talk of love and death but only of love. His smothered words, "Half silenced in a darkness of warm hair," assure her that love will outlast the stars, that time is nothing, that tonight is all.

VIII. Late this summer morning, Tristram leaves wet- and sleepy-eyed Isolt, walks through a forest and past a sea-like field, untrampled yet by men and horses, and plunges into the sea to splash and swim like a fish. Her violet eyes seem to laugh when he emerges for air. The laughing, whispering trees seem to tell him to be content here for a time. Security stands vigil over Joyous Gard for many days. Summer is fading. He talks to Isolt, stroking her as though she might be a cat, about her beautiful face, which, he says, if joy fattened it, would still inspire his love. She replies at great length: Were she deformed, he would return to Brittany; they aren't meant for old age together; she will die young; he mustn't suffer on her account; his world of "fame and banners" is for him alone; he'll soon return to Brittany. Isolt demands and receives a kiss. Then silence. She says she'll pretend to believe his pledge of love regardless, then expresses fear of rich Mark's long reach. Despite Tristram's vows of constancy, she smiles, shakes her head, and this time looks at him with uniquely shadowed eyes.

Autumn finds Tristram happily riding, singing with fishermen, finding new scenery in brief "manful" escapes while seeing but not hearing other women, and always returning to her, feeling her, and hearing his heart's music. Joyous Gard holds "heaven and all but God / To welcome him."

One day, laden with flowers for Isolt, Tristram rides back, passes strange men at the gate, and enters one room after another throughout their house, calling for Isolt in vain. She is gone. Frozen in fear, he stands like an unbreathing "man of bronze," stumbles, finds a chair in a shadowy corner, and sees Gawaine, fated to smite him with bad news.

Gawaine explains that Brangwaine just told him that Mark, freed for a time, sent his men to Brittany, where they found his queen sitting by the shore "Alone and happy," and are even now returning her by ship to Cornwall. Gawaine warns Tristram against trying to recapture a king's wife and instead encourages him to start a new life. All these words cause Tristram to fall like a log. Gawaine, Brangwaine, and Gouveneril put him on a couch and wait a week while the wordless fellow mends a trifle. Gawaine and Brangwaine leave for Camelot. Sad to learn that sweet Brangwaine was leaving, Gouvernail sighs and thinks that if love does all this to Tristram — now insane, deadened, or whatever — he'd rather live alone on a rock, drink seawater, and eat himself.

Gouvernail stays a month with wooden Tristram, then conveys a report to him from Camelot: Isolt is alive in Cornwall. Tristram

tells Gouvernail not to get involved. They wait some days. Then comes a letter to Tristram from Morgan: Isolt is in Cornwall; in his place, she would prove fate right by galloping there. Tristram tells Gouvernail that tomorrow he will head for something perhaps more than a mere journey and that Gouvernail should return to Brittany with this message: He remembers; won't lie to "her"; something more than himself was between him and her. Gouvernail says he'll deliver those words but not tomorrow, since he purposes to accompany Tristram on that trip of his.

IX. Isolt, in Cornwall a month, looks one afternoon from a parapet in Cornwall at a ship on the sleepy sea. Mark, repenting, tells her this: "I shall do no more harm to either of you / Hereafter, and cannot do more to myself." Although it was natural, he adds, to get her back, he's now unsure of himself and fate. He says she's free but wants not to see Tristram again. Mark's mercy surprises Isolt, who calls him good and kind, and says she will no longer fear either him or Andred, that fawning dog, who, she adds, once insanely loved her. Mark says Morgan has been toying like a cat with the seemingly love-struck fool.

Isolt's sorrowful thoughts for Mark, "foredoomed to be himself," are interrupted by Brangwaine. Tristram is here. Mark takes Brangwaine away. Tristram enters, embraces Isolt, sits, holds her hands, and concludes that she persuaded Mark to be generous. When he says that she could get the devil to unbar hell's doors, she replies that she and Tristram are in heaven while he is here — and when gone, he will be here still. She is sorry Mark must be Mark, wonders if she and Tristram should lament their natures, says her one summer with him was enough to ask of God. She wants only his happiness; he, only hers. She says their season of love was so full that time forgot them. In these words he senses "an unwilling / And wistful intimation of things ended." So he says that when he becomes God he'll create stars to shine for her to see.

While couched, Isolt fixes her violet eyes on Tristram so calmly that they hurt him and yet they could also gently tell him lies. She predicts that he will return to Brittany, to that other Isolt, perhaps become king there, may be king of his Lyonesse, and will when old "remember this — this afternoon."

Tristram agrees he'll return to Brittany later; maybe nothing much remains there for him; women do change, and more should, probably. Isolt counters at length: Many women resemble birds that think they have broken wings and can't fly, but find their wings weren't broken and therefore do fly; also, broken wings can heal and mend; some have wings for one flight only; finally, "One will have wings to fly again; / And that is best for him."

He not only sees her lying there, before him, but also mulls her thoughts. She is fair, will vanish, "dark and white / And violet"; must die, and it is best so; he will fly as he wills. He says that what is best, really, is her face, her love, and their flight off England to where time forgot them. She wishes that they could wing together over the still and windless sea, adds that fate has been merciful to him alone, queries whether her "all" was enough for him, and notes that he "told Isolt it was enough" and prays that "she be no burden."

He says he should at first have insisted on separation. She says that he lived while she didn't, that their being together "was too much like always to be time," and that "no more . . . was enough / And . . . all there was." Cradling him, she feels him more as one hurt by fire than by fate. It seems best, while "her . . . peace and wisdom frightened her," to "see . . . / Unseen," and silently "to forget and to remember." Meanwhile, neither sees dark rocks, fate's dark shadow followed by "evil dressed as man," or Andred's flashing knife. Isolt shouts to God. Tristram, glad it wasn't Mark, offers thanks to Andred. Tristram and Isolt both die.

Andred laughs. Brangwaine, Mark, and Gouvernail rush in, all late. Andred kneels, clasps Mark's knees, and gloats of serving Mark the master and of being a lizard no more. Mark half-strangles him, hurls him away, throws his knife into the sea, and then stands sadly above the silent couple. Gouvernail notes the distant ship and the unusual silence of the sea. Mark remembers Isolt's words about such stillness after life but unlike death, perhaps peace. He stares absently at madly ecstatic Andred as though he were an "unreal" sea creature; then

ponders Andred's deed, God's evaluation of it, the silent couple's impossible future, and the certainty that "this is peace."

X. Mark soliloquizes on the parapet: Those two lying within, with no future, are better dead, would not welcome life renewed; fate is stronger than I; I'll not know such incredible love as theirs; I learned too late that I'll never know certain darknesses; perhaps those two victoriously tore "life from time" like a flower full of death; perhaps Morgan guided the knife of that "sick misshapen grief"; I don't know what this probably "more than random issue," bringing peace for two, brings me and what comes later for me.

The distant ship disappears. Mark goes inside, to be worn out by Gouvernail and silence, until he finds more silence, darkness, and peace.

Meanwhile, in Brittany the white-handed Isolt waits and looks for a ship and waits. One day Gouvernail arrives and reports to her father, King Howel, who, with Gouvernail's concurrence, tells her that Tristram, permitted by Mark, saw Queen Isolt once more before her death, planned to proceed to Brittany, but was killed by a mad kinsman named Andred. Howel hopes his Isolt will recover. But that night she wept and mumbled. After many a silent day, her father finds her sitting by the cold waves. They whisper "Tristram" to her, just as, unknown to her, they once whispered a different name to him. Her aging father gently lectures her: It has been two years since Tristram married you while loving another; you mustn't live with a ghost until you die, ahead of me; remember you are beautiful and famous; quit having expensive dreams; you'll soon be queen, and after my death "all you are will shine for me."

Isolt replies that she may be a queen "Of Here or Hereafter" later, that she must be allowed to dream first, that she knows Tristram once went away but will be with her always now, and that no one can learn wisdom at another knees — "Not even a father's" — since

Wisdom is not one word and then another,
Till words are like dry leaves under a tree;
Wisdom is like a dawn that comes up slowly
Out of an unknown ocean.

Howel chides Isolt that some wisdom drops into darkness, to be followed by a "new dawn"—one, say, for her. He predicts she will change, because, just as the last two years changed her, so the next two will as well.

Isolt's answer: My present wisdom sinks; I will die, but not alone; I would have been all in all for Tristram but was naught to the man, whom "an almost visible doom" accompanied, who seemed too strong to die but was too ill-"mingled" to survive long; something in him and in me "that died for him" was unearthly; if he hadn't died, he would have been kind and sweet while pitying me; if in his arms later, I wouldn't have been aware of his distance from me; now, when sleepless, I will "know where he is." Her father caresses her hair, hopes his treatment of her was wise, studies her gray eyes, and leaves her.

Isolt watches the sea. No ship could bring gold worth the agate he gave and then forgot. She imagines the unseen castle where he had been with and died for another, not, perhaps, thinking of his Isolt of the white hands. He was her all but never returned, alive, to her, even but briefly.

> It was like that
> For women, sometimes, and might be so too often
> For women like her. She hoped there were not many
> Of them, or many of them to be, not knowing
> More about that than about waves and foam,
> And white birds everywhere, flying, and flying . . .

And Isolt kept watching the birds over Breton waters until her very thoughts turn white.

Esther Willard Bates* says that the working title for *Tristram* was *Tristram and Isolt* until the typescript was sent to the publisher. According to Ruth Nivison,* her mother Emma Robinson* saw so many parallels between Isolt and Tristram on the one hand, and herself and ill-starred Robinson on the other, that she indignantly asked him how he could ever publish such a revelation; Nivison adds that Robinson's reply was that no one in Gardiner, Maine, would ever make the connection. Chard Powers Smith* reports that Elizabeth Sparhawk-Jones* regarded Isolt of the white hands as partly modeled on herself.

Literary sources Robinson used for *Tristram*, and also for *Merlin* and *Lancelot*, both of which preceded it, are *Le Morte d'Arthur* by Sir Thomas Malory, *Tristram and Iseult* by Matthew Arnold, *Idylls of the King* by Alfred, Lord Tennyson, *Tristram of Lyonesse* by Algernon Charles Swinburne, and part of the French version that Swinburne followed. Robinson would have nothing to do with the tragic lovers' relationship being triggered by the original love potion, which figures in *Tristan und Isolde* (1865) by Richard Wagner. Robinson attended several performances of this opera and others by Wagner, and also studied the *Tristan und Isolde* libretto. Smith says *Tristan und Isolde* was Robinson's favorite opera. But Robinson wrote (July 29, 1925) to Lewis Montefiore Isaacs* that "Even with Wagner's music, the love potion makes the whole story silly for me." Charles T. Davis (1969) compares and contrasts Wagner's and Robinson's handling of the powerful love story. Andred's actions as murderer were Robinson's invention.

In 1930 Charles Cestre* was the first non-American critic to praise *Tristram* in detailed professional terms. Noting its "beauty and pathos" at the outset of his commentary, Cestre goes on to say that its "exceptional merit . . . is due to the wistful thoughtfulness of the characters in the grasp of an irresistible passion, to the decorous intensity of the feelings, to the perfect art of composition and the subdued glow of the style—in a word, to the classic artistry which decks the old romantic tale with proportionate and equable beauty." As for Robinson's restraint in adumbrating consummated passion, Cestre applauds the fact that he "resorts to indirection and suggestion—within the limits of his wonted reserve—to depict a situation where the modern school of the sex-appeal would seize on every opportunity to pile up crudities." Frederic Ives Carpenter in an early, major essay (1938) on *Tristram* summarizes critical responses to the poem already gathering, suggests its continuity following Robinson's previous works (notably *Merlin* and *Lancelot*), contrasts Robinson's Tristram with previous treatments of the famous love story, relates ideas in it to the Transcendentalism of Ralph Waldo Emerson, and concludes that far from denying and refuting Transcendental traditions it embodies them well. Hoyt C. Franchere, after identifying Robinson's principal sources for *Tristram*, helpfully analyzes its structure, dramatic dialogues, transitions, central and minor characters, lyricism, and sensuousness. Louise Dauner, who has examined Robinson's whole gallery of women, regards the Isolt of Cornwall as "perhaps the loveliest and most moving of Robinson's feminine creations." E. Edith Pipkin says that "*Tristram* is tragic, but the tragic element lacks the grim austerity of *Merlin* and *Lancelot*," and adds that "the poem is a glorification of love, and Isolt gives expression to its dominant idea" by saying her love for Tristram is more important than her life itself. In an analysis of the three leading lover in *Tristram*, Glauco Cambon compares Tristram to Robinson himself: Robinson is held in tension between the cultural heritages of his Old World and his New World, just as Tristram hovers between Isolt of Brittany (Continental, watery, diurnal, temporal) and Isolt of Cornwall (farther to the West, fiery, nocturnal, eternal). S. L. Clark and Julian N. Wasserman define the uniqueness of the love of Tristram and Isolt of Cornwall: "For Mark, and for the other members of society in this poem, love is time-bound. One can look back upon its occurrence or posit its recurrence, but one can never escape its essential temporality. For Tristram and Isolt, however, love occurs in time but goes beyond time." Emery Neff suggests that in naturalistically describing Tristram's frustration at the thought of his precious Isolt with goatish King Mark, Robinson "broke the sex taboo" which had already been weakened earlier by some of his favorite French authors. Nathan Comfort Starr, giving Mark short shrift, feels that his "coarseness is but little redeemed by his stunned comprehension at the final tragedy." Ellsworth Barnard observes that "*Tristram* also [as in *Merlin*] draws its significance and derives its appeal from the changes in the characters," with Tristram and Isolt becoming humble, Mark ceasing to hate, and the other Isolt turning tragically simple. Laurence Perrine presents evidence to show "that Andred stabbed only Tristram and that Isolt died, almost simultaneously, of the shock and of her love," and therefore concludes that

"Isolt's love-death is one of the most carefully prepared-for incidents in *Tristram*."

Louis Coxe calls Robinson's *Tristram* "the only meretricious performance of his career," because the poet admittedly regarded it as "a conscious appeal to a wide public." Does that make the result "meretricious"? In evident agreement, Robert Mezey calls *Tristram* the "flabbiest" of Robinson's Arthurian efforts. More engagingly, Charles T. Davis (1961) notes that the sea imagery in *Tristram* suggests not only what is forceful, unfathomable, and indifferent in the natural world, but also what at last leads one mostly to a resigned, peaceful acceptance. The sea tortures but later pleases Tristram, educates Isolt of the white hands, but, to be sure, puzzles Mark.

Robinson dedicated *Tristram* "To the Memory of Edward Proby Fox." Herman Hagedorn* and Richard Cary report that Fox was Robinson's uncle by marriage on his father's side, that Fox worked for the Riverside Press in Cambridge, and that he had negotiated for the publication of *The Torrent and The Night Before*—with the $52 cost to be borne by the poet. Robinson wrote *Tristram* painstakingly, often in a mood akin to agony. It is Robinson's longest poem. It is 4,127 lines and in the standard *Collected Poems* 135 pages. Shakespeare's two narrative poems, *Venus and Adonis* and *The Rape of Lucrece*, together total only 3,049 lines, thus comprising only three-quarters the length of Robinson's *Tristram*.

The Literary Guild, in the planning stage from 1921, was officially organized in 1927. This was fortunate for Robinson, whose *Tristram* the guild selected for distribution and ordered 12,000 copies for starters. Bacon Collamore* provides details of an evening honoring Robinson at New York's Little Theatre on May 8, 1927. Collamore quotes from a letter (May 2, 1927) in which Robinson cutely says that the program may merit inclusion in the recipient's antique collection. Robinson predictably declined an invitation to read from his *Tristram*; but Mrs. August Belmont, i.e., the actress May Robson (1865–1942), was happy to do so. Collamore adds that the Literary Guild edition and the Macmillan trade edition enjoyed 20 printings, sold 75,000 copies the first year, and made Robinson such a celebrity that he grew embarrassed. The next two years of royalties, mostly from *Tristram* but partly from small continuing sales of his *Collected Poems*, came to at least $30,000, according to Smith, who adds that *Tristram* sold steadily through America's Great Depression. Francis Murphy says that before Robinson's death *Tristram* sold more than 100,000 copies. William Rose Benét contends that *Tristram* earned Robinson $80,000. (Sources: Barnard, 109–10; Bates, 19; Benét, 54; Cambon, 66; Carpenter; Cary [1974], 25–26; Cestre, 12, 110; Clark, 112; Collamore, 36; Coxe, 123; Dauner, 156; Davis [1961], 384–85; Davis [1969], 97–99; Franchere, 116–17, 127–33; Hagedorn, 106; Lacy; Mezey, xl; Murphy, 4; Neff, 224; Perrine [March 1949]; Pipkin, 194, 195; E. Robinson, 18; *Selected Letters*, 145; C. Smith, 53, 262, 347–48; Starr [1954], 79).

Tryon, James L. (1864–1958). Author. James Libby Tryon met Robinson at Harvard, in the fall of 1891, at a small reception in the home of Fréderic César de Sumichrast,* a professor who had been assigned as adviser to both young men. Tryon, in his junior year, and Robinson, just beginning as a special student, became close friends until Robinson withdrew from school (1893). Tryon later wrote books concerning the United States and Canada, the League of Nations, international justice, and international peace. He delivered a speech extolling Robinson at a Colby College Phi Beta Kappa chapter meeting (April 16, 1940) and published his remarks as a 16-page pamphlet entitled *Harvard Days with Edwin Arlington Robinson* (1940). In it Tryon quickly establishes his tone by defining Robinson as "constant in friendship, with a charity that envieth not and a chivalry that halloweth criticism." (Source: Tryon, 3–4)

"Twilight Song" (1902, 1968). Poem. The persona says that he and his comrades have marched long and hard, through sunshine and in rain. Together, they have also laughed, wept, and "tossed the King's crown." Some of his friends have died. So, this evening, it's time to sing a while. A long time ago, a sign appeared in the sky, and they grew fearful, because the King was nearby. At night, they had dreams, which daylight came and destroyed. But there's a road ahead now, because the King has died. There may be danger ahead, but they've all cooperated. Also,

> We may laugh down the dream,
> For the dream breaks and flies;
> And we trust now the gleam,
> For the gleam never dies.

They can now unburden themselves, because of knowledge of the future. Yes, they've laughed and wept, fought and died, but also "burned the King's bones." So, they will now sing again and soon confront "Where the road leads along / Through the shine, through the rain."

In two additional stanzas, originally deleted, the persona, aware that he and his friends have worked, played, loved, and sung together, recalls specific actions — about winning, resting, watching the curling leaves, seeing a boy and a girl with the King and the Queen, and hearing the King's knell.

Hermann Hagedorn* reports that Robinson encountered great trouble in composing "Twilight Song," which he called "a long-legged lyric." Hagedorn adds that Robinson said that it would be regarded as obscure, that he meant it to be impressionistic, that William Vaughn Moody* persuaded him to cut 24 lines, and that he asked Josephine Preston Peabody* to cut another two dozen if she could. This poem has three main prosodic virtues. First, it is composed in easy, sing-song anapestic lines, dimeter in essential stress. Second, it has a captivatingly simple rhyme scheme, *ababcdcd-eaea*. Third is the neat way in which, refrain-like, the first line and the last line of the first stanza are identical ("Through the shine, through the rain") and are exactly echoed in the fourth stanza, while the eighth line of the first stanza is repeated in the eighth line of the fourth stanza ("Ere the night flies again").

Richard Cary presents evidence that Theodore Roosevelt,* upon receipt of *Captain Craig* (rev. ed., February 10, 1915), in which "Twilight Song" reappeared, wrote Robinson that he was fond of many poems in it but perhaps "Twilight" most. Ellsworth Barnard finds "Twilight Song" to be "an unexpectedly buoyant representation . . . of humanity's march across the ages." The composer Daniel Gregory Mason* set the opening lines of "Twilight Song" to music as a chorus of mixed voices (1934). The lines are "Through the shine, through the rain, / We have shared the day's load." Mason sent a copy to Robinson, who replied (May 14, 1934) that he and a musical friend had gone over it together with pleasure. That letter was Robinson's last one to his old friend. (Sources: Barnard, 74; Brower, 119–20; Cary [1975], 47, 182; Cary [1974], 276; Hagedorn, 169, 178; Mason [Spring 1937], 240)

"Two Gardens in Linndale" (1910).

Poem. Oakes and Oliver are a pair of gentle, loving brothers. They have inherited land, which they divide with a fence and will turn into separate gardens. Oakes says he feels born to raise artichokes. Oliver cautions that their father warned them that artichokes wouldn't grow in this soil. But Oakes perseveres. Oliver, respecting Oakes's "vision," hopes God will help him. Each attends his own "enterprise," with Oliver's being implicitly more conventional. Hoping for mutual success, the two plan to rejoice and sing together, and meanwhile "lived along in innocence." Years pass, and no artichokes. One day "the Stranger," who is also "a Gardiner," comes between the brothers, remains only a short time, "and then / The land was all for Oliver." Oliver sows and harvests successfully, all the while listening for his sleeping brother's songs, which prove to be "undreamed of and unknown." Mostly Oliver hears his brother's dawn-time songs when nearby "Birds ring the chorus of the light." Although Oliver, this "gentle anchorite," can't sing without Oakes's accompaniment, he remains worshipfully patient, since he was selected to be the "heir of age and pain." He sits, smokes, and wonders who will "by God's grace" eventually inherit these two Linndale gardens. Oliver often sees Oakes's ghost restlessly digging up "Soft, shadowy flowers in a land / Of asphodels and artichokes."

Emma Robinson* and Ruth Nivison* label this poem a lyrical satire, the subject of which is the Palmer brothers in Pittston. But it is far more. Louis Coxe says that it "is about art,

about poetry"; he retreats, however, to add that he "do[es] not mean to suggest that the poem . . . is solely or even primarily about poetry . . . [but] that 'poetry' here becomes a symbol of man's devotion to a great endeavor impossible of achievement, one which uplifts him as man and brings him close to both his forebears and his brothers, and in so doing creates a grace beyond the reach of art." Ellsworth Barnard says that the poem "support[s] . . . the principle that every human being has the right to live his own life, so long as he does no injury to another."

The simple format of "Two Gardens in Linndale" suits a story about two gentle brothers. Each of its 19 stanzas has five lines, each in iambic tetrameter, and each rhyming *aabba*. The heroes' proximity to the soil is suggested by their names: Oliver suggests the functional "olive" tree, while Oakes reminds the reader of a tree perhaps more magnificent. (Sources: Bernard, 247; Coxe, 84, 85; E. Robinson, 15)

"Two Men" (1897).

Poem. Robinson says he would like to know about the activities of Melchizedek and Ucalegon. He knows Melchizedek "praised the Lord, / And gave some wine to Abraham"; and he knows Ucalegon "lost his house / When Agamemnon came to Troy." But that's all. Anyone who knows more about the former is very learned; if he knows more about the latter, he deserves great joy. Those two men "chase" the frustrated poet everywhere he goes.

For Melchizedek, see Gen. 14:18–20, Ps. 110:4, Heb. 5, 6, 7. In Genesis, where he first appears, he is the king of Salem, priest of God, meets Abram, brings him bread and wine, blesses him, and receives tithes from him. Later references to him, few in number, are surprising and mysterious. For the one and only mention of Ucalegon in the classics, see Virgil's *Aeneid*, II, 311–12: Agamemnon's men have burned out Deiphobus, and "iam proximus ardet / Ucalegon" (even now his neighbor Ucalegon blazes).

"Two Men" is a quasi-nonsense poem in which Robinson comes as close as he ever did to writing something pleasantly valueless. Laura E. Richards* remembers that when Robinson was 10 or 12 years old, he and Alice

Jordan and her brother Augustus Jordan, two of his closest childhood friends, used to find and shout unusual words at each other. "Melchizedek" was one such word. (Source: Richards [1936], 11)

"Two Octaves" (1897). Two eight-line poems, both numbered.

I. We aren't so much scared by griefs, which keep us from recognizing "righteous omnipresence," as we are by common ordinary upsets, the purpose of which is to make us stronger in these shameful times.

II. The sun's looking down on lazy, sweating, cursing men makes the poet think that God is looking reproachfully at the poet's "arrears" and "unprofitable thoughts." (Source: Cary [1975], 44, 180)

"Two Quatrains" (1897). Poem. Two numbered quatrains.

I. Just as vast problems are epitomized in brief, so mundane little items foreshadow much.

II. We want to live but don't do so until breath stops; we imagine death but don't encounter it until we "quit the road."

"Two Sonnets" (1896). Sonnets. Two, both numbered.

I. Robinson wonders why the person he is addressing waits to see again what is past, and also why he or she is so doubtful of God's love as to "shudder . . ." before "the Unseen." Robinson says he lacks not only the addressee's backward-looking faith to seek God in dead men's names but also that person's "ingenious" belief that we should "cherish" the "features of dead friends" "in the life that is to come."

II. Until we are spiritually "strong enough / To plunge into the crater of the Scheme," "redeem / Love's handsel," and shed our experience-tormented "reptile skins," we will never "get / Where atoms and the ages are one stuff." Neither we will understand "the cursed waste / Of life" amid blessed but sinfully misused "starlight," "sunlight and soul-shine," until "we have drunk, and trembled at the taste [of], / The mead of Thought's prophetic endlessness."

In a letter (April 21, 1897) to Edith Brower,* Robinson expresses annoyance at the "unconscious agreement" of reviewers of *The Torrent and the Night Before* to avoid all mention of "Two Sonnets," which appeared in that volume. In an earlier letter (December 7, 1896), to Harry de Forest Smith,* Robinson declines to lament the death of his mother, Mary Robinson,* instead merely saying that "She has gone ahead and I am glad for her." He continues: "I have come to look on death as a deliverance and an advancement (vide 'Kosmos,' 'Two Sonnets,' etc.) and I am very glad to be able to stand up and say that I am an idealist."

William J. Free explains that the rhetoric of the sestet of the second sonnet aims "to express Robinson's passionate dedication to belief in a numinous world." (Sources: Brower, 39; Free, 18; *Untriangulated Stars*, 264)

"Uncle Ananias" (1905). Poem. Of all the elderly Robinson remembers from his childhood days, the one he labels Uncle Ananias was the most outstanding. This true-hearted fellow, whose words were "magic," was welcome everywhere, and — by the poet, at least — was "crown[ed] . . . loveliest" among "all authoritative liars." In springtime, the old man expressed "faith in everything." In the summer, the poet and his buddies sat at the codger's knees under apple trees, where his magnificently sinful fibs made "the day sublime." When the foliage turned an autumnal russet, his words, "winged with a feathery flame / Like birds of paradise," created whirling visions before the children's eyes. Throughout the seasons, he fearlessly wore "The laurel of approved iniquity," and children nearby and from far away all "love[d]" him faithfully."

Emma Robinson* and Ruth Nivison* identify the local Ananias as William Morrell, the Robinsons' neighbor on Lincoln Street, Gardiner, Maine. His wife was Mary Morrell.* Their son Harry Morrell and Robinson enjoyed listening to his stories. The Ananias of the Bible (Acts 5:1–5), having lied to the Holy Ghost and to God, was rebuked by Peter and fell dead.

Hermann Hagedorn* and Chard Powers

Smith* report that Robinson was at a low point, financially and professionally, in New York, when on March 24, 1905, he sold "Uncle Ananias" to Richard Watson Gilder,* editor of *Century Magazine.* It was his first sale since Lippincott's bought his sonnet entitled "For a Copy of Poe's Poems" 10 or so years earlier, and his success was owing to the pressure Theodore Roosevelt* had put on Gilder. In a letter (October 2, 1905) to Edith Bower,* Robinson reveals his annoyance that his "Uncle Ananias," though earning him $20, was set in small type and published alongside comic writing. (It appeared in the *Century* department entitled "In Lighter Vein.") But why should Robinson have complained? After all, the poem is about a colorful village prevaricator, who may have delighted kids, to be sure, and yet was not, frankly, a completely acceptable role model. Evidently disliking such sobersided thinking, Ellsworth Barnard opines that "Uncle Ananias" pleases readers at "the thought of the discomfiture . . . of the town's solid citizens [on encountering the fibber], whose inherited Puritan assumption that happiness is a reward for industry and truthfulness is here so blithely challenged." (Sources: Barnard, 185; Brower, 151; Cary [1974], 163; Hagedorn, 212; C. Smith, 216; E. Robinson, 15)

"The Unforgiven" (1915). Poem. A certain man is "the unforgiven." When he first saw a certain woman, he was smitten by her voice, eyes, and fair hair. Her charming glances smote him, and made him blind and glad, humble and mad. A long account of the relationship "would be neither good nor bad." Now behold "Where properly the play begins." There's nothing lurid, nothing sinful, and we don't know "whether man or woman wins." Nor do we know what will follow after this quiet, farcical domestic drama of two broken lives ends. Meanwhile, staring under "his hard half of the cross," he regards love as a coin toss; "she, the unforgiving," greets his smile with a "cold hush" and reviles him more because of lacking something than because of losing something. He assuages his indecisiveness with a touch of pride, remembers when he wasn't her prisoner, and tries to resurrect

the "vision" of her he must have had once. But though waiting, he can never again locate that face, which ruined his aim in life. He doesn't hold her accountable, and she remains silent. In their drama, he is not cast as a Bluebeard. Outsiders calmly reckon that there must be a way out for the two of them. But "there will be no change to-day."

"The Unforgiven" is a bleak narrative in eight seven-line stanzas, with the following complex rhyme scheme: *ababbab,* and — for an added challenge, splendidly met — every *a*-rhyme being feminine.

Ruth Nivison,* following the lead of her mother Emma Robinson,* suggests that this poem depicts the wrecked marriage of her parents, Emma and Herman Robinson,* and that it is presented from the latter's point of view. Chard Powers Smith* partly agrees, saying that the poem "portrays the old tragic impasse between Emma and Herman." Robert Mezey also endorses this interpretation, calling it "on the mark." Robinson in a letter (November 16, 1915) to Edith Brower* says that the poem shows that he has "a better opinion of men than 'The C[linging]. V[ine].' may have led you to fancy." Louis Coxe says that the poem "seems to put a case for divorce." I. D. MacKillop points out that "neat malice becomes a rhetorical scorn in some of the more ambitious character poems [by Robinson,] . . . for instance, . . . [i]n 'The Unforgiven' his rhythm seems to deliver blows at the couple saying almost that the husband has *merely* [MacKillop's emphasis] fallen into one of the many traps that await self-deluding humanity." Robert D. Stevick contrasts "The Unforgiven" and "Eros Turannos," to the disadvantage of "The Unforgiven." Denis Donoghue, on the other hand, regards "The Unforgiven" as "one of the greatest [poems]" in which Robinson depicts frustrated lives; then Donoghue defines its two miserable characters as "not only beyond praise or blame . . . [but] beyond speech itself." (Sources: Brower, 164; Coxe, 133; Donoghue, 33, 35; MacKillop, 297–98; Mezey, 230; E. Robinson, 4; C. Smith, 240; Stevick [1969], 55–59)

"Unquestionable Genius" (1928). Essay. An encomium for Percy MacKaye.* When

MacKaye was turning 50, *Percy MacKaye: Symposium on His Fiftieth Birthday*, a collection of congratulatory essays, was published by the Dartmouth Press, in 300 copies. Robinson's item is on page 44, according to Bacon Collamore.* (Source: Collamore, 46)

Untermeyer, Louis (1885–1977). Man of letters. Untermeyer was born in New York City. At 15, he left school to work for his father, a prosperous jewelry manufacturer. He rose to be vice president of his father's company. Meanwhile, he published humorous verses (from the early 1900s); was a contributing editor of the socialist journal *The Masses* (1911–1917); in his ——— [*sic*] *and Other Poets* (1916) greatly advanced public awareness of Robinson by including a cute parody of him; and co-founded *The Seven Arts* (1916–1917), which published early works by many rising stars, among them Robert Frost (his closest literary friend); and compiled *Modern American Verse* (1919). Retitled *Modern American Poetry* (1921), it enjoyed many revised editions. Untermeyer's later anthologies incorporated modern British poetry. After his father's death, Untermeyer could afford to live in Austria (1923–1925). In 1906 he had married the poet Jean Starr (1886–1970; they had one son). Returning home, Untermeyer obtained a non-binding Mexican divorce; in 1926 married the poet Virginia Moore (b. 1903; they had a child); reunited with Jean Starr Untermeyer (1927) and when their son committed suicide (1930) adopted two children with her; then obtained another Mexican divorce and married a lawyer named Esther Antin (1933).

Untermeyer continued his frenetic life. He lectured widely and was a poet in residence in colleges and universities, often controversially, given his socialist leanings (1937–1940); did editorial work for the federal government during World War II; was the bigamist husband of an editor named Bryna Ivens (beginning in 1948) until their union was legalized (1951); was a panelist on "What's My Line? (CBS's television quiz program) from its inception (1950) until he was ousted (1952) by pressure against liberals inspired by Senator Joseph McCarthy; worked again for the federal government at home and abroad; and, as a consultant

on poetry for the Library of Congress, supervised an exhibit of Robinson's books and manuscripts (1963). Untermeyer's nearly one hundred titles include serious verse, silly pieces, clever paraphrases, a biography of Heinrich Heine (1937), a biblical redaction, critical studies long and short, children's books, items concerning fables and fairy tales, and two autobiographical volumes, *From Another World* (1939) and *Bygones: The Recollections of Louis Untermeyer* (1965). Over many productive decades, Untermeyer complained against Victorian gentility and corporate greed.

In *The New Era in American Poetry* (1919), Untermeyer lauds Robinson's poetry. In *Modern American Poetry* (1921), he included Robinson's "Vain Gratuities," and in later editions of this popular anthology he reprinted additional poems by Robinson. The two men socialized beginning about 1935 at the MacDowell Colony* (see "Too Much Coffee"). Over the years, Untermeyer continued to write favorably about Robinson, at times superficially. One wonders, had Robinson known Untermeyer more thoroughly, what kind of dark poetic narrative he might have created out of his friend's personal, political, and creative adventures. (Sources: Cary [1974], 295–96; Untermeyer)

"Vachel Lindsay" (1932). Essay. Robinson says it is easy but unnecessary to repeat what is commonly known, that the characteristic poetry of Vachel Lindsay (1879–1931) is unlike that of any other poet, dead or alive. It is hard to predict what place later critics, harsher than critics used to be, will assign him, and his contemporaries as well. Lindsay was a unique combination of sincere, wandering evangelist and troubadour. Like that of other people's work, most of his is likely to be forgotten. However, his best would have appealed to cave dwellers and will be accepted by future unsophisticated readers. According to Bacon Collamore,* this one-page tribute appeared in *The Elementary English Review* (May 1932), a memorial number devoted to Lindsay. (Sources: Cary [1975], 112–13, 194; Collamore, 55)

"Vain Gratuities" (1920). Sonnet. She is

the only woman who doesn't regard him as really, truly ugly and grim. Other women all hope she's philosophical, since God has given her a full "chalice" all right. Now that she has been with him some 20 years, they say it's "No wonder that she kept her figure slim / And always made you think of lavender." However, if, "demure as ever, and . . . fair," she had heard their gossip, she would have laughed and it would have impressed her about as much as foam on a silent "island shore / Where there are none to listen or to care."

Louis Coxe notes that "the world outside," which figures in "Vain Gratuities" and elsewhere in Robinson's writings, "has its views and makes its false judgment." (Source: Coxe, 134)

"The Valley of the Shadow" (1918). Poem. In this negative and dreary poem, Robinson begins by saying that "There were faces to remember in the Valley of the Shadow." He catalogues the unwanted, friendless, frustrated, neglected, enslaved, misguided, prematurely aging, gloomy, vehement, alcoholic, falsely flashy, envious, sinful, darkness-seeking, unanswered, and ignorant. He concludes to the effect that "the children of the dark" in the valley could be "builders of new mansions" if they were not "dying" or "blinded" or "maimed."

When readers look at the title "The Valley of the Shadow," most of them probably think of "Yea, though I walk through the valley of the shadow of death, I will fear no evil" (Psalm 23:4). But Robert Mezey says that, "for all its Dantesque vision of some circle of hell," the poem may "not . . . [be] about the afterlife," and "might well have been called *The Valley of the Shadow of Life.*"

Given the date of first publication of this poem, victims of the First World War would be literally included among the mortally ill, the blinded, and the maimed. Wallace L. Anderson summarizes "The Valley of the Shadow" when he says that in it Robinson "brought together as general types some of the 'scattered lives' he had been writing about for years: 'the broken . . . the weary . . . the baffled . . . the shamed' [ellipses Anderson's] and others who for one reason or another find themselves lost, their hopes shattered, their identities gone." Although the metrical form of "The Valley of the Shadow" is mainly rippling heptameter and octameter lines, with iambic and trochaic feet producing nice rhythms, in truth many of its 72 lines read like conversational prose; for example, "Where they saw too late the road they should have taken long ago." Each stanza has a curious rhyme scheme—*abcbdefe*—but, with almost every line stretching to 16 syllables, the rhymes are often sounded faintly. (Sources: W. Anderson [1968], 136; Mezey, 231)

Van Doren, Carl (1885–1950). Author and educator. Carl Clinton Van Doren was born in Hope, Illinois, earned a B.A. at the University of Illinois (1907) and a Ph.D. at Columbia University (1911). While he was a member of the Columbia faculty (1911–1930), he also did editorial work on *The Cambridge History of American Literature* (4 vols., 1917–1921), was literary editor *The Nation* (1919–1922) and of *Century Magazine* (1922–1925), and wrote many pioneering studies of American authors, among other works. He was a founder of the Literary Guild and its first editor (1927–1934), and helped manage (1926–1936) the ongoing and huge *Dictionary of American Biography*. He collaborated with his younger brother Mark Van Doren (1894–1972) on several literary projects. In later years, Carl Van Doren combined his ongoing professional career, capped with a popular biography of Benjamin Franklin (1938), with personal sorrows. He had married Irita Bradford (1912; they had three children but divorced in 1935) and married Jean Wright Gorman (1939; they divorced in 1945); in addition he was long ambitious to be a novelist, failed with *The Ninth Wave* (1926), but too tardily abandoned that dream.

Van Doren accepted "Mr. Flood's Party" for publication in *The Nation*, after *Collier's Weekly* rejected it because old Eben Flood drank too much; later he also accepted "Lost Anchors" for *The Nation*. Still later, he accepted "Haunted House" for *Century Magazine*. Van Doren's autobiography, *Three Worlds* (1936), details a beautiful career. In it, he discusses his long friendship with Robinson, his and his colleagues' choice of *Tristram* to be the third offering of the Literary Guild (May 1927), his persuading his brother Mark to write a 90-page booklet about Robinson to accompany guild shipments of *Tristram*, his organizing a Sunday reading at New York's Little Theatre (May 8, 1927) of parts of *Tristram* by the actress May Robson (1865–1942), and the shy poet's attendance at a reception afterwards. (In his booklet, Mark Van Doren's praise of Robinson is routine and unexceptional in content but was influential through being eloquently phrased.) After Robinson predicted adverse responses by Literary Guild members to his *Tristram*, Carl Van Doren selected a hundred letters out of many hundreds from happy fans and had them copied and sent to him. Van Doren, who regularly reviewed Robinson's works favorably, may have gone overboard when he called *Tristram* "the greatest poem . . . by an American" (*Century*, June 1927). (Source: Brower, 191)

Van Zorn: A Comedy in Three Acts (1914). Drama.

Act I. Weldon Farnham, a successful, self-satisfied painter, 32, in his studio in Macdougal Alley, New York, shows Otto Mink, a young author, his portrait of lovely Villa Vannevar, to whom he is engaged. George Lucas, a sad-looking poet, 29, enters. (It is later revealed that Villa has known Lucas from childhood.) He is greeted by his long-time friend Otto, who calls him Phoebus. Lucas is surprised to learn of Farnham's engagement, congratulates him, and asks for and has some whiskey.

Farnham leaves to run an errand for Mrs. Lovett, Villa's aunt. (Her husband drank himself to death.) Talk between Otto and Lucas establishes this: Lucas came to New York four years ago; he and Villa were once in love; Van Zorn, a multi-millionaire who believes in destiny, is influencing Farnham. Mrs. Lovett and Villa enter, and look at Villa's portrait. Villa dislikes it.

Enter Van Zorn, 32, powerful, engaging, mysterious. Otto introduces him to Mrs. Lovett and Lucas. Villa and Van Zorn recall when they, with Farnham and Otto, visited Van Zorn's boat before his world cruise a year

ago. (Van Zorn first met Villa then, was then gone four years, went to India.) Farnham returns, asks his guests' opinions of his portrait, but dislikes their criticism. Van Zorn looks seriously at Lucas, as Otto is taking him out for gin. Van Zorn and Villa stare at each other, then her aunt whisks her to a luncheon party.

When Farnham becomes frivolous, Van Zorn gets serious, asks about Lucas, says the fellow seems at a cross-roads, and feels he and Lucas are linked somehow. Farnham says this: Lucas's mother died early; his father was a city rounder; Lucas is able but ineffective; we can't defeat "Destiny." Van Zorn agrees but adds that Destiny can make us improve. Pressed about Farnham's engagement to Villa, Van Zorn says, "I may not see life as it is, but I see it as I see it," then warns Farnham that marriage to Villa will make three people unhappy. Farnham asks how long Van Zorn has been planning to marry Villa. Van Zorn says for about four years but time is rather meaningless; he will interview Villa this afternoon, and will be in touch.

Act II. Later that day, Mrs. Lovett is in her comfortable home with Villa, who tells her Otto and Lucas think her marriage to Farnham would be a mistake. The two dispute about Van Zorn, soon to visit, and also about Lucas, whose surprising arrival the maid Jenny announces.

Alone with Villa, Lucas mentions Van Zorn's interest in and concern for him. Lucas says he's going away, from her, from the confining city, maybe forever. Villa admits they made mistakes. Jenny announces Van Zorn. Villa asks Lucas to remain, and says it may be fate that he and Van Zorn are here together.

Van Zorn enters, learns of Lucas's plans, and wants him not to leave New York. Mrs. Lovett enters but escorts Villa out when Van Zorn asks permission to speak with Lucas privately. Van Zorn tells Lucas he wants him to be part of a New York business scheme, gives him a check, persuades him to have dinner with him at his hotel, and accepts a vial of poison from him. Lucas turns serious and leaves.

Villa returns. Van Zorn becomes friendly, and says she looks troubled. When Villa says Lucas is good, Van Zorn counters thus: One of their group ought to be "fortunate"; the others probably won't be; she controls the happiness of three people; he asked Farnham's permission to interview Villa; he may possibly not see her again. When Villa hints that Van Zorn, supposedly Farnham's best friend, is interfering, he hints back, concerning "destiny," warns that her "unalterable will" will make two people and herself unhappy, says years of darkness await her. Villa admits she and Farnham are heading toward fearful dark and wonders if that would be destiny. Van Zorn says yes. Jenny announces Otto.

Otto, having this morning promised Villa a copy of his latest book, hands it to her, bores Van Zorn by reminding her that they boated on the Hudson River, then says that a few minutes ago Lucas, shouting about being born again, refused a gin drink with him along Broadway. Villa is pleased; Van Zorn, not. She hints he caused Lucas's reformation. Van Zorn says Farnham told him about Lucas's father's drinking. Villa suggests Farnham couldn't have known much about that. Apologizing for causing Villa's vexation, Otto leaves.

Van Zorn, when Villa calls him unusual, offers to go. She wants to tell him something first. He declines to take advantage of her sad confusion. She says she is courageous because she trusts him, wonders about waiting until she knows him better. Saying she never will, he quotes John Milton: "They also serve who only stand and wait." She weeps; he leaves.

Act III. That evening Farnham is in his studio. Van Zorn rings, is admitted. After some chit-chat, Van Zorn says he dined with Lucas earlier. Surprised at this, Farnham is further surprised upon learning Lucas didn't get drunk, asks about Van Zorn's so-called destiny. Van Zorn says his is good but someone else's is better, sadly for himself. Farnham is concerned about Van Zorn's interview with Villa at Mrs. Lovett's. Van Zorn counters by saying that he and Lucas are becoming mutually helpful, and that, despite Farnham's distress, Lucas now figures largely. Van Zorn warns Farnham not to gripe about Destiny, says that Lucas was also at Mrs. Lovett's, adds that Farnham will be more fortunate than Van Zorn. He returns to Farnham his engagement ring from Villa and solemnly adds this: Villa

and Lucas, at her request, are this hour together; they will come here in a moment, stay briefly; Farnham and Van Zorn will then talk; all these events would have occurred without Van Zorn, though less suddenly.

Villa and Lucas ring and are admitted by Farnham, who is puzzled. Villa says their engagement was driving her mad; she did something, is responsible, but asked Van Zorn's aid; he was initially reluctant; she has asked Lucas to marry her. Farnham is surprised; Van Zorn also, momentarily. Asked by Farnham to speak, Lucas says Villa has solved a difficult problem. Farnham calls everything an "impetuous farce." Villa calls it "ordained," among other things. Lucas adds that she would have returned Farnham's ring in any event. Farnham blames Van Zorn, who says no human being worked it thus. Villa tells Farnham their marriage would have ruined their lives. When he replies that if lives are ruined so easily, "some of us would be ruined before we were born." Van Zorn comments, "Some of us are." Villa says this: She and Lucas were born for each other, have long known each other, belong to each other; she told this long ago to "Auntie," who volubly didn't like Lucas's father. Farnham does some goading. Lucas replies that he has delayed accepting Villa's proposal in order to do so in Farnham's presence. Van Zorn replies that earlier he merely told Lucas that Villa wanted to see Lucas at about eight o'clock. He tells Farnham, for his art's sake, not to cling to ruins. Villa tells Farnham he's happy to be rid of her. Smiling, he says women's problems are sometimes "simple." At this, she looks at Lucas, then at Van Zorn.

Otto rings, enters, says he saw Farnham's light and came over. The others chatter about seeing the light. Villa asks Otto to congratulate her and Lucas on their engagement. Otto shakes some hands and tells Farnham it's "a kind of destiny." Villa asks Lucas to escort her to Auntie's. First, Otto recites a popular song he has written about a man robbing his baby's piggybank. The young couple leave. Otto helps himself to Farnham's whiskey, hints he may die soon, and heads for what he calls his "mousy garret."

Farnham offers Van Zorn a cigar. They light up. When Farnham mentions destiny, Van

Zorn says this: Otto may have one; Lucas's will probably combine unrealized ambition but also happiness; Farnham will do well. Growing completely serious, Van Zorn says that he himself has truly lost, has lost belief in life; that whereas others face others he faces only himself and is talentless. Farnham suggests that the "Van Zorn and Lucas" commercial business should raze old tenements and build some "sanitary and ornamental" family dwellings. Van Zorn seems receptive. Farnham asks about Lucas's afternoon meeting with Mrs. Lovett. Van Zorn's sole response: Lucas was planning to leave town; his change of mind wasn't caused by Farnham's ring or the woman wearing it. Van Zorn gets Farnham to give him his painting of Villa, calls it "charlatanry," and burns it in the fireplace. To Farnham's slight protest, Van Zorn orders him not to toy with these "extravagant" times but to meet them halfway. Confessing former unawareness of Van Zorn's earnestness, Farnham extends his hand. The men shake, separate, watch the fire. Farnham smiles, seems doubtful.

Robinson was short of money in 1905 and therefore spent the next four years trying to write profitable dramas. The results were *Van Zorn* and *The Porcupine*. Neither was successful. His effort to turn *Van Zorn* into a novel (1910) also failed. The play was published in book form (1914), dedicated to Hermann Hagedorn.* *Van Zorn* was performed for a week by a Brooklyn community theatre group (1917) but did not move elsewhere. (For Robinson's comments on his drama-writing inability, see *The Porcupine*.)

The plot of *Van Zorn* puzzled its few reviewers. Esther Willard Bates,* Robinson's typist, says that she wrote him that she did not understand *Van Zorn* and that he replied to this effect: Van Zorn believes he found his fate in Villa Vannevar, but learns in Act II that he has been unknowingly working for Lucas, who is also ignorant; by now Villa is aware that Van Zorn loves her; this, plus her awareness that she is going to have Lucas, disturbs her. Robinson added that he was probably trying to achieve too much in his play for it to be comprehended. In several letters to Edith Brower,* Robinson complains at the obtuseness of readers of *Van Zorn*, comments on their

interpretations without giving away his own, but also criticizes himself.

Van Zorn is a closet drama lacking confrontational action, is replete with stage directions indicating body language, but is also full of hairsplitting talk, much of it advancing by one character's picking up a word or two from another and adumbrating possible meanings. Robinson often makes his characters bookishly reveal his own literary and musical favorites. The following are mentioned in the play: Lord Byron's *Childe Harold*, Frédéric François Chopin, Samuel Taylor Coleridge's "The Ancient Mariner," Gilbert and Sullivan's *H.M.S. Pinafore*, Alexandre Charles LeCocq's *La Fille de Madame Argot*, William Shakespeare, and Richard Wagner's *Lohengrin*. Irving D. Suss, after calling *Van Zorn* "neither . . . complex . . . nor . . . opaque," analyzes its style and structure. Michael C. Hinden demonstrates that "[p]receding publication of *The Cocktail Party* [1950] by better than three decades, *Van Zorn* anticipates [T. S.] Eliot's play in key aspects of plot, structure, character, setting, mood, tone, and theme." (Sources: Bates, 8–9; Brower, 157–69 passim; Hinden, 463–64; Suss, 353 and passim)

Vannah, Kate (1855–1933). Friend. Letitia Katherine Vannah was born in Gardiner, Maine, the daughter of Isaac G. Vannah, the local hardware merchant, and Eliza C. Rafter Vannah. A precocious child, she gave public piano and organ performances at age nine. She presented the valedictory poem at the time of her high-school graduation (1872). After studying elsewhere, she returned to Gardiner, was the organist for St. Joseph's Catholic Church there, gave recitals, and composed more than two hundred musical scores. Many of her songs are, or at least once were, widely played and cherished, including "Goodby, Sweet Day!" (1891) and "From Heart to Heart" (1893). Two of her books of poetry are *Verses* (1883) and *Poems* (1911).

Hermann Hagedorn* reports the following: Kate told him she could write a sonnet in 10 minutes but Robinson sometimes required six weeks to do so (and therefore one of them was crazy); Kate said Robinson said he would rather live in New York City on four dollars a week than remain in Gardiner (1897); and Kate shocked Gardiner by converting to Catholicism (in the early 1890s). (Sources: Erskine; Hagedorn, 96, 118, 104)

"Variations of Greek Themes" (1915).

Eleven verse translations from 10 Greek poets, in *The Greek Anthology*. Each poem is numbered and titled, with the author parenthetically identified.

I. "A Happy Man (Carphyllides)." The man is happy to say that, now dead and resting among the blest, he had a happy married life, left several children, including three sons, whose sons he "rocked at night."

II. "A Mighty Runner (Nicarchus)." Charmus raced with five others and came in seventh, because a fur-coated friend ran alongside shouting useless encouragement.

III. "The Raven (Nicarchus)." The raven is deadly looking; but when Demophilus sings, it dies.

IV. "Eutychides (Lucilius)." Eutychides wrote songs, has died, and is proceeding to hell with his lyres and songs. Where are the "poor tortured soul[s]" to go who are already there?

V. "Doricha (Posidippus)." You are gone to dust, as has your "scented garment" that you let Charaxus cling to. However, because of Sappho, your beloved name will remain memorable as long as ships "return / Again to Naucratis and to the Nile."

VI. "The Dust of Timas (Sappho)." When Timas, now dust, died "almost on her wedding day," many a maiden wept and cut off her curls.

VII. "Aretemias (Antipater of Sidon)." When you set foot on the shore of Cocytus in Hades, fair Dorian women cried to see you with only one child. You explained that Euphron, your other child, still lives and mourns you.

VIII. "The Old Story (Marcus Argentarius)." Women loved you but only until you lost your wealth. Women who used to speak sweetly to you ask others for information about you now. Are you uniquely tardy in learning that one "who has nothing has no friend?"

IX. "To-morrow (Macedonius)." Tomor-row is virtually all you have to promise me. Other days will belong to another. Oh, you'll see me this evening? "What evening has there been, / Since time began with women, but old age and wrinkled skin?"

X. "Lais to Aphrodite (Plato)." Lais says that when she was beautiful, lovers were aplenty. But, old now, she offers the goddess a mirror of no use to her any more.

XI. "An Inscription by the Sea (Glaucus)." The message is from a shipwreck victim entombed in "this unending sea," without dust, without a grave, and in a place only "the seabirds know."

The Greek Anthology is a collection of about four thousand Greek epigrams, epitaphs, rhetorical exercises, and songs, mostly in elegiac couplets but also in a variety of other meters. Some of the poems are as early as the seventh century B.C.; others were written in A.D. 1000 and a little later, by Christians in the Byzantine Empire. Most of the poems have little but historical value, but several hundred have exquisite literary charm.

Antipater of Sidon was late second century B.C. Carphyllides (Karphyllides, Karpyllides) may predate 90 B.C., or may be second century A.D. Glaucus (Glaukos of Nikopolis) is not datable. Lucilius was mid-first century A.D. Macedonius was late fifth to early sixth century A.D. Marcus Argentarius was first century B.C. to perhaps first century A.D. Nicarchus (Nikarchos) is the name of two poets, one first century B.C., the other mid-first century A.D. Plato the poet, known as Plato the younger (first or second century A.D. or later), was the philosopher's namesake. Posidippus was born c. 310 B.C. Sappho was late seventh to early sixth centuries B.C.

Robinson knew very little Greek and therefore relied on translations into English, which he then recast into his own poetic lines. He wrote Lilla Cabot Perry, the wife of Thomas Sergeant Perry,* that for these translations he used *Select Epigrams from the Greek Anthology* (1890), chosen and translated in prose by John William Mackail (1859–1945). Henry Rushton Fairclough praises Robinson's translations, which he says "reproduce in admirable fashion the wit, humor, and pathos of . . . those charming originals." Robert Mezey provides

Mackail's translations of all 11 of these brief poems. (Sources: Cary [1974], 281; Cary [1975], 182–83; Fairclough, 15; Jay; Mezey, 221–25)

"Variations of Greek Themes, V" (1915). Poem, subtitled "With Sappho's Compliments." The poet gloats that his addressee is dead. He was brainless, had good looks, never read the poet's work, and is hiding with "ignoble shades." The poet won't depress the person's spirit, though, because "you are dead now — and I'm glad."

This poem is not a translation from anything in *The Greek Anthology* but is Robinson's own improvisation. It appears in *Captain Craig* (rev. ed., 1915), but Robinson excluded it from the other "Variations of Greek Themes" in his *Collected Poems* (1921). (Source: Cary [1975], 49, 182–83)

Variell, Arthur Davis (1868–1940). Physician and businessman. Variell was born in Gardiner, Maine, attended school there, graduated from the Bowdoin Medical School (1894), and worked for two years in Portland, Maine, and New York, London, and Paris. Variell returned to the United States, and practiced in Watertown, Connecticut (1896–1907), and Waterbury again later (1908–1916). He went into business in Waterbury (1916–1928). Though nominally still active in commercial ventures, he also traveled and did significant medical research in Asia, Africa, the Balkans, and Syria.

Robinson, who knew Variell, renewed his friendship with him at the MacDowell Colony* (1922). Richard Cary (1974) reports that Variell gave Robinson (1926) a three-volume set of *Oeuvres* by François Villon. Variell, surviving Robinson, died in Miami Beach, Florida. Cary, who did research on Variell and his association with Robinson, suggests that Variell was yet another man whom Robinson knew well despite the poet's unwarranted reputation for aloofness. Cary (June 1974) proves this assertion by use of the 53 letters and one postcard Robinson wrote and sent to Variell (1922–1929). (Sources: Cary [1974], 42; Cary [June 1974])

"Verlaine" (1896). Sonnet. Robinson angrily asks critics to stop digging "like long-clawed scavengers" for details concerning the life of this fellow, who admittedly "fled / The uplands for the fens" in order to "riot . . . / Like a sick satyr with doom's worshippers." Would-be biographers should let grass grow over the poet's grave and "leave his verse / To tell the story of the life he led." His poetry shuffles off his sins, which are forgiven when his art is remembered. Only laurel remains "For long" on "the stricken brow" touched by the Muse. Only a permanent hell could "blot the star that shines on Paris now."

Paul Verlaine (1844–1896) was a leading French poet of the symbolist and decadent movements. Louis Coxe, after listing several prose writers who might have influenced Robinson's early publications, says that "[i]f any poet can be said to have had a direct influence . . . , it might be Verlaine," then names "Luke Havergal" and concludes that "Verlaine . . . may possibly have influenced it." Edwin S. Fussell observes that in the "Verlaine" sonnet Robinson "says nothing about the nature of Verlaine's poetry, merely insisting on separation of aesthetic and biographical judgments." Fussell also notes that in early letters Robinson never refers to Verlaine. Can Fussell be sure? (Sources: Coxe, 46, 49; Fussell [1954], 198)

"Veteran Sirens" (1916). Poem. If beautiful Ninon's ghost should see these faded women, she wouldn't laugh. They crisply try to fight off time. They aren't as comely as some old women are. They are cognizant of their "maimed allure." While "others fade and are still fair," these crones are ardently patient while "unpursued." Their vanity combines quaintness and bravery. Their folly illustrates sturdy self-deception. They are "far from Ninon and. . . . near the grave"

Ruth Nivison* quotes the following from a copy of Robinson's *Collected Poems* that her mother Emma Robinson* owned: "The women at Peterborough in pursuit of man — so says Carty Ranck" (see Ranck, Edwin Carty).

An early, careless reviewer distressed Robinson because while discussing "Veteran Sirens" he misquoted the phrase "Poor flesh," by which the poet describes his subjects here, and instead wrote "Poor fish," which the poet would never call sirens, young or old.

But what sort of females are these old sirens? Yvor Winters calls them "old prostitutes." Laurence Perrine proves his contrary claim that "the poem deals rather . . . with middle-aged or elderly spinsters who refuse to accept either their age or their spinsterhood gracefully, but continue to invoke rouge, lipstick, nailpaint, hair dye, bright clothes, and artificial gaiety in an effort to simulate youth and attract men." Scott Donaldson says that "[s]ome [critics] have read this poem as a satirical portrait of ancient flirts in salon society, pitifully trying to stave off the ravages of time"; then he adds that "Time has treated these women frivolously, . . . and it is age that will occupy the throne in their salon, not a reincarnation of Ninon." Ninon, named twice in the poem, is Anne Lenclos (1620–1705); known as Ninon de Lenclos, she was the witty, wealthy, never-aging, beautiful courtesan popular in French salons during the time of King Louis XIII, Cardinal Richelieu, and Madame de Sévigné. Edwin S. Fussell notes a contrast between the eternally beautiful girls on the urn in "Ode on a Grecian Urn," by John Keats, and Robinson's ladies. Fussell comments: "Keats' maidens are pursued, but will never be caught; Robinson's will never be caught because they are no longer pursued." Robert Mezey calls Robinson's description of time as bestowing "malicious mercy" "a trenchant oxymoron," but Mezey is also naughty when he too labels these lady veterans "old prostitutes." (Sources: Brower, 182 n. 2; Donaldson [1969], 50, 51; Fussell [1954], 82; Mezey, 230; Perrine [1947], 13; E. Robinson, 5; Winters, 33)

"Vickery's Mountain" (1910). Poem.

Bright-eyed Vickery sits in the twilight, "dream[ing] of honor and wealth and fame." The mountain to his west is blue. He is happy because he has a secret "golden word" and an ever-invisible "gift." He is pleased because he recalls that a sick stranger visited him once, stayed a while, was "troublesome," but revealed that he and the mountain yonder "shall make / A golden man" of Vickery and enable him to help "a friend" and inspire "hundreds." So, be-

fore dying, the stranger adjures Vickery to "take the way that's clear, / And be a man of gold."

Vickery continues to gaze at his mountain, and he also laments discomfited "worthy men." Twenty years pass. He remains content, aware of "what sands / Are golden at its [the mountain's] base." He anticipates his eventual success and renown, all the while reckoning he has plenty of time. Meanwhile "unseen hands" keep him "at home" like a singing, "life-caged linnet." He has that unshared word and gift — destined for "some one else — / And Vickery not to know."

Robinson sufficiently explicates "Vickery's Mountain" in a letter (March 15, 1914) to Edith Brower* when he says, "I merely meant that the gold was waiting for him [Vickery], but that the Fates and devils wouldn't allow him to accumulate sufficient sense and energy to go and get it."

Gold here can mean something as mundane as wages earned but more likely suggests spiritual enrichment. Scott Donaldson believes that "a message in Robinson's poetry" may be that "we are probably happier if we remain ignorant of the hell that is life on earth, but that any such happiness is hollow and meaningless"; he cites "immobile Vickery . . . [as an] example" verifying that belief. Ellsworth Barnard opines that "*Vickery's Mountain* is not a sermon against idleness." But if not that, what is it? To be sure, Barnard in his own defense quotes an earlier letter by Robinson (July 20, 1910) to Louis V. Ledoux* to the effect that when Robinson contemplated a mountain near Chocorua, New Hampshire, he began to feel that Vickery's thought processes were reliable. Still there's nothing wrong in a poet's briefly not living up to his own sermonizing. In a letter (July 11, 1917) to Lewis Nathaniel Chase,* Robinson implicitly reduces the poem about Vickery to a presentation of inertia, which in Vickery's case is overpowering. (See also "My Methods and Meanings.") Daniel Gregory Mason* wrote a parody of "Vickery's Mountain," called it "Chickory's Fountain," and sent their mutual friend Ridgely Torrence* a copy (1910). (Sources: Barnard, 177, 297; Brower, 155; Donaldson [1966], 225, 226; Mason [1938], 142; *Selected Letters*, 66, 104)

"Villanelle of Change" (1891). Poem. Villanelle. Much time has passed since the Athenians defeated the Persians at Marathon. Yet "ghostly" war trumpets still shake the "ancient plain" at night, just the way Helicon "swayed with rapture" long ago. Now, however, "The glory of Greek shame" has fallen "into soundless Acheron," and the sun of Hellas has set.

Some present-day readers may wish to be reminded that the Athenian army defeated a segment of the Persian army at Marathon (400 B.C.); Helicon, a mountain range in Greece, was an abode of the Muses; Acheron in Greek mythology was the river in Hades across which Charon ferried departed souls; and Hellas is equivalent to Greece. For a definition of the villanelle, see "The House on the Hill." In "Villanelle of Change." Robinson uses rhymes of "Marathon" and "fast" to achieve the required two-rhyme rhyme scheme, while the two repeated lines, also required, are "Since Persia fell at Marathon" and "Long centuries have come and gone."

"The Voice of Age" (1914). Poem. This silver-haired lady would look at the poet and his friends as sternly as Rhadamanthus if she were able to do so. Her face, however, is gentle, and in addition her "mystical serene address" combines "age . . . with loveliness." She does have opinions concerning their behavior and feels that they might well find "Less insane things . . . to do." They also ought to avoid imitating "Belshazzar [, who] couldn't read." They also should be guided spiritually by something better than their "self-kindled aureoles." She seems acquiescent when they explain that they are generous to others. When she hears certain things, she is wont to frown, shake her old head, and seem apprehensive. Although she says "grown-up children" ought to be more observant, she won't reveal any "rose-leaf ashes of romance" from her past.

Rhadamanthus, the son of Zeus and Europa, was inflexibly honest and therefore became a judge of the dead in the lower world. Belshazzar, the last king of Babylon, needed Daniel to interpret the handwriting on his palace wall, which prophesied his overthrow (see Dan. 5:5–31). In a letter (January 1915)

to Edith Brower,* Robinson referred to "The Voice of Age" as "my 'Old Lady.'" Emma Robinson* and Ruth Nivison* identify her as probably Laura E. Richards.* The pace of "The Voice of Age" is made a little more rapid by its form: four eight-line stanzas, in iambic tetrameter couplets. Couplets in iambic pentameter would have elevated the lacy old lady to unseemly heroic stature. (Sources: Brower, 161; E. Robinson, 8)

Walsh, William Thomas (1891–1949). Biographer and playwright. Robinson met Walsh, a devout Catholic, at the MacDowell Colony* at Peterborough, New Hampshire (1929). The two became friends, and each admired the other's intellect. Some years after Robinson's death, Walsh wrote an essay in which he reminisces about their conversations, includes letters from Robinson to him, and provides the following information about Robinson: Robinson called Marian Nivens MacDowell* the "Vittoria Colonna of the twentieth century." Thornton Wilder, also at the colony, called Robinson "a sublimated Yankee." Robinson read and praised Walsh's *Isabella of Spain* (1931). Robinson "had a little streak of Manichaeanism in him." Robinson considered "Rembrandt to Rembrandt" "one of his best [poems]." Walsh's evidently unpublished play, *Thirty Pieces of Silver*, which Robinson read in a smudged carbon manuscript copy, influenced his "Nicodemus." Walsh adds that "Robinson himself was a sort of Nicodemus, secretly attracted to Christ, venerating him enormously but a little afraid of his own veneration, afraid to analyze it too much." Walsh contends that he persuaded Robinson to change the man comforting Ponce de Leon, in the draft of his poem "Ponce de Leon (Havana, 1521)," from a priest to a physician, since no priest would advise a dying murderer to seek hope only by listening to the waves. Robinson wrote a letter to Walsh (November 23, 1931) after *Matthias at the Door* was published, in which he said that the entire earth was too dark for any religion to lighten it much but that the Catholic church was "the only real Church that is left." (Source: Walsh, 522, 524, 527, 530, 705, 710, 711)

"Walt Whitman" (1896). Poem. Robinson commends Walt Whitman, recently deceased. "Last night it was the song that was the man, / But now it is the man that is the song." Whitman's poetry was too piercing, eternal, pure, powerful, loving, and triumphant for many to hear it well. But some do, and "he shall sing to-morrow for all men, / And . . . all time shall listen." Whitman's name will survive forever.

Richard Cary (1974) summarizes Robinson's conflicting responses to Whitman over the years. For one example, Hermann Hagedorn* reports that Robinson, when he heard Mowry Saben* read Whitman's "When Lilacs Last in the Dooryard Bloom'd" aloud, said that if "that's not poetry, it is something greater than poetry." For another example, Winfield Townley Scott (1910–1968), the Massachusetts-born New England man of letters who visited Robinson in Peterborough, New Hampshire (1929), said that Robinson told him this about his Whitman poem: "I was very young when I wrote it, but I knew all the time I was writing it that I didn't really mean it." Scott Donaldson comments on Winfield Scott's friendship with Robinson. (Sources: Cary [1974], 57–58; Cary [1975], 31–32, 178; Donaldson [1969], 52–53; Hagedorn, 73; Scott, 167)

"The Wandering Jew" (1919). Poem. The persona, despite "the newness" of his present New York location, knows this strange, lonely man, with his remembering eyes, from earlier, from childhood even. He might have been Abimelech, Lamech, Nathan, Noah, or, more than any of these, Melchizedek. The persona finds unforgettable revealings in the man's "endless eyes." Did he in turn find in the persona's eyes "Compassion that I might regret"? No; rather, what he wants is for the persona to pay him "The tribute of a tempered ear / To an untempered eloquence." Before the persona can figure out details of the fellow's past, he anathematizes and scorches the very world. The persona wonders what in his background caused him to feel abandoned by humanity. The persona had little time to ponder on future ruinations before his inner vision conjured "Mirages of remembered scenes" utterly lost. The gloom that had obscured the man lightens and exposes his anger.

His old troubles have expired, while new ones oppose him now, even as he remains ignorant that the old ones were horribly destructive. His present world, which anguishes him, he regards as dead, promising nothing, and "fit [only] for devils." The persona asks himself whether the man "Saw nothing good, as he had seen / No good come out of Nazareth?"

The man becomes completely silent, as though he saw "A Presence that would not be gone." This is awesome for the man to deny. He looked at the persona the way "others might have looked and [then immediately] died," but he looked and kept on living. Then, as though remembering, his eyes looked like those of a person who had stared into the eyes of "One who never dies." He saw what life holds but what is also "to be lost." Was this presence in front of the persona "man or ghost"? It was possible that he was too rebelliously proud ever to be free. Maybe "The Second Coming came and went," but in vain for him, because an onset of humility was too tentative. The persona doesn't know whether the man is still defiantly angry and for that reason is assigned to a timeless chaos. Anyhow, this is how the persona understood him. Perhaps, while he is still wandering among the living, his same "old, unyielding eyes may flash, / And flinch — and look the other way."

Ivor Winters calls "The Wandering Jew" a poem "perhaps as great as one can easily find." He contends that it "should not be construed . . . as an attempt to evaluate Jewish character . . . [but as] an attempt to examine a spiritual vice which may occur in any group at a fairly high intellectual and spiritual level. The vice [Winters continues] is the vice of pride in one's own identity, a pride which will not allow one to accept a great wisdom from without even when one recognizes that the wisdom is there and is greater than one's own; the result is spiritual sickness." Donald E. Stanford also regards "The Wandering Jew" as supremely fine, for its handling of the legend of the Wandering Jew, the psychological symbolism of the poem, its literary qualities, and elements in it more personal to the poet. Robert Mezey calls "The Wandering Jew" "one of Robinson's four or five greatest poems" (without, however, naming the others). He also comments on the five Old Testament figures mentioned in the second stanza: "Nathan" was a prophet ordered by God to predict Israel's future greatness; "Lamech" was the father of "Noah" (Genesis 5:25–30); "Abimelech" was warned by God (Genesis 20; he was given Sarah by the apprehensive Abraham); "Melchizedek," probably a Canaanite, was a high priest (Genesis 14:18–20). Mezey cites his biblical sources for Lamech, Noah, Abimelech, and Melchizedek, but not for Nathan, who was also ordered to bless David (2 Samuel 7:2, 3, 17; 12:1–12). Although Louis Coxe "glancingly" equates the Jew with Alfred Hyman Louis,* he is obviously more than the subject of a personal character sketch, and becomes, indeed, a myth figure. (Sources: Coxe, 56; Mezey, 232; Stanford [1978]; Winters, 38, 38–39)

Wendell, Barrett (1855–1921). Man of letters and educator. He was born in Boston, graduated from Harvard (1877), taught English there (1880–1921), and helped to found the *Harvard Monthly* (1885–1917). In addition to books on Cotton Mather (1891), William Shakespeare (1894), European literature from Homer to Dante (1920, and other subjects, this traditionally oriented professor wrote texts entitled *English Composition* (1891) and *A Literary History of America* (1900), the latter being a standard literary history for decades.

According to Hermann Hagedorn,* Wendell told Robinson he was fortunate to have escaped Harvard without remaining long enough to get a degree. In a letter (February 24, 1895) to Harry de Forest Smith,* Robinson asked rhetorically about Wendell's book on composition: "Was there ever a more interesting book written on the subject?" In another letter (June 9, 1895) to Smith, Robinson says that a mutual friend regarded Wendell's book on Shakespeare "characteristic of the author, paradoxical, impertinent, and little"; Robinson added that "these three adjectives . . . [are] almost like magic" (in defining Wendell). In a letter (January 17, 1901) to John Hays Gardiner,* then teaching at Harvard, Robinson called Wendell's book

on American literature "a most prodigious compilation." (Sources: P. Cohen; Hagedorn, 138; Morison, 351, 374–75; *Selected Letters*, 37; *Untriangulated Stars*, 210, 229)

"When We Can All So Excellently Give" *see* **"Sonnet"** ("When we can all so excellently give")

"Where Does a Dead Man Go?" (1938). Octave. The dead man dies, enjoys "a thrilled invisible advance," and is free "of memory." We should stop crying and rejoice instead that he has gone. Robinson gave this poem to his friend Hermann Hagedorn* in 1897, and it remained unpublished until it appeared in Hagedorn's 1938 biography of Robinson. (Source: Hagedorn, 119)

"The Whip" (1910). Poem. The narrator stands before a body in a coffin and speaks. Everything is past now, especially the doubt you resisted, your cynicism, domination, wrong, ruin. "The coffin has you fast, / The clod will have you next." Ever since the river gave you a gift, "The mistress and the slave / Are gone . . . , and the lover." After leaving "the two to find / Their own way to the brink," you blindly plunged and sank. You hardly needed to die because of your bitter disappointment. If we had been in your place, I wonder if we could have done what you did, could have pursued as you did, could have felt the way you did. But wait; you have "a welt" on your face. Some have sought help in "ropes of sand" but not "Of water." Ah, you were only "a neck behind" when she struck you. "You saw the river flow — / Still, shall I call you blind?"

"The Whip" is one of Robinson's most difficult poems. Bernard Duffey, disliking it, cites it, among other poems, as proof "Robinson could blunder often enough into plain confusion." Ellsworth Barnard brands "The Whip" "notorious." Is the man pursuing a woman? His wife? Is the welt from a physical blow? Were the three principals in a boat? Did the casualty let himself drown? Robinson hardly helped when, according to William Rose Benét, he made two comments about

"The Whip." First, Robinson said that the whip symbolized the margin in stock-market investing and that the lover was meant to represent Anthony Comstock (1844–1915; campaigner against obscene literature). Second, he said that the poem is perhaps improperly obscure but that its action is to be taken literally. David Moran regards "The Whip" as "a little masterpiece of mystery and subsequent revelation." Henry Pettit suggests that the narrator of the poem might be the surviving lover of the tragic triangle.

When Robinson says in the poem that "some ropes of sand" were "Recorded long ago" but that nothing has been written about ropes of water, his rope-of-sand conceit derives from "The Collar" by George Herbert (1593–1633). In it, the poet, restive because of a collar (whether clerical or, more likely, any restraint he wishes to slip free of), says to himself,

> forsake thy cage,
> Thy rope of sands,
> which pettie thoughts have made[,]

but then "me thoughts I heard one calling, Child: / and I reply'd, My Lord." (Sources: Barnard, 290; Benét; Duffey, 181; Moran [2003], 3233; Pettit)

"The White Lights" (1907).

Poem. It is parenthetically subtitled "Broadway, 1906." When Delos increased the wealth of Pericles, and when Euripides and Aristophanes were writing beautifully, "Here ... / There were some islands and some hills" that the Greeks knew nothing about. When Roman armies were plundering too far, when Flaccus was speaking to his Leoconoë, and when Maro was writing, here "there was neither blame nor praise / For Rome, or for the Mantuan." And when a certain "One" was inspired beside the Avon, "Here, where the white lights have begun / To seethe a way for something fair," no prophet was around who could predict from past performances "That there was something in the air."

Some present-day readers may appreciate being reminded that Delos alludes to the Delian League (478–404 B.C.), which enabled Pericles (c. 490–429 B.C.) to enrich Athens

and thus help enable Athenians to enjoy the dramas of Euripides and Aristophanes; that Flaccus and Leoconoë figure in Horace; and that the full name of Virgil, born near Mantua, was Publius Vergilius Maro. Obviously the Avon reference is to Stratford upon Avon, where William Shakespeare was born. Robert Mezey faults Robinson for mentioning Avon and Avalon in the last stanza, "since [Mezey notes] Shakespeare made no use of Arthurian legend."

Emma Robinson* and Ruth Nivison,* and Hermann Hagedorn* also, state that "The White Lights" is a generous tribute to Robinson's friend and rival poet William Vaughn Moody,* on the occasion of the popular 1906 Broadway production of Moody's play *The Sabine Woman*. The work was staged again, in 1909, as *The Great Divide*. Edwin S. Fussell rightly, if harshly, points out that "The White Lights" may "be cited to show up Robinson as a false prophet," since no American dramas he ever saw may be favorably compared to literary works by Aristophanes, Euripides, Horace, Shakespeare, or Virgil. Still, Ellsworth Barnard praises the structure of "The White Lights." It is in three eight-line stanzas, with each line in iambic tetrameter, and with a tight *ababcdcd* rhyme scheme. The first six lines of the first stanza concentrate on Periclean Athens; the first six lines of the second, on Augustan Rome; and the first four lines of the third, on Elizabethan England. The last lines of the first and second stanzas depict, Barnard notes, "the wilderness that was New York," while the last four lines of the third stanza are alive with New York's white-hot lights and what they augur. (Sources: Barnard, 112; Fussell [1954], 9; Hagedorn, 242; Mezey, 225; E. Robinson, 15)

"Why He Was There" (1924).

Sonnet. The poet enters the room, which seems pretty much the way a certain man "left it when he went from us." It also still seems to contain "something of him," since he had been there such a long time. A remnant of him "should be seen, / Or felt." The poet turns, and there the man is, sitting "in his old chair," "laconic," thin as before, "and as cadaverous." He was calm, just the way he was when the poet and others "were young." While the man is "gazing at the pallid flame," the poet asks himself "how far will this go on?" As though he heard, the man smiles and replies: "I was not here until you came; / And I shall not be here when you are gone."

According to Emma Robinson* and Ruth Nivison,* "Why He Was There" is a mental image of Edward Robinson,* the poet's father, during his final sickness. However, the poem also addresses a larger concern and suggests that those who have left us are with us still, when we return to their haunts and evoke their ghostly presence. (Source: E. Robinson, 21)

"The Wife of Palissy" *see* **"Partnership"**

"The Wilderness" (1896). Poem. Resolute explorers and travelers, far from home and endangered, explain that they are hearing this refrain-like appeal: "Come away! come away!" The marshes show frost. The cold wind "shakes the dead black water" and moans through the trees. Its "dirge" urges the men "back to the arms of those that love us." Lazy summer was followed by an autumn now in ashes, and glory has fled to "other valleys and . . . other shores." The men are urged to "roam no more" but instead to return to home "scenes" made empty by their departure. Alluring songs heard this night, and the winds carrying them, have been going on for "ten thousand years"; but the men are certain now of nothing but "the joy that waits us / In the strangeness of home-coming, and a woman's waiting eyes." The only thing of comfort now is "love's road home," beyond which are "a window that gleams" and "a warm hearth . . . within." If they don't stop boasting and don't return soon, "the roving-fiend" will clutch them forever. They would be like willow leaves that the frost misses but soon returns to blight, and they couldn't escape an unseen "doom." Some men are frozen dead already. Yet their strident laughter, shrieking, sinking, and whimpering, continues to mingle with the rushing wind.

Yvor Winters detects the influence of Rudyard Kipling in "The Wilderness." Its form is curious, having long, irregularly accented lines without rhymes, comprising six stanzas, of which the first, third, and fifth have eight lines each, while the others, all in italic type, have four lines each. The poem is not in counterpoint, however, because the message in every stanza is the same — avoid continued danger and return to a welcoming home. Emery Neff anticipates the worst for the "explorers, . . . [whose] inexorable passion for wandering . . . sends them to their doom." He notes that "[t]he changes of pace in 'The Wilderness' serve admirably the changes of mood from the opening dactyls and anapests to the split rhythm of the final line: 'And the long fall wind on the lake.'" "The Wilderness" and "The Klondike" have opposite messages, although their meters are similar. (Sources: Neff, 66, 72; Winters, 22)

"The Wise Brothers" (1910). Poem. It is in dialogue. First Voice: Were "heaven and earth . . . framed amiss" to such an extent that we drifted and have now come dreadfully aground? Second Voice: Is it possible that we have been so "accursèd" that there's no point in going forward? Third Voice: Even though no harbors are visible now, can we not, like others in trouble, by still "going far, go right"?

Emma Robinson* and Ruth Nivison* contend that here Robinson is contrasting his two brothers, Dean Robinson* and Herman Robinson,* and himself. (Source: E. Robinson, 15)

"The Woman and the Wife" (1902). Sonnets. Two titled and numbered dramatic-monologue sonnets.

"I — The Explanation." She remarks that the two of them can say little. She wants him not to throw himself away because he loves her. They must be strong. Love is going to make them pay. Every day and every song end in darkness and silence. She can't lie. God never created her to become his wife. He must agree.

"II — The Anniversary." She asks him to speak truly. He is the one to do so. Although they are now married, she asks: Was there not "More marriage in the dream of one dead kiss / Than in a thousand years of life like this?" It seems that pride locked up passion and now holds the key. She asks him to remember that "Love . . . fed with lies" remains hungry, and not to expect her to "take moonlight for the sun."

Ruth Nivison* suggests that in this poem her mother Emma Robinson* is speaking to Emma's husband Herman Robinson.* In a letter (February 1902?) to Laura E. Richards,* Robinson called "The Woman and the Wife" "the best I have ever done or am likely to do," but added that he might discard it later. Bacon Collamore* quotes a manuscript note by Robinson to the effect that friends admire "The Woman and the Wife" but magazine editors seem not to. Emery Neff observes that the poem "shatters the sentimental commonplace, more often uttered in 1900 than today, that a man should refuse to release a reluctant woman from her engagement because his devotion will teach her to love him after marriage." (Sources: Collamore, 10; Neff, 120; E. Robinson, 13; *Selected Letters*, 50)

"The World" (1896). Poem. The world is composed of a variety of people. Some are brotherly. Some are blinded by hate of our "unguarded fate." Some delight in heavenly music, beneath which, however, are hellish "curses and cries of men gone mad." Although some bask in love's light, others anticipate chaos. The poet concludes that "what we are . . . makes for us / The measure and the meaning of the world." (Source: Cary [1975], 31, 178)

"A Wreath for Edwin Markham" (1922). Poem. Time writes on Markham's face in vain, because Apollo rubs away every trace.

Apollo is the god of light and poetry. Robinson contributed this four-line ditty, also called "Quatrain," to *A Wreath for Edwin Markham: Tributes . . . on His Seventieth Birthday* (1922). No biographical evidence seems to exist revealing any personal friendship between Robinson and Edwin Markham (1852–1940); they were fundamentally different poets. Richard Cary (1974) reprints "Robinson, My Hand to You" (New York *American*, February 13, 1909), a one-page notice by Markham of Robinson's "The Man Who Came" (see "The Master"). Also, in *The Book of Poetry* (1927), an anthology Markham edited, he included Robinson's "Flammonde," "The House on the Hill," "Many Are Called," "The Master," "Miniver Cheevy," and "Richard Cory." After Robinson's death, Markham sent a letter to Cyril Clemens (1902–1999), the (third) cousin (twice-removed) of Mark Twain, and the editor of the *Mark Twain Quarterly*. In the letter, published in the *Mark Twain Quarterly*, Markham said that Robinson "was a great poet, and his death is an incurable disaster to American letters." (Sources: Cary [1974], 206; Cary [1975], 52, 184; Markham, 17)

"Young Gideon" (1932). Poem. It is in 11 iambic-pentameter quatrains, each rhyming *abcb*. Gideon, the young Israelite, is forced to work in his father's fields simply to feed the Midianites, who have dominated Israel. The eyes of the Midianites penetrate Gideon's very "heart and brain," until his anger enslaves him and he has been sapped of all ambition and desire. Why does he work when his only pay is shame? Is "Jehovah's wrath" unaware? Gideon waits "for the word within him" to prompt him to suicide; instead, he hears "the Voice." After doubting for a time, he knows what he must do. God, finding Gideon young, gave him knowledge outfacing fear, and faith superior to knowledge. Meanwhile, he is sadly aware of future casualties among the Israelites. Still, once aware of his ability, he hears the bell of freedom and fearlessly loosens "the Midean yoke." Nevertheless, "a second morning finds him / Fearing to find the dew upon the fleece."

Robinson cites "Judges, 6" in a parenthetical subtitle. His narrative closely follows that of his poem "Sisera" and like it is placed at a time in history when the Israelites were dominated by foreigners because they had neglected to worship a consequently vindictive Jehovah. God's choosing Gideon to lead the Israelites to defeat the Midianites causes the young man's response which Robinson expresses in his poem. He varies from the biblical account by having yet another of his existential heroes flirt with the idea of suicide, only to abandon the notion confidently, upon hearing "the Voice," "the Word," or the like. The reference to "dew upon the fleece" makes sense only to those aware that in the Bible (Judges 6:37–40) may be found the following: Gideon asks God to give him a sign one morning by having his fleece wet with dew but the ground dry; God does so; Gideon asks for another sign, this time having the fleece dry but the ground dewy; it so came to pass the next morning. But not in Robinson's poem. As Nicholas Ayo explains, "With this dramatic volte-face Robinson ends the poem. Gideon in the final stanza reverts to the fearful Gideon in Judges" — this because, if the fleece were wet, Gideon would feel abandoned by God. Ayo, who presents evidence of Robinson's extensive use of the Bible in many of his poems, says that the poet "alters details" from the Bible "only in 'Young Gideon,' and [thus] in some respects . . . rewrites the Gideon story." (Source: Ayo, 174–75, 215)

"Zola" (1896). Sonnet. People "loathe him" for several reasons. He places "the compromising chart / Of hell" in front of them. He tells them how costly their innocence is. As for their "squeamish and emasculate crusade" in opposition to his "grim" writings, he is aware of God's humane evaluation thereof. Only when "we" so-called Christians overcome our reluctance to "scan / The racked and shrieking hideousness of Truth" will we be able "To find," amid all of his self-defensive unsavoriness, "Throbbing, the pulse, the divine heart of man."

Laura E. Richards* quotes a letter (June 1929) from Robinson to her in which he calls his sonnet on Zola "rather pinfeatherish" and says that when he wrote it he had read nothing by Zola except *L'Assommoir* (1887) and only one more book by Zola since then. Edwin S. Fussell traces Robinson's changing attitude toward the powerful French naturalist Emile Zola (1840–1902). At first, Robinson said that Zola's treatment of sex lacked moral content (1893). Next, he deplored the conflation of love and lust in works by French writers in general (1894). Also, he approved of Max Nordau's strong criticism of Zola (1895). But then, conversation with an unidentified intellectual in Gardiner, Maine, persuaded him to admire the truth at the base of Zola's smut (1896). Soon came the sonnet "Zola," in which, according to Fussell, "Robinson was blending New England's transcendentalism with the realism of modern French fiction at the outset of his career." In a letter (April 4, 1897) to Harry de Forest Smith,* Robinson announces that "Zola is the greatest worker in the objective that the world has ever seen, and someday he will be recognized for what he is." Henry W. Wells notes that Robinson "in his sonnet to Zola . . . glances at his own style when he speaks of 'the grim dominion of his [Zola's] art.'" (Sources: Fussell [1954], 123; Richards [1936], 14; *Untriangulated Stars*, 282; Wells, 92)

Appendix:
Robinson's Writings by Category

Poems

LONG NARRATIVE POEMS

Amaranth
Avon's Harvest
The Book of Annandale
Captain Craig
Cavender's House
Genevieve and Alexandra
The Glory of the Nightingales
King Jasper
Lancelot
The Man Who Died Twice
Matthias at the Door
Merlin
Roman Bartholow
Talifer
Tristram

SONNETS

"Aaron Stark"
"Afterthoughts"
"Alma Mater"
"The Altar"
"Amaryllis"
"Another Dark Lady"
"As It Looked Then"
"Battle After War"
"Ben Trovato"
"Calvary"
"Caput Mortuum"
"Charles Carville's Eyes"
"Christmas Sonnet"
"The Clam-Digger"
"The Clerks"
"Cliff Klingenhagen"
"Credo"
"The Dead Village"

"Dear Friends"
"Demos"
"Discovery"
"Doctor of Billiards"
"En Passant"
"L'Envoi"
"Erasmus"
"An Evangelist's Wife"
"Firelight"
"Fleming Helphenstine"
"For a Book by Thomas Hardy"
"For a Copy of Poe's Poems"
"For Arvia"
"For Some Poems by Matthew Arnold"
"The Garden"
"The Garden of the Nations (1923)"
"George Crabbe"
"The Growth of 'Lorraine'"
"Haunted House"
"Horace to Leuconoë"
"How Annandale Went Out"
"'I Make No Measure of the Words They Say'"
"If the Lord Would Make Windows in Heaven"
"Inferential"
"Isaac Pitman"
"Job the Rejected"
"Karma"
"Kosmos"
"The Laggards"
"Leffingwell"
"Lingard and the Stars"
"The Long Race"
"Lost Anchors"
"A Man in Our Town"
"Many Are Called"
"Maya"
"Menoetes"
"The Miracle"
"Modernities"

"Monadnock Through the Trees"
"New England"
"The New Tenants"
"Not Always"
"On the Night of a Friend's Wedding"
"The Pity of the Leaves"
"Plummer Street, Gardiner, Maine"
"The Rat"
"Recalled"
"Reuben Bright"
"Reunion"
"The Sage"
"Shadrach O'Leary"
"The Sheaves"
"Silver Street"
"A Song at Shannon's"
"Sonnet — Oh for a poet..."
"Sonnet — The Master..."
"Sonnet — When we can..."
"Souvenir"
"The Story of the Ashes and the Flame"
"The Sunken Crown"
"Supremacy"
"The Tavern"
"Thalia"
"Thomas Hood"
"The Torrent"
"Two Sonnets"
"Vain Gratuities"
"Verlaine"
"Why He Was There"
"The Woman and the Wife"
"Zola"

DRAMATIC MONOLOGUES
AND DUOLOGUES

"Ben Jonson Entertains a Man from Stratford"
"The Clinging Vine"
"Demos and Dionysus"
"An Evangelist's Wife"
"How Annandale Went Out"
"An Island"
"John Brown"
"John Gorham"
"London Bridge"
"Nicodemus"
"The Night Before"
"Nimmo"
"Partnership"
"The Prodigal Son"
"Rahel to Varnhagen"
"Tasker Norcross"
"The Three Taverns"
"Toussaint L'Ouverture"

OCTAVES

"The Idealist"
"Octave"
"Octaves [I–III]"
"Octaves [I–XXIII]"
"Two Octaves"
"Where Does a Dead Man Go?"

POEMS OF SHORT OR
MODERATE LENGTH

"Annandale Again"
"Archibald's Example"
"As the World Would Have It"
"Atherton's Gambit"
"Aunt Imogen"
"Au Revoir"
"Ballade by the Fire"
"Ballade of a Ship"
"Ballade of Broken Flutes"
"Ballade of Dead Friends"
"Ballade of Dead Mariners"
"Bewick Finzer"
"Bokardo"
"Bon Voyage"
"A Book of Verses Underneath the Bough"
"Boston"
"Broadway"
"The Burning Book"
"But for the Grace of God"
"Calverley's"
"Cassandra"
"The Children of the Night"
"The Chorus of Old Men in 'Aegeus'"
"Clavering"
"The Companion"
"The Corridor"
"Cortège"
"The Daffodils"
"Dionysus in Doubt"
"Doubts"
"Eros Turannos"
"Exit"
"The False Gods"
"The Field of Glory"
"Flammonde"
"The Flying Dutchman"
"For a Dead Lady"
"For Calderon"
"Fortunatus"
"Fragment"
"The Gift of God"
"Glass Houses"
"Hannibal Brown"
"Hector Kane"
"Her Eyes"

"Hillcrest"
"The House on the Hill"
"In Harvard 5"
"Isaac and Archibald"
"John Evereldown"
"The Klondike"
"Late Summer"
"Lazarus"
"Leonora"
"Limericks"
"Lisette and Eileen"
"Llewellyn and the Tree"
"Look at Edward Alphabet"
"Luke Havergal"
"The Man Against the Sky"
"The March of the Cameron Men"
"The Master"
"The Mill"
"Miniver Cheevy"
"Mr. Flood's Party"
"Modred: A Fragment"
"Momus"
"Mortmain"
"Mulieria..."
"Neighbors"
"Normandy"
"Old King Cole"
"The Old King's New Jester"
"An Old Story"
"Old Trails (Washington Square)"
"On the Way"
"Pasa Thalassa Thalassa"
"Peace on Earth"
"The Pilgrims' Chorus"
"The Pilot"
"A Poem for Max Nordau"
"Ponce de Leon"
"The Poor Relation"
"The Return of Morgan and Fingal"
"The Revealer"
"Richard Cory"
"Romance"
"Sainte-Nitouche"
"Shiras"
"Shooting Stars"
"Siege Perilous"
"Sisera"
"The Spirit Speaking"
"Stafford's Cabin"
"Tact"
"Tavern Songs"
"Theophilus"
"There Was a Calm Man in Sabbatis"
"Three Quatrains"
"Too Much Coffee"
"Triolet"

"Twilight Song"
"The Town Down the River"
"Two Gardens in Linndale"
"Two Men"
"Two Quatrains"
"Uncle Ananias"
"The Unforgiven"
"The Valley of the Shadow"
"Veteran Sirens"
"Vickery's Mountain"
"Villanelle of Change"
"The Voice of Age"
"Walt Whitman"
"The Wandering Jew"
"The Whip"
"The White Lights"
"The Wilderness"
"The Wise Brothers"
"The World"
"A Wreath for Edwin Markham"
"Young Gideon"

Translations

"The *Antigone* of Sophocles"
"The Galley Race"
"Horace to Leuconoë"
"Palemon — Damoetas — Menaclas"
"Variations of Greek Themes"
"Variations of Greek Themes, V"

Plays

The Porcupine
Van Zorn

Essays, Reviews, and Editorials

"The Arthurian Trilogy and 'Rabbi Ben Ezra'"
"Autobiographical Sketches: Harvard"
"The Balm of Custom"
"A Book of Verses That Is Poetry"
"The First Seven Years"
"For Harriet Moody's Cook Book"
"Foreword to *The Mountain*"
"Franklin Schenck (1856–1927)"
"Introduction to *The Letters of Thomas Sergeant Perry*"
"MacDowell's Legacy to Art"
"Music and Poetry"
"My Methods and Meanings"
"A New England Poet"
"The New Movement in Poetry"
"A Note on Myron B. Benton (1834–1902)"

Works Cited

Adams, Richard P. "The Failure of Edwin Arlington Robinson." *Tulane Studies in English* 11 (1961): 97–151.

Adams, Stephen J. *Poetic Designs: An Introduction to Meters, Verse Forms, and Figures of Speech*. Toronto: Broadview Press, 1997.

Aiken, Conrad. "Three Reviews." In *Edwin Arlington Robinson: A Collection of Critical Essays*, edited by Francis Murphy, 15–28. Englewood Cliffs, NJ: Prentice-Hall, 1970.

Allen, James L., Jr. "Symbol and Theme in 'Mr. Flood's Party.'" *Mississippi Quarterly* 15 (Fall 1962): 139–43.

Amacher, Richard. "Robinson's 'New England.'" *Explicator* 11(March 1952): Item 33.

Anderson, Hilton. "Robinson's 'Flammonde.'" *Southern Quarterly* 7 (January 1969): 179–83.

Anderson, Wallace L. "E. A. Robinson's 'Scattered Lives.'" *American Literature* 38 (January 1947): 498–507.

———. *Edwin Arlington Robinson: A Critical Introduction*. Cambridge: Harvard University Press, 1968.

———. "The Letters of E. A. Robinson: A Sampler." *Colby Library Quarterly* 16 (March 1980): 51–62.

Ayo, Nicholas. "Robinson and the Bible." Ph.D. dissertation, Duke University, 1966.

Baker, Carlos. "'The Jug Makes the Paradise': New Light on Eben Flood." *Colby Library Quarterly* 10 (June 1974): 327–36.

Barnard, Ellsworth. *Edwin Arlington Robinson*. New York: Macmillan, 1952. Reprint, New York: Octagon Books, 1969.

Barstow, James S. *My Tilbury Town*. Np: 1939.

Bates, Esther Willard. *Edwin Arlington Robinson and His Manuscripts*. Waterville, ME: Colby College Library, 1944.

Beach, Christopher. *The Cambridge Introduction to Twentieth-Century American Poetry*. Cambridge: Cambridge University Press, 2003.

Beem, Edgar Allen. "The Mayor of Tilbury Town." *Down East: The Magazine of Maine* 49 (October 2002): 66–69, 97.

Benét, William Rose. "The Phoenix Nest." *Saturday Review of Literature* 26 (February 20, 1943), 18; 26 (April 17, 1943), 54.

Berthoff, Warner. "The 'New' Poetry: Robinson and Frost." In *Edwin Arlington Robinson: A Collection of Critical Essays*, edited by Francis Murphy, 117–27. Englewood Cliffs, NJ: Prentice-Hall, 1970.

Bloom, Harold, ed. *The Best Poems of the English Language*. New York: HarperCollins, 2004.

Brashear, Thomas L. "Robinson's 'Mr. Flood's Party." *Explicator* 29 (February 1971): 45.

Brien, Dolores E. "Edwin Arlington Robinson's 'Amaranth': A Journey to 'The Wrong World.'" *Research Studies of Washington State University* 3 (June 1968): 143–50.

Brookhouse, Christopher. "Imagery and Theme in *Lancelot*." In *Edwin Arlington Robinson: Critical Essays*, edited by Ellsworth Barnard, 120–29. Athens: University of Georgia Press, 1969.

Brower, Edith. *See Edwin Arlington Robinson's Letters to Edith Brower*. Edited by Richard Cary. Cambridge: Belknap Press of Harvard University Press, 1968.

Brown, David. "A Note on *Avon's Harvest*." *American Literature* 9 (November 1937): 343–49.

Brown, Maurice F. "Moody and Robinson." *Colby Library Quarterly* 5 (December 1960): 185–94.

Brown, Rollo Walter. *Next Door to a Poet*. New York: D. Appleton-Century, 1937.

Burton, David H. "Edwin Arlington Robinson and Christianity." *Spirit: A Magazine of Poetry* 37 (Spring 1970): 30–35.

———. "Edwin Arlington Robinson and Morris Raphael Cohen." *Colby Library Quarterly* 14 (December 1978): 226–27.

———. "Theodore Roosevelt and Edwin Arlington Robinson: A Common Vision." *Personalist* 49 (Summer 1968): 331–50.

Burton, Richard. "Robinson as I Saw Him." *Mark Twain Quarterly* 2 (Spring 1938): 9.

Cahill, Daniel J. *Harriet Monroe*. New York: Twayne, 1973.

Cambon, Glauco. *The Inclusive Flame: Studies in American Poetry*. Bloomington: Indiana University Press, 1963.

Carley, James P. "Introduction" to *Arthurian Poets: Edwin Arlington Robinson*. Woodbridge, Suffolk: Boydell Press, 1990.

Carpenter, Frederic Ives. "Tristram the Transcendentalist." *New England Quarterly* 11 (September 1938): 501–23.

Cary, Richard. "'The Clam-Digger: Capitol Island.'" *Colby Library Quarterly* 10 (December 1974): 505–511.

———. *Early Reception of Edwin Arlington Robinson: The First Twenty Years*. Waterville, ME: Colby College Press, 1974.

———. "The First Publication of E. A. Robinson's Poem 'Broadway.'" *American Literature* 45 (March 1974): 83.

———. "Mowry and Edwin Arlington Robinson." *Colby Library Quarterly* 9 (December 1972): 482–97.

———. "Robinson's Friend Arthur Davis Variell." *Colby Library Quarterly* 10 (June 1974): 372–85.

———. "Robinson's Notes to His Nieces." *Colby Library Quarterly* 5 (December 1960): 195–202.

———, ed. *Uncollected Poems and Prose of Edwin Arlington Robinson*. Waterville, ME: Colby College Press, 1975.

Cestre, Charles. *An Introduction to Edwin Arlington Robinson*. New York: Macmillan, 1930.

Chant, Elsie Ruth Dykes. "The Metrics and Imagery of Edwin Arlington Robinson, as Exhibited in Five of His Blank Verse Poems." Ph.D. diss., University of New Mexico, 1930.

Childers, William C. "Edwin Arlington Robinson's Proper Names." *Names* 3 (December 1955): 223–29.

———. "Robinson's 'Amaryllis.'" *Explicator* 14 (February 1956): Item 34.

Clark, S. L., and Julian N. Wasserman. "'Time Is a Casket': Love and Temporality in Robinson's *Tristram*." *Colby Library Quarterly* 17 (June 1981): 112–16.

Clum, John M. *Ridgely Torrence*. New York: Twayne, 1972.

Cohen, Morris Raphael. *A Dreamer's Journey: The Autobiography of Morris Raphael Cohen*. Glencoe, IL: Free Press, 1949.

Cohen, Paul E. "Barrett Wendell and the Harvard Literary Revival." *New England Quarterly* 52 (December 1979): 483–99.

Cohen, S. A. "Robinson's 'Lost Anchors.'" *Explicator* 24 (April 1966): 68.

Collamore, Bacon, and Lawrance R. Thompson. *Edwin Arlington Robinson: A Collection of His Works from the Library of Bacon Collamore*. Hartford: n.p., 1936.

Cowley, Malcolm. "Edwin Arlington Robinson: Defeat and Triumph." *New Republic* 119 (December 6, 1948): 26–30.

Coxe, Louis. *Edwin Arlington Robinson: The Life of Poetry*. New York: Pegasus, 1969.

Crowder, Richard. "Redemption for the Man of Iron." *Personalist* 43 (January 1962): 46–56.

———. "Robinson's 'An Old Story,'" *Explicator* 4 (December 1945): Item 22.

———. "Robinson's *Talifer*: The Figurative Texture." *Boston University Studies in English* 4 (Winter 1960): 241–47.

Current-García, Eugene. "Josephine Preston Peabody: Poetic Drama and the Feminist Movement." *Southern Humanities Review* 28 (Summer 1994): 233–46.

Daniels, Mabel. "Edwin Arlington Robinson: A Musical Memoir." *Radcliffe Quarterly* 46 (November 1962): 5–11.

Dardis, Tom. *The Thirsty Muse: Alcohol and the American Writer*. New York: Ticknor & Fields, 1989.

Dauner, Louise. "The Pernicious Rib: E. A. Robinson's Concept of Feminine Character." *American Literature* 15 (May 1943): 139–58.

Davis, Charles T. "Imagery Patterns in the Poetry of Edwin Arlington Robinson." *College English* 22 (March 1961): 380–86.

———. "Robinson's Road to Camelot." In *Edwin Arlington Robinson: Critical Essays*, edited by Ellsworth Barnard, 88–104. Athens: University of Georgia Press, 1969.

Deckert, Peter. "He Shouts to See Them Scamper So: E. A. Robinson and the French Forms." *Colby Library Quarterly* 8 (September 1989): 386–98.

Dickey, James. "Introduction." In *Selected Poems of Edwin Arlington Robinson*, edited by Morton Dauwen Zabel, xi–xxviii. New York: Macmillan, 1965.

Domina, Lyle. "Fate, Tragedy and Pessimism in Robinson's 'Merlin.'" *Colby Library Quarterly* 8 (December 1969): 471–78.

Donaldson, Scott. "The Alien Pity: A Study of Character of E. A. Robinson's Poetry." *American Literature* 38 (May 1966): 219–29.

———. "The Book of Scattered Lives." In *Edwin Arlington Robinson: Critical Essays*, edited by Ellsworth Barnard, 43–53. Athens: University of Georgia Press, 1969.

———. "Robinson and Music." *Colby Library Quarterly* 16 (1980): 63–72.

Donoghue, Denis. "A Poet of Continuing Relevance." In *Edwin Arlington Robinson*, edited by Harold Bloom, 29–53. New York: Chelsea House, 1988.

Drinkwater, John. *The Muse in Council*. Boston: Houghton Mifflin, 1925.

DuBois, Arthur E. "The Cosmic Humorist." *Mark Twain Quarterly* 2 (Spring 1938): 11–13, 14.

Dudley, Dorothy. "Wires and Cross-Wires." *Poetry: A Magazine of Verse* 24 (May 1924): 96–103.

Duffey, Bernard. *Poetry in America: Expression and Its Values in the Times of Bryant, Whitman, and Pound*. Durham, NC: Duke University Press, 1978.

Dunn, N. E. "Riddling Leaves: Robinson's 'Luke Havergal.'" *Colby Library Quarterly* 10 (March 1973): 17–25.

———. "'Wreck and Yesterday,' The Meaning of Failure in *Lancelot*." *Colby Library Quarterly* 9 (September 1971): 349–56.

Dzwonkoski, Peter, ed. *American Publishing Houses, 1638–1899*. 2 vols. *Dictionary of Literary Biography*, vol. 49. Detroit: Gale, 1986.

Edwards, C. Hines, Jr. "Allusion and Symbol in Robinson's 'Eros Turannos.'" *Colby Library Quarterly* 20 (March 1984): 47–50.

Edwin Arlington Robinson's Letters to Edith Brower. Edited by Richard Cary. Cambridge: Belknap Press of Harvard University Press, 1968.

Erskine, Robert J., et al. *The Gardiner Story: 1849–1949*. Gardiner: City of Gardiner, 1949.

Fairclough, Henry Rushton. *The Classics and Our Twentieth-Century Poets....* New York: AMS Press, 1967.

Fisher, John Hurt. "Edwin Arlington Robinson and Arthurian Tradition." In *Studies in Language and Literature in Honour of Margaret Schlauch*, edited by Mieczyslaw

Brahmer, et al., 117–31. Warsaw: Panstwowe Wydawnictwo Naukowe, 1966.

Foy, J. Vail. "Robinson's Impulse for Narrative." *Colby Library Quarterly* 8 (March 1969): 238–49.

Franchere, Hoyt C. *Edwin Arlington Robinson*. New York: Twayne, 1968.

Frazer, Winifred L. *Mabel Dodge Luhan*. Boston: Twayne, 1984.

Free, William J. "The Strategy of 'Flammonde.'" In *Edwin Arlington Robinson: Critical Essays*, edited by Ellsworth Barnard, 15–30. Athens: University of Georgia Press, 1969.

Frost, Robert. "Introduction" to *King Jasper*, by Edwin Arlington Robinson, New York: Macmillan, 1935.

Fussell, Edwin S. *Edwin Arlington Robinson: The Literary Background of a Traditional Poet*. Berkeley and Los Angeles: University of California Press, 1954.

———. "A Note on E. A. Robinson's 'Credo.'" *Modern Language Notes* 66 (June 1951): 398–400.

Garvin, Harry R. "'Comprehensive Criticism': A Humanistic Discipline." *Bucknell Review* 10 (May 1962): 305–27.

Genthe, Charles V. "E. A. Robinson's 'Annandale' Poems." *Colby Library Quarterly* 7 (March 1967): 392–98.

Gibran, Jean, and Kahlil Gibran. *Kahlil Gibran: His Life and World*. New York: Interlink Books, 1991.

Gierasch, Walter. "Robinson's 'Luke Havergal.'" *Explicator* 3 (October 1944): Item 8.

Gilman, Owen W., Jr. "Merlin: E. A. Robinson's Debt to Emerson." *Colby Library Quarterly* 21 (September 1985): 134–41.

Goodrich, Norma Lorre. *Merlin*. New York: Franklin Watts, 1987.

Graff, Gerald E. "Statement and Poetry." *Southern Review*, n.s., 2 (Summer 1966): 499–515.

Gray, Richard. *American Poetry of the Twentieth Century*. London: Longman, 1990.

Gregory, Horace, and Marya Zaturenska. *A History of American Poetry 1900–1940*. New York: Harcourt, Brace, 1946.

Griffith, Benjamin W. "A Note on Robinson's Use of 'Turannos.'" *Concerning Poetry* 4 (Spring 1971): 39.

Grimm, Clyde L. "Robinson's 'For a Dead Lady': An Exercise in Evaluation." *Colby Library Quarterly* 7 December 1967): 535–47.

Gross, Harvey, and Robert McDowell. *Sound and Form in Modern Poetry: A Study of Prosody from Thomas Hardy to Robert Lowell*.

Rev. ed. Ann Arbor: University of Michigan Press, 1996.

Hagedorn, Hermann. *Edwin Arlington Robinson: A Biography*. New York: Macmillan, 1938.

Harlow, Virginia. *Thomas Sergeant Perry: A Biography and Letters to Perry from William, Henry, and Garth Wilkinson James*. Durham, NC: Duke University Press, 1950.

Hepburn, James G. "E. A. Robinson's System of Opposites" *PMLA* 80 (June 1965): 266–74.

Hinden, Michael C. "Edwin Arlington Robinson and the Theatre of Destiny." *Colby Library Quarterly* 8 (December 1969): 463–71.

Hirsch, David H. "'The Man Against the Sky' and the Problem of Faith." In *Edwin Arlington Robinson: Critical Essays*, edited by Ellsworth Barnard, 31–42. Athens: University of Georgia Press, 1969.

Holland, Norman N. "The Miller's Wife and the Professions: Questions about the Transactive Theory of Reading." *New Literary History* 17 (Spring 1986): 423–47.

Howe, Elizabeth A. *The Dramatic Monologue*. New York: Twayne, 1996.

Howe, Irving. *The Critical Point on Literature and Culture*. New York: Horizon Press, 1973.

Hudson, Hoyt H. "Robinson and Praed." *Poetry* 61 (February 1943): 612–20.

Isaacs, Lewis M. "E. A. Robinson Speaks of Music." *New England Quarterly* 22 (December 1949): 499–500.

Jarrell, Randall. "Fifty Years of American Poetry." *Prairie Schooner* 37 (Spring 1963): 1–27.

Jay, Peter, ed. *The Greek Anthology and Other Ancient Greek Epigrams*. New York: Oxford University Press, 1973.

Joyner, Nancy Carol. *Edwin Arlington Robinson: A Reference Guide*. G. K. Hall, 1978.

Justice, Donald. "Afterword," in *The Torrent and the Night Before*, by Edwin Arlington Robinson. Gardiner, ME: Tilbury House Publishers, 1996.

Kaplan, Estelle. *Philosophy in the Poetry of Edwin Arlington Robinson*. New York: Columbia University Press, 1940.

Kavka, Jerome. "Richard Cory's Suicide: A Psychoanalyst's View." *Colby Library Quarterly* 11 (September 1975): 150–59.

Kelly, David, et al. "Richard Cory." Vol. 4, *Poetry for Students*, 115–24. Edited by Mary K. Ruby. 19 vols. Detroit: Gale, 1999.

Kerby, Steve. "Robinson's 'Hillcrest.'" *Explicator* 51 (Spring 1993): 172–75.

Lacy, Norris J., and Geoffrey Ashe. *The Arthurian Handbook*. New York: Garland, 1988.

Lagorio, Valerie M. "Edwin Arlington Robinson: Arthurian Pacifist." Vol. 2, *King Arthur Through the Ages*, 165–79. Edited by Valerie M. Lagorio and Mildred Leake Day. 2 vols. New York & London: Garland, 1990.

Landini, Richard G. "Metaphor and Imagery in E. A. Robinson's 'Credo.'" *Colby Library Quarterly* 8 (March 1968): 20–22.

Latham, G. W. "Robinson at Harvard." *Mark Twain Quarterly* 2 (Spring 1938): 19.

Latham, Harold S. *My Life in Publishing*. New York: E. P. Dutton, 1965.

Ledoux, Louis V. "In Memoriam: Written in 1935." *Mark Twain Quarterly* 2 (Spring 1938): 10.

Letters of Edwin Arlington Robinson to Howard George Schmitt. Edited by Carl J. Weber. Waterville, ME: Colby College Library, 1943.

Levenson, J. C. "Robinson's Modernity." In *Edwin Arlington Robinson: A Collection of Critical Essays*, edited by Francis Murphy, 164–81. Englewood Cliffs, NJ: Prentice-Hall, 1970.

Lie, Ulf. "A Poetry of Attitudes: The Speaker Personae in E. A. Robinson's Early Dramatic Poetry." Vol. 4, *Americana-Norvegia*, edited by Britta Seyerstad, 193–210. Oslo: Universitetsforlaget, 1973.

Lippincott, Lillian. *A Bibliography of the Writings and Criticisms of Edwin Arlington Robinson*. Boston: Faxon, 1937.

Locklear, Gloriana. "Robinson's 'The Mill.'" *Explicator* 51 (Spring 1993): 175–79.

Lowe, Robert Liddell. "A Letter from Edwin Arlingotn Robinson to James Barstow." *New England Quarterly* 37 (September 1964): 390–92.

Lowell, Amy. "A Bird's Eye View of E. A. Robinson." *Dial* 72 (February 1922): 130–42.

———. *Tendencies in Modern American Poetry*. New York: Macmillan, 1917.

Lucas, John. "The Poetry of Edwin Arlington Robinson." In *Edwin Arlington Robinson*, edited by Harold Bloom, 137–53. New York: Chelsea House, 1988.

MacDowell, Mrs. Edward. "Robinson at the MacDowell Colony." *Mark Twain Quarterly* 2 (Spring 1938): 16.

McFarland, Ronald E. "Robinson's 'Luke Havergal.'" *Colby Library Quarterly* 10 (June 1974): 365–72.

Macgowan, Christopher. *Twentieth-Century American Poetry*. Oxford: Blackwell, 2004.

MacKillop, I. D. "Robinson's Accomplishment." *Essays in Criticism* 21 (July 1971): 297–308.

MacLeish, Archibald. "On Rereading Robinson." *Colby Library Quarterly* 8 (March 1969): 217–19.

Manheimer, Joan. "Edwin Arlington Robinson's 'Eros Turannos': Narrative Reconsidered." *Literary Review* 20 (Spring 1977): 253–69.

Markham, Edwin. "Dean of American Poets Pays Tribute." *Mark Twain Quarterly* 2 (Spring 1938): 17.

Martin, Jay. "A Crisis of Achievement: Robinson's Late Narratives." In *Edwin Arlington Robinson: Centenary Essays*, edited by Ellsworth Barnard, 130–56. Athens: University of Georgia Press, 1969.

Mason, David Gregory. "Early Letters of Edwin Arlington Robinson: First Series." *Virginia Quarterly Review* 13 (Winter 1937): 52–69.

———. "Edwin Arlington Robinson to Daniel Gregory Mason: Second Series." *Virginia Quarterly Review* 13 (Spring 1937): 223–40.

———. *Music in My Time and Other Reminiscences*. New York: Macmillan, 1938.

Matthiessen, F. O. "Society and Solitude in Poetry." *Yale Review* 25 (March 1936): 603–04.

Maynard, Theodore, "Edwin Arlington Robinson." *Catholic World* 141 (June 1935): 266–275.

———. *Our Best Poets: English and American*. London: Brentano's, 1924.

Merton, John Kenneth. "A World His Own." *Commonweal* 26 (May 14, 1935): 79–80.

Mezey, Robert, ed. *The Poetry of E. A. Robinson*. New York: Modern Library, 1999.

Miles, Josephine. "Robinson's Inner Fire." In *Edwin Arlington Robinson: A Collection of Critical Essays*, edited by Francis Murphy, 110–16. Englewood Cliffs, NJ: Prentice-Hall, 1970.

Miller, John H. "The Structure of E. A. Robinson's *The Torrent and The Night Before*." *Colby Library Quarterly* 10 (June 1974): 347–64.

Mims, Edwin. *The Christ of the Poets*. New York and Nashville: Abingdon-Cokesbury Press, 1948.

M[onroe], H[arriet]. "Robinson's Double Harvest." *Poetry* 18 (August 1921): 273–76.

Monteiro, George. "'The President and the Poet': Robinson, Roosevelt, and *The Touchstone*." *Colby Library Quarterly* 10 (December 1974): 512–15.

Moran, Ronald. "*Avon's Harvest* Re-examined." *Colby Library Quarterly* 6 (June 1963): 247–54.

———. "Edwin Arlington Robinson." Vol. 6, *Critical Survey of Poetry*, 2nd rev. ed., 3227–35. Edited by Philip K. Jason. 8 vols., continuously paged. Pasadena: Salem, 2003.

———. "Meaning and Value in 'Luke Havergal.'" *Colby Library Quarterly* 7 (March 1967): 385–91.

———. "The Octaves of E. A. Robinson." *Colby Library Quarterly* 8 (September 1969): 363–70.

Morison, Samuel Eliot. *Three Centuries of Harvard: 1636–1936*. Cambridge, MA: Belknap Press of Harvard University Press, 1964.

Morris, Celia. "E. A. Robinson and 'The Golden Horoscope of Imperfection.'" *Colby Library Quarterly* 11 (June 1975): 88–97.

Morris, Charles R. "Robinson's 'Richard Cory.'" *Explicator* 23 (February 1965): 52.

Murphy, Francis. "Introduction" to *Edwin Arlington Robinson: A Collection of Critical Essays*, edited by Francis Murphy, 1–7. Englewood Cliffs, NJ: Prentice-Hall, 1970.

Neff, Emery. *Edwin Arlington Robinson*. New York: William Sloane, 1948.

Nitze, William Albert. *Arthurian Romance and Modern Poetry and Music*. Chicago: University of Chicago Press, 1940.

Nivison, David. "Does It Matter How Annandale Went Out?" *Colby College Quarterly* 5 (December 1960), 174–75.

Notopoulos, James A. "Sophocles and 'Captain Craig." *New England Quarterly* 17 (March 1944): 109.

Parini, Jay. "Robert Frost and the Poetry of Survival." In *The Columbia History of American Poetry*, edited by Parini and Brett C. Miller, 260–83. New York: Columbia University Press, 1993.

Parish, John E. "The Rehabilitation of Eben Flood." *College English* 55 (September 1966): 696–99.

Parker, George Lawrence. "Robinson Meets Nicodemus." *The Christian Register* 113 (June 27, 1935): 425.

Parlett, Mathilde M. "Robinson's 'Luke Havergal.'" *Explicator* 3 (June 1945): Item 57.

Payne, Leonidas Warren, Jr. "The First Edition of E. A. Robinson's *The Peterborough Idea.*" *University of Texas Studies in English* (July 8, 1939), 219–31.

Peabody, Josephine. *The Diary and Letters of Josephine Preston Peabody.* Edited by Christina Hopkinson Baker. Boston and New York: Houghton Mifflin, 1925.

Pearce, Roy Harvey. *The Continuity of American Poetry.* Princeton, NJ: Princeton University Press, 1966.

Peltier, Florence. "Edwin Arlington Robinson, Himself." *Mark Twain Quarterly* 1(Summer 1937): 6, 11–14.

Perrine, Laurence. "Robinson's 'Eros Turannos," *Explicator* 8 (December 1949): 20.

———. "Robinson's *Tristram.*" *Explicator* 7 (March 1949): 33.

———. "Robinson's 'Veteran Sirens.'" *Explicator* 6 (November 1947): 13.

———. "The Sources of Robinson's Arthurian Poems and His Opinions of Other Treatments." *Colby Library Quarterly* 10 (June 1974): 336–46.

———. "Tennyson and Robinson: Legalistic Moralism vs. Situation Ethics." *Colby Library Quarterly* 8 (December 1969): 416–33.

Perry, Bliss. *And Gladly Teach: Reminiscences.* Boston and New York: Houghton Mifflin, 1935.

Pettit, Henry. "Robinson's 'The Whip.'" *Explicator* 1 (April 1943): Item 50.

Pipkin, E. Edith. "The Arthur of Edwin Arlington Robinson." *English Journal* 19 (March 1930): 183–95.

Power, Sister Mary James. *Poets at Prayer.* New York and London: Sheed & Ward, 1938.

Powys, John Cowper. "The Big Bed." *Mark Twain Quarterly* 2 (Spring 1938): 2.

Pringle, Carleton. *Theodore Roosevelt, a Biography.* New York: Scribner, 1958.

Rand, Edward Kennard. *The Magical Art of Virgil.* Cambridge: Harvard University Press, 1931.

Raven, A. A. "Robinson's 'Luke Havergal.'" *Explicator* 3 (December 1944): Item 24.

Redman, Ben Ray. *Edwin Arlington Robinson.* New York: Robert M. McBride, 1928.

Richards, Laura E. *E.A.R.* Cambridge, MA: Harvard University Press, 1936.

———. *Stepping Westward.* New York: D. Appleton, 1931.

Robbins, J. Albert. *American Literary Manuscripts: A Checklist of Holdings in Academic, Historical, and Public Libraries, Museums, and Authors' Homes in the United States.*

2nd ed. Athens: University of Georgia Press, 1977.

Robinson, Emma L., and Ruth R. Nivison. Untitled typescript, 1939, in the Collections of the Gardiner Library Association, Gardiner, Maine.

Robinson, W. R. *Edwin Arlington Robinson: A Poetry of the Act.* Cleveland: The Press of Western Reserve University, 1967.

Rodnick, Lois Palken. *Mabel Dodge Luhan: New Woman, New Worlds.* Albuquerque: University of New Mexico Press, 1984.

Roosevelt, Theodore. *The Letters of Theodore Roosevelt.* Selected and edited by Elting E. Morison. 8 vols. Cambridge: Harvard University Press, 1951–1954.

Rothert, Otto Arthur. *The Story of a Poet: Madison Cawein: His Intimate Life...* Louisville: J. P. Morton, 1921.

Satterfield, Leon. "Bubble-Work in Gardiner, Maine: The Poetry War of 1924." *New England Quarterly* 57 (March 1984): 25–43.

Schmitt, Howard George. *See Letters of Edwin Arlington Robinson to Howard George Schmitt.* Edited by Carl J. Weber. Waterville, ME: Colby College Library, 1943.

Scholnick, Robert L. "The Shadowed Years: Mrs. Richards, Mr. Stedman, and Robinson." *Colby Library Quarterly* 9 (June 1972): 510–31.

Scott, Winfield Townley. *Exiles and Fabrications.* Garden City, NY: Doubleday, 1961.

Selected Letters of Edwin Arlington Robinson. Edited by Ridgely Torrence. New York: Macmillan, 1940. Reprint, Westport, CT: Greenwood Press, 1979.

Sherman, Dean. "Robinson's 'Battle After War.'" *Explicator* 27 (April 1969): Item 64.

Sinclair, May. "Three American Poets of To-Day [William Vaughn Moody, Edwin Arlington Robinson, Ridgely Torrence]." *Atlantic Monthly* 98 (September 1906): 325–35.

Skupin, Michael. "Merlin in the Works of Edwin Arlington Robinson and Laurence Binyon." Ph.D. diss., University of Houston, 2003.

Slote, Bernice. "Robinson's 'En Passant.'" *Explicator* 15 (February 1957): Item 27.

Smith, Chard Powers. *Where the Light Falls: A Portrait of Edwin Arlington Robinson.* New York: Macmillan, 1965.

Smith, Danny D., and Earle E. Shettleworth, Jr. *Gardiner on the Kennebec.* Dover, NH: Arcadia, 1996.

Smith, Herbert F. *Richard Watson Gilder*. New York: Twayne, 1970.

"Some Other Recent Acquisitions." *Colby Library Quarterly* 4 (February 1956): 99.

Somkin, Fred. "Tocqueville as a Source for Robinson's 'Man Against the Sky.'" *Colby Library Quarterly* 4 (June 1963): 245–47.

Spear, Jeffrey L. "Robinson, Hardy, and a Literary Source of 'Eros Turannos.'" *Colby Library Quarterly* 15 (March 1979): 58–64.

Squires, Radcliffe. "Tilbury Town Today." In *Edwin Arlington Robinson: Centenary Essays*, edited by Ellsworth Barnard, 175–83. Athens: University of Georgia Press, 1969.

Stanford, Donald E. "Classicism and the Modern Poet." *Southern Review* 5 (Spring 1969): 475–500.

———. "Edwin Arlington Robinson's 'The Wandering Jew.'" *Tulane Studies in English* 23 (1978): 95–107.

Starr, Nathan Comfort. "Edwin Arlington Robinson's Arthurian Heroines: Vivian, Guinevere and the Two Isolts." *Philological Quarterly* 56 (Spring 1977): 253–58.

———. *King Arthur Today: The Arthurian Legend in English and American Literature 1901–1953*. Gainesville: University of Florida Press, 1954.

———. "The Transformation of Merlin." In *Edwin Arlington Robinson: Centenary Essays*, edited by Ellsworth Barnard, 106–19. Athens: University of Georgia Press, 1969.

Steele, Timothy. *All the Fun's in How You Say a Thing: An Explanation of Meter and Versification*. Athens: Ohio University Press, 1999.

Stevick, Robert D. "The Metrical Style of E. A. Robinson." In *Edwin Arlington Robinson: Centenary Essays*, edited by Ellsworth Barnard, 54–67. Athens: University of Georgia Press, 1969.

———. "Robinson and William James." *University of Kansas City Review* 25 (June 1959): 293–301.

Stovall, Floyd. "The Optimism Behind Robinson's Tragedies." *American Literature* 10 (March 1971): 1–23.

Sullivan, Winifred H. "The Double-Edged Irony of E. A. Robinsin's 'Miniver Cheevy.'" *Colby Library Quarterly* 22 (September 1986): 185–91.

Super, R. H. "Robinson's 'For a Dead Lady.'" *Explicator* 3 (May 1945): Item 60.

Suss, Irving D. "The Plays of Edwin Arlington Robinson." *Colby Library Quarterly* 8 (September 1969): 347–63.

Sutliffe, W. Denham. "The Original of Robinson's 'Captain Craig.'" *New England Quarterly* 16 (September 1943): 407–31.

Sweet, Charles A., Jr. "A Re-Examination of 'Richard Cory.'" *Colby Library Quarterly* 9 (September 1972): 579–82.

Tanselle, G. Thomas. "Robinson's 'Dark Hills.'" *CEA Critic* 26 (February 1964): 8–10.

Thompson, Lawrance, ed. *Tilbury Town: Selected Poems of Edwin Arlington Robinson*. New York: Macmillan, 1953.

Thompson, W. R. "Broceliande: E. A. Robinson's Palace of Art." *New England Quarterly* 43 (June 1970): 231–49.

"'Torrent' Number Sixty-Six." *Colby Library Quarterly* 4 (August 1955): 64.

Tryon, James L. *Harvard Days with Edwin Arlington Robinson*. Waterville, ME: n.p., 1940.

Untermeyer, Louis. *Edwin Arlington Robinson: A Reappraisal...* Washington: Library of Congress, 1963.

Untriangulated Stars: Letters of Edwin Arlington Robinson to Harry de Forest Smith 1890–1905. Edited by Denham Sutliffe. Cambridge: Harvard University Press, 1947.

Van Norman, C. Elta. "Captain Craig." *College English* 2 (February 1941): 462–75.

Wagenknecht, Edward. *Gamaliel Bradford*. Boston: Twayne, 1982.

Waggoner, Hyatt H. *American Poets from the Puritans to the Present*. Boston: Houghton Mifflin, 1968.

Walsh, William Thomas. "Some Recollections of E. A. Robinson." *Catholic World* 155 (August–September 1942): 522–31, 703–12.

Weeks, Lewis E., Jr. "Edwin Arlington Robinson's *Antigone*." *Colby Library Quarterly* 20 (September 1984): 137–51.

———. "Maine in the Poetry of Edwin Arlington Robinson." 8 (June 1969): 317–34.

Weil, Eric A. "Robinson's 'The Tree in Pamela's Garden.'" *Explicator* 51 (Summer 1993): 230–32.

Wells, Henry Willis. *New Poets from Old: A Study in Literary Genetics*. New York: Columbia University Press, 1940.

Williams, Alice Meacham. "Edwin Arlington Robinson, Journalist." *New England Quarterly* 15 (December 1942): 715–24.

Winters, Yvor. *Edwin Arlington Robinson*. New York: New Directions, 1971.

Wolf, H. R. "E. A. Robinson and the Integration of the Self." In *Modern American Poetry: Essays in Criticism*, edited by Jerome

Mazzaro, 40–59. New York: David McKay, 1970.

Zietlow, Paul. "The Meaning of Tilbury Town: Robinson as a Regional Poet." *New England Quarterly* 40 (June 1967): 188–211.

Index

Page references to main entries are in **boldface**.